D1008718

THE MITFORDS

ALSO EDITED BY CHARLOTTE MOSLEY

A Talent to Annoy:
Essays, Articles and Reviews by Nancy Mitford, 1929–1968

Love From Nancy:
The Letters of Nancy Mitford

The Letters of Nancy Mitford and Evelyn Waugh

THE MITFORDS

LETTERS

BETWEEN

SIX

SISTERS

Edited by Charlotte Mosley

HARPER

An Imprint of HarperCollins*Publishers*

www.harpercollins.com

HarperCollins books may be purchased for educational, business, or sales promotional use. For information please write: Special Markets Department, HarperCollins Publishers, 10 East 53rd Street, New York, NY 10022.

First published in Great Britain in 2007 by Fourth Estate, an imprint of HarperCollins Publishers.

FIRST U.S. EDITION

Library of Congress Cataloging-in-Publication Data is available upon request.

ISBN: 978-0-06-137364-0
ISBN-10: 0-06-137364-8

07 08 09 10 11 OFF/RRD 10 9 8 7 6 5 4 3 2 1

CONTENTS

BIOGRAPHICAL NOTES

NANCY

(28 November 1904–30 June 1973)
'Naunce(ling)', 'The Old French Lady', 'The Lady', 'Dame', 'Susan', 'Soo'.

Married to Peter Rodd, 1933–58. No children. Studied briefly at the Slade School of Art before embarking on a writing career with *Vogue* and *The Lady.* Worked in London at Heywood Hill bookshop during the war. Fell in love with Free French officer Gaston Palewski in 1942, moved to Paris in 1946 to be near him and remained in France, an ardent Francophile, for the rest of her life. Flirted with socialism and fascism before becoming a staunch Gaullist after meeting Palewski. Achieved fame with her post-war novels and repeated the success with four historical biographies. Author of the novels *Highland Fling* (1931), *Christmas Pudding* (1932), *Wigs on the Green* (1935), *Pigeon Pie* (1940), *The Pursuit of Love* (1945), *Love in a Cold Climate* (1949), *The Blessing* (1951) and *Don't Tell Alfred* (1960), and of the historical biographies *Madame de Pompadour* (1954), *Voltaire in Love* (1957), *The Sun King* (1966) and *Frederick the Great* (1970). Editor of a collection of letters of nineteenth-century Mitford cousins, *The Ladies of Alderley* (1938) and *The Stanleys of Alderley* (1939), and of a volume of essays and journalism, *The Water Beetle* (1962). Her notorious article on 'U and Non-U' (upper- and non-upper-class usage) in *Encounter* magazine (1954) was reprinted in *Noblesse Oblige* (1956).

PAMELA

(25 November 1907–12 April 1994)
'Pam', 'Woman', 'Woo', 'Wooms', 'Woomling'.

Down-to-earth in her tastes and interests, she was a superb cook and happiest living in the country in the company of her dogs. From 1930 to 1934, she managed the farm at Biddesden in Wiltshire for Diana's first husband, Bryan Guinness. Married to physicist Professor Derek Jackson, 1936–51. No children. When married, she lived at Rignell House, Oxford, before moving to Tullamaine Castle, Ireland, in 1947. In 1963, she settled in Zurich and shared her life with two women, Giuditta Tommasi and Rudi von Simolin. Returned to England in the mid-1970s to live at Woodfield House in Gloucestershire, which she had bought in 1960. She became an acknowledged expert on rearing poultry. Entertained the idea of writing a cookbook but never found time to finish it.

DIANA

(17 June 1910–11 August 2003)
'Cord(uroy)', 'Bodley', 'Honks', 'Nard(y)'.

The acknowledged beauty of the family. Married to Bryan Guinness, 2nd Baron Moyne, 1929–34. Two sons, Jonathan and Desmond. Married fascist leader Sir Oswald Mosley in 1936. Two sons, Alexander and Max. A visit to the 1933 Nuremberg Nazi Party Rally ignited a lifelong admiration for Hitler. Imprisoned in Holloway in 1940 under Defence Regulation 18B. Released in 1943, reunited with her children, and held under house arrest until the end of the war. Moved to Ireland in 1951 and lived between Co. Galway, Co. Cork and France. Settled permanently outside Paris in 1963. Until Mosley's death in 1980, she devoted herself to the furtherance of his comfort and happiness. Edited and contributed to *The European*, 1953–60, a monthly magazine to advance Mosley's ideas of a united Europe. Reviewed for *Books & Bookmen* and the *Evening Standard*. Author of an autobiography, *A Life of Contrasts* (1977), pen portraits of friends, *Loved Ones* (1985), and a biography, *The Duchess of Windsor* (1980).

UNITY

(8 August 1914–28 May 1948)
'Bobo', 'Boud(le)', 'Bird(ie)'.

Artistic, rebellious and keen to shock, she became a supporter of the Nazis after attending the Nuremburg Parteitag with Diana in 1933. Moved to Munich in 1934. Met Hitler in February 1935 and continued to see him frequently until the outbreak of war. Attempted to commit suicide in 1939 when war was declared between England and Germany. She lived on as an invalid, cared for by her mother, until her death aged thirty-three.

JESSICA

(11 September 1917–23 July 1996)
'Decca', 'Hen', 'Henderson', 'Boud', 'Susan', 'Soo', 'Steake', 'Squalor'.

Became a socialist in her teens and eloped, aged nineteen, to civil-war-torn Spain to marry her cousin Esmond Romilly. Moved to America in 1939. Esmond joined the Canadian Air Force and was killed in 1941. Two daughters, Julia (died at five months) and Constancia ('Dinky'). Married American attorney Robert Treuhaft in 1943. Two sons, Nicholas (died aged ten) and Benjamin. Active member of the American Communist Party, 1944–58, and energetic campaigner for civil rights. The success of her autobiography, *Hons and Rebels* (1960), enabled her to make a living from writing. Prolific investigative journalist and author of *Lifeitselfmanship* (1956), *The American Way of Death* (1963), *The Trial of Dr Spock* (1969), *Kind and Usual Punishment* (1973), a second volume of memoirs, *A Fine Old Conflict* (1977), *The Making of a Muckraker* (1979), *Faces of Philip, A Memoir of Philip Toynbee* (1984), *Grace Had an English Heart* (1988) and *The American Way of Birth* (1992).

DEBORAH

(31 March 1920–)
'Debo', 'Hen', 'Henderson', '9', 'Stublow', 'Miss'.

Married, in 1941, Lord Andrew Cavendish, who succeeded his father as 11th Duke of Devonshire in 1950. One son, Peregrine, two daughters, Emma and Sophia. Immunized by her sisters' fanatical views, she remained firmly apolitical all her life. An astute and capable businesswoman, she was largely responsible for putting Chatsworth, the Devonshire family home, on to a sound footing after she and her husband moved back into the house in 1959. Accused by Nancy of illiteracy, she was suspected by her family and friends of being a secret reader. Diana believed that unlike most people who pretend to have read books that they have not, Deborah pretended not to have read books that she had. She took to writing late in life and produced *The House: A Portrait of Chatsworth* (1982), *The Estate, A View of Chatsworth* (1990), *Farm Animals* (1991), *Treasures of Chatsworth* (1991), *The Garden at Chatsworth* (1999), *Counting My Chickens* (2001), *The Duchess of Devonshire's Chatsworth Cookery Book* (2003) and *Round About Chatsworth* (2005).

INDEX OF NICKNAMES

Al	Alexander Mosley, Diana's son
Bird/Birdie	Unity
Blor	Laura Dicks, the Mitfords' nanny
Bobo	Unity
Boud/y	Unity
Cake	Queen Elizabeth, the Queen Mother
Cha	Charlotte Mosley, Diana's daughter-in-law and editor of these letters
Colonel, Col	Gaston Palewski
Cord	Diana
Count/y	Jean de Baglion
Cuddum	Communist
Deacon	Elizabeth Cavendish, Deborah's sister-in-law
Debo	Deborah
Decca	Jessica
Diddy	Ellen Stephens, the Devonshires' nanny
Dink/y/Donk	Constancia Romilly, Jessica's daughter
Duch (my)	Mary, Duchess of Devonshire, Deborah's mother-in-law
Em	Emma Tennant, née Cavendish, Deborah's elder daughter
Farve	Lord Redesdale
Fat Friend (F. F.)	President John F. Kennedy
Fem	Lady Redesdale
French Lady	Nancy
Hen/Henderson	Deborah or Jessica
Honks	Diana
Id/Idden	Ann Farrer, a first cousin of the Mitfords
Jonnycan	Jonathan Guinness, Diana's eldest son

Kit	Oswald Mosley
Lady	Nancy
Leader/Lead	Oswald Mosley
Little gurl	Sophia Cavendish, Deborah's younger daughter
Loved One	President John F. Kennedy
Maggot	Margaret Ogilvy
Mrs Ham	Violet Hammersley
Muv	Lady Redesdale
Nard/y	Diana
Naunce/Naunceling	Nancy
Oys	James and Chaka Forman, Jessica's grandsons
P's/Parent Birds	Lord and Lady Redesdale
Prod	Peter Rodd, Nancy's husband
Recs	Chickens
Revereds	Lord and Lady Redesdale
Rud/Rudbin	Joan Farrer, a first cousin of the Mitfords
Sir O	Oswald Mosley
Squalor	Jessica
Sto/Stoker	Peregrine Hartington, Deborah's son
Tig	Anne Tree, née Cavendish, Deborah's sister-in-law
TPOF	Lady Redesdale, 'The Poor Old Female'
Tud/Tuddemy	Tom Mitford
Uncle Harold	Harold Macmillan
Wid/Widow	Violet Hammersley
Wife	Lady Mersey
Woman/Woo/Wooms	Pamela

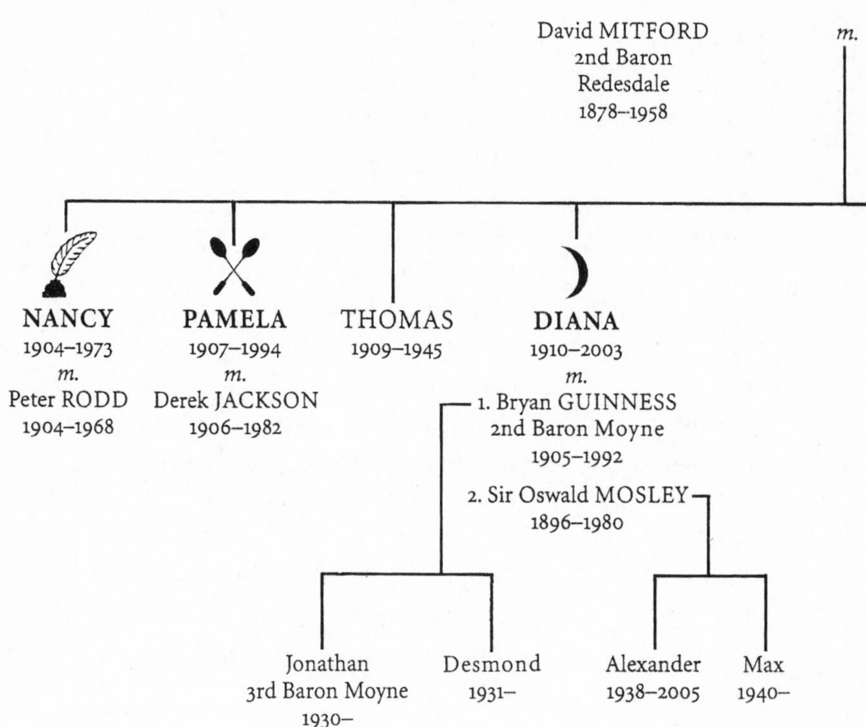

Symbols above the sisters' names precede their letters throughout the book and are for quick identification.

The Mitford Family Tree

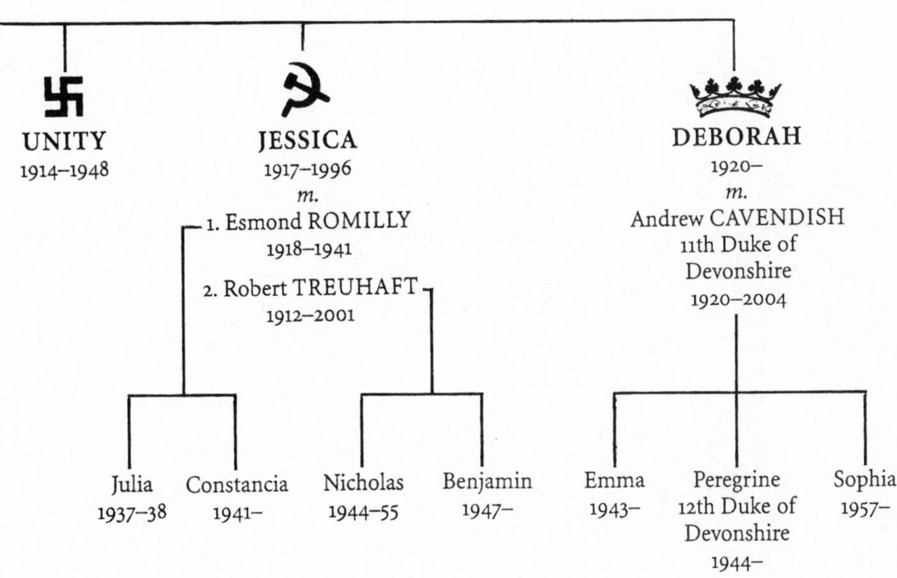

EDITOR'S NOTE

The correspondence between the six Mitford sisters consists of some twelve thousand letters – over four million words – of which little more than five per cent has been included in this volume. Out of the fifteen possible patterns of exchange between the sisters, there are only three gaps: no letters between Unity and Pamela have survived, and there are none from Unity to Deborah. The proportion of existing letters from each sister varies greatly: political differences led Jessica to destroy all but one of Diana's letters to her, while the exchange between Deborah and Diana, the two longest-lived sisters, runs to some three thousand on each side.

The Mitfords had a brother, Tom, who was sent away to school aged eight while his sisters were taught at home. Although he composed many dutiful letters to his parents, Tom rarely wrote to the rest of the family. Unlike his sisters, for whom writing was as natural as speaking, he took no pleasure in the art of corresponding. (In 1937, in a brief note added to the bottom of one of Unity's letters to Jessica, he deplored his 'constitutional hatred' for letter-writing.) Perhaps his later training as a barrister also made him wary of committing his thoughts to paper. Nancy often wrote to Tom before she married and although over a hundred of her letters to him have been preserved, as have a handful from his other sisters, the correspondence is so one-sided that no letters to or from Tom have been included in this volume.

Letters make a fragmentary biography at best and I have not attempted to present a comprehensive picture of the Mitfords' lives; those seeking a more complete account can turn to the plentiful books by and about the family. In order to weave a coherent narrative out of the vast archive and link the six voices, I have focused my choice of letters on the relationship between the sisters. I have also selected striking, interesting or entertaining passages, as well as those that are particularly relevant to the story of their lives. While some letters have been included in their entirety, more often I have deliberately cut them, sometimes removing just a sentence, at other times paring them down to a single paragraph. To indicate all these cuts would be too distracting and they have therefore been made silently.

As in many families, the Mitfords used a plethora of nicknames and often several different ones for the same person. While the origins of most of these are long forgotten, the roots of a few can be traced. Sir Oswald Mosley, Diana's husband of forty-four years, who was known as 'Tom' or 'the Leader' before the war and 'Sir O', 'Sir Oz' or 'Sir Ogre' after the war, was nearly always called 'Kit' by Diana. In private she admitted that the name came from 'kitten' but, realizing its inappropriateness for such a powerful character, she wrote in her memoirs that she could not remember how it had originated. Deborah knew him as 'Cyril' because as a young girl she had asked her mother how she should address her new brother-in-law and misheard her terse answer, 'He's Sir Oswald to me'. Nancy often referred to Mosley as 'Keats', a derivation of 'Kit'. Deborah's husband, Andrew Devonshire, was known as 'Ivan' (the Terrible) or 'Peter' (the Great), according to his mood. He was also called 'Claud' because when his title was Lord Hartington, before he inherited the dukedom, he used to receive letters addressed to 'Claud Hartington Esq.' To make matters even more complicated, Nancy and Jessica addressed and signed letters to each other as 'Susan' or 'Soo', for reasons now forgotten; Deborah and Jessica called each other 'Hen', and by extension 'Henderson', inspired by their passion for chickens; Jessica and Unity were to each other 'Boud', from a private language they invented as children called 'Boudledidge'. Nancy addressed Deborah as '9', the mental age beyond which she claimed her youngest sister had never progressed.

I have left unchanged the sisters' numerous nicknames for one another as they are intrinsic to their relationships, but for clarity I have standardized other nicknames and regularized their spelling. The only other editorial changes that have been made to the text are the silent correction of spelling mistakes – except in childhood letters; the addition of punctuation where necessary; and the rectification of names of people, places and books. In my footnotes and section introductions,

I have referred to people variously by their first name, surname or title, aiming for quick recognition rather than consistency. Foreign words or phrases have been translated in square brackets in the text; the translation of longer sentences has been put in a footnote.

As a child, Nancy invented a game in which she played a 'Czechish lady doctor' and adopted a thick foreign accent. This voice endured and the letters are scattered with 'wondair' for 'wonderful', 'nevair' for 'never mind', and other phonetic approximations of Mitteleuropean English. After Nancy moved to France, should she ever use a French word in conversation, Deborah, who did not admit to speaking the language, would interject with 'Ah oui!' or 'Quelle horrible surprise', expressions that have found their way into the letters. Deborah was also the instigator of the frequent plea 'do admit' – not something any Mitford did willingly – which was an attempt to catch the attention of one of her siblings and get them to agree with her. The exaggerated style of writing that the sisters used, a continuation of the drawling way in which they spoke, began in childhood and originated in part from their brother Tom's 'artful scheme of happiness', a particular tone of voice that he employed when trying to wheedle something out of someone. 'Boudledidge', which Jessica and Unity often used in their letters to each other, was a derivation of this way of speaking. 'Honnish', a language invented by Jessica and Deborah, was derived not from the fact that as daughters of a peer they were Honourables but from the hens that played such an important part in their upbringing. Their mother, Lady Redesdale, had a chicken farm from whose slim profits she paid for the children's governess and the sisters each kept their own birds and sold their eggs to their mother in order to supplement their pocket money.

The Mitford sisters all wrote in longhand, except for Jessica who learned to type at the beginning of the war. Their handwriting is clear and legible, and, as a rule, they dated their letters. Pamela, who was probably dyslexic, kept a dictionary at hand and her spelling is usually accurate. Her occasional use of unorthodox capitalizations and spelling has been retained. The sisters' letters to each other are held in the archives at Chatsworth, where they have been collected by Deborah, with the exception of those written to Jessica which are in the Rare

Books and Manuscripts Library at Ohio State University. The letters in this volume are previously unpublished, except for a dozen that were included in *Love from Nancy* and three times that number in *Decca*.[1]

At a certain point, the sisters became aware of the value of their letters and of the possibility that they might one day be published. In 1963, Nancy advised Deborah to throw nothing away because the correspondence of a whole family would be 'gold for your heirs'. Pamela, who until then had discarded most of her letters, began to preserve them, and Jessica started keeping carbon copies of her correspondence in the 1950s. It is nevertheless abundantly clear that the sisters did not write with an eye to posterity; the frankness, immediacy and informal style of their communications bear this out. Only when I had begun editing these letters did the idea of publication at times inhibit the two surviving sisters. A few months before she died in 2003, Diana wrote to Deborah, 'I've started this letter and for the first time in my life I can't think of anything to say. My old mind is a blank. If this had happened sooner it would have saved Charlotte a lot of trouble.' Happily, it did not.

1 *Love From Nancy: The Letters of Nancy Mitford*, edited by Charlotte Mosley (Hodder & Stoughton, 1993); *Decca: The Letters of Jessica Mitford*, edited by Peter Y. Sussman (Weidenfeld & Nicolson, 2006).

INTRODUCTION

The Mitford sisters first began to make headlines in the late 1920s and have rarely been out of the news since. Between them they were close to many key figures of the last century. They knew Winston Churchill, John F. Kennedy and Hitler; were friends of Lytton Strachey, Evelyn Waugh and Maya Angelou; sat for Augustus John, Lucian Freud and Cecil Beaton; entertained the Queen, the Duchess of Windsor and Katherine Graham; were guests of Lord Berners, Goebbels and Givenchy. They lived out their lives in very different spheres, from the London of the Bright Young Things, pre-war Munich and cosmopolitan Paris, to rural Ireland, left-wing California and the deep English countryside.

How did these six sisters, offspring of parents whose highest hopes for their daughters were that they should make good wives, achieve such fame? Some clues can be found in the personalities and careers of their forebears. Talent often misses a generation and the sisters' grandfathers on both sides of the family were notable in their day. Bertram Mitford, the 1st Baron Redesdale, was a diplomat, politician and author. His memoirs were admired by Edmund Gosse and his collection of popular Japanese stories, *Tales of Old Japan*, is still in print today. The Mitfords' maternal grandfather, Thomas Gibson Bowles, was a politician and journalist who started the popular weekly satirical magazine *Vanity Fair* (unrelated to its modern namesake) and *The Lady*, founded in 1883 and still famous for its classified columns advertising for domestic help. A combative and opinionated self-made man, Bowles used *Vanity Fair* and his position as a Member of Parliament as weapons to bring down his opponents. Never afraid of saying what he thought, he relished being a gadfly to the Establishment and engaged in a constant guerrilla warfare of press campaigns and court cases. His energy, wit and what *The Times* described as a 'temperamental dislike of compromise' passed down in generous measure to his granddaughters, who also inherited his interest in politics and a gift for writing.

While the sisters' enduring reputation owes much to their originality, forceful opinions, and good looks, the turbulent times in which they grew up provided the catalyst for their highly publicized exploits. The decade leading up to the Second World War was one of ideological extremes and, like many of their contemporaries, they were drawn to radical politics which they saw as the answer to Europe's ills. Their beliefs spanned the political spectrum, from fascism, Nazism and communism, to socialism, Gaullism and Conservatism, politics dividing the family as surely as religion had done in former centuries, political absolutism replacing religious absolutes. The causes they took up were closely connected with the men who embodied them, with the difference that Unity and Jessica chose men whose politics corresponded with their own natural ideological tendencies, while Nancy and Diana's political beliefs were sustained by the men they loved.

For a family that is regarded as quintessentially English it is interesting that all the sisters, except Deborah, spent much of their lives abroad. Consciously or unconsciously, the desire to set themselves apart from their siblings, to stand out as individuals and not just as one of the 'Mitford girls', drove them not only into opposite political camps but also to different parts of the world. What the sisters shared, however, was stronger than that which divided them. In spite of their differences, and however little their daily lives might have in common, they needed to keep in touch; recounting their lives to each other was a vital part of their existence. Only Jessica broke this chain by completely severing ties with Diana before the war, when political antipathy replaced her childhood love for her 'favourite person in the world', and when too much bitterness made meeting on the basis of sisterly fondness 'unthinkable'.

A family correspondence of this scope and size is rare; for it to include four such gifted writers makes it unique. Nancy, Diana, Jessica and Deborah were all published authors, their books international bestsellers that are mostly still in print. Even Unity, whose suicide attempt effectively cut off her development in her mid-twenties, and Pamela, who was slowed down by a bout of childhood polio, wrote with natural, distinctive voices.

Eighty years separate the earliest surviving letter between the sisters – a note written in 1923 by nine-year-old Unity, who was on a seaside holiday in Sussex, to thirteen-year-old Diana who had stayed at home – and the last – a fax sent in 2003 by 83-year-old Deborah from her home in England to 93-year-old Diana who was dying in Paris. The letters began as a trickle while the sisters were still living at home, swelled in number in the 1930s as they gradually went out into the world, and reached a flood after the war when they settled in different countries and saw each other less often. Although they started using the telephone in the 1950s – Diana and Deborah used to ring regularly on Sunday mornings and when Nancy and Diana were both living in France they spoke almost daily – telephoning remained of secondary importance; letters were their principal means of keeping in touch. The post and everything that touched on it played a key part in their lives: Jessica left $5,000 in her will to her local postman; Deborah's idea of contentment in old age was to be the postmistress of a small village; and at the end of her life Diana was reconciled to moving from a house and garden in the suburbs to a flat in Paris mainly because it was situated immediately above a post office. While the sisters' correspondence with one another represents just a fraction of their total output – they rarely left a letter unanswered and kept up with many hundreds of other correspondents – it is unique because it was sustained over a lifetime.

The strength of feeling amongst the sisters was intense: childhood love, sympathy, generosity and loyalty were mixed with hate, envy, resentment and exasperation – sentiments that remained with them to a greater or lesser extent throughout their lives and give their letters to one another an adolescent quality which persist even in old age. During their childhood, alliances were formed and broken, common enemies fought then sided with. As they grew up, politics hardened their positions and determined which camp they chose to support. In a family where overt demonstrations of love were avoided and where the English upper-class code of frowning on any public display of emotion was observed, teasing was a relatively safe way of dealing with sibling rivalry and of expressing affection. The joking relationship between them acted as a safeguard, creating an environment in which tensions could be defused before they grew too serious. Nancy, as the eldest, was usually the instigator of these practices which she carried on even in later life, partly in commemoration of schoolroom custom but also because her jealousy of her sisters was never fully resolved and her feelings towards them remained ambivalent. Teasing, in her hands, could become a cruel weapon, while for the others it was a way of deflating self-importance or relieving the tedium of long winter evenings when they had only each other for company. Their father, Lord Redesdale, disliked having people to stay, and when there were guests he did not always make them feel welcome. Once when the house was full of Nancy's friends, he shouted down the table to his wife, 'Have these people no homes of their own?'

Jessica described having sisters as 'a great toughening and weathering process' which prepared one for later life. When Nancy once ventured that she thought sisters were a protection against life's cruel circumstances, Jessica countered that, as a child, her sisters *were* the cruel circumstances. Diana wrote that she regarded it as a fault of their upbringing that it should be considered unthinkable to admit to 'weakness, misery or despair'. Certainly all six sisters had the capacity to withstand private tragedy and public opprobrium with unusual resilience – often appearing insensible to other people's opinions – and were practised at putting on a brave face and hiding their vulnerability behind a lightly worn armour of flippancy and self-deprecation. They wore this protective shield not just with the outside world, where it was often taken for ruthlessness, but also with each other and, with few exceptions, rarely shared their most intimate confidences. While avoiding emotional depth and turning everything into a joke is a widespread English custom, the sisters' comic genius transformed a national character trait into an art form.

Less inhibited than their memoirs and more intimate than the biographies that have been written about them, the sisters' correspondence explores the kaleidoscopic pattern of their shifting relationships and exposes less-well-known sides of their complex and contradictory characters. Unlike many books about the Mitford family that have focused on the years when the sisters' exploits intersected with historical events, their letters cover their whole lives, revealing how triumphs and tragedies wore down their youthful fanaticism.

The sisters wrote to each other to confide, commiserate, tease, rage and gossip but above all they wrote to amuse; when something made them laugh, half the fun of it was to relate it to a sibling. Beneath their contrasting personalities they shared a common temperament: unconditional in their loves and hates and passionate about the causes they embraced, they also possessed the ability to laugh at themselves and to make light of even the darkest predicaments. It is this indomitable spirit, fierce courage and irrepressible enjoyment of life that make their letters so powerful, eloquent and entertaining.

I had letters from you & the Lady* & Henderson** today, wouldn't it be dread if one had a) no sisters
b) sisters who didn't write.

Deborah to Diana, 21 July 1965

* Nancy
** Jessica

ONE

1925–1933

The Mitford children in 1921: Unity, Pamela, Deborah, Tom,
Nancy, Jessica and Diana.

There are few letters to record the Mitford sisters' childhood and early youth, and such letters as they did write were mostly to their mother and father. Nor are there many letters dating back to the eight years covered in this section. By 1925, only Nancy, aged twenty-one, and Pamela, aged eighteen, had gone out into the world; the four youngest children were still in the nursery or schoolroom. Nancy's main family correspondent at the time was her brother Tom, and Pamela – who confided mostly in Diana – was the least prolific writer of the sisters.

When the letters begin, the family had been living for six years at Asthall Manor, a seventeenth-century house in the Cotswolds, which the sisters' father, Lord Redesdale, had bought when he sold Batsford Park, a rambling Victorian pile that he had inherited in 1916 and could not afford to keep up. Before the First World War, David Redesdale, or 'Farve' as he was known to his children, lived in London where he worked as office manager for *The Lady*, the magazine founded by his father-in-law. Life in the country was far better suited to this unbookish, unsociable man, whose happiest moments were spent by the Windrush, a trout river that ran past Asthall, or in the woods where he watched his young pheasants hatch. Unluckily for his family, country sports did not exhaust his energies and Asthall, which the children loved, was not to his liking. In 1926, they moved to Swinbrook House in Oxfordshire, a grim, ungainly edifice that Lord Redesdale had built on top of a hill near Swinbrook village. All the sisters except Deborah, who was six when they moved, disliked the new house, which was cold, draughty and impractical. Worst of all, unlike Asthall where the library had been in a converted barn some distance from the house and where the children were left undisturbed, there was no room at Swinbrook that they could call their own. The younger children found some warmth and privacy in a heated linen cupboard, later immortalized in Nancy's novels as the 'Hons' cupboard', while the older children had to share the drawing room or sit in their small bedrooms. Lord

Redesdale was hurt by the family's dislike of his dream project and began to spend more time at 26 Rutland Gate, a large London house overlooking Hyde Park that he had bought when Asthall was sold.

The sisters were in awe of their father. Strikingly handsome, with the brilliant blue eyes that passed down to his children, he was kind-hearted, jovial and the source of much of the fun that was had in the family. Deborah remembered him as 'charming, brilliant without being clever' and uproariously funny when in a good mood. She wrote that when he and Nancy started sparring they were better than anything she had ever seen on stage, 'a pair of comedians of the first order'. But he could also be impatient and had a violent temper. The smallest transgression – a child spilling her food or being a minute late – could send him into a towering rage. His anger was all the more alarming for being unpredictable: he would turn with sudden fury on one of his daughters and then, for no apparent reason, decide to single out another. Their way of standing up to him, and of drawing his un-wrathful attention, was to catch their father in one of his sunnier moods and tease him, which he took in good part. Jessica used to call him 'the Old Sub-Human' and pretend to measure his skull for science or would gently shake his hand when he was drinking a cup of tea to give him 'palsy practice' for when he grew old. Nancy's caricature of him in her first novel, *Highland Fling*, as the jingoistic, hot-tempered General Murgatroyd – a precursor of the formidable Uncle Matthew in her later novels – was an effective way of reducing this larger-than-life figure to less alarming dimensions. As they grew up, the sisters rarely seem to have resented Farve and looked back on his autocratic eccentricities with affectionate amusement. The inclination to hero-worship is foreshadowed in their relationship with their father; like the other powerful men who were to come into their lives, he could do no wrong.

Their resentment – and that of Nancy and Jessica in particular – against the perceived shortcomings of their upbringing was reserved for their mother. In contrast to her moody, volatile husband, Sydney, or 'Muv' as her children called her, was cool and detached. Her own mother had died when she was seven years old and at the age of fourteen she had taken on the responsibility of running her father's household. This had taught her financial prudence and to be a good manager – qualities that came in useful later when raising a family of seven on never quite enough money – but it also created a certain rigidity in her attitude to her children when they were growing up; an inflexibility that fuelled her daughters' rebellious behaviour and their desire to shock.

From her father, Lady Redesdale had inherited definite opinions about health and diet, believing that the 'good body' would heal itself more effectively without the intervention of doctors or medicine. An early campaigner against refined sugar and white flour, she made sure that her children ate only wholemeal bread, baked to her recipe. Physically undemonstrative, she rarely exhibited outward signs of maternal warmth and seldom hugged or cuddled her daughters, who had to compete fiercely for the scarce resource of her attention. In 'Blor', an essay on her childhood, Nancy described her mother as living 'in a dream world of her own', detached to the point of neglect. In her fictional portrait of her as Aunt Sadie, she depicted a more sympathetic character but one that was nevertheless remote and disapproving. But the aloofness that some of her daughters complained of also had its positive side, enabling their mother to remain calm in the face of an unpredictable husband and to deal impartially with six boisterous and constantly feuding girls (her ambition had been to have seven boys). She was also fair, principled, direct, selfless and honest to the point of innocence. As the sisters grew up and their escapades sent their mother reeling from one calamity to the next, her unshakeable loyalty and acceptance of their choices in life showed that she cared for her daughters very much indeed.

Like most girls of their class and generation, the sisters were educated at home. Lady Redesdale taught all her children until they were eight, after which the girls moved to the schoolroom to be instructed by governesses and Tom was sent away to boarding school. Nancy and Jessica blamed their mother for this lack of formal education, even though Lord Redesdale was just as opposed to sending his daughters to school. 'Nothing would have induced him to waste money on anything so frivolous', wrote Deborah. He also worried that they might develop thick calves from being made to play hockey. Neither parent believed that girls should be educated beyond basic literacy and regarded intellectual women as 'rather dreadful'. The Redesdales' views were not uncommon at the time but their children's response was more unusual. Nancy's bitterness at not having received what she considered a proper education was enduring and runs as a refrain throughout her correspondence. Jessica wrote that the dream of her childhood was to be allowed to go to school, and that her mother's refusal to countenance it had burned into her soul.

It is questionable, however, whether the sisters would have been better educated had they gone away to school. At the time, fashionable establishments for girls taught social rather than intellectual skills, preparing pupils for marriage and the drawing-room rather than the workplace. When the Redesdales eventually allowed Nancy, at the age of sixteen, to go to Hatherop Castle, a small private school for girls from 'suitable' families, the mainly non-academic curriculum concentrated on music, dancing and French, whereas at home, the sisters were free to make use of their grandfather's first-rate library and Nancy and Diana became bookworms at an early age. It was perhaps the boredom of being confined at home with only siblings for company that rankled with Jessica and Nancy as much as their lack of formal schooling. Not until they left home and had to earn a living – they were the only two sisters who did not marry rich men – did they have cause to view their rudimentary education as a handicap.

The age gap between the Mitford children meant that they formed almost two separate generations. In 1925, the year that opens this collection of letters, the older children, Nancy, Pamela, Tom and Diana, ranged between the ages of twenty-one and fifteen. The youngest three, Unity, Jessica and Deborah, were aged eleven, eight and five. Nancy had 'come out' when she was eighteen and had followed her first season as a debutante with three further years of weekend parties and balls. She had met the right people, made many friends and quite enjoyed herself, but she had failed to do the expected thing and find a husband. With very little money and no immediate prospects, she was living at home, taking out her frustration on her sisters. The three youngest looked up to her like a remote star: her vitality, cleverness and supreme funniness lit up the family atmosphere, as did her determination to turn everything into a joke, but she was too caustic and indiscreet to be the recipient of anyone's confidences. In Unity's copy of *All About Everybody*, a little book of printed questions that she asked her family and friends to fill in, Nancy put as her besetting sin 'disloyalty', a trait that could make her incomparably good company but an uncertain ally.

Nancy's usual victim was Pamela, whose unguarded nature made her an obvious target for teasing. Diana, however, presented more of a challenge; she was fully Nancy's intellectual equal, with just as determined a character, and was able to stand up to her sister's bullying. Occasionally Nancy managed to exert her seniority and successfully torment her younger sister. When she was sixteen, she formed a company of Girl Guides, appointed herself captain and tried to make ten-year-old Diana salute her. On another occasion, she pretended to have heard the Redesdales discuss sending Diana to boarding school, an idea that filled her little sister with horror. But they both enjoyed reading, which drew them together, as did a similar sense of humour and a longing to escape the confinement of Swinbrook. As they grew up, they became, according to Diana, great friends. But underlying the friendship was a deep current of envy on Nancy's part towards a younger sister who was already a great beauty and the instant centre of attention with the undergraduate friends that Nancy brought home. These feelings were exacerbated when Diana, aged eighteen, married the extremely rich and good-looking Bryan Guinness and became a sought-after London hostess.

Shortly before Diana's engagement to Bryan in 1928, Pamela accepted a proposal of marriage from a neighbour of the Mitfords, Oliver Watney. The prospect of having two younger sisters married before she was may help to explain Nancy's unwise decision to become unofficially engaged to Hamish St Clair-Erskine, a friend of Tom's from Eton who was younger than her and homosexual. Her infatuation with Hamish dragged on for five unsatisfactory years, causing her a great deal of unhappiness. During this period she started to write her first articles for *Vogue*, and in 1930 was taken on as a regular contributor to cover social events for *The Lady*. This brought in a little pocket money, as did her first two novels, *Highland Fling* and *Christmas Pudding*, light satires on upper-class life that sketched out the world she would so successfully depict in her accomplished post-war novels.

Nancy used to say that the first three years of her life were perfect, 'then a terrible thing happened, my sister Pamela was born' which 'threw me into a permanent rage for about 20 years'. Her affront at being supplanted in the nursery was compounded by an insensitive nanny who immediately shifted all her love and attention to the new baby. By the time Nancy was six and Pamela three, they might have overcome their differences and played together, had not Pamela contracted polio which affected her physical and mental development. She was in constant pain from an aching leg, and often tearful and sad. Her illness was doubtless a strain on Nancy: 'you've *got* to be kind to Pam, she's *ill*', was dinned into her unceasingly. Instead of narrowing, as it normally would, the age gap between the two sisters widened. Pamela, who was the least able to defend herself, became Nancy's scapegoat. She learnt to keep her head down and seems never to have shown any ill will towards her tormentor. She loved jokes as much as the rest of the family, and laughed about her own limitations, but she refused to retaliate or compete in the teasing. Her sisters nicknamed her 'Woman' because, like a symbolic character in a medieval Mystery Play, she epitomized the womanly virtues of simplicity and goodness. From her mother, she inherited dignity, common sense and the talent for making a comfortable home; from her father, a love of the countryside, where she was at her happiest. In 1925, when these letters begin, Pamela was a shy seventeen-year-old debutante, confiding to Diana her nervousness about going out into the world.

Unlike Nancy, who was a late developer and drew out her adolescence well into her twenties, Diana, by the time she was thirty, had been twice married, given birth to four sons and experienced the most eventful decade of her life. When these letters begin, she was a precocious fifteen-year-old, dreaming of independence. Her closest companion in the family, both in age and interests, was Tom, and when he was home for the holidays the two were inseparable. Diana admired her brother's musical and intellectual talents and delighted in the company of his sophisticated friends. These glimpses of a world of art, music and intelligent conversation increased her yearning to escape the restrictive family atmosphere. The 1926 General Strike, sparked off by the grim working conditions in the coal mines, made a deep impression on her, kindling her social conscience and fostering a lifelong interest in politics. Whereas Nancy treated the national emergency as something of a joke and disguised herself as a tramp to frighten Pamela who was running a canteen serving food to strike-breaking lorry drivers, Diana felt the injustice of the miners' situation acutely. Her interest in politics was also fuelled by visits to Chartwell, Winston Churchill's family home in Kent. Churchill's wife, Clementine, was a first cousin of Lord Redesdale, and two of the Churchill children, Diana and Randolph, were much the same age as Tom and Diana.

In 1927, Diana spent six months studying in Paris, where she said she learnt more than in six years of lessons at Asthall. For the first time in her life she was free of the strict chaperoning imposed by her parents and of having to jockey for position among her sisters. The painter Paul-César Helleu, a friend of Thomas Gibson-Bowles, was an important influence during her visit. He took her to the Louvre and Versailles, introduced her to his artist friends and admired her looks, making her aware for the first time of the effect of her exceptional beauty. When she returned to Swinbrook, Diana was more impatient than ever to get away from its schoolroom atmosphere. The following year, at the end of her first season, a proposal of marriage gave her the chance to escape. Bryan Guinness, the sensitive and diffident elder son of Lord Moyne and heir to a brewing fortune, fell deeply in love with her. A poet and novelist, Bryan was part of a group of Nancy's Oxford friends that included Evelyn Waugh, John Betjeman, Roy Harrod, Harold Acton, James Lees-Milne, Henry Yorke and Robert Byron, young men whose interests represented everything that Diana aspired to. She and Bryan were married in January 1929 and divided their time between London and Biddesden, a fine eighteenth-century house in Wiltshire, where Diana was able to give free rein to her talent for decorating and entertaining. Unity, Jessica and Deborah often went to stay with the young couple and in 1930 Pamela settled in a nearby cottage to run the Biddesden farm. Nancy was a less frequent visitor. Caught up in her unhappy affair with Hamish and very short of money, it was galling to see Diana settled in a splendid house, surrounded by a loving husband and two healthy babies. However, the picture of happiness that Diana and Bryan presented was not as bright as it appeared. Although they were undoubtedly in love, there was a basic incompatibility between them that soon made itself felt. Increasingly, Bryan wanted to stay at home with only his family for company while Diana, who was eager to travel and fill her house with friends, found this domesticity all too reminiscent of the life she had so recently managed to escape.

In the spring of 1932, Diana sat next to Sir Oswald Mosley at a dinner party in London. The former Conservative MP and Labour Minister, whose New Party had been resoundingly defeated in the previous year's general election, was preparing to break with parliamentary politics and launch the British Union of Fascists (BUF). Diana fell under the spell of this seasoned womanizer and compelling talker who seemed to her to have all the answers to Britain's problems. In Mosley, she found the combination of a powerful man she could love and a cause to which she could dedicate herself, a pattern that Unity and Jessica – and to a lesser extent Nancy – were to conform to in their different ways. Mosley was married and made it clear that he would not leave his wife. Undeterred, and encouraged by Mosley, Diana decided to divorce Bryan in order to be available for her lover whenever he could spare the time from politics, family and the other women in his life. By throwing in her lot with Mosley, Diana was prepared to sacrifice her social position, distance herself from her beloved Tom, who disapproved of her leaving Bryan, alienate her parents – who refused to allow her two youngest sisters to visit her – and even risk losing her sons. She once wrote of her decision, 'I probably ought to have behaved differently but I never regretted it'. Of the family, only Nancy supported Diana's choice and became a regular visitor to the house in Eaton Square that Diana took after her divorce. It was no doubt easier for Nancy to be close to her sister when she was unpopular than when she was at the height of her success.

Unity was described by her mother as a sensitive, introverted little girl, who used to slip under the dining-room table if anything was said at meals that upset or embarrassed her. By the time she was eight, and had graduated to the schoolroom, she had become naughty and disruptive, her shyness concealed beneath a tough shell of sullen defiance. More solemn than her sisters, she lacked their quick wit and enjoyed practical rather than verbal jokes. In an effort to stand out, she behaved outrageously. When she was fourteen, partly because she was so difficult at home and partly because she wanted to go away, Lady Redesdale decided to make an exception among her daughters and sent Unity to boarding school. The three establishments she attended were no more successful at controlling her than her governesses had been and she was expelled from all of them. In 1932, she followed her older sisters and was launched into society: 'a huge and a rather alarming debutante', according to Jessica. Social life bored her and she had not grown out of the need to draw attention to herself. The only party she enjoyed was a Court ball, where she distinguished herself by stealing Buckingham Palace writing paper. In early 1933, to fill in the months before another Season, she enrolled at a London art school. Diana's house in Eaton Square was forbidden to the two youngest Mitfords because of the scandal of her divorce and involvement with Mosley, but Unity, freed from parental supervision, was able to call on her sister whenever she liked. On one of her visits she met Mosley and became an instant convert to his ideas. The fascist cause had the attraction of being disapproved of by her parents, as well as providing her with the thrill of being connected to its charismatic leader. For Diana, who at the time was cut off from most of her family, Unity's enthusiastic support was reassuring.

During the eight years covered by these early letters, Jessica, the second-youngest sister, went from being a cheerful, mischievous eight-year-old to an angry, rebellious adolescent. While there was nothing unusual about this – her sisters had also gone through periods of teenage moodiness – the boredom of home life and the frustration of not being allowed to go to school instilled in Jessica a lasting sense of grievance. Although in her memoirs of 1960, *Hons and Rebels*, she may have exaggerated the fortress-like aspect of Swinbrook and overlooked the laughter and genuine companionship that existed between herself, Unity and Deborah – whom she likened to 'ill-assorted animals tied to a common tethering post' – there is no doubt that life there for the three youngest Mitfords was more circumscribed than Asthall had been for the eldest four. A few months after Diana, who had always been her preferred older sister, left home to get married, twelve-year-old Jessica's determination to rebel took a tangible form and she opened a 'running-away' account at Drummond's Bank. In her memoirs, she recalled that by this time her social conscience had been awakened by newspaper accounts of the economic depression gripping Britain. She dated her interest in socialism to reading, at the age of fourteen, Beverley Nichols' pacifist novel, *Cry Havoc!*, and noted that it was she, not Unity, who first became interested in politics. Nichols' book was not in fact published until 1933, the year Jessica turned sixteen, by which time Unity had taken up fascism and the struggle between the two ideologies was already being played out on a wider stage than the Swinbrook schoolroom. But no matter which of them was the first to take up an extreme position, Unity and Jessica had, like many sisters, quarrelled relentlessly as children and their political disagreement was in many ways a continuation of earlier squabbles. Beneath their rivalry, however, was a deep and lasting affection which remained intact, even after they had embraced diametrically opposite sides in the conflict of the day.

After their disappointment at her birth – the Redesdales had been hoping for another boy – Deborah was the only one among the sisters never to cause her parents any heartache, and was probably their favourite daughter. She was a contented child with a loving nature, for whom the idea of school was anathema. She was happy so long as she was with the ponies, dogs, goats, guinea pigs and other animals that were as important to her as the human inhabitants of Swinbrook. While she possessed just as passionate and resolute a nature as her sisters, the key to Deborah's well-adjusted disposition was the ability to accept life as she found it. The youngest of a large family, she soon learnt, as she wrote in a memoir of her childhood, that 'as everything in life is unfair, perhaps the sooner it is realized the better', and unlike her politically engaged sisters she never felt the urge to go out and right the injustices of the world. Unencumbered by spite or malice, Deborah possessed a cheerfulness and buoyancy of spirits that never deserted her. As a small child, she worshipped Nancy and sought out her company, only to be teased or treated with amused condescension in return. Her staunchest ally against her eldest sister's persecution was Jessica; the two remained very close throughout childhood and adolescence, when they shared an easy, happy relationship, expressed through 'Honnish' jokes, songs and poems.

PAMELA to DIANA
24 July 1925

Asthall Manor
Burford
Oxfordshire

My dear Diana,

You must have had an awful time poor dear![1] Didn't it hurt most horribly? Anyway I am sure you will be very happy at Bexhill-on-Sea. We have just got the telegram to say that you got there alright, not that I quite see what could have happened to you unless it might have been a train accident. But it is the custom to send telegrams whenever one arrives safely anywhere.

Pat[2] has arrived, he came at tea time. Mary[3] came yesterday and so far no one else has arrived. I *do* so wish that you were here. You see I feel so stupid because every one invited Togo[4] to tea on Sunday to play tennis and Mary keeps telling everybody that she has asked him for me and that everybody is to fade away and leave us two together! If you were here you would of course also join in and I should not feel so young. However I shall have to get over feeling shy and this weekend is sure to help me in doing so. I should really much prefer to be at Bexhill with you.

We want to do some table turning one night but we are so afraid that Farve[5] might find us at it. That would be awful of course.

Much love from Pam

1 Diana had just had her tonsils out and was convalescing at the seaside.
2 Patrick Cameron; a dancing partner of Nancy and Pamela, and a frequent visitor at Asthall.
3 Mary Milnes-Gaskell; a friend of Nancy from schooldays. Married Lewis Motley in 1934.
4 Oliver (Togo) Watney (1908–65). Member of the brewing family and a country neighbour of the Mitfords. He was briefly engaged to Pamela in 1929. Married Christina Nelson in 1936.
5 David Mitford, 2nd Baron Redesdale (1878–1958). The sisters' father believed that Asthall was haunted by a poltergeist, which was one of the reasons he eventually sold the house and built Swinbrook.

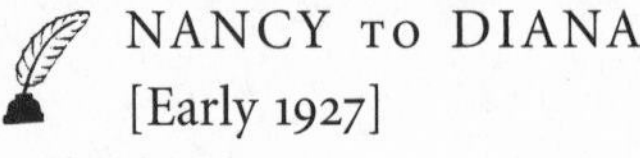

NANCY TO DIANA
[Early 1927]

Women's Union Society
University College
London WC1

Dearest Ling

Isn't this too grand?[1]

So awful, I *ought* to be drawing but the professor has been so beastly to me in a piercing voice, everyone heard & I rushed away to hide my shame in the writing room. Very soon I shall have to go back & face my brothers & sisters-in-art.

They are so awful to you, they come up & say What a *very* depressing drawing, I wonder how you manage to draw so foully, have you never had a pencil in your hand before. They burble on like this for about ½ an hr & everyone else cranes to catch each word. Luckily they are the same to all. I now burst into loud sobs the moment one comes into the room, hoping to soften them.

Very soon it will be lunch time & then I shall be seated between an Indian & a Fuzzy-Wuzzy[2] degluting sausage & mash oh what a treat. I'm learning Italian here now which I enjoy. In fact I love being here altogether, it's the greatest fun.

I hope you are in rude health & enjoy your matutinal cold bath.[3]

So awful, the head of the whole university had us all up the other day & said there is a lady thief among us. I tried not to look self conscious but I'm sure they suspect me. I now leave my old fur coat about everywhere, I long for the insurance money.

Love, Naunce

1 After much wrangling with her parents, Nancy had been allowed to enrol at the Slade School of Fine Art. She had little artistic talent, received small encouragement from her teachers and left after a few months.

2 University College London, of which the Slade is a part, was the first university in England to welcome students regardless of their race, class or religion.

3 Diana was in Paris learning French and staying in lodgings where the only bath was a shallow tin of water brought to her room twice a week.

JESSICA TO DIANA
[1927]

*[26 Rutland Gate
London SW7]*

Dear ould 'Al,

I expect you wonder why I haven't sent you that Toblerone? Well, you see, it is like this: I bought a 4/6d dove, in a 16/6d cage, which made £1 1s, and I only had £1, so I had to wait *two weeks without pocket-money!* and so forgot about the toberlerone. But as

perhaps you'll forgive me.

We have started an 'Industry Club' and we've got a Mag, called the 'Industries', and I pronounce it 'in*dust*ries' which annoys Boudle.[1] But I wondered if you'd like it whenever it comes out; and if you would please write and tell me, and I'll send you one.

Yours *fairly* affectionately, DYAKE

1 Unity in 'Boudledidge' (the first syllable pronounced as in 'loud'), the private language invented by Jessica and Unity. This was incomprehensible except to themselves and Deborah who, although she understood it, would never have dared venture on to her older sisters' territory and speak it.

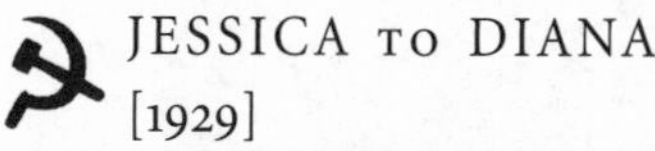

JESSICA TO DIANA
[1929]

*[Old Mill Cottage
High Wycombe
Buckinghamshire]*[1]

Darling Cortia,

Thank you *SO* much for that *marvellous* little satin bed-coat, it has been my one prideandjoy. Nurse and Nanny[2] simply love it, too, and actually let me wear it sometimes instead of keeping it up and hoarding it in drawers. I had my stitches out yesterday (one of which I enclose). There were five altogether. Debo has bought one for 6d,

I've sent one to B. Bamber, a school friend. I'm keeping my appendix in methylated spirits to leave to my children.[3]

I hope poor little Bryan[4] is better, give him my love & show him the enclosed stitch. He can have half of it.

Love from Decca

1 A weekend cottage that Lady Redesdale had rented before the First World War when the Mitfords were living in London. After the war, she bought it and the family lived in it during the Depression while Swinbrook was let.

2 Laura Dicks (1871–1959). The daughter of a Congregationalist blacksmith who went as nanny to the Mitfords soon after Diana's birth in 1910 and stayed until 1941. Known

'Blor', the Mitfords' much-loved nanny, Laura Dicks. *c.*1930.

as 'Blor' or 'M'Hinket', she provided a steady, loving presence during the sisters' childhood and was the model for the nanny in Nancy's novel *The Blessing* (1951).
3 In her memoirs, Jessica remembered selling her appendix to Deborah for £1 (£50 today) and that it was later disposed of by their nanny. *Hons and Rebels* (Victor Gollancz, 1960), p. 39.
4 Bryan Guinness, 2nd Baron Moyne (1905–92). Diana had finally overcome parental opposition and became engaged to Bryan in November 1928. He trained to be a barrister but left the Bar in 1931 when he realized that his wealth was preventing him from being given briefs. His first novel, *Singing Out of Tune*, was published in 1933, followed by further volumes of poetry, novels and plays. Married to Diana 1929–34, and to Elisabeth Nelson in 1936.

NANCY TO PAMELA
[May 1929]

Castle Grant
Grantown
Strathspey

Darling Pam

Oh I am so sorry how beastly for you poor darling.[1] Never mind I expect you'll be rewarded by marrying someone millions of times nicer & obviously Togo would have been a *horrid* husband. Are you going to Canada? I hope so, that would be lovely for you.[2]

Best love & don't be too miserable, I am, dreadfully, about it but one must make the best of things.

Heaps of love, Naunce

1 Pamela's engagement to Oliver Watney had been broken off shortly before they were to be married. Pamela was not in love, and Togo was tubercular and probably impotent, but it was a disappointment nevertheless.
2 To help her get over her broken engagement, Pamela accompanied her parents on one of their regular visits to prospect for gold in Canada where Lord Redesdale hoped, in vain, to restore the family fortune.

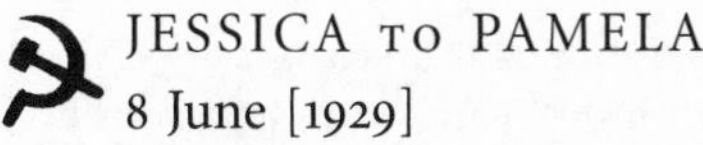

JESSICA TO PAMELA
8 June [1929]

Old Mill Cottage
High Wycombe

Darling Pam,

Thank you so much for the letter. I am so glad you did not feel sick on the ship. The parrot is very well, and is often let out in the garden. We are going to stay with Diana[1] at Littlehampton a week yesterday, and will probably be there when you get this letter. Nancy is staying in London with a person called Evelyn,[2] and they will do all their own housework like you and Muv.[3]

Love from Jessica

1 Diana and Bryan had been lent Pool Place, a seaside house in Sussex belonging to Lord Moyne.
2 Evelyn Gardner (1903–94). Married to Evelyn Waugh in 1928. Nancy's spell as her guest was short-lived; soon after her arrival the two Evelyns separated and later divorced.
3 Sydney Bowles (1880–1963). While they were prospecting for gold, Lady Redesdale and her husband lived in a simple cabin where she did the cooking and cleaning.

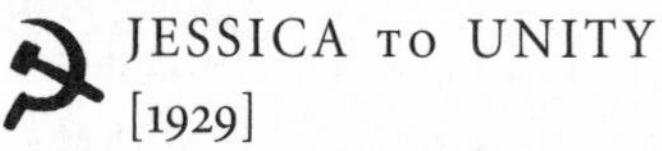

JESSICA TO UNITY
[1929]

Langley House
118 Lansdowne Place
Hove, Sussex

Dee Droudled Boudle,

It is rather fun here, but it is a bore having to miss ½ term in London. Debo has been rather cross part of the time. Day before yesterday at lunch she told the maid she wanted 'a *very* little ham', and she was furious with Nanny for saying afterwards she wanted 'a very, very little ham'. She said 'What's the use of my saying I want a very little ham if you go and say I want a very, very little ham?'[1]

Yesterday morning, too, she wanted to go out directly after breakfast, but poor Nanny had to go to the lavatory, and Debo was furious again, and said 'When Muv was here we didn't have to do all this silly going to the lavatory'. Nanny said very crossly 'I shall go to the lavatory when I want to'.

Love from DECCA Je Boudle

I swear it's quite true about the ham & lavatory, don't believe Debo.

1 Lady Redesdale, whose father brought her up according the dietary laws of Moses because he believed they were healthy, forbade her own children to eat rabbit, shellfish or pig. 'No doubt very wise in the climate of Israel before refrigeration, but hardly necessary in Oxfordshire,' Deborah wrote in a childhood memoir, *Counting My Chickens* (Long Barn Books, 2001), pp. 168–9.

Pamela with Lord and Lady Redesdale at 'the shack', prospecting for gold in Swastika, Ontario. 1929.

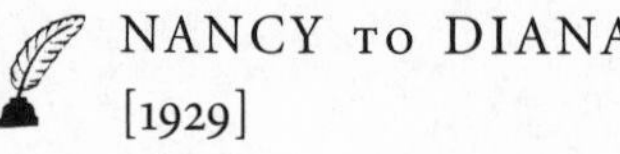

NANCY TO DIANA
[1929]

10 Buckingham Street[1]
London SW1

Darling Bods

After 2 hrs solid of thinking I have at last analysed my feelings.

I *am* in love with H[2] but as you know the one thing in the world I admire is intellect so I am in the position of someone who is out to marry money & falls in love with a poor man.

I think this is quite the true state of my mind & sounds more sane than my rather hysterical conversation this evening. So frightfully tired.

Love, N

1 Diana and Bryan's London house.
2 James Alexander (Hamish) St Clair-Erskine (1909–73). Nancy's unhappy relationship with the flighty, homosexual son of the Earl of Rosslyn was in its second year and although she considered him her fiancé, they were never officially engaged.

JESSICA TO NANCY AND DIANA
16 January 1930 [postmark]

[Pontresina
Switzerland][1]

Dear Nancy & Corbish,

Last night I went to a party & danced with M. Chaliapine.[2] He *IS* so sweet he jumped about with me and hummed in a sweet voice to the band. I have struck up an acquaintance with his two daughters at the Pontresina Hotel. They are good and nyang [sweet] – aged 8 and 17. It is snowing and a blizerd today.

Love from Decca

1 All the sisters except Nancy and Diana were on a winter holiday with their parents. The Redesdales were both keen skaters and used to take the family to the Oxford ice rink every Sunday. It was once suggested that Deborah should train for the British skating team, a proposal that Lady Redesdale immediately rejected.
2 Feodor Chaliapin (1873–1938). The great Russian operatic bass had left the Soviet Union in 1921 and was based in Paris.

Deborah, Tom, Pamela, Unity, Jessica and 'Muv', in one of the rare photographs of Lady Redesdale smiling. Pontresina, 1930.

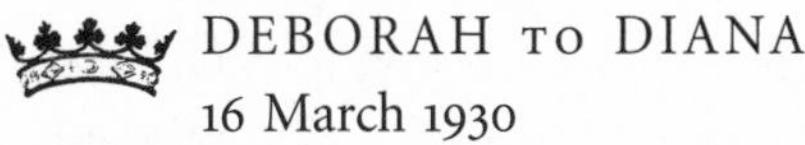

DEBOROAH TO DIANA
16 March 1930

Old Mill Cottage
High Wycombe

Darling Honkite

We were so excited when Nan woke us up at six o'clock to tell us about Baby G.[1] What is his name? We are coming up to see him as soon as nurse lets us. Won't it be fun? There isn't much more to say except to heartily congratulate you!

Much love (and to the baby) from Debo

1 Jonathan (Jonnycan) Guinness, 3rd Baron Moyne (1930–). Diana's eldest son became a writer and banker. Author, with his daughter Catherine, of *The House of Mitford* (1984), a history of three generations of the family. Married to Ingrid Wyndham 1951–63, and to Suzanne Lisney in 1964.

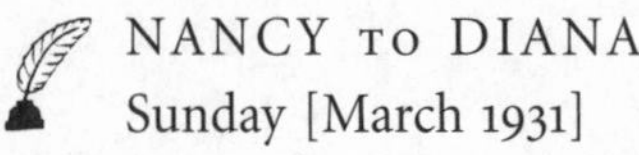

NANCY to DIANA
Sunday [March 1931]

[Swinbrook House
Burford
Oxfordshire]

Darling Bodley[1]

Oh I am having such an awful time. First poor little Decca who happily does seem to be more or less all right.[2] Now today a huge picture of me in the *Sunday Dispatch* saying that my book[3] is dedicated to Hamish who I'm engaged to. And there is the most appalling row going on. Muv & Farve spent the whole morning telling me that my friends are all drunkards, that I'm ruining my health & my character, hinting that I have taken to drink myself. I simply don't know what to do. They say if I go to London this summer it will be the end of me & I've practically promised not to go.

Then dear Uncle George,[4] to whom I sent an advance copy, has written to Muv saying it's awfully indecent but he hopes it will sell & I gather Aunt Iris[5] wrote in the same vein. Farve says it is killing Muv by inches.

Why did I dedicate the beastly book at all, as I said to Muv *other* people can dedicate books without this sort of thing happening but she & Farve appear to think I did it to annoy them. Then they say that as I'm nearly thirty I ought to stop going out at all. Why? And what should I do if I did stop. I can't make out what they really want me to do. Live permanently in the country I suppose.

Oh dear I do feel miserable.

Best love, N

1 When she was a baby, Diana's head was thought to be too big for her body and was nicknamed 'The Bodley Head' by Nancy, after the publishing company of that name.
2 There is no record of what was wrong with Jessica.
3 Nancy's first novel, *Highland Fling* (1931).
4 George Bowles (1877–1955). Lady Redesdale's elder brother was manager of *The Lady*, the family magazine to which Nancy contributed her first articles. Married 1902–21 to Joan Penn and to Madeleine Tobin in 1922.
5 Iris Mitford (1879–1966). Lord Redesdale's younger sister was the archetypal maiden aunt, loved by all but very censorious. General Secretary of the Officers' Families' Fund, she devoted her life to charitable works.

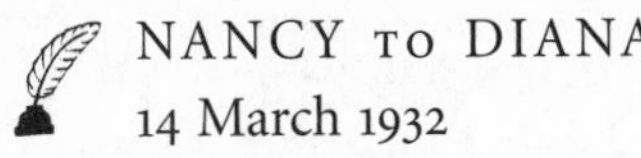

NANCY TO DIANA
14 March 1932

Swinbrook House
Burford

Darling Bodley

I am so unhappy for you on account of this terrible tragedy.[1]

I can't help thinking that for her it must have been best, as she didn't do it on an impulse *when* he died it shows she must have considered it & decided that life without him was & always would be intolerable. But for you & all her friends it is a terrible loss, I am so so sorry darling.

Please give my love & sympathy to Bryan.

V. best love, Naunce

1 Dora Carrington (1893–1932). The Bloomsbury painter, a friend and neighbour of Diana at Biddesden, had shot herself with a gun that Bryan had lent her to hunt rabbits. Two months previously, Lytton Strachey, the love of Dora's life, had died aged fifty-one.

UNITY TO DIANA
Friday [May 1932]

31 Tite Street
London SW3

Darling Nard

I thought I would just write & tell you that I went to court last night & enjoyed it very much, though when I came into the PRESENCE my heart failed me & I was almost too nervous to curtsy, though I managed to in the end.[1] *Everyone* admired my dress, and it really is too *lovely*, how can I ever thank you enough, I shall never wear anything else at dances now. I was entirely dressed by you – dress, bag, fur coat, & bracelet. It was great fun waiting in the Mall, we waited about two hours. I shouldn't have enjoyed it *nearly* as much if I hadn't had such a lovely dress.

Please give my love to Bryan & Tom.[2]

Best love from Bobo

1 The London Season opened with a ball at Buckingham Palace at which debutantes were presented to the King and Queen. Unity would have been required to walk up to the royal couple, curtsey twice and retreat backwards gracefully.

2 Thomas (Tom) Mitford (1909–45). The sisters' only brother, nicknamed 'Tud' or 'Tuddemy' (to rhyme with 'adultery' because of the success his sisters believed he had with married women), was studying to be a barrister in London.

Unity, 'a huge and rather alarming debutante', dressed for presentation at court, 1932.

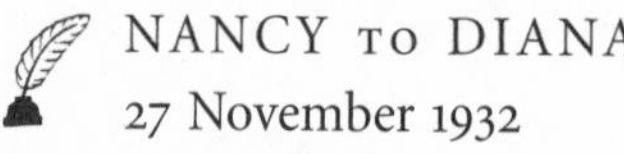

NANCY to DIANA
27 November 1932

Swinbrook House
Burford

My Darling Bodley

Thank you for the lovely week I had, I enjoyed myself to the full.

Mitty[1] & I spent the whole of yesterday afternoon discussing your affairs[2] & are having another session in a minute! He is horrified, & says that your social position will be *nil* if you do this. Darling I do hope you are making a right decision. You are SO young to begin getting in wrong with the world, if that's what is going to happen.

However it is all your own affair & whatever happens *I* shall always be on your side as you know & so will anybody who cares for you & perhaps the rest really don't matter.

With all my best love, Nance

1 Tom Mitford.
2 Diana had told her family that she was planning to leave Bryan.

DIANA TO NANCY

[November 1932]

Biddesden House
Andover
Hants

Darling Naunce

You are divine to me, I don't know what I would do without you.

I have read your book[1] and it is simply heavenly and beautifully written and I read a lot of it to the Leader[2] and we laughed so much we couldn't go on reading.

Bryan has now arrived and is in a state of airy bliss and longing for me to start work on his flat.[3] He is in a magnanimous mood and I told him about the stock of country shoes and crepe de chine[4] I am laying in and he was all for it. He says I can have the pick of Cheyne Walk furniture and in return I am giving him two or three pictures. The future appears to me to be roseate specially now he is so gay and bright.

I ought to get you a diamond necklace – last chance!

All love, Diana

1 Nancy's second novel, *Christmas Pudding* (1932).
2 Sir Oswald Mosley (1896–1980). Diana's affair with the leader of the British Union of Fascists (BUF) had begun earlier in the year. Mosley was married to Lady Cynthia Curzon 1920–33 and to Diana in 1936.
3 Bryan was so distraught by the break-up of his marriage that he could not face the resulting upheaval in domestic arrangements. He asked Diana to pack up their London house in Cheyne Walk and find him a flat.
4 Diana had joked to Nancy that she was going to stock up on 'a trousseau' of expensive clothes while she could still afford them.

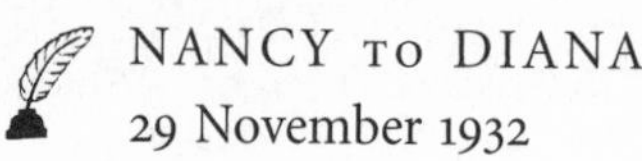

NANCY TO DIANA
29 November 1932

Swinbrook House
Burford

Darling Bodley

Oh I feel as if I were sitting on a volcano (thank you, by the way, a million times for the life saving gift of £5 THE LAST). You know, back in the sane or insane atmosphere of Swinbrook I feel convinced that you won't be allowed to take this step. I mean that Muv & Farve & Tom, Randolph,[1] Doris,[2] Aunt Iris, John,[3] Lord Moyne[4] & in fact everybody that you know will band together & somehow stop it. How, I don't attempt to say.

Oh dear I believe you have a much worse time in store for you than you imagine. I'm sorry to be so gloomy darling.

I *am* glad you like the book, so do Robert[5] & Niggy,[6] it is a great comfort. But so far there's not been *one* single review – is this rather sinister? I think I had quite a lot in the first week of *H. Fling*.

Mitty says £2,000 a year will seem tiny to you & he will urge Farve, as your trustee, to stand out for more.

Do let me know developments, I think it better in every way that I should stay here at present but if you want me at Cheyne Walk I'll come of course. Only I think I can do more good down here. I wish I felt certain it *was* doing good though, it would be so awful later to feel that I had been, even in a tiny way, instrumental in messing up your life. I wish one had a definite table of ethics, for oneself & others like very religious people have, it would make everything easier.

Much love always darling, Naunce

1 Randolph Churchill (1911–68). Winston Churchill's only son was related to the Mitfords through his mother, Clementine. He was a great friend of Tom and had a crush on Diana as a teenager. In 1932, he began his journalistic career covering the German elections for the *Sunday Graphic*. Married to Pamela Digby 1939–46 and to June Osborne 1948–61.

2 Doris Delavigne (1900–42). Beautiful, uninhibited daughter of a Belgian father and English mother. Married the gossip columnist Viscount Castlerosse in 1928.

3 John Sutro (1904–85). Talented mimic, musician and film producer from a well-off Jewish London family. A lifelong friend of Nancy and Diana, he was best man at Nancy's wedding and Jonathan Guinness's godfather. Married Gillian Hammond in 1940.

4 Walter Guinness, 1st Baron Moyne (1880–1944). Diana's father-in-law, a distinguished soldier and politician, was assassinated in Cairo by members of the Stern gang, a Jewish terrorist group.
5 Robert Byron (1905–41). Travel writer whose best-known book, *The Road to Oxiana* (1937), was a record of his journeys through Iran and Afghanistan. Nancy counted him as one of her dearest friends and mourned him for many years after his death at sea.
6 Nigel Birch (1906–81). A tart and witty friend of Tom who became a Conservative MP after the war. Married Esmé Glyn in 1950.

DIANA TO NANCY
25 December 1932

96 Cheyne Walk
London SW3

Darling Naunce

The detectives are *extraordinary* and just like one would imagine.[1] It is really rather heavenly to feel that they are around – no pick-pockets can approach etc. Isn't it all *extremely* amusing in a way. I mean there is such a great army of them and it is all so expensive for Lord Moyne (may he burn in hell).

I have shirked the Grosvenor Place party[2] because I was advised it would be better not to go. They *ALL* cried when I wouldn't & I gave as an excuse 'Grosvenor Place is such a big house to surround so thought it more friendly to save half a dozen men & stay at home'.

Darling you are my one ally. But it is vastly lying to suggest you encouraged my sot [foolish] behaviour;[3] you *always* said it would end in TEARS.

Do come here soon. I am not hurrying to leave because if Bryan leaves *ME* the onus is on *HIM* and so he will.

All love darling, Diana

1 Diana's father-in-law had hired private investigators to gather evidence that could be used in the divorce hearing.
2 A Christmas party at the Moynes' London house.
3 The Redesdales and Tom blamed Nancy for supporting Diana's decision to leave Bryan.

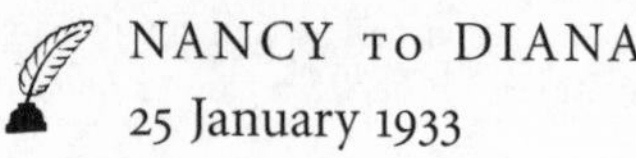

NANCY TO DIANA

25 January 1933

96 Cheyne Walk, SW3

Darling,

At last a moment to write you – & now my fingers are too cold to hold the pen! Oh the cold is awful, luckily the 'tectives have made themselves an awfully cosy little wigwam outside with a brazier & are keeping themselves warm & happy taking up the road. Bless them.

Saw Bryan yesterday, he was pretty spiky I thought, keeps saying of course I suppose it's my *duty* to take her back & balls of that sort. Henry Yorke[1] told him you had gone to Mürren with Cela.[2] Would I either confirm or deny? I said I thought it very doubtful if Henry knew anything about it & that I would forward a letter to you if B cared to write one.

I may say that the Lambs[3] seem to have turned nasty, apparently they told B they were nearly certain you had an affair with Randolph [Churchill] in the spring.

Lunched with Dolly [Castlerosse] & Delly.[4] Delly said I don't mind people going off & fucking but I do object to all this free love. She is heaven isn't she?

I had a long talk with Mrs Mac[5] who refuses to stay with Bryan. She says you are the one she is fond of. I told her it would mean no kitchen maid but she doesn't seem to mind that idea at all. You must see her as soon as you get back. B & Miss Moore[6] both told her (a) you couldn't afford her & (b) you wouldn't be entertaining at all, but living in a very very quiet retirement.

Rather wonderful old ladies in fact.[7]

John [Sutro] had a long talk to the Leader & is now won over. Next tease for John, 'Why even Mosley can talk you round in half an hour'.

Best love darling, Nancy

1 Henry Yorke (1905–73). Author, under the pseudonym Henry Green, of nine highly original novels, including *Blindness* (1926), *Living* (1929) and *Doting* (1952). Married Adelaide (Dig) Biddulph in 1929.

2 Lady Cecilia Keppel (1910–2003). A childhood friend of Diana. The Redesdales had asked her to invite their daughter to Switzerland in the hopes that removing her from Mosley would make her change her mind.

3 Henry Lamb (1883–1960). A founder member of the Camden Town Group who had

Diana *(right)* with her childhood friend Cecilia Keppel in Mürren, Switzerland, 1933.

painted a portrait of Diana the previous year. Married, in 1928, to Lady Pansy Pakenham (1904–99).

4 Adele Astaire (1897–1981). Older sister and original dance partner of Fred Astaire with whom she starred on stage until 1932, when she married Lord Charles Cavendish, second son of the 9th Duke of Devonshire and uncle of Deborah's future husband.

5 The cook at Biddesden.

6 Bryan Guinness's secretary.

7 At about this time Nancy wrote a privately circulated short story, *The Old Ladies*, loosely based on herself and Diana. The two old ladies lived in Eaton Square and had a friend, the Old Gentleman, who was based on Mark Ogilvie-Grant.

TWO

1933–1939

HOTEL KAISERHOF BERLIN

BERLIN W 8 24th Oct. 1935

Darling Nard,

Thank you for your letter, which came this morning.

Oh dear, I have been telling everybody, including the Führer and Ribbentrop, that the Leader is standing in the election. And now he isn't. They will think I am stupid not to know.

I will tell you about our Berlin visit. It has all been quite dull except for yesterday. We dine every night in Haus Vaterland, which I only knew about because you had told me about it, we are very grateful to you, the food is delicious & altogether the Lokal

Letter from Unity to Diana.

By mid-1933, to all appearances, the three eldest Mitford sisters were settling down. At almost thirty, Nancy had at last reached the end of her affair with Hamish and was engaged to Peter Rodd, a clever, handsome banker, son of the diplomat Lord Rennell, who seemed on the surface a far better prospective husband than Hamish. Pamela was living in a cottage at Biddesden and managing the Guinness farm. Diana's affair with Oswald Mosley was still regarded with disapproval by her parents, but her divorce from Bryan and the sudden death of Mosley's wife had weakened the Redesdales' opposition. The three youngest Mitfords were giving no outward cause for worry. Unity had become a keen member of the British Union of Fascists but this had been kept secret from her parents and they had no reason to suspect her growing fanaticism. Jessica, who was going to Paris for a year to learn French, was about to have her first taste of longed-for freedom. Thirteen-year-old Deborah was content in the Swinbrook schoolroom.

But beneath the deceptively calm surface, personal choices and political events combined to make the years leading up to the war a period of turmoil in the sisters' lives. Nancy had accepted Peter's proposal of marriage on the rebound, just a week after Hamish, desperate to extricate himself from their sham engagement, had pretended to be engaged to another woman. Peter, or 'Prod' as he soon became known in the family, was no more in love with Nancy than Hamish had been, but, like her, he was nearing thirty and was under pressure from his parents to marry. Peter's career before meeting Nancy was as inglorious as his record after their marriage: he had been sent down from Oxford and was then sacked or had resigned from a succession of jobs, mostly found for him by his father. He was not only a drinker and a spendthrift, but pedantic and arrogant to boot. For Nancy, however, his proposal came as balm after the humiliation of being jilted by Hamish and she remained blind to his shortcomings. They were married at the end of 1933 and settled in Rose Cottage, a small house near Chiswick, where Nancy, in love with being in love, played for a while at being happy, writing to a friend, with no apparent irony, that she had found 'a feeling of shelter & security hitherto untasted'. Since Pamela's engagement to Oliver Watney had been called off, Nancy was now the only married Mitford – a not unimportant consideration as the eldest daughter. It was not long, however, before her determination to be amused by Peter's inadequacies began to falter and her ability to overlook his unfaithfulness, neglect and over-spending was severely tested. In 1936, they moved into London, to Blomfield Road in Maida Vale, which suited Nancy because it brought her closer to her friends. But with no children – she suffered a miscarriage in 1938 – her marriage was increasingly unhappy.

Nancy could never take politics very seriously. Peter had left-wing leanings and she too became a socialist for a while, 'synthetic cochineal' according to Diana. When they returned from their honeymoon Peter and Nancy went to several BUF rallies, bought black shirts and subscribed to the movement for a few months. In June 1934 they even attended Mosley's huge meeting at Olympia, which must have led Diana to hope that another sister was being won round to the cause. But Nancy was beginning to find Unity and Diana's fanaticism distasteful. It was not just their political opinions that she disliked, she also deplored the seriousness with which they defended them. The posturing and self-importance that accompanied extremism went against her philosophy that nothing in life should be taken too seriously. Characteristically, she responded with mockery and wrote *Wigs on the Green*, a novel that satirized Mosley, fascism and Unity's blind enthusiasm. Its publication in 1935 angered Diana: Mosley and his movement were one area where jokes were unacceptable and she regarded any attack on him as an act of betrayal. She broke off relations with Nancy and the two sisters hardly saw or wrote to each other until the outbreak of war four years later. Unity also threatened never to speak to Nancy again if she went ahead with publication but failed to put her threat into action. Nancy's letters to Unity, written in the same mocking tone that she used in her novel, betrayed an underlying affection for her wayward younger sister in spite of her aversion to her politics.

Pamela ran the Biddesden dairy farm until the end of 1934. After her broken engagement she had many suitors but formed no deep emotional attachments. John Betjeman, the future poet laureate, proposed to her twice but, although fond of him, she was not in love and turned him down. Her hobby was motoring; she was a tireless driver and made several visits to the Continent in her open-topped car, travelling as far as the Carpathians in Eastern Europe. In 1935, Derek Jackson, a brilliant physicist with a passion for horses, who worked at the Clarendon Laboratory in Oxford and hunted with the Heythrop hounds in the Cotswolds, began to court her. He had known the Mitfords for some years and, according to Diana, was in love with most of them, including Tom. Pamela was the sister most readily available and he proposed to her. Fifteen-year-old Deborah, who had a crush on Derek, fainted when she heard the news. Pamela and Derek were married at the end of 1936 and set off for Vienna for their honeymoon. On arrival, they were greeted with the news that Derek's identical twin, Vivian, also a gifted physicist, had been killed in a sleigh-riding accident. Part of Derek died with his brother, who meant more to him than anyone – including Pamela – ever could. Derek's speciality, spectroscopy, the study of electromagnetic radiation, was, unsurprisingly, a closed book to Pamela and she did not share his interest in painting and literature. Their joint passion was for their four long-haired dachshunds and the dogs may have gone some way towards making up for the children Derek did not want and which Pamela never had. Derek had inherited a large fortune from shares in the *News of the World* and was a generous man. They settled at Rignell House, not far from Swinbrook, where Pamela's housekeeping talents made them very comfortable. Pamela's few letters that survive from this period are written to Jessica, after Jessica's elopement with Esmond Romilly, and to Diana to thank her for visits to Wootton Lodge, the house in Staffordshire that the Mosleys rented between 1936 and 1939. Derek got on well with Mosley and shared many of his political opinions. Nancy attended Pamela's wedding but saw little of her until after the war; she did not like Derek and he in turn resented her treatment of Pamela.

In May 1933, Mosley's 34-year-old wife, Cynthia, died from peritonitis, a month before Diana was granted a divorce from Bryan. Diana records that both she and Mosley were shattered by Cimmie's unexpected death. Mosley threw himself into building up the BUF, which was growing increasingly militaristic and disreputable in the eyes of the general public, and embarked on an affair with Alexandra (Baba), Metcalfe, his wife's younger sister. That summer, while the man for whom she had sacrificed so much was on holiday with another woman, Diana received an invitation to visit Germany from Putzi Hanfstaengl, Hitler's Foreign Press Secretary, whom she met at a party in London. The British press had been criticizing the Nazis' attacks on the Jews, and the BUF's anti-Semitic stance was bringing it into conflict with British Jewry. When Diana questioned Hanfstaengl about the German regime's attitude to Jews, he issued a challenge: 'You must see with your own eyes what lies are being told about us in your newspapers'. In August, while her two sons – Jonathan was now three and a half and Desmond nearly two – were spending the holidays with Bryan, Diana left for Germany, taking with her nineteen-year-old Unity whose allegiance to Mosley made her a natural ally. Hitler had been elected Chancellor at the beginning of the year and the sisters' arrival coincided with the annual Nuremberg Party Congress, a four-day celebration of the Nazis' accession to power. The gigantic parades impressed Diana and demonstrated that fascism could restore a country's faith in itself. Although Hanfstaengl's promise of an introduction to Hitler did not materialize on this visit, she saw that links with Germany could be useful for furthering the interests of Mosley, whose career and welfare had now become the centre of her existence. At the end of 1934, with Mosley's encouragement, she returned to Munich for a few weeks to learn German.

Unity had been in Germany since the spring of that year. She too had been enthralled by the Parteitag parades and her burning ambition was now to meet Hitler, whom she considered 'the greatest man of all time'. Confident that she would succeed, she persuaded the Redesdales to allow her to live in Munich, where she set herself to learn German so as to be able to understand the Führer when they eventually met. From then until the outbreak of war, Unity lived mostly in Germany. Heedless of the inhumanity of the regime, she embraced the Nazi creed unquestioningly and let it take over her life. Hitler became her god and National Socialism, as she wrote exultantly to a cousin, 'my religion, not merely my political party'. When she discovered that the Führer often lunched informally at the Osteria Bavaria, a small local restaurant, she started going there daily, sitting at a table where he could see her, and waited to be noticed. In February 1935, her patience was rewarded when Hitler invited her over to his table, spoke to her for half an hour and paid for her lunch. Over the next five years she was to see him more than a hundred times. She was rarely alone with him and, in spite of what has often been speculated, there was no love affair. Just to be in her idol's orbit was sufficiently intoxicating and gave Unity a sense of importance which led her to imagine that she had a role to play in Anglo-German relations.

Unity spent her first months in Munich lodging with Baroness Laroche, an elderly lady who ran a finishing school for young English girls; she then lodged in a students' hostel and a succession of flats before moving, in June 1939, into accommodation in Agnesstrasse found for her by Hitler and belonging, she wrote insouciantly to Diana, 'to a young Jewish couple who are going abroad'. All the other members of the Mitford family, except Nancy, eventually made their way out to Germany. The Redesdales, who had initially disapproved of Nazism, were eventually won round to Unity's point of view – permanently so in the case of Lady Redesdale.

Diana also met Hitler for the first time in the spring of 1935 and she remained loyal to their friendship for the rest of her life. In her view, the Second World War and its horrific consequences could have been avoided. Of all the sisters, the contradictions in Diana's character are perhaps the most difficult to reconcile. The latent anti-Semitism and racism of pre-war Britain, assumptions that she never questioned, were at odds with her innately empathetic nature. Her admiration for a barbaric regime, whose essential characteristic was dehumanizing its opponents, jarred with the qualities of generosity and tolerance that led her family and many friends to cherish her. Endowed with originality and intelligence, and priding herself on intellectual honesty, she never acknowledged the reality of Hitler's criminal aims. While her pre-war sympathy with Nazism can be accounted for by her witnessing the economic transformation of Germany under National Socialism, Diana's post-war defence of Hitler can be mainly explained by her devotion and undeviating commitment to her husband. Mosley's links with the Nazis and his opposition to the war brought his political career to an end and led to his and Diana's imprisonment for three and a half years – years of social ostracism and public vilification during which they were separated from their young children. Diana, who possessed all the Mitford obduracy, sacrificed so much for Mosley that forever afterwards she had to go on defending his cause or admit that the losses and privations she had suffered were for no purpose.

Diana made several visits to Germany before the war and in 1936 she and Mosley were secretly married in the Berlin house of Nazi leader Joseph Goebbels, with Hitler as a guest. Ostensibly the secrecy was to protect Mosley's political image but the main purpose was to keep the press from discovering the reasons for Diana's frequent trips to Germany. The British Union of Fascists was in urgent need of funds and, with the help of a member, Bill Allen, who was an advertising magnate, Mosley had developed a scheme to set up a commercial radio station on German soil from which to broadcast to southern England. (No advertising was allowed on British wireless at the time and companies had no means of promoting their goods on the airwave.) Diana's friendship with Hitler and other Nazi officials placed her in an ideal position to negotiate a deal, but it was essential that the connection between the proposed radio station and Mosley was not made public since the BUF's unpopularity would almost certainly have led advertisers to boycott the project. It also suited Mosley to keep his marriage secret because he was still carrying on an affair with his sister-in-law. At the end of 1938, Diana successfully obtained Hitler's agreement to the project and the station would have started broadcasting the following year had war not put an end to the venture. The birth of the Mosleys' first son, Alexander, in November 1938, coincided with the signing of the contract and precipitated public disclosure of their marriage.

Diana's closest confidante in the family during this period was Unity and they wrote to each other regularly during the pre-war years. Their correspondence, especially Unity's, forms the bulk of surviving letters from the late 1930s. Incongruously written in the gushing tones of breathless excitement normally reserved for romantic fiction, the two sisters' letters about Nazi Germany unavoidably dominate this section.

In the autumn of 1933, sixteen-year-old Jessica and her first cousin Ann Farrer travelled to Paris. Here they attended classes at the Sorbonne and lived with a Madame Paulain who was conveniently lax about chaperoning her charges and allowed the girls to slip out unobserved to nightclubs and the Folies-Bergère. In letters to her mother Jessica was careful not to mention these escapades but she did describe the riots that broke out in Paris following the sacking of the city's right-wing police chief. She quoted from the communist daily, *l'Humanité*, as well as from the *Daily Mail*, and expressed regret that her *quartier* had been much too quiet during the unrest. On returning to England, she endured a season as a debutante, a custom that went against her progressive principles but which she confessed to have been 'rather guiltily looking forward to'. In 1935, Jessica read two more books that influenced her deeply: *The Brown Book of the Hitler Terror*, published in 1933, which detailed the horrors perpetrated after the burning of the Reichstag when communist and other opponents of the Nazis were rounded up, savagely beaten and in some cases murdered; and *Out of Bounds: The Education of Giles and Esmond Romilly*, written by two rebellious young cousins of the Mitfords. The Romilly brothers were the sons of Clementine Churchill's sister, Nellie, and nephews by marriage, therefore, of Winston Churchill. Esmond's contribution to *Out of Bounds* enthralled Jessica because his attitudes and opinions were so similar to her own. As a schoolboy at Wellington College, Esmond had interrupted Armistice Day commemorations by distributing anti-war leaflets, started a subversive magazine attacking public schools and, aged sixteen, had run away to work in a left-wing London bookshop. Jessica had followed his exploits – the subject of scandalized family gossip – for several years and hero-worshipped her cousin from afar, judging her own revolt against parental authority trivial by comparison.

In early 1937, Jessica and Esmond met by chance at the house of a cousin. Esmond had recently come back from Spain, where he had been fighting with the International Brigades and where he was planning to return as correspondent for the *News Chronicle*. For nineteen-year-old Jessica, this was the chance to translate her romantic idealism into reality and she begged Esmond to take her with him. They improvised a plan to trick the Redesdales into believing that Jessica was on holiday with friends, drew the money out of her 'running-away' account and disappeared to Spain. It was two weeks before their ruse was discovered. Nancy and Peter, to whom it was thought Jessica would be most likely to listen, went out to try to persuade her to come home but the attempt ended in a bitter row. Jessica had made up her mind and she and Esmond were married in Bayonne on 18 May, with Lady Redesdale in attendance. If there was any residual element of playfulness about Jessica's politics – Nancy used teasingly to call her a 'ballroom communist' – it was eradicated by her marriage to Esmond, which also marked the beginning of a hardening in her feelings towards her family. Esmond was not amused by Unity's friendship with the 'sweet' Führer, and although Diana had sided with Jessica over her elopement, Esmond's hatred of fascism was unconditional.

Jessica's break with Diana was final and, except in 1973 when Nancy was dying, they did not meet or correspond after 1937. Whenever Unity was in England, however, Jessica would arrange to see her – without Esmond's knowledge – and although few of their letters from the period have survived, they continued to write to each other up to, and after, the war. That Jessica never broke with Unity as she had done with Diana – Nazism, after all, was no less abhorrent to her than fascism – highlights the complexity of the relations between the sisters. In a letter to her mother, Jessica wrote that she considered Diana a dangerous enemy and the fact that she 'was once related' to her made no difference to her feelings, yet in the very same letter she sent her love to Unity. In Unity's last letter to her parents before she tried to kill herself, she sent 'particular love' to Jessica. Perhaps the close ties Jessica and Unity had formed as children were too strong to break, or perhaps Unity's childishly boastful behaviour masked her sincerity of purpose and meant that Jessica could never take her seriously. Or did Jessica recognize in Unity a fellow zealot whom she could respect, even though they were at opposite ends of the political spectrum? Whatever the reasons, Unity's espousal of Nazism remained an unsolvable riddle to her sister. 'Why had she', Jessica mused, 'to those of us who knew her the most human of people, turned her back on humanity?'

In February 1939, Jessica and Esmond left for the United States. They had expected a storm of indignation to greet Chamberlain's signing of the Munich Agreement, which handed over part of Czechoslovakia to Germany, and when it did not materialize the spectre of a completely Nazified Europe no longer seemed remote. Esmond looked to America for a new adventure, somewhere to explore while waiting to see whether Britain would fight. Money difficulties also contributed to their decision to leave the country: they had run up debts on their London flat and were being hounded by bailiffs. When Jessica came into a trust fund of £100 on her twenty-first birthday, rather than pay the bills they decided to spend it on one-way tickets to New York.

For Deborah, alone among the sisters, the sale of Swinbrook in 1936 was a lasting sorrow and spelt an end to what she regarded as an idyllic childhood. Lord Redesdale's fortunes had not recovered from the Depression and he could no longer meet the cost of maintaining a large house and estate. Although Lady Redesdale had grown fond of the village and enjoyed living in the country, she went along with her husband's decision. They moved to the Old Mill Cottage on the outskirts of High Wycombe, some thirty miles from London, taking with them Jessica and Deborah, the only two sisters still at home. The picture in the public mind of the Mitfords' childhood is largely formed by Jessica's first volume of memoirs, *Hons and Rebels*, and by Nancy's novels. Both Jessica and Nancy remembered their childhood essentially as a period of unhappiness and discontent, and their parents as cold and unloving. Deborah had a much easier time than her older sisters; she found Lady Redesdale no stricter than other mothers and was fond of her father. The shock waves sent out by the escapades of her older siblings reached her as distant disturbances and were not sufficient to undermine the security of her well-ordered life, in which lessons with a succession of governesses alternated with long hours in the stable and on the hunting field. There was also a single term at The Monkey Club, a London finishing school from which Lady Redesdale quickly removed her when Deborah told her that it was full of communists. Jessica's elopement, however, came as a complete surprise and, following closely after the sale of Swinbrook, shook her profoundly. It was a betrayal of the complicity she thought she shared with her beloved childhood companion and it brought an end to their intimacy. Jessica, who envied Deborah's beauty and her position as their parents' favourite, never realized how much she had meant to her youngest sister or understood how deeply her disappearance had upset her. To add to Deborah's distress, the Redesdales forbade her to go to Jessica's wedding and would not allow her to visit the Romillys when they returned to England. Although Deborah managed to see her sister a few times in secret, the visits were not a success. She did not get on with Esmond, did not like his communist friends, and found being in their company a 'lowering experience'.

Deborah's adolescent letters show that she could be quite as sharp and funny as Nancy but without her eldest sister's spiteful streak. She adopted an apolitical stance early on, partly because she had seen the damage that extremism had inflicted on her family and partly because, unlike her sisters, politics simply did not excite her. When she visited Germany in 1937 and had tea with Hitler, she dismissed him as one of the 'sights', and was far more interested in a handsome musician in a band. Like Nancy, she deplored the fact that politics made people lose their sense of the ridiculous and she poked fun at Unity and Diana's earnest involvement. Deborah looked forward to being a debutante, enjoyed her London Season, and, shortly after her 'coming-out' dance in March 1938, fell in love with Lord Andrew Cavendish, younger son of the Duke of Devonshire, to whom she soon became unofficially engaged.

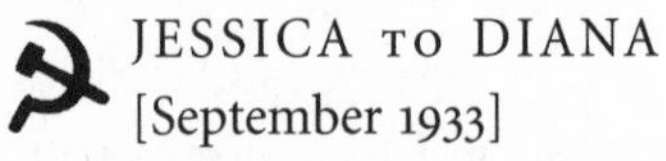

JESSICA TO DIANA
[September 1933]

Swinbrook House
Burford

Darling Corduroy,

You really are the most brick like girl I know. Thank you a *MILLION* times for the *divine* pound which I found here last night when I arrived back from the Isle of [Wight] nearly crying with tiredness, and I nearly died of joy when I saw the £1 because naturally I thought that the £10 was meant for my birthday you *are* a brick. We had a lovely time at the Widow's[1] except that Muv & Debo had to do her knitting for her all the time so that wasn't too good. Debo found a copy of Farve's letter[2] to you in TPOF's[3] bag, poor Corda you do have bad luck, but the worst of the storm of fury fell before you came back, & was braved by Tuddemy,[4] who softened them both down a heap. Boudy is in top-hole form & has told me all about her semi romance with Putzi,[5] at least I call it a semi romance.

Idden[6] & I went on the Sunday school outing to Southsea, & had some romance with (a) a Frenchman who we picked up on the Prom, & (b) two men on a switchback & one of them asked Idden to go to Blackpool with him for a week but I don't think she's going. It *was* fun.

Give my love to TPOL[7] & Jonathan & Demi[8] if they are there.

Much love & millions of thanks from Decca

1 Violet Williams-Freeman (1877–1964). A childhood friend of Lady Redesdale, 'Mrs Ham' was also a favourite with those she called the 'Horror Sisters'. The butt of many of their teases, she could be querulous and demanding but her intelligence and sympathy ensured that she remained a cherished friend. After her husband Arthur Hammersley's death in 1913, she became known as 'the Widow' or 'Wid', which suited her pessimistic outlook. She lived between Tite Street, Chelsea, and Wilmington, Totland Bay, on the Isle of Wight.

2 When Lord Redesdale learnt that Diana had taken Unity to the Parteitag, the annual Nazi Party Congress in Nuremberg, he wrote her a furious letter saying that he and Lady Redesdale were 'absolutely horrified' that they should accept hospitality from 'people we regard as a murderous gang of pests', and begged her to avoid embroiling Unity 'with matters & people you know we cannot tolerate'. (Lord Redesdale to Diana, 7 September 1933)

3 The Poor Old Female, i.e. Lady Redesdale.

4 Tom Mitford.

5 Ernst (Putzi) Hanfstaengl (1887–1975). The Harvard-educated German-American who first encouraged Diana to visit Nazi Germany had been made Foreign Press Secretary in 1931. Alienated from Hitler in 1937, he left Germany for England and later lived in the United States. Married to Helene Neemeyer 1920–36.

6 Ann (Id, Idden) Farrer (1916–95). A first cousin of the Mitfords and lifelong friend and correspondent of Jessica. Worked as an actress and married the actor David Horne in 1941. Author, under the pseudonym Catherine York, of *If Hopes Were Dupes* (1966), an account of her nervous breakdown.

7 The Poor Old Leader, i.e. Mosley.

8 Desmond Guinness (1931–). Diana's second son. President of the Irish Georgian Society 1958–91 and author of books on architecture. Married to Princess Mariga von Urach 1954–81 and to Penelope Cuthbertson in 1985.

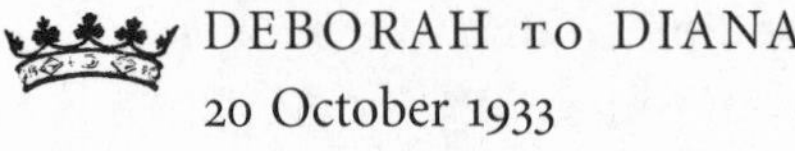

DEBORAH to DIANA

20 October 1933

Swinbrook House
Burford

Darling Honks

Thank you *SO* much for the HEVERN eveninger,[1] Blor was 'dumfounded' when Nancy told her what it cost. I honestly never seen anything quite so lovely in all my.

I even forgive you being a fascist for that.

Thanks ever so much.

Best love from Debo

1 'A heavenly evening bag'; a sophisticated present for a thirteen-year-old.

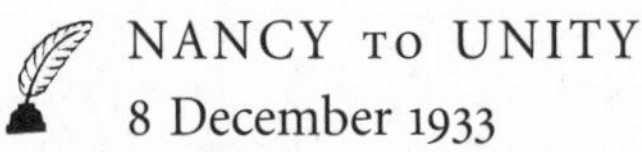

NANCY to UNITY

8 December 1933

[167 Via Giulia
Rome]

We are having a fine time though very sorry to miss all the fun at home. We hear such dreadful accounts of the weather that we really couldn't face the journey. Why do people say they don't enjoy honeymoons? I am adoring mine.[1] You must come out here soon it is wonderful & everyone is so nice & kind.

Best love, NR

1 Nancy had married Peter (Prod) Rodd (1904–68) in London on 4 December. They were honeymooning in his parents' flat in Rome.

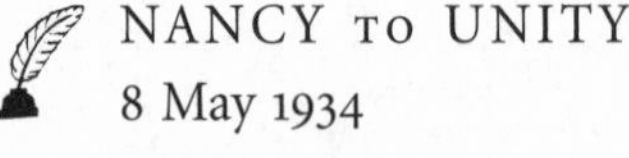

NANCY to UNITY

8 May 1934

Rose Cottage
Strand-on-the-Green
Chiswick

Darling Forgery

The book[1] about you is going to be extraordinary, your grandparents who you live with are called Lord & Lady Tremorgan (TPTPOF)[2] & you are called Eugenia let me know if you would rather not be.

I will finish this later.

Oh deary. Aunt Sport[3] came & said some wonderful things & the

ROMANCE OF PEER'S DAUGHTER.—The Hon. Nancy Freeman-Mitford, Lord Redesdale's eldest daughter, whose engagement to the Hon. Peter Rodd (right), son of Lord Rennell, was made known yesterday.

Nancy's engagement to Peter Rodd was announced in July 1933.
They were married five months later.

chiefly wonderful was in Kew. She wanted to find out why her camellia drops its buds, so went up to a gardener & said 'Good afternoon. Bud dropping by a camellia please?' The gardener just said 'Overfeeding' & went on with his work. It was funny.

Much love, NR

WRITE

1 *Wigs on the Green* (1935). Nancy's satirical novel, which poked fun at Unity and Diana's extremism, was the only one of her books never to be reissued after the war. She wrote to Evelyn Waugh, 'Too much has happened for jokes about Nazis to be regarded as funny or as anything but the worst of taste.' *The Letters of Nancy Mitford and Evelyn Waugh*, edited by Charlotte Mosley (Hodder & Stoughton, 1996), p. 249.
2 The Poor Tremorgan Poor Old Female.
3 Dorothy Cordes (1887–1967). Married Lord Redesdale's younger brother Bertram (Tommy) in 1925.

卐 UNITY TO DIANA
12 June 1934

[Königinstrasse 121]
Munich

Darling Nard

I'm so *dreadfully* sorry to hear you are so ill & couldn't go to the great meeting,[1] I think it's too awful for you to have missed it. It does sound such heaven. What an outcry in the papers, though! As to Bill Anstruther-Gray,[2] I'm longing to see him thoroughly beaten up. He does deserve it. Was Nancy at the meeting?

Poor Nard, how awful, your illness costing you such a lot. I do hope you're better by now, & not in pain. It sounds horrid.

Such a terribly exciting thing happened yesterday. I saw Hitler.[3] At about six last night Derek[4] rang me up from the Carlton Teeraum & said that He was there. Derek was having tea with his mother & aunt, & they were sitting *just* opposite Him. Of course I jumped straight into a taxi, in which in my excitement I left my camera which I was going to take to the shop. I went & sat down with them, & there was the Führer opposite. The aunt said 'You're trembling all over with excitement', and sure enough I was, so much that Derek had to drink my chocolate for me because I couldn't hold the cup. He sat there for 1½ hours. It was all so thrilling I can still hardly believe it. If *only* Putzi had been there! When he went he gave me a special salute all to myself.

Do write & tell me whether or not you think Olympia was a success? Does the Leader think so? I suppose all these absurd attacks in the papers are bound to do the Party a certain amount of harm. The accounts in the German papers were marvellous.

I do *love* hearing stories about the kits[5] in your letters, do *always* tell me if they say anything funny.

With best love from Bobo

1 Mosley had addressed a huge audience at Olympia, Kensington, where violent fights broke out between Blackshirts and communists. Diana was unable to attend the meeting because she had a high fever.
2 William Anstruther-Gray (1905–85). Conservative MP who co-signed a letter to *The Times* accusing the uniformed Blackshirts at Olympia of 'wholly unnecessary violence'.
3 Adolf Hitler (1889–1945). Eighteen months after his appointment as Chancellor, the Führer's Nazification of Germany was well under way.

4 Derek Hill (1916–2000). Painter, notable for his portraits and landscapes, who was studying stage design in Munich.
5 'The kittens'; i.e. Diana's two sons, Jonathan and Desmond.

卐 UNITY TO DIANA
Sunday, 1 July 1934

Königinstrasse 121
Munich

Darling Nard

Thank you so much for your letter, & the cutting about Tilly's divorce.[1] I'm *so* glad Edward won, although I hardly know him, because I do think she was a little brute to say such horrid things about him.

Thank you so much too for sending me the cutting about Putzi[2] – I never see the *Express* here. I wonder if it's true or if the *Express* put it in out of spite – I should think it is probably true, it's just the sort of thing Putzi would do. Members of the Party are furious about it & I don't wonder, they don't like their high-up members making themselves ridiculous abroad. I saw to it that the cutting was shown all round the Brown House.[3] I hope Putzi is coming back in about a fortnight, or even sooner, I hope he won't bring Miss Olive Jones here, I would be cross.

The excitement here over the Röhm[4] affair is terrific, everyone is horrified. No-one knew about it until last night. I heard rumours after dinner & immediately went into the town, where there were printed accounts of it stuck up in the chief squares. I couldn't believe it at first. I went to the Brown House, but the street was guarded by SS men so I couldn't get near. I waited in a huge crowd in a square near for two hours, they were all waiting to see Hitler & Goebbels[5] come away from the Brown House. While we stood there several huge columns of SS, SA & Stahlhelm marched past us to the Brown House, & huge lorries full of sandbags with SS or Reichswehr sitting on top, & there were SS men dashing about the whole time on motorbikes & cars. It was all very exciting. Then word was passed round that Hitler & Goebbels had left by a back entrance & were already flying to Berlin, so I came home. Today no-one can talk of anything else, & there is a rumour that Schleicher[6] & his wife, Röhm

& Heines[7] have all killed themselves. I wonder if it is true. I am so *terribly* sorry for the Führer – you know Röhm was his oldest comrade & friend, the only one that called him 'du' in public. How anyone could do what Röhm did I don't know. It must have been so dreadful for Hitler when he arrested Röhm himself & tore off his decorations. Then he went to arrest Heines & found him in bed with a boy. Did that get into the English papers? *Poor* Hitler. The whole thing is so dreadful. I must now go into the town & find out what has happened since last night.

With best love to you & the Kits & Nan from
Bobo

1 Ottilie (Tilly) Losch (1907–75). Austrian dancer and actress who had been a girlfriend of Tom. Married the capricious poet and collector Edward James in 1931 and sued for separation in 1934, charging him with homosexuality among other things. James scandalized everyone by counter-suing, accusing her of adultery with Prince Serge Obolensky.

2 The *Daily Express* was waging a vendetta against Hanfstaengl for expelling their Munich correspondent, and reported that on a visit to America he had fallen in love with a nightclub hostess and invited her to Germany where he would 'personally supervise' her career. (20 June 1934)

3 The Nazi Party headquarters in Munich.

4 Ernst Röhm (1887–1934). Chief of Staff of the Sturmabteilung (SA), a large, unruly army that constituted a potential threat to Hitler's dictatorship. On 30 June, in the Night of the Long Knives, Röhm and members of his staff were dragged from their beds and shot, ostensibly for plotting a coup.

5 Josef Goebbels (1897–1945). Minister for Public Enlightenment and Propaganda since March 1933. Married his secretary, Magda Ritschel-Friedländer, in 1931.

6 Kurt von Schleicher (1882–1934). The former Chancellor of Germany and his wife were murdered by the SS in Berlin on 30 June.

7 Edmund Heines (1898–1934). The SA commander who, like Röhm, was a homosexual, was also executed for his part in the alleged plot.

UNITY TO NANCY

[Munich]

[July 1934]

Darling Nancy

Thank you ever so for your letter. How *lovely*, are you really going to give a party when I get back? I hope it will be as lovely as the one before I went. I actually return next Thursday the 19th, but have to go straight to Swinbrook, and please give me time to have my one-&-only evening dress altered by Gladys[1] so it fits me, otherwise I couldn't possibly come. So could it be about 1½ weeks after my return?

Now seriously, about that book.[2] I have heard a bit about it from Muv, & I warn you you can't *possibly* publish it, so you'd better not waste any more time on it. Because if you did publish it I couldn't *possibly* ever speak to you again, as from the date of publication. And as for the article in the *Vanguard*[3] I'm furious about it. You might have a little thought for poor me, all the boys know that you're my sister you know.

The Passion Play[4] was very long. So was the opera we went to last night. It's fun having TPOF & Decca & Ann [Farrer] here, only TPO isn't in a *very* good temper. I am though.

You must come to Swinbrook when I get back, as you will be wanting to see my 304 postcards of the Führer I'm sure. Poor sweet Führer, he's having such a *dreadful* time. Well now I must go. But I must tell you one thing first. You see there is a monument in the town to the Nazis who were shot down in 1923, & everyone must salute while they pass it. I took the old Fem[5] past it once & she wouldn't salute, & the next time we passed it she went round a different way alone. So to pay her out, Decca & Ann & I dashed for a tram, & went home, & left her in the town quite lost & not being able to speak a word of German & that was in the morning, & poor old girl she didn't find the way back until dinner time! Wasn't it a good pay-out.

Heil Hitler! Love Bobo

P.S. No I didn't fumble with Röhm at the Brown House. He preferred men you know.

1 Lady Redesdale's maid who ran up the sisters' evening dresses for £1 a time.

2 *Wigs on the Green.*

3 Nancy had written an ambivalent article in which she began by decrying Britain's 'decaying democracy' that could be saved only by a 'great Leader', before going on to lampoon Mosley in the same mocking tones that she had used in *Wigs on the Green*. 'Fascism as I See It', *Vanguard*, July 1934.

4 Unity, Jessica and Lady Redesdale had attended the 300th anniversary performance

Jessica (*left*) on her second visit to Germany, with Unity.
Weilheim, 1935.

of the *Passionsspiel*, the annual re-enactment of Christ's Passion performed at Oberammergau, where Hitler was also present.
5 Lady Redesdale.

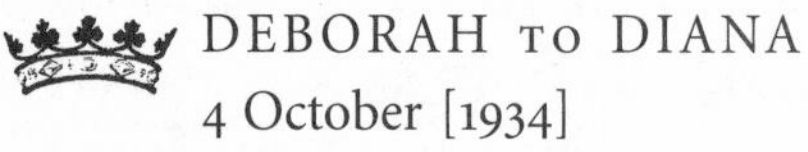

DEBOROAH TO DIANA
4 October [1934]

Swinbrook House
Burford

Darling Honks

Could you possibly send the belt of the wonder gown as I'm going to wear it soon. I expect you heard the story of me leaving school after two days.[1] I had to see the headmistress for two hrs and she lectured me about stone walls not making a prison, and I said of course not if you've got a horse that'll jump them. She was furious.

Best love from Debo

I argue for fascism at school as all the girls are Conservatives. Please tell Mr. Maize.[2]

1 Lady Redesdale considered it too expensive to keep a governess just for Deborah and had enrolled her as a day girl at Wychwood, a weekly boarding school in Oxford, where she lasted for just one term.
2 A newsreel at the cinema was showing a short interview with Mosley. Diana complained that in order to see it twice she twice had to sit through a boring documentary called *Amazing Maize.*

NANCY TO UNITY AND DIANA
6 November 1934

Rose Cottage
Strand-on-the-Green

Darling Eugenia Fitzforgery (& Bodley)

Tell Bodley I couldn't go to the case[1] as my car is quite smashed up again & we are frightfully in the dee pend in many ways. We fear we shall have to do without a car in fact. But it appeared the Lead was a *wonderful* witness, everyone is talking about it & as the case has been reported in full & as he has managed to make nearly all of 'the speech' during the course of it, I expect it will do the Party a heap of good.

I met a friend of Serge[2] last night, she says the whole summer Serge was madly in love with Woman [Pamela]. So it looks as if the old thing didn't play her cards very well.

The book is getting along – 34,000 words so far with 60,000 to do so only another 17,000. It is funnier than it was because there is more about E.U.G.E.N.I.A. – Eugenia.

Well do come home soon oh do.

My best love to Nard & you, NR

1 Mosley had brought a libel case against the *Daily Star* for reporting that his movement was ready to 'take over government with machine guns when the moment arrived'. He was awarded £5,000 damages.
2 Count Serge Orloff-Davidoff (d.1945). Married Elisabeth Scott-Ellis in 1935.

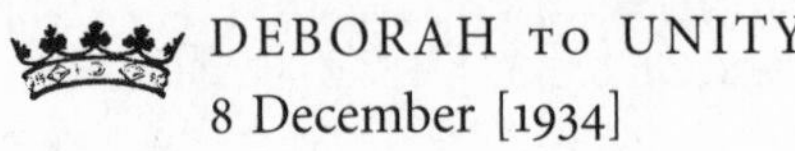

DEBORAH TO UNITY
8 December [1934]

Swinbrook House
Burford

Darling Birdie

Oh what a thrill! The Hill Top[1] is coming to the dance – at least I hope he is. I took great care to see that he was asked. I am really dying for it because it has been so dull and *AWFUL*.

This is what I am giving to Filthy Rodd for Xmas

They are links called 'road to ruin' and are ballet girls, cards, drink and racing. I am giving Tuddemy a pair of 6d Woolworth little boy's shorts with an opening in front and nothing to do it up with!!

Best love from Dawly

1 Derek Hill.

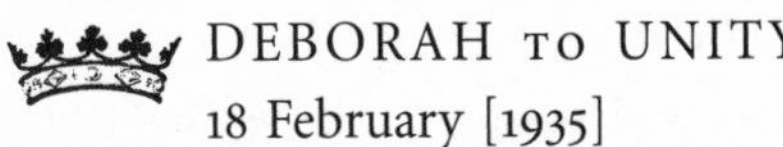

DEBORAH TO UNITY
18 February [1935]

Lowndes House
London SW1

Darling Bird

I have a French gov this afternoon who, since she has seen her, has never stopped raving over the beauties of Diana. If one mentions Muv, she says 'Et la fille!' meaning Diana, or if you mention Decca she says, 'Et la soeur!', or Jonathan she says 'Et la mère!' It makes Muv say Orrhhn when she flatters all of us!!! She thinks you look like heaven from your photograph.

Best love from Dawly

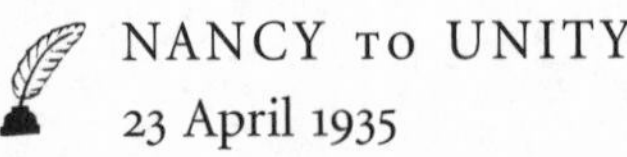

NANCY TO UNITY
23 April 1935

Swinbrook House
Burford

Darling Boud

See! I write to you –!

Your Boud[1] read *Wigs on the G.* & said that it quite inclined her to join the movement. I swear that's true. So please don't stone up or

Where brain should be – bone
Where heart should be – stone

will sum you up all too truly.

I went over to see Penelope Betjeman[2] & her German maids were thrilled to see the Sister of One who knew Hitler & asked me a lot about him. I told them about how wonderful he is & all about Hannibal[3] & they sent him a post card for his birthday. When they heard that I know Mrs Wessel[4] quite well too they were beside themselves with delight & excitement. I told them I would try & get a lock of her hair for them.

What d'you think I have found in a Witney curio shop? A church, about eighteen inches high & with a steeple about two foot made *entirely* of white quills & pins. It is wonderful & you would absolutely adore it. We thought you might make one of brown quills just like the B House. The doors, Gothic windows, & even a clock in the tower are really marvellous & all for 30/– (in a glass case). I am too poor alas to buy it.

Tom has been awful, disappointing Farve by not coming, & resultant tempers very distressing for all.

I go back to Rose Cot on Fri but shall soon be coming over to see

Head of Bone
Heart of Stone

bone
stone
rubber truncheon
hobnail foot for trampling on jews.

So au revoir till then

Love, NR

1 Jessica.
2 Penelope Chetwode (1910–86). Writer and traveller. Married the poet John Betjeman in 1933. They lived at Uffington, not far from Swinbrook.
3 Unity had presented Hitler with a collage she had made of Hannibal crossing the Alps.
4 Nancy's nickname for Unity. Horst Wessel (1907–30) was an SA storm trooper murdered by communist sympathizers in a private quarrel. Goebbels exploited his death and transformed him into a martyr. A poem written by Wessel and set to music became the marching song of the SA and later the official song of the Nazi Party.

卐 UNITY TO DIANA
25 April 1935

Kaulbachstrasse 49
Munich

Darling Nard

The last two days have been wonderful. On Tuesday evening Muv & Miss Fenwick[1] & I went to your hated Platzl,[2] they loved it, I came away in the middle & went to the Osteria, & the Führer was there.[3] He sent Brückner[4] to invite me to his table, & I went & sat next to him, & on my other side was Gauleiter Forster of Danzig, who was *very* nice & invited me to visit Danzig. The Führer was sweet & stayed a long time & talked a lot about all these Notes.[5] He said he would like to see Muv. The next day (yesterday) Brückner came to the Osteria to invite us to tea with the Führer at the Carlton at 6. We went, & there he was, and he said I must be interpreter, but as you can imagine it was very embarrassing as no-one could think of anything to say. After a bit, when Werlin[6] came, the conversation warmed up a bit. Muv tactfully went away after about an hour, I stayed on & after that of course all went swimmingly, he stayed until ¼ to nine. Of course it was bound to be embarrassing with Muv, as she can't speak German, that is always rather a wet blanket. Whenever I translated anything for either of them it always sounded stupid translated. On Tuesday by the way he asked after you, & sent you Grüsses [greetings]. I *do hope* you will come soon Nardy, don't forget to. I fear the whole thing was wasted on Muv, she is just the same about him as before. Having so little feeling she doesn't feel his goodness & wonderfulness radiating out like we do, & like even Farve did. She still says things like 'Well I'm sure he is very good for Germany, *but*' and then she enumerates the things she disapproves of. The most

Collage of Hannibal crossing the Alps made by Unity for Hitler's birthday.

she will admit is that he has a very nice face. She is going back to England this evening.

Last night I went out with Stadelmann,[7] he also sent you many greetings. He has been skiing & is dark brown, can you imagine it.

Do write soon & tell me all about what it is like where you are. And *DO* come soon to Munich.

Heil Hitler!

Best love from Bobo

1 Cecily Fenwick; a friend of Lady Redesdale.
2 A noisy beer hall with a rustic cabaret that performed Bavarian dances.
3 On 9 February, Unity had met Hitler for the first time at the Osteria Bavaria.
4 Wilhelm Brückner (1884–1954). Hitler's chief adjutant.
5 It is not clear which notes Unity is referring to.
6 Jakob Werlin (1886–1958). An SS regional commander and manager of Daimler-Benz in Munich who supplied Hitler with Mercedes cars.
7 Julius Stadelmann; one of Hitler's junior adjutants.

卐 UNITY TO DIANA
12 June 1935

Kaulbachstrasse 49
Munich

Darling Nard

I got your letter yesterday but couldn't answer it at once as Tom didn't go until last night, and as you know when there is someone here one never has a moment. I think he enjoyed his stay, the heat was terrific the whole time. We lunched with the Führer twice – Saturday & yesterday – and although I didn't want him to meet him I am quite pleased now.[1] He *adored* the Führer – he almost got into a frenzy like us sometimes, though I expect he will have cooled down by the time he gets home – and I am sure the Führer liked him, & found him intelligent to talk to. So really I think no harm is done, though on Saturday as we went to his table my heart sank. If it hadn't been for the Führer's sudden habit of lunching early it would never have happened.

Did you like Ribbentrop?[2] Did he remember me? He was at Berchtesgaden with the Führer for the week-end.

Tom quite loved the Good Girl,[3] yesterday we took her out to a

Tom Mitford, from Unity's album. Munich, 1936.

café. They had a long argument – though of course GG took no notice of his arguments – and GG has requested him to keep her informed, on postcards, about the relations between America, Japan, Russia & Europe!

Heil Hitler!

With best love from Bobo

1 Unity had been apprehensive about introducing Tom to Hitler as he was anti-Nazi – or lukewarm towards Nazi policies at best – and was not an anti-Semite. Although Unity tried to reassure Diana that Tom had been won over by meeting Hitler, Diana remained uncertain of her brother's allegiance. When Hitler extended an invitation to Tom for the 1936 Parteitag, Unity wrote to Diana, 'Oh Nardy please don't think it's my

fault because it really isn't, it was his [Hitler's] own idea.' A year later, however, she wrote to Diana that she was composing a verse to celebrate Tom's conversion.
2 Joachim 'von' Ribbentrop (1893–1946). Hitler's foreign affairs adviser since 1933. Appointed ambassador to London in August 1936 and Reich Foreign Minister in 1938. Unity and Diana both disliked him and regarded him as a poor choice for ambassador.
3 Erna Hanfstaengl; Putzi's sister, whom he once referred to as 'a good girl', worked in the family shop selling prints of Old Masters. She often invited Unity to stay at her cottage at Uffing near Munich.

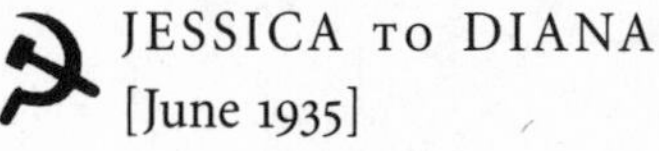

JESSICA TO DIANA

[June 1935]

Swinbrook House
Burford

Darling Corduroy,

Many Happy Returns of the Day. I'm sorry this present is so beastly. I got it (*as* usual) at The Little Shop.[1]

You *are* lucky to have been out to Germany to see my hated Boudle. Did she write & tell you how she saw the Führer, of whom she writes as 'Him' with a capital H, as for Christ or God!! I love my Boud in spite of all.

Love from Decca

1 A Burford antique shop.

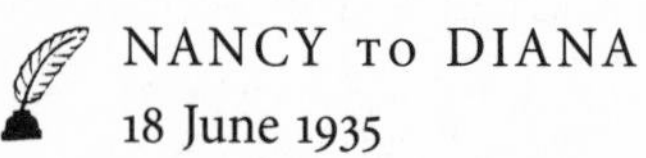

NANCY TO DIANA

18 June 1935

Highfure
Billingshurst
Sussex

Darling Bodley

My book comes out on the 25th inst:, & in view of our conversation at the Ritz ages ago I feel I must make a few observations to you.

When I got home that day I read it all through & found that it would be impossible to eliminate the bits that you & the Leader objected to. As you know our finances are such that I really couldn't afford to scrap the book then. I did however hold it up for about a month (thus missing the Spring list) in order to take out everything which directly related to Captain Jack, amounting to nearly 3 chap-

Diana and Jessica in 1935, two years before politics separated them for ever.

ters & a lot of paragraphs. There are now, I think, about 4 references to him & he never appears in the book as a character at all.

In spite of this I am very much worried at the idea of publishing a book which you may object to. It completely blights all the pleasure which one ordinarily feels in a forthcoming book.

And yet, consider. A book of this kind can't do your movement any harm. Honestly, if I thought it could set the Leader back by so much as half an hour I would have scrapped it, or indeed never written it in the first place.

The 2 or 3 thousand people who read my books, are, to begin with, just the kind of people the Leader admittedly doesn't want in his movement. Furthermore it would be absurd to suppose that anyone who was intellectually or emotionally convinced of the truths of Fascism could be influenced against the movement by such a book.

I still maintain that it is far more in favour of Fascism than otherwise. Far the nicest character in the book is a Fascist, the others all become much nicer as soon as they have joined up.

But I also know your point of view, that Fascism is something too serious to be dealt with in a funny book at all. Surely that is a little unreasonable? Fascism is now such a notable feature of modern life all over the world that it must be possible to consider it in any context, when attempting to give a picture of life as it is lived today.

Personally I believe that when you have read the book, if you do, you will find that all objections to it except perhaps the last (that my particular style is an unsuitable medium) will have disappeared.

On darling I do hope so!

Always much love from NR

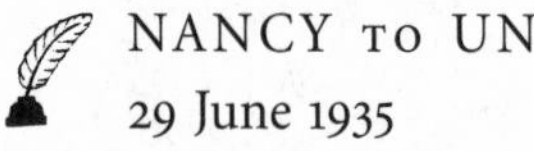

NANCY TO UNITY
29 June 1935

Rose Cottage
Strand-on-the-Green

Darling Stony-heart

We were all very interested to see that you were the Queen of the May this year at Hesselberg.[1]

> Call me early, Goering dear.
> For I'm to be Queen of the May.[2]

Good gracious, that interview you sent us, fantasia fantasia.

5 July. I have been too busy in the giddy social whirl to finish this but will do so now – or never.

We are off to Amsterdam tomorrow so shall be nearer to you in body if not in spirit. By the way aren't you going abroad, to England, quite soon. Well then I shan't bother to send this to the nasty land of blood baths & that will save me 1d.

We were asked to stay with somebody called Himmler or something, tickets & everything paid for, but we can't go as we are going to Venice & the Adriatic for our hols. I suppose he read my book & longed for a good giggle with the witty authoress. Actually he wanted to show us over a concentration camp,[3] now why? So that I could write a funny book about them.

We went to Lord Beaverbrook's[4] party last night, it was *lovely* & I told him about how Goering called you early & he roared.

I must say you are a wonderful noble girl, & everyone who has read my book longs to meet you.

Well, I hope to see you when we get back from Amsterdam.

Love from your favourite sister, NR

1 Unity had addressed the annual Nazi festival at Hesselberg where she expressed sympathy with the German people and admiration for the Nazis' treatment of the Jews. She also gave an interview to a Munich newspaper about the BUF and its anti-Semitic stance.
2 Hermann Göring (1893–1946). The most powerful man in the Third Reich after Hitler was present at the Hesselberg rally. Nancy was parodying Alfred Lord Tennyson's 'The May Queen' (1833): 'You must wake and call me early, call me early, mother dear . . . For I'm to be Queen o' the May, mother.'
3 Germany's first concentration camp had been opened at Dachau in March 1933 by Heinrich Himmler (1900–45), head of the Gestapo and Waffen-SS. The first prisoners were political detainees, rounded up after the burning of the Reichstag.
4 William Maxwell Aitken, 1st Baron Beaverbrook (1879–1964). The politician, financier and newspaper proprietor campaigned for appeasement with Germany.

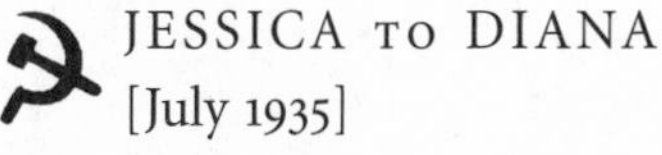

JESSICA TO DIANA
[July 1935]

Swinbrook House
Burford

Darling Cord

I *was* sad to hear about your accident,[1] you can't *think* how sorry we all were. I do hope you're better now & not in too much agony, it sounded *too* frightful, poor Cord, having stitches in while you were still conscious (at least that's what Farve said, I hope it wasn't true).

All the Farrers wrote & sent you their love & sympathy.

Have you had any results from the chain letter yet, I've had about 3/– I think which, after all, although it isn't exactly £312 isn't too bad for 6d is it.

Much love from Decca

1 Diana had been involved in a car crash in which her face was badly injured.

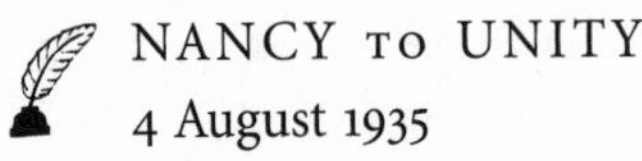

NANCY TO UNITY
4 August 1935

39 Bryanston Square
London W1

Darling Forge

This is to wish you many happy returns of your 21 birthday. I hope you will have a lot of lovely presents, & enclose a miserable cheque to buy yourself some pretty little Nazi emblem with.

Well much love from NR

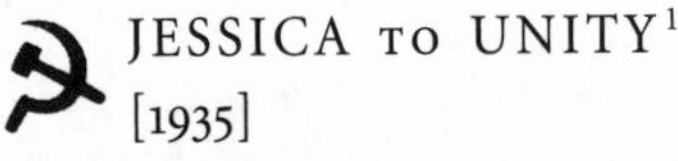

JESSICA TO UNITY[1]
[1935]

Darling Boud

I've saved up £4 towards the Tour,[2] it's in the bank, I expect to add another £6 at the end of the month. When shall we go? About the beginning of October do you think? Also are we definitely going?

This is the new Honnish poem (to be pronounced in true Honnish)[3]

For into bed she sped
And in her bed she read
And while she read
A lump of lead
Fell on her head in bed.

Well Boud, write soon to your old Boud who loves her Boud in zbeed udj al[4] and it's in zbeed of a good deal.

P.S. I went to see poor Cord after her operation, she looked terribly ill. I kept nearly having to leave the room because she and Muv would keep talking about an awful thing called the after-birth.[5]

1 This letter was transcribed in Lady Redesdale's unpublished memoir of Unity. The original has not been found.
2 Jessica and Unity left on a ten-day sightseeing tour of Germany on 24 September.
3 Although they both knew the invented language, it was unusual for Jessica and Unity to communicate in Honnish rather than Boudledidge.
4 'In spite of all.'
5 For the second time in two years, Diana had aborted a child she was expecting with Mosley.

卐 UNITY TO DIANA
19 September 1935

Kaulbachstrasse 49
Munich

Darling Nard

I'm afraid you must have had an *awful* journey. Even I, travelling only as far as here, was frozen when I arrived; and when I woke up yesterday morning and heard the wind whistling I thought of your poor crossing.

Well now I have a lot to tell you. Yesterday about 12, on my way to the hairdresser, I was walking up the Ludwigstrasse & just going to cross one of the side streets & there was a large Merc in it waiting to be able to cross the Ludwigstrasse & to my astonishment in front sat the Führer. I stood for about ½ a minute saluting about 5 feet from him, but he didn't see me. When I got to the hairdresser I felt quite faint & my knees were giving, you know how one does when one sees him unexpectedly. But I was so pleased, because it was the first time I had seen him like that, quite by chance, in the street. Hardly any of the other people recognised him.

I went to the Osteria, & found Erich[1] & Heemstra[2] & Micky[3] there, I made them sit in the garden & I sat alone inside. He came about 2.30, & smiled wonderfully as he shook hands, but then I waited & waited & no-one came. I was in despair, I thought he wasn't going to ask me. Rosa[4] came & told me she had heard he wasn't in at all a good mood, so then I thought he certainly wouldn't invite me. However at last, at about 3, Brückner came & asked me to go to him. I feel sure the Führer had pains,[5] which I know he sometimes does have. For one thing he didn't stand up when I came to the table, which he *always* does. Also the skin round the outside corners of his eyes was yellow. And then he couldn't seem to keep still, he moved backwards & forwards the whole time, with his hands on his knees, you know how he does. I was so unhappy about it, it is so terrible to think of him being in pain. However he was in the most divine mood imaginable, I think he was almost sweeter yesterday than I have ever known him. We talked a lot about the Parteitag, he was terribly pleased at the way it had all gone off. He said he felt terribly flat now that it's all over, & that it was so depressing driving away from Nürnberg, a few people in the street for about 100 yards & then no-one. I explained to him why that was, that they all thought he was going to the Flughafen [airport] and I think that cheered him up, but he was sad that the people had waited so long & hadn't seen him. He told me where we had sat at both the Congresses, and said he had seen me at the opera, but of course that was you. He put his hand on my shoulder twice & on my arm once. I told him about having to go to Paris, & he was sorry for me, but then he said 'But in Paris you will see real Life, and then Munich will seem like a rocky island to you'. (He said the word 'island' in English.) I said no, Munich will always be my Paradise.

Now Nardy I am going to tell you a thing that will make you *so jealous*. We came to speak of the English National Anthem, and he *whistled* it *all* the way through. Wasn't it *wonderful*. Hoffmann[6] showed him a book of photos of him (Hoffmann) as a child, in different costumes – artist, soldier, sailor etc – and the Führer simply *roared*. I must say, although I don't much like Hoffmann now, he was a most divine looking & lovely child, even at about 14. There were only Brückner, Dietrich,[7] Hoffmann & the Doctor [Goebbels] at the table, & Dietrich left half-way through. After a bit the Führer sent to see if he was telephoning, but they said he had gone, and the Führer said quite sadly 'einfach weggelaufen'.[8] You would have *loved* him when he said that. Apparently he talked to Lord Rennell[9] on Tuesday, and was full of praise of him. He was very surprised to hear he is a sort of relation of ours. He thinks he is wonderful. I asked him to sign my belt, and he laughed like anything, he didn't do it very well but you can see it. I think it is the first time he has ever signed a belt. I have definitely arranged to go to Berlin in November, and he is going to take me on the Wannsee in Dr Goebbels' ship. There was no one else in the garden except Erich & co & one old woman, who presently came up to the Führer & with a trembling voice asked if she might greet him, she had never seen him & this was the second time she had come all the way from Dresden to see him, the first time she hadn't succeeded. He stood up & gave her his hand & she said 'God bless you mein Führer. This is the schönster Augenblick meines Lebens'.[10] Then she was so overcome she went away, but he called her back to sign a postcard she had in her hand. It was really wonderful. He asked where you were, & whether you were coming back. Have you sent your letter? I wrote one & sent it, I do hope he will understand what I mean, I think he will.

Well Nardy this letter is already far too long, so now I will stop. But I thought you would like to hear some of the little details of my lunch with the Führer.

I do hope your journey wasn't too bad. Please give my love to all Kits.

V Best love, German greetings & Heil Hitler!
Bobo

1 Erich Widmann; Unity's SS boyfriend who worked in a photography shop.

2 Ella van Heemstra (1900–84). Dutch-born mother of the actress Audrey Hepburn. She and her English husband, Joseph Hepburn-Ruston, were both keen BUF members at the time.

3 Michael Burn (1912–). A young reporter on the *Gloucester Citizen* who had met Unity in London. An initial enthusiasm for Hitler soon turned to disenchantment. He was imprisoned in Colditz during the war and became a convert to Marxism.

4 A waitress at the Osteria Bavaria.

5 Hitler suffered from a chronic stomach condition.

6 Heinrich Hoffmann (1885–1957). Hitler's official photographer and author of *The Hitler Nobody Knows* (1933).

7 Otto Dietrich (1897–1952). Hitler's press chief 1933–45.

8 'Just ran away.'

9 James Rennell Rodd, 1st Baron Rennell (1858–1941). Nancy's father-in-law was a diplomat, poet and scholar. Married Lilias Guthrie in 1894. He and his wife attended the 1936 Olympic Games.

10 'The most beautiful moment of my life.'

JESSICA TO DIANA
[November 1935]

8 Avenue Charles Floquet[1]
Paris VII

Darling Cord,

I *did* mean to write ages ago but somehow time really *flew.*

It is so lovely being in Paris again, we are all enjoying it terrifically, specially me. Do try & get the Boud not to come as I don't think she'd like it, one doesn't want a really *huge* wet blanket in such a small flat.

Cordy it *was* kind of you to lend me that beautiful fur, it's naturally made the whole difference to the coat.

We went to Molyneux dress show, where we saw several lovely things, and we are going to Worth's & Vionnet's if the Fem can get a card for that one. Yesterday we went to tea with Princess F Lucinge,[2] she *is* a spamp[3] I must say, & her house is too fascinating & wonderful for words.

Are you coming to Paris soon? You did say so. Nancy's coming on the 25th for a bit. Hm.

Muv saw in the papers that the filthy old Boud has been putting posters in people's cars saying 'The Jews take everything, even our names' (it didn't actually *say* Boud, but of course we guessed).

Didn't it seem awful & in a way unnatural Lady A.S. & the Duke of[4] having rose petals sprinkled over them. I see it said in the *Tatler*, '*PART* of the h.moon is bound to be delightful as it's being spent in hunting country'. Well Cord goodbye, I *DO* hope you will *SOON* come.

Much love from Decca

1 Lady Redesdale had taken Jessica and Deborah to Paris for a few weeks.
2 Liliane (Baba) d'Erlanger (1902–45). A girlfriend of Tom Mitford. Married Prince Jean-Louis de Faucigny-Lucinge in 1923.
3 A Mitford word for spaniel, hence anything very sweet.
4 The Duke of Gloucester (1900–74), third son of King George V, and Lady Alice Montagu-Douglas-Scott (1901–2004) were married on 6 November 1935.

JESSICA to UNITY
[1935]

Swinbrook House
Burford

Dee Droudled Boudle,

Well here I am back again. What agony to leave Paris. You *can't* think what a *lovely* time we had, but still I am *thrilled* for my dance which is fairly soon. I *do* think you might come back for it. I gave Diana a present for you, I am afraid it's beastly & anyhow I hope you will throw it from you with disgust as it was made by enemies of Germany.

This is the new Boud song, Id[1] came in to my room in Paris one day & found me singing it to myself. I will write it in English as it is easier to understand & takes up less space.

I went down to St James' infirmary
I saw my Boudle there
Stretched out on a long white table
So cold so beastly so fair
I went up to see the doctor
'She's very low', he said;
I went back to see my Boudle
Good god!!! She's lying there *DEAD*
Let her go, let her go, God bless her;
Wherever she may be
She can search the whole world over
And never find a sweet Boud like me.

It has actions, too.

We are going to see Womb [Pamela] today, & stay there a night. Diana has given me a HEAVENLY evening dress.

Give her my love, & hate to Hitler
Lodge Vrudub, Je Boudle[2]

1 Ann Farrer.
2 'Love forever, Your Boud.'

卐 UNITY to DIANA
23 December 1935

Pension Doering
17B Ludwigstrasse
Munich

Darling Nard

I must write again, because such a lot seems to have happened since I wrote.

Firstly DO write & say when you are coming. Everyone keeps asking. I will get you a room here when I know.

I didn't expect to see the Führer, as he apparently hasn't been to the Osteria for weeks. However today at last he came, it was wonderful, & he was tremendously surprised to see me. He immediately asked me, as he came in (himself, for the first time), to go & sit with him. A bit later Max Schmeling[1] came with Hoffmann, & sat on the Führer's other side. He remembered you & me from the Parteitag. The Führer was *heavenly*, in his best mood, & very gay. There was a choice of two soups & he tossed a coin to see which one he would have, & he was *so* sweet doing it. He asked after you, & I told him you were coming soon. He talked a lot about Jews, which was lovely. News from Abyssinia & Egypt kept on coming through on the telephone, which was rather exciting. The Führer stayed in the Osteria for two hours, wasn't it lovely. After he went Werlin drove me to see his new shop, which is wonderful.

The most amazing piece of news of all is – Baum[2] is out of the Partei! She was in the Osteria yesterday, & Rosa told me. According to Stadelmann she was discovered to be a half-Jüdin [Jewess]. Isn't it *amazing*. She also hasn't any work poor thing, as there was a big row in her Mütterheim at Starnberg & she was kicked out. I am really sorry for her, as the Partei & her hate for the Jews were really all she had.

This evening I went to the Christmas party in Hössl's[3] Clinic, it was terribly pathetic, with all the little lupus-faced children dressed up as angels. The grown-up patients were very pathetic too. I think you would have hated it. The head doctor rushed up to me & thanked me profusely for all my kindness to the children, I felt awful as all I have ever done is to club with Armida & Rosemary[4] & send them a Prinz-Regenten-Kuchen [cake]. So I sent them another today.

Hössl, of course, sends you best love. He walked all the way home with me this evening, & I must say he is sweet.

Luckily Stadelmann has got hols now, so he stays around most of the time as a sort of Adjutant. Erich comes to-morrow evening.

Come *SOON*.

With best love & Heil Hitler! Bobo

1 Max Schmeling (1905–2005). German world heavyweight boxing champion 1930–32. In June 1936, he beat Joe Louis in his first fight against the black American heavyweight champion.

2 Eva Baum was a keen Nazi who taught German to Unity. Having been friends, they fell out when Baum reported Unity to the SS, claiming, amongst other things, that she was bloodthirsty and had an 'hysterical' passion for Hitler. She also reported that Unity was having 'a real affair' with Erich Widmann and that she was not a suitable friend for an SS member. (Unity to Diana, 8 February 1935) The rumour that Unity had in turn denounced Baum for being Jewish is not borne out by this letter.

3 An SS doctor who ran a children's clinic in Munich.

4 Armida (1917–) and Rosemary (1918–) Macindoe were English sisters studying German in Munich.

卐 UNITY TO DIANA
Saturday 8 February 1936

Pension Doering
Munich

Darling Nard

Yesterday the Führer was in the Ost, he came about 3 & left at 5 & was in a wonderful mood, quite different from last week. He told me that Lord & Lady Londonderry & the youngest daughter[1] had visited him in the Reichskanzlei last week. I felt bound to say that I was horrified that he should receive such people, and that he would soon find that practically all his English acquaintances were in concentration camps. He also admitted to having seen Beaverbrook, which horrified me even more. You know Nardy he must have a very bad adviser as to which English people he receives. I think this time it wasn't Ribbentrop. After all, he isn't like an ordinary politician, who has to receive anyone who is important. Visits to him should be reserved for those who have deserved it, by doing something for his cause or at any rate for really loving him, regardless of titles & money & importance, don't you think. I mean, to my mind it would have been much better to receive your Mrs Newall,[2] who really does adore him, than Lady Londonderry, who will simply go back & say just as nasty things as ever. If they want to get on the right side of some important person, they should take them to see Hess[3] or Goebbels or Goering or anyone, but not the Führer. We talked about it quite a lot, and he seemed to understand. Of course it's impossible for him to know whom to receive, but he should be better advised. However he said that to make up for it, whenever you & I are in Berlin, he will give an 'Abend [evening]' for us in the Reichskanzlei. So that is lovely, isn't it. We must go. He said he had never seen such jewels as Lady L wore.

He talked a lot about England & Germany, & said that in 2 years time the German army will be the strongest, not only in Europe but in the WORLD. Isn't it wonderful. And he said that with the German army & the English navy we could rule the world. Oh if we could have that, and what wouldn't be worth doing to help the cause of friendship between the two countries even a little.

He is going to invite Mary[4] & me to tea in the Wohnung [flat] tomorrow, isn't it wonderful. To a 'kleine Gesellschaft'.[5] Herr & Frau Hoffmann were also at lunch yesterday, & he invited them too. I am thrilled. And Oh Nardy, what do you think, he mentioned his SISTER.[6] Wasn't it thrilling. He said he had wanted to send for her to come to Munich, but couldn't get hold of her. I am so miserable, because if she had been in Munich PERHAPS she would have come to the kleine Gesellschaft.

The curse came today, & I have a pain, thank god it didn't come tomorrow. Mary is in a quandary as she hasn't anything to wear. I shall wear my white fur blouse & black skirt.

Tonight is the Osteria Faschings ball, it is wonderfully decorated. Hess & Frau are going to the 2nd one. Now I must scram. Do write soon, & we must go to Berlin.

With best love & Heil Hitler! Bobo

1 7th Marquess of Londonderry (1878–1949). Until 1938, the former Air Minister was an admirer of Hitler and worked for rapprochement with Germany. His wife, Edith,

was more sceptical and saw that 'to live in the upper levels of National Socialism may be quite pleasant, but woe to the poor folk who do not belong to the upper orders'. (Quoted in Anne de Courcy, *Circe*, Sinclair-Stevenson, 1992, p. 270) After their visit to Germany, the Londonderrys and their fourteen-year-old daughter, Mairi, left bearing photographs of the Nazi leaders in silver frames, which may have made Unity jealous.
2 Mary Pollen (1892–1983). Married Colonel J. D. Macindoe in 1915 and K. W. Newall in 1933. Contrary to what Unity believed, the mother of her friends Armida and Rosemary was not an admirer of Hitler.
3 Rudolf Hess (1894–1987). Deputy leader of the Nazi Party since 1933.
4 Mary Wooddisse; an exact contemporary and close friend of Unity who was also studying German in Munich.
5 'A small gathering.'
6 Paula Hitler (1896–1960). Hitler's younger sister was the only one of his five full siblings to survive to adulthood.

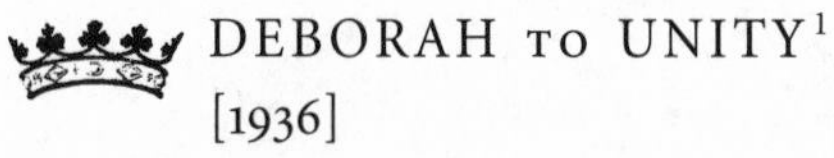

DEBORAH TO UNITY[1]

[1936]

*[Old Mill Cottage
High Wycombe]*

Darling Birdie

Thanks ever so much for the postcard.

I am here quite alone except at weekends which gets rather boring. My gov is quite nice and I haven't done any arithmetic since she came (don't tell Muv) I can't imagine why.

I don't think Decca is enjoying her season much but don't tell Muv.

Are you excited for the Cruise thing we're going on?[2] I'm not because we're probably going to Greece and there are going to be lectures on the Greek one which I'm not going to attend if I can help it. I *hate* lectures. Besides, I thought the whole point of a cruise was the romance on it, not *lectures*. I shall be having romance while you and the others go to the beastly lectures.

Love from Dawly

1 Lady Redesdale transcribed this letter in her unpublished memoir of Unity. The original has not been found.
2 Lady Redesdale was taking Unity, Jessica and Deborah on a cultural cruise of the Mediterranean.

Deborah, 1936.

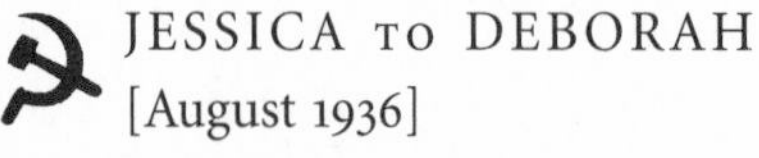

JESSICA TO DEBORAH
[August 1936]

Hôtel des Panoramas
Saint-Briac[1]

Dearest Cheerless,

Thank you for your letter dear, it was quite funny in parts. But poor young gelding what a dull time you must be having. When are you scramming to Scotland?

Everyone in our party has gone from here except us & the slavers.[2] The male slaver has taken a terrific hate on me because I told him a lot of lies. Yesterday we went to an extraorder nightclub in a town near here, run by an ex-Folies Bergère lady called Popo (or Pot-pot perhaps). And there are notices on the walls saying things like 'Popo a soixante ans, elle est garantie pour cent.'[3] And she did a dance & took off her jersey. Wasn't it extraorder. And then she waltzed with Mary Sewell. Nancy didn't come because she thinks nightclubs boring, & the Sewells (evidently) thought it was because she was shocked by them, & on the way home kept saying 'I wonder what NANCY would have thought of it!' Wasn't it killing.[4]

I got a 'gram this morning saying I can't go down the Danube with Tom & Boud, will you tell whoever sent it it was j.n. or jolly nice of them to spend an extra 5d on saying 'very sorry'?

There are some lousy people called the Grevilles here & the other day they asked Chris & me to go on a picnic with them. But when the time came they simply went without us, wasn't it rude of them. So we pretended to the others that we had been on the 'nic & that it was heaven with champagne & everything. But when I saw the slaver's killing old père de famille-ish face believing it all I couldn't contain my giggles so it all came out. So the s. was simply horrified at me telling such a lie & he said his faith in human nature was shaken. So now we're always telling him lies like 'we saw two people fall out of a boat this morning' & then he says 'did you *really*' & we say 'no!' It teases like mad.

Love from Tarty

1 Jessica was on holiday in Brittany with Nancy and Peter.

2 As children, Jessica and Deborah imagined that Anthony Sewell, a neighbour at Rutland Gate, was a white-slave trader – their nanny having warned them that London was the centre of the traffic. Sewell was married, 1930–45, to Mary Lutyens, daughter of the architect Sir Edwin Lutyens.

3 'Popo is sixty, she is guaranteed for a hundred.'

4 It is more likely that Nancy stayed at home because her husband and Mary Sewell were having an affair.

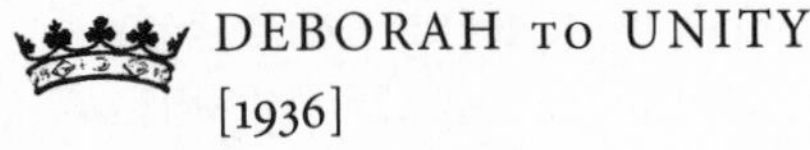

DEBORAH TO UNITY
[1936]

[Old Mill Cottage
High Wycombe]

Dear Bird

Would you send me a letter with a German stamp & an Olympic Games stamp on it like you sent to Muv because Sex Hay[1] longs for one. *DON'T FORGET.*

I've started a new National Movement & its slogan is FOOD & DIRT. That's what we stand for. There are 3 members. It started with Peter Ramsbotham[2] & me & then Sex joined.

It's called Nourishilism.

It's a very swell movement.

Goodness the weather.

What a silly muddle about the Danube thing. Poor old Squalor will be disappointed again I suppose.[3] The whole family is abroad except me. Typical.

Jaky[4] sends his love.

Sex has been staying here. Ivan[5] has got a job about anti-aircraft intelligence at the Home Office. Isn't it killing, I mean the intelligence bit. I'm afraid poor England will be beaten in a war if we have Ivan as chief.

Isn't it wicked about the bombing of the Alhambra. If only all the Spaniards could be converted to Nourishilism it would never have happened. THE BRUTES.

Well *DON'T FORGET* about the Olympic stamp.

Hail Food!

Hail Dirt!

Hail our leader Ramsbotham!

Yours in National Nourishilism, Dawly

1 Alexandra Cecilia Hay (1922–91). A friend of Deborah who did lessons with her at Swinbrook.

2 Peter Ramsbotham (1919–). The future distinguished diplomat had made friends with the sisters during their Mediterranean cruise.

3 Unity had cancelled her plan to travel down the Danube and on to Constantinople with Tom and Jessica because the Redesdales had forbidden Jessica to go.

4 Deborah's dachshund.

5 Ivan Hay (1884–1936). Cecilia's father.

Diana with Joseph Goebbels, the Nazi Propaganda Minister; Heinrich Hofmann, Hitler's official photographer; and Albert Speer, the Reich's chief architect. Haus Wahnfried, Bayreuth, 1936.

DIANA TO UNITY
17 September 1936

Hotel Kaiserhof
Berlin

Darling:

I have *so* much to erzähl [tell] and as I can't sleep I have got up to erzähl it. When I arrived here I felt so ill that I went to bed and took a lot of aspirin, and then I rang up Magda[1] and arranged to meet her the next morning, and I rang up the Kit[2] and told him about everything being put off.[3] Next morning Bill[4] came round, and then he left and Magda and I took all the papers and went to the police etc. While we were talking she happened to let it out that the Führer was in Berlin, but she added it would be impossible to see him because he was just off to the manoeuvres. Then she rang up Brückner and said she would like to talk to the Führer for a minute about my affair. We went shopping to get her clothes for Greece and while she was trying on a message came, would she ring Brückner up. She only did so an hour later, it was pure agony because I kept thinking the Führer would have scrammed. However we were asked to go round at 7.30, and in the end we stayed for dinner and saw a lovely film with Lillian Harvey.[5]

But now I must tell you how *sweet* the Führer was. He came into the room and made his beloved *surprised* face, and then he patted my hand and said 'Es hat mir *so* eine Freude gemacht, dass Sie sind zum Parteitag gekommen und jeden Tag im Kongress gewesen sind'[6] or words to that effect, and he was so wonderful and really seemed pleased we had gone every day, and he said specially to the Schluss-kongress, so I said we had been freuing [enjoying] ourselves over that the whole week. He asked after Tom and I said 'Der Judenknecht is fast National-sozialist geworden'[7] and he roared with laughter and said 'Ihr Bruder ist ein fabelhafter Junge'[8] twice over. Isn't Tom *lucky.* Then I said we loved the wonderful parades and he said it was the best Parteitag he had ever had because *everything* had geklappt [worked]. He had noticed Janos.[9] He sent you his love; and darling everything is arranged for the *6th*, and it is to be in Schwanenwerder[10] and the Führer is giving up his day to it and everything is to be done without Joan Glover[11] I am so happy now because it all seemed to be hopeless without talking to the Führer first, but now it is all perfect, and not too late for you, is it? I terribly want to bring J[onathan] & D[esmond] over, what do you think? They needn't know what is going on but I would so love them to be blessed by a glimpse of the Führer. He has gone off last night to the manoeuvres at Kiel or somewhere. He looks in blooming health & his skin is peeling from so much sun.

All love darling, Nardy

Magda is being an *angel*, and she can talk of nothing but your marvellous attack on Joan Glover and how pleased they all were with you for doing it, that day you know.

1 Magda Ritschel-Friedländer (1901–45). The ideal of German motherhood married Dr Joseph Goebbels in 1931 in order to be close to Hitler, whom she idolized. Her first marriage in 1921 to Gunther Quandt, a rich industrialist, ended in 1929.

2 'Kitten'; Diana's nickname for Mosley.

3 Diana's marriage had been postponed until 6 October while the official paperwork was being arranged.

4 W. E. D. Allen (1901–73). Chairman of an advertising company and Ulster MP for

West Belfast who resigned his seat in 1931 to take up a senior post in Mosley's New Party. He may also have been reporting back on the Mosleys to British intelligence services.

5 Lillian Harvey (1907–68). The English-born actress spent her youth in Germany before moving to Hollywood in 1933. She released two films in 1936, *Glückskinder* and *Schwarze Rosen*.

6 'It has given me such pleasure that you came to the Party Rally and that you have attended every day.'

7 'The lackey of the Jews has almost become a National Socialist.'

8 'Your brother is a splendid young man.'

9 Count Janos von Almasy (1893–1968). An Hungarian friend of Tom who lived at Bernstein Castle in the Austrian province of Burgenland. Tom introduced him to Unity who often stayed at Bernstein and became Janos's lover. Married Princess Maria Esterhazy in 1929.

10 Goebbels had recently bought a villa in the fashionable Berlin suburb and it is there that the Mosleys' wedding lunch was given.

11 Ribbentrop. Tom Mitford had made up the nickname, inspired, for no particular reason, by the medieval song, 'Go to Joan Glover, and tell her I love her and at the mid of the moon I will come to her'.

DIANA to UNITY — *Berlin*
7 October 1936

Darling

I am sitting in a bower of orchids envying you, because I expect you are still in the Führer's train. Yesterday was the loveliest and at the same time the most terrible day for me. The wedding itself was so beautiful, and the blick [sight] out of Magda's window of the Führer walking across the sunny garden from the Reichskanzlei was the happiest moment of my life. I felt everything was perfect, the Kit, you, the Führer, the weather, my dress, Magda, the Standesbeamter [registry clerk], the Doktor, and even Bobbie[1] and Bill [Allen]. The Führer's orchids and Widemann's roses, and the Kit's orchids, and the ceremony, and the Führer's wonderful present,[2] and the drive to Schwanenwerder, and the wonderful *essen* [food], and Magda's and your sweetness, and Maria's[3] sweetness too; and then your present and the detective reading a detective novel, and the Standesbeamter's heart beating so loud because he was so happy to see the Führer; but in any case, I could write for ever about that part of the day.

The other part I cannot describe, how they spoilt the meeting for me, and made me late for dinner at the Reichskanzlei, and the Kit's awful childish behaviour, and the way in which he tried to say everything he could to wound me.[4] He succeeded in a way because I had been so happy and excited. However, it is all over now and I shall be frightfully busy today; and tomorrow I shall go to England.

I thought the Führer's speech was wonderful[5] and it was a perfect ending to the day when I blotted out of my mind the sad part.

Well darling, I can never thank you enough for all your sweetness and we will have such a lot to talk over at home. I will send the money.

All love & masses of kisses, Nardy

1 Robert Gordon-Canning was best man at Mosley's wedding. Joined the BUF in 1934 before breaking with it in 1938 on personal grounds.
2 Hitler presented Diana with a large signed photograph of himself in a silver frame.
3 Maria Goebbels; Dr Goebbels' younger sister lived with her brother until she married the film director Max W. Kimmich in 1938.
4 Diana was unable to remember the exact reasons for this quarrel but could only suppose that Mosley was irritated by her admiration for Hitler. In her appointment diary for 10 October 1936, four days after her wedding, she noted, 'We discuss H and the wedding, He compares H with Ramsay MacDonald. I am furious. We quarrel.'
5 Hitler had addressed a meeting of the Winterhilfswerk, a Nazi charity that raised money to help the poor during the winter months.

卐 UNITY TO DIANA
7 October 1936

Regina Palast Hotel
Munich

Darling Nard,

I did so hate having to leave you in such a hurry last night & there were such a lot of things to discuss. I do hope the Kit is less nasty by now; but all the same he didn't succeed in spoiling the day did he, it was a lovely day wasn't it. And wasn't the Winterhilfswerk *wonderful*, I simply thought the Führer's speech was one of the best I ever heard him make. He was sweet in the train last night & we had a lot of jokes, he went to bed about 2 but I stayed for ages talking to Gauleiter Wagner[1] whom I love like anything, and Hoffmann got terrifically drunk & started telling me how cold English women are. He said he had been ages in England & had only had one affair!

I do hope you will be coming south some time soon when I return. I may not arrive in London till Monday, as the Kreistag lasts till then & Wagner has promised me tickets for everything. I shall hear Frau Scholtz-Klink[2] speak, aren't I lucky.

Well I do hope the Kit is being better now.

With best love & Heil Hitler, Bobo

1 Adolf Wagner (1890–1944). Nazi provincial chief of Munich and Upper Bavaria; Bavarian Interior Minister from 1933.
2 Gertrud Scholtz-Klink (1902–99). Reich Women's Leader and the only woman to reach ministerial status in the Nazi Party.

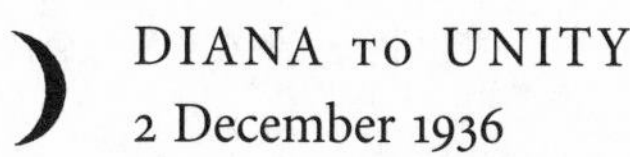

DIANA TO UNITY
2 December 1936

Hotel Kaiserhof
Berlin

Darling:

I did not mean to write but I am so bored and miserable that I feel I must. I have been here a week tomorrow and I have been alone the entire time.[1] The Führer is here but he is frightfully busy and I haven't seen him. The only person who has been beloved is Wagner, he is so wonderfully sweet and he said he will ring us up in England just to say 'Good night sleep well'. But he has gone, ages ago, back to Munich. The real reason why I am writing is because I am worried about Jonathan. He looked so sad when I left and it must seem very long to him. Please darling will you write to him. I can't you see.[2] I have got them their Reichswehr uniforms and a few other things. It is very odd you know but in the summer I spent 10 weeks on end without seeing them, and I didn't worry about them, but I can hardly bear it this time, I feel sure they think I have forgotten my promise to be back in a very few days.

There was snow when I arrived but now it is warm and horrid. I thought I would come back on Sunday, but now it looks more like being *next* Sunday.

This letter is as boring as I feel, I am afraid. When I do get back I will ring up, but I expect I shall go straight to the Unexpected.[3] I have missed seeing the Kit, he will be there tonight & tomorrow during his tour. Now I shall not see him for more than a week. Altogether everything is vile.

Please wish me luck.

By the way do you remember how we thought we would hate it if the Führer called us good souls? Well Wagner said to me 'Sie sind ja eine gute Seele'[4] and it made my day.

Well goodbye darling, and please write to little Jonathan and say I send him love and a hug and everything; and to Desmond too, though I don't think he misses me very much. I miss them *both* so terribly much.

All love darling & Heil Hitler! Nardy

1 Diana was in Berlin trying to get Hitler's agreement to Mosley's plan to set up a commercial radio station in Germany to broadcast to Britain.
2 It is not clear why Diana could not write to her son at the time.
3 Wootton Lodge. An article in *Country Life* had described the house as 'the home of the unexpected'.
4 'You certainly are a good soul.'

UNITY TO JESSICA
3 March 1937

26 Rutland Gate
London SW7

Darling Boud

Peter Rodd is going off to try & find you[1] so I am writing this on the chance. I *do* hope he will find you. I expect you will have realized what agonizing worry the whole family has been in ever since we heard. It was really as if there had been a death in the family when I arrived – it still is, people are always coming round to condole or sending flowers, the house is a bower.

I was in Munich when I heard, oh I *was* sad, it seemed like my old Boud had died or something, of course I came scramming back at once, but thank goodness I saw my friend[2] before I left & he was a perfect angel & comforted me like anything, tho' he was terribly sad himself about it. When I returned I couldn't *believe* that my wool-gathering Boud wouldn't be on the doorstep to greet me. I miss my Boud *terribly* – more than I would anyone else in the family. Debo keeps saying she is 'bidding her messengers ride forth, E. & W. & S. & N., to summon her cenoi'.[3] Oh Boud *do* come back & see us all, even if it's only for a bit. It would make everything so much better. You see ever since you left Muv & Farve haven't slept, Muv cries all night & Farve has to make her tea, and they both look 10 years older, & Blor's face has gone all grey & she divides her time between crying & saying 'Jessica has only taken two pairs of knickers & they are both too small for her & I'm afraid they will burst'. Tom is here nearly all day & when he's not here he's ringing up. Poor little Debo has had a dreadful time & misses you dreadfully. *DO* come back Boud, no one wants to prevent you from marrying Esmond,[4] & they are all so unhappy, so is *your* Boud. I'm dying to see Esmond, & hear all about him, Tina[5] knows him so I have heard some. Tina sends her love.

With best love from your Boud

1 The news of Jessica's elopement had at last reached the Redesdales, two weeks after her disappearance.
2 Hitler.
3 'Hen' in 'Honnish', Jessica and Deborah's private language.
4 Esmond Romilly (1918–41). In her memoirs, Jessica described Esmond when she first met him as 'a star around which everything revolved . . . He represented to me all that was bright, attractive and powerful'. *Hons and Rebels*, p. 105.
5 Clementine Mitford (1915–2005). Posthumous daughter of Lord Redesdale's eldest brother, Clement. Married Sir Alfred Beit in 1939.

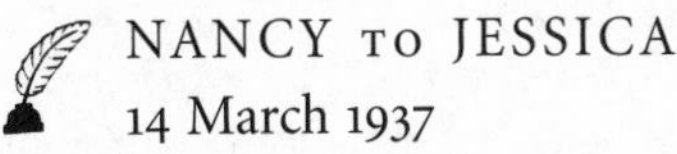

NANCY TO JESSICA
14 March 1937

12 Blomfield Road
London W9

Darling Sue

I got back to find such a mass of things to do that I haven't time for a long letter.[1]

I saw the family yesterday & they are miserable. Susan it isn't very respectable what you are doing & I see their point of view I must say.

Oh dear you were stupid on the platform, those men were quite bamboozled until you got back on the train – battering on my door & asking if you were there. Why didn't you stop in the cabinet?[2]

Here is a letter from Rodd. I am inclined to agree with it – after

Express

...DED BY LORD BEAVERBROOK

NORTHERN EDITION

...DAY, MARCH 1, 1937 — ONE PENNY

Peer's Daughter Of 17 'Elopes,' Spain Search

'YARD' JOIN IN THE SEARCH FOR HER

Daily Express Staff Reporter

A PEER'S 17-YEAR-OLD DAUGHTER IS BELIEVED TO HAVE ELOPED TO SPAIN IN AN ATTEMPT TO MARRY HER 18-YEAR-OLD COUSIN.

Scotland-yard and the Foreign Office are searching for the Hon Deborah Vivien Freeman-Mitford, daughter of Lord and Lady Redesdale, who disappeared from Dieppe.

Her cousin, Esmond Romilly, is a nephew of Mr Winston Churchill, and was recently fighting on the Madrid barricades in the Spanish Government's international column.

He is believed to be making for Bilbao, Government stronghold, now cut off by insurgent troops.

Miss Mitford was believed by her parents to be staying at Dieppe, where Colonel and Mrs Romilly have a house. Last week a messenger brought them a letter dated from Bayonne on the Franco-Spanish border, stating that she might attempt to marry Romilly in Spain.

Lord Redesdale at once made every possible attempt to intercept his daughter and bring her home. His solicitors sought the aid of Scotland Yard, the British Foreign Office, the consular service, and the Spanish Embassy.

It was found that the girl had not visited Colonel or Mrs Romilly. They did not know she had fled from Dieppe.

The first trace of the girl was found at Bordeaux, where she apparently stayed during her flight to Spain.

Then she made a brief halt at Bayonne, last large town before the Spanish border. There she sat down and wrote the letter to her mother.

The Hunt

"I do not know where my daughter is," Lord Redesdale said last night. "If I did know I would go to Spain at once, or get somebody to go and bring her home. We think she may be in Bilbao."

All the British Consul posts in Spain and near the border have been given a description of the girl. Spanish Embassy officials have advised Lord Redesdale that they will do all they can to trace his daughter and let him know her whereabouts.

Miss Mitford's family fear that the couple may attempt to marry under Communist laws. Such a marriage could be made without previous notification or any residential qualifications.

A registered Communist official could marry them in the same way as a registrar in this country. Such a marriage declaration would be signed and stamped.

The Spanish Embassy, however, have advised the family that such a marriage would be illegal and unrecognised in Spain. For the couple to marry under Spanish laws it would be necessary for them to give 32 days' notice of their intention.

Miss Mitford is the youngest of Lord Redesdale's four daughters.

Exactly three years ago Esmond Romilly ran away from Wellington College, where he was at school with his brother. It was stated then that he was deeply under the influence of a group of London Communists. A few days later he met his mother by arrangement in Hyde Park, London.

He went to Spain and [illegible] Government forces in the [illegible] days of the Spanish war.

THE HON DEBORAH FREEMAN-MITFORD (left), aged 17, and her sister Jessica.

MISS FREEMAN MITFORD, Daughter of Lord Redesdale.

SEARCH IN SPAIN FOR YOUNG COUPLE

ESMOND ROMILLY AND A PEER'S DAUGHTER

THE Foreign Office have asked British Consular officials at Bilbao and Bordeaux to endeavour to discover the whereabouts of the Hon. Jessica Lucy Freeman-Mitford, aged 19, and Mr. Esmond Romilly, aged 18.

Mr. Romilly is a nephew of Mr. Winston Churchill, and the girl is a daughter of Lord and Lady Redesdale.

The Hon. Jessica Freeman-Mitford

The Consular agents have been notified that these young people are both under age and may be contemplating matrimony.

It is believed that they have been at Bordeaux within the last week, and it may be their intention to go to Bilbao.

Edited a Magazine

Esmond Romilly has had a remarkable career. Three years ago he left Wellington College, and reappeared in London to edit a students' anti-war magazine "Out of Bounds."

Last year he suddenly decided to throw up his job in London. Next news of him came from Spain. He was reported to be a member of the International Brigade, fighting for the Spanish Reds.

Short, square-jawed and courageous, red-headed Romilly returned to London last month for a short holiday before rejoining the Brigade.

The *Daily Express* named the wrong 'peer's daughter' and had to pay £1,000 to Deborah for compromising her prospects of marriage.

all one has to live in this world as it is & society (I don't mean duchesses) can make things pretty beastly to those who disobey its rules.

Susan do come back. No Susan. Well Susan if anything happens don't forget there is a spare room here (£4.10. bed).

Love from Sue

1 Nancy and Peter had returned from Bayonne where they had tried, unsuccessfully, to convince Jessica to come home.
2 Nancy had endeavoured to persuade Jessica to hide in the train lavatory to avoid the press.

DIANA TO UNITY
30 March 1937

Wootton Lodge
Ashbourne
Staffordshire

Darling:

Thank you *so* much for your lovely long letter. I am so terribly sorry for Muv over everything and I do not blame her for not letting Debo come.[1] It is obviously no good to argue that no one need know she has been here. I have left it and did not answer her letter at all because I could not think what to put; but I answered her long and marvellously ausführlich [detailed] letter about her visit to Decca, without mentioning Debo's visit.

I suppose they will let them be married and I suppose it is better so. Apparently (the Wid rang up and told me this) poor Muv is again plunged in melancholy gloom.

In the mean time the Kit and I spent the long Easter weekend here in a sort of delirium of happiness. You know how that sometimes happens quite unaccountably. We were so happy, the weather was so fine, the landscape so beautiful, the horses such fun, the flowers so pretty, our walks and rides so delightful, and the food so delicious, that really it seemed like Heaven on earth.

I was depressed last week about the Debo thing (as I expect you noticed in my letter) and so it was all the more lovely in a way. After all, my darling Kit is more to me than all the visitors who are not allowed to come here.

You will see from the enclosed Private Document that Beckett & Joyce[2] have been too vile for any words. All the others (102 of them) have behaved nobly and written the most wonderful loyal letters etc, but these two are really disgusting rats. I am sending it to you so that if anyone of importance asks you will know the facts. Keep it carefully or send it back.

Do write all about Frank,[3] I am sure he is frightfully marling [embarrassing] but I expect he has got a personality – in fact of course he must have. Mr Holme[4] wrote me a very terrible marling letter which I must answer.

How *LOVELY* the new Führer-stamps are. Oh darling I wish you were here there is so much to tell & to hear.

All love Nardy

1 The Redesdales refused to allow seventeen-year-old Deborah to visit Diana while her marriage to Mosley was still a secret and in the eyes of the world she was 'living in sin'.
2 John Beckett (1894–1964), ex-Labour MP, and William Joyce (1906–46) had been dismissed from their positions in the BUF, which was in financial trouble and was sacking many of its employees. After the war, Joyce (Lord Haw-Haw) was accused of high treason for broadcasting from Germany – where he had fled to avoid arrest – and was executed.
3 Frank Buchman (1878–1961). Founder of the Oxford Group, a fundamentalist religious movement renamed Moral Rearmament in 1938. In 1936, Buchman had publicly thanked heaven for the existence of Hitler as a defence against communism.
4 Reginald Holme; author of memoirs, *A Journalist for God* (1995).

卐 UNITY TO JESSICA
3 April 1937

Pension Doering
Munich

Darling Boud

Jung va ja leddra.[1] I'm glad the stockings are useful.

Your letter is really so *extraorder*, on reading it over again I can hardly believe you wrote it yourself, it's so unlike you. However I suppose my good Boud has been changed by recent events.

It's really hard for me to describe how Aunt Iris & everyone reacted to your scramming, as you ask. You see I didn't return until after they first heard of it, & when I saw them they were mostly only thinking of the poor Fem & Male & how miserable they were & how they could possibly comfort or help them. But the vile Aunt Weenie[2] was heard to remark that it would be better if you were dead! But I know she *thinks* that about Diana & me too, & has probably often said it.

Boud how *extraorder* of you to say did I know that Muv went out to see you, of course I knew, a) because otherwise how could I have sent you the stockings and b) there was a terrific family conference about it beforehand, & no-one talked of anything else, & at first the idea was that I should go too, of course I wanted to awfully to see my Boud, but then it was decided that as Esmond is by way of hating the idea of me so, it might do more harm than good. So I came here instead, in the new car Farve gave me.

I met the Führer by great good luck last Tuesday, I was driving along in my car & met him at a street corner driving in *his* car, he hadn't known I was back & seemed very pleased to see me & got out into the street to speak to me & everyone rushed from all directions shouting 'Heil!' when they saw him. He asked me to go back to tea with him & I followed his cars to his flat & sat with him for 2½ hours alone chatting. He wanted to hear *all* about you & what had happened since I saw him last. He had forbidden it to appear in the German papers which was nice of him wasn't it – at least perhaps you won't think so as Nancy says Esmond adores publicity. However he got enough of it in other countries.

I think Rodd was boring about the whole thing, right from the beginning he wanted to arrange everything & adored it, & he was dying to be the Heroic Brother-in-Law who rushed out to France (expenses paid by Farve) to bring you back. Also it was his silly & expensive idea to make you a ward in Chancery. I don't suppose, either, that you much loved his interview to the *Daily Mail* – or perhaps you didn't see it – in which he said that you only became a communist in order to 'get even' with me.

Well I wonder when your wedding will be, I don't suppose I shall be invited but still.

Bedsd Lodge Vruddemb[3], Je Boudle

1 'Thanks for your letter.'
2 Dorothy (Weenie) Bowles (1885–1971). Lady Redesdale's disapproving younger sister. Married Percy Bailey in 1907.
3 'Best love from.'

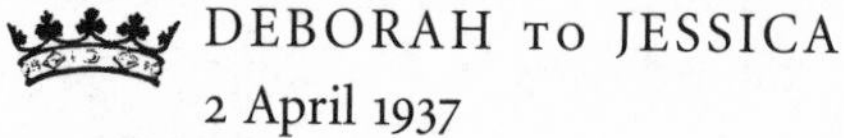

DEBOROAH TO JESSICA
2 April 1937

Old Mill Cottage
High Wycombe

Dear Madrigal[1]

I was pleased to get my old Hen's letter. I thought I should never hear from her again.

A good many things seem to have happened since you left, but nothing of much importance.

It's pretty dull down here without a Hen to chat to. Muv & Farve have been so depressed since you left, it's made them look quite ill.

The cruise would have been so good for Muv but it's rather natural she doesn't want to go any more.[2] She said all the fun would have gone without you & I think she meant it. I do hope you have enough to eat & everything. I envy you the coffee you must get there.

Do write & give an exact description of Esmond. It's so fascinating to think of my old Hen in love that I must hear everything about him.

The hunting all the winter has been fun, & now I am training a horse.

The Grand National was marvellous, but Derek's[3] horse got knocked over by a loose horse which was disappointing. Lord Berners[4] had a horse in for the first time in his life & the Mad Boy[5] said to us before the race 'If it falls at the first fence Gerald will be broken hearted'. And it did! Wasn't it *awful*. But luckily he is very short-sighted & he thinks it was the second fence so all is OK.

Well dear, do write & if you want anything in the way of clothes just write to your Hen & she'll get them for her Hen. Or anything else in fact.

Do write often to Blor. It would cheer her up. She has gone to Hastings for a week as I'm going to Castle Howard next week.

Much love from Scott Wallace

1 Deborah could not remember the origin of the rush of fantastic nicknames she and Jessica used in their letters to each other at the time of the elopement. They were perhaps a way of trying to re-establish their relationship which had been so shaken by Jessica's disappearance.
2 Lady Redesdale, worried that Jessica seemed depressed, had been planning to take Deborah and her on a world cruise in March.
3 Derek Jackson (1906–82). Distinguished physicist, amateur jockey and heir to the *News of the World*. Married Pamela, as the second of his six wives, in December 1936. They were divorced in 1951. In 1940 he joined the RAF, winning the Distinguished Flying Cross in 1941. The following year he transferred to Fighter Command and was decorated with the Air Force Cross.
4 Gerald Tyrwhitt, 14th Baron Berners (1883–1950). Composer, painter and writer. A friend of both Nancy, who depicted him as Lord Merlin in *The Pursuit of Love* (1945), and Diana, who wrote an appreciation of him in *Loved Ones* (1985). He lived at Faringdon House, Berkshire.
5 Robert Heber-Percy (1911–87). Known as the 'Mad Boy' because of his wild behaviour. Married twice, to Jennifer Fry, 1942–7, and to Lady Dorothy Lygon in 1985, but his liaisons were mostly with men, principally with Gerald Berners whom he met in 1932 and with whom he carried on a stormy relationship for eighteen years.

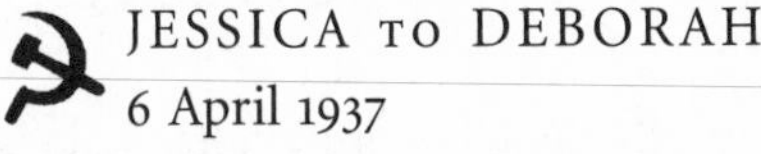

JESSICA TO DEBORAH
6 April 1937

Hôtel des Basques
Place St André
Bayonne

Dear Henri Heine,

Thanks for your letter, I did like getting it. I expect you are at Castle Howard now. If so will you ask George[1] what was in his Greetings 'Gram that Nancy brought out with her among my letters? I opened it & saw some message about Dolly[2] but I didn't really take it in as I was so busy reading all the other letters, & now it's lost. Anyway tell him that jokes about Dolly are rather 'vieux jeu' [old hat] now, & give him my love!

Well here's a description of Esmond which you ask for. He has got blue eyes & beige hair about the colour of mine and he talks rather like Michael Farrer[3] only with a slight cockney pronunciation – for instance he says riowd instead of rood for rude. Also he can do awfully good imitations of people like Winston Churchill[4] & he talks French so well you'd take him for a Frenchman, because once a Frenchman said to him 'vous êtes Alsacien, Monsieur?' which proves it. (He is frightfully good at languages altogether & has already learnt enough Spanish to talk in quite easily, but your poor old Hen can hardly speak a word.) I expect you know most about his doings such as scramming from Wellington etc from seeing it in the papers so won't bother to tell you. Didn't you guess slightly what your old Hen was up to in London the week before I left, for instance when I hurriedly rang off when you came into the room one day & you asked me why I did & I was cross?

Now dear about my clothes; it's very cheery & Hen-like of you to say you'll get them for me etc in fact you are the only one to have made a nice suggestion like that. I'll tell you what though; you know my Worth satin dress that's been dyed purple? Well I don't suppose I shall need a dress like that for ages by which time it'll be out of fashion; so I wonder if you could very kindly try & sell it for me? Being Worth & just newly cleaned & dyed it might fetch quite a lot. I suggest you should take it to Fine Feathers or somewhere & try & get about three to five pounds for it. It would really be most Beery of you if you could dear & I would be grateful. I don't actually need any of my other clothes at present but when the hot weather comes I'll write to you for them.

I wonder if you could write me a really delicious long letter telling among other things exactly what account the Rodds gave of their visit out here. Rodd wrote me a long & incredibly boring letter with points numbered 1), 1(a), 2), etc!!! about how silly it was of me not to come home & I think they were rather cross because we were not impressed by it! I had a letter from Boud the other day in which she said 'Nancy says Esmond adores publicity', which seems to me to be absolutely incomprehensible considering we spent the whole time in St Jean de Luz frantically trying to escape reporters; so if everything she said has been as untrue as that I wish she'd never come out here. Not that it matters, but it seems so stupid of her. Do tell me any other bits of fascinating gossip that you have heard.

Well Dear I long to see you; we may be coming to England about the end of Sept so I'll see you then.

Love from (Stone) Henge

P.S. Your letter was much the nicest I've had for ages.

1 George Howard (1920–84). A cousin of both Esmond Romilly and the Mitfords. Chairman of the BBC 1980–83.
2 Dolly Wilde (1895–1941). Witty lesbian niece of Oscar Wilde. The sisters used to tease their mother by pretending to be in love with her.
3 Michael Farrer (1920–68). A first cousin of the Mitfords.
4 Winston Churchill (1874–1965). The statesman was related through his wife, Clementine Hozier, to both Esmond Romilly and the Mitfords. There was also a rumour in some circles that he was Esmond's father.

卐 UNITY TO DIANA
8 April 1937

Pension Doering
Munich

Darling Nard

Fancy you being in Berlin again, I was so surprised to get your letter. I imagine the Führer is there isn't he?

Do come here for the weekend, everyone has been asking when you are coming, it's such ages since you were here. The Baroness[1] would be so thrilled – you know how she hates me & adores you.

I think I gave the impression that our conversation about the party was more important than it was. Only he said very emphatically, & enlarged upon it quite a lot, that he thought it *might* have proved a fatal mistake in England to call them fascists & Blackshirts instead of something typically English, and suggested that if he had been starting a party in England he would have gone back to Cromwell & perhaps called his SA 'Ironsides'. I thought that rather a sweet idea don't you.

Well let me know when & where you arrive & I will meet you in the car.

Best love from Bobo

P.S. Have you seen Frau Doktor [Magda Goebbels]? She really wrote such a sweet letter about Decca.

1 Unity had kept in touch with Baroness Laroche with whom she lodged when first in Munich.

卐 UNITY TO JESSICA
11 April 1937

Pension Doering
Munich

Darling Boud

Thanks so much for your letter, I was so pleased to get it.

About Esmond's feeling for fascists (actually I prefer to be called a National Socialist as you know) I will explain how I feel about it, & I don't really see why he should feel any different. I hate the communists just as much as he hated Nazis, as you know, and it naturally wouldn't occur to me, nor would I want, to make friends with a lot of communists, if I had no reason to. But I don't see why we shouldn't *personally* be quite good friends, though politically enemies. Of course one can't separate one's politics & one's private life, as you know Nazism *is* my life & I very much despise that democratic-liberal-conservative-English idea of walking about arm-in-arm with one's opponent in private life and looking upon politics as a business or hobby; but I do think that family ties ought to make a difference. After all, violent differences of opinion didn't prevent you & me from remaining good friends did they. My attitude to Esmond is as follows – and I rather expect his to me to be the same. I naturally wouldn't hesitate to shoot him if it was necessary for my cause, and I should expect him to do the same to me. But in the meanwhile, as that isn't necessary, I don't see why we shouldn't be quite good friends, do you. I wonder if he agrees.

As to me turning against my Boud as you say, how could you think I would. On the contrary I was one of the *very* few who always was on your side, all through. The only other ones who *always* stuck up for you, & who I never heard say anything against you or blame you in any way, were Diana & Tom. (And Muv of course, but that was a bit different.) I am longing to see you & tell all about the different attitudes, I expect you are longing to hear too aren't you.

I hear from the old boy that the judge says you can marry, that is good news.

Oh dear I *would* love to see you & have a good chat – there are so many things one can't really ask or discuss in a letter, if one did one would spend the whole day writing.

Mrs Ham is coming on Friday, it *will* be funny having her here & showing her round, somehow the idea of the Wid in Munich is so incongruous.

I wonder what you do in Bayonne all day, & what it's like. Does Esmond speak French well.

By the way I think the only person who thoroughly enjoyed the family crisis was Mrs Ham. She used to come round to Rutland G about five times a day to see one or other of the family, she always insisted on seeing each of us alone so as to get all our individual slants on the affair. Do you remember she used to call you the ballroom communist?

Well Boud *do* write again at once, I long to hear from you. I plan to return to England about the 25th April & stay for the coronation.[1]

Do you remember P. Nevile's ridiculous demonstration for Edward VIII?[2] If I didn't think him so odious I should really be sorry for him. He must be congratulating himself, by the way, on making quite a bit out of your affair. I should claim it if I were you.[3]

Well Boud *do* write soon.

Best love fruddem, je Boudle

1 King George VI, who succeeded to the throne after the abdication of his brother Edward VIII, was crowned on 12 May 1937.
2 In 1936, Peter Nevile, a friend of Jessica and Esmond, tried to stage a demonstration in favour of Edward VIII at a time when the government was putting pressure on the king to give up Wallis Simpson or abdicate.
3 When the publicity surrounding Jessica's elopement was at its height, Peter Nevile sold an interview with Esmond to the *News Chronicle*. Esmond and Nevile shared the proceeds.

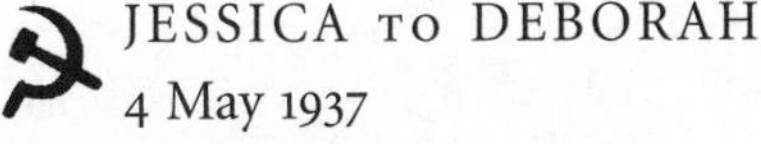

JESSICA TO DEBORAH
4 May 1937

Hôtel des Basques
Bayonne

Dear Hengist & Horsa,

Your old Hen *is* sorry she hasn't written for such an age, she has kept meaning to & is always starting letters to her Hen & then losing them. You *were* kind to take all that trouble about my dresses at Fine Feathers, & I *was* pleased with the £2.10. I know what a bore it is seeing about that sort of thing, & thank you so much for doing it. I certainly don't think I shall sell the Worth for so little. As for the white chiffon dress, I don't think it's worth anything at all as it's so badly made; why don't you get Blor to make you a smart evening shirt out of it to go with your navy moiré coat & anyway, I don't want it any more.

Are you coming to your old Hen's wedding with Muv on the way to Italy? I do hope so. At least I'm afraid it'll be very dull for you being at the Consulate. But do come all the same. Was it fun at Cortachy? I saw in *Vogue* that there was a list of 'important debutantes' (such as Gina,[1] & Iris Mountbatten[2]) & a list of beauties, & Jean[3] was in a horrid sort of side list which included neither!

Peter Nevile has been out here for a few days on his hol, he told all about his visit to Rutland Gate & seemed to admire you very much – we played 'Which would you push out of bed' with him & he kept you for nearly everyone!

Two other English people have been out here, they are *absolute* torture, (a married couple), the wife writes in *Woman & Beauty*, & kept saying how she is an attractive woman & hopes still to be so when she is 35! Somehow we couldn't get rid of them, you know how one can't with English acquaintances in foreign towns.

I saw a dachshund just like Jaky today, & suddenly realized I had completely forgotten his existence. Is he still alive? Der mann, der pet.

I'm sorry this letter is so short & boring, but anyway I hope to see you soon. Give my love to Muv & Boud.

Love from an old Ho Hon

P.S. *Sweet* Blor sent me a weddinger of £1, isn't she an angel.

1 Georgina Wernher (1919–). Daughter of Sir Harold Wernher of Lubenham Hall, Leicestershire, one of the richest men in England, and Lady Zia, daughter of Grand Duke Michael of Russia. Married Harold Phillips in 1944.

2 Lady Iris Mountbatten (1920–82). Great-granddaughter of Queen Victoria.

3 Lady Jean Ogilvy (1918–2004). A cousin of the Mitfords and the eldest daughter of the 12th Earl of Airlie, who lived at Cortachy Castle in Scotland. Married 2nd Baron Lloyd in 1942.

DEBORAH TO JESSICA
8 May 1937

Old Mill Cottage
High Wycombe

Dear Anglo Saxon

Thank you so much for your letter, I was pleased to get it.

I am having rather a fascinating time. For instance I went to London to see Jean & Gina in their dresses before they went to the court. All the Wernhers' servants from Lubenham came up & the stud groom was rather drunk & lay full length on the sofa whistling!! It was a scream.

There is going to be a terrific party on coronation night with the Ogilvys & the Lloyd Thomas's & Wellesleys & Astors. It will be a riot. Maggot[1] & I are going to Florence on Friday.

I *do* so wish I was coming to your wedding, it cuts into a Hen's heart not to be at her Hen's wedding.

I know I shan't enjoy Florence because I shall be wishing I was at your wedding.

Well dear, do write often, the letters will be forwarded to wherever we are.

Love from Sack of Rome

1 Lady Margaret Ogilvy (1920–). Daughter of the 12th Earl of Airlie and a great friend of Deborah. Married Sir Iain Tennant in 1946.

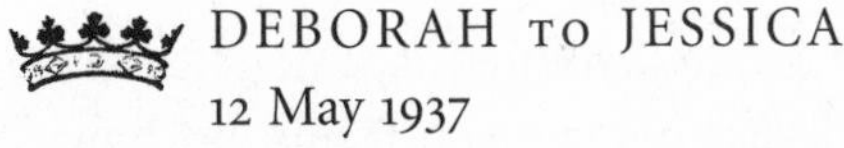

DEBORAH TO JESSICA
12 May 1937

Marlborough Club
Pall Mall, SW

Dear Henry Hall

Dear, you can't imagine how terribly sad I am about not coming to your wedding. You must know that *I* want to come & I certainly don't think that going to Florence with Maggot is a good enough excuse but you know how hopeless the parents are when they get something into their heads. I am writing this on mourning paper, because of not coming.

I *did* like ringing you up last night.

I am sitting in the Marlborough Club waiting for the coronation.[1]

We got up at 5 this morning & helped Muv dress. She was so killing because she went to Phyllis Earle's[2] yesterday to be made up & she slept on her makeup & I must say she looked wonderful this morning. The robes are *too* wonderful & she looked marvellous in her jewels.

Tud[3] came to breakfast at 6 & he looked a knockout in his uniform, really wonderful. We got here by tube with the old boy. The crowds are terrific & they cheer everything that goes by, even fainting people on stretchers so I sing 'cheer cheer what shall we cheer'.

Love from Jack Harris

Oh dear, I *do* wish I was coming to Bayonne. I can't tell you how *furious* I am about it.

Dear, *do* write when we go abroad.

1 From the windows of the Marlborough Club, Deborah could watch the coronation procession on its way to Westminster Abbey. As a peer of the realm, Lord Redesdale attended the service with Lady Redesdale, who was dressed in coronation robes of ermine-trimmed crimson velvet with a three-foot train.
2 Phyllis Earle; a hairdresser and beauty parlour in Dover Street.
3 Tom Mitford.

UNITY TO JESSICA

16 May 1937

Old Mill Cottage
High Wycombe

Darling Boud

This is to wish you happiness & a lovely wedding, I don't suppose it will get to you in time but still. The Fem started off this morning, and she is taking with her a gram[ophone] which is a club present from Tiny [Deborah] & your Boud, I hope it plays all right, it seemed to when I bought it.

PLEASE write & tell your Boud all about your wedding, & what presents you have had & everything, I am dying to hear. The Fem told me she had bought you a wedding dress.

Oh dear it *will* be extraorder to think of my Boud being married, and you can't think how much I miss her. I *DO* hope you will come back a bit before the autumn. I would like to motor from Munich to see you, but I suppose I should skeke [hardly] be very welcome among the comrades at Bayonne.

Well Boud I *DO* hope you will be very happy, and I shall think of you all day on your wedding day, & wish I was there.

I drove Blor over to Egham yesterday for her hol.

Farve sends his best love.

With very best love from your Boud

JESSICA TO DIANA
Thursday [May 1937]

16 rue des Fontaines
Dieppe

Darling Cord,

A delicious looking tin parcel arrived for me this morning with postmark Ashbourne, so it must have been your present.[1] I did long to open it but the awful thing was there was 500 francs customs to pay on it. So I asked the postman if there was any way of getting out of paying it & he said only by returning it to the sender. So I thought perhaps that would be the best, although I hated seeing it go without even opening it, but as we may be returning to England in the autumn perhaps I can have it then? Anyway thank you millions of times for sending it. I *am* excited to have it. The others told me it was a lovely necklace & I am *so* longing for it. The only other way I could have it would be if anyone going to Paris or somewhere could send it to me from there.

We are staying in Cousin Nellie's[2] house, it is too lovely here & we adore it. We are going back to Bayonne (Hôtel des Basques) on Friday, as Csn Nellie & Bertram are coming here.

Well thank you again so much for the weddinger.

Love from Decca

1 A necklace and earrings of pearls and amethysts.

2 Nellie Hozier (1888–1955). Esmond's mother was a first cousin of Lord Redesdale and a sister-in-law of Winston Churchill. Married Bertram Romilly in 1915.

Daily Express

TODAY'S WEATHER: COOLER. RADIO PROGRAMMES: PAGE 19.

WEDNESDAY, MAY 19, 1937 ONE PENNY

MR. ESMOND ROMILLY

MARRIED IN BAYONNE TO PEER'S DAUGHTER

From Our Own Correspondent

BAYONNE, Tuesday.

Mr. Esmond Romilly, a nephew of Mr. Winston Churchill, and the Hon. Jessica Freeman-Mitford, daughter of Lord Redesdale, were married at the British Consulate at Bayonne this morning.

Mr. Romilly wore a brilliant red carnation in his buttonhole and a red handkerchief in the breast pocket of his navy blue suit.

Miss Mitford had a brown three-quarter-length coat over a rainbow-coloured skirt and a native damaged hat with the Basque yellow, red and green cockade.

Lady Redesdale and Mrs. Romilly acted as witnesses. Miss Mitford's age was given as 19 and that of Mr. Romilly as 18.

News Chronicle

ESMOND ROMILLY MARRIED

19 May 1937

From Our Own Correspondent

BAYONNE, Tuesday.

Mr. Esmond Romilly, 18-year-old nephew of Mr. Winston Churchill, and Miss Jessica Freeman-Mitford, 19-year-old daughter of Lord and Lady Redesdale, were married by the British Consul at the Consulate here today.

Lady Redesdale and Mrs. Romilly were present.

"This marriage is purely a formality, and doesn't make any difference to our plans," Mr. Romilly told me.

"We shall return to Bayonne after our holiday to continue our work and shall stay here until the end of the summer."

It was in March that the young couple eloped to Bilbao. Mr. Romilly previously had been fighting with the International Column on the Madrid front.

NO KISSES AS JESSICA IS MARRIED

Daily Express Staff Reporter

BAYONNE, Tuesday.

NINETEEN-YEAR-OLD Mrs. Esmond Romilly—Miss Jessica Freeman-Mitford, daughter of Lord Redesdale—rushed excitedly from a room in the British Consulate here today.

Then, her beige straw hat decorated with buff, red and green—the Basque national colours—swinging in her hand, she went off with her husband. They had been married ten minutes.

Romilly, eighteen-year-old ex-international trooper, nephew of Mr. Winston Churchill, married with the consent of his parents, Colonel and Mrs. Romilly; Miss Jessica with that of Chancery.

Permission—necessary because both are minors—was brought by their mothers, Lady Redesdale and Mrs. Romilly, the only official witnesses.

Before the wedding I asked Mrs. Romilly, smartly dressed in black and white, if the marriage, at first forbidden, now had the full approval of all the parents.

She answered: "Neither Lord Redesdale nor my husband will be present, but both Lady Redesdale and myself wish the young couple every happiness."

Jessica looked radiant in a brown ensemble, bought an hour before.

Marriage, Official

The marriage itself was simple, official, in a sunless, lamplit room.

Formalities were finished by M. Bendedlin, bearded, courteous British Vice-Consul:

"*By warrant of the Secretary of State for Foreign Affairs I hereby make known that according to the law of England you are man and wife.*"

Good wishes from the consul, a red box of chocolates with the Basque arms from Senor Orueztabala, Basque Government representative at Bayonne, and Jessica left the consulate as Mrs. Romilly.

No kisses were exchanged, no ring used. Jessica's hands were covered throughout the ceremony by brown gloves.

Mr. and Mrs. Esmond Romilly, I understand, will divide their honeymoon between Paris and "somewhere in the Pyrenees." Mr. Romilly intends to finish a book on Basque life. "But this time," he said, "I shall not be doing anything very ..."

Nineteen-year-old Miss Jessica Freeman-Mitford, Lord Redesdale's daughter, was married by the British Vice-Consul at Bayonne, France, yesterday, to ex-International trooper Esmond Romilly, nephew of Mr. Winston Churchill. No kisses were exchanged at the ceremony; no ring used.—*Wired picture. Story on Page Eleven.*

Hon. Jessica Freeman-Mitford   Esmond Romilly

Page from Lady Redesdale's scrapbook with cuttings about Jessica's wedding to Esmond Romilly.

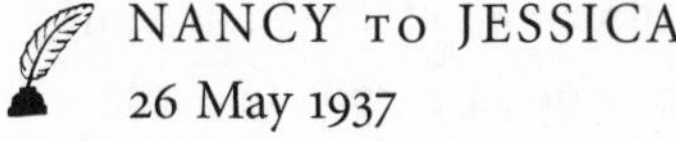

NANCY TO JESSICA
26 May 1937

12 Blomfield Road, w9

Darling Sooze

Really Susan it was your turn to write – or not? Anyway I would have written for your wedding only the typical Fem never told me until the day before or so & I didn't note on my mantelpiece 'Col & Mrs Romilly request the honour (pleasure) of your company at the wedding of their son' etc etc but perhaps it slipped down the back, all my invites do.

Life here is very hectic & I am having a good time. In August we go to Naples, why don't you come? The German Amb. invited us to a party in German which is very rude so Rodd refused in Yiddish but I took the letter away because of my weak mind & not wanting to be tortured when the G's have conquered us.

Love to Esmond & you, Susan

P.S. I hope you got our wedding telegram all right. The Fem didn't seem to think so.

DEBORAH TO JESSICA
3 June 1937

In the train from Vienna to Salzburg

Dear Hen whose Hen has by now given up all hope of her Hen writing to her Hen

Well dear we are in the train doing a horrid long journey of 6 hours from Vienna to Salzburg to meet Birdie.

Yesterday we went to stay with Janos [von Almasy] & Baby[1] took us in her car. We found Mrs Janos in a great state because Janos had been taken off by the gendarmes because he was thought to be plotting for the Nazis & the soldiers had been through all his papers & writing desk & they had found the picture of Bobo & H. & were in a state about it.

Baby has got the most fascinating collection of Angela Brazil[2] school stories I have ever seen.

How are you getting on with your honeymoon & when are you going back to Bayonne.

I must say I have enjoyed myself in filthy abroad although I am longing to get back to the old homeland. (Angela Brazil almost.)

I am in a frenzy because I can't find out what has won the Derby although it happened yesterday.

Bobo – the brute – has started an anti the WID league & Diana has joined. So I have started a pro one & Tom & Nancy & Muv are joining.

Will you too? If so I will send you the forms, & the conditions are (i) that you will always pay her taxis etc for her & (ii) that you will always give her any clothes that she asks for & (iii) that you help her with her packing or whatever is worrying her at the moment & (iv) that you will always buy her clothes off her at 4 times their price.

The subscription is £500 a year which will go towards her upkeep.

Love from Embittered Hen

1 Countess Francesca (Baby) Palffy-Erdödy, a girlfriend of Tom Mitford, and her older sister, Johanna (Jimmy), were friends of Unity and lived at Kohfidisch, Austria.
2 Angela Brazil (1868–1947). Prolific author of racy books about schoolgirls.

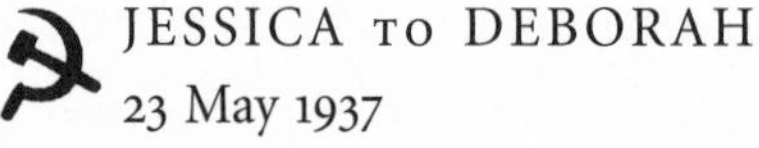

JESSICA TO DEBORAH
23 May 1937

16 rue des Fontaines
Dieppe

Dear Miss Girdlestone or Geldedstone,

I got your letter[1] on arriving here last night, forwarded from Bayonne. It must have taken *ages* getting here, & what's more I'm afraid you won't get this for ages as I've only got your address up to the 23rd which seems to be today. Oh how cheerless. Dear I simply *can't* thank you enough for the absolutely *HEAVENLY* gramophone, oh I do adore it you really *are* a cheery young tart to send me such a marvellous present. It's easily one of the nicest we've had. I wrote to my Boud thanking her too. The following are what I've had so far: Muv, lovely brush set with JLR on the back, a ruby & diamond ring which is *absolute* heaven & I can't stop looking at my hands on account of it; Tello,[2] killing hideous black bag with rosebuds on it ('at least three pence, Sydney')[3] but wasn't it sweet of her to send it; Woman, cheque; Derek, cheque; Tuddemy, cheque (goodness how nice). That isn't all but I can't remember all the others now. *Sweet* Peter Ram's bottom wrote asking what I wanted & apologising for not sending a present out to Spain!! So I thought of suggesting records, which I've asked George for, too.

I expect Muv's told you all the low down on the wedding so I won't bother to enlarge on it. It really was great fun, & we nearly giggled from nerves during the ceremony. Afterwards we went to Paris where we jollied ourselves up in nightclubs etc for two days, it *was* fun but rather tiring & it's lovely to be here for a bit. Dieppe is full of the most extraorder people, they all seem about 70 but according to Cousin Nellie never stop having affairs with each other, chiefly as far as I can make out in the darkened corners of the Bridge club.

Being a married Hen is not at all unlike being an unmarried Hen has been during the last few months, except it seems rather extraorder to have a wedding ring & a mother in law & everything. Well Henderson dear I must thank you again *millions* of times for the phone, it was too sweet of you to give me such a lovely expensive gift.

Best love from Decca

P.S. Maggot sent me a photo of a statue of a naked gentleman: do thank her for it if she is with you. Cousin Nellie has got *The Well of Loneliness*[4] here, your poor old Hen is reading it but goodness it is boring, she can skeke [hardly] get through it.

1 A letter from Deborah sent on 16 May from Florence.
2 Henrietta (Tello) Shell (1864–1950). Governess to Lady Redesdale and her siblings when they were children. After their mother's death in 1887, she became their father's mistress, bore him three sons and assumed the name Mrs John Stewart. In 1894 she became editor of *The Lady*, a position she occupied for twenty-five years.
3 Lady Redesdale's unusual Christian name came from one of her father's half-sisters, Sydney Isabella, who was a goddaughter of Sydney, Lady Morgan, the nineteenth-century Irish novelist.
4 Radclyffe Hall's lesbian novel was banned on publication in 1928 and not republished in Britain until 1949.

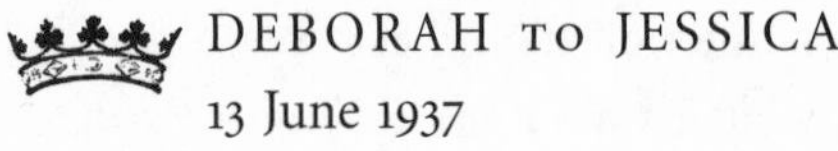

DEBORAH TO JESSICA
13 June 1937

Pension Doering
Munich

Dear Straight Eight or Racing Eight

What a kind old Hen to write her Hen at last. I thought I'd give you some of your own bread or whatever it's called & not write for ages but then I thought I must tell you about the fascinator I have fallen in love with.

There is a wonderful band led by the most wonderful & sweet man called Barnabas von Géczy[1] & they play at a delicious café called the Luitpold. Dear, there is a man in that band who simply makes your hair stand on end to look at him. We don't know his name but he plays the violin the 2nd from the right so that is what we've called him. He is the personification of my type – awfully like Franchot Tone[2] & he sometimes makes the most fascinating faces like Maurice Chevalier.[3] We go there every night so I can sit & stare at him & it makes Muv furious. The terrible thing is that he smiled twice at Bobo last night & not once at me but I think that was partly because I didn't dare look at him much. Géczy himself is a perfect love & he always roars when he sees us. I bought two gramophone records of his yesterday, they are wonderful.

We have had quite a nice time here & we've had tea with Hitler & seen all the other sights.

We are going to try & get Géczy for my dance next March if he comes to London. But I expect he would be much too expensive & anyhow dance music isn't his line so much as wonderful Hungarian tunes.

I have bought a delicious locked diary to note down all about the 2nd from the right in.

We are going home tomorrow. I am quite pleased although I have enjoyed myself like anything. If it hadn't been for Géczy & the 2nd from the right I should have longed to go ages ago. I think Munich is no end nice all the same. If I had to live anywhere abroad I should certainly live here.

We have been away for a whole month, a record almost. I miss My Man & Studley[4] so much that it is really them that I long to get home to.

I am going to Jean's dance on the 23rd, & Elizabeth Wellesley's[5] &

Gina's. The King & Queen are going to be at Gina's which will be wonderful because everyone will be dressed in their best. But I am terrified because I haven't been asked to any dinner party & it will be terrifying just arriving at a dance like that.

Do write dear. Write to Wycombe.

Love from Poor Hen
who swarms for the 2nd from the right.

1 Barnabas von Géczy (1897–1971). Hungarian-born leader of one of the most popular swing orchestras of the time. Deborah's admiration for him was reciprocated: when Unity saw the band the following year, Géczy whispered into her ear, 'Wheer ees Debo?' (Unity to Lady Redesdale, 12 July 1938).
2 Franchot Tone (1905–68). Suave American actor who starred in *Mutiny on the Bounty* (1935). Married to Joan Crawford 1935–9.
3 Maurice Chevalier (1888–1972). Actor who played the quintessential Frenchman in 1930s American cinema.
4 Deborah's whippets.
5 Lady Elizabeth Wellesley (1918–). Daughter of the 7th Duke of Wellington.

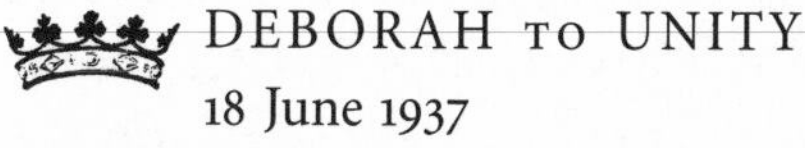

DEBORAH to UNITY

18 June 1937

Old Mill Cottage
High Wycombe

Dear Bird

My case[1] came on yesterday & there is a long account of the apology in *The Times* & a furious one in the *Daily Express*.

Muv wouldn't allow me to go for some unknown reason, I was simply furious. It would have been so exciting, the first case I had ever been to to be my own, like one's own wedding being the first one has ever been to. (Rather involved I'm afraid.)

Did the Führer go through Munich on his way to Berlin? If so I suppose we missed him by a day. Typical.

Muv was simply wonderful at Ascot yesterday, the things she said. Luckily I had my Femmerism note book with me so I wrote them down. The first was this: there were fifty aeroplanes going overhead practising for the display & I said 'wouldn't it be *terrifying* if they were enemy ones & we were being attacked from the air'. So the Fem said quite slowly and unconcernedly 'Orrhhn, well I should always expect them to miss me'. But the way she said it – in her best Mae West style.

As we were getting out of the crowd she made her best remark for weeks. She said 'I always think that if one had any sense one would always bring stilts to this kind of thing & just hop up on them.' You must say that beats nearly everything. Of course they don't look half as funny written down as they do when they are said. The important thing is to get just the right pause between 'this kind of thing' and 'just hop up on them'.

Love from Tiny

1 Deborah had sued the *Daily Express* for saying that she, not Jessica, had eloped with Esmond. The case was settled out of court and Deborah was awarded £1,000.

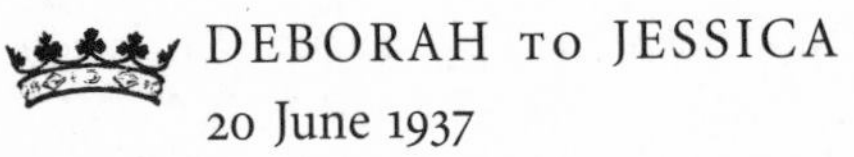

DEBORAH TO JESSICA
20 June 1937

[The Mill Cottage][1]
Swinbrook

Dear Crackinjay

We arrived here yesterday for the first time & it is really very nice if very cold. The fishing is terrific, we caught five trout last night. As Muv & Farve are always going on about how they love housework I leave it all to them to serve them right. All I have done so far is to make a Mitford Mess – tomatoes & potato fried in oil – which is the only thing I can cook & is it delicious.

It is more than ever like a Russian novel here because Farve has taken terrific trouble to buy things he thinks Muv will like & she goes round putting all the things away that he has chosen. The worst of all was when she went to her bedroom for the first time & saw two wonderfully hideous lampshades with stars on them & she said 'I certainly *never* bought these horrors' & Farve's face fell several miles. It is simply pathetic.

Last night a child was murdered at Capps Lodge & they haven't arrested the man yet so I am terrified that he will be after us & I keep thinking I see his face at the window. He was the chef from the Lamb Inn at Burford.

Pam came to lunch the other day & they talked for 2½ hours about servants. Pam has had her hair dyed orange & it makes her look like a tart.

Bobo & Terence O'Connor[2] are having a terrific get off, but I am going to steal a march on her at his cktl pty on Wednesday as Birdie is in Germany.

The Hitler tea party was fascinating. Bobo was like someone transformed when she was with him & going upstairs she was shaking so much she could hardly walk. I think Hitler must be very fond of her, he never took his eyes off her. Muv asked whether there were any laws about having good flour for bread, wasn't it killing.

Well dear do write often, there is nothing yr Hen likes better than a letter from hr Hen.

Love from André Gide

1 After the sale of Swinbrook, Lord Redesdale rented a cottage in the village so that he could continue fishing on the Windrush.
2 Terence O'Connor (1891–1940). Conservative MP and Solicitor-General 1936–40. A keen follower of the Heythrop, he died after straining his heart on the hunting field. Married Cecil Cook in 1920.

DIANA TO NANCY
21 June 1937

Wootton Lodge
Ashbourne

Darling Nancy

I only got your letter this morning because it was sent to me in a packet and then followed me back here. It was so sweet of you to write darling, and wish me happiness. Driberg's story was all wrong and from the date on your letter I was here and not in Berlin when he offered you a free call![1] There was no such romantic reason for my going as he told you. When you get back I will tell you the story or Muv & Farve can. Farve says the press telephone him constantly and ask him for TPOL's[2] address, and he says 'But I don't know it, I've never met him' isn't it wonderful. I expect he adds: 'the damned sewer'.[3]

So for the present I am Mrs G and intend to remain so for some time.

Best love from Bodley

1 Tom Driberg (1905–76). Labour MP, author and journalist. Since 1933 he had been the 'William Hickey' gossip columnist on the *Daily Express*. The press suspected that

Diana and Mosley were married but were unable to find proof. Of the family, only the Redesdales, Unity and Tom knew about the marriage; Nancy, who was incapable of keeping a secret, had not been told.
2 'The Poor Old Leader', i.e. Mosley.
3 Lord Redesdale's favourite term of abuse derived from 'suar', meaning 'pig' in Hindi, a word he learnt when he worked as a tea planter in Ceylon.

UNITY TO JESSICA

3 July 1937

Old Mill Cottage
High Wycombe

Darling Boud

We sit all day playing a sad tune called 'Somebody stole my Boud' (alternatively 'Somebody stole my Hen').[1]

Love, Your Boud

1 From a popular song of 1937, 'Somebody Stole my Gal'.

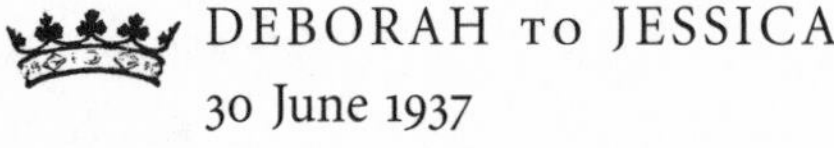

DEBORAH TO JESSICA

30 June 1937

4 Rutland Gate Mews
London SW7

Dear Hen's Egg

Well dear, the dances have begun in earnest. I must say they are *exactly* like what you said always – perfectly killing. I have *never* seen anything like the collection of young men – all completely chinless & all looking exactly alike. Last night was the Wellesleys.

According to everyone it was a really typical deb dance. Rather a small square room to dance in & many too many people in the doorway & on the stairs. I thought I should be alright & then they started to cut my dances till, in the end, in desperation I had to go home. Tuddemy has been to all the ones I have, luckily for me. He is simply *wonderful* & literally waits around till I haven't got anyone to dance with & then comes & sits on a sofa or dances with me. I must say it is terribly nice of him. My conversation to the debs' young men goes like this:

The chinless horror 'I think this is our dance.'

Me (knowing all the time that it is & only too thankful to see him, thinking I'd been cut again) 'Oh yes, I think it is.'

The C.H. 'What a crowd in the doorway.'

Me 'Yes isn't it awful.'

The C.H. then clutches me round the waist & I almost fall over as I try & put my feet where his aren't.

Me 'Sorry.'

The C.H. 'No, my fault.'

Me 'Oh I think it must have been me.'

The C.H. 'Oh no, that wouldn't be possible.' (Supposed to be a compliment.)

Then follows a long & dreary silence sometimes one of us saying 'sorry' & the other 'my fault'. After a bit we both feel we can't bear it any longer so we decide to go & sit down.

The C.H. 'Got off camp this time, told them it was a sprained ankle, look at the bandages, ha ha'. (I look & see no bandages so suppose it must be a joke & say 'ha ha' too.)

Then one hears the drums rumbling & one knows that is the end of the dance & goes hopelessly back to the doorway hoping for the other chinless horror to turn up & of course he doesn't so one scrams thankfully off to bed.

Yesterday one young man told me the same funny (?) story three times. At least I think it was the same young man but one can't possibly tell.

Well dear, Family Life seems to go on in the same old way & I never see any of the sisters except sometimes Bobo, & the boredom of Wycombe is absolutely unbelievable. One never dares ask any of one's friends for fear of the family taking against them & being fearfully rude 'like only Mitfords can'. Bobo has just come back from Germany. She is going back again soon. I wish I was going with her. I should at least be able to go every night to listen to the band with the man I love in it. When she goes I shall be absolutely alone again which I hate so. There isn't anyone to talk to because you know how the parents simply don't listen.

Pam comes over sometimes which is awful. When Derek comes too it is worse. I never see Diana & very seldom see Nancy or Tom.

So altogether it isn't much fun. We have got to be at Wycombe for three months now. Lord only knows what I shall find to do all that time.

Everyone does the same old things here. Farve goes off to *The Lady* & the House of Lords & Muv paints chairs & reads books called things like 'Stalin: My Father' or 'Mussolini: The Man' or 'Hitler: My Brother's Uncle' or 'I Was In Spain' or 'The Jews – By One Who Knows Them' etc etc etc. I haven't read a book for eight months now.

I never can remember what jokes you've heard & what you've missed, but I know you can't have heard this one. It's a summing up of the Fem's character by Bobo & me. It goes like this 'Nelson, bread of my life, meet me tonight without any doctors or any medicine under the kitchen table'.[1] You must say it's a wonderful summing up. Well dear, hotcha.

Love from Yr Hen

1 Lady Redesdale, whose admiration for Nelson was as great as her distrust of the medical profession, used to give lectures at the Women's Institute on bread-making.

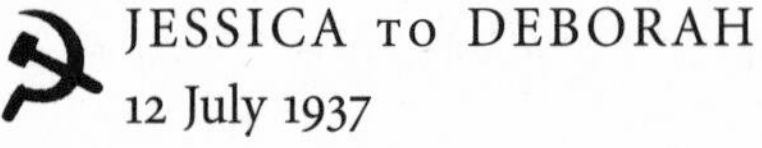

JESSICA TO DEBORAH
12 July 1937

Hôtel des Basques
Bayonne

Dear Henderson,

Thanks v. much for amusing letters

Have you been to any more dances? I gather from your letters that you more or less loathe most of them, I must say deb dances aren't the cheeriest form of entertainment. But it seems all the more marvellous when one doesn't have to go any more; Esmond says that's the same as being at a public school or remand home, that always afterwards you think how lucky you are not to be there still. Anyway I expect next year it really *will* be more fun; I call the middle of July an extraorder time to come out, you might have liked it more if you had come out at the beginning of the summer.

Couldn't you cheer off abroad somewhere, e.g. to Italy with the

Rodds, or Germany with the Boud? Or even France with your Hen. Where are you all going to be in the winter – R Gate or the cottage? Your Hen will be in London then, we are coming back after our Tour to live there for a few months while your Hen has her baby etc. Shall I call it Henderson, or even Hon Henderson & everyone'll think it's *the* Hon(ble) Henderson. Did you know your old Hen was in pig.[1] Yes dear, you had better be training as a young midwife, as soon as possible. I hope you will be its Henmother (Honnish for Godmother) anyway. Do write to your Hen & say if you are interested about it. Your poor Hen never stopped sicking up *all* her food for about three months on account of it, which was so cheerless.

Peter R[amsbotham] & George Howard have sent us an absolute *mass* of phone records which is such bliss of them. Do impress how grateful I am if you see them, there's such a terrific lot.

Love from Henry

1 When one of the Mitford children's guinea pigs was pregnant, the sisters called it 'in pig', as 'in foal', and used the expression for humans and animals alike.

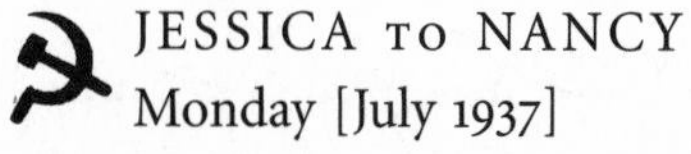

JESSICA TO NANCY
Monday [July 1937]

Hôtel des Basques
Bayonne

Darling Susan,

Thanks for yr. letter. All *is* oke now really, but Susan I must just remind you of a few things you seem to have forgotten! Susan *how* can you say you & Rodd were pro Esmond & me living together when you wrote saying how unrespectable it was & how Society would shun me, & Rodd wrote saying how French workmen would shun me. In fact what you actually wanted us to do was to come home to England, in which case I should have been caught by the P's[1] & narst old Judge & altogether teased in every way. So what you were really against was *both* us getting married *and* us living together not married. Do you admit, Susan. Do you also admit it *was* a bit disloyal just as I was thinking you were the one I could count on to be on my side through thick and. Anyway it's all such ages ago now I expect you've forgotten a bit what you did do, &, as you say, now we *are* married there's no point in [illegible].

I am going to have a baby in January (1st to be exact, oh Susan do you remember poor Lottie's[2] agonies, & I expect it's much worse for humans), yes Susan some of us do our duty to the community unlike others I could name. Shall I call it Nancy? I think skeke [hardly] as I have a feeling it's going to be a boy, & being called Nancy might prove a handicap to it throughout life. I do hope it will be sweet & pretty & everything. Goodness I have been sick but I'm not any more now.

The bathing here is *absolute* heaven, we go to Biarritz nearly every day. Well Soose. End of paper.

Love from Susan

1 'The Parent Birds', i.e. the Redesdales.
2 Nancy's French bulldog.

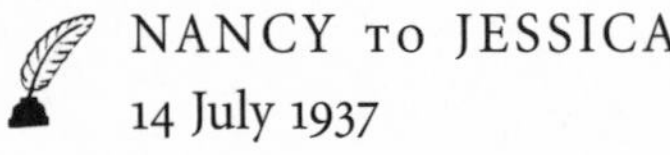

NANCY TO JESSICA — *12 Blomfield Road, w9*
14 July 1937

Darling Sooze

Oh thank goodness what a weight off my mind. Well Susan now I know that all is OKE I am sending you a) a narst little diamond ring as I know it is nice to have things of popping value even if only for a few pounds & b) which you will like *much* more *Busman's Honeymoon*[1] which must be the funniest book ere written. And I daresay some cash will be forthcoming in Jan. when needed. Susan fancy you with a scrapage. I don't think you are fit to bring one up after your terribly awful behaviour but what luck that you will always have dear old aunt Nancy at hand to advise & help.

Love from Sooze

1 Dorothy L. Sayers' eleventh thriller featuring Lord Peter Wimsey (1937).

JESSICA TO DEBORAH
3 August 1937

Select Hotel
Dieppe

Dearest Henderson,

It *WAS* lovely seeing you & Blor, you can't think how *terribly* pleased I was you could come. I only wish you were still here, it seemed such an awfully short time.

I do hope you weren't bored & I didn't talk about Esmond all the time like Woman does about Derek, but you know it seems such an *AGE* since he went, however he's coming back today for certain.

I think I only really realized, from seeing you, what things had been like at home; it is so extraorder how people can make themselves so miserable when there's nothing to be miserable about, & of course I'm dreadfully sorry they were so unhappy. It seems such a tease that one can't be what one likes without causing all that misery. The more I think of it the less I can understand it.

Best love from Squalor

It's early Spring in January, because I'm in pig.

DIANA TO UNITY
3 August 1937

Wootton Lodge
Ashbourne

Darling:

I would have written ages ago, but we are having a heat wave of terrific proportions and it is really *boiling* and I spend the days in a pair of bathing pants and a shirt. I am reading *Mein Kampf*.[1] Everything looks unbelievably beautiful.

4th August. I have got a lot to erzähl [tell] about the Oxford Group. Annemarie[2] said could she come here, so I said yes (I was alone) and she came needless to say with Mr [Reginald] Holme & Miles Phillimore.[3] They arrived for lunch and made an onslaught which lasted till 10.45, trying to persuade me to go back to Oxford with them for the weekend. It was a very special weekend with very important people, and Frank [Buchman] had said would I come etc. I did not want to go in the least but as I was alone here I had no reason. When they saw I was set against it they tried a sort of mixture of flattery ('you could change the world') and blackmail and threats ('you are afraid of being converted. You are not a revolutionary if you don't give us a fair trial'). 'Why not?' is the answer I think!!

Anyway it ended with a Quiet Time. I did not write anything on the bit of paper they gave me although I thought of lots of jokes. They all read out their guidance and it consisted mostly of God saying he wanted me to go to Oxford. In the end they went off in despair. I suppose Frank had told them to bring me back. But during the day I got a terrific nausea for the whole silly affair, and when they said Frank had changed the world and prevented industrial disputes etc I asked how long he had been at it; they replied since 1921, so I said that was as long as the Führer, leaving them to make the comparison. I said in order to change anything properly in the modern world you had to have a political organization and several thousand people willing to give their lives and some machine guns. I said why the hell didn't Frank stick to America and try and change that, because the industrial disputes there were the horror of the whole world.

They were very hurt and made all kinds of lame answers.

6 August. So then I said you will never get me for your sort of 'revolution' because I am a realist and we must have a framework first in England. Miles Phillimore, 'We are realists too, and after all when I had been in New Zealand a year, the Prime Minister said "the Oxford group is the only policy for the world".' And what difference has it made him saying that?

But the thing that makes me angriest is when they harp on the fact that Frank said publicly 'thank God for Adolf Hitler'. They tell one that as if it were gleichzeitig [at the same time] very brave and a terrific compliment for the Führer.

I am sorry for all this boring outburst but I longed for you to be there at the time. Although I am really fond of Annemarie I shall not lift a finger for her to see the Führer while she is with that ghastly Frank.

It is so lovely and calm here with Kit. We don't even ride, but just lie in the sun and listen to the wireless, and fish, and row in a tiny little boat he has brought. I am so happy. At the end of next week Vivien[4] & Nicky[5] come, and then it will be less peaceful. The boys are coming too and I am perfectly dying for them.

This letter has gone on so long it must be a birthday letter now darling, so many happy returns, and I enclose the usual dull-but-useful.

I wish you were here. Kit wants you to come & bring the Princesses Wrede[6] with you!!

All love, Nardy

P.S. Miles & co kept being guided to use my telephone for trunk calls! They all ring up nearly every day but I say I am away. They are nothing daunted by my firmness. Of course they are mad to get to see the Führer. But then who isn't?

1 Hitler's autobiography, *My Struggle*, was first published in two volumes, in 1925 and 1926.

2 Annemarie Ortaus; a keen German follower of Moral Rearmament whom Diana had met in Munich.

3 Miles Phillimore (1915–72). Author of *Just for Today*, a Moral Rearmament pamphlet (1940).

4 Vivien Mosley (1921–2002). Diana's stepdaughter. Married Desmond Forbes-Adam in 1949.

5 Nicholas Mosley, 3rd Baron Ravensdale (1923–). Diana's stepson became a novelist and biographer. His books include *Accident* (1964), *Julian Grenfell* (1976), *Hopeful Monsters* (1990) and a two-volume life of his father, *Rules of the Game* (1982) and *Beyond the Pale* (1983). Married to Rosemary Salmon 1947–74 and to Verity Raymond in 1974.

6 The Princesses Edda and Carmen von Wrede were twin daughters of a German father and Argentinian mother. They lived at Schloss Fantaisie near Bayreuth and had been friends of Unity's since 1935.

卐 UNITY TO DIANA
4 August 1937

Pension Doering
Munich

Darling Nard

Thank you so much for your letter. It arrived just after I had posted my letter to you, with the photo

I quite forgot to thank you for the lovely photos of the boys,

I *was* so pleased with them & I shall stick them in my family book when I go to England.

Erna is most terribly aufgeregt [excited] about 'Entartete Kunst',[1] she says that the artists in it are the *only* good ones in Germany today and the whole world envies Germany for them. She has stopped working in her shop because her brother is afraid the SS will come & smash the windows if she is caught selling reproductions of modern pictures (that sounds unlikely doesn't it) and she sits at home in Solln all by herself getting aufgeregter & aufgeregter. I spent a whole afternoon & evening with her & she didn't speak of anything else at all, just a torrent of Aufregung [excitement]. She goes to the exhibition every day, & she says that all the really artistic people in Munich are freu-ing [enjoying] themselves like anything because they say, never before have we had a chance of seeing all these wonderful pictures collected together in one Ausstellung [exhibition], & they go every day, & noch dazu [what's more] the entrance is free. She says all the Americans come to her & say 'If only we could have this wonderful collection in America, wouldn't they let us take it over?' I asked Erna to let me go to it with her but she refused but at last I persuaded her & we went, I feel I learnt quite a lot by it. She has small pictures by two of the artists, which they gave her themselves, hanging in her house, in fact she has three pictures by Nolde. [incomplete]

1 The celebrated exhibition of 'Degenerate Art', comprising pictures that had been removed from state collections, was designed to educate the Germans on the 'evils' of modern art. Works by Max Beckmann, Chagall, Otto Dix, Max Ernst, Kandinsky and Nolde attracted five times as many visitors as a show of Nazi-approved art held at the same time.

卐 UNITY TO JESSICA
10 August 1937

Pension Doering
Munich

Darling Boud

I have been wanting to write to you for ages but I didn't know your address, now Muv has sent me the Dieppe one & says it will find you. I hope it will. Do write to your Boud soon.

I did envy Blor & Tiny going to see my Boud, I *do* hope I will soon. I hear you had a tooth out without anaesthetic, *poor* Boud how *awful*. How is the baby, I hear you can feel it kicking already. It is so exciting, I *do* envy you. I think I really must have a darling little Bastard, it would be so sweet & I should love it. Do you hope for a boy or a girl? What will you call it?

Clementine [Mitford] & I went with the Führer to Bayreuth for the festival, we were there ten days, it was lovely. Kukuli von Arent[1] was in Bayreuth, & she hadn't heard about you, she was perfectly amazed when I told her & kept on saying 'Aber die Decca war doch so nett! Sie war doch so lustig und reizend![2] Do you remember when the two SS men here called you 'die lustige Kommunistin'? Clementine went to England from Bayreuth, & I returned here. I have seen the Führer a lot lately which has been heaven, only now he has gone back to his mountain for a bit.

I do hope you are having lovely weather for your motor tour. We have been having a heat wave here for a week, but today alas it's raining. The other day when it was boiling hot I found a secluded spot in the Englischer Garten[3] where I took off all my clothes & sunbathed, luckily no-one came along. While I was lying in the sun I suddenly wondered whether Muv *knew* I was sun-bathing naked, like when she *knew* that you were bathing naked, & I laughed till I ached, if anyone had come along they would have thought me mad as well as indecent.

Well Boud *pray* write to your Boud as soon as you get this, she does so long to hear from her Boud.

Best love from *Yr* Boud

1 The wife of Benno von Arent (1898–1956), Hitler's favourite theatre designer.
2 'But Decca was so nice! She was so funny and charming!'

3 The city park in the centre of Munich where two years later Unity attempted to commit suicide.

DIANA TO UNITY

14 August 1937

Hotel Kaiserhof
Berlin

Darling:

I have got a lot to erzähl [tell] about a wonderfully typical day I spent at Schwanenwerder yesterday. After discovering that the people I have come to see are all away, I rang up Magda on the chance and she asked me to come at once. Kukuli was there, radiant after spending a week with her loved one, her idyll was spoilt later in the day by Benno von Arent who bullied her to go back to her Kinder [children]. The Doktor was there and the food, conversation and whole set-up was so exactly like last year that I kept thinking it *was* last year. Magda wanted to play Animal Vegetable or Mineral, and when we chose something for her to guess she always complained either that it was, 'Wirklich zu dumm, viel zu leicht'[1] etc. Or if she couldn't guess it, it was 'a frightfully unfair one'. When it was one of our turns she kept saying, 'Aber Sie müssen nur logisch denken, ich hätte das in zwei minuten gefunden'.[2]

It was pure heaven. Then we played Analogies which I taught them. Magda got the hang of it in a moment, and we had a heavenly time doing Helldorf, Frau Funk, Frau Hoffmann and so on. Then the Doktor joined us and we, or rather he, did the Führer for Kukuli. Here is what he said (we all helped and this was the result)

Animal:	Pure-bred Arab stallion
Colour:	Feuerrot[3]
Drink:	Ein schwerer Wein[4]
Flower:	Madonna lily*
Style:	Michaelangelo – Renaissance*
Landschaft:[5]	Top of the Alps
Weather:	A hot storm*
Frau:	Eine grosse schöne blonde Frau[6]

*I have marked my own contributions with a star.

Needless to say although Harald[7] who came halfway through kept saying, 'Aber Kinder, ganz klar, es gibt nur einer',[8] Kukuli failed to guess, and when she was told said, 'Ich habe die ganze Zeit an den Führer gedacht, aber er trinkt doch nur Wasser!'[9] Whereupon both Goebbels rounded on her so cruelly that she nearly cried. I must say it was rather dotty because we had told 23 times it had nothing to do with what the person liked, or wore etc. Well I was pleased when the Doktor said, 'Eine grosse schöne blonde Frau'.

The lovely part of the day was a *wonderful* film called *Entscheidende Tage* [*Decisive Days*] and it is only real-life films, of the war, the Versailles Treaty, the revolution here, the coming of the Führer, 1923 Parteitag, meetings, Schlageter[10] being shot, Jews, Nazis, the 1929 Parteitag, Machtübernahme [taking power], Aufbau [rebuilding], 1936 Parteitag. It was pure heaven, except that the Doktor schimpfed [railed] all the way through at the man who had spent eight months making it. I must say he was perfectly right because it was an awful muddle and terribly hard to know what was going on. The Doktor said he himself didn't know half the time although he lived it all. So it has to be entirely altered, but darling the *material* is simply thrilling.

There was a lovely moment when the Doktor said, 'Ich stelle mich meine Mutter vor; sie hätte fast nichts davon verstanden; es muss absolut klar sein für die einfachsten und dummsten Leute.'[11]

There is the most heavenly picture of the Führer at the 1929 Parteitag, laughing and throwing flowers at the SA as they march vorbei [past]. *Oh* how I wished we had been there, it makes me cry with rage to think we were alive and yet missing *everything*.

Do you really think the Führer might come here? I thirst for only a glimpse of him. I know he's at Nürnberg today because the Doktor is meeting him there. If you see Wiedemann[12] give him my fondest love and tell him I am here, could you darling.

MASSES of love, do write again, Nardy

1 'Really too stupid, much too easy.'
2 'But you've only got to think logically, I'd have guessed it in two minutes.'
3 'Fiery red.'
4 'A full-bodied wine.'
5 'Landscape.'

6 'A tall, beautiful blonde woman.'
7 Harald Quandt (1921–67). Magda Goebbels' son by her first marriage.
8 'But children, it's obvious, it couldn't be anyone else.'
9 'I was thinking of the Führer all along, but he drinks only water!'
10 Leo Schlageter (1894–1923). A Nazi martyr executed by the French for resisting their forces in the Ruhr.
11 'I'm thinking of my mother; she'd have understood hardly anything; it must be absolutely clear for the simplest and stupidest people.'
12 Fritz Wiedemann (1891–1970). Hitler's immediate superior during the First World War and subsequently one of his military aides and policy advisers.

卐 UNITY to DIANA

1 September 1937

Pension Romana
Akademiestrasse 7
Munich

Darling Nard,

I had lunch with the Führer in the Ost the day before the Duce[1] came, & said goodbye to him as I shan't see him again. The little Doktor was there. We had rather a stormy scene as all of them, except the Führer, set on me because I said I didn't like Musso, & bullied me till I was almost in tears, it was dreadful. I thought I wouldn't be able to prevent myself crying. However the Führer took my part (without of course saying anything against Musso) & he was perfectly sweet. Of course the one that led the attack was Dr Brandt.[2]

Two days before Musso's visit Wardie[3] & Randolph [Churchill] arrived here. I met them at the plane & spent the whole three days with them, it was great fun. Randolph never stopped complaining because I didn't get him an interview with the Führer & grumbling about the lack of 'facilities' whatever that may be, but he was very nice. Altogether, the three days were great fun & I adored it in spite of the misery of Musso coming.

May I come to Wootton for a few days when I get to England?

Best love, & to the boys, Heil Hitler, Bobo

P.S. Have you read *Gone with the Wind*?[4] It is the most fascinating book ever written. I read it in under a week although it's got 1036 pages & you know what a slow reader I am, so that just shows. One can't put it down.

Unity on the cover of a news magazine, November 1937. Hardly a week went by during the 1930s without one of the sisters making headlines.

1 Mussolini's state visit to Germany, during which Hitler put on a massive display of military power, was instrumental in convincing the Italian dictator to join forces with Germany.
2 Karl Brandt (1904–1947). Surgeon who joined the Nazi Party in 1932 and served as Hitler's doctor 1934–44.
3 George Ward Price (1886–1961). Munich correspondent for the *Daily Mail* and author of *I Know These Dictators* (1937), a sympathetic portrait of Hitler and Mussolini.
4 Margaret Mitchell's bestseller had been published the previous year.

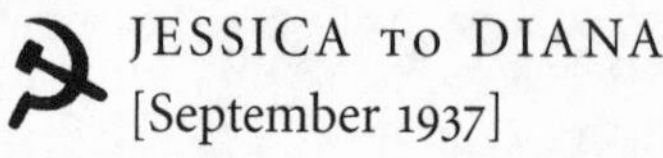

JESSICA TO DIANA
[September 1937]

41 Rotherhithe Street
London SE16

Darling Cord

Thank you *so* much for the delicious cheque for £5, I *was* pleased to get it, & it arrived on my birthday, too.

We went to Biddesden the other day for the wknd, it was a scream, Bryan made everyone slave away from morning till on the farm, & he kept saying to his wife 'would you like to come for a bicycle ride?' although it was only a week before the baby was born![1] We have got a house looking over the river, which is heaven, I think I shall be staying here for the baby.

Thank you again for the lovely birthday gift.

Love from Decca

1 Rosaleen, Bryan and Elizabeth Guinness's first child, was born on 7 September 1937.

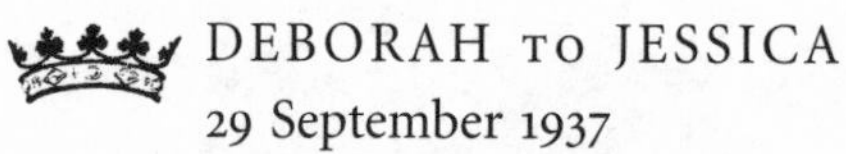

DEBORAH TO JESSICA
29 September 1937

Cortachy Castle
Kirriemuir, Angus

Dearest Crackinjay

Oh goodness the Bridgetness[1] of it! She is being *so* awful that I would really like to be very rude to her if it wasn't for Maggot. This afternoon she said 'Of course I think it is so awful for gals not to play games like tennis & golf because not only are they left out of everything but they are a fearful bore to have in the house & it is very selfish of them because they ruin everybody else's good time'. Don't you think it is the damn rudest thing you have ever heard when I was sitting there & she knows I can't (& won't) do anything like that. I was simply furious.

She says that 'gals' never get asked anywhere unless they are good at games. I hate the idea of being asked somewhere to 'make up a four at tennis'. I'd much rather not go away to stay anywhere if I thought I was being asked to make even numbers for tennis of all blasted games. Why they can't sit & talk like normal humans I can't imagine. They are always driving you to 'do something'. Goodness it does make me angry. I hate Bridget more than I ever have before. She is perfectly bloody.

Tom is back from Germany & has been down to Wycombe.

Well dear, do write.

The Forfar ball is on Friday. I hope it will be nice.

Much love from Henderson

1 Lady Bridget Coke (1891–1984). Mother of Deborah's great friend Margaret (Maggot) Ogilvy. Married the 12th Earl of Airlie in 1917.

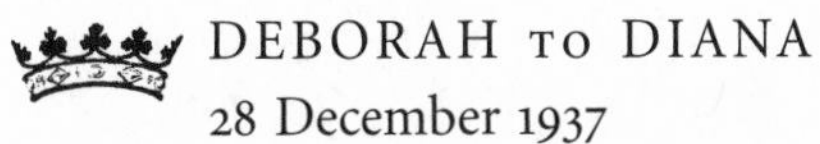

DEBORAH TO DIANA
28 December 1937

Old Mill Cottage
High Wycombe

Darling Honks

Thank you *so* much for the really wonderful gift, they are things I have always longed for but I have never afforded them as Blor always makes me buy woollen combies. They are such heaven, thank you a *million* times.

I had measles all through merry Xmas. It *was* so awful I nearly died of the horror of it.

This letter has been disinfected by Blor putting it in the oven, at least it will have been by the time you get it. The one I wrote to Bridget I specially didn't have done.

You are kind to have sent the gorgeous gift, goodness you are.

Tuddemy says they are pretties, like the adverts.

Much love from Debo

I am still in bed for seven days as the doctor says I shall get bronchitis if I get up which makes Muv furious. I have also had some glorious medicine.

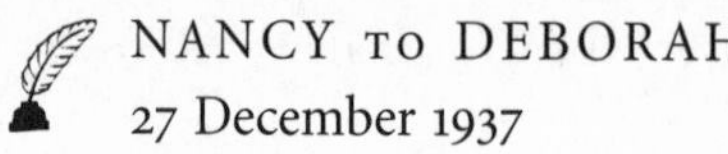

NANCY TO DEBORAH
27 December 1937

West Wycombe Park
Bucks

Dear Miss Measles

Oh those *little* armless hands* I simply adore them. Rodd thinks they are awfully sinister & they terrify him but I wear them the whole time.[1] It was kind of you.

Poor Miss how awful about yr blindness, of course one can't help wondering what sort it is when remembering yr awful reputation.[2]

Yes it is very nice here – Rodd spends his time making hats for Helen,[3] & SHE WEARS them. So we are happy.

Love from Get on & get out of here.[4]

* The little armless hand
It lies upon the land
It cannot hold
It cannot mould
Nor rub an aching gland

It lies alone & makes no moan[5]

1 Deborah's Christmas present to Nancy was a bracelet of Hand of Fatima charms.
2 The attack of measles had affected Deborah's eyes. The sisters used to tease each other about syphilis, which can lead to blindness in its later stages.
3 Helen Eaton (1899–1989). Nancy's nickname for her hostess at West Wycombe was 'Hell Bags'. Married Sir John Dashwood in 1922.
4 'Get on', Deborah's way of addressing Nancy, was an interpretation of the sort of

growl that the Mitfords' groom used to greet people with. Deborah took it up as a way of fighting back at her eldest sister.

5 When Deborah was small, Nancy used to tease her with a rhyme that never failed to make her little sister cry: 'A little houseless match, it has no roof, no thatch / It lies alone, it makes no moan, that little, houseless match'. She put the poem into *The Pursuit of Love*, where it induced 'rivers of tears' in the heroine, Linda.

☭ JESSICA TO DEBORAH
28 December 1937

41 Rotherhithe Street, SE16

Dearest young Hen,

How I do love your delicious gift of face cream, it really is just what I wanted dear thank you *so* much.

I was amazed at your letter in the Fem's writing, it seemed so extraorder to see Honnish terms in a non-Hon's handwriting.

How *simply* wretched for you having measles, poor old Hohon.

The baby[1] is terribly strong already & you could have seen it and me any time if you hadn't been a young germ carrier.

We had the most *heavenly* Xmas you can image. Yr Hen had in her stocking: E. Arden bath salts & hand lotion, L. Philippe lipstick, Atkinson scent, Turkish delight, two boxes of chocolates, a book and 1s worth of cream which she drank down at one gulp. The poor Babe hung its sock but didn't get a damn thing! Luckily it didn't seem to notice.

Dear you can't *imagine* how sweet it is, I long for you to come & see it. She hasn't got any of the disadvantages of so many babes such as excessive redness & baldness & smelling of sick.

Yr Hen is *loving* her delicious time in bed, tho of course it isn't nearly such heaven now as over the Xmas hol when Esmond was here all the time;[2] but Id is coming today & I hope lots of people will be scramming down here.

Well dear
Not much news
So cheer ha.

Love from Beery

1 Jessica's daughter, Julia, was born on 20 December.

2 Esmond had found work as a copywriter with a London advertising agency.

卐 UNITY to DIANA
16 February 1938

Kohfidisch
Burgenland
Austria

Darling Nard

I had great fun my last week in Vienna, Heine Bleckmann took me out a lot, & I also met some other friends who I went out with; so I saw quite a lot of the life in Vienna.

Of course hopes are high here about the Reichstagsrede;[1] and the evening on which it came out that Schuschnigg[2] was with the Führer, Vienna was in an uproar. No-one could think of anything else, & the first thing everyone – taxi-men, shop assistants or friends – said to one was 'Haben Sie gehört? Der Schuschnigg ist beim Führer!'[3] I *do* hope the result won't be a disappointment. Poor Austria is such a tragic country, & the people here really such heroes, I had never realized how really heroic the Kampf [struggle] here is until my time in Vienna. I have never met such fanatics in Germany as I have here. Several times young men have come up to me & said, 'May I kiss the hand the Führer has touched?' – not at all in a gallant or complimentary way, but merely because they do really so worship him, rather like a Christian might kiss a bit of wood which Christ had touched. And they all talk of 'draussen im Reich'[4] with bated breath, as if they were talking of Heaven.

Do write – to [Pension] Doering.

Best love from Bobo

1 The foreign policy speech that Hitler made four days later gave encouragement to the Austrian Nazi Party.

2 Kurt von Schuschnigg (1897–1977). Anti-Nazi Chancellor of Austria since 1934. Hitler threatened to invade Austria unless concessions were made to the Nazi Party. Schuschnigg resigned and in March 1938 Germany annexed Austria.

3 'Have you heard? Schuschnigg is with the Führer.'

4 'Over there in the Reich.'

JESSICA TO DEBORAH — *[41 Rotherhithe Street, SE16]*
31 May 1938

Dearest Hen,

Thank you so much for writing.[1]

We are going tomorrow morning, so I do hope you will write to yr hen. Please give my love to Muv, & thank her for her letter & for offering to help with the house, but as a matter of fact Esmond has already arranged for Peter Nevile to try & let it for us. If any of you hear of a likely person, would you let him know? They would have to keep Rose on at £1.1.3 a week (the 1/3d is insurance).

Love from Henderson

1 Jessica and Esmond's baby daughter, Julia, had just died from measles, aged five months. They had decided to go to Corsica for three months to try to recover.

DIANA TO DEBORAH — *Hotel Kaiserhof, Berlin*
2 June 1938

Darling Debo

Last night the Führer was talking about which of us was going to the Parteitag, and he says he *specially* wants you to go. Isn't it wonderful. I told what a marvellous rider you are and he thinks you are so beautiful and wants you to see the Parteitag while you are young. So of course I said you would be thrilled and he arranged it all, on the spot. Isn't he kind and sweet. He talked a lot about Farve and his speech[1] and said he should thank him very specially when he sees him at Nürnberg.

I must rush off now, but I know you will be excited when you get this.

Lots of love from Honks

1 Lord Redesdale's visits to Germany to see Unity had led him to revise his opinion of Nazism and, until Hitler invaded Czechoslovakia in March 1939, he was sympathetic to the regime. In a speech to the House of Lords, he had announced that the Anschluss was the 'sincere desire' of a large majority of Austrians and that the gratitude of Europe was due to Hitler for averting bloodshed.

卐 UNITY TO JESSICA *26 Rutland Gate, SW7*
26 June 1938

Darling Boud

You can't *think* how thrilled your Boud was – in fact we all were – to read your letter to the Fem, the Fem was out when it arrived & your Boud *died* to open it but she managed not to. I am so glad you are in Corsica because ever since we went there I have thought it the most heavenly place in the world – do you remember the *attractive* French officer Yobboud fell in love with in that fortress in Ajaccio, and is he still there?[1]

Boud ee ub je eedjend vegudden je Boudle[2] because she thinks the whole time about you. I was so terribly sad to be coming back knowing my Boud wouldn't be there, and altogether your Boud has been so much in despair about it all & so miserable that she couldn't write until now.

I feel sure you are having the most wonderful time & I envy you all the sun & bathing like anything.

Baby [Erdödy] is here, she came back to England with me in my car & we both return to the Continent next week. She sends you lots of love. I think she is quite enjoying it here. Yesterday Aunt Puss[3] took us both to a play & was killing as usual. The Widow adores Baby & wants her to go to Totland Bay. The other day there was a huge headline in the *E. Standard* – 'BLACK WIDOWS DOOMED IN CASE OF WAR'. Naturally we all supposed it included the Widow but it turned out that it means the Black Widow spiders at the Zoo, because their bites are fatal & they intend killing them at once in case a bomb or something might break their cage & let them loose. Isn't it killing. The Widow stayed here for two nights she was a scream, she wore a shiny green satin blouse which Farve insisted on calling her 'imperméable', he also kept saying she had a 'coiffure à la jolie femme'.[4] We all shrieked.

Well Boud I have enjoyed writing to you because I almost feel as if we had had a chat.

Very best love from Yobboud

1 Unity had flirted with the French officer when the sisters visited Corsica during their cruise of the Mediterranean in 1936.
2 'Boud, I hope you haven't forgotten your Boud.'
3 Frances Mitford (1875–1951). Lord Redesdale's eldest sister who was popular with all her nieces. Married Alexander (Alec) Kearsey in 1907.
4 'A pretty woman's hairstyle.'

UNITY TO DIANA

[No address]

18 July 1938

Darling Nard

It *is* a shame you can't come to Bayreuth, & also to the Berg[1] tomorrow, I am really awfully excited for that because it's the only side of his life which I don't know at *all*. Magda will be sorry you're not in Bayreuth, won't she.

What I couldn't tell you on the telephone was this. You remember my little friend from Vienna who you said was like an Indian, & his pretty blonde fiancée who asked the Führer for an autograph in the Osteria. Well yesterday she telephoned & said could she come & see me for five minutes, but her fiancé mustn't know anything about it. So this morning she came, & she was here when you telephoned. You know Heinz, her fiancé, was a member of the SS in Vienna – I believe since 1932. He was a *tremendously* enthusiastic Nazi & really risked everything for the cause during the Schuschnigg Regime. Well it seems that just after the Machtübernahme[2] his father, also a member of the Partei, who had brought him up to be very 'national-denkend' [nationalistically minded], told him that both his (Heinz's) mother's parents were Jewish. Of course poor Heinz was completely erledigt [shattered] when he heard it, & wanted to shoot himself at once, which it seems to me would have been the best way out. Though, officially, he doesn't count as a Jew as both the grandparents were baptized. But for Heinz, being a real Nazi 'aus Überzeugung' [by conviction], that naturally made no difference. His father made him promise not to do anything until they had had a reply to their Ersuch [request] to the Führer, but so far there has been no reply, & in the meanwhile of course he is having what is practically a nervous breakdown. Well it seems that there are several half-Jews who have, at one time or another, been allowed to remain in the Party on account of special Verdienste [services]. So they *hope* that he also will, though of course this will anyhow, from his own point of view, have ruined his life. So she came to ask me if I would help her, & I told her that if she would write a personal letter to the Führer I would give it to him personally. Isn't it *awful* for them, poor things. I must say it gave me an awful shock when she told me.

At lunch, a man who was there, said the Osteria was just like an Italian Osteria, 'nur viel sauberer'.[3] At that the Führer looked at me out of the corner of his eye & then started to blither [giggle] quite uncontrollably, & when he had sufficiently regained his composure he said 'Das hört sie gern'.[4] I think the man was amazed. When he left he said, 'come to the Berg any day you like between now & the 20th'. Later I rang up & said might I come today, but he sent a message to say that today he has Besprechungen [meetings] but would I come tomorrow. It *is* a shame you're not here.

Well now I will run out & post your dress. I will finish this letter after my Obersalzberg visit, so I can tell you about it.

Later. I have just returned from posting your dress, and just as a matter of interest I must tell you what it was like, & I think you might speak to your Minister O.[5] about it. Well I had to fill in *six* long & quite unintelligible forms, and then take one of them to the Reichsbank in the Briennerstrasse. Of course, all this didn't matter at all to me as I have all the time in the world & a motor; but imagine some wretched person who had to work hard & had no motor! I think it really might be changed, do speak to the Minister about it.

20th July. Well I arrived back late last night from the Berg, & will tell you about it. It was really *simply heavenly.* Well the drive up takes about 20 minutes, & when I arrived at the house, there were the Führer & Wagner waiting for me on the balcony or terrass. I was taken to them through the house, & they both said, 'Wo ist die Schwester?'[6] so I explained. Well I must say I never in my life saw such a view as one sees from that house, the whole chain of mountains lying at one's feet so to speak. Well the Führer & Wagner & Schaubchen[7] & I went & had tea in the big room or hall. It is simply huge & hung with wonderful pictures & tapestry, & at one end it has a raised platform with a big round tea table & a huge Kamin [chimney], & at the other end the whole wall is one huge window. The effect is simply extraordinary. The window – the largest piece of glass ever made – can be wound down like a motor window, as it was yesterday, leaving it quite open. Through it one just sees this huge chain of mountains, and it looks more like an enormous cinema screen than like reality. Needless to say the génial [brilliant] idea was the Führer's own, & he said Frau Troost[8] wanted to insist on having *three* windows. Well after tea he showed me the whole house, even the kitchen & the maids' bedrooms & bathrooms, and I must say it is perfectly lovely, I know you will think so. After seeing the house, which took quite a time, we went & sat in the terrace & chatted to Werlin & Dietrich & his little daughter Gisela, then the Führer said would I like to go for a walk so I said yes. Just as we were starting off, the Führer's new huge car arrived from the Mercedes works, so of course we examined it all over. When told it went easily 150 km.p.h., he said something so typical: 'Das ist natürlich für mich ein Nachteil, denn wenn ich so schnell fahre, bin ich 20 Minuten früher da, und muss 20 Minuten länger im Hotel oder in meiner Wohnung sitzen.'[9] Well we started on our walk, which turned out to be a pretty long one: he & I in front, & the others following us a good way behind. We walked down the mountains, quite slowly, & the view is too lovely for words. The 'Ziel' [aim] of our walk was a little teahouse he has built on a projecting piece of hill, it is too pretty for words inside, round, with a big round table & very comfy armchairs all round, & flat marble pillars round the walls, & a pretty fireplace with a lovely 18th-century clock on it. We sat & had tea & he talked about politics for about an hour, in his best style, & then we walked down to where the cars were standing below the teahouse, & he put me in my car & then got into his & we drove through the new Bauernhof that is being built & then he drove back up the mountain, & I down to Berchtesgaden at about 9.

Well now I must scram out, I will write to you from Bayreuth. My best love to the boys.

Best love from Bobo

1 The Berghof was Hitler's mountain retreat at Obersalzberg, which he had converted from a simple Alpine house into a residence suitable for receiving foreign dignitaries.
2 The annexation of Austria.
3 'Only much cleaner.'
4 'She's delighted to hear you say that.' Unity's dislike of Italians was a running joke between her and Hitler.
5 Wilhelm Ohnesorge (d. 1962). German Minister of Posts and Telegraphs who was sympathetic to the Mosleys' plan to set up a radio station.
6 'Where is your sister?'
7 Julius Schaub; Hitler's personal adjutant and former head of his bodyguard.
8 Gerdy Troost (1904–2003). Interior designer and a confidante of Hitler. Married to Paul Ludwig Troost (1878–1934), one of Hitler's favourite architects.
9 'Of course it's a disadvantage for me because if I drive that fast I get there twenty minutes early, then I have to sit and wait in my hotel or at home for twenty minutes.'

卐 UNITY TO DIANA
28 July 1938

Zeppelinstrasse 1½
Bayreuth

Darling Nard

I have been meaning to write to you for several days but there hasn't seemed to be much to tell. I am living, as you see, in the same house as always. It's terribly hot & one can hardly sleep, & the heat is *awful* in the opera.

On Sunday – the morning after I arrived – I drove over to Eger to an SdP[1] demonstration at which Konrad Henlein spoke. When I arrived I was met by Wollner,[2] who said he could only stay five minutes 'denn ich muss den Führer ausholen'.[3] I was amazed. I was taken to the Rathaus [town hall] where there was to be a Begrüssung [reception] & there we waited & at last everyone said, 'Der Führer kommt! Der Führer kommt!'[4] & in came Konrad Henlein, followed by Wollner & others. Well the mayor began his Begrüssungsrede, 'Mein Führer! Es ist für mich eine Freude und Ehre, Sie, mein Führer, begrüssen zu dürfen'[5] etc etc. I *was* amazed. Afterwards I was presented to Konrad Henlein, but there was no time to chat because we had to go out to the demonstration, & I had to leave early to be in time for *Tristan*.

At dinner, the Führer & the Doktor & Kannenberg[6] were all in their best form, so you can imagine we had a riotous evening. But I think the Führer teased Kannenberg dreadfully by saying that the food in the Quirinal & also in Florence was *much* better than his (K's) food, and that he would *never* be able to achieve such perfection.

The next evening, the Führer got into quite a rage twice; the first time with Kannenberg, for whom I felt heartily sorry! The second rage, however, was over Reichsminister Gürtner[7] & the new laws he is making. He got angrier & angrier, & at last thundered – you know how he can – like a machine-gun – 'Das nächste Mal, dass die Richter so einen Mann freilassen, so lasse ich ihn von meiner Leibstandarte verhaften und ins Konzentrationslager schicken; *und dann werden wir sehen, welches am stärksten ist, the letter of Herr Gürtner's law oder MEINE MASCHINEN GEWEHRE!*'[8] It was wonderful. Everyone was silent for quite a time after that.

I have been having rather a terrible time on account of a young man I met in Munich just after you left – Wolfgang Hoesch by name, no relation to the Ambassador[9] – has been pestering me with marriage proposals, & to my horror followed me here! I do have an awful time with 'Wolfgangs' don't I. I have a terrible time getting rid of him here, in fact I have to get up early & drive off somewhere for the day. However thank god he has to go tomorrow anyway.

Well I will now close because I feel I *must* go for a walk. My love to the boys – did they get my P.C.s?

Best love & Heil Hitler! Bobo

1 The Sudeten-German Party of Czechoslovakia, led by Konrad Henlein (1898–1945) who was instrumental in preparing the way for Hitler's occupation of his country in 1939.

2 Georg Wollner; Gauleiter of Reichenberg.

3 'Because I have to bring the Führer out.'

4 'The Führer is coming! The Führer is coming!'

5 'It is a pleasure and an honour for me to greet you, my Führer.'

6 Willy Kannenberg; Hitler's cook.

7 Franz Gürtner (1881–1941). Reich Minister of Justice since 1932 who opposed Nazi brutality but was unable to stand up to Hitler.

8 'Next time the judges let that sort of man free, I'll have him arrested by my bodyguards and sent to a concentration camp; *then we'll see who is stronger, the letter of Herr Gürtner's law or my machine guns!*'

9 Dr Leopold von Hoesch (1881–1936). German ambassador to London 1932–6.

卐 UNITY TO DIANA *Zeppelinstrasse 1½*
Thursday, 4 August 1938 *Bayreuth*

Darling Nard

Thank you for your letter forwarded from Munich. I didn't *mean* for you to feel guilty about the dress, I only told you as a matter of interest & I didn't *mind* at all a bit. But of course as a matter of fact you *always* feel guilty, don't you.

Well I had meant to write before but the fact is, I have had flu since Friday. I felt queer Friday night on coming home very late from the Führer's, after *Walküre*. The Führer, however, had said he would take me with him to Breslau, & of course I would rather have died than miss that. So on Saturday I stayed in bed till 5, & then got up & packed, & the Sonderzug[1] left at 7. By the time it started I felt like death, & dreaded being called to dinner. You know how one sometimes can't even raise one's hand to comb one's hair. However when I was with the Führer I felt sort of stimulated like one does, & he was in a sweet mood. We sat at a table with the Reichsärzteführer Wagner.[2] Of course eating was agony & yet I had to because I couldn't say I was ill. Luckily the Führer had to have a Besprechung [meeting] with an officer after dinner, so I got to bed early, feeling frightfully sick. We arrived at Breslau at the unearthly hour of 7.30 A.M. We drove in Kolonne [procession] to a hotel which had been abgesperrt [closed]. One of the Führer's secretaries had come too so that I shouldn't be the only female on the train, & she was my sort of Begleitung [chaperone]. The hotel was full of Greatnesses of course, & Seyss Inquart[3] was there. Tschammer-Osten[4] gave us Ehrenkarten [free tickets] & a man to go with us, and we walked to the square where the march-past was to be, which was next-door to the hotel. Already the sun was almost unbearably hot – before 8 A.M. – so you can imagine what the next 4 hours were like, & I had a high temperature. We sat on the front row of the Tribüne, just behind the Führer's little jutting-out box. Behind us were Wollner & the other Sudetendeutsch leaders. I think Wollner was terrifically impressed that I had come with the Führer, though I think he only believed it *sometimes*. Well then the Führer arrived & the march-past began – 150,000 people (i.e. half as much again as the SA & SS Vorbeimarsch in Nürnberg) but they marched in three columns, the middle one going in the opposite direction from the other two. At first came the Reichsdeutsche from the various Gaus [regions]; then the Sudetendeutsche. I never expect to see such scenes again as when the Sudetendeutsch women arrived. You will have read about it in the papers but the accounts I saw seemed to bear no relation to what actually happened. Really everyone was crying & I thought they would never sort out the muddle when the marchers broke ranks & surrounded the Führer in a seething mass, & those who had already passed came running back to try & see the Führer once more, & they were all sobbing & stretching out their hands & some of them managed to shout in chorus 'Lieber Führer, wann kommst Du zu uns?' and 'Führer, wir schwören Dir aufs Neu, wir bleiben Dir auf ewig treu'.[5] Henlein stood beside the Führer and it must have been his greatest day.

Well after that was over we went into the hotel & I went up to a room & lay down. The lade with me was in her element, as she is very pretty & very loud & coy with the Umgebung & Begleitung [staff] & calls them all 'du', from Sepp Dietrich[6] to the chauffeurs. I was able to sleep till 3 & then we had to leave for a stadium outside the town where there were very wonderful demonstrations of Leibesübungen, etc, including a dance by 5,000 women & club-swinging by 15,000. We had to leave early so as to get to the Flugplatz [airport] before the Führer, our planes left at 8, I didn't go in the Führer's because I was suddenly terrified I would give him my flu. We landed at Nürnberg & drove in Kolonne in ten huge cars to Bayreuth. After we arrived a car was sent round to take me to dinner but of course I felt like death & couldn't go. Well ever since then I have been in bed, & have missed *Siegfried* and *Götterdämmerung*. *Siegfried* I would have missed anyhow as it was the day we started for Breslau.

On Monday night – the last night he was here – when the Führer heard I was ill, he sent me the most lovely huge bouquet of roses, & the next morning he sent round to enquire how I was. Then he left by plane for Berlin. It seems that when he left he told Frau Wagner[7] I was ill & would she look after me a bit & send a doctor. Also, that he wanted *all* bills to be sent to him. Isn't he really too sweet for words.

Someone even came – I don't know who – to say I was to be given back all the money I had spent on oranges etc. I am really so terribly grateful to him.

Well yesterday Frau Wagner came & brought the hugest & most lovely bouquet of garden flowers I ever saw, evidently picked by herself, & it makes my room smell like a garden. She was awfully nice & motherly, & said she would send a doctor.

A large bouquet arrived tied with two broad red satin ribbons with Hakenkreuzes [swastikas] on them – the sort of thing one puts on Horst Wessel's grave – from the Lord Mayor of Bayreuth, whom so far as I know I have never met. All the flowers make one much more cheerful. Also Wollner came & brought a large bunch of gladioli.

Well this letter has got awfully long & may be frightfully dull but I do love writing to pass the time, now that I can sit up. My salvation has been *A Passage to India*[8] which thank goodness I hadn't read before, what a wonderful book, only much too short. I am so grateful to you for telling me about it. Alas I have finished it.

Please give my best love to the boys – did they get my postcards from Breslau? I hope so because they were quite special.

The Führer asked in the train how you were, I said I thought very well, I hope you are.

Well I will now close this weighty letter.

Best love & Heil Hitler! Bobo

1 Hitler's special train.

2 Gerhardt Wagner (1888–1938). Reich Medical Leader who was instrumental in formulating the infamous Nuremberg Laws that established anti-Semitism and euthanasia as official Nazi policy.

3 Arthur Seyss-Inquart (1892–1946). Leader of the Austrian Nazi Party and keen supporter of Austria's union with Germany, who became governor of Austria after the Anschluss.

4 Hans von Tschammer-Osten (1887–1943). Reich Sports Leader and president of the German Olympic Committee in 1936.

5 'Dear Führer, when are you coming to us?' and 'Führer, once again we swear undying loyalty to you'.

6 Joseph (Sepp) Dietrich (1892–1966). Hitler's close associate and head of his SS bodyguard.

7 Winifred Williams (1897–1980). The English-born wife of Richard Wagner's son,

Siegfried, had been a friend and ardent admirer of Hitler since 1923. In 1930, she became head of the Bayreuth Festival and ran it until the end of the war.
8 E. M. Forster's novel was first published in 1924.

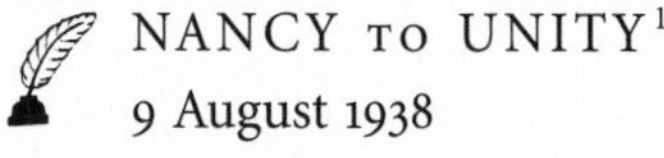

NANCY TO UNITY[1] *[12 Blomfield Road, w9]*
9 August 1938

The B[urden] of my S[ong] is I am awfully sorry you are ill. I always think to be ill abroad is most un-hochworthy. I hope there is an agreeable Gesellschaft [society] in the town to go and see you, anyway the Fem has gone now. I remember being ill in Napoli and a bearded Doctor laid his bearded face on my bosom which was his old world way of taking my temp. I thought luckily that it was only part of my delirium.

I am getting on well with my German. I know Herrschaft, Tisch and pfui; Pfennig, gemütlich and Rassenschande.[2] Six words which would get one a long way if made good use of. Oh and mit mir [with me]. Did Muv enjoy her flight? She must be enchanted by the injections you describe. I fear modern science means o to her.

Well, head of bone, heart of stone – here is a little poem to show you what a lot of German I know.

Rassenschande is my joy
(Tisch Tisch and a merry go round)
Gemütlich is my hochgeboren [highborn] boy.

My hochgeboren love sits mit mir
(Tisch Tisch and a merry go round)
With all our Pfennigs we buy delicious beer.

And Rassenschande we do all day
(Tisch Tisch and a merry go round)
For my lover is a geboren Malay.

Pretty good, eh what?

P.S. I saw Bernstein[3] who remembered sitting next to you at Emerald's[4] and saying, 'I hate you, I don't know why' and you replied 'But I know why'.

1 This letter was transcribed in Lady Redesdale's memoir of Unity. The original has not been found.
2 'Power, table and ugh; penny, cosy and racial disgrace' (i.e. interracial sex).
3 Henry Bernstein (1876–1953). French boulevard-theatre playwright.
4 Maud Burke (1872–1948). American-born widow of Sir Bache Cunard, the shipping-line magnate, whom she married in 1895. Changed her name to 'Emerald' in 1926 and was one of London's leading society hostesses between the wars.

卐 UNITY TO DIANA
14 August 1938

Klinik Dr Treuter
Bayreuth

Darling Nard –

Your *wonderful* cheque arrived today from Pension Doering – you shouldn't have sent me so much, it's *much* too much, but you can imagine how thrilled I was to get it. You are so kind, thank you a million times.

This is the first letter I have been able to write but can't sit up hence the scrawl. The doctors say I may not be able to go to the Parteitag, so you & I may be in the same boat – tho' you get a lovely prize for it[1] & I get nothing. I hope however that I may get well quicker than they think & be able to go. The old doctor[2] the Führer sent me looks like the Aga Khan, he cured the Führer of indigestion. The Führer rang him up in the middle of the night & said he must leave for Bayreuth at *once*, so he arrived here at 3 A.M. & examined me at once & phoned the Führer. He had to leave several patients in Berlin including – who do you think? – your lover Joan Glover![3] The Führer rings up several times a day from the Berg & speaks to the doctor, & two days ago a phone was brought into my room & *I* spoke to him, wasn't it heaven. He sent me a sweet telegram & masses of flowers for my birthday.

Oh dear I envy you all at Wootton, it is so dull here but thank goodness the Fem is here. She flew out, to Farve's horror. Please give the boys my best love. I do hope I will see them soon.

Best love & Heil Hitler, Bobo

1 Diana was expecting a baby in November.
2 Theodor Morell (1886–1948). Hitler's private physician.
3 Ribbentrop.

DIANA TO UNITY
18 August 1938

Wootton Lodge
Ashbourne

Darling:

How simply dreadful to have had pneumonia; we were *so* sorry about it. The Führer is the kindest man in the world isn't he? I bet Joan is teased at his doctor being snatched away. He looks as if he might die any minute I must say. What is the matter with him? Do ask the Doc.

The boys have gone off to Biddesden, looking very well. Kit and I are here alone now. The day before the boys went we were all down by the lake, Kit was fishing, when all of a sudden Debo appeared! Kit had never seen her before. He stayed where he was and Debo and I walked back to the house, and hiding a few hundred yards away were two friends of Debo's, Lord Andrew Cavendish[1] and a troglodyte of sorts. They had been to some races. They stayed literally ten mins and then scrammed. They all looked as if they had seen a ghost, Debo said they were frightened they might be shot at. Apparently the day before they had come within a few yards of the house and then been too afraid to approach. It seems so odd to think they are *grown up*; they seemed incredibly babyish and so shy. (Not Debo of course.)

Kit has got such a lovely new rod for spinning minnows, he caught a huge trout last night with it. We are having such *heavenly* hols.

How too awful if you have to miss the Parteitag, but thank goodness it is the same year as me. I expect you will go but *don't* overdo it darling. Come back *soon.*

You know the grey flannel dress and coat you gave me; well Nanny has let the dress out and it makes the *most* wonderfully concealing garment for best. I shall have to give it back when you have one. You can't think how I bless you every time I wear it.

All love darling from Nard

1 Lord Andrew Cavendish (1920–2004). Succeeded as 11th Duke of Devonshire in 1950. Deborah's future husband was a student at Cambridge when they first met.

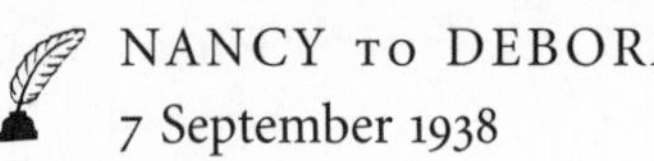

NANCY TO DEBORAH *12 Blomfield Road, w9*
7 September 1938

Dear Miss

Poor Boud got beaten up in the *Express*, did you see (I know you read the papers from cover to cover all except the news, the book reviews or anything of interest). I must say I think it was silly not to write the letter herself but then Boud always is silly.[1]

Love from NR

The dr just been says that for two months I mayn't go in any sort of vehicle, isn't it deadly. I mayn't even take a taxi & go out to lunch.[2]

1 Unity had written to the *Daily Express* to deny an article in 'William Hickey' which said that 'those members of Britain's governing class whose Aryanism has been okayed by Unity Mitford are packing their bags for Nuremberg'. (2 September 1938) A photograph of her letter accompanying the article shows that it had been signed by Unity but was in Lady Redesdale's handwriting.

2 After more than four years of marriage, Nancy was at last expecting a child but in spite of carefully following her doctor's instructions, she miscarried a few weeks later.

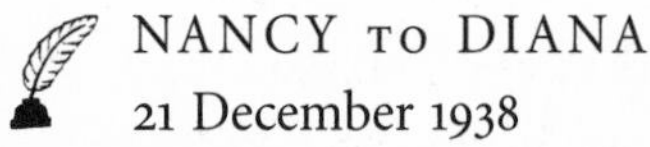

NANCY TO DIANA *12 Blomfield Road, w9*
21 December 1938

Darling Diana

Wasn't it funny – the very day your baby[1] was born I was transcribing letters about Alice Stanley's's[2] baby & she called it Alexander St George. I recommend St George to your attention, I think it's so pretty.

I expect you will have a lovely Xmas in bed which I envy you in every way.

Much love from Nancy

I am going to Roy[3] & Billa tomorrow, did you know they are having a baby also the David Cecils.[4]

1 Diana's son, Alexander (Al) Mosley (1938–2005), was born on 26 November.

2 Nancy was editing the letters of her ancestors Maria Josepha, Lady Stanley of Alderley,

and Henrietta Maria Stanley. Published as *The Ladies of Alderley* (1938) and *The Stanleys of Alderley* (1939).

3 Roy Harrod (1900–78). Influential economist who taught at Christ Church, Oxford. Married Wilhelmine (Billa) Cresswell in 1938.

4 Lord David Cecil (1902–86). Biographer and professor of English Literature at Oxford 1948–70. Married Rachel McCarthy in 1932. Their son Jonathan was born in 1939.

UNITY TO DIANA
29 March 1939

Margeritenstr. 6
München-Solln

Darling Nard

Thank you for your letter.

I had lunch with the Führer on Sunday & Monday, & he asked me to send you viele Grüsse. Both days he was in his very sweetest mood, particularly on Monday, he held my hand most of the time & looked sweet & said 'Kind [child]!' in his sympathetic way because he was so sorry about England & Germany being such enemies.[1] However he said nothing but wonderful things about England & he completely gave me faith again that it will all come right in the end.

Yesterday I visited the new English Consul, he is awfully funny & rather nice.

There is still snow on the ground here, but it's getting a bit warmer.

Do write soon.

Best love from Bobo

1 Hitler's occupation of Czechoslovakia on 15 March violated the Munich Agreement and had brought all efforts at appeasement to an end.

UNITY TO DIANA[1]
9 July 1939

[Agnesstrasse 26
Munich]

Well, I had lunch with Wolf[2] today. We are invited to Bayreuth, I don't know when it begins but will let you know later. He was in his least forthcoming mood, you know, all preoccupied.

He asked after you and Alexander and when I told him Alexander was bald, he said 'Other people lose their hair through wisdom. He is wise from birth.' So when I said 'Let's hope so' he said 'Let's hope *not*. It's better to have hair than wisdom. Weisheit hilft nichts.'[3]

1 This extract was transcribed in Lady Redesdale's memoir of Unity. The original has not been found.
2 The cover name used by Hitler at the beginning of his political career and adopted as a nickname by his intimates. Neither Unity nor Diana used the name to his face but from 1938 often referred to him as 'Wolf' in letters.
3 'Wisdom is no help.'

卐 UNITY TO DIANA
2 September 1939

[Agnesstrasse 26 Munich]

Darling Nard

Your letter of the 30th just arrived. You can't think how thrilling it is every time I hear the letterbox click, as I always expect every letter to be the last that will get through.

I listened in to the English news last night, it seems *quite* hopeless doesn't it.[1] I wonder if this letter will get through.

I think Chamberlain & co are criminals & should be hanged.

In case you didn't hear the Führer's speech, this is what he said about England. 'Ich habe England immer wieder eine Freundschaft und, wenn notwendig, das engste Zusammengehen angeboten. Aber Liebe kann nicht nur von einer Seite angeboten werden, die muss von der anderen ihre Erwiderung finden.'[2]

I tried to ring you up last night but was a few hours too late – no more calls to England allowed.

Last night we had blackout for the first time, the streets were so pitchy black one had to feel one's way. Today I covered all my windows with black paper.

I fear I shan't see the Führer again. Nardy if anything should happen to me, & the English press try to make some untrue story out of it against W, you will see to it that the truth is known won't you.

When the war is over, do try to get Boy[3] back, I am so worried about him. Baby knows where he is.

Very best love, to you & the boys, from Bobo

I *do* hope you will feel better soon. It must be awful to be feeling ill just now.

1 On the previous day, the German army had invaded Poland. Hitler ignored Britain and France's ultimatum to withdraw and on 3 September Neville Chamberlain, the British Prime Minister, declared war.
2 'I have proposed friendship to England again and again and, when necessary, the closest collaboration. But love cannot be all one-sided, it must be reciprocated.'
3 Unity's Great Dane, given to her by Diana.

THREE

1939–1945

Unity, Tom, Deborah, Diana, Jessica, Nancy and Pamela, 1935.

On the afternoon of 3 September 1939, the day that Britain and France declared war on Germany, Unity went to the English Garden in the centre of Munich and put a pistol to her head. The bullet lodged in her brain, failed to kill her but inflicted irreversible damage. She was taken to a Munich hospital were she lay unconscious for several weeks. Communications between England and Germany were difficult in the early part of the war and on Hitler's orders no report of Unity's suicide attempt appeared in the German press. It was two months before the Redesdales received any definite news of their daughter and a further two months before they were able to fetch her home from a clinic in neutral Switzerland where Hitler had arranged for her to be sent. In January 1940, Lady Redesdale and Deborah travelled to Bern and found Unity still seriously ill, paralysed, with her hair matted and untouched since the day she had tried to shoot herself. They brought her back to England in an ambulance and Lady Redesdale took on the distressing task of looking after her daughter, who was left with the mental age of a twelve-year-old and in whom religious mania had replaced Hitler mania. Unity's behaviour was unpredictable, alternating between bouts of fury and moments of pathetic vulnerability, and she was untidy, clumsy and incontinent at night. The Redesdales' marriage was already under stress from political disagreements – when Hitler invaded Czechoslovakia Lord Redesdale reverted to being violently anti-German while Lady Redesdale continued to regard the Führer as Germany's saviour – and it deteriorated further with the strain of Unity's infirmity. Lord Redesdale withdrew to Inch Kenneth, a small island off the coast of Mull in the Inner Hebrides which he had bought after selling Swinbrook House, taking with him Margaret Wright, the parlourmaid, who became his companion and remained with him until the end of his life. Lady Redesdale took Unity to Mill Cottage in Swinbrook, where they lived for most of the war.

Nancy spent the 'phoney war', the months between the declaration of war and Hitler's invasion of Norway and Denmark in April 1940, working in London at a first-aid post and writing her fourth novel, *Pigeon Pie*, a comic spy story that did not sell well. Peter joined up, 'looking very pretty' in his uniform, and they had a brief *retour de flamme* which resulted in a second miscarriage for Nancy. It was a depressing time and in her unhappiness she lashed out at her sisters: Deborah was 'having a wild time with young cannon fodders at the Ritz'; Jessica was attacked for living in America: 'You must be *mad* to stay there & like all mad people convinced you are sane'; Unity, whose suicide attempt had not yet reached the ears of her family, was rumoured to be in a concentration camp which was 'a sort of poetic justice'; Pamela was living at Rignell, 'in a round of boring gaiety of the neighbourly description'. Where Diana was concerned Nancy exulted when 'Sir Oswald Quisling' was imprisoned but thought it quite useless 'if Lady Q is still at large'. Her hostility towards Diana did not stop at angry words. In June 1940, she was summoned by Gladwyn Jebb, an official at the Foreign Office, to give information on what she knew about Diana's visits to Germany. She told him that she considered her 'an extremely dangerous person'. 'Not very sisterly behaviour', she admitted to a family friend, 'but in such times I think it is one's duty?' According to an MI5 report of the time, Nancy also informed on Pamela and Derek who she thought should be kept under observation because of being 'anti-Semitic, anti-democratic and defeatist'.

Although Diana would probably have been interned regardless of Nancy's character reference, her sister's testimony must have lent support to the government in their decision to detain her. She was arrested on 29 June 1940 and sent to Holloway, a women's prison in north London. Diana did not learn of Nancy's act of disloyalty until 1983, ten years after her death. Had she known, it is likely that she would have cut Nancy out of her life for ever. Even if she had wanted to keep up some kind of communication with her, it is certain that Mosley would have forbidden it. In the event, once Diana was in prison, the five-year estrangement between the two sisters, that had started with *Wigs on the Green*, began to heal. After the novel's publication, Nancy had written just twice to Diana, to congratulate her on the births of her two Mosley sons, which, by painful coincidence, had occurred within a few weeks of Nancy's two miscarriages. While Diana was in Holloway, prison regulations restricted her letter-writing but when she was released in 1943 and was living under house arrest the correspondence between them resumed. This was in spite of Nancy having once again performed her patriotic duty by going to the authorities when the Mosleys' release was announced and volunteering that in her opinion Diana should not be let out of prison because she 'sincerely desires the downfall of England and democracy generally'. Diana was never to know about this second betrayal as the government papers in which it was recorded were not made public until four months after her death.

During the first two years of the war, Nancy worked in a canteen for French soldiers evacuated from Dunkirk and later looked after Jewish refugees billeted at Rutland Gate. In 1942, she found a job more to her liking at Heywood Hill, a bookshop in Mayfair, which soon became a meeting place for her London friends. In the same year she met Gaston Palewski, a Free French officer who was General de Gaulle's right-hand man in London and who very quickly became the love of her life. This cultivated, sophisticated and amusing man was a passionate lover of women and a fiercely loyal supporter of de Gaulle – qualities that made up for his lack of physical charm. The 'Colonel', as Nancy always called him, worked the same powerful effect on her as Hitler, Mosley and Esmond had on her sisters. She became as indiscriminately pro-French as Unity had been pro-German; as ready to swallow her pride and put up with Palewski's infidelities as Diana was with Mosley's; as convinced that Gaullism was the answer to France's problems as Jessica was that communism would solve the world's injustices. Although Palewski was not in love with Nancy – and never pretended to be – he made her feel desired in a way that no other man had. The eight months that their affair lasted before he left to join de Gaulle in Algeria were among the happiest in her life and inspired *The Pursuit of Love*, the novel that made her famous. It is not clear when Nancy told her sisters about the affair; Palewski is not mentioned in her surviving letters until after the end of the war.

Oswald Mosley's message to his supporters on 9 May 1940 to 'resist the foreign invasion with all that is in us' did not forestall his arrest.

On 23 May 1940, he was sent to Brixton Prison under Defence Regulation 18B, which enabled the government to detain without trial anyone suspected of being a threat to the country. Diana, an 'extremely dangerous and sinister young woman' according to the Home Office official who signed her detention order, was arrested a month later. In October, she appeared before an Advisory Committee appointed to decide whether she should remain incarcerated. Diana treated her hearing with contempt, as 'an absurd and insulting farce', an attitude that she later admitted to regretting. Her loyalty to her friendship with Hitler and her refusal to repudiate Nazi policies led to the recommendation that she be kept locked up. On her arrest, Diana left her two youngest sons, Alexander, who was eighteen months old and Max, who was just eleven weeks and not yet weaned, with their nanny. Lady Redesdale would have taken them to live with her but she was fully occupied caring for Unity, so the children went to live at Rignell with Pamela, whose nickname 'Woman' belied the fact – unluckily for the little boys – that she was the least maternal of the sisters. After a year and a half at Rignell, they went with Nanny Higgs as paying guests to the new owners of Swinbrook House. Diana missed her four children terribly and their occasional brief visits were overshadowed by the anguish of having to part with them. But her greatest complaint was being separated from Mosley. Other couples detained under 18B had been moved to married quarters and the Mosleys began to press for permission to be housed together. At the end of 1941, they were reunited in Holloway and lodged in a flat in the prison grounds where they spent two further years in detention. In the autumn of 1943 Mosley contracted phlebitis and the prison doctors reported that his life could be in danger. The Mosleys were released in November and settled at Crux Easton, near Newbury, where they remained under house arrest until the end of the war. The government's decision to release them was met with a storm of protest and countrywide demonstrations.

Nancy was not the only sister to remonstrate against the decision to free the Mosleys: Jessica wrote to Winston Churchill to demand that they be kept in jail because their release was a 'direct betrayal of those who have died for the cause of anti-fascism', and she sent a copy of her letter to the *San Francisco Chronicle*. In her second volume of memoirs, *A Fine Old Conflict*, Jessica wrote that on re-reading this letter thirty years later, she found it 'painfully stuffy and self-righteous', and noted that Nancy had written condemning her action as 'not very sisterly' – the very same words that Nancy had used for her own behaviour when she denounced Diana in 1940. Jessica's views, as she herself honestly admitted, were mixed with a 'goodly dash of familial spitefulness' and with bitterness over Esmond's death in action in 1941. There is no evidence that Nancy ever told Jessica that she too had denounced Diana, or conceded that in performing her 'duty' she might also have been acting with a not insignificant dash of sisterly spite – and without Jessica's justification of having lost a husband in the fighting.

The Romillys spent their first months in America scraping a living in various occupations; Jessica worked as a salesgirl in a dress shop before landing a job selling Scottish tweeds at the New York World's Fair of 1939. A clutch of letters of introduction from family and friends helped the couple to make contacts, some of whom, such as Katherine Graham of the *Washington Post*, were to become lifelong friends. They went to Washington, where Esmond worked as a door-to-door silk-stocking salesman, and then on to Miami, where Jessica found a job selling costume jewellery and Esmond became part owner of a bar with a $1,000 loan from Katherine Graham's father, the wealthy financier Eugene Meyer. When Chamberlain resigned and Churchill formed a National Government, Esmond decided to join the war effort and signed up with the Canadian Royal Air Force, applying for a commission as a pilot officer. In June 1941, four months after their daughter Constancia was born, Esmond was posted to Britain as an air force navigator. Six months later, a few days before Jessica was planning to join him in England, Esmond was declared missing after his aircraft went down over the North Sea. Winston Churchill, who was on a visit to America to meet Roosevelt, saw Jessica and gave her details of Esmond's disappearance. He made it clear that there was not the slightest chance that Esmond was being held prisoner of war but Jessica continued to hold out hopes of his survival and it was months before she could accept that he was dead. There are no letters to her sisters to tell of her devastating loss, and in *Hons and Rebels* his death is recorded in a mere footnote. Jessica buried her grief as her upbringing had taught her and refused to give in to misery or despair. She turned her anger on Diana and her 'precious friends'. Where previously she had felt revulsion for her sister's politics, her hatred was now personal. Unity escaped any share of the blame, perhaps because her pitiful state made her impossible to hate.

After Esmond's death, Jessica decided to stay in America and eventually found a job in the Office of Price Administration, a federal agency established to prevent wartime inflation, where she fell in love with Robert Treuhaft, the son of Jewish immigrants from Hungary who was working as an enforcement attorney and who shared her commitment to radical causes. They were married in the summer of 1943 – in secret, like the Mosleys. After the hounding she had received from the press when she first arrived in America, Jessica was anxious to preserve her new-found anonymity in San Francisco. She wanted to be considered on her own merits and not merely as one of the Mitford girls. In 1944, she forfeited her British citizenship in order to join the American Communist Party and threw herself into tireless fund-raising and recruiting on its behalf. Although Lady Redesdale wrote to her regularly, keeping her informed of family news, Jessica's contact with her sisters was sporadic. She had made a conscious effort to break away and was carving out a life for herself in deliberate opposition to the world of privilege and prejudice she felt her family represented. Her deep well of feelings for her sisters remained intact, but mistrust had entered their relations and behind the long-standing jokes and teases was a wariness that was never dispelled.

Pamela spent the war years at Rignell where – like Lady Redesdale who in Unity's little book of questions *All About Everybody* had put as her favourite occupation 'woman at the till' – she kept a close eye on expenditure. Her housekeeping and farming skills came in useful when coping with wartime rationing and labour shortages. In the bitterly cold winter of 1942 when the water tanks for her cattle froze, the youth who had replaced her cowman told her that there was no need to fetch fresh water for the cows since they could eat the snow. Pamela's experience of running the Biddesden dairy farm had taught her otherwise. 'How do you know what they want?' she scolded. '*You've never been an in-calf heifer.*' As a leading scientist, Derek would have been exempt from active service but he was determined to join up and volunteered for the Royal Air Force. He went into action in 1941 in a night-fighter squadron and finished the war as a heavily decorated wing commander. When the Mosleys were released in 1943 and had nowhere to live – the lease on Wootton had been surrendered in 1940 – Pamela and Derek immediately offered to take them in, just as they had taken in their two boys at the beginning of the war. Diana never forgot Derek and Pamela's loyalty, and it brought her closer to her sister than she had been since Biddesden days.

The beginning of the war was a particularly miserable time for nineteen-year-old Deborah. She had travelled with her mother to Switzerland to collect Unity after her suicide attempt and suffered the shock of finding her a completely changed person. She was witness to the increasingly bitter political arguments between the Redesdales and their decision to separate. When Unity came out of hospital, Deborah, except for a few months when she worked in the forces canteen at St Pancras Station, was cooped up with her sister and mother in the small cottage at Swinbrook, or stayed at Inch Kenneth with her grim and physically diminished father. In April 1941, Andrew Cavendish, to whom she had considered herself unofficially engaged for some time, formally proposed and they were married the following month, both aged just twenty-one. Deborah spent the first two years of her marriage following Andrew, who was in the Coldstream Guards, to his different training grounds across the country, living in small pubs and, occasionally, rented houses. She bore three children during the war, two of whom survived: a daughter, Emma, and a son, Peregrine. In 1943, while Andrew was fighting with his battalion in Italy, she moved to The Rookery, a house on the Derbyshire estate of her parents-in-law, where she spent the rest of the war.

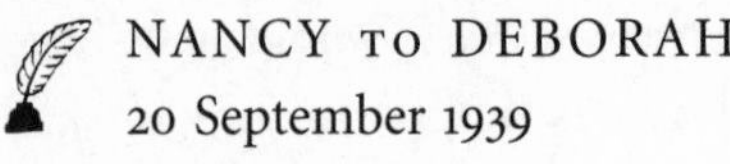

NANCY TO DEBORAH
20 September 1939

S.M.H. 1st Aid Post
Praed Street
London W2

Dear Deb Dahlia

Haven't had a letter from you for ages, what has happened? How are the P[arent Bird]'s – everyone I see asks if they are interned & poor Ld Londonderry has had to deny publicly that he is.

Tell Muv I have written to the Duchess of Aosta & asked her to find out from the wop consul in Munich how & where Boud is. This is very round about & will take time but it should work.

I suppose they are pleased about having the Russians on their side[1] – do note the reactions. Dear me *how* I regret not having taught you how to write. And what about Hitler's weapon, is it the Russian air force or some awful gas or bomb? Do they know?

Now be tactful & don't tell the P's I asked the trend but I do simply so *die* to know.

Where is Squalor? Coming home or not or what. I long to write to her & don't know where.

I am learning to shoot with Rodd's revolver so that I can be like the Polish grandmothers when the Germo-Russians turn up here which I suppose they will do *soon*.

Give my love to Blor & mind you write soon.

Love from NR

P.S. Everybody here is being inoculated for all the diseases they can remember as they think H's policy is bacteriological warfare. I have quite refused as it always makes me so ill.

What is your policy? Now *TACT* Dahlia & tear this letter up for laud's sake.

1 The Nazi–Soviet non-aggression pact was signed on 23 August 1939.

NANCY TO JESSICA
21 September 1939

S.M.H. 1st Aid Post
Somewhere in Praed Street

Darling Susan

Here I sit in this awful dark cellar all day from 11–7 & no day off not even Sunday & this is the sixteenth day I've been here & I feel as if it were seven years already. It is gas &, therefore, air proof & one has a racking headache after the 1st half hour. I *hope* you are harrowed.

Susan Stalin how could you let him. Honestly Soo I had such an awful dream, that I was in Harrods & I saw a big crowd so I thought it was the Queen & Q. Mary & when I went to look it was Adolf & Uncle Joe. I woke up yelling.

Peter has a commission in the Welsh Guards. He was offered a job in propaganda but says he must kill Germans. Luckily he won't go abroad for two months at least. Tud is quartered quite near here & he & Nigel [Birch] come to dinner quite often.

Susan the P's. The day war broke out I was leaving the Island[1] & Muv was taking me to the station & I said something only fairly rude about Hitler & she said 'get out of this car & walk to the station then', so after that I had to be honey about Adolf. Then later I said Peter had joined up so she said 'I expect he'll be shot soon', which I thought fairly tactless of her.

Altogether she is acting *very* queer. Farve has recanted in the *Daily Mirror* like Latimer.

Poor Boud I do wonder. Fleet St says she has been put on a farm for Czech women – we have written to the Duchess of Aosta to find out what has really happened to her & if she is awfully miserable she could perhaps go to Italy. Probably she is on top of the world though.

Susan Hitler's secret. Well if he wipes us all out with it *PROMISE* you'll take a dose over there in revenge. I absolutely trust you to.

Do write & tell the American form. I imagine they just don't want to think about the war like us & the Abyssinians & heavens I don't blame them.

RSVP

Love from NR

1 Inch Kenneth.

NANCY TO DEBORAH
25 September 1939

S.M.H. 1st Aid Post, W2

Dear Miss

I see you have *learnt* to *write* in a *single night.*

Really, the Fem! She always thinks anybody who isn't a hide-bound Tory is a communist – if she knew the trouble *I* have with the C[ommunist] P[arty], & that the Labour Party have always hated them worse than anything – but these little niceties seem to have escaped her! Actually, I have always said that there wasn't a pin to put between Bolshies & Nazis except that the latter, being better organized, are probably more dangerous. It's the Fem herself who was always writing articles trying to point out the (invisible) differences.

Rodd has got his commission & goes off on Friday & we are having a GRAND BALL on Thursday, white ties & ball dresses & dinner for 30 people at Blomfield. Ambitious?

Write again soon. I wish I was on the Island. I too have been digging up my lawn, oh the hard work. I am going to keep recs.[1]
I had a very grumbly letter from Woman.

Love from NR

1 Chickens. As a small child, before she could spell, Deborah thought that chickens on the lawn on a cold morning looked like wrecks at sea.

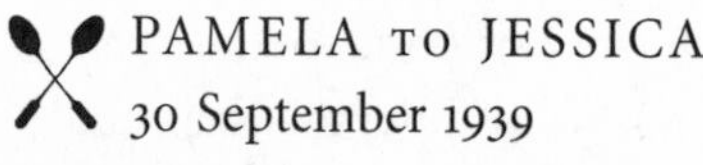

PAMELA TO JESSICA
30 September 1939

Rignell House
Deddington
Oxon

Darling Steake[1]

I wonder so much how you are both getting on now & if you like your new jobs. Do write & tell me all about your holiday & where you went.

Our flying journey home was wonderful but it was rather frightening when we took off.[2] The plane seemed far too small to battle all across the Atlantic. We came down at Botwood in Newfoundland & were able to go for a walk while the plane was being filled with petrol. The next stop was at Foynes in Ireland. The whole journey only took 28 hours! Derek had a special job for three weeks on research for the Air Ministry & now expects to go off again soon for a similar job. Muv, Farve & Debo are all still up at the Island & say it is lovely there. Uncle George, Aunt Madeleine & their two children[3] are going to stay up there for two weeks with them. Nancy is working at a casualty depot & has of course had nothing to do. I heard from her a few days ago & she said she had been given an indelible pencil to write on the foreheads of her dead & dying & what would she do if a black man was brought in!!! So Nancy-like.

We had a refugee family in one of our cottages but they left at the end of the week because they found it too far from the public house. We are more or less full here: Tello & her granddaughter[4] were here for three weeks but have now left. We have a friend's baby with his nurse, & they come (the parents) every weekend. So far food has not been rationed but it is going to be. And we may only have ¾ the amount of coal. Petrol is very severely rationed & we only get fifteen gallons a month for the two cars. As I have to fetch nearly all the food from Banbury because the shops also have very little petrol the fifteen gallons will not last very long.

We can never get into Banbury for the cinema these days partly on account of the shortage of petrol & partly because it is so horrid driving in a blackout. We went to London for a night last week & saw the barrage balloons[5] for the first time. They are so very beautiful & make a wonderful decoration.

I am sorry to have been so long before writing but I have been so terribly busy the last five weeks that I have not had a moment to spare for writing. One of the most difficult things has been blacking out this house. We have had to make black curtains for *all* the windows. Even if a pin prick of light shows through the police come rushing down on you!

There is no more family news at the moment but I will write again soon & I do long to hear from you.

Much love to you both from Woman

1 There was no particular reason for the nickname which was pronounced 'Stee-ake' in an exaggerated way.

2 Pamela and Derek had returned from New York where he was involved in top-secret work, and where they had visited Jessica and Esmond. Their return journey by seaplane was the second-ever commercial flight to cross the Atlantic.
3 Julia and Thomas Bowles were seven and five years old respectively.
4 Madeleine (Madeau) Stewart (1921–2006). A cousin of the Mitfords. Daughter of Oliver Stewart, Henrietta Shell's illegitimate son by Thomas Bowles. Producer for the BBC and author of *The Music Lover's Guide to the Instruments of the Orchestra* (1980).
5 Large silver balloons that were raised in the skies as an anti-aircraft device during the Blitz to prevent enemy planes from making low-level attacks.

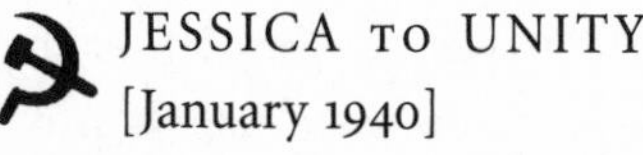

JESSICA TO UNITY
[January 1940]

268 S.W. 1st Street
Miami
Florida

Darling Boud,

Your Boud is *so* sorry you are ill, I've written to you very often but I think the letters may have gone astray. I've been so longing for news of you & am awfully glad you are back home again with Blor & everyone to take care of you.

Esmond & I have got jobs in a Miami bar, you must admit rather 'fascinating'. The other people there are *heaven* (mostly Italian & Spanish) & we have all our food there which is wonderful, because it's the most delicious food I've e'er noted. We've got to know the most amazing people here; for instance, I have one friend whose only interest in life is birth control, & when I go to tea with her she takes me round in her car for free handouts of contraception to nigger families. Miami's rather like the South of France or Venice, all the people here have got something extraorder about them. Well Boud I'll write again soon, & *do* get well quickly.

Very Best Love, Yr Boud

卐 UNITY TO JESSICA
20 February 1940

Old Mill Cottage
High Wycombe

Darling Boud

When I got your letter, I nearly went off my head! You SEE, I had ached for your, because I do love you so much.

Oh, Boud, I have a Goat! The Fem gave her to me & I *LOVE* her. Oh Boud, I *AM* so sorry to be short, but will write again soon!

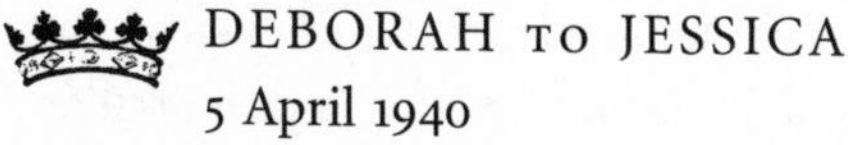

DEBORAH TO JESSICA
5 April 1940

Rignell House
Deddington

Dearest Cheerless

Well dear, I'm here for the weekend and although it's very comfortable, it's pretty bloody in some ways because Woman will keep telling one to keep one's dogs off the daffodils etc & one feels that if one settles down with one's book someone will say something & interrupt one.

Birdie is here & is so terribly pathetic, it really makes one miserable to see her. I can hardly bear the idea of this summer because she & Muv & I will be all boxed up at Swinbrook together & when Muv gets gloomy it's awful. Actually she is wonderful, I believe I would have gone mad if I had been with poor Bird all this time. She is like a completely different person, it is extraordinary & awfully horrifying. She has stages of doing things, really like a child, I mean she has now got a habit of standing up till everyone in the room has sat down, & is *furious* if anyone starts eating before the Fem has started. The whole thing is really so awful it doesn't bear thinking of. I wish you could see her, I long to know what you would think. She is very apologetic & funny in that way, always says 'I'm awfully sorry' before she says anything else.
[Incomplete]

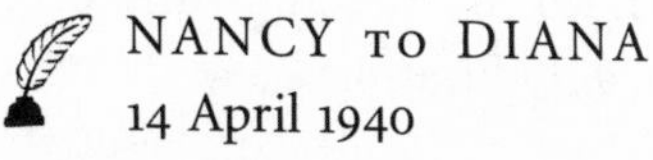

NANCY TO DIANA
14 April 1940

[The Mill Cottage]
Swinbrook

Darling Diana

So pleased to hear of another 10lb son (Maximilian[1] this time I suppose). I hope it wasn't too much trouble in spite of the size.

I stayed with Sachie & Georgia[2] last weekend & S told me such a typical Sitwell story – it seems that ages ago they had to stay two people who knew you & Bryan very well & one who had never met you & for some reason the only topic the whole weekend was you & B. By Sunday night the man who didn't know you was joining in & saying no that was the weekend Bryan & Diana went to Bailiffscourt, it was the one after they rode over to see Lytton Strachey,[3] because by then he knew you so intimately. *Of course* Sachie couldn't remember who any of them were. Weston is heaven, have you seen it?

I am here chaperoning Debo & Andrew you must say good-natured of me. They are so funny, rush at the papers & turn *quickly* to the racing news. The Germans will have to march down the village street before they notice anything.

Cecil[4] was also there, he now does 0 but photograph Cab ministers wouldn't you love to see him at it.

Much love & to the beautiful BOY. NR

1 Diana's fourth son, Max, was born on 13 April.
2 Sacheverell Sitwell (1897–1988). The writer, traveller, poet and youngest of the celebrated literary trio lived at Weston Hall in Northamptonshire. Married Georgia Doble in 1925.
3 Lytton Strachey (1880–1932). Diana first met the author of *Eminent Victorians* when she was eighteen and saw him often when they were neighbours at Biddesden. She included an essay on him in *Loved Ones*.
4 Cecil Beaton (1904–80). The photographer of society beauties and royalty had begun a series of portraits of ministers and war leaders.

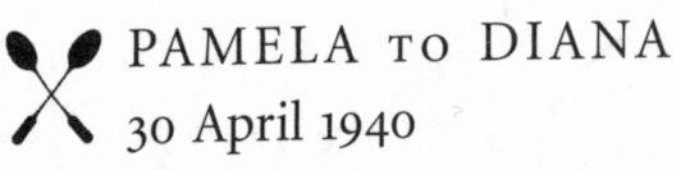

PAMELA TO DIANA
30 April 1940

Rignell House
Deddington

Darling Nardy

I am so pleased that you feel really well this time, it must make the whole difference of course. Are you feeding him for a few months? And what is his name?

I am in an anxious state as Derek is determined to join the Air Force if he can, as a gunner! But of course he must do what he thinks most useful, although it is heaven having him safe in Oxford.

Hoping to see you soon – in haste to catch the last 1½d post!

Much love to you all from Woman

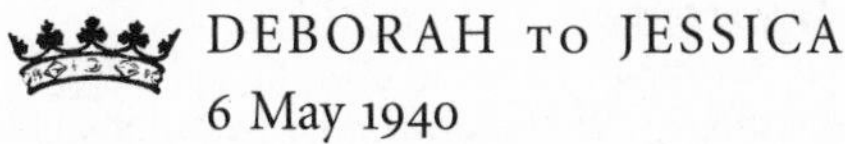

DEBORAH TO JESSICA

6 May 1940

[The Mill Cottage]
Swinbrook

Dearest Cheerless

I did *adore* getting your letter, I forget whether I got it before I wrote last.

You do sound to be having a lucky time. It's all right here at least more or less. I have been here a month now without going away which is terrific for me. I have got very what Stiegson[1] would call 'keen on the garden' isn't it extraorder, in fact I'm going to lunch with Aunt Sport [Dorothy] tomorrow to get more plants, would you believe it.

Muv & Bobo are getting awfully on my nerves, I must go away soon I think. There was a dreadful row at breakfast this morning & I swore at Muv in front of Mrs Timms[2] & Farve shook me like he did you after you'd been to Mrs Rattenbury's trial.[3]

I think Bobo is a bit better but I don't know. All outsiders think she is, but she certainly is very odd. Things like this happen – Colonel Buxton came here this morning & she dashed at him thinking he was the Dean & he looked rather surprised when she kissed him. Today we went to tea at Ditchley with the Trees[4] & the Duff Coopers[5] were staying there & for one ghastly moment I thought she wasn't going to shake hands however she just did.

Lots of my friends are in France & some in Norway so I don't think it sounds much fun in London. How that will make you roar. I always think while I'm writing how terrifically you despise my life.

It is such a pity we can't go to the Island, I think Muv & Bobo would like it better.

I expect you know that Honks produced another ten pound boy the other day, she really does make a habit of it. She & the Leader really do get on well, a terrific tease on everyone.

Well dear I can't think of anything else, *do* write. Goodness I do sometimes wish you were around here, you can't think what a difference it would make when lividry is the note with the others.

Love from Yr Hen.

1 Amy Hussey; one of the Mitfords' many governesses.
2 The wife of Lord Redesdale's foreman.
3 Alma Rattenbury (1897–1935). A musical prodigy from Canada who was accused of murdering her husband and acquitted after a sensational trial. Tom Mitford worked on the case in a lowly capacity.
4 Ronald Tree (1897–1976). Marshall Field department-store heir and Conservative MP 1933–45. Married Nancy Field in 1920 and Marietta Peabody in 1947. His son Michael married Deborah's future sister-in-law Anne Cavendish. Owner of Ditchley Park in Oxfordshire where Winston Churchill held secret meetings during the war.
5 Alfred Duff Cooper, 1st Viscount Norwich (1890–1954). Politician, diplomat and writer. Ambassador to Paris 1944–7. Married Lady Diana Manners in 1919.

DEBORAH TO NANCY
1 July 1940

Inch Kenneth
Gribun, Oban
Isle of Mull

Get on.

What with one thing or another I've come here. Bobo has become quite impossible, she gets absolutely furious whatever I do & Muv is fed up so I left, just when the STOCKS I GREW FROM SEED (tease on you because you always said they never would) were beginning to flower.

I got here on Saturday after a terrifically easy journey[1] on account of going 1st class which I'd never been before & now I would rather not go than go 3rd. My dear ones[2] slept on my bed all night & none made a murmur. The train doesn't stop during air raids so it's never very late.

There is masses to do here, the kitchen garden is a mass of weeds & all where the field was ploughed for oats & potatoes needs hoeing & things & there is no servant here at all so I have to make my bed & cook. Luckily Peter[3] washes up so it's not too bad. We have our meals in the kitchen at the same time, but at a different table, as the men, so that puts a bar on any conversation but as Farve only says 'what' it doesn't make much difference. The first morning I came down to breakfast about 10 & found the kitchen full of stale smoke (Farve had been smoking there since 6) & him peeling onions to put in a vile looking stew. However I've put a stop to all that because I *won't* eat my breakfast in a sort of 3rd class smoking carriage.

The new boat is a dream. We are going to Salen[4] to try & buy a goat this afternoon, I don't much take to tinned milk.

Do write. I rang you up in London but of course you weren't there.

Far the most awful thing ever happened at Swinbrook last week. Nina had been on heat & I thought all was o'er & let her out & it was a Saturday night & the inn was full of air force gentlemen & when I went out what should I see on the road in front of *everyone* but my dear ones stuck together for life but standing back to back & everyone pointing & roaring. I didn't dare tell Muv because I knew she'd be so livid so I had to get the car & Studley had to get in backwards. They stayed together for about ½ an hour. So of course she'll pig, isn't it awful.

How is Milly & where is Abbey.[5]

Isn't it awful about Honks,[6] & isn't it wonderful about Tim.[7]

I wonder what you would think of Birdie now, she really is impossible to live with because she flies into these fearful rages & it really is terrifying.

I wish you would come here, why don't you?

WRITE.

Love from Dahlia

1 The journey to the Redesdales' Hebridean island was laborious, involving a night on a sleeper train, a morning's wait at the mainland port of Oban, a crossing by ferry-steamer to Mull, and a ten-mile drive to Gribun before transferring to a rowing boat to reach the island.

2 Deborah had taken her dogs with her on the long-drawn-out journey to Scotland.

3 Husband of the cook at Inch Kenneth.

4 The village on the west coast of Mull where the ferry to the mainland docked.

5 Nancy's French bulldogs.

6 Diana had been arrested and was being detained in Holloway Prison.

7 Timothy Bailey (1918–86). The Mitfords' first cousin, who had been declared missing, was discovered to be a prisoner of war. Two of his brothers, Christopher and Anthony, were killed in action.

DIANA to PAMELA
No. 5433 [passed by prison censor 16/7/40]
13 July 1940

F. Wing
Holloway Prison
London N7

Darling Pam

I read your letter over and over again – thank you *so* much for it and for being so angelic about having the babies[1] and for taking Jonathan out and for sending me Bromo and pillow and towels. I do hope Alexander will soon get less screamy, I think it is a phase they all go through. I wonder if he enjoyed the drive to Rignell, I expect he did. How splendid that Max has done well on his new food; I miss him terribly sometimes and would give anything to hear him say 'Agee', and Alexander doing what Kit calls his morning broadcast. I *do* hope that Bryan will let Desmond and Miss G[2] go to you – I don't think Biddesden suits him at present. If possible I want his tonsils out – if Sir Frederic still advises it, which I am sure he will.

If you or Nanny or Muv writes 'the' letter[3] to me do enclose letters from the boys, I am allowed to have them in the same envelope. I had a letter from Kit yesterday, he is quite cheerful. It is such hell not being able to see him.

Could you write to Miss Gillies and give her my love and explain that I am not allowed to write more than one letter (one goes to Kit of course) and ask her to tell you just how Desmond is getting on so that you or Muv can tell me. I am asking the Governor's permission to see Desmond and if he says yes I will put his name on the visiting pass which I will send to Muv. If he can't come of course it doesn't matter but I will write his name in case he can. Please tell Muv not to bother to come all the way to see me if it is a trouble; I *adore* having a visitor but I feel it is such a business for her. I am perfectly well again. If anyone comes I would love a few country flowers; also a Woolworth cup & saucer, & a bowl or dish (for salad or anything I may cook). No food is allowed to be brought or sent, although we may order once a fortnight. When the hols start I will put Jonathan's name on the pass. If Desmond & Miss Gillies come, it would be better if no one else came as we only have 15 mins. Do write again, or Nanny, and put everything about the babies, no detail is too insig-

Max Mosley, Desmond and Jonathan Guinness, Alexander Mosley, 1940. Diana kept this photograph of her four sons with her while she was in prison.

nificant, I so long to hear *all* about them. Give them and Nanny all my love, & Horse[4] if you see him.

All love darling from Nardy

1 Alexander and Max were staying with Pamela at Rignell, looked after by Nanny Higgs.

2 Jean Gillies, Jonathan and Desmond Guinness's governess, was reporting on Diana to Lord Moyne who passed the information to MI5.

3 When she was first arrested, Diana was allowed to send and receive only two letters a week, one of which was always kept for communicating with her husband. After some months this restriction was relaxed.

4 Derek Jackson.

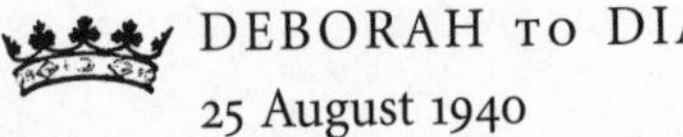

DEBORAH TO DIANA

Inch Kenneth
Gribun, Oban

25 August 1940
[passed by prison censor 29/8/40]

Darling Honks

Muv writes saying one can write to you at last, oh I do so long to see your cell. I haven't seen you or your pigs for such ages that I've almost forgotten what you look like what with one thing and another.

I've been here for three weeks with Farve & it's terribly gloomy because it *never* stops raining so the result is that Lilah McCalmont[1] who has come to stay, & I *never* stop cooking for one minute, we stiffly whip all day. I have made a wonderful improvement on Béarnaise by putting equal amounts of wine, lemon juice & vinegar. I hear you cook like a mad thing too, I do hope you are given eatable ingredients. As for poor Sir O, is *he* allowed to? I suppose not, *horrors*, what would Pat[2] say.

I suppose it isn't any good me coming to see you because you can see your pigs nearly always can't you, or anyhow old women who can tell you about them.

We're coming back next week & I suppose I shall have to work in London, I can't live at Swinbrook it's too tricky, so if ever you were short of a visitor I would come hurrying to Holloway, hurry*ing* to Hollo-*way*.

I can't think of anything fascinating, nothing much occurs here. Farve is either in fits of gloom or terrific spirits, apparently for no reason. I hope he won't live here alone in the winter because gloom is usually the form & what it must be like here then I can't imagine. Lividry sets in when my goat eats his creepers etc exactly like it always did, he is an eccentric old fellow.

When we were climbing around the caves here the other day I heard the most terrifying sound just like a hermit tearing calico, it so horrified me that we haven't been round there since. It has become the stock joke & thing to be frightened of, oh the horror.

I wonder what Muv's form is now, I mean whether she's in a good temper or not. Her favourite thing is going to see you, she always writes 'I'm going to see D', or 'I've just been to see D' usually from the tea room at Paddington. She will be the death of me.

Much love. I would adore to come & see you if you thought it a good idea from Debo

1 A friend and contemporary of Deborah.
2 A Cordon Bleu teacher who had given cookery lessons to Deborah, Diana and Mosley.

DIANA TO PAMELA — *Holloway Prison, N7*
5433 F 4/5 [passed by prison censor 30/8/40]
29 August 1940

Darling Pam

I am asking permission to send you this letter instead of the visit – I did not send a pass because there have been so many air raid warnings and I thought it would be so awful if you came all the way here and then there was a warning and you could not see me after all. I am sending you a pass in this letter; but *please* don't come unless you more or less must come to London – *don't* come on my account because I know it must be such a trouble. Will you thank Muv millions of times for her visit and for bringing Jonathan with her, I *did* love seeing him, it has made such a difference. How I wish Desmond could come, but I suppose he is not strong enough yet.[1] Please thank Nanny for her sweet letter; Kit always asks all details about Stodge and Weedom[2] and we both *long* to see them, do ask her to write again *soon*, and do tell Miss Gillies she can write to me now ('tho I can't reply) about Desmond. Will you ask Muv to send £1 to Desmond from me for his birthday; I am also getting Harrods to send him a few little things.

Now darling I wonder if you can possibly imagine *how* grateful I am to you for all you are doing for the babies, I feel so overwhelmed by all your wonderful kindness. I do long to see you all *so* much, and the sweet little foals. The vegetables from last week are still lasting, they are heaven. I made saucisses au vin blanc today for tea. Do send some more lovely DILL, Enid[3] & I adore it. I am very well, only wish we were out more in this divine weather, we are only let out 8.30–9.30 and 6.30–7.30 – early and late. Heavens what a lot there will be to tell when I get out – there is very little one can put in a letter. It is rather cold and chilly in the prison and one *longs* for more sun. Tell Nanny to get any clothes she needs for Alexander and Max before the purchase tax is imposed. Also, if she sends me wool and pattern, I would knit anything – for instance, knickers to go over Max's nappies (!) Have you seen the dress I knitted for myself? Would you like me to make you one? *Do* write soon – every detail enchants me.

All love darling & *so* many thanks from Nard

Kisses to Alexander & Max.

1 Desmond Guinness had had his tonsils out.
2 Alexander and Max.
3 Enid Riddell (1903–73). A member of Captain Ramsay's Right Club who was detained in Holloway for propagating fascist views.

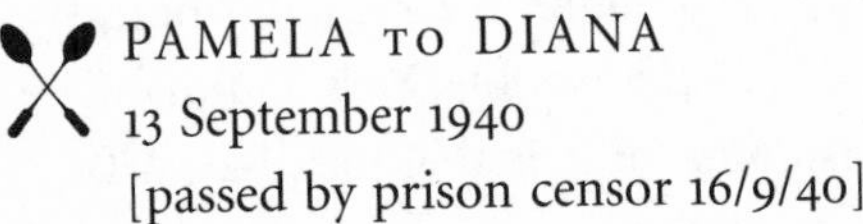

PAMELA TO DIANA
13 September 1940
[passed by prison censor 16/9/40]

Rignell House
Deddington

Darling Nardy

I hope no bombs have dropped on the Prison yet. Max & Alexander are very well, except that Max has rather taken to not sleeping much in the day time. Nanny thinks he may be getting some teeth. He is now having milk from an Ayrshire herd in the village which is not only T[uberculosis] T[ested] but also Attested which is the very best that it could be. The other day I was out blackberry-ing with Alexander in his push chair & the most peculiar looking Aircraft came over which looked just like a huge toy one, it was so old fashioned. It was *very* low & at first I thought I saw figures standing between the double wings & holding on to the wires in readiness to jump off. When it arrived closer I could see that there were no figures & that it was English. It made a wonderful Nanny tease &

I told her that I put Alexander well out in the open so that he could be plainly seen in his white coat & that I rushed into the hedge & hid! Nanny has to be teased a good deal, she enjoys it. Of course the darling dogs are a very good teasing subject, she thinks I take far too much notice of them & not nearly enough of her babies. She always comes into the library with me after dinner to hear the news & do some knitting. Alexander is to have a scarlet woolly coat made. His blue one looks lovely & I do hope you are not too cold; we can send you some warmer things if you want them.

In haste to get to Banbury & catch the post.

Love from Woman

DEBORAH TO DIANA
4 October 1940
[passed by prison censor 4/10/40]

[The Mill Cottage]
Swinbrook

Darling Honks

We are going to Woman's next week, my wonderful plan of Birdie going away for two weeks has fallen sadly through because Muv & I have got to go instead. It is awful because she *so* hates me that life here has become almost impossible. The sitting room is so small & two enormous tables in it belong exclusively to her & if one so much as puts some knitting down on one for a moment chaos reigns because she hies up & shrieks 'bloody fool' very loud. I think in some ways she's better though but she seems to have completely lost her sense of humour & never roars at the funniest thing.

Muv seems always to be in rather a way about me, doing things she doesn't allow, really I should have thought what with one thing & another there isn't much point in being seen to as though one was three.

Isn't it killing about the Jews in Rutland Gate.[1]

Farve has gone to Southend & taken Margaret the-maid-who-has-a-young-man-who-took-her-to-Ascot-in-a-Rolls-Royce.[2] I expect he will have a gay time.

I had lunch with the Wid the other day. She was alone because the Baileys had gone to lunch with the Dulvertons who hadn't asked the Wid – none of the neighbours do! Mrs McCalmont told me she was very surprised when shopping one morning in Stow she saw an Egyptian figure approach dressed in a cape & turban & said 'Tell me, what do you think of Dakar?'[3] The Baileys have got printed notices all over their house to say 'There is no gloom in this house'. And the Wid is living there!

I must go & milk my good goat.

Much love from Debo

1 The Redesdales' London house was requisitioned to provide temporary accommodation for Polish Jews evacuated from Whitechapel.
2 Margaret Wright, the Redesdales' parlourmaid. She later married her young man, a Mr Dance.
3 An unsuccessful attempt by the Allies to capture the French West African port of Dakar had ended in heavy French and British losses. Violet Hammersley, who relished bad news, was invariably swathed in scarves, shawls and veils.

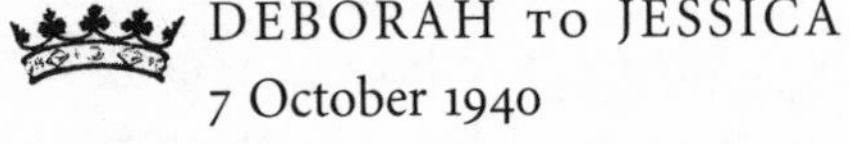

DEBORAH TO JESSICA
7 October 1940

[The Mill Cottage]
Swinbrook

Dear Cheerless

Well dear I am sorry I haven't written but I thought my old hen would be bored with long accounts of aching around with everyone you don't know & you know how you despise my life anyhow.

I spend most of my life in taxis going to & from Sandhurst because Andrew is there learning to be an officer which takes 5 months of appalling hard work & never a night off which you must say is a long time. Philip Toynbee[1] is there too & they all like him & are suitably amazed by his filthy habits.

We are going to Woman's tomorrow which is a great move for me because wherever I go I have to take two dogs, my goat & my pony & cart.

It is wonderful of Esmond to have joined the airforce I do think.

If you ever come across the Kennedys (the ambassador here) do take note of Kick,[2] she is a dear girl, I'm sure you'd like her. (Though of course you'd despise her like you do me.)

Well dear, do write.

Best love from Henderson

1 Philip Toynbee (1916–81). Left-wing friend and great admirer of Esmond Romilly, who became a novelist and critic on the *Observer*. In her memoir of him, *Faces of Philip* (1984), Jessica wrote that when young he was 'unkempt in the extreme', would get outrageously drunk and proposition any young girl in sight. Married to Anne Powell 1939–50, and to Frances Smith in 1950.

2 Kathleen (Kick) Kennedy (1920–48). Daughter of Joseph Kennedy, US ambassador to London 1937–40, and younger sister of President Kennedy. Married Andrew Cavendish's older brother, William (Billy), Marquess of Hartington, in 1944.

DIANA TO UNITY
15 November 1940

Holloway Prison, N7

Darling Bobo

I am using a letter this week to write to Nanny and you, she will send it on to you. I *wish* I could do it more often, but it is not possible.

How are you darling; I always get your messages from Muv, how I wish I could see you. Perhaps before very long I shall be let free, wouldn't that be Paradise. If not quite free, what we want more than anything is for Kit and me to be imprisoned together. Please get anyone who sees MPs and so on to press for this. It has never even been suggested that any charge could be brought against either of us or that we have ever done anything illegal.

You can't imagine what a joy Muv's visits are to me, please do tell her so. I only wish I could write to her as well, but as I see her I thought she would understand. She brings me such lovely things and does such boring boredoms for me. I am quite clean and comfortable again as we now have hot water to wash in and gas to cook on again.

Isn't it horrible about Jonathan having an appendix operation – I *do* hope they will let me out to go & see him. Do write to Desmond if you have time, because when Nanny cuts this part of the letter off all the ends of the words will be teased – however the point of this letter is to say how *much* I think of you and long to see you. Do write to Tom and thank him so much for going all the way to Brixton, I wish it had not been *umsonst* [in vain]. It was divine of him.

Do ask Muv to visit Kit the week after next, he would so love it. It was HEAVEN seeing him the other day at the Law Courts.[1]

All love darling from Nard XXXXXXX

1 The Mosleys had successfully sued the *Sunday Pictorial* for saying that they led a life of luxury in prison. Diana spent her share of the damages on a fur coat to keep her warm in her cell.

DIANA TO UNITY

Holloway Prison, N7

D. Mosley 5433 F3/23
19 December 1940
[passed by prison censor 19/12/40]

My darling Boud:

We have just been told that we may write one extra letter (for Christmas) so of course I shall use mine for you. You can imagine how much I shall be thinking of you all at Christmas; it will be simply hateful being in jail for it but never mind, next year perhaps everything will be wonderful again. Darling I *do* hope you are feeling really better; my Christian Scientist friend always asks so much about you, and she spends her entire life praying for people (you know how they do) and dozens of prayers are for you. Aren't you pleased? Tell Muv, the butter she brought will last ages and it is literally the joy of my life, and do thank her for the eggs and the lovely delicious brioche. Kit writes to say that he hopes they may soon give us better prison conditions, and imprison us together. If we had each other it would make *all* the difference of course, and if Muv could ask Choiney[1] to press for that it would be an immense help.

I do so love the green scarf you made me and I often wear it on my head and look like a mad Turkish lady. I haven't opened your Xmas pres yet, I am keeping it for the day, of course I won't be able to write and thank, but I am *thrilled* about it. Please will you send a message to Nanny, not to hoard food[2] (for the babies). I don't suppose she *would* but Kit suddenly had a nightmare that she *might*. Send her and Blor, and everyone and the babies *all* my love, and Debo, and specially Muv and you. I *do* hope the boys will spend some of the hols with you, please spoil them from me, and make them eat a lot and get fatter. I get so homesick at times, but perhaps it won't be much longer now. Tell Muv to get Hansard of December 10th, all about us;[3] if she can't I will send you mine. I am reading *Die Jungfrau von Orleans* (Schiller) it is so beautiful. If you want a *heavenly* novel get Goethe's *Wahlverwandtschaften*.[4] I adored it, and so did Kit. Well goodbye darling, I *wish* I could write to you more often, but there it is. I think of you every day.

All Christmas love darling from Nardy xxxxxxxxx

P.S. Tell Muv if she gets what looks like a letter from me it will only be *dull* old rent bill to pay! Wish I *cd* write to her.

1 Sir James Edmondson (1886–1959); the Redesdales' local MP.
2 Hoarding was a crime punishable by up to two years' imprisonment.
3 In a debate in Parliament, Richard Stokes, Labour MP for Ipswich, had raised a question concerning the legality of detainment under Regulation 18B and the treatment of detainees in prison.
4 *Elective Affinities*, Goethe's novel about love and adultery, was first published in 1809.

卐 UNITY TO DIANA

29 December 1940
[passed by prison censor 1/1/41]

[The Mill Cottage]
Swinbrook

Darling Nard,

Oh, Nard, I *WAS* surprised to get your lovely letter – I never thought you *COULD* write!! Oh Nard, I do so *HOPE* you had a lovely and beautiful Christmas, I prayed about it a terrific lot. Nard, I am going to be confirmed. Of course, I shall be a Christian Scientist, but my wonderful Christian Science lady, Miss Taylor, says I must if it helps me, and it *DOES* help me, a terrific lot.

Oh Nard, thank you *SO* much for your lovely pound, I liked it best of all my presents.

Nard, I am in the Choir!! In the church, of course. Aren't I lucky!!!! I'm afraid all this sounds nonsense to you, only you see how I am SO bored here.

Well, Nard, I am afraid I must stop, you don't know how slowly I do write!! So goodbye, Nard.

Best love, Nard, from Bobo

NANCY TO DIANA

26 Rutland Gate, SW7

7 January 1941

[passed by prison censor 9/1/41]

Darling Diana

I had no idea I was allowed to write – as I now hasten to do – & thank you for your kind present. I have bought myself some much needed facial condiments with it & am most grateful – actually managed to find a Guerlain lipstick in an obscure chemist's shop which must have given me the same sensation a bibliophile would have on coming across a 1st folio of Shakespeare.

I sent the Wid a box of soap called Modestes Violettes & she wrote back 'Coming downstairs in a rather specially sad mood . . .'

No wonder she is rather specially sad, freezing at Maugersbury & Aunt W[eenie] *won't* pick the war over with her – 'I said I hear that Holland House has quite gone & she said come on let's have luncheon, *much* more interesting.' Can't you see it.

I saw your little Alexander the other day he *is* a darling how I wish they were living with me – I had almost forgotten what heaven Nanny is.

Much love from Nance

PAMELA TO DIANA

Rignell House
Deddington

27 February 1941

[passed by prison censor 28/2/41]

Darling Nardy

Both Alexander & Max are extra well. Apparently Alexander was heard calling this last night when he was meant to be going to sleep

'Trude, Trude, dogs, dogs, dogs!' & as far as he could he was copying my voice. Isn't it extra tüm [sweet]? I do wish you could have them, I always feel so awful when I can see as much as I like of them & you are unable to do so. I may seem not to understand how awful it is for you when I am actually talking to you but that is only because we have to get through so much in such a horribly short space of time. I must tell you that I spend hours at night sometimes worrying about it & I always feel so gloomy when the visit is over & there is still so much we have not been able to discuss. I only pray it may now only be for a short while longer.

I saw Nancy yesterday. She is going to leave Rutland Gate & hopes to get a little house at Wimbledon so as to be with Peter. Derek is still in Scotland but I much hope will be down here again in about two weeks' time. Muv & Bobo arrive to stay today & I will tell them news of you.

Much love & to Kit from Woman

DEBORAH TO DIANA
3 March 1941
[passed by prison censor 4/3/41]

Rignell House
Deddington

Darling Honks

It *is* so exciting because Andrew & I are going to be married, such a tease on Bridget [Airlie] who always said we never would. His parents have been so wonderful about it, I didn't know people could be so nice, they really seem pleased. It would be awful getting married if everyone hated it, but as it is it's perfect. It was only arranged between us for two days before the papers started telephoning, they really are like magic. We went to get a ring, it was such fun & I was terrified someone we knew would come in & see us at it because no-one was meant to know till it was in *The Times*. The awful thing is that when a soldier gets married he has to tell his Colonel & of course Andrew hadn't when it was in the paper so I hope lividry hasn't set in.

I expect we shall be terrifically poor but think how nice it will be to have as many dear dogs & things as one likes without anyone to say they must get off the furniture. I *do* so wish you weren't in prison, it will be sad not having you to go shopping with, only we're so poor I shan't have much of a trousseau on account of everything being so expensive.

Poor Andrew is hating every moment of it & keeps saying how embarrassing it all is & how he wishes he could go away. He's at Elstree for this week, learning something, which is a great tease because we wanted to go out the night it's announced but as it seems to be in all the papers already it doesn't seem much point.

I am so excited for it. We haven't decided on a church, all the nice ones have been bombed. Anyhow it isn't for nearly two months so there isn't any hurry. Your nanny was killing & said 'You'll be wanting all our baby clothes'. I can't get over how wonderful the Devonshires were, they never said *anything* against, not even how young he is, because he's only just had his twenty-first birthday, I do think it was nice of them.

I don't know where we shall live or anything, it all depends on where he is sent, I should think some boarding house or something.

Much love, Debo

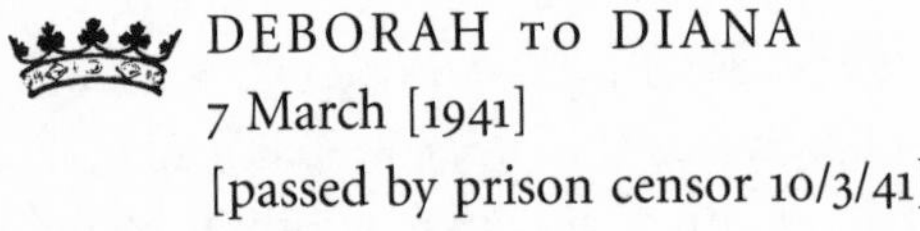

DEBORAH TO DIANA
7 March [1941]
[passed by prison censor 10/3/41]

[The Mill Cottage]
Swinbrook

Darling Honks

Thank you so much for your heavenly letter, it was bliss of you to write. You can't think how exciting it all is. The only tease is you not being out, you are the only person who is taking *proper* interest. I keep on at Muv about the dress etc. & she only looks at the ceiling and says, 'Ohrrr, I think we want some new paint'. I will show you my ring which everyone except me & Mrs Bunce[1] thinks very mivvy [stingy]. Nancy was rather teasy about it & said, 'You *can't* go to *Cartier*, it's well known to be *hopeless*', when we'd already been. However *I* like it & I hope you will.

Nancy is going to ask Cecil Beaton where to have my dress made by a theatrical person because it wouldn't be so expensive as a proper shop. It's going to be masses & masses & masses of white tulle, tight bodice & sleeves, a skirt such as has never been seen before for size. I don't mind if that is the fashion or not, it's what suits me. And the train will come out of the skirt & be *enormous* with great ruches of tulle all down, otherwise the skirt will be quite plain. What to wear on my head I don't know & I *know* Miss Stevens will wreck my hair but I couldn't go to anyone else. Then if the actual wedding dress doesn't cost too much we could go a bit of a bust on the going away one, have it from Worth or Molyneux or somewhere. Oh Honks, it is so exciting. I'm going to begin on my underclothes next week. Lady Dashwood said I could choose something at Lydia Moss & put it down to her account, so that will be heaven. If you are *really* going to give me something, I would *adore* a little jewel – I'm sure I won't get any. Only you're *not* to spend too much because it is the war & all.

Andrew is away on a course this week so I haven't seen him for ages but shall on Sunday & I expect we'll fix when to get married then. It will be about the middle or end of next month I expect. The thing is, which church? Some say St Maggots [Margaret's], some say the Smithfield one & I rather think St Martin's-in-the-Fields but I must go & study-dear this week. If only one knew how many people would come, I *do* hope masses. As for the reception, the Wid has kindly offered Tite St but I'm secretly hoping the Salisburys will say Arlington St, but Muv says I'm not to say that in case they don't. I had twenty-four letters & telegrams yesterday, wasn't it wonderful. On top of all this, Nina is going to have puppies next week, isn't it a worry.

I roared about the 'cris de joie', when I cook there is nothing but groans. Poor Andrew doesn't know what he's in for. I wish I knew how much dough we shall have, not much I suppose on account of the war. The Wid was wonderful & wants to be a bridesmaid draped in black. She said, 'Tell me dear, will you be *IMMENSELY* rich?'

I'm coming to London in my £14 car tomorrow, it does go so well, you can't imagine. I'm only having £200 for my trousseau, but I suppose it will buy the essential though certainly not linen.

Everything is so terribly expensive but I hope I shall be able to get *something* nice.

Well Honks I do long to see you & tell you all though Muv says it's terribly dull for other people, isn't it vile of her. All Farve said when I told him was something about the insurance of my car. He is hopeless.

All love, Debo

1 Mrs Bunce held the licence for the Swan Inn at Swinbrook.

UNITY TO DIANA

24 April 1941

[The Mill Cottage]
Swinbrook

Darling Nard

Well, Nard, about the Wedding!!!! Well, it was quite heaven. Debo's dress was quite too lovely, and she looked *MARVELLOUS*. The only person who looked ghastly was dear old Farve; he looked so sad. He was wearing his Home Guard Uniform ('Rompers') which was also rather depressing as it wasn't even long enough. Horrors!!

12 May Well, Nard, I am continuing this letter, I didn't finish it before because of my poor paralysed hand. Nard, I want to tell you something important. Nard, I am not allowed to visit you. You know, I am sure, how much I would love to come & see poor you. But it's not possible.

I see the Germans have bombed the House of Commons – how awful.

Nard, I must tell you about my sorrow. Five of my very best English friends, and one foreign one, have died in the last year. How can I bear it?

The Fem sends you her love.

V best love, Nard, from Bobo

Mary Ormsby-Gore, Unity and Pamela at Deborah's wedding. London, 19 April 1941.

卐 UNITY TO JESSICA
10 May 1941

[The Mill Cottage]
Swinbrook

Darling Boud

I *am* so sorry, Boud, not have written about the Babe,[1] but the fact is, I write *so* slowly still. Never mind, I write faster now than I did earlier. You know, I think, why I was ill; so I can explain it to you. You know I got shot in the head. Well, that paralysed my right arm & right leg. Understand?

Well, Boud, I was *so thrilled* by your cablegram – or, was it really yours? – I telephoned the Fem immediately, and, do you know, Boud,

I heard her crying with complete joy!!!! As for darling Blor – well, well. Boud, what are you going to call her? *Do* write & say.

Boud, I must tell you something fearfully sad. Dolly Wilde has died. Oh, Boud, I know you will be unhappy. I was, fearfully unhappy.

Peter Rodd is going off to Africa. Poor, poor Nancy.

Well, Boud, I will stop, as I can't write Fast!!

Give your baby a kiss from Aunt Me!!

V. Best Love, Boud

1 Jessica's daughter, Constancia (Dinky, Donk) Romilly, was born on 9 February.

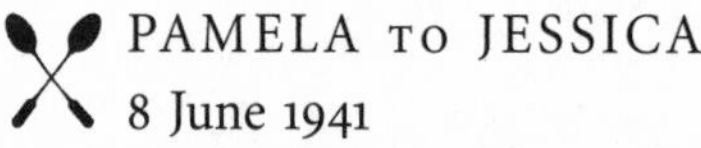

PAMELA TO JESSICA
8 June 1941

Rignell House
Deddington

Darling Decca

I wonder how you & your baby are getting on now, also Esmond. I hear you have been in Canada to see him. Do you think he will come over here soon or is he to remain in Canada? I do wish we could see you all again, it seems such ages since we were in New York for the World Fair.

Derek is now operational flying & has been for about eight weeks. He has just been home for six days leave which he badly needed as going up most nights is very exhausting. The Air Force blue suits him so well & I expect it suits Esmond also with his blue eyes. What is your baby like & what are you naming her? Do send me a photograph of her if you have one. Diana's two children are here still, it will be a year at the end of this month since they arrived. Nanny is kept very busy looking after them both, we cannot get a nursery maid to help, they have all gone into munitions. Also it is impossible to get housemaids & parlour maids so we now only have a cook & a little girl who seems to do everything. We are now rationed for clothes as I expect you have seen. A mackintosh takes fourteen coupons! The total number of coupons is sixty-six a year. Luckily for me I still have plenty of summer clothes from last year & so will not have to use any coupons just yet.

We see quite a lot of Bobo. She & Muv often come over & stay here for a few nights. Also darling Blor often comes here, she showed me a photograph of you & your baby.

On account of the difficulty of getting food for cattle I am having to give up my herd of Aberdeen Angus. It is very sad because I had bred some really beautiful ones. However they will make good beef. The Bull, Black Hussar, has already been sent to the butcher. Poor Black Hussar!

Please give Esmond my love when you next see him.

Much love from Woman

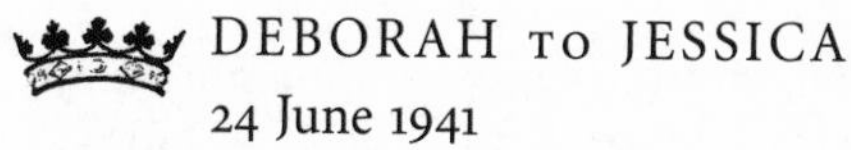

DEBORAH TO JESSICA
24 June 1941

Compton Place[1]
Eastbourne
Sussex

Dear Cheer

Well dear, I've smacked my ovary and taken it to Madame Bovary and the result is I'm in pig, I shan't be like my old Hen and not tell anyone because although it's not going to be born for nigh on a year I have to tell people on account of being sick and feeling so awful.

Well dear, do write an account of exactly what you felt like and exactly how embarrassed you were when you went to see the dr because I really nearly died when he pulled at the budding bust and said I must get a point on it whatever that may mean. I am glad to see in the papers that pregnant ladies are going to have some more clothes coupons otherwise think how awful it would be with everything splitting when one got huge. Think of a name for it there's a good old Hen, I *do* hope it's a girl. It ought to be exactly a year younger than your one, it's supposed to be born on the 10th of Feb.

The idea of Andrew being a dad is so killing that I think of nought else. I hardly ever see him because he is always in some remote place and country hotels are so full now that you usually can't get a room. He is going to be near Biddesden soon so I shall ask myself there. I have been here for three weeks and it's been lovely and hot and there are masses of strawberries but even they taste disgusting, did things used to taste disgusting with you?

Cheer yourself along and write to yr old Hen if you can be bothered. I do long to hear what you're up to.

Birdie hates me so dreadfully, I really can't think why, it makes it almost impossible to go to Swinbrook. You can't think how awful it is to see her now because although one is quite used to it because she's been like that for nearly two years now it's simply awful when one suddenly remembers what she used to be like. I don't believe she will ever get quite normal again, it really is a nightmare when one thinks of her future. She has got a terrific religious thing on now and if you say even 'damn' she gets quite furious and says it [is] wicked to swear.

I was among the girls being called up to work at some horrid job for 48 hours a week but now I'm in pig I don't have to do it and you know how I hate work so it's very lucky.

Well dear do cheer and write to me. Swinbrook is the best address.

Love from Yr Hen

1 An eighteenth-century house belonging to the Devonshires which became a school in 1954.

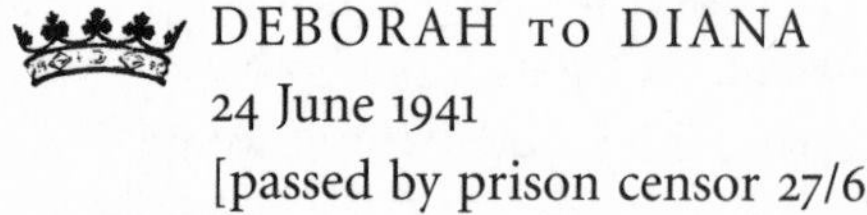

DEBORAH to DIANA

24 June 1941

[passed by prison censor 27/6/41]

Compton Place
Eastbourne

Darling Honks

It is awful of me not to have written to you before for your birthday, anyhow I do hope you had a nice one, I hear your pigs went up to see you. I saw in the paper that you had arrived in the Isle of Man with 50 suitcases and you had to carry them all yourself![1] I did so roar. I went to see Mr Gilliat[2] on account of being in pig and I've never been so embarrassed as I was by the things he did, it really was torture, how did you manage it? And how *did* you manage to have four pigs, were you very sick with all of them because it really does poison life, I go about with my hand over my mouth.

It's heaven here in many ways, people are allowed to bathe in the sea at one place and I've been several times as the doc seems to think it O.K.

The trouble about married life is never seeing one's husband. He is going on a course for all July to Netheravon. *How* I wish you were still at Biddesden. I've written to Woman to ask if she thinks one could possibly ask oneself there for a weekend or two because she used to go when Derek was near them. Otherwise I shan't see him for weeks and weeks and it was such a waste having the Regent's Park house done up because so far I've spent exactly one night in it! Eddie Marsh[3] lives here now, he is such a silly old man and eats a terrible lot. His best friend is Ivor Novello[4] who is acting in Brighton and has just been over here for the day. The children[5] got giggles at lunch when he said something was 'divine' for the 10th time, it *was* awful. I'm going to Swinbrook for July, I do hope Bird won't kill me, she does hate me so!

My good goat is giving ten pints of milk a day and Muv has been making cheeses, you must say it's good. That wonderful ring you gave me is the admiration of everybody, it makes my engagement ring look perfectly stupid.

Did I tell you about when Jonathan and Desmond came over to lunch about a month ago and I said 'Do go & see Pam Timms'[6] & Desmond went bright red & said he didn't want to and Jonathan said 'she's like an old toy you've no more use for and have thrown away'. Tom was there, I never saw anyone roar so much.

Much love from Debo

1 Fanciful stories about the Mosleys appeared regularly in the British newspapers.
2 William Gilliat (1884–1956). Obstetrician and for more than twenty years gynaecologist to the royal family.
3 Edward Marsh (1872–1953). Civil servant, patron of the arts, private secretary to Winston Churchill. He was knocked down in St James's Street, London, during the blackout and was taken to nearby Pratt's Club where Deborah's father-in-law took pity on him and invited him home to recuperate. He stayed a year and a half with the Devonshires, irritating Deborah.
4 Ivor Novello (1893–1951). The songwriter, playwright and matinee idol was touring with his musical *The Dancing Years* (1939).

5 Deborah's sisters-in-law: Lady Anne (Tig) Cavendish (1927–), who married Michael Tree in 1949, and Lady Elizabeth (Deacon) Cavendish (1926–), who never married but in 1951 became the close companion of John Betjeman.
6 The daughter of Lord Redesdale's foreman and granddaughter of Mrs Bunce who owned the pub in Swinbrook.

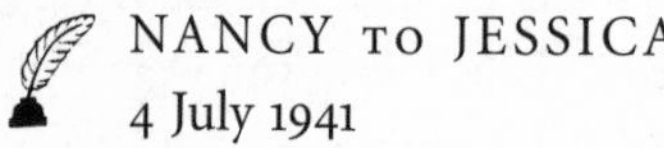

NANCY TO JESSICA

4 July 1941 *12 Blomfield Road, w9*

Darling Sue

Many thanks for a long & most interesting letter dated 20 May. Oh dear I do wish I could see you & (such a charming name) Constancia she sounds such heaven.

Boud. Well I promise that I am quite confident about her now. When I first saw her I had to go away & cry for hours because I felt sure she would be mad, but now, although quite dotty as she always was, she is heaven to be with & a happy person again. Muv has been *too* wonderful with her & absolutely given up her whole life – Farve simply beastly, hardly goes near her & has never been there to relieve Muv & give her a change to have a little holiday. Poor TP, one keeps off the war with her but she is, I fear, very unsound at heart. But she never mentions it.

About sending things, one mayn't ask, you know, but really we have everything so don't bother. Food is plentiful although rather dull. I have yet to feel in the least hungry or to have a craving for anything special.

Rodd has gone, I can't say where, which is very dull for me & goodness knows when one will see him again.

I have a simply splendid maid called Gladys,[1] she has been with me now a year. She really enjoys the raids & is awfully funny about everything, she is the *greatest* comfort in my life.

I go to work now all day, a paid job thank goodness. I find country holidays for A[ir] R[aid] P[recautions] workers – it is jolly nice as they come back saying how the wife & I couldn't have been better treated if we had been the King & Queen. They are such heaven.

The other people in the office seem to think I'm a sort of joke

(Susan how queer) & when there's a quiet moment do imitations of me on the telephone.

Robert [Byron] has been drowned I am very miserable about it. I must go to sleep – will write again soon.

Much love, Susan

1 A different Gladys from the one who made dresses for the sisters when they were debutantes.

UNITY TO DIANA
15 October 1941
[passed by prison censor 17/10/41]

[The Mill Cottage]
Swinbrook

Darling Nard –

Well, I can hardly tell you my news! I am being allowed to go & see – you! you! I'm *SO* happy & wonderfully contented! Oh, Nard! Oh, Nard!

With love from Bobo

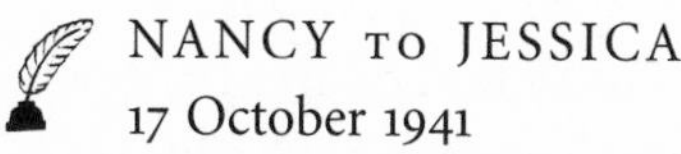

NANCY TO JESSICA
17 October 1941

12 Blomfield Road, w9

Darling Soo

Did you get my letter thanking for the parcel, it was wonderful & now I know it took such hours I really feel grateful. Kind little miss.

I haven't seen Boud for months, you see I WORK Susan also Sat mornings & then one is asked not to travel but if one does do so one has the drunken & licentious soldiery pressed to one's bosom the whole way except for very occasional weekends.

I never note Rodd's graph[1] at all & it is 5 months since he left & there is no leave & most people think the war will last another 5 years. So – you see. Also my dear old mother in law has stopped my allowance in order to build a ballroom in memory of my pa in law. I keep saying how I wish she were religious, a nice marble X would cost far less (tho less practical of course).

Well Soo write soon your last was very short.

Love from NR

1 'N[ancy] & I were travelling . . . and I picked up the *D. Telegraph* & said, "I must just note the graph". For some reason N. thought that very funny so it was used for ever – as, for example, "I long to note your graph" meant "I long to see you".' (Jessica in a letter to the editor)

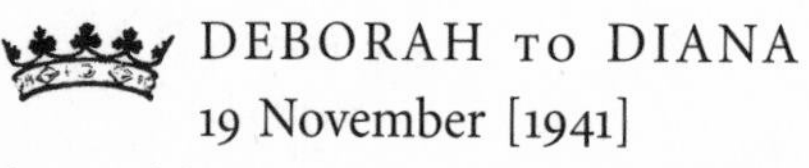

DEBORAH TO DIANA
19 November [1941]
[passed by prison censor 20/11/41]

Carnarvon Nursing Home Ltd.
The Glebe, Hadley Common
Barnet, Herts.

Darling Honks

It was heaven of you to write your precious letter and all. You can't think how much better I feel now, really quite alright.[1] The comfort of this place is unbelievable and blissful nurses. It is so odd I'd never even had a bedpan before. Oh Honks, never Gilliat again, I have completely lost confidence in him. He never turned up till ages after he was wanted and when I was lying there with everything over he came in and all the nurses said '*Here's* a friend to see you' and if I'd had the strength I really would have kicked him or at least asked him where he had been all the afternoon.[2] What was rather awful was that I'd had a temperature of 103 for four days beforehand so I really wasn't feeling like an effort. However all one can say is that it can't have been one quarter so bad for me as it was for Decca because I never knew the baby though it was so alive when it was born that I felt a sort of glimmer of hope though I knew it wasn't any good. Muv was quite wonderful and Andrew stayed with me till it was nearly born, it was so wonderful to have him. He finishes his leave tomorrow which is terribly sad because he has been here such a lot this week. My duch[3] and everyone have been absolutely wonderful.

Lady Carnarvon[4] embraced Muv wasn't it wonderful.

Poor Nancy sounds rather bad with her appendix and ovary.[5] I wish she could come here. I think when you first get out of prison you ought to come here for ages, the difference would be so wonderful.

(Everything seems to be wonderful in this letter though it isn't really.)

Anyhow it was heaven of you to write, I do so long to see you, it is such a tease.

I'm afraid they won't let me get up for two more weeks which will seem rather long but perhaps be the best in the end.

Much love from Debo

1 Six days earlier Deborah had given birth to a premature son who died almost immediately.
2 The obstetrician not only arrived too late to assist at the birth but upset Deborah by saying, 'You didn't expect it to live, did you?'
3 Deborah's mother-in-law.
4 Almina Wombell (*c.*1877–1969). Wife of the 5th Earl of Carnarvon who led the expedition to open King Tutankhamun's tomb. Lady Carnarvon took a close interest in medical matters and in the patients admitted to her nursing home.
5 Nancy had suffered an ectopic pregnancy after a brief affair with a Free French officer, Roy Desplats-Pilter (1904–45).

NANCY TO DIANA
22 November 1941
[passed by prison censor 28/11/41]

University College Hospital
London WC

Darling Diana

Thank you so much for the wonderful grapes, you are really an angel & grapes are so good for me. I have had a horrible time, so depressing because they had to take out both my tubes & therefore I can never now have a child. I can't say I suffered great agony but quite enough discomfort – but darling when I think of you & the 18 stitches in your face[1] it is absolutely nothing.

The Rodds have been wonderfully true to form – my mother in law was told by the surgeon I shld be in danger for 3 days, & not one of them even rang up to enquire let alone sending a bloom or anything. I long to know if they bothered to look under R in the deaths column, very much doubt it however.

I never hear from Peter or he from me it is too depressing like the grave. Also he never gets his pay.

Muv was wonderful, she swam in a haze of bewilderment between me & Debo. When my symptoms were explained to her she said 'ovaries – I thought one had 700 like caviar'. Then I said how I couldn't bear the idea of a great scar on my tum to which she replied 'But darling who's ever going to see it?'

Poor Debo it must be wretched, the worst thing in the world I should think – except losing a manuscript of a book which I always think must be *the* worst.

Have you read *Mémoires d'outre tombe*[2] it is so wonderful. I've had a heavenly time reading my books in peace, such a change from rushing off to the office at 8.30.

I've left my address book at home so must send this to Muv.

Nigel [Birch] has just been to see me rather optimistic in mood which is entirely new for him, I nearly fell out of bed.

I spent the week end before I got ill (in considerable pain most of the time) with Roy & Billa [Harrod]. They have an ideal child called Hen[ry] – I think the prettiest, most amusing little boy I ever saw.

Oxford society is very pleasant I think, everybody so amiable & nice, most unlike what one would imagine such a small highly cultivated world to be. Gerald [Berners] has taken up his residence there. Apparently he has a mania for tea-shop life & Billa says it is a kind of task, undertaken in turns, to face Gerald across rather grubby check tablecloths at mealtimes.

Much love darling
& many more thanks for the grapes, Nancy

1 After Diana's motor accident in 1935.
2 François René de Chateaubriand's autobiography (1849–50).

UNITY TO DIANA
20 November 1941
[passed by prison censor 23/11/41]

[The Mill Cottage]
Swinbrook

Darling Nard

Well, Nard About the 1st December. I could come then, again. May I come? *Do* say yes, do. Because, Nard, I do love visiting you, I do, really. And, you know now I am well again, I can't bear life. I mean, this war!

You see, when I first came back, I thought all this was a play, and I was looking on. Now, I know I have a part to play, & I can't bear acting it!

Next week am going to stay with Woman, which will be fun, I shall see Max! Oh, Nard, I love, adore Max!

V Best Love, Nard, from Bobo

DEBORAH TO DIANA
11 December 1941
[passed by prison censor 13/12/41]

Churchdale Hall[1]
Bakewell
Derbyshire

Darling Honks

I thought I would just write and say how completely better I am although you couldn't possibly be interested. I came up here in the most glorious luxury with a nurse and I was wheeled in a chair across St Pancras to the train! I am still in bed but getting up tomorrow, I can't face getting up today as I should be alone with that awful old Eddie M[arsh].

I was terrified that Gilliat would say I wasn't to start another pig for two years but thank goodness he said six months rather grudgingly and even that depending on my kidney. I write long letters to Muv about my medicines and things but I'm sure she says 'Orrhhn' and doesn't read them.

I do hope what I saw about Sir O in the paper is true, I was so excited for you, it will make a difference.[2]

It is so absolutely dreadful about Esmond isn't it,[3] I don't know what to say to poor Squalor, I don't even know how to begin the letter because I can't start Dearest Cheerless like I usually do. Thank goodness she has got her pig anyhow. It is so much worse for her because of her being so queer one feels she would mind even more than most people.

I do die to see you again. I'm home till the beginning of January when we move into a new house at Stanmore. At least that's what we mean to do but it all depends on getting a maid which seems literally impossible.

Andrew can't get away for Xmas which is sad but he is coming up for one day next week. He *was* so wonderful when I was actually having the baby and stayed with me till the last moment.

Much love, Debo

1 Deborah was staying with her parents-in-law.
2 After a separation of eighteen months, and on the instructions of Winston Churchill, Diana was joined by her husband in Holloway where they remained imprisoned together for a further two years.
3 Jessica's husband had been reported missing on 30 November.

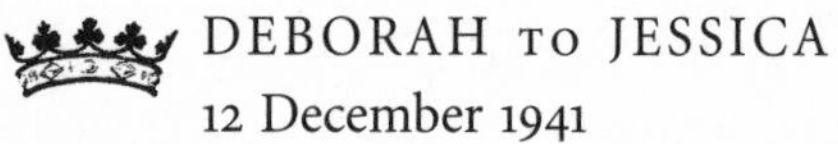

DEBORAH TO JESSICA
12 December 1941

Churchdale Hall
Bakewell

Dearest Hen

I am so appalled by the news I heard from Muv that I simply don't know what to say or even how to begin. It must be so absolutely dreadful for you waiting for news. I have sometimes tried to imagine what it would be like if anything happened to Andrew and I can almost guess what you must be going through. I am so hopeless at writing, but I have been thinking the whole time of you, and I do so long to see you, it seems such ages that I've almost forgotten what you look like and I do long to see Constancia.

This is a hopeless letter but I can't make it any better because of being so hopeless at explaining what I mean.

Much love, Hen

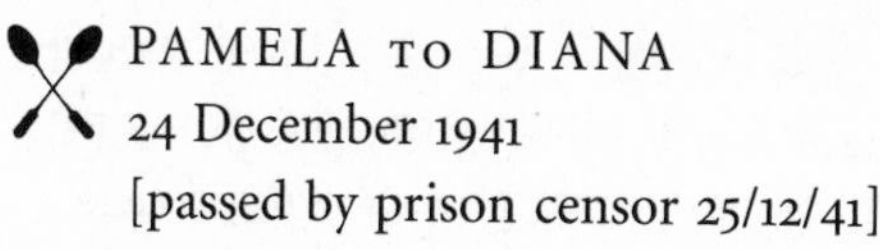

PAMELA TO DIANA
24 December 1941
[passed by prison censor 25/12/41]

Rignell House
Deddington

Darling Nardy

Oh! How much I wish you could be with us here for Christmas. These two hankies are instead of a Christmas card – the boys each wanted to buy one for Bobo & actually four went to the coupon so I had these for you. I believe you actually have Kit with you now, how marvellous that it has happened in time for Christmas; it will at least make all the difference to you both. I am in a terrible haze because we will be a huge party with almost nothing to eat, at least that is how it seems now. I suppose it will be OK in the end. We will be eight in the dining room, Muv, Tom, Bobo, Captain & Mrs Fox, the boys & myself. The usual four in the nursery & three in the kitchen. I hope the one turkey will go round & leave something for Friday!!! Poor Derek had to go back yesterday. I can't even go down & have Christmas lunch with him tomorrow because he will be 'on' today & tomorrow.

There is no more news but I will write again soon.

Much love & best wishes from Pam to you & Kit

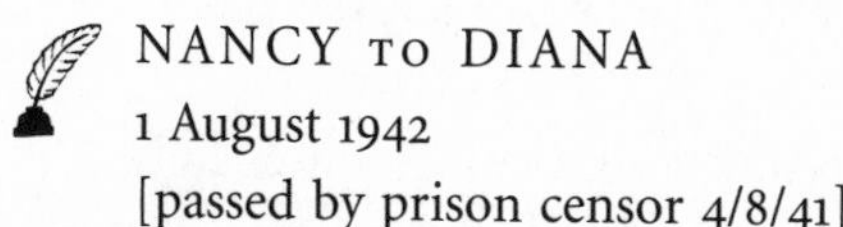

NANCY TO DIANA
1 August 1942
[passed by prison censor 4/8/41]

[The Mill Cottage]
Swinbrook

Darling Diana

I've just seen your charming babies. I think Max is a peach. Alexander didn't like me much I think. I was very disappointed but I suppose it would be all right if he got used to one. Max has terrific poise hasn't he. It was heaven to see Nanny.

Henry Yorke would love to visit you. He said I was to ask, & not tell him if you would rather not. It would have to be this month as he is on leave from his fire fighting.

Bobo is being very reasonable. She was too naughty when she was with me. I took her out to luncheon in a place where by bad luck I happened to know two other people lunching & she put on a completely mad act, announcing to the room at large 'I'm going to have my *feet* off, Nancy' & really being *too* naughty. She did much the same with poor Gladys who nearly died of it! Here however she is much more normal, though inclined to be rather bad tempered.

Goodness the prettiness of the country after months of London also it is bliss to be out of that pitch-dark shop,[1] much as I like the work.

Much love from NR

1 Nancy had begun working at Heywood Hill's Curzon Street bookshop in March 1942.

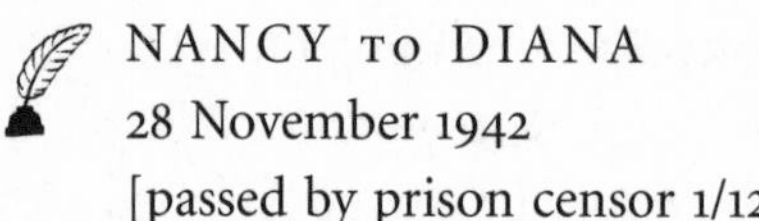

NANCY TO DIANA *12 Blomfield Road, w9*
28 November 1942
[passed by prison censor 1/12/42]

Darling Diana

How *could* you be so wonderful it brings tears to the eyes. You can't imagine the horror of the stocking situation in a book shop where one is forever on one's knees & I spend my weekends darning. Anne Hill[1] wears black & white check wool ones but I somehow can't –

Bobo enjoyed my party. She brought a ghastly old dress full of moth holes so I crammed her into my only good black one which we left undone all the way down the back & she kept on a coat so all was well but it was rather an awful moment when I saw what she did propose to wear. Then she refused to make up her face but the adored Capitaine Roy[2] took her upstairs & did it for her. So in the end she looked awfully pretty.

Cecil [Beaton] came into the shop 'such an oasis' & roared with laughter for an hour. The shop is really very gay now, full of people all day, & I am installed *in* the gas fire so manage to keep fairly warm.

Fancy favourite aunt how blissful. I can't think why as I am completely tongue tied by children, even yours, & at a loss how to behave. I long for a niece, can't you provide one.

It would be fun to see you with Dig & Henry [Yorke] as I hear you suggest though *slight* waste not to see you alone.

Goodness I feel old, going grey & bald & look terrible. I've been doing far too much & need a week in bed.

Much love, NR

1 Lady Anne Gathorne-Hardy (1911–2006). Married Heywood Hill in 1938 and worked in the bookshop with Nancy.
2 André Roy was the *nom de guerre* of Nancy's lover Roy Desplats-Pilter.

DEBORAH TO DIANA
11 September 1943
[passed by prison censor 14/9/43]

The Rookery
Ashford, Bakewell
Derbyshire

Darling Honks

Your blissful Blor and Pig life arrived safely yesterday, it is *utter* bliss having them you can't imagine how wonderful all the Blors are together, they talk about rations and girls and the weather and they are too wonderful about 'helping' as we've only got one servant in this vast house so it's altogether glorious but if *only* you were here it would just be more glorious.

Max and Alexander are so terribly funny. The first thing they said was, 'What is *your* neem?' which was a wonderful start. They both told me not to talk at table. Max is in a permanent furious rage.

We eat all our meals in the kitchen, it's so much easier and the food is hot, I hope they don't mind. Max keeps saying, 'This is a very odd nursery', which of course it is.

Much love and to Sir O, Debo

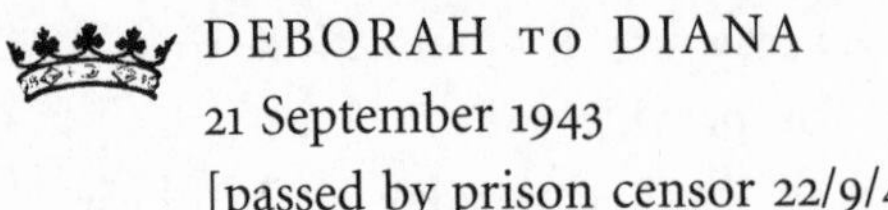

DEBOROAH TO DIANA

21 September 1943

[passed by prison censor 22/9/43]

The Rookery
Ashford

Darling Honks

Thank you so much for your letter. I am so *adoring* the children, they are a roaring success wherever they go and no wonder. I hope they aren't finding it too dull though.

Billy[1] has been on leave and came down to entertain them. They asked him to draw things for them like lions running which he found very difficult. They both drew very complicated systems of pipes with a so-called tap at the end. They are obviously going to be sanitary engineers. They went to tea at Churchdale yesterday and Max told the duke not to smoke at table. I wasn't there as Andrew and I went to Belvoir for the weekend. I think they enjoyed it, my duch *adored* them and they didn't get back till ¼ past 7. We went for a picnic to Chatsworth[2] in the pony cart which was great fun. We went into the strong room to see the gold plate but the children were only interested in the bars across the window.

All the nannies are so wonderful together and help each other to tea like mad. It's so good for Em,[3] my nanny says, to have other children, can you imagine at her age!! They are awfully good and it really is utter heaven having them, I shall never have more glorious guests.

If only you were here it would be perfect.

Best love to Sir O.

All love, Debo

1 William (Billy), Marquess of Hartington (1917–44). Andrew Devonshire's older brother and heir to the dukedom was a major in the Coldstream Guards. Married Kathleen Kennedy in May 1944.

2 During the war Chatsworth, the Devonshire family seat, was occupied by Penrhos College, a school for girls.

3 Lady Emma Cavendish (1943–). Deborah's six-month-old daughter.

VISITING ORDER
(VALID FOR 28 DAYS ONLY)

H.M. Prison Holloway.

13-11-1943.

Reg. No. 5433 Name Lady Mosley

has permission to be visited by Lady Redesdale,

Swinbrook, Oxford.

1 The visit to last only 30 minutes 15 mins Sat. 10.30 am to 11.30 am.
2 Visitors admitted only between the hours of 1-30 p.m. and 3-30 p.m.
3 No visit allowed on Sundays, Christmas Day, or Good Friday
4 Such of the above-named friends as wish to visit, must all attend at the same time, and produce this order

for GOVERNOR

Lady Redesdale's permit to visit Diana in Holloway.

DEBORAH TO JESSICA
30 September 1943

The Rookery
Ashford

Dearest Hen

It *is* so wonderful about you getting married, do write and tell if Mr Treuhaft[1] is a Hon, I'm sure he must be a tremendous one, I do die to see him or even a photograph, do try & send *something*, we all so die to see. Have you fully instructed him about Honnish embraces, Andrew has become quite good and will show everyone all the time.

Oh dear I do long to see you measuring trees, do write & tell. And as for investigating I wish you'd come and investigate about the huge rent here.[2]

We've moved in here for the war, at least I say we but it's me & Em really as Andrew hasn't been able to get away to see it although we've been in for 4 weeks. I hope he'll get a short weekend soon but they work so hard I doubt even that. He is on the Yorkshire moors now, bitter cold poor soul. Otherwise everything goes on as usual, London is rather drear though, no one much there and everything v. expensive. We have tremendous pony cart life here as there is no petrol.

Kick Kennedy is in London, it is lovely to have her back, did you like her, I do awfully.

I long to see Constancia, she must be so fascinating, that photograph of you & her was heaven. Do send some more. The difficulty here is one can't get films, perhaps it's difficult with you too?

Well dear if anything of note or interest occurs I'll write again. Be an old Hen & write to yr Hen.

Will you stay in San Francisco now or will you go lumbering off to Seattle? Do you remember how poor Bird always longed to go there.

Farve's operation was a miracle almost, it was too dreadful to see him quite blind.

Well dear cheery cheer, Henderson

1 Robert Treuhaft (1912–2001). New York-born lawyer who met Jessica when they were both working for the Office of Price Administration. They were married on 8 June 1943.
2 Jessica's work at the OPA involved checking that regulations on building materials, including lumber, were being met.

DIANA to NANCY
28 November 1943

Rignell House
Deddington

Darling Nancy

Many happy returns darling. The present was mingy beyond belief, I rather wish it had got lost in the post.

Woman is being simply too killing, we are besieged by hordes of pressmen & photographers[1] & every now and then she rushes out and says, 'I dislike you intensely' or when photo-ed, 'You foul man'. She doesn't in the least realize what a wonder-working woman she is being. We ourselves just stay in the house with the curtains drawn and I would rather be us than *them* because it is the most frightful weather. I hope you all go to the demonstration in Trafalgar Sq this afternoon, I wish I could go.

It is such paradise just not to be in gaol that it is indescribable. Did you see Bernard Shaw in *D. Express.*[2]

Could you keep the Wieland[3] just till I know where we are going or is it a great trial to you – being so many vols I rather dread it in our luggage.

Desmond tells me that one master at Summer Fields says I ought to be shot. 'Yes' said Jonathan, 'he is an old *menace*'.

I do LONG for a chat with you but of course I shall never be able to come to London.

Best love, D

1 Mosley's poor health had led to his and Diana's release from prison. They were placed under house arrest and prohibited from going to London or having any contact with politics. After a few days with Pamela they moved to the Shaven Crown inn at Shipton and later bought Crux Easton, near Newbury.
2 In an interview in which he supported the Mosleys' release, Bernard Shaw wrote, 'We are still afraid to let Mosley defend himself. And we have produced the ridiculous situation in which we may buy Hitler's *Mein Kampf* in any bookshop in Britain, but we may not buy ten lines written by Mosley.' *Daily Express*, 26 November 1943.
3 Diana had ordered works by Christoph Martin Wieland, the eighteenth-century German poet and translator of Shakespeare.

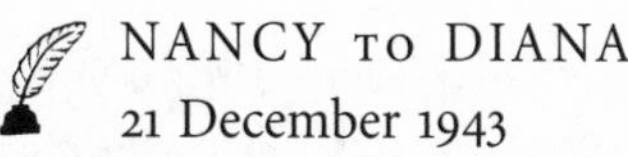

NANCY TO DIANA
21 December 1943

G. Heywood Hill[1] *Ltd*
17 Curzon Street
London W1

Darling,

A girl I know was in Trafalgar Sq that day trying to get to the tube. In order to do so she was obliged to join a queue & shout in unison '*Put Him Back*'. If you didn't shout you were flung out of the queue & no chance of getting to the Underground! Then she had to stop twice & sign things – also in order to keep her place. After which she was very late for tea. You must say.

Just had a wonderful weekend at Faringdon. I hear Gerald [Berners] is going to stay with you.

Best love, NR

1 (George) Heywood Hill (1907–86). Bookseller who opened his Mayfair shop in 1936, where Nancy worked 1942–5.

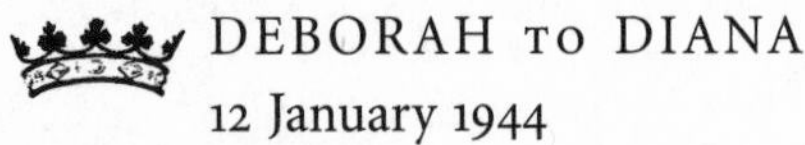

DEBORAH TO DIANA

12 January 1944

Compton Place
Eastbourne

Darling Honks

I *do* think it's so wonderful about Nicky getting the MC,[1] Sir O must be nearly dying of excitement.

I do disgusting work now, do feel sorry for me. It's in the YMCA canteen and it's v. embarrassing because they all copy my voice.

No more news of Andrew – I *do* hope he comes soon.

All love & millions of congratulations on Nicky's wonderfulness. Debo

1 Diana's stepson, Nicholas Mosley, who was serving in Italy with the Rifle Brigade, had been awarded the Military Cross for capturing a strategic farmhouse held by the Germans.

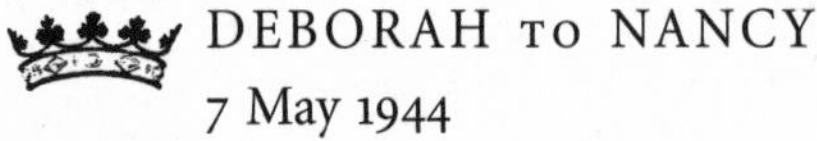

DEBORAH TO NANCY

7 May 1944

Churchdale Hall
Bakewell

Get on

I don't appreciate the SHORT NOTES I have received from you, my frail fingers are well able to open a VERY LONG letter so kindly write one.

Well Mornington[1] is too comic for words, he is fast going bald but the nurse still tries to make a parting and the result is he looks exactly like his grandpapa Devonshire. I went dry after two days. I *meant* to feed him but I'm quite pleased now as I shan't be tied. Muv looked v. disapproving when we decided to give up the unequal struggle. It was too wonderful having her here.

Oh the fury on all sides about the baby's names. The dowager duch has been heard to say she wouldn't be surprised if the Duke of Wellington sued us for using his name. But surely if Mrs Cannon

William (Billy) Hartington, Deborah's brother-in-law, and Kathleen (Kick) Kennedy were married on 6 May 1944, despite opposition from both sets of parents.

could call her son Morny why shouldn't I.[2] Anyhow they are Andrew's choice so all the critics can go to hell. I am calling him Morny but I expect Andrew will call him Peregrine. I haven't heard from him that he's heard but hope to this week.

Isn't it a do about Billy getting off, I am so pleased & so is Andrew and I can't get over the wonderful luck of having Kick for a sister-in-law as she is far the nicest girl ever. Poor things they must be thankful to have actually got spliced after all these years.[3]

It is boiling out today. I can see it is but I suppose I shall have to stay in bed a bit longer.

Tig & Elizabeth[4] are coming up tomorrow, I shall hear all about Rodd no doubt. Elizabeth said he was *fascinating* but *terrifying* and Tig said he was fascinating about Abyssinia, we all know what that means, toll-gating[5] with a vengeance. They obviously thought he was heaven. I do die to see you, perhaps I shall come down before long for the dentist and to have a *change.*

I have got to page 652 in *C*[6] & there are only 741, what shall I do

when it's finished, I really never will read any more beastly books they are only an extra complication to one's pathetic life.
WRITE.

Love from Dahlia

1 Deborah's son, born on 27 April, was christened Peregrine Andrew Morny but was soon known as 'Stoker' or 'Sto'.
2 Mrs Cannon was mother of a famous jockey, Mornington Cannon. The courtesy title of the Duke of Wellington's eldest grandson is the Earl of Mornington.
3 Kathleen Kennedy had fallen in love with Billy Hartington when her father was posted as ambassador to London. Both sets of parents refused to allow them to marry because the Devonshires were firm Protestants and the Kennedys entrenched Catholics. Kathleen was sent back to the US but returned in 1943, determined to get her way.
4 Deborah's sisters-in-law, Anne and Elizabeth Cavendish.
5 Peter Rodd was notorious among the sisters for his lengthy monologues on the tollgate system of England and Wales.
6 Maurice Baring, *C* (1924). A popular saga of Edwardian society.

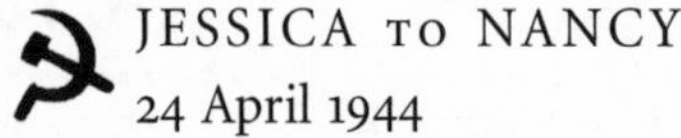

JESSICA TO NANCY
24 April 1944

1350 Haight St
San Francisco
California

Darling Susan,

Thanks so much for your letter. I do keep meaning to write but as you say it becomes increasingly impossible to note other people's graphs from this distance. I write to the P[arent Bird] quite often as she seems to like to get letters though Lord knows why, I can never think of anything to say.

I am sending a picture of Constancia taken by Bob, also a family group of me & Bob & Constancia.

As you can see, Constancia is our pride & joy, she really is the prettiest child ever seen & has a frightfully nice character, there's not a trace of Mitford in her.

I left the OPA job & am working at the Joint Antifascist Refugee Committee, v. interesting & pleasant. I am now an American citizen, which is nice.

Are you planning to come to America after the war? Otherwise

I shall probably never see you. Do come Susan, I long to note you not getting on with Americans.

Love from Susan

JESSICA TO DEBORAH
22 May 1944

1350 Haight St
San Francisco

Dearest Hen

We seem to be running neck & neck – I just had a baby boy too. His name is Nicholas Tito,[1] & he weighs 9 lbs 1½ oz (or did at birth. He is now 6 days old). Bob sent Muv a telegram but she may have found it rather confusing as he just said 'Nicholas Tito born today'. She probably thought it was a dog or something. He is simply beautiful with slanting eyes like Bob, & a terrific eater. Unfortunately I can't nurse him because he needs 5 oz per feeding. Are you going to stop smacking your ovary & sending it to Madame Bovary after this? Or can't you on account of the Cavendishes being religious?

I'm still in the hospital so the Donk hasn't seen Nicholas T. yet, but she telephones me every day & is awfully excited about him. Is Emma excited or is she too young to note? I had a wonderfully easy time. They have a thing called caudal anaesthesia; they stick a needle into your spinal cord which numbs from the waist down, & you are completely conscious all the time but feel no pain. I saw him come out all red & slimy & bloody, it was so exciting. It only took minutes. I didn't even have to have stitches. Bob was there all the time except the last 7 minutes in the delivery room. I'm sure the Fem would disapprove terrifically of *Orrhhn* sticking a nasty needle into the Good Body, but it was wonderful. She sends me a fascist mag. called *Truth* in which there are weekly letters by Uncle Geoffrey[2] on 'murdering milk' by pasteurizing it, they make Bob simply roar.

Well old Hen it's time I blew my Honnish whistle for the bed pan. Give my love to the Fem & Blor, I'll write to them soon.

Love from Your Hen

1 Jessica wrote to Nancy that she had named her son 'after Lenin & Marshal Tito' to annoy her parents.
2 Geoffrey Bowles (1879–1968). Lady Redesdale's eccentric and reclusive older brother was an early advocate of the health-food movement and spent much of his time writing letters to newspapers inveighing against 'murdered food'.

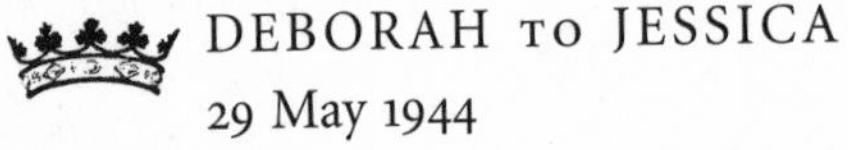

DEBOROAH TO JESSICA
29 May 1944

Compton Place
Eastbourne

Dearest Hen

It is *too* wonderful about you pigging again, isn't it quaint that yours and mine should have been born within two weeks of each other. I do hope they will have a Honnish meeting one of these days, and goodness I do long to see Donk and for you to see Em who is becoming heaven and walks about like mad, but she doesn't talk yet. She is enormously fat. Her face is exactly like the photographs of you and Nancy at that age only her hair is as straight as any poker. We are calling the baby Peregrine as that is what Andrew chose, and Morny after a jockey. I don't know which we are going to actually call him, I am waiting for Andrew to say. He is still in Italy, poor him. He's been away nearly seven months, it seems endless.

When I go home next month I am going to have the babies photographed and I'll send you one. I do so long to see a picture of your Honnish Husband, do send one. Donk looks such a fascinator in the last ones you sent Muv.

We are all going to the Island in August.

It is bliss here. The air activity is extraordinary, one can lie in the garden and count anything up to 900 aeroplanes going to France and this house rattles and shakes most of the night with explosions from across the channel.

There is no actual news. I live in a house called The Rookery in Derbyshire and I am here on hol.

Do write and tell all about the baby, I do so long to hear. Were you very pleased it was a boy.

Mine only took an hour & a half to be born, wasn't I terrifically lucky.

Andrew, Deborah, Emma and Peregrine, 1944.

Mabel[1] came up to cook for us while I was in bed and talked of nothing but you like she always does.

Do write.

Much love, Henderson.

1 Mabel Woolvern; the Redesdales' parlourmaid.

NANCY TO JESSICA
26 May 1944

G. Heywood Hill Ltd
17 Curzon Street, W1

Darling Soo

So very glad to note yr graph at last & also to hear from Muv that you have another baby. I am *so* pleased. My heiress[1] is wonderful & I die to see her but Susan *no* I couldn't go to America, even for you. The cruelty of the A[merican]s to me here in this tiny bookshop (which they call a *store*, as tho it were Selfridges) is something too inhuman – & then they are such fascists Soo. Not in your set, perhaps – or do they put it on to tease? I asked one of them why they were so unkind & he said 'Well of course they see you in a bookshop & probably don't know who you are' – but that doesn't seem quite right to me? Susan do explain.

Well Prod has reappeared – he walked into the *store* one day when I thought he was in Italy & I felt quite faint. Three years he was away. So you can imagine there was some wonderful toll-gating. He is toll-gating round the place now to the army & completely blissful the dear old fellow & a *Colonel* Susan. 'Is the Colonel in to dinner?' You must say it's funny.

I'm going to send you Peter Rabbit books as they take up no room. Don't forget I've got masses of furniture of yours – should you want some money any time we could sell it for you. Meanwhile I am using it – I mean it's not put away somewhere damp to moulder.

I heard about Constancia packing her bag.[2] I did so roar – do you remember saving up for a bed-sitter?

Susan isn't work dreadful. Oh the happy old days when one could lie & look at the ceiling till luncheon time. I feel I shall never be right again until I've had trois mois de chaise longue[3] – & *when* will that be? Susan I can see you shrieking so will now be off. Please give my love to Bob & Constancia. I note their graphs far more now I've seen their photag's. Send me more sometime.

Susan I do simply so *long* for you sometimes, you can't think.

NR

1 In 1941, Nancy had written to Jessica to say that in her will she had left Constancia a diamond brooch and £20 in war savings.

2 Jessica had written to Lady Redesdale that she thought Constancia had 'running-away blood' in her as she would threaten to run away whenever scolded.

3 'Three months on a chaise longue.'

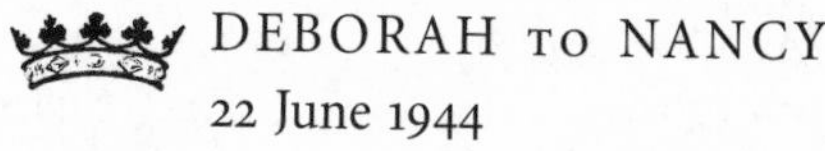

DEBOROAH TO NANCY

22 June 1944

Churchdale Hall
Bakewell

Get on

I *adored* the picture of the Rookery & so did Mornington Rose though he couldn't see it very well on account of he can't see very well.

I am utterly trusting in you coming to stay. Are the bombs frightening? Do write descriptions. Are they as bad as the raids used to be? They have seen a lot at Eastbourne but I gather they haven't been aimed at them so it's not so frightening.

Do you listen to a German programme called *D Day Calling*. It happens at 7.30 A.M. & 7.30 P.M. and there is a heavenly tune called 'Invasion', it's the signature tune & it's bliss.

Andrew was in Rome the day after it fell, no one kissed him, he *was* in a bait. Someone threw a dead rose into his jeep and three very small children shook him by the hand.

Goodness, Diddy[1] has had a day out and I have been struggling with Mornington and Em, struggle is the word.

Think of the horror of my future, I've got *four* fêtes to open, the first one is this Saturday and in my speech I've got to thank a lady called Mrs Pottinger, you must say that is asking too much. I am dying at the thought.

I had a v. successful Oaks,[2] lucky me. The cheque hasn't come yet, I'm getting in a do as I owe masses to two gentlemen who backed the horse on my account.

Well, the point of writing is to make sure you're coming on the 12th, you absolutely must for the sake of morale at The Rookery.

I can't get over about Tud coming home it *is* so exciting.

Love from Debo

What can I read? I sit here with a vacant stare and no book.

1 Ellen Stephens; nanny to Deborah's children 1943–63.
2 Deborah had backed a winner in the Classic race for three-year-old fillies held on Epsom Downs.

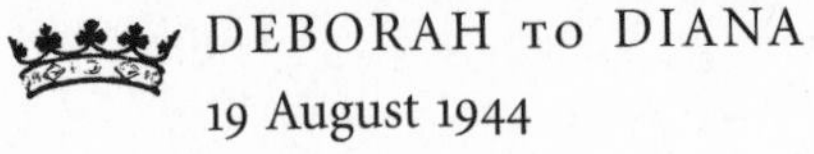

DEBORAH TO DIANA

Inch Kenneth
Gribun, Oban

19 August 1944

Darling Honks

Oh Honks, I *DO* so wish you were here, I am utterly at a loss to know what to do or say but one thing is certain and that is that the awful girl[1] *must* go. It's like nothing you can imagine. The house doesn't seem to be Muv's at all, she is treated like a guest. Nobody speaks at meals, except when I do to Muv or Farve, and everything is as difficult as you can possibly imagine. Farve looks very ill I think, he is terribly thin and everything worries him, even the smallest little things about the boats & the house etc. He never sits with us in the drawing room but helps Margaret in the kitchen.

I haven't had a chance to chat to him at all yet and if & when I do I'll write you what he says but it seems to me that underneath he must know he's in the wrong & that Muv and all of us are more important than her but all the same he is so dreadfully difficult and cross and quite unapproachable.

It was evidently owing to the idea that there would be too much for her to do that the babies were put off from coming because I think he would have liked to have them. Of course it's perfect nonsense as she only has to cook and do nothing else as Muv does the housework and it seems to me that Farve is a sort of scullery maid. Then of course there is the news which Farve has at 7, 8, 10, 1, 3, 6 & 9 & midnight and Muv won't listen to it, so Farve & Margaret listen together and she makes maddening comments.

Oh Honks you don't know what it's like, the wonderful country and the enormous sense of peace make it all the more agonizing. Tud's advice was for Muv to simply stay here and make it so unpleasant for M that she will have to leave but I really believe she has got some reason for staying as it can't be any more comfortable for her than for the rest of us except that Farve is on her side.

The calling up thing isn't very hopeful as she has got a doctor's thing to say she is ill, whether she is or not I can't say. Tud evidently had it out with Farve but he'll have to do more as it really can't go on like this much longer, Muv is so miserably unhappy. Uncle George is coming soon I hope, he is the very best person because although he is such a great friend of Farve's he is really on Muv's side. Bird makes everything even more complicated as Farve is very touchy with her and she's not much help to Muv. Please don't let on that I've written you all this, but if you see Tud do impress on him how very unhappy Muv is, though he must have seen for himself.

She is so furious about the babies not coming but can't say anything as Farve flies into a temper so easily. I wish I could stay here longer because I think an extra person is a good thing but I've got to be home by the first September at the latest.

I am pinning great hopes on Uncle G and can't wait for him to come. Oh Honks the misery of it.

Much love, Debo

1 Margaret Wright had originally gone to work for the Redesdales as parlourmaid, but as relations between the Redesdales deteriorated, she had gradually taken over Lady Redesdale's role. The sisters disliked her – she was tactless, bossy and gave herself airs – but their father found her an ideal companion and lived with her until he died.

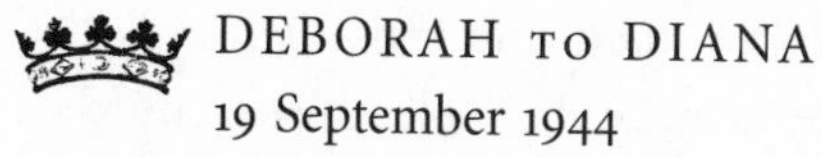

DEBORAH TO DIANA
19 September 1944

Compton Place
Eastbourne

Darling Honks

I can't tell you how wonderful they are being here.[1] I am the only one who is hopeless, I really can't bear to see them, they are pillars of strength to everyone else and last night you would hardly have known that anything was wrong but they have got such strained faces. The girls are wonderful, I am put to shame when I see them! My duch's relations are all coming in relays, it will make a great difference. I think though nothing can really make any difference.

Oh Honks there is nothing but misery. What will poor Andrew do, I am terrified that he will go right under for a time. The only consolation is that all soldiers, and everybody who has been fighting in their lives, say that it is different when you are fighting yourself. They don't hold out any hopes of getting him home till the war is over. The Duke was trying to get Charlie Lansdowne[2] home so he has been into it all and says that it is not possible. Perhaps something will turn up all the same, I do pray it will, it would make the whole difference to them to have him here.

You were so wonderful and so was Sir O, I wouldn't have heard the news anywhere else but I'm afraid it was beastly for you. I did so *love* my weekend. Thank you *SO* so much and please thank Sir O for being such a Hon.

Much love, Debo

1 Deborah was staying with her parents-in-law after their eldest son, Billy, had been killed by a sniper's bullet while serving with his regiment in Belgium. His death made Andrew heir to the dukedom and the Devonshires' vast estates.
2 7th Marquess of Lansdowne (1917–44). Served in the Royal Wiltshire Yeomanry and was killed in a tank explosion in Italy on 20 August.

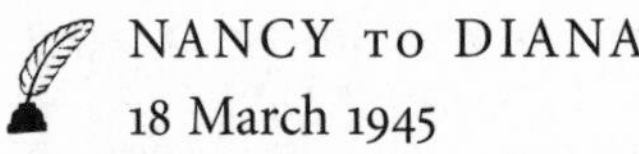

NANCY TO DIANA
18 March 1945

The Rookery
Ashford

Darling Diana

Oh the Royal Family – just one cloud of myosotis. I'm sure they ought to try & be more glamorous but then, with those figures & those faces, how? Never would they acquire the Doll Waist so much advocated by the couturiers unless by such tight lacing as to make them scarlet in the face & utterly breathless.

Heaven here. Debo & I so roared at the baby chicks smothered in scarves. I can't wait to see you, only it is v difficult to work with sisters about, one so longs to chat all day. The book[1] must be a success as I'm living on my savings & they must be replenished!

You can't imagine the *heaven* of hols after a three year solid grind in that shop.

Much love, NR

1 Nancy was writing *The Pursuit of Love*, which was published in December 1945.

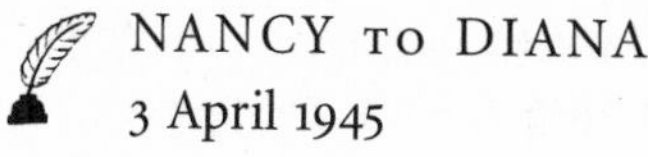

NANCY TO DIANA
3 April 1945

Faringdon House
Berkshire

Darling

Gerald [Berners] & I, who seem to be doing a sort of honeymoon tour (we go to Violet Trefusis[1] from here), would like to come if all right on the 20th. I absolutely die for it. Oh don't rub salt into my wounds I *can't* bike – if you knew what a misery this has been the whole war, struggling in bus queues etc you would never mention it. Perhaps you will teach me (it's getting on & specially off I can't do, I think I could wobble along all right).

Debo's Emma is a dream, too good to be true & oh dear how nice Debo is, she really is *heaven.* The boy gives me the creeps but you know how I feel about babies! I suppose a thin man is wildly signalling to get out just like in Cyril's[2] book. I *long* for your boys, it is exciting.

Much love, NR

P.S. Just heard about Tom how too horribly worrying oh poor Farve.[3]

1 Violet Keppel (1894–1972). Novelist best known for her elopement with Vita Sackville-West. Married Denys Trefusis in 1919.

2 Cyril Connolly (1903–74). In *The Unquiet Grave* (1945) the corpulent literary critic noted ruefully, 'Imprisoned in every fat man a thin man is wildly signalling to be let out.'

3 Lord Redesdale had received a telegram advising that Tom, who was fighting in Burma, was badly wounded. He had in fact died on 30 March, six days after being shot in the neck and chest. He was buried in the military cemetery at Rangoon.

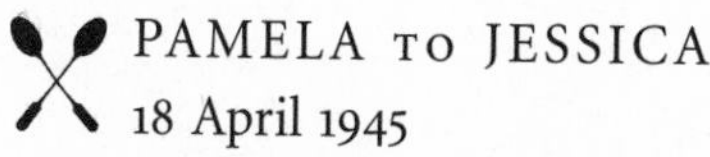

PAMELA TO JESSICA
18 April 1945

Rignell House
Deddington

My darling Decca

We have all been thinking so much of you just lately & wished you had been with us all. It has been such a ghastly blow about Tom. Poor Muv was on the Island when she received the news and at first it was too rough for her to get over to the mainland. It must have nearly driven her mad.

Nardy came to London just for a few hours & came to the Mews to see Farve. She had not seen him for about six years. Darling Nanny was there too, she had come up from Egham. Peter [Rodd] and Andrew also came to see Muv & Farve. Derek is in America so was unable to be there. I am not quite sure how much longer he will be away but hope he will be back in about three weeks time.

With very much love from Woman

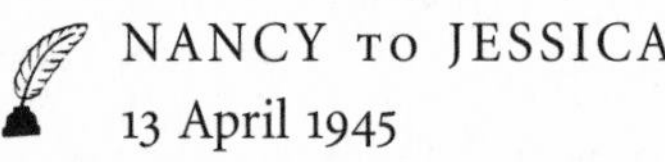

NANCY TO JESSICA *12 Blomfield Road, w9*
13 April 1945

Darling Sooze

I thought you would like a line to say Muv & Farve are being simply wonderful & much much better than we had feared at first. But it is almost unbearable oh *Tud* if you knew how sweet & nice & gay he has been of late & on his last leave. That is a comfort, it shows he was happy & I know he enjoyed the journey out very much. But I shall miss him dreadfully, I'd seen a lot of him during the war.

Old Rodd often thinks of you. The other day his mother said to him if I leave you some money who will you leave it to & he said Decca's children so now of course she won't as she wants it for her own grandchildren! But I was so surprised & really touched & thought you would be. Dear old thing, I'm thankful to say he's in England for the moment.

I'm writing a book about us when we were little, it's not a farce this time but serious – a novel, don't be nervous!

More photographs please. Oh Susan I shall never see you again & I would so like to.

Much love from Sooze

JESSICA TO NANCY
[April 1945]

956 Clayton Street
San Francisco

Darling Sooze,

Thanks for your letter. You must all have been having a miserable time, I am so terribly sorry and I do wish I were there. It seems like a lifetime since that day in 1939 when Tuddemy saw us off at the station – he & Nanny & Aunt Puss – and he was one of the few people in England I really looked forward to seeing again. Are you bringing into your book about church services at Swinbrook, when we used to make Tud blither by nudging him in the parts about not committing adultery?[1]

Tell Rodd I appreciate his thought about his mother's dough (which I really do) but why did he tell her who he was going to leave it to, he might have guessed that would ruin all.

You would love the amazing Donk, now called Constancia in her new school. Also the beautiful, new improved walking & talking & self-feeding Nicholas Tito. We would come to England if we could afford it. If we do come, can we stay with you? I've lost track of who else I'm on speakers & stayers with. At the moment I'm not working because my lade who took care of the children has left. So I'm trying to look after them. Luckily Constancia helps a lot by washing up, making beds etc. She's not at all like we were as children, but is in some ways a typical nursery-school product. Any chance of you & Rodd coming to America? I know you hate foreigners specially Americans but you would adore Bob & Constancia & Nicholas.

Do write again soon, and if you ever see Id or Rud[2] give them my love.

Yr loving Susan

1 'During the reading of the Ten Commandments . . . we'd wait for the signal: "Thou shalt not commit adultery", then nudge all down the row to where poor Tom was sitting, desperately trying to suffocate giggles. We were sure he led a glamorous life of sin abroad and in his London flat, and needed emphasis on this particular Commandment.' *Hons and Rebels*, p. 22.

2 Joan (Rud/Rudbin) Farrer (1913–93). The Mitfords' first cousin, and sister of Ann (Id), was a debutante at the same time as Unity. Married to Guillermo de Udy 1936–41, and to Paul Rodzianko in 1949.

FOUR

1945–1949

Those Mitford Sisters

The Aristocratic Mitford Sisters Traveled, Individually, This Way and That, With the Perverse Hand of Fate Guiding Them Into Channels That Brought Embarrassment to Their Parents.

upon a time there lived
ngland a lord and lady
might have been called
t parents in all the land.
re Lord and Lady Redes-
ie Freeman-Mitford.
ere six beautiful daugh-
Mitford home, bearing
names: Unity, Jessica,
ela, Diana and Deborah.
ion there was one son,
have been called a special
this tranquil household.
e day, politics crept down
of this ideal home. In-
rious "isms" pried into
of the household and
the lives of the Mitfords.
son, who had great sta-
rently escaped the clutches
rines, but he later gave
e war.
ith the fanatic devotion
ed for Hitler, was the
able political casualty.
he got a disabling bullet

at unhappy beginning,
glamorous British sisters
ve run the gamut from
to Fascism.
as only recently rocked
oundations by contribut-
to the London Daily
ommunist paper.
who is the wife of the
Rodd, son of Lord and
l, and a prominent Brit-
contributed her bit to
centricity when she pub-
lampooning the British

of Happiness" deals with
mily almost as impetuous
wn turned out to be.
Pamela married the
onet in 1928.
the youngest, married
enant Lord Andrew Cav-
Coldstream Guards, and
uke and Duchess of De-
ly in the war, and lives
a Marchioness can.
iana, Unity and Jessica
ut into the spotlight of
eccentricity, dragging
d father and their Vic-
r along with them. Unity
lunching with a paper-
d Hitler in Munich one
rnoon 15 years ago.
after that Unity, whose
was Walkyrie, was seen
with the Nazi bigwigs.
her elder sister Diana,
n married to the son of
in as ornate a wedding
Mayfair ever saw, but
l him later on grounds
joined her in Berlin.
all, beautiful, blond sis-
e toast of Berlin, each
e swastikas signed on
itler himself. They even
eir father and mother
Nazi Congress at Nur-
na was married secretly
of Propaganda Minister
ir Oswald Mosley, of the
British Union of Fascists.

When the war broke out, Lady Mosley was in England. She and her husband were detained by British wartime regulations, and lived together with her children, now three, in an apartment in Holloway jail.

Unity, however, stayed in Germany with her ideal, Adolf. This sojourn in her beloved enemy's country was cut short, however, by a mysterious bullet. Though denying all knowledge of it, the Nazis cared for her by Hitler's direct command. The two warring governments soon afterwards made arrangements to get Unity home. Her father met the boat, took the muffled figure in charge, and sent her to an isolated community in Scotland.

Lord Redesdale, convinced of his mistake in following his daughter's political ideas, returned to London in spite of the blitz.

That leaves Jessica. In 1937 she was the storm center of three countries, as members of her family, the consular service, and reporters followed her trail. Jessica had eloped with Esmond Romilly, who already had developed a reputation as a left-wing warrior and writer, and was on her way to war-torn Spain.

The various entourages finally caught up with the lovers in Bayonne, France. There Jessica, in an old hat and brown suit, was married to Romilly, in the British consulate. The bride and groom took off right away for Dieppe, where they honeymooned and Romilly wrote a book on Spain in two weeks.

Later they came to America, where both got jobs, and lived happily and quietly until the war. Romilly immediately joined the Royal Canadian Air Force, and was shot down over the North Sea.

Jessica's whereabouts were a secret to strangers until the strange bequest of money to the Communist paper was revealed. Then it was learned that she had married Robert Treuhaft, had lived in the Greenwich Village section of New York until two years ago, and had a son named for Marshal Tito of Yugoslavia.

Now they are living in San Francisco, where Jessica has been an OPA investigator. Treuhaft, an attorney, is a member of a firm which represents CIO unions. Both are active in the National Citizens Political Action Committee, which is somewhat more left than the CIO's PAC.

Illustrated by JOHN FLOHERTY

r 27, 1946

THE AMERICAN WEEKLY

Article in *The American Weekly*, 1946.

Tom's death in action, aged thirty-six, in the very last weeks of the war dealt a blow to the Redesdales from which they never recovered and was a loss that his sisters mourned all their lives. Unable to settle the differences that had kept them apart during the war, Lord Redesdale retreated to Redesdale Cottage, one of the last properties still owned by the family on their ancestral Northumberland estate. Here he was looked after by Margaret Wright, who had become his companion after his separation, while Lady Redesdale took Unity to Inch Kenneth. Unity's condition had improved to the point where she could undertake simple household tasks but she was still as demanding as a small child and could not be left on her own for long. In May 1948, while she and her mother were on Inch Kenneth, Unity contracted an infection from the old bullet wound which quickly developed into meningitis. A storm was blowing and it was several days before a doctor could reach the island, by which time her condition had become critical. She died on 28 May, aged thirty-three, and was buried in the churchyard at Swinbrook.

Perhaps because all the sisters except Jessica were together at the funeral, Unity's death is hardly mentioned at the time in their letters to one another. In *Hons and Rebels*, Jessica wrote that she had already thought of Unity as dead when political differences had parted them, but according to her daughter, Constancia, she was heartbroken when the news of her sister's death reached her. Thirty years later, Jessica wrote to Deborah, 'To this day sometimes I dream about her, arriving fresh from Germany in full gaiety.' Nancy wrote to Eddy Sackville-West at the time, 'I am *very* sad, I was so fond of her as you know & it seems such a dreadful waste of the charming beautiful & odd creature that she used to be. A victim of these terrible times . . .' In her memoirs, Diana described the funeral as the saddest day of her life.

The first tangible result of Nancy's affair with Gaston Palewski was *The Pursuit of Love* which she wrote, in a burst of inspiration, in the opening months of 1945. Starring Palewski as Fabrice, duc de Sauveterre, and featuring the Mitfords – minus the politics – as the Radlett children, the book was a paean to the man who had transformed her life and was her first truly accomplished novel. It was an instant success, selling in huge numbers, and almost for the first time the name 'Mitford' appeared in the press unattached to scandal. There are no letters between the sisters to record their reactions to Nancy's fictional rendering of their childhood but Lord Redesdale was said to be delighted with the portrait of himself as Uncle Matthew and to have cried at the end of the book. On the proceeds of her bestseller, Nancy moved to Paris to be close to 'the Colonel', living for the moments he could snatch between political obligations and his other girlfriends. But however little time Palewski might have for her, Nancy was happy to be in Paris, to be part of the social and cultural explosion that took place in the city after the Liberation, and to have money to spend on herself for the first time in her life. She moved between small hotels and rented flats on the Left Bank – always close to Palewski's apartment in the rue Bonaparte – while searching for a permanent home. She became an habituée of the British Embassy, presided over by Duff and Diana Cooper; indulged her love of couture clothes; and made lifelong friends among the cosmopolitan café society and Parisian *gratin*. Her enjoyment was only clouded by the intermittent appearance of Peter, who would turn up to cadge money and who refused to give her a divorce. Diana became Nancy's preferred correspondent immediately after the war. In over two hundred marvellously vivid letters that survive from the period, she regaled her sister with descriptions of the parties she had been to, the beautiful clothes she was ordering and the fascinating people she had met – her enjoyment heightened, no doubt, by recounting all this to a sister who could not travel because her passport had been confiscated and whose horizons at the time were limited to the domestic concerns of her immediate family in the austere atmosphere of post-war Britain.

Diana's letters to Nancy are more guarded. She knew nothing, of course, of Nancy's two wartime denunciations and invited her to stay at Crux Easton as soon as peace was declared. However, she was well aware that Nancy was capable of disloyalty and that she did not like

Mosley. Juggling her allegiance to her husband and enjoyment of her sister's company was a feat that Diana managed to keep up for many years. Crux Easton was sold at the end of 1945 and the family moved to Crowood, an eighteenth-century manor house near Ramsbury in Wiltshire, which came with 1,100 acres of land that Mosley settled down to farm. He had not given up political ambition or abandoned the dream that he would one day be called upon to rescue his country at a time of national crisis. In 1948, he returned to politics as leader of the Union Movement with a programme promoting a centralized European nation. Diana never lost faith in Mosley's ideas. She continued to believe in his political diagnoses but she was under no illusion that his policies would ever be adopted or that he himself would be called upon to play an active role. This was not an opinion she could share with her husband – he depended too heavily on her faith in him – and she herself had invested so much in sustaining him that to admit defeat, even to herself, was unthinkable. Keeping tight control of the image she presented to the world and blocking out any areas of pain – the cult of perfection was a key element in Diana's life and 'perfect' a recurrent word in her conversation and letters – she sacrificed her own interests and put all her energy into creating a life that would keep her restless and demanding husband entertained. Mosley was forty-nine when the war ended and lived for a further thirty-five years. Although his name never lost the power to inflame British public opinion, he remained a marginal political figure until the day he died.

Jessica had very little communication with her sisters for five years after the war. In 1946, she provoked the family by trying, unsuccessfully, to leave her share of Inch Kenneth – which under Scottish law the sisters inherited after Tom's death – to the Communist Party, in order, she wrote to her mother, 'to undo some of the harm our family has done particularly the Mosleys and Farve when he was in the House of Lords'. Her sisters, who had all agreed to hand over the island to Lady Redesdale for her lifetime, were angered by Jessica's gesture, but their mother refused to be drawn into the controversy. At the beginning of 1948, Jessica's seven-year-old daughter, Constancia, wrote to Lady Redesdale asking her to stay with them in America, an invitation which, to Jessica's consternation, her mother immediately accepted. The visit was a success; it dissipated Jessica's resentment of her mother and kindled a growing appreciation of her qualities. She was 'a marvellous and accommodating guest', Jessica wrote, 'appreciative, uncritical and determined to make friends with her estranged daughter and her family'. Jessica's relations with Nancy were tentatively re-established through Robert Treuhaft's mother, Aranka, who made annual trips to Paris to buy stock for her New York hat shop.

In 1947, the Treuhafts moved from San Francisco to Oakland, where Robert worked for a left-wing law firm and Jessica became involved in the Civil Rights Congress (CRC), an organization created after the war by communist leaders principally to establish civil liberties for American blacks. Jessica became branch secretary and threw herself with energy and commitment into defending her black neighbours against police brutality and false accusations of crimes, the only one of the sisters actually to go out and work for her political beliefs. In a context very different from that in which it had evolved, the Mitford love of teasing came to the fore in Jessica's battles against racial prejudice. In her memoirs she described the 'spectacular tease' she managed to pull off by helping a black family buy a house in an exclusive all-white area, right across the street from her arch enemy, the bigoted local District Attorney.

Pamela and Derek stayed at Rignell for two years after the war. Derek returned to his scientific work and was appointed Professor of Spectroscopy at the Clarendon Laboratory, the physics department of Oxford University which under Professor Lindemann had become a major research facility. Pamela pursued her domestic and farming activities. The Mosleys at nearby Crowood were close enough for the sisters to call on each other easily. In a letter written to her mother in 1946, Diana described a visit from the Jacksons during which Pamela launched into one of her 'sagas', for which she was famous in the family, dwelling on how pleased she was with her new cook, how she did everything for him, 'lighting the stove etc', before rushing home after tea with Diana 'in case the cook should feel lonely'. In 1947, driven out by the super-tax levied on the rich by the Attlee government, the Jacksons moved to Tullamaine Castle, near Fethard in County Tipperary, Ireland, where Derek was able to indulge his love of hunting and steeple-chasing. He was an amateur jockey who rode twice in the Grand National. Although he had some contacts with a laboratory in Dublin and a regular visiting professorship at Ohio State University in Columbus, he cut back on his scientific research and concentrated on horses.

The death in action in 1944 of Deborah's brother-in-law, William Hartington, had made Andrew Cavendish heir to the dukedom and to an inheritance which included estates in England, Ireland and Scotland. In 1946, Deborah and Andrew moved with their two young children from The Rookery to a house in Edensor, a small village on the Chatsworth estate less than a mile from Chatsworth House, the family's magnificent late-seventeenth-century seat in the Peak District of Derbyshire. The great house, which had not been redecorated since the First World War and had been occupied by a girls' school during the Second, was in a sorry state. Andrew's parents never considered moving back but in 1948 they began the immense task of clearing and cleaning it. The following year, the gardens and the main rooms – which had been open to visitors ever since the house was built – were reopened to the public. Andrew, whose greatest interest was politics, stood as a Conservative candidate for Parliament in 1945 and 1950, unsuccessfully both times. In 1945, Labour, with a policy of radical social reform, inflicted a crushing and unexpected defeat on the Tories who had banked on the heroic stature of their leader, Winston Churchill, to win. Deborah went canvassing just once with her husband, which in the immediate post-war election could be very rough. They were tripped up, spat upon and their car nearly overturned, which did little to dispel her distaste for politics. She decided, 'Never again'.

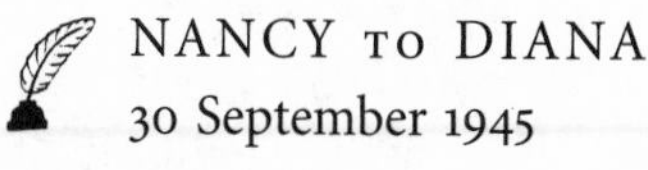

NANCY TO DIANA
30 September 1945

20 rue Bonaparte
Paris VI

Darling,

My life is now a bedroom farce. Going (shockingly late) to the kitchen yesterday morning to cook up my pannikin of washing water I observed an EGG which certainly had never been there before. It

Deborah canvassed with Andrew once and swore 'Never again'.
Chesterfield, Derbyshire, 1945.

gave me quite a jump, quite like R Crusoe & I awaited developments in some disquiet. Presently a dear little Frenchman appeared & announced that he also lives here (nobody had told me). He had arrived at 12.30 the night before & he said made a fearful noise bumping into things. I sleep with all doors open so can't think why I didn't hear him I must say. I think I'd have died of fright if I had! Then of course the Col[1] rang up & was far from pleased at hearing a male voice, which couldn't be very satisfactorily explained with its owner in the next room! So altogether as I say it gets more like a French play every minute. But the egg – you can't think how somehow unsettling that was!

I'm doing well, writing for French mags, they pay like anything & as one knows one is safe from the mocking eye of you & Gerald one can go ahead unselfconsciously.

The terrifying Swiss lady returns tomorrow & may drive me out I feel. I have to share a bathroom with her which leads out of my bedroom & I think that will be rather hell for both. The weather is divine again, boiling, & I so long to stay on – Col goes away for three days this week which is sad if it's my last. But perhaps I shall stay a bit longer. I'm going to Laval's trial[2] if I do. Except for seeing you & a few buddies I absolutely *dread* leaving, you can imagine. Business going like wildfire, only rather damaged by the fact that nobody in London is the least interested. Heywood [Hill] doesn't answer my letters & the others just complain it makes more work for them.[3]

I went to see Baba [de Lucinge] – she is dreadfully sad about Tom. The odd thing is she had heard four years ago he was killed & when she saw him in London last Nov. she thought it was a ghost. When she was told again he was killed she said that's an old story, I've heard it before.

I see H. Hamilton[4] advertises poor Linda as a screaming farce, I knew he would. The Col thinks it's more serious than *Brideshead*[5] – though he has many faults to find. Greatly tickled at his own portrait.

Let me know if you die for a swansdown powder puff (I can't do without them but some people don't mind) they are very plentiful here. Scent is £5 a bottle which really seems too much. Oh the Printemps and all those shops, one can hardly drag oneself through them everything is so tasty. I think I'm safe to be here another week as the actual mechanics of getting away take that – permits & so on.

What shall I do in London, simply die I should think, the idea of all that gloom weighs me down like a ton of bricks.

Somebody asked the Col what he thinks of the atom bomb to which he replied 'Comme amateur de porcelaine –'[6]

Much love, NR

1 Gaston Palewski (1901–84). Always called by Nancy the 'Colonel', or 'Col', after his rank in the army. Joined General de Gaulle in London in 1940 and remained as head of his cabinet 1942–6. Elected Deputy in 1951, he was vice-president of the National Assembly 1953–5, ambassador to Rome 1957–1962, and president of the Constitutional Council 1965–74.

2 Pierre Laval (1883–1945). As a senior member of the Vichy government, Laval was tried for collaboration. After a failed suicide attempt, he was executed on 15 October 1945.

3 Nancy had justified her move to Paris by ostensibly going to buy books for Heywood Hill.

4 Hamish (Jamie) Hamilton (1900–88). Nancy's publisher from 1940 until her death and the publisher of Diana's memoirs, *A Life of Contrasts* (1977).

5 Evelyn Waugh's novel *Brideshead Revisited* came out in May, six months before *The Pursuit of Love*.

6 'As a lover of porcelain –'.

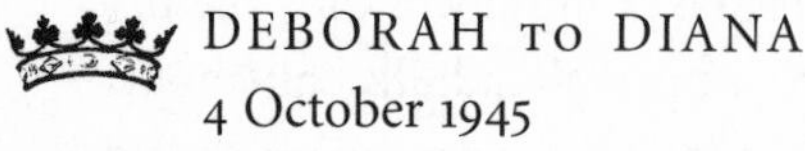

DEBORAH TO DIANA
4 October 1945

Inch Kenneth
Gribun, Oban

Darling Honks

I have been here for a week with Elizabeth & Anne [Cavendish] and at first Muv was really quite cheerful and so was Bobo, but after a day or two when they got used to us being here Birdie became *furious* with everyone and everything and Muv became silenter and silenter and she seems so *sad* and everything seems so pointless for her, oh dear it is so terribly sad, I don't know what to think about it all. Her plan to go to Wycombe is quite a good one I think but I have an awful feeling that Farve won't go as he really seems to hate her now, and he certainly won't stay there much as Bobo irritates him so much.

I think Muv would be more or less alright looking after Bobo if only Bobo wasn't so *beastly* to her, she never leaves her alone for a minute and as you know, is exactly like a child in that she has to be entertained the whole time and poor Muv can never sit down to read or enjoy herself for a moment. I do think we all ought to try and help her make some arrangement about Bobo which would leave Muv free, even for a few weeks or months, as I really do think the strain on her is too much, she looks so thin & tired & utterly miserable.

Her plan about Bobo having a cottage of her own is the best I think, but it depends entirely on getting a sort of Mrs Stobie[1] to look after her. Oh goodness I wish I knew what would be the best thing.

We are going back tomorrow to The Rookery for the weekend & then to Eastbourne till the end of Jan. Do write.

I'm in such a worry about Muv, I know something ought to be

done & it is only us who can do anything as Farve takes no responsibility for Bobo which I think is awful of him.

I hope your move isn't too agonising, of course they can't really be anything else.

Masses of love to Sir O & Nanny & the boys,
Debo

Em talks properly now & says things like 'Everyone in the graveyard is dead'.

1 Lady Redesdale's cook for many years who went to help out when Unity returned from Germany after her suicide attempt.

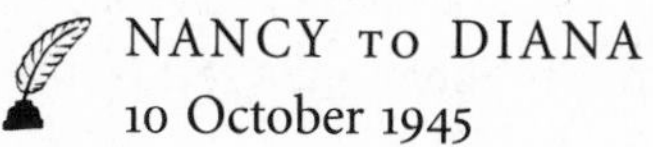

NANCY TO DIANA
10 October 1945

20 rue Bonaparte, VI

Darling,

My life has resolved itself into a mule-like struggle not to leave this spot (Paris I mean). Miss Chetwynd,[1] owner of the flat, wrote & said when M. de Seyres arrives you must instantly go as he is very sad, has lost his wife, & *must* be alone.

I'm ashamed to say I haven't gone & am leaving here, for an hotel, only on Sunday, a week after I got her letter. I blush at my awful behaviour. But the Col rushed off to Brussels & I hardly saw him between Rhineland & that, & must stay & say goodbye. So I made his secretary find me a room, but there wasn't one until Sunday anywhere in Paris. Now I *hope* to stay until after the elections which has always been my real aim! The weather is boiling like June, really too divine & the trees are all yellow – just the time for Paris.

Little Marc de Beauvau[2] turned up & took me round the night-clubs. I said 'Marc what time does the metro end?' 'At one – but (hopefully) it begins again at 5'. However I was firm, & at 3 we were dragged home by a groaning man on a bike. He charged about £1 a groan, but even so I found it embarrassing. Marc said 'If I come to London in Nov. will you find me a wife exactly like you?' I can only think of the utter fascinators[3] but perhaps they're not *exactly*. But perfect for rank of course. He is awfully dotty but I am very fond of him I must say.

Oh the move. Poor you – still it will be the last for ages.

I went to a huge, madly enthusiastic meeting of MRP[4] at the 'Vél[odrome] d'Hiv[er]'. In the middle of the 'Marseillaise' (not a dry eye) the record ran down. They all simply shrieked with laughter. I do think the French are heaven.

From what I observe I should say Gaulle[5] was almost certain to be all right but I believe they aren't v. optimistic themselves. Electors are funny things as we all know. The lists are going up all over Paris – on one of them is three déportés one aveugle [blind man] & about two other equally lugubrious categories, can it be a joke? I'm inclined to think everything here is a joke really, like Mitford life, one of the reasons I so long to live here! The déportés wear a kind of centipede in their button holes & one is supposed to give them one's seat in the metro.

Must go out into the heavenly sun.

Much love, NR

1 Elizabeth Chetwynd (d.1961). An English bluestocking who reviewed for the *Times Literary Supplement*. Her flat was handy for Nancy as Palewski lived in the same street.
2 Prince Marc de Beauvau-Craon (1921–82). A Free French officer and friend of Palewski. Married Laure de Rougemont in 1972.
3 Anne and Elizabeth Cavendish.
4 Mouvement Républicain Populaire, a Christian Democrat party formed in 1944.
5 Charles de Gaulle (1890–1970). The General had been President of the provisional government since 1944 and was re-elected in November 1945.

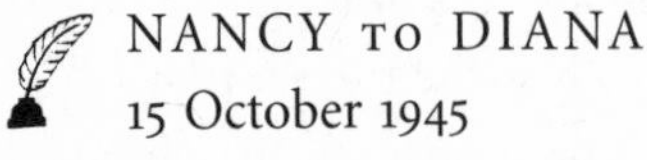

NANCY TO DIANA
15 October 1945

Hotel Pont Royal
Paris VII

Darling,

I think I shall come home today week. The weather has taken a chilly turn & so much of my time is spent waiting about (which now I am driven to doing in my dreary bedroom as out of doors is too cold to sit & read). The Col is wildly busy & sometimes I don't see him at all. When he got back from Germany he rang up at 2 A.M. to say he was in terrible agony & they had found an abscess in his spinal column. Imagine if I had a fit. He was given penicillin & was perfectly well & working again in twelve hours. Had it happened a year ago he would either have died or been paralysed. How would Muv explain this?

Oh I wish you could have heard a conversation at Baba's about Denise Bourdet[1] & how over her bed (where she insisted on keeping her dead hubby for a week) there hang two pictures of him dead & a death mask. Baba said 'after all she is young & beautiful & soon she will start a love affair & then – will she have it under poor Edouard's very nose?' Jacques Février:[2] 'Never will Denise have another affair'. Baba – to me in a loud aside 'Don't pay any attention to him, he thinks of nothing but boys'. Aren't French people wonderful. Apparently Mme B held endless receptions over the dead body & Baba arrived from England not knowing he had died & suddenly SAW. Think if it had been us! She said 'Of course Denise always has been rather provincial'.

I've just had a letter from the French consul in London saying there is no hope of a visa for me to come here for at least six more months!

See you very soon now I hope.

Much love, NR

1 Denise Rémon (1892–1967). Parisian literary and café-society figure. Married the French dramatist Edouard Bourdet (1887–1945) as her second husband.
2 Jacques Février (1900–79). Pianist, and a close associate of the composer Francis Poulenc.

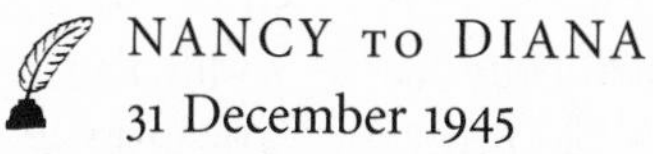

NANCY TO DIANA *12 Blomfield Road, W9*
31 December 1945

Darling

Poor Gladys,[1] sobbing loudly, was removed today in an ambulance, with scarlet fever. Oh I do pray I don't get it – it means one month on your back apparently. I should go mad.

The Colonel rang up & says the Windsors[2] are giving my book to everybody for Xmas, which tickles me very much. Violet T[refusis] says Emerald [Cunard] will never be the same again & I have ruined her few remaining years as she feels she has missed something. Everybody I see says how can they get a French lover.

My situation is deplorable, strict quarantine for a week. Luckily my old mad Norwegian[3] is faithfully feeding me or I should starve to death. I shall have to take a fancy to housework but I *do* so hate it, & I never know where G hides dusters etc. Oh *bother.*

Best love darling, NR

1 Nancy's maid.
2 The Duke and Duchess of Windsor settled in France after the war.
3 Sigrid, Nancy's ex-maid.

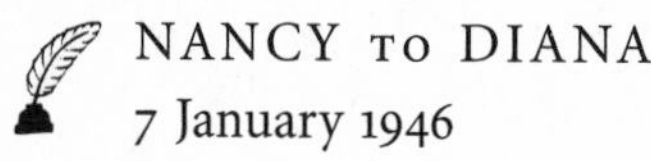

NANCY TO DIANA *12 Blomfield Road, W9*
7 January 1946

Darling,

Out of quarantine which is a comfort as every time I sneezed or felt shivery I thought it was that!

Fancy, Mrs Keppel's[1] favourite joke in my book is the chicken's mess (A's jewel).[2] I was so pleased, never thought anybody would see that one.

Darling, housework. I make my bed & wash up a coffee cup & then I go to bed & sleep the sleep of utter exhaustion until dinner time. What does it mean & how can people manage? I never attempt the Hoover or lighting the stove or any of the moderately tough things

Pam Chichester[3] was in a baker's shop & all the women began saying 'Oh! it's disgusting' & making a fearful fuss & she suddenly realized they had seen Boud who was ambling down the street, & then one she knew came in & said '*Your* friend Unity Mitford is outside' & she was nearly lynched. Isn't it lucky they never do it to her – but as Pam said, how can they recognise her? Rather fascinating. SW7 mentality of course.

Much love, do come up soon again, NR

1 Alice Edmonstone (1869–1947). Edward VII's mistress during his last years. Married George Keppel in 1891.
2 In *The Pursuit of Love*, Louisa's fiancé gave her a replica of King Alfred's jewel which Linda, the heroine of the novel, compared to a chicken's mess, 'same size, same shape, same colour'. Nancy based this episode on an actual remark she made to Pamela when Oliver Watney had given her a replica of the jewel as an engagement present in 1929.
3 Pamela Peel (1900–62). Married to Charles Chichester 1924–8, and to John Wrench in 1934.

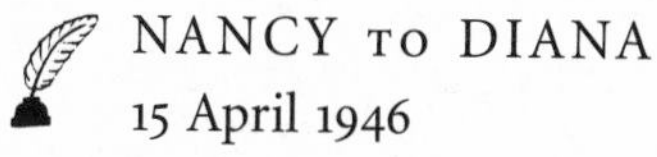

NANCY TO DIANA
15 April 1946

Hotel de Bourgogne
Paris VII

Darling

You are not to say you are infamous & unfashionable it hurts my feelings. Anyway *nobody* so beautiful & beloved.

Spent yesterday at Versailles with my Col. I can't get over having hours & hours of his company like this, it has never happened before except once in London when the Gen. sacked him for a week. Versailles at this time of year is magical – have you seen it?

Went to tea with two old French Comtesses, friends of a friend, to whom I took a parcel. They were exactly, & even to look at, like Aunt Iris, & I couldn't resist teasing & when they said how dreadful it is here with nothing to eat I said, 'I don't call pâté de foie gras – then lobster – then beef steak – then camembert – which I had for lunch (quite true) nothing to eat.' They were utterly furious & Aunt Iris-like, it was just like teasing her.

Poor Woman – I feel they are having rather a down in life at the moment. But surely they didn't expect to win & he's done awfully well in other races hasn't he?

I've sold Linda here for £100 in francs, which I get straight away, & I hear she's been taken in Sweden too, so I might go for a holiday there but I think it would be a bore.

Much love darling – write sometimes if poss. NR

NANCY TO DIANA

Hotel de Bourgogne, VII

26 April 1946

Darling,

Randolph [Churchill] has appeared & roars at me for articles. So the Col writes them & I translate them & Randolph pays & we go out to a restaurant as a change from le High Grade.[1] The articles are so good, you can't think, & the Col gets very cross at them being under Randolph's name, like *Cyrano*. But he won't do them under his own, & R has to think they are by me – it is all vastly complicated. By the time I have translated them & R has turned them into American the Col wouldn't recognise one word, but this I keep from him!

More thousands for the book, two more to be exact. So I've simply let go everything & buy whatever takes my fancy, it is heaven. Also, one of the thousands is from Johnen, & he offers me £50 a week to work on the film[2] while it is being made so I don't think H. Hill & Co will see me for a while but don't *dare* tell Molly[3] this as I fear she would mind dreadfully.

Randolph won't go to Nuremberg, he disapproves of it. I wonder if his dad does too.[4]

Noël Coward[5] is here, he called the Col 'Chéri', greatly to the latter's surprise. In fact the town is full of English & on the Right Bank one hears nothing else spoken at all.

Off to Violet [Trefusis] for the weekend.

All love, NR

1 Gaston Palewski's American friends sent him tins of high-grade pork from time to time.

2 John Sutro's plan to film Turgenev's *Torrents of Spring* never got off the ground.

3 Molly Friese-Green (1909–2005). Assistant at Heywood Hill who managed the accounts. Married Handasyde Buchanan, a partner in the bookshop, in 1949.

4 Observing the Nuremberg trials, Winston Churchill commented to Lord Ismay, 'It shows that if you get into a war, it is supremely important to win it. You and I would be in a pretty pickle if we had lost.' *The Memoirs of Lord Ismay* (Heinemann, 1960), p. 157.

5 Noël Coward (1899–1977). The playwright was in Paris working on the French version of *Blithe Spirit*.

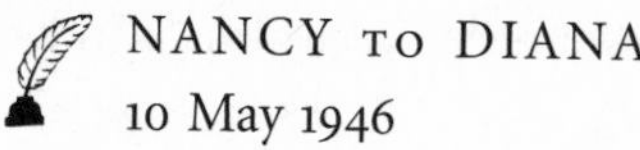

NANCY TO DIANA
10 May 1946

Hotel de Bourgogne, VII

Darling

I've had a terrible letter from Molly to whom I wrote saying I hear you look tired, saying it's not tiredness it's sadness & my throat is sore all day from trying not to cry. I believe she was in love with that infinitely dreary blond young man who has now left. Oh *dear.* I've begged her to try to come here but I'm sure she won't. Isn't she a worry. If it wasn't for the Col I would hasten back, but I feel if once I leave I shan't get back here again & I couldn't bear it. I live from week to week without making any plans & always hoping some miracle will occur which would force us to live here, but of course it won't. Oh for pre-war days when one could choose where one lived.

Oggie[1] has appeared – tremendous Lesbian reunion last night at Marie-Louise's[2] jour. When I heard them all telling Oggie how beautiful she is, it took me down a peg or two –! But oh how pleasant that one can look forward at Oggie's age & weight to still being told one is beautiful – only here, never in London that land of sober truth.

All love darling, NR

1 Olga Lynn (1882–1961). Diminutive opera singer and singing teacher.
2 Marie-Louise Vallantin (1890–1977). Hostess who held a literary and artistic salon from the beginning of the First World War until shortly before her death. Married to the playwright Jacques Bousquet.

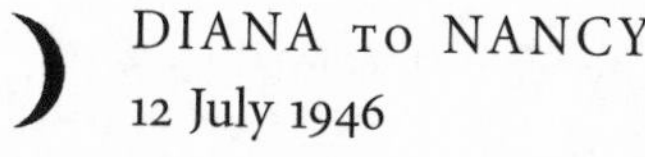

DIANA TO NANCY
12 July 1946

Crowood House
Ramsbury
Wiltshire

Darling

Thank you so much for your letter – we also are having glorious heat at last & that's why I haven't written, you know how one rushes out at every spare moment. Also I have had Debo's babies for the last eleven days, oh the sweetness of them.

I took Emma to London to be a bridesmide, as she calls it, to Maggot [Ogilvy]. The wedding was yesterday & Muv wore my new hat as she hadn't got one and she looked wonderful in it. It is a straw bonnet with black velvet ribbon.

The night I was in London I went (by myself) to *La casa de Bernarda Alba*,[1] it is all about Muv and us. You must see it if they do it in Paris. I told Muv the story to see if it rang a bell and she said at once, 'Oh yes, I *know*, those late visits, how it reminds one, etc.' I shrieked and said of course *Nancy* would say it was about us, like the Barretts being about Farve.[2] At the play I found myself sitting beside Oggie, so we chatted & I said 'I hear you were the belle of Paris.' 'Who told you that?' 'Nancy.' 'Well', said Oggie, 'she really *is* the belle of Paris.'

Goodbye darling

All love from D

1 *The House of Bernarda Alba* (1936), Federico Garcia Lorca's last play, was the story of a widowed mother and her five daughters whom she cloistered in the house after her husband's death and ruled with a rod of iron.
2 The father of the poet Elizabeth Barrett Browning (1806–61) was a tyrant who tried to prevent any of his children from marrying.

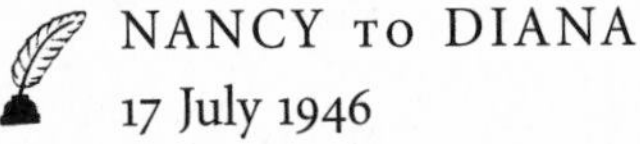

NANCY TO DIANA
17 July 1946

Hotel de Bourgogne, VII

Darling,

I took the chance of Peter going back to send you one of those woolly coats for a birthday present. Of course it's not for this weather exactly, but I think they are a comfort as one can't be cold in them & yet they look summery!

Eat the truffles & let me know truthfully what they are like & if *really* good I'll bring more.

Big dinner for Winston last night at the Embassy. Dinner very brilliant, of twenty-four, succeeded by a party of nearly all English in their thin Debenham georgettes & their Cromwell Road hair. 'Oh Lady Diana, do you *like* waking up in all this red brocade? I'm afraid *I* shouldn't'.

The Colonel & I dined. Diana rang him up & said 'Viens dîner avec la légitime'.[1] Which very nearly did me out of a lift there in his car. Winston sat between Mme Pol Roger,[2] who is the prettiest & gayest woman in Paris, & M. Blum[3] who looks an absolute love I must say.

I've been with Alvilde[4] two or three days as the Col went down to the Gen. Although she is only twenty minutes from Paris her house is in the deepest quietest country you could possibly imagine. I wonder if I would like to have one there eventually & not in Paris – it might be better. I must say I think Paris society people are too vicious to play a real part in one's life. I'm not a prude am I? But it's all too much for me & too open, I find there's something to be said for British hypocrisy after all.

How funny it is about Cecil & Greta Garbo.[5]

Saw Daisy[6] & Ld S[7] on their way to the South & they talked of o but you.

Don't know about coming back. I'm so frightened of not getting a visa to re-enter France. Also the Col now talks of spending August here & I see so much more of him now the town is emptier, it seems waste to go away & he makes a great fuss if I suggest it.

Is it entendu [agreed] for Jonathan in the Xmas hols? I do long for that. My flat is now definite, six months from Oct.

V. Best love darling, NR

1 'Come to dinner with your legitimate companion,' i.e. 'wife'.

2 Odette Wallace (1911–2000). Married to Jacques Pol-Roger of the champagne firm. She was introduced to Winston Churchill by Duff Cooper in 1945 and thereafter Churchill insisted that she be invited whenever he visited Paris.

3 Léon Blum (1872–1950). First Socialist Prime Minister of France 1936–7. Imprisoned by the Germans during the war, he emerged after the Liberation as one of the country's leading veteran statesmen.

4 Alvilde Bridges (1909–94). A protégée of Princess Winnie de Polignac, rich lesbian patron of the arts, who was living at Jouy-en-Josas near Paris. Expert on gardening and garden design. Married to Anthony, 3rd Viscount Chaplin 1933–50 and to James Lees-Milne in 1951.

5 Cecil Beaton's romance with Greta Garbo had been interrupted after the photographer published several portraits of the actress in *Vogue* without her permission.

6 Marguerite (Daisy) Decazes (1890–1962). Often described as one of the best-dressed and sharpest-tongued women of her day. Married to Prince Jean de Broglie 1910–18 and to Reginald Fellowes in 1919.

7 Hugh Sherwood (1898–1970). Liberal MP. He had a long affair with Daisy Fellowes who used to refer to him as 'H.L.' (Hated Lover). Married to Patricia Chetwode 1942–8.

NANCY TO DIANA

Hotel de Bourgogne, VII

3 August 1946

Darling

There has been a series of dreadful attacks on the Col in a paper called *l'Aurore* & he is quite got down by them so I said I would go & shoot the editor. He says when Mme Cailloux did so the sub editor rushed into the room & hors de lui cried, 'Madame vous êtes une – une – mal élevée!'[1] Words he was never after able to live down.

The Stanleys. You know B. Russell[2] wrote to me & said unless he had actually read those letters no power on earth would have made him believe that Hen[rietta], whom he remembered as an utter ogre, could ever have been so plaintive & submissive. I suppose those women were only kept under control by their sexual instincts & for as long as they were functioning. Great Granny was so *exigeante* in that way that Airlie had to go abroad for months every year.

Evelyn[3] talks of reissuing the two books in one volume, I wish he would. When they came out there was a super slump for books & they were not a financial success. But I believe now they would 'go'.

Much love, NR

1 'Madame, you are a – a – rude woman.' In 1914, the editor of the *Figaro* was shot by the wife of the politician Joseph Cailloux, about whom he had been running a series of exposés.

2 Bertrand Russell (1872–1970). The philosopher descended, like the Mitfords, from the Stanleys of Alderley and was, therefore, a distant cousin.

3 Evelyn Waugh (1903–66). The novelist was on the board of Chapman & Hall, the publisher of Nancy's edition of the Stanley letters.

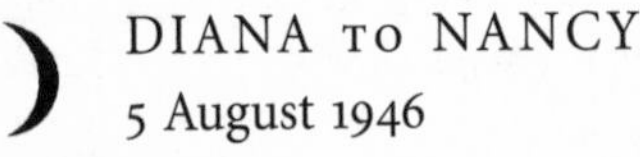

DIANA TO NANCY

Crowood House
Ramsbury

5 August 1946

Darling

Isn't Aunt Weenie an old meanie and aren't the minds of *virtuous* people utter sinks of abominable filth.[1] The part about it that annoys me most is that Kit is one of the few people who have taken trouble to be kind to poor Boud & considering his character & how easily bored he is it was really very good of him, & now this! It shows what comes of behaving in a kind Christian disinterested manner – absolutely fatal. Although the whole story was a tiresomeness on Boud's part I don't blame her a quarter as much as these old horrors, because after all they are supposed to be in their right minds.

Yesterday Gerald came over with dear Harold,[2] I was *so* pleased to see him, and Robert [Heber-Percy] & a friend. They came for lunch & stayed till 6 & we had a wonderful chat. Harold talked brilliantly and Kit took a tremendous fancy to him & said when he was gone 'I adore Harold'. He talked a lot about you and says your elegance is unbelievable (with a glance at my cotton dress) and that you are the best dressed woman in Paris, and my *dear* looking so *radiant*. I made him tell about his whiff being shattered to atoms,[3] as well as my favourite of all Harold stories when his American cousins say to him 'Harold, how *English* you have become'. Isn't he far the best company of all our contemporaries.

Muv telephoned last night & I have arranged to go there for a night next Monday. Of course she is still mourning for Tom but Aunt Weenie's thing is great nonsense as she has cheered up very much and gets better all the time. She has not *lost interest* in the least but is simply very sad, but it has no bitterness in it (her sadness). At least that is what I think.

All love darling, *do* come soon – we all *pine* for you. D

1 The sisters' aunt Dorothy Bowles had told Nancy that Mosley had tried to seduce Unity.
2 Harold Acton (1904–94). The writer had been a friend of the family, and of Nancy and Diana in particular, since the late 1920s. After living in China before the war, he returned to Italy where he divided his time between Florence and Posillipo.
3 In *Memoris of an Aesthete* (1948), Harold Acton described being tipped out of his whiff while sculling on the Thames and seeing his craft swept downstream where it 'shattered to splinters'. Nancy and Diana loved hearing him retell the story in his Italianate accent which made even ordinary observations seem amusing.

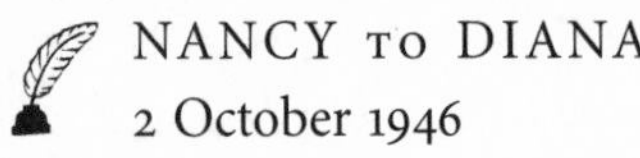

NANCY to DIANA
2 October 1946

Inch Kenneth
Gribun, Oban

Darling

The more I see of Muv the more I feel that the one absolutely insuperable obstacle to happiness for her is Boud. Now it seems to me that as, when Muv dies, something will have to be arranged for Boud, it would be better if it could be done now so that poor Muv's last years can be spent in peace. But what? We simply must think – if it's a question of money surely you & I & Debo could give a pound or two a week – we shall probably have to eventually in any case. As far as I can see, on vague lines, the solution is a separate establishment in some built-up area, with an attendant & an ample supply of bed linen. What about saying all this quite brutally to Boud herself – I believe Muv gets on her nerves quite as much as she on Muv's.

I know it's all very well for me to talk like this when I'm off to live abroad & can't really help & my point is though that if Muv died tomorrow it would *have* to be done, wouldn't it be better to do it now so that she can have a little peace & quiet before she dies. Is it any good saying all this to Farve? *Oh* for Tom.

Say what you think, & I'll talk to Muv before I leave. I think she would welcome *anything* & also it would set her mind at rest if she could more or less see Boud settled. I believe she half thinks Boud will be on the streets like a poor stray dog when she dies.

I do hope I shall see you once more – shall be in London 10–15 Oct unless I go to Woman.

Much love, NR

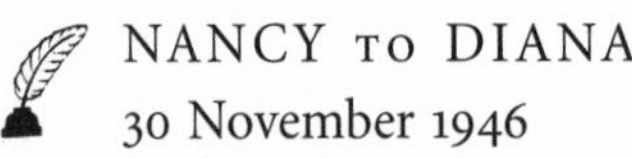

NANCY to DIANA
30 November 1946

20 rue Bonaparte
Paris VI

Darling

I had a dinner on my birthday, rather spoilt by old Col Mitford[1] arriving an hour late – he'd been down to see the Gen & the communists had sawed half way through something which caused a back wheel to fly off which it duly did when they were doing cent à l'heure.[2]

The Colonel unmoved but very late & I was in a fit thinking something awful must have happened – anyhow this drive once a week, 4½ hours each way, is fit to kill him. I keep saying there must be lots of nice generals who live nearer Paris he could get to know.

Mrs Harrison Williams[3] is here with ginger hair. I've utterly now decided against dyeing – all right for blondes but my colour always goes red & that I can't face.

I hear Debo had a miscarriage.[4] Flying nearly always does it, you'd think people would know by now, but perhaps really she's pleased.

I've had such a darling little coat made from yr black velvet, a sort of Victorian riding jacket – so warm & useful.

Much love darling, NR

1 Gaston Palewski. 'Violet Trefusis says the Colonel is getting so English he ought to be called Colonel Mitford while I get more foreign every day & should be La Palewska.' (Nancy to Deborah, 23 August 1946)
2 'A hundred kilometres an hour.'
3 Mona Travis Strader (1897–1983). Elegant beauty from Kentucky who wed her way to fame and fortune. Her husbands included the billionaire financier Harrison Williams, Count Edward von Bismarck and Umberto de Martini, an Italian doctor.
4 Deborah had miscarried one of the twins she was expecting.

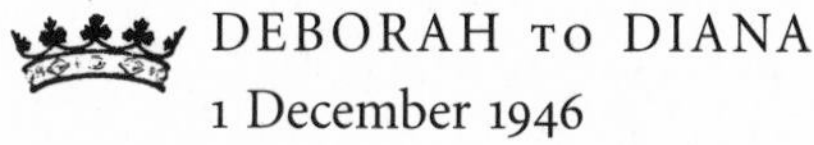

DEBORAH TO DIANA
1 December 1946

Edensor House
Bakewell
Derbyshire

Darling Honks

Oh goodness, have you really got a turkey for us, how utterly dreamlike, I can't tell you how wonderful that will be only you *must* let us pay for it this time. I wonder what the best way of getting it would be. I think we shall be in London for a party on the night of the 19th, would it keep all that time, tell what you think.

I am weighed down with Xmas shopping, my mind is a positive blank when it comes to actually thinking of something for everyone.

Muv and Birdie are coming here I hope but Farve says he can't because he hasn't any clothes, what nonsense. There are forty-nine children coming to the Tree so that will be fun. Andrew says he insists on having the Tree either before Birdie comes or after she's gone as she embarrasses him so much with the clergymen as she always asks them (a) why they became clergymen (b) if they wish they had been made a bishop and (c) if they enjoy sleeping with their wives. I must say I do see.

I am coming to London next week on Wed till Fri evening, do phone if you are there (May 4770). The Wid has been in Mount Row for the last ten days, entertaining intellectuals. The horror of it.

We went to dinner at Buckingham Palace for a ball last week, I sat next to the King, he is a terrific Hon. Andrew sat between the Queen & Princess Thicknesse,[1] wasn't he glamorous.

Oh the turkey.

Much love, Debo

1 Deborah's sister-in-law, Elizabeth Cavendish, was sometimes nicknamed 'Thicknesse'. The name was extended for a while to all Elizabeths.

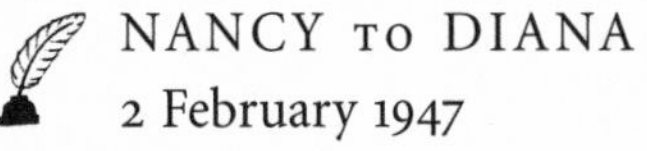

NANCY TO DIANA
2 February 1947

Le M. Chaplin
Jouy en Josas
S et O

Darling,

Fancy being Boud's favourite. I fear it's simply a matter of never seeing her! When I'm there – 'Well I do really hate you, Nancy'.

Violet rang up & said 'I've decided to leave Saint Loup[1] to you in my will'. So I was suitably impressed. Later she rang up & said 'You're not to tell anybody'. So I said 'Now listen Violet, for one thing it's no good telling me secrets because I can't keep them, & to go on with I'm not going to have my life made a burden on account of Saint Loup – I'm sure I shall die ages before you do'. I know she's just doing a Volpone – she's hinted to the Col she would leave it to him. Then she said 'I'm making it a condition you should marry the Colonel'. 'Then save yourself the trouble my dear Violet, I am married already.' She's a sort of second Boud in one's life you know, & quite as dotty, & such a trouble maker. All the same I do rather love her.

Lunched with the Chabillons – the Marquis turned to me & said did I know Emily Brontë – he had just finished *Les Hauts de Hurlevent.*[2] The Colonel was there & a hateful little writer, Jean Tharaud,[3] began a sort of pro-Vichy lecture – the Col laid in to him (I've never heard him do this before). Afterwards the twittering little Comtesses there began saying to each other, 'Tu savais que Palewski était communiste – moi pas'.[4] *Oh* the dottiness!

I said to the Col, 'Do you know it's 4½ years now?' 'Am I not a faithful Colonel?' he replied smugly. Well, fairly faithful.

Their head spy, Rémy, has just written an account of all the secret stuff – I've never read anything so fascinating. It's called *Mémoires d'un agent secret*, I don't know if it has come out at home but if it does you must read it – I hurry back to the flat to get on with it.

I'm here with Alvilde alone – deep snow has fallen at last (the first time) & it is much warmer. Snow always reminds me of Batsford.

Much love from NR

1 Violet Trefusis's house outside Paris which she willed to so many people that Nancy suggested they form a union.
2 *Wuthering Heights* (1847).
3 Jean Tharaud (1877–1952). Journalist and prolific author who wrote books with his older brother, Jérôme (1874–1953).
4 'Did you know that Palewski was a communist? I didn't.'

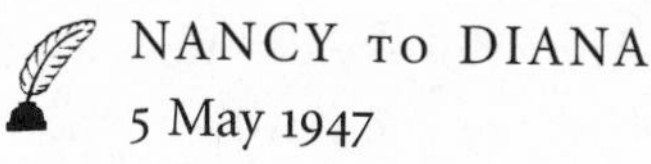

NANCY TO DIANA
5 May 1947

Madison Hotel
Paris VII

Darling,

The Last Hours of Garth[1] made me utterly sob oh you must so MISS him. It seems to me really the point of children is when they are puppies & that rather consoles me for not having any – afterwards it is struggling for boots & school trunks & must be less amusing.

The Moulin.[2] I wonder if I was mad not to. The Col so very much against it & indeed would I ever have set eyes on him – here he rings up when he has ½ an hour & round I go, you know. But the times when he would have two hours & a car available are so much more limited – also he refuses to see Peter so when he was at home that would make another complication. I've been to see about flats – you pay £1,000 a room roughly. Of course compared to that the Moulin at £5,000 with ⅓ paid on mortgage is for nothing – cottage & quite a lot of land. It's still unsold. Oh dear.

I really can hardly say it, you must be so bored with me & my plans, but I still *may* come home. Will say no more on this subject!!

When they brought my Dior suit to try on they held up the skirt saying 'Quel joli coup de taille'[3] after which noises like the last moments of Heath[4] were heard while they tried to do it up!! It's come now & is a dream I must say.

Peter brought a ham from Andorra weighing 34lbs so all our friends are benefiting – all thrilled as there is no meat to be had for love *or money.*

As you will see, the political situation is highly complicated & goodness knows what will happen. The English journalists are furious because London papers give no space to their stories, it must be maddening for them. A man called Walewski has murdered his mistress called Linda which struck me as a curious thing. Colonel shrieking!

It is being such fun here, masses of English buddies – Momo,[5] Cyril [Connolly], Peter Derwent[6] & so on & heavenly weather.

Much love darling, NR

I reopen to say Hervé Alphand[7] just back from Moscow describes a dinner at which Stalin sat glowering & only spoke one word – at the end he lifted his glass & said *Truman.* I love him for that!

1 Diana's eight-year-old son Alexander, nicknamed after the *Daily Mirror* comic-strip hero, had been sent to boarding school. 'It was pure torture. He was dressed up as for market and his new clothes so stiff he could only walk in that way children do when they are teed up. I had to leave him behind among terrifying strangers. They didn't seem cruel, but *so* vague.' (Diana to Nancy, 2 May 1947)

2 Nancy had considered buying the Moulin de la Tuilerie, a house near Paris, from the painter Drian. It was later bought by the Duke and Duchess of Windsor.

3 'What a slim waist.' Nancy had ordered the model 'Daisy' from Christian Dior's first 'New Look' collection.

4 Neville Heath; a murderer who had been hanged the previous year.
5 Maud (Momo) Kahn (d.1960). Elder daughter of the legendary American financier Otto Kahn and a close friend of Nancy. Married General Sir John Marriott in 1920.
6 3rd Baron Derwent (1899–1949). Diplomat and writer. Engaged to be married to Carmen Gandarillas.
7 Hervé Alphand (1907–94). French politician and diplomat who was Deputy Foreign Minister at the time.

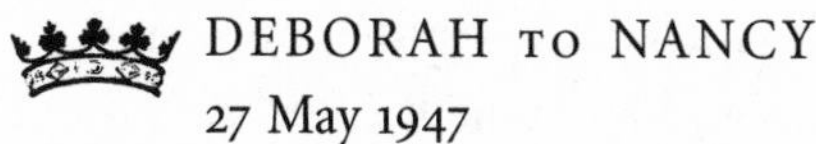

DEBORAH TO NANCY
27 May 1947

Edensor House
Bakewell

Get on

Thank you so much for your letter which I shrieked at.

I am quite alright and long to get up as I can see I am missing the only bit of sun of all the summer.

Having babies successfully seems to be the most difficult thing in the world,[1] I can't think how some people manage to pull it off every time. This time it was pure bad luck as it was quite alright when it was born, although it was six weeks too soon, & when it was eight hours old it suddenly had a haemorrhage in its brain and died at once. The doctor said if they ever do recover from that they are always either cripples or dotty, so it was really a mercy.

The village nurse came for the birth and was too heavenly for anything and called me Your Ladyship all the way through the most undignified parts.

Muv is coming tomorrow which will be bliss.

Andrew has been too wonderful. We are going either to Italy or the South of France or somewhere hot for the first two weeks of July, so what about Paris on the way?

Please write and do come up here any time. I have got about another two weeks in bed & then I suppose a week of pottering & then we may go to Eastbourne so I do hope to see you somehow or other.

Much love, Debo

1 After losing this baby – the second twin she had been expecting – Deborah gave birth to a stillborn child in 1953, bringing to four the number of children she lost.

NANCY TO DIANA *As from 20 rue Bonaparte, VI*
22 July 1947

Darling,

I'm still shrieking over a letter from Muv which ends 'I gaze out over wild flowers & white goats, how disgusting of one to be hermaphrodite, love from Muv'. Of course for ages I thought one meant ONE. Really Muv's goats! Also a letter from Farve saying the prices he got for everything have been terrible.[1] Oh that one could say told you so & serve you right. Were they so bad? I fear the books will be no better, the bottom has dropped out of that market weeks ago.

I went last night to Prod's Sudan film given at the Embassy & whom should I see but Sex Hay, looking quite wild with flowers in her hair like Ophelia (a very fat myopic Ophelia, some clever producer's new idea). She works here!

Have you ever been over Chantilly? I spent Sunday doing an American tour with the Sergeant.[2] Oh the treasures are beyond belief. Then we went to the house of some vulgar Americans at Senlis – they were all, eight of them, playing Bridge *indoors* & evidently had been for hours, & when they finally emerged there were Duff & fat chuckling Bob.[3] So it was rather fun. Then Diana came over in trousers (flannel, boiling day) with Balmain the dressmaker & John Julius.[4]

I was very depressed by Debo's appearance – she was in low spirits evidently not a bit well – not even looking pretty but yellow & her eyes quite small. Then she had bought in Cannes a really terrible black taffeta dress which she wore the whole time – so stuffy & hot looking. Oh dear, & there are such pretty cottons to be had! I took them to dine with the Col & would you believe it Andrew (supposed to be so much interested in politics, hurrying home for a rally) never asked *one single* question. Doesn't it seem strange when there we were, just the four, & the best informed man in France, probably, waiting to be agreeable. I was really astounded.

Andrew seemed sulky & out of spirits but I think was worried about her. He spent the whole afternoon, while she rested, in the

Travellers Club of which Pete had made him a member, watching strangers play Bridge.

Well, the world is certainly composed of oddities!

All love, NR

P.S. Re reading this sounds catty about D & A which I do not intend – it was *heaven* seeing them & they were really sweet & so appreciative.

Just lunched with dear Hog.[5] I'm really so fond of him, he looks too desperately ill & seems rather poor!

1 Lord Redesdale had held one of his frequent sales of furniture and objects.
2 Stuart Preston (1915–2005). Art critic on the *New York Times* whose friends called him by his rank in the American army during the war.
3 Robert Boothby (1900–86). Conservative Unionist MP 1924–58. His career as Parliamentary Secretary to the Minister of Food came to an end in 1941 when he was accused of improper dealings over Czechoslovak gold.
4 John Julius Cooper, 2nd Viscount Norwich (1929–). Only son of Duff and Lady Diana Cooper. Travel writer, historian and broadcaster.
5 Peter Watson (1908–56). Stylish heir to a margarine fortune who underwrote and edited *Horizon*. As a young man, he was once bold enough to ring up Nancy. Lord Redesdale answered and, without moving his mouth from the telephone, shouted, 'Nancy, it's that hog Watson wants to speak to you.'

NANCY TO DIANA *20 rue Bonaparte, VI*
28 August 1947

Darling,

You can imagine if I'm in a terrible fuss over the foreign travel thing because do you think they can make me go home? I've enough dollars to last me nearly two years but then what will I do – & another thing, can they force me to give up my dollars even in spite of being a foreign resident? It seems they can do anything. I feel like a rat in a trap.[1]

Do say what you think – will they drag me home? I shan't dare put my head in the lion's mouth now in September. Of course everybody thinks I'm too awful not to want to live in England but you know it's only the Col – although evidently life *is* more agreeable here, people are nicer to one. Still that is all offset by no relations etc.

But I *can't* live without that military gentleman. 'Are you under my thumb?' he always says, & of course I am. If only he were rich I could borrow indefinitely from him but he's an utter church mouse, it is unlucky.

Oh dear I'm sorry to inflict this wail on you but you do see – I can think of o else. Do ask Kit how long it's all going to last & if he thinks it's real or just the Tory papers' tease? I *am* being selfish – only just seen about petrol, is that *death* to you?

Best love, NR

1 The British government had set rigorous limits on overseas travel and no currency was to be made available for travel outside the sterling area unless approved by the Exchange Control.

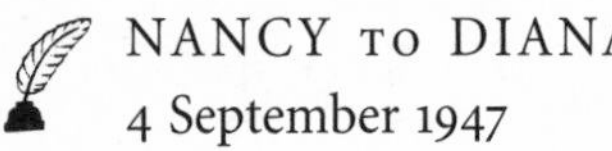

NANCY TO DIANA
4 September 1947

Hotel Jacob et d'Angleterre
Paris VI

Darling,

Yesterday I stood at Dior for two hours while they moulded me with great wadges of cotton wool & built a coat over the result. I look *exactly* like Queen Mary – think how warm though! I see that for customers they don't make them quite to the ankle. Ad[1] says all the English papers are on to the long skirts, & sneer. They may, but all I think of is now one will be able to have knickers over the knee. Now I'm nearly fifty I've decided to choose a style & stick to it, & I choose Dior's present collection.[2] Simply, to my mind, perfect.

Fancy I nearly sent Woman some rice – it would have been waste. I only sent to people who I know have good cooks otherwise pointless.

Snooty letter from Aunt Iris about deserting the old country & saying do I not wish to share in the austerity. Well it seems exaggerated actually to *wish* such a thing – & as I pointed out somebody else can have my lovely rations & live in my house if I'm not there. I do feel it would be different if I could go to the coal face or something, but just sharing austerity seems pointless.

I'm like a cat wanting to have kittens with my book[3] – can't wait to get settled & begin. I only wish I could talk it over with you – there's to be a chapter of Sheila-Poppy-Molly-Sonia etc, you know at a house party, which I hope will greatly tease.

Some French paper has said that Queen Mary's dress for THE wedding[4] is to have a huge pocket over the stomach – what can she be going to put there. Diana [Cooper] says a baby kangaroo. By the way I hope you'll have seen my darling old Marie-Louise [Bousquet], (at Daisy's). I long to know what you think of her.

Went to the opening of the Louvre – oh the beauty. Instead of rust & choc the huge gallery is pink & white & grey & gold. *Would* you'd been here – oh & tomorrow for Gen de G. I never can find shriekers to do things with now the Col is so taken up, it is such a bore – I've been asked to a reception before the speech & can't go alone, what I need is Brian Howard[5] really. (Think of the Col's face!) I've been reading about the Régent – he's so like the Col & his last words, to a pretty Duchess, were 'Alors racontez'[6] & fell dead. The Col persecutes me with racontez & I have to take all your letters to read to him to try & keep him amused – he's an utter slave driver.

Do tell every detail of the wedding I can't have enough. I hope your house is on the route – or is there an 18B stand? Remember I never see an English paper – once a week perhaps.

V best love, NR

1 Adelaide Stanley (1906–81). A cousin of the Mitfords and girlfriend of Peter Rodd. Married Maurice Lubbock in 1926.

2 Christian Dior's second collection kept the nipped waist of the 'New Look' but had even longer lengths and fuller skirts.

3 *Love in a Cold Climate* (1949).

4 Princess Elizabeth's marriage to Prince Philip, which took place on 20 November 1947.

5 Brian Howard (1905–58). Writer who reached a peak of brilliance at Oxford then dissipated his talent in drugs and drink. He committed suicide after the accidental death of his lover.

6 Philippe d'Orléans, nephew of Louis XIV, was Regent during the minority of Louis XV. Like Palewski, who began his morning telephone calls to Nancy with, 'Alors, racontez', and Sauveterre in *The Pursuit of Love* who expected Linda to keep him amused with stories, the Regent was a famous libertine whose last words, 'Well, tell', revealed his love of gossip.

UNITY TO NANCY
8 November 1947

Old Mill Cottage
High Wycombe

Darling Nancy

I *LOVE* your gift. Just the right colour. Thank you.

Well, Nancy, I'm working at last! In the Hospital. 2 till 5, but *DON'T* laugh – washing up & serving tea! The first day I thought I should die. Now, I enjoy it.

Do write to me.

V best love, Bobo

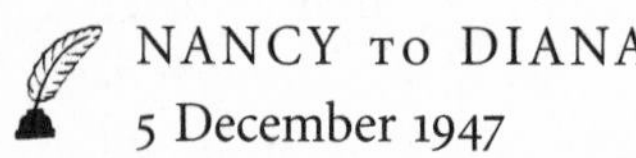

NANCY TO DIANA
5 December 1947

19 quai Malaquais
Paris VI

Darling,

I'm so excited about my flat.[1] I've just spent two hours with the owner & the *sweet* Marie,[2] an utter love. I said if you *could* leave enough linen for two beds? 'Well there is three dozen of everything. This is the silver – I suppose you won't be more than fourteen at dinner?'! It is an 18th-century pavilion exactly the same both sides.

One faces into a garden & the other the prettiest *cour* you ever saw – I have the ground floor. The furniture is an odd jumble, hideous at first sight, of utter horrors & pieces from the Petit Trianon. I think with a little rearrangement it will be terribly nice. All for £25 a month – *aren't* I lucky. In the rue Monsieur. If Audrey[3] allows I move in before Xmas but I must consider her as she has been so kind. I shall be glad to leave this flat & spoilt millionaire's servants – it simply eats money & very little to show for it – not even very warm. A simply rotten cook, I daren't invite people.

No more news as I wrote this morning.

All love, NR

P.S. Just come from the Embassy – all the people beginning to arrive for the Ball[4] – it's so exciting, like a house party for a hunt ball when one was young & loved them only magnified a hundred times. Also made more strange by the streets – blackout, search lights playing, huge mounds of refuse everywhere & armoured cars dashing through the serried ranks of limousines.[5] The *idea* of coming home when all this is going on – you seriously see, don't you? Dined with Derek Hill – I think the ball will be literally nothing but pansies.

1 Nancy moved into 7 rue Monsieur on 19 December 1947; it remained her home until 1967.
2 Marie Renard stayed with Nancy as cook and housekeeper for twenty-two years.
3 Audrey Evelyn James (1902–68). Married to Marshall Field III 1930–34 and to Peter Pleydell-Bouverie 1938–46. She was the sister of Edward James and had lent Nancy her flat on the quai Malaquais overlooking the Seine.
4 A farewell ball given by the Coopers who were leaving the embassy after three years *en poste*.
5 Strikes had closed down public services in Paris, including rubbish collection and power supplies, and troops had been brought in to deal with communist riots.

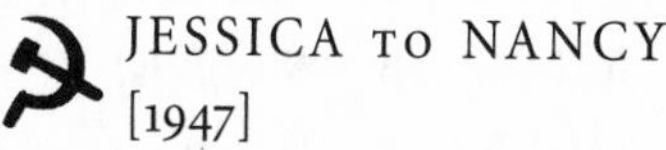

JESSICA to NANCY
[1947]

675 Jean Street
Oakland
California

Darling Susan

No wonder I never write because you always seem to be staying in hotels so I don't know what your address is. This probably won't reach you.

I told Constancia about your being her Madame but she doesn't want to go, probably she has you mixed up with wicked Aunt Diana who would melt us all down for soap if she could catch us, most likely. I bet she would, too.

We have another Baby, born Oct 18th, called Benjamin. He weighed 9lbs 3oz & I didn't have any anaesthetic, it was terrific. He is very sweet & looks like Nicholas Tito.

Are you going to Hollywood for the films? If so it is quite near here. I wish you would.

Tim [Bailey] is coming next wknd he'll be the first relation I've seen in about six years or more.

Goodbye Susan. Don't be weak-minded about Diana or I shall have to be off writers again for several years.

Love from Decca

P.S. Do you have a Fr. lover like the girl in *Pursuit of*? Do tell about him, if so.

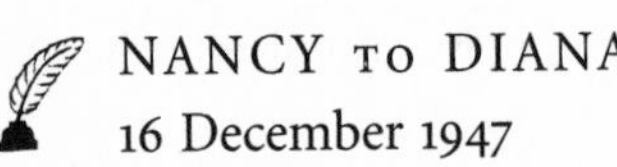

NANCY TO DIANA
16 December 1947

19 quai Malaquais, VI
after Friday 7 rue Monsieur, VII

Darling,

Oh *don't* be depressed count your blessings, you *must*, though of course without a hot bath it's more difficult I do see.[1] Also a depressing house is dreadful, this one, though so rich, so cosy, & so near the Col, is positively on my nerves – he can't understand why but it's inexplicable & true.

A letter from Decca saying that when the new baby was born Tito went about saying 'now I'm a father' – oh how funny. I think she hates me though at heart, we've become sort of bogy-men to her. What a bore – in a way, though really *less* boring than cheerful American goodwill towards all.

I don't suppose you remember how Johnny L.[2] talks exactly like Harold [Acton]. We went to a screamingly funny ballet called *Sylvia* (Delibes) & there is a statue which comes to life, so he said 'Heow could that ma*nn* have remained oall that w*h*ile – *motionless*?' He thought the ballet less funny I think than I did, I literally gasped with giggles – there is a seduction scene with a drunken caveman & Sylvia, all roses in a cavern which *must* be meant to be funny, he (the image of Hog Watson) leaps after her with a hatchet & she archly plies him from a goblet. Oh heavens. Not one soul laughed except me – it's even funnier than *Lakmé* & that's saying something. How awful it will be when the modern world finally does away with the genre opéra comique – happily it is packed every night so it won't be just yet awhile.

The Col's mother out of danger thank goodness. If I come over in Jan. shall you be at Crowood or up & down to London? When would be the best time to come? I suppose I could go to the mews for a few days. I just want to see you & Muv & Gerald & I suppose ought to go to Redesdale, he writes rather pathetically. Once I'm settled in my new house I can come any time.

V. best love, NR

1 Diana was staying in a rented house in Belgravia where there was no hot water.
2 Prince Jean-Louis de Faucigny-Lucinge (1904–92). Anglophile author of a volume of souvenirs, *Un Gentilhomme Cosmopolite* (1990).

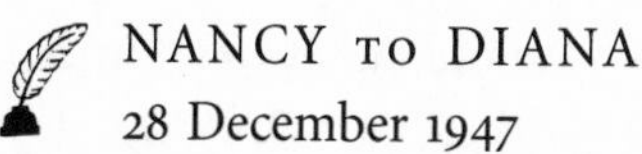

NANCY TO DIANA
28 December 1947

7 rue Monsieur, VII

Darling

Colonel was cinema'd yesterday for *March of Time*[1] so perhaps you'll see him one day. Noël C[oward] who is here said, 'Now you are a vedette [star] Gaston, always remember that whether an audience claps or boos it always makes the same noise. Terrifying.'

I was so glad to get your letter on Xmas Eve – I always think I don't care about Xmas & then the first chords of 'Stille Nacht' & I am in floods!! I went to Alvilde for the actual day. I'm getting up a tremendous hate against her, really I mustn't as she's my only English buddy here – she's very like Helen Dashwood, greedy & possessive, fond of one & yet never stops denigrating, hinting that the Col is treating me badly & so on. You know, perpetual pricks. Such a bore.

My book is getting on again which is a comfort,[2] it's having a more settled establishment of course.

Write soon, all love, NR

1 The American weekly newsreel series.
2 Nancy was finding *Love in a Cold Climate* more difficult to write than *The Pursuit of Love.*

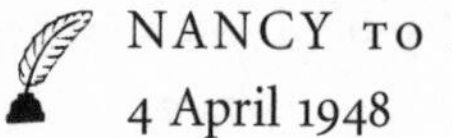

NANCY TO DIANA *7 rue Monsieur, VII*
4 April 1948

Darling,

Great to-do over the wedding of Marie's nephew. Marie (who is only 53 but looks 73) said she couldn't go as she had no New Look clothes. So I gave her a black dress which made new look on her, being tiny. Then she has six sisters all with vast families – darling, only one from each family could go because they could only afford one N.L. dress in each. Marie said 'Je vous assure Madame que la mode actuelle empêche les gens de sortir'.[1] Stuff is such a terrible price, when you think Marie earns 6,000 a month & even cotton is 1,200 a metre.

I heard the following blissful remark – one old count to another old count about a third: 'Mon cher, *très* à gauche, il est Orléaniste'![2] And the same ones about the Dsse de Vendôme whose death has plunged the Faubourg into widows' weeds, 'Well she must be in heaven *by now*' as if she had caught a tram. Oh how funny they are.

Dined with Sauguet[3] two nights ago but all was spoilt by a dreadful Reventlow[4] (Hutton husband) being there & S never got going properly.

V best love darling, NR

1 'Believe me, Madame, fashion today makes it impossible for people to go out.'

2 'My dear, *very* left-wing, he's an Orleanist.' Although there had not been a king of France for a hundred years, Parisian society still argued about who the rightful heir to the throne would be were there still a monarchy. The Orleanists supported the claim of the descendants of Louis-Philippe, who reigned as the last king of France, 1830–48.

3 Henri Sauguet (1901–89). Composer of the Diaghilev ballet *Les Forains* (1945) and a brilliant mimic.

4 Count Curt Haugwitz-Reventlow (1895–1969). Danish-born second husband of Woolworth heiress Barbara Hutton.

DIANA TO NANCY
2 May 1948

39 South Eaton Place
London SW1

Darling

Yesterday was May Day & Kit had a meeting in the E. End[1] it wasn't a great success because the police (Cossacks) kept everyone away friend & foe alike, they rode me & Alexander down several times, at last a man got us through. Then as they have banned marches in E. End we all went to the edge of the banned area to watch the march but of course missed the way & I found myself accompanied by three not very tough men (one of them was Nicky [Mosley]) and Alexander & several old women (Londoners who knew the way) and we always seemed to be almost *in* a terrifying procession of young & very strong looking Jews who were chanting 'Down with Mosley'. As Alexander had been very conspicuous at the meeting shouting 'Bravo' and saluting with an outstretched hand on which he wears a *ring* (so unlikely for him somehow) I kept fearing we might be recognized & overwhelmed. However all ended well, outside Holloway prison, and a good time was had by all except me. I believe we must have walked at least six miles. It was just like Scotland as we were soaked to the skin & then walked so long that we got bone dry again.

Muv is back,[2] I rushed round. She was suffering rather from Birdie who had spent a guinea on some dead roses for her & then was taking it out of her like mad by saying she had a temp of 103, awfully tiring for Muv after her long flight. She gives a good account of Decca & says Mr T is a good husband & father and not such a rabid red as Decca is! Mustn't he be surprised when he thinks over his fate.

All love darling, D

1 Mosley's new party, the Union Movement, held its first meeting in London's East End, an area where Mosley had found support before the war.

2 Lady Redesdale had been to San Francisco to visit Jessica, the first time they had seen each other for nine years.

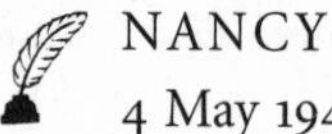

NANCY TO DIANA *7 rue Monsieur, VII*
4 May 1948

Darling,

Thank goodness Muv is back – I was so worried by all that sickness as it sounded so like her heart not standing up to the journey. Then of course one knows communists can never pull any strings & whereas any of us would have got her onto the *Queen E.* they clearly never could. However all is well & she seems to have enjoyed it enormously.

Now darling are you going to the Island at all? Because I must go away for a month, Marie's hols, & think I had better kill two birds or even three, seeing Muv & finishing my book in peace. If you were going to be there it would be absolute heaven of course. Otherwise perhaps I could go to dull old [Crowood] on the way. I thought last fortnight July & first in Aug. It's nice for my Col when I'm here in August as nobody else is. My Colonial life very much complicated by the return, apparently for good, of Peter whom the Col refuses to see. A *great* worry because coming here is a little rest for him & it's not at all the same when I go to his flat, full of secretaries & callers. I'm beginning really to wish I could marry the Col, for the first time, but I suppose it always comes to that. But for a hundred reasons it isn't possible so no use thinking of it.

Harold's book.[1] Of course I shrieked the whole way through – wasn't it lovely having the *whiff* – but I find everybody else including I hear Emerald thinks it dull. How can they? Of course he doesn't know English really & it reads like a translation but that makes it, anyhow if you know Harold, so extra funny & nice.

Tell me when you move to Chapel St as I've got a little present for you for Peter to take when he goes over.

All love darling, NR

1 Harold Acton, *Memoirs of an Aesthete.*

NANCY TO DIANA
23 June 1948

7 rue Monsieur, VII

Darling,

The Colonel (whose speeches are given more & more space every day in the press here) says that he & Debo are the two Mitfords who are doing best at the moment!

Oh my life with Prod – he is so vague – invites people & forgets all about it, fills the house with terrible drinkers who spend their time telephoning & going to my loo. You know. The trouble is I have become old maidish. However I'm rubbing well in the horrors of married life to the Col so it's not all in vain. I tell all about the broken glasses & so on & he trembles for his china. Daisy asked him on Sunday too but he has a meeting, how sad. He says it's always heaven there.

Do tell what Cairns said, I'm so anxious to hear.[1]

Great interruptions. I'll write again soon.

V. best love, NR

1 After Unity's death on 28 May, Lady Redesdale had consulted Hugh Cairns (1896–1952), the professor of neurosurgery who had attended her after her suicide attempt, to find out more about the causes of her last illness.

NANCY TO DIANA
7 July 1948

7 rue Monsieur, VII

Darling,

After Monday I shall be at Château de Saint Firmin, Chantilly, Oise. Better put aux bons soins[1] of the Coopers[2] as I'm not certain if that's *quite* correct but c/o them will find it.

A letter from Wid *complaining* that you are utterly unchanged & unbowed by misfortune. How she hates happiness – & doesn't mind saying so what's more.

The horror of the weather – I've got a ravishing grey spotted cotton dress & haven't worn it once – & I feel that next year it will be utterly out of fashion.

Oh yes the Wid. Went to see Gerald [Berners] '& we had a long talk about breakdowns, Sanatogen[3] & the like'. Jolly it sounds. I'm very doubtful about Prod's pills[4] tell Gerald. Diana C who knows quite a lot about nursing says it's such a tiny dose it wouldn't kill a mouse – furthermore that morphia is a tricky way of doing it as people are so often sick – & also it goes off as in the case of poor old Laval.[5] I'm sure the only thing is strychnine. But I don't see what there is to worry about in England – the Russians can't get over the water surely, if even the Germans couldn't & they had a navy. Reading Mme de Dino in 1848 – she says 'what between war in the East & communism in the West we are crushed between two colossi – all one can hope for is to die in one's bed et encore cela paraît beaucoup éxiger'.[6] She also says there isn't a corner of the world where one could hide & be safe – rather comforting you must say.

I've laid in ten tons of wood at a cost of £50, I simply dread this winter remembering what the last one was like after a cold summer.

Went to Versailles for the Grandes Eaux, it is a fairy story – I'd no idea it was so wonderful. The terrific crowds seem to make it even prettier somehow. Ran into Margaret [Wright] there (!) who said 'Oh I *would* like to have been somebody's mistress in those days' which I thought disingenuous. She has had a wow of a time. Farve rings up, I gather, & writes every day. I can't help thinking it is wonderful the old boy is fixed up with somebody he really likes but then I am always pour [for] love, & one can't say there was ever much of that from Muv who really didn't even like him particularly – not that I blame her.

A David exhibition.[7] I see him to have been a really *terrible* painter – isn't it funny how one sees so much better the moment they are all together. But the details – furniture, clothes & so on very amusing.

All love darling, do write, NR

Where is Muv? Not one word since I got back, but I suppose she is still engulfed in Bobo letters.

1 'Care of.'

2 Duff and Diana Cooper had returned to France to live in the house they had rented for weekends while he was ambassador.

3 A vitamin and mineral supplement.
4 Following the Soviet blockade of Berlin, anti-communist hysteria and fear of a Russian invasion was at a height. Some people were contemplating suicide rather than risk falling into Russian hands.
5 Pierre Laval, the Vichy politician, tried unsuccessfully to commit suicide on the morning of his execution by firing squad.
6 'And even that seems a lot to ask for.'
7 An exhibition of the paintings of Jacques-Louis David (1748–1825) was showing at the Musée de l'Orangerie.

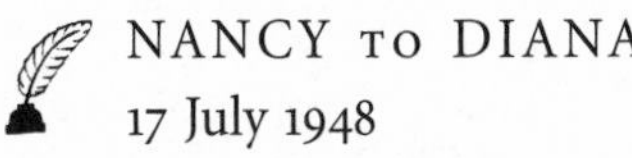

NANCY TO DIANA
17 July 1948

Château de St Firmin
Vineuil, Oise (Coopers)

Oh darling your boat invitation[1] – I do die for it but now I *must* finish the book. I think another break would be fatal, you see each time I leave off I terribly lose interest & now it is swimming along – seven hours a day. Diana is wonderful, just like Gerald used to be, & shoos me back. She said once what is your favourite colour & of course I said pink & she has had a little room in an out house done up pink for me to work in. You must say.

Also I don't want to go too far from Paris. I'm in a great fuss about the Colonel – he had a sort of attack very like Gerald, fainted & was sick, & for two days he stayed in bed very weak & I took him all his meals – on the third day he got up, had a fourteen-hour day journey to Tarbes to address a meeting where they half killed the chairman & he only escaped by a miracle. Now he is speaking every day in a different place, returns to Paris on Sunday.

Oh politics, do I *loathe* them!

Although I hardly see him he likes the idea of me being in or near Paris & complains bitterly if I go away.

I've got masses to tell only the book stops letter writing – but I must 'take' Mrs Kliot, Decca's mother-in-law.[2] Well she arrived the day I was to leave for here so very nobly I put off coming & spent all day with her, luncheon & dinner, went round the hat shops, changed her dollars, I don't know what else – rather wonderful of me? She *is* Madame Rita,[3] the image, & she never stopped groaning about Decca. 'Why can't she dress like you – why is she such a slattern – what will happen to the children – she & Bob are *sure* to go to gaol.

My Bob never thought of being a communist till he met her, & then he was doing so well, but now he only works for coloured people who can't pay. You never go there but they've got coloured people as house guests' & so on. I saw her point *vividly.* She said when she first saw Decca she cried for a week – so dirty. She had had a letter from them, saying 'Tito will be known as Nicholas until the situation is clarified'!! So I wrote to Decca & said 'I hear Tito has changed his name by *deed of poll* to Dimitrov'.[4]

Oh yes 'My Bob used to be so smart he was called the Duke – I wish you could see him now – terrible'.

Mrs Kliot is going to Hungary & Prague so perhaps she'll meet Jonathan.[5] She said 'I hope you never see the Mosleys', I said of course I do I *live* for them. This threw a froid [damper].

I've been reading the letters of Madame[6] – almost more fascinating than St Simon. I see Versailles was an absolute Eton as far as Sodomy goes. She says after forty years in France she can't get used to the horror of French food.

I must go back to Polly.[7] *Do do* write – perhaps to rue Monsieur in case I leave here next week.

All love darling, NR

1 Since the Mosleys' passports had been confiscated when they were imprisoned and the authorities had refused to issue new ones after the war, they were planning a trip to the Channel Islands where passports were not required.
2 Aranka Hajos (d.1975). Robert Treuhaft's mother was married first to Albib Treuhaft and to Albert Kliot in 1944. She owned a hat shop in New York and went to Paris regularly for the fashion shows.
3 A milliner in Berkeley Square.
4 Marshal Tito had fallen out with Stalin but the Bulgarian premier, Georgi Dimitrov, was still in favour.
5 Jonathan Guinness had been planning to travel to Czechoslovakia.
6 The correspondence of Louis XIV's sister-in-law, Elizabeth, Princess Palatine (1652–1722), was first published in the nineteenth century.
7 The heroine of *Love in a Cold Climate.*

DIANA TO NANCY
21 July 1948

21 Chapel Street
London SW1

Darling:

Of *course* I understand about the book, I am so glad it is swimming along, the bliss of it. The boat would be horrid, I only hoped to lure you out of selfishness.

We screamed with laughter about the Treuhafts, Kit says after all the talk & trouble only *ONE* Mitford has ever done any harm to a Jud [Jew] – Decca. I adore where he was known as the Duke, won't Debo be interested.

Did you see the article in *Time* about Evelyn, it says you can see his progress as a social climber by the dedications in his books, starting with Evelyn G[ardner] and ending in the topmost pinnacle – you![1]

I said to Alexander 'Is there anything Mr Watson[2] would like for a present?' So he said 'Yes & I know what it is because I once asked him what he would wish for if he got a wish & he replied "For a clear mind"'. I asked him myself after that & we have got him a hearth rug.

All love darling, I will write on the boat, D

1 Evelyn Waugh's novel *The Loved One* (1948) was dedicated to Nancy.
2 The Mosley boys' tutor.

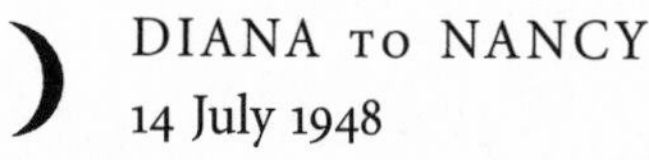

DIANA TO NANCY
14 July 1948

21 Chapel Street, SW1

Darling:

Just a line to say that Debo popped in yesterday and (this is between ourselves) it seems that Muv has got an idea that you think she oughtn't ever to have taken Boud far away from Prof Cairns – of course I *knew* this had never crossed your mind but if you could write and put something comforting about how wonderful it was that Birdie was able to go about here & there, and not be a hospital case all those years – or you will think of something much cleverer than that, but do write her a line. She was such a saint to Bobo, I can't imagine how she could have *any remorse*, but the fact is almost all deaths bring remorse, isn't it odd.

All love darling. D

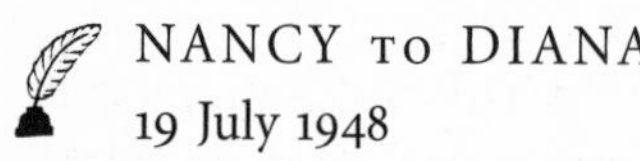

NANCY TO DIANA
19 July 1948

Château de St Firmin
Vineuil

Darling,

I am dreadfully teased by what you say & don't quite know what to do. Not only *never* did such an idea cross my mind, but I couldn't *imagine that anybody* could think such a thing. I vaguely remember that under the stress of great emotion & after that dreadful journey (I was really *ill* with it you know) I said 'Oh but didn't you send for Cairns' which I see now was very tactless – but like that & no more than that, & said 'Oh of course, naturally' when Muv explained why not. Do you think she's brooding over that, poor Muv? I can't bear her to think I feel that anything different should have been done. I will ponder over it all & write what I think best.

I always thought except for you & the Col I shouldn't *mind* anybody but you see one never can tell. I am terribly sad about Bobo.

V. best love darling, NR

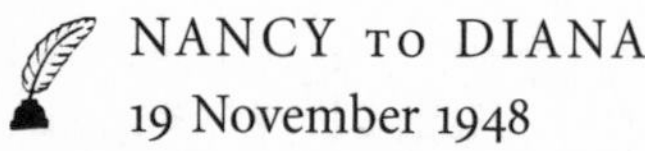

NANCY TO DIANA
19 November 1948

7 rue Monsieur, VII

Darling,

I've just acquired a mammoth Bécuve to heat my drawing room. As Peter plans to spend the winter here & we can't both huddle in my bedroom I have to make an effort – I guess it will cost £100 in wood. Oh *dear* – & at Noël's first night my pocket book was stolen *out* of my bag! And I'm so poor anyway, it was a blow. I feel very low about Prod, I can see he never intends to do another stroke of work as long as he lives, & in the winter it is twenty times more difficult somehow to see the Col in his flat, the cold makes everything such an effort doesn't it. However he – Prod – has got me in a cleft stick with no possible means of escape. Marriage, the horror of it!

I've just been to the Musée Rodin – what a lot of English people he sculpted, I'd no idea. What a wonderful artist & how sad he lived then really, he can't quite avoid awful bad taste can he?

All love darling – write write, NR

My back aches terribly again do you think it is Farve's complaint[1] or ovaries?

1 Lord Redesdale broke his pelvis after falling from a horse.

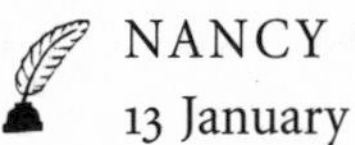

NANCY TO DIANA
13 January 1949

7 rue Monsieur, VII

Darling,

I am haunted by the idea of you leaving Crowood – where will you go?[1] I had an awful dream about you packing last night – everything lost – one of those nightmares! You know they say here 'Trois déménagements = un incendie'.[2] And Mr Watson? Oh the horror of husbands!!!

Here we are all greatly dashed by the sudden death of Peter Derwent. He just lay down for a little rest after luncheon & never woke up again – a happy death for him. But for Carmen [Gandarillas] I feel it is the end – she was so so happy, had her wedding dress & they were to be married 6 Feb – did you ever hear such a tragedy?

Now a letter from Evelyn speaking of my 'horrible sins'. Altogether I am quite low this morning only consoled by *Clèves*[3] which I am very much enjoying. Of course it is twice as easy as Balzac – you were so brave to tackle that.

What have you done about titles? One must say King & Queen. One can say Duke of X but one can't say Miss of Chartres. I can't decide. You must have come up against it in the *Duchesse*.

Oh the death of Peter has *shaken* me, to think people can walk out of the world like that. I suppose it's because we are older, but how people do seem to die nowadays.

Now St François has begun its funeral bell, the last straw, I must get up.

Love darling, NR

1 The Mosleys did not sell Crowood until 1951 but Mosley was restless and often talked about moving house.
2 'Three moves = one fire.'
3 Nancy was translating Mme de La Fayette, *La Princesse de Clèves* (1678) for Euphorion Books, a publishing company set up by the Mosleys after the war, initially to publish Oswald Mosley's *My Answer* (1946). Diana's translations of Balzac's *La Duchesse de Langeais* and *Le Curé de Tours* were published by Euphorion in 1950.

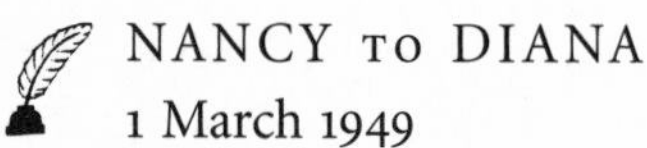

NANCY TO DIANA *7 rue Monsieur, VII*
1 March 1949

Darling,

Peter & Ad[1] have arrived from a huge motor TOR of Italy & Sicily. Ad has now gone home & Peter will take me to Dieppe on the 10th which makes the journey ever so much cheaper.

Then Debo appeared with a sister-in-law (the thin fascinator)[2] & a bald young man, making no sense at all & such clothes darling, so awful one couldn't think how anybody could *have* such things in the cupboard even. Oh dear I do wish she were a little tidier I must say because then she would be perfection – I do so feel it's a duty for people like her to be a little bit elegant. Never mind it was heaven to see her, & perhaps if she were different in that respect she would become pompous which would be far worse.

Oh dear, a note from Edward in six different coloured chalks saying that since I wore a black beard everybody thinks I'm his sister. Alas I did look exactly like him.[3] So now I must ask him to something – *and* Audrey [Pleydell-Bouverie] is here *and* Helen [Dashwood], Tony[4] just arrived. Rather a struggle as they all expect such hours of time & then there's Ed Stanley's daughter said to be *very* shy & *very* critical, what to do with her?

Much love darling, NR

1 Adelaide Lubbock, Peter Rodd's current girlfriend.
2 Anne Cavendish.
3 'I went to the ball in black tights & a black beard hoping to have a success with the chaps. But they thought I was Edward James & *fled*.' *The Letters of Nancy Mitford and Evelyn Waugh*, p. 119.
4 Antonio de Gandarillas (1886–1970). Opium-smoking, gossip-loving Chilean diplomat.

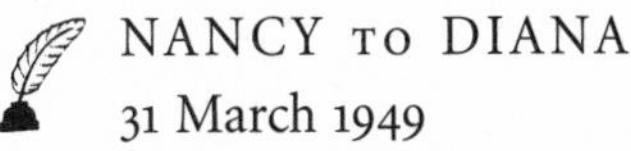

NANCY TO DIANA *7 rue Monsieur, VII*
31 March 1949

Darling,

Fog in Kent, foghorns *all* the way over the Channel, fog in the Pas de Calais – blazing sunshine here & the chestnuts out. Now you've had it!

Oh the bliss of seeing the Col again. I said on the telephone 'I've had a wonderful time, I've got a present for you'. 'I don't quite follow your argument.'

Darling I can never thank you enough for being so wondairfool & having me so long, an *imposition* really. I enjoyed myself terrifically, felt less tired than I generally do, hardly at all in fact & it was heaven being with you. If we could live in the same town my happiness would be complete.

My camellia is out, Marie has done terrific cleaning & the flat is a dream – also the lawyer says he has good news for me & I'm to hear it tomorrow. I feel almost too much on top of the world – how nice it is to be happy in middle age after a wretched youth instead of the other way round.

Oh I *do* adore my scented bath flannel. I'm having a day in bed, bliss. Do be careful won't you & *not* do too much. Sometimes you look tired, but less than last time I was there I thought but you go to bed late & really ought to rest more in the day – now *please* take these words to heart.

I got all my stuff over without trouble & thankful I did because all that in the papers about rations here being off is *pure lies* & it was very bien reçu [well received] by Marie specially the oil.

Millions more thanks for everything – love, NR

Darling the key oh what can I say, *worse* than Jonathan. And I don't like to post it. I see too that I left my beast of an umbrella, but I have one here so if you could bear to keep it in some rubbish room or other that would be perfect. Oh I have been *awful* – only just seen the key.

DIANA TO NANCY *21 Chapel Street, SW1*
4 April 1949

Darling:

Just got your letter, the KEY doesn't matter a bit, I have got dozens & am always having more made (don't tell Kit). I will keep your umbrella and thought I might get Heywood to pack up your slippers with Weizmann?[1] I have read every word, it is engrossing, and now I wish I were a Jew, well not *now* perhaps, I should hate a settlement but it must have been wonderful to be Chaim. His chief hates are Venetia's husband and B. Baruch,[2] & do note the 'old English gentleman', some Montefiore who spoke o but German.

Yesterday our Captain came, it made the voyage seem so lovely & near.[3] He told such tales of calm (being rocked by swell until the crew go off their heads) that I now rather hope for *storms.*

All love darling, D

1 Chaim Weizmann, *Trial and Error*; the autobiography of the first President of Israel was published in 1949.
2 Edwin Montagu, Venetia Stanley's husband, and Bernard Baruch were both anti-Zionist Jews, opposed to the establishment of a Jewish state.
3 Mosley had discovered that although no ship or aeroplane would take him without a passport, he could not be stopped from entering or leaving England at will. He had bought a boat and was planning to sail to Spain and Portugal, where he had been given permission to land.

DIANA TO NANCY
27 May 1949

707 Hood House
Dolphin Square
London SW1

Darling

No, not gone yet, but *wonderful* news – PASSPORTS. Kit discovered that you get turned out of the United Nations or something unless you allow your citizens the four freedoms or whatever it is called & one of them is that people shld be allowed to leave & return to their country at will – of course you *can* if you can spend thousands on a yacht but I don't suppose that was meant. Anyway Bob [Boothby] teased with the freedoms and now they have given in at long last & at the last moment. Isn't it bliss; I couldn't help dreading all the difficulties we might have had everywhere. Oh darling I can't wait to get there. We are off I hope on Whit Monday, we had to put it off a few days as Max has had his adenoids out, he got terribly deaf again so the specialist rushed him to Gt Ormond St & did it. He seems better already.

Muv & Debo are in London which is lovely.

We met (at Daisy's) the editors of *Woman's Home Journal* or whatever it is & I said I couldn't *believe* they hadn't serialized your new book[1] as it was such heaven. So Mr Gould,[2] who is a terrific prig, said the subject was rather *unsavoury*, something about a fairy, so I said 'unsavoury, why in Europe we love them & always choose them out for friends'. He said what were you like & I lost my head & said 'Oh she's wonderful, just like me'. Then he said wouldn't Cedric have a very limited appeal here so I teased by saying well it is Book Society Book of the Month AND *D. Mail*. He was shaken I could see. I wish I could think I had done some good. He said all those little kiddies in the first book, why they were just *delightful*.

All love darling, D

1 *Love in a Cold Climate*, in which Nancy introduced Cedric Hampton, a composite portrait of her homosexual friends.

2 Bruce Gould (1898–1989). Editor of *Ladies' Home Journal*, 1935–60.

DIANA TO DEBORAH
26 July 1949

Alianora
Cannes

Darling Debo

We do long for you more than words can express.

Daisy is here on her boat which is a sort of floating Donnington[1] for glamour. Nancy is with us, and we expect Jonathan who is in trouble with the army for parading in his (I am sure *filthy*) pyjamas, & for some reason has got ten days leave! Cannes is as beastly as ever & I want to move as soon as possible to Antibes or Monte Carlo, but we must stay a moment because of various business.

Darling, Spain was such fun, I long to go with you to Madrid. It is solid with dukes and they all ask one to boar hunts. The boys went to a bullfight & saw a matador tossed, Max said, 'we enquired after him next day, but' (very disappointed voice) 'he was quite well again.'

All love darling, *DO* come (both if poss), Honks

1 Daisy Fellowes' house, Donnington Grove, Berkshire, was famous for its luxurious comfort.

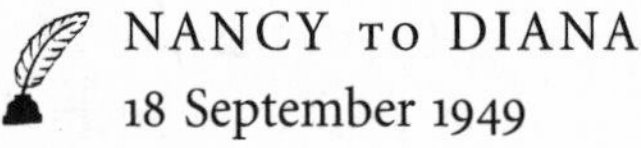

NANCY TO DIANA
18 September 1949

7 rue Monsieur, VII

Darling,

What day do I expect you? I *utterly utterly* die for it & only hope you won't be too uncomf. We shan't be able to have all meals here because by *great* bad luck I am without a charwoman for the time being for reasons which I will explain (or won't, being not Woman) but you'll probably want to go out a bit.

Can you believe it, *Les Oeufs de l'autruche*[1] is on again, I am so thrilled for you to see it.

I'm doggo, not answering telephone & working ten hours a day[2] – all day in fact. Saw the Wid approaching yesterday & hid in a cupboard but it was no use she soon had me out. She insisted on taking my only pair of country shoes & then said 'Child they give a very curious sensation – I feel as if I were walking *backwards*'. She'll be here when you are & is full of plans & projects. She said it would be better for me to give up all thought of work until you've gone, I said 'yes but the point is I must *finish* before they *come*' – which I must, my preface. I shan't begin the other[3] until you're gone – if at all. I'm flinching from it rather, but egged on by Col.

Much love, love to Kit & Debo. NR

Saw Gerald who read me your letter. He is quite well I think but furious if one says so!

1 A comedy by André Roussin first performed in 1948.
2 Nancy was writing the preface to her translation of *La Princesse de Clèves.*
3 Nancy had undertaken to produce a film treatment around the idea of a boy who does his best to keep his divorced parents apart. Her script was refused but she developed the story into a novel, *The Blessing*, which was subsequently bought by MGM and made into a film.

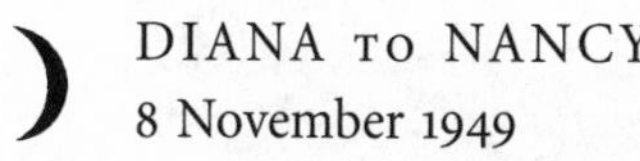

DIANA TO NANCY
8 November 1949

707 Hood House
Dolphin Square, SW1

Darling

I had such a fright about Gerald, I couldn't go over because the motor was away being mended, and on Sunday I telephoned & Robert [Heber-Percy]'s mother evidently thought him very bad, and then on Monday morning Robert rang up and said do come over, so we rushed there on our way to London. When I saw him I thought him no worse and perhaps a shade more cheerful. He adored your letter about Sir S. Cripps's walk from the Gare du Nord,[1] and at that, & one or two things, he said I screamed with laughter and Kit, who was in the drawing room with Mrs Heber Percy, said he heard nought but peacock shrieks & I believe he thought I got him over there just because I wanted a good laugh (I was in floods on the way over because of Gerald being worse).

It is so hard for some people to understand that laughter doesn't always mean cheerfulness – just something funny. The odd thing is that the doctors say there is nothing much the matter with him now, but he lies like a log with two nurses and all the paraphernalia of terrific illness and I believe he dreads getting better for fear of his depression coming back (he is not awfully depressed now). We talk of him coming to Crowood and he says he *longs* to, but you know he won't even open his eyes![2]

All love darling, D

1 Nancy wrote that Sir Stafford Cripps, the Chancellor of the Exchequer, renowned for his harsh economic policies, had told the embassy staff not to meet him when he arrived in Paris. 'They all thought that he must be doing it for austerity but it was really because he needs a good walk every day, so he & his wretched secretary arrived on foot from the Gare du Nord (*miles* as you know).' (Nancy to Gerald Berners, 30 October 1949)

2 After months of illness, Gerald Berners died on 19 April 1950, mourned by Nancy and Diana, who wrote, 'I loved him better than anyone outside the family. I am so sad, but for myself and not for him.' (Diana to Lady Redesdale, 21 April 1950)

A photograph of Lord Berners taken by Diana in the Munich Botanical Garden, 1933.

FIVE

1950—1959

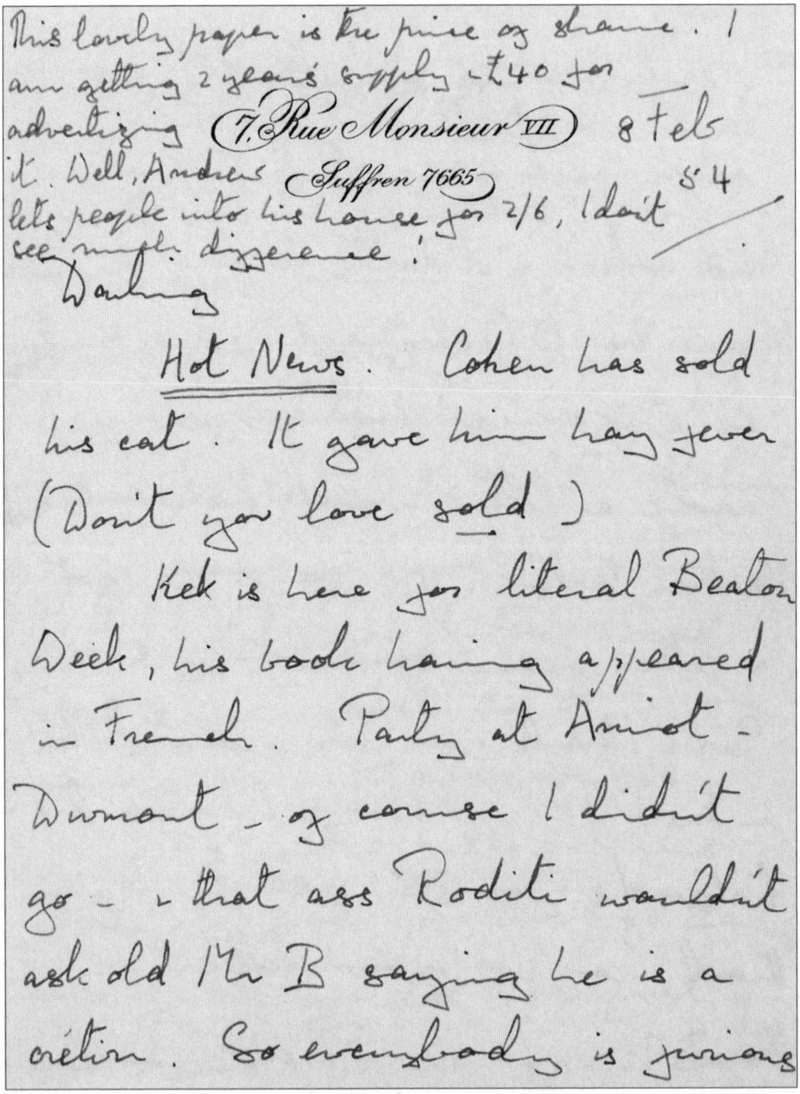

This lovely paper is the prize of shame. I am getting 2 years' supply - £40 for advertising it. Well, Andrews lets people into his house for 2/6, I don't see much difference!

7, Rue Monsieur VII

Suffren 7665

8 Feb 54

Darling

Hot News. Cohen has sold his cat. It gave him hay fever (Don't you love sold)

Kek is here for literal Beaton Week, his book having appeared in French. Party at Amiot-Dumont - of course I didn't go - & that ass Roditi wouldn't ask old Mr B saying he is a crétin. So everybody is furious

Letter from Nancy to Diana.

Nancy's love of Paris never waned and her wild Francophilia, which extended even to the weather, was a running joke among the sisters. She was as much in love with Gaston Palewski as ever and suffered as much as ever from not being loved in return. In 1958, Peter Rodd finally agreed to give her a divorce but it brought her no closer to marriage with the Colonel. He was a busy man: elected a Deputy in 1951, he was sent as ambassador to Rome in 1957 where he stayed until 1962. He was also deeply involved with Violette de Pourtalès, a married woman, whose flat was inconveniently close to Nancy's and who eventually became his wife. Nancy often preferred to stay at home in the evenings rather than run the risk of seeing him with another woman. While her emotional life may have been unfulfilling, the success of her career helped to make up for the Colonel's absences. The 1950s was a golden decade for her writing: two novels, *Love in a Cold Climate* and *The Blessing*, became international bestsellers; the *Sunday Times* commissioned her to write a regular column about Paris, which led to many more offers of journalism; and *The Little Hut*, her adaptation of a French comedy, was a box-office sell-out in London and brought in generous royalties. When she found she no longer had the inspiration to write novels, she embarked on *Madame de Pompadour* and *Voltaire in Love*, meticulously researched biographies written in the easy, conversational style of her novels. She also perpetrated her most successful tease ever with an article on the English aristocracy in which U and non-U – for upper and non-upper class – was introduced into the English language.

Success brought Nancy a financial security and confidence that helped to ease the lingering jealousy she felt towards her sisters and towards Diana in particular. In 1951, this was put to the test when the Mosleys bought a property on the outskirts of Paris and settled there for much of the year. In spite of Nancy's dislike of Mosley – a feeling that was reciprocated – the sisters enjoyed each other's company too much not to see each other often. Nancy did her best to keep Palewski away from the Mosleys – although they became friends after her death – and in spite of Diana being the sister Nancy came closest to confiding in, she never admitted the extent of her unhappiness over her one-sided relationship with the Colonel. Because she and Diana saw each other so often and spoke on the telephone most mornings, they now exchanged far fewer letters. By the mid-1950s, Deborah had replaced Diana as Nancy's favourite correspondent.

In 1951, after fourteen years of marriage, Pamela and Derek were divorced. Their move to Ireland had not been a success; after a while Derek had become bored with a life that revolved around horses and dogs, and he missed his scientific work. He had also fallen in love with another woman, Janetta Kee, née Woolley, whom he married as the third of his six wives soon after his divorce from Pamela. Until 1960, Pamela stayed on at Tullamaine, sharing her life with Giuditta Tommasi, an expert with horses who worked at a riding school near Dublin. Of Pamela's relationship with Giuditta, Diana told a friend, 'I don't know if they were lovers but it really was a kind of marriage.' Jessica was more forthright and wrote to her husband in 1955 that her sister had become 'a you-know-what-bian'. Pamela made frequent trips to the Continent to visit her close friend Rudi von Simolin in Bavaria, stopping off on the way to see Diana and Nancy.

The Mosleys' move from Crowood in 1951 was sad for Diana and a terrible wrench for her sons Alexander and Max, aged twelve and ten, for whom it was their first settled home. They bought a seventeenth-century bishop's palace in Clonfert, Ireland, and the Temple de la Gloire, a Directoire folly in Orsay, fifteen miles outside Paris, which had been built for Napoleon's General Moreau. The move was prompted by Mosley's realization that social and official hostility in Britain would not dissipate in a hurry and that life would be more congenial abroad. For the next nine years, the Mosleys would divide their time between Clonfert, the Temple de la Gloire, a flat in Paris and a flat in London. Alexander and Max met their parents for holidays in France or Venice but stayed in Ireland with a tutor until they were sent to boarding school in 1954. For Mosley, the early 1950s was a period of reflection. In 1953 he started a monthly magazine, *The European*, which was principally a vehicle for his political ideas. Diana edited the magazine during the six years of its existence, contributing regular book reviews and a diary, which gave her a platform from which to take swipes at her bêtes noires: the British Establishment, democracy, left-wing politicians, America, schools, churchmen and the other villains in her canon. Mosley returned to active politics in the general election of 1959 when he unsuccessfully contested the London borough of North Kensington, campaigning against Commonwealth immigration.

Jessica devoted most of the 1950s to working for the CRC and the Communist Party, fighting for civil rights and championing victims of social injustice. In 1951, she travelled to Mississippi to help organize a campaign to save Willie McGee, a black truck driver who had been condemned to death for raping a white woman. As a result of their involvement in the case, the Treuhafts were subpoenaed by the House Committee on Un-American Activities and Robert was branded by Joseph McCarthy one of the most subversive lawyers in the country. In 1958, after fourteen years of membership, Jessica left the Communist Party. Unlike many comrades who resigned after the Soviet invasion of Hungary and the disclosure of Stalin's crimes, Jessica's decision to leave the party was based on her frustration with an organization that had failed to develop a form of communism adapted to the realities of American life and which had become 'drab and useless'. As blind to the inhumanity of Soviet rule as Unity and Diana had been to the cruelty of the Nazi regime, Jessica considered herself a communist until the end of her life, convinced that it was the 'decent and logical solution to political life' and that its demise in Russia was a misfortune.

In 1955, aged ten, the Treuhafts' eldest son, Nicholas, was knocked off his bicycle while doing a paper round and was killed instantly. The cable that Jessica sent to her mother giving her the news has survived, but there are no family letters of condolence after the boy's death – the fifth tragedy to scar Jessica's life after the loss of her baby daughter, Julia, and the deaths of Esmond, Tom and Unity. Nicholas's death is not mentioned in her memoirs and was never referred to in letters to her sisters.

Later that year, after difficulties in obtaining passports that mirrored the Mosleys' experiences in England, Jessica and her family made their first visit to Europe. Except for Deborah, who visited the Treuhafts in 1952, it was the first time that Jessica had seen any of her sisters for sixteen years and the reunion brought out all the ambivalence between them. She took her family to Inch Kenneth to see Lady Redesdale, stayed several days with Deborah at Edensor, saw Pamela in London and spent a week in Paris with Nancy. In her memoirs she wrote of these visits, 'I had longed to see them yet found myself constrained in their company, awkwardly separated by the twin gulfs of time and outlook. They were wonderful hosts and I was not a good guest.' When Diana heard that Jessica was coming to Europe, she wrote to her mother, 'I'm afraid she won't see me though; of course I should *adore* to see her'. The two sisters did not meet. Jessica wrote in her memoirs that she 'could not have borne to see Diana again'. Nor did she visit her father. She told her mother that she would be prepared to see him if he undertook not to roar at her family; Lady Redesdale replied that since she had imposed conditions it would be better for them not to meet.

Lord Redesdale died in 1958, without being reconciled with Jessica. His death is hardly mentioned in the sisters' letters, perhaps because 'the odd, violent, attractive man' who had played such a central part in their childhood had disappeared long ago leaving, in his own words, 'someone putrefying and going quite grey, very violent but quite harmless'. Deborah and Diana had been with him on his eightieth birthday, a few days before he died, and all his daughters except Jessica attended his funeral at Swinbrook. Lord Redesdale cut Jessica out of his will because of her attempt to leave her share of Inch Kenneth to the Communist Party. His gesture did not surprise Jessica but Nancy felt that she had been unfairly treated and made over her share of the island to her younger sister. In the 1950s, at a time when the Treuhafts' finances were shaky, Lady Redesdale and all the sisters – including Diana – contributed to a small annual allowance to help Jessica and her family. In 1959, Jessica came into a Romilly inheritance, and with it she offered to buy out her sisters' share of Inch Kenneth and let Lady Redesdale, who could no longer afford to keep the island, stay on rent-free for her lifetime.

In 1950, Andrew's father, the 10th Duke of Devonshire, died of a heart attack aged fifty-five, leaving the family with death duties amounting to eighty per cent of his estate. Negotiations with the Inland Revenue dragged on for seventeen years and the final payment was not made until 1974, twenty-four years after the duke's death. In order to raise money to pay off the debt, Andrew sold thousands of acres in Scotland and Derbyshire, as well as important works of art, including paintings by Rembrandt, Holbein, Memling, Claude and Rubens. Hardwick Hall, which had been in the family for fifteen generations, went to the National Trust in lieu of duty. In 1955, it became clear that the best way of preserving Chatsworth for future generations would be for the family to move back into the house and develop it as a business. Inspired by her mother's example, Deborah decided to do the decoration herself, a massive undertaking in a house with some 175 rooms, 24 bathrooms, 21 kitchens, 3,426 feet of passages, 400 windows and 17 staircases. Nancy, who was one of Deborah's first guests, for once praised her youngest sister unreservedly, writing to Diana, 'I think she has been *géniale* with the house & nobody else could have done it as well'.

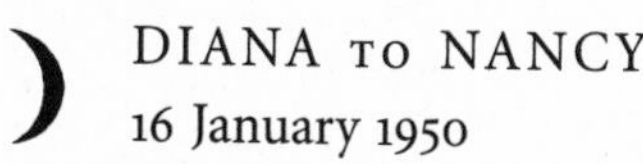

DIANA TO NANCY
16 January 1950

707 Hood House
Dolphin Square, SW1

Darling

Alexander has been so extraordinary lately, this was the conversation between him & Max.

A. You know Mohammedans don't have to be baptized, you just say the creed and then you *are* a Mohammedan.

M. Oh *do* say it.

A. I believe in Allah & Mahomet his prophet.

M. Well then, now you're a Mohammedan!

A. Oh no. You have to hold the index finger to the brow as you say it.

Then as we climbed the dentist's stairs where there were several astonished patients he went on in his loud voice, 'You can have no idea of the sensations of ease, refreshment and elation as you leave the hammam. That is the Turkish bath you know Max'.

And yesterday Kit had a sex talk with him because his songs and rhymes are so awful, beyond a joke, & K thought he would try to show him how beautiful love could be and then told him if later on he terribly wanted to it cd probably be arranged whereupon he said 'I can't stand harlots' and later on I saw him in his bath and he said in dramatic tones 'I have been having a talk with Daddy, it is not suitable for your ears though Mummy, I never guessed the *dark reality* before, and I must say I am shocked, because I am a bit of a prude you know.' Considering he has nearly driven Nanny & co out of the house with his disgusting rhymes not bad?

I won't bother you with the page proofs,[1] Muv and I will read them as you say. I am so longing for the book to be ready, of course they are being dreadfully slow.

The *Duchesse [de Langeais]* is now held up for binding, we didn't bind many to begin with.

All love darling, D

1 Of Nancy's translation of *La Princesse de Clèves.*

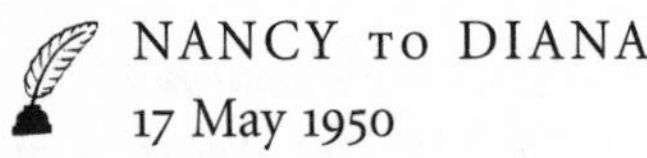

NANCY TO DIANA *7 rue Monsieur, VII*
17 May 1950

Darling,

Oh dear I've just had a morning with my dressmaker – an evening dress now can't be made even by her under a tout dernier prix de £50.[1] Isn't it dreadful, it seems such a lot of money. And that includes using an old one as foundation. She says 30–40 yards is the minimum if it's not to look skimpy & I know she's right. The dresses have never been so vast & elaborate. So I don't know what to do & meanwhile have to refuse all dinners as I've o to wear – I do think it's the *limit*! Still, better concentrate on the day [dresses] which is really far more important.

Evelyn [Waugh]'s visit was terrible & wonderful & wore me out. I took him to see Marie Laure[2] & he said afterwards 'while I was looking at that lady's pictures I found a Picasso, so I hid it – it will be months before they find it I hope'. Just a leetle beet mad.

All love, NR

Loving *Nothing*[3]

1 '£50 at the very cheapest.'
2 Marie-Laure Bischoffsheim (1902–70). Poet, novelist, patron of the Surrealists and fashionable Parisian hostess. Married Viscount Charles de Noailles in 1923.
3 Henry Green, *Nothing* (1950). A comedy of upper-class life set in post-war London.

JESSICA TO DEBORAH
4 June [1950]

675 Jean Street
Oakland

Dearest Hen,

Thank you so much for your letter, sorry I didn't answer before but you can't imagine how frightfully busy I am. Our wonderful built-in sitter has left for one thing. The first week she left, little mounds of honey & sugar began accumulating on the furniture & floor (left by the children) & the second week, bits of hair & fluff began to adhere to the bits of sugar & honey, nothing ever seems to get cleaned up any more.

We are longing for our tour to start. Dinky is terribly excited specially about seeing Emma & Boy.[1]

We hope to go to Paris & possibly Prague if one can get there, as well as England. The only thing still needed is passports, we're seeing about them next week.

Sorry not to have written for several years but as a matter of fact I didn't know your address – or your name, so am addressing this to Hon. Henderson, hoping it will get there.

I am sure Dinky & Emma will be amazed at each other, I can't wait to see them together. In some ways I wish we were bringing Nicholas & Benjamin, they are so extraorder, but it will be more peaceful without them.

Yr loving Hen

1 Deborah's six-year-old son, Peregrine.

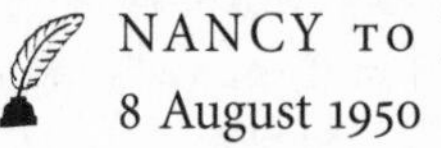

NANCY TO JESSICA
8 August 1950

Redesdale Cottage
Otterburn
Northumberland

Darling Sooze

It is a *bitter blow* to hear you're not coming.[1] I was so dying & dying to note the graph with you.

I am on a tor. Well it is a tor of all the most disgusting towns in the Br Isles, with a play I've adapted into English called *La Petite Hutte.*[2] Not very good, but funny I think. So I'm here with the poor old boy for the weekend before we go to Newcastle.

This play will probably go to New York in the autumn & they want me to go but I don't think so. I've had about enough, & you don't go to N.Y. do you? If I thought I'd see you I might think again.

So odd, Farve thinks of literally nothing now but cocktail parties. 'We've sold the cows because milking time is cocktail time' & there is one literally every day. 'Cocktail party at the camp this afternoon', he says looking at his engagement book. So it's rather terrible for me who hates them more than anything in the world.

Yesterday we went to one given by 2 Lesbians to see a large oil painting of Margaret [Wright] in black velvet. It was a yell Susan.

Oh dear, I would like to see you.

All love, Nancy
(In case you've forgotten my writing)

1 Jessica had cancelled her trip to Europe because the McCarran Act, an anti-communist law that was passing through Congress, might have made it difficult for her to leave the US and would almost certainly have prevented her from returning.
2 Nancy's adaptation of André Roussin's boulevard comedy *The Little Hut*, directed by Peter Brook, ran for four years in England.

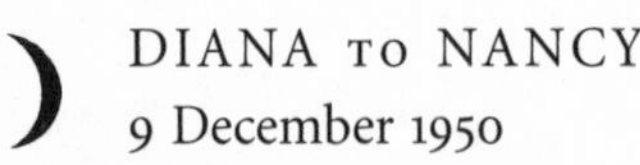

DIANA TO NANCY
9 December 1950

Crowood House
Ramsbury

Darling

We flew round to say goodbye but you had gone out.[1]

We all dined with the Mogens's[2] also Daisy [Fellowes], and the talk turned on noses (just as you say it always does when Dolly is about) and after lyrical descriptions of what can be done by operations, Dolly said in a sad way, 'Peut-être je devrais faire opérer le mien?' Daisy: 'Mais non, ça ne vaut pas la peine'[3] (very sweetly). It *was* so awfully sad.

Yesterday I spent the morning with Muv & Debo, Debo is preparing for poverty,[4] it upset me & I said we would all subscribe to keep her in the luxury to which she is accustomed.

Well darling thank you so much for all. I am so terribly excited for the little Temple. By the way Kit has given his word he will do no politics while he is in France, they will be his treat *here*.

All love darling, D

1 The Mosleys had been staying in Paris. It was on this visit that they decided to buy the Temple de la Gloire, an abandoned nineteenth-century folly at Orsay, which remained Diana's home for nearly fifty years.
2 Mogens Tvede (1897–1977). Danish architect and painter. Married Dolores (Dolly) Radziwill in 1932.
3 'Perhaps I should have mine operated on?' Daisy: 'Oh no, it's not worth it.'
4 The 10th Duke of Devonshire had died on 26 November, leaving huge death duties.

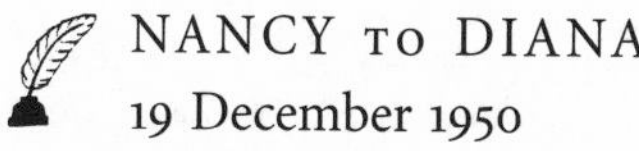

NANCY TO DIANA *7 rue Monsieur, VII*
19 December 1950

Darling,

The panicking here has reached such a pitch that even I have got a bit windy.[1] It's just like I remember London in 1940, everybody showing you their pills. (As you know I'm never as frightened as most, but feel in a bad position here being a foreigner.) I dined with Mogens, Dolly & Geoff[2] & really the talk – you know how I love old Geoff, but my gorge does slightly rise when I hear him say 'well my life is arranged so that in between the wars I can be *very comfortable* & during them only rather bored'. The Col however keeps my pecker up, he is quite unmoved by it all. What do THEY (such as Bob [Boothby]) say in London?

I must hear every word about the Connollys please. I've got him in my book[3] – he runs a highbrow theatre called the Royal George, all those terrible girls are the crew & he's called the Captain. The heroine of the book goes to a performance of *Phèdre* brought up to date by an Indian, with Aricie a dancing boy called Hari-See (psychologically sounder, I must say).

Have you read *The Novel in France*?[4] It's very lowering for a writer of my class to read – in fact what between that & the general feeling of hopelessness in the air I've done pretty badly the last week or so. It's awfully riveting.

So glad Woman is to roll.[5] Derek asks everybody 'what does Nancy think?' Geoff says she's never mentioned it & Hamish [Erskine] 'She doesn't mind one way or the other', both of which make him furious!

All love, NR

1 President Truman had proclaimed a state of emergency in the US because of the escalating war in Korea.
2 Geoffrey Gilmour (1907–82). Rich English collector who divided his time between an elegant Parisian flat in the rue du Bac and the Argentine.
3 Cyril Connolly inspired the character of Ed Spain in *The Blessing*.
4 By Martin Turnell (1950).
5 Pamela had received a generous divorce settlement from Derek.

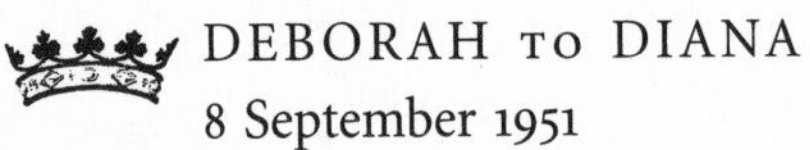

DEBORAH TO DIANA
8 September 1951

Edensor House
Bakewell

Darling Honks

I got yr middle of Aug letter when I got back here, idiots hadn't forwarded it.

It *was* sad you had gone from Venice, I did mind, as I half hoped you'd still be there instead of all those impossible people.

I must say it was fascinating in its way, & the ball[1] itself a real amazer. The *richness* of everything, from every dress to each small detail of the dance like food and the jewelled things to pull the gondolas in, was a positive revelation. The women were more beautiful than anything I ever saw & the men more revolting. The foreign women are so clever at making up and all the rest of the things that make people look nice, & the clothes seemed to be made of such wonderful stuff. Anyhow the whole effect was really beautiful, so much to look at. The Entrées were frightfully comical in a way, though they must have taken such a lot of thinking out, they walked once round a room & finished. Someone standing next to me said they were a series of one-act plays, I did shriek as that reminds one of the W.I.[2] Daisy Fellowes looked very good (though a bit like Beatrice Lillie)[3] and as for the Empress of Russia's lovers, *well* the only three I knew were Chips Channon, Count de Chambrun and Peter Coats, so poor her.[4] Honks Cooper looked a bloody fool sitting up on a dais with F. Fred de Cabrol bowing away at each lot, though one must admit she looked beautiful.[5] The standard of English looks was v. high as there was her & Liz Hofmannsthal[6] & Clarissa Churchill[7] & Rose Paget & Tig[8] looked her utter best. The Deacon[9] was an 18th-century housemaid, poor look out for the dusting.

It was a gloat. The prettiest part was arriving in a thick mess of gondolas shouting & jockeying for position to land the people on a platform covered with a wonderful Savonnerie carpet.

The rest of Venice was quite jolly. Elizabeth Winn[10] said she'd seen you which she had loved.

We got back three days ago. I must see you soon, what will you be doing, staying in France or going to Ireland again? Do write & tell & then one can act according.

All the mags will be full of the ball as there were lots of press photographers.

Goodness the foreigners are jokes. Your sweet little friend, the Spaniard Domingo,[11] always says Goodbye when he means Hello. It muddled me properly and about the 10th time he did it I said 'Oh dear are you going' and of course he wasn't. He took Nancy Lancaster[12] on a sight-seeing tour & when they were gazing at a picture of the Virgin in a church he said 'Chic, huh?' which surprised her a bit.

Terribly wet here, no harvest in. Blor & Mabel are coming to stay on the 17th. I must ask Nanny Higgs to stay, do you think she would come.

Muv is loving having Max. Em will love the shell, how clever of him to get it. Oh Honks I do long to see you, please tell where you'll be.

Much love to all, Debo

I found Mrs Fellowes on the Piazza & gave her your letter, I think she thought I was a tramp, begging.

1 The celebrated masked ball given by Charles Beistegui at Palazzo Labia, Venice, on 3 September 1951. Deborah went as Georgiana, wife of the 5th Duke of Devonshire, in a dress copied from the John Downman portrait at Chatsworth.
2 The Women's Institute, founded in 1915 to expand the horizons of women living in rural areas of England, often produced amateur theatrical events. Deborah had been a member of the WI since she was fourteen.
3 Daisy Fellowes and her party went as 'America' from Giambattista Tiepolo's frescoes of *The Four Continents* in the Würzburg Residenz. The comic actress Beatrice Lillie had rather masculine good looks.
4 Princess Elizabeth Chavchavadze went as Empress Catherine the Great. Her three 'lovers' all preferred men.
5 'Honks', Diana's childhood nickname, was later adopted by Evelyn Waugh and applied to Lady Diana Cooper. Lady Diana greeted guests at the ball dressed as Cleopatra, inspired by the Tiepolo frescoes at Palazzo Labia, and was accompanied by Baron Frédéric de Cabrol dressed as Mark Antony.
6 Lady Elizabeth von Hofmannsthal and her sister Lady Rose Paget went to the ball both dressed as the eighteenth-century ballet dancer Marie de Camargo.
7 Clarissa Spencer-Churchill (1920–). Niece of Winston Churchill. Married in 1952 Anthony Eden, Prime Minister 1955–7.
8 Anne Cavendish.
9 Elizabeth Cavendish.
10 Elizabeth Winn (1925–). Interior decorator and friend of Deborah and Diana.
11 The Marquess of Santo Domingo.
12 Nancy Perkins (1897–1994). Virginian-born arbiter of taste who bought the interior decorating firm Colefax & Fowler after the war. Married to Henry Field 1917–19, to Ronald Tree 1920–47, and to Claude Lancaster in 1948.

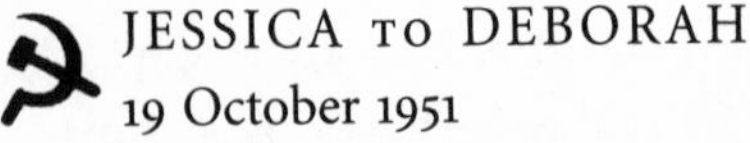

JESSICA TO DEBORAH
19 October 1951

730 59th Street
Oakland
California

Dearest Hen,

Thanks very much for your letter. I think it's a wonderful idea about you coming out here, I long to show you the children, I'm sure they are quite unlike yours. However, before you take the plunge, I must warn you of a few things.

1. We lead an *extremely* un-Duchessy life here. For instance, if you stay with us you would have to sleep on a couch in the dining room, we don't have a spare room here. Of course you could stay in a hotel, only how to pay for it? Which leads me to:

2. You can't bring more than $25 out of the country, so you would be completely at our mercy once here. We'd *love* to have you, but wouldn't be able to afford to pay for a hotel. However people often do come to stay on one's couch, so maybe you would do that.

3. Our life becomes daily more uncertain. A lot of our friends have been thrown in prison & one never knows who's next. (Not that we expect to be, at least not before February, but I'm just warning you.)[1]

Now you've heard the worst, I *DO* hope you'll still come. There is one more thing: I work quite hard, in fact night & day. If you come I would plan to take off for a week or two, but then if some emergency should arise I might have to scram back to work.

I'm sorry not to have written lately but we *ARE* so busy all the time. How about Andrew, couldn't you possibly bring him? I've never even met him, you know. He'd probably loathe the couch, that's the only trouble.

By the way please don't do what TPOF did: she sent me a telegram saying 'Am considering smuggling some things into US to sell, please suggest best things to bring'. Of course I wired back saying 'all wires & phones tapped by FBI, don't smuggle things, won't be responsible'[2] but I was terrified all through her visit that the Customs people would be raiding the house. However I'm sure Andrew being the type to stand for Parliament is also very law-abiding & will advise you on such things.

So do come. Let me know in plenty of time so I can try to arrange about taking off from work. I'm sending some pictures of the children, looking like Angels, they are not at all like this in real life but are quite dirty most of the time as well as noisy & spoiled. This is not their fault, we never seem to have time to really bring them up, poor things. However they are all beautiful & clever, which makes up for their faults.

We are longing to see you, write soon & let us know your plans.

Yr Loving Hen

1 Under the Smith Act, which made it a criminal offence to belong to an organization suspected of wanting to overthrow the US government, the Treuhafts, as members of the Communist Party, risked being arrested.
2 It is unlikely that Lady Redesdale's intentions were dishonest. At the time, Jessica had written to her mother, 'When I got your telegram it was all mixed up, so I got the impression you were planning to smuggle some English goods into the country in order to get dollars.' *Decca, The Letters of Jessica Mitford*, edited by Peter Y. Sussman (Weidenfeld & Nicolson, 2006), p. 129.

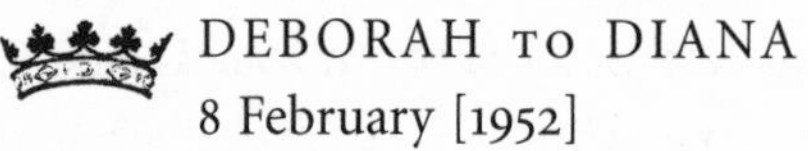

DEBORAH TO DIANA
8 February [1952]

Hotel Claremont
Berkeley
California

Darling Honks

I have just arrived and must write quickly. Don't take too much notice of it all as first impressions are sometimes so misleading and *don't tell anyone.*

I got off the aeroplane after all night and was walking to where you go out and a figure appeared who somehow was Decca and yet *completely* different. Oh dear it was frightening and in a way so terribly sad, I couldn't believe that this complete American could ever have been her. I was so overcome I simply stared at her and I must say so did she so perhaps she was equally amazed at changes in me.

So we went into the restaurant and there was Bob and the youngest child. Oh Honks. Decca has lost all colour even her eyes look different but I suppose people do change between twenty & thirty-four, and also this dreadful airless climate must be bad for people. The accent is what struck me most, I still can't believe it, she not only does the accent but says completely American sentences like when I asked her how old Bob was she said 'Pushing forty'. The house is a little suburban house, they seem very pleased with it. It is a sort of box painted like a child would, red doors in one room, blue in another. It had a very peculiar smell and they said they had a negro family in the basement so of course that was it. The Negress is a woman on the dole which Decca says is a good thing as she can do more work for the whatever it is she works for. Then Nicholas came in, he is very black looking & like any poor child in an American film but rather sweet, but as for Dinky she is *heaven*. She has got a beautiful face and fat body but she really is sweet, so enthusiastic. She booked my room in this amazing super hotel and came with me and arranged everything.

All this is very much first impressions, I may think quite differently about it all tomorrow, but somehow it is awfully frightening seeing someone like that after so long, and I feel that her blasted cause has become so much part of her that she can never forget it for a minute. She said 'Of course I stopped writing to Nancy the minute I heard she was living with a Gaullist'. But it's the voice that I can't get over. Please don't say any of this to anyone, specially not Muv, only I had to write to tell as I got such a turn. As I say I may change my mind about a lot of things in a day or two.

We are going on a trip tomorrow with all the children in the car & stay somewhere by the sea till Tues when we come back here to go to a dinner party some of her friends are having for us, what will it be like, anyhow terribly kind of them. I expect most of them will be black. I am so thankful to be in this luxurious hotel. I suppose one is tired a bit by the journey anyway.

I'll write again.

I do wonder how Clonfert is going.[1]

Much love, Debo

1 Clonfert Palace, the old bishop's house in Co. Galway which the Mosleys had just bought, needed many repairs.

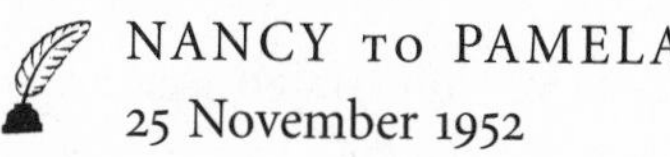

NANCY TO PAMELA *7 rue Monsieur, VII*
25 November 1952

Derel

I never remember birthdays until I see the date & then I say to myself Gog[1] or whatever it is.

How are u? I don't seem to have heard for ages.

I hear all your dogs had children while you were away – *what scenes* there must have been on your return with twenty dogs all rushing out hunting, all more idiotic than ever, & you in hot pursuit, hairnet on head & whip in hand.[2]

I bought *The Best of Boulestin*[3] but the agony of translating for Marie really makes it rather useless.

I hear you can't come to France any more for fear of being Drummonded by Diana & me for The Will.[4]

Victor Cunard[5] would like to marry you but we have had to forbid it – people sometimes ALTER their wills when they marry.

Dereling, many happy returns. No more now as I have much work to do.

I am told you can kill dogs painlessly & *quite* cheaply by gas, do think it over.

Love from N

1 George (Gog) Farrer (1909–44). Eldest son of the Mitfords' Aunt Joan. He was killed on active service in India.
2 When the Mitfords were living at Asthall, Pamela had come down to dinner one day wearing a hairnet and Tom came up with the rhyme, 'The Woman, the Woman, the brave and the fairnet / When she came down she was wearing a hairnet.'
3 A book of recipes by the famous London restaurateur Marcel Boulestin (1878–1943).
4 After her divorce settlement, the matter of Pamela's heir was a running joke among the sisters, who all banked with Drummond's in Charing Cross, London.
5 Victor Cunard (1898–1960). A homosexual friend of Nancy whose malice and extra-dry humour appealed to her. Correspondent for *The Times* before the war, he settled in Venice for most of his life.

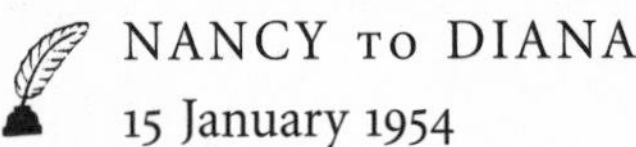

NANCY TO DIANA — *7 rue Monsieur, VII*
15 January 1954

Darling,

The posts are still very odd to tell the truth – one day from Ireland & seldom less than six from London. *Sunday T* wrote a very urgent letter asking for 800 words on Willy Maugham,[1] which took a week. I had to refuse, & I fear it will leave a short time to somebody else. He lunched here today – *most* agreeable. I was rather nervous as he can be so crusty, but he had a great click with Marie-Louise [Bousquet] while Lolotte[2] faisait la cour à *me*[3] (gel gel [jealous]?). Luncheon absolutely delicious I must say, Marie at her best.

A letter from Aunt Weenie ordering me to go to London for Muv's golden wedding in Feb. It's too farcical & I won't – anyhow I can't face the journey. But are we expected to send telegrams or something? I should have thought a tactful silence was indicated. (Fancy having the date of one's wedding – I haven't the vaguest idea, have you? I mean I know the year but literally not the month.) Do say what you intend to do. Flowers? *R.S.V.P.* (!!) and if so, to one or both or all three. It must be his silver with Margaret by now.

Colonel has sent you, c/o me, a teasing Xmas print – you know the sort. Guilty giggles of course! Brute.

Much love – so glad you are having a good rest, N

1 W. Somerset Maugham (1874–1965). The writer had been a friend of Nancy since before the war.
2 Marquis Louis de Lasteyrie (1881–1955). A descendant of General Lafayette who owned the General's Château La Grange outside Paris.
3 'Was paying court to *me*.'

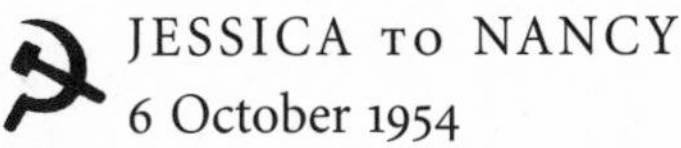

JESSICA TO NANCY
6 October 1954

574 61st Street
Oakland
California

Darling Susan,

Please note my address, your letter took almost a month.

Why don't you come, at least for a week and one $5,000? Or shall I go to H.wood & pretend to be you?[1] I wonder if we are still exactly alike? I'm sending along a picture so you can see.

The graphs *are* rather different, but I still note them a bit. I thought you going to Russia was *frightfully* unfair, you *are* so lucky.[2] I note you thought they were governessy, I expect you thought they would be Mme de Pompadourish[3] but you know that isn't their form, in fact their main pnt is not being. I expect you would find me a bit governessy too but so would you if you had 3 children & no governess. By the way, are you still leaving the Donk some jewels? I came across some old letters, round the time she was born, where you said you would.

Well Sooze I can't think of anything to write, it's been too long since I've seen you – (16 years? or more?) so you'd better come, I can see I won't ever get to Europe now because they won't let us have a passport.

Best love from Susan

P.S. I can't imagine you & Aranka [Kliot] specially liking each other, I was simply amazed when she & Muv liked each other. Do write & tell what she says about me & Bob, or better still, come & tell.

Give my love to Muv, & Idden if you ever see her, I haven't written to her for years but keep meaning to.

1 Nancy had turned down an offer from MGM of $6,000 a week to work in Hollywood on the script of *Marie Anne*, from the novel by Daphne du Maurier.
2 In May 1954, Nancy spent two weeks in Moscow as the guest of Sir William Hayter, the British ambassador in Russia.
3 Nancy's biography of Madame de Pompadour, the elegant mistress of Louis XV, was published that year.

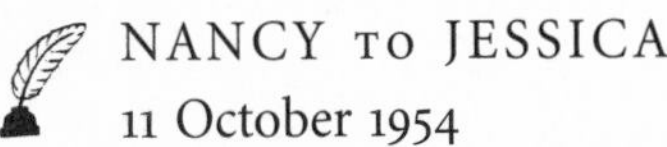

NANCY TO JESSICA *7 rue Monsieur, VII*
11 October 1954

Darling Sooze

I was excited to note yr handwriting. Oh dear, if I could have come for a short time it would have been different, but it had to be from three to six months & I couldn't face it.

I loved the photographs & riposte with one of me in Russia which seems rather suitable.

About the Donk. I haven't any jewellery, only trinkets, & I haven't much money to leave, but what I have got is the furniture of this flat, all of which is valuable. I love fine furniture more & more & when I have a little money that is what I buy. I have left it to Diana for her boys but now she has sent them to school in Germany where their greatest friend is young Krupps, & it's too much even for me to swallow. If I left it to the Donk, with enough money to take it to America would she like it do you think? Oh dear how difficult – it is all rather fragile, & might be spoilt by the central heating which I hear is terrific there. We must think about it.[1]

What about the Donk learning French? When she is older will you send her here to go to a *cours*? If so I'll alter my existence, arrange a room for her & have her to stay. Only I suppose she ought to know a bit of French first, before being plunged among French girls all day.

Aranka. Well I absolutely love her, she is a *dear.* Also she's the only person who gives me news of you, so I eat her up whenever she comes. She simply thinks the world of you. She says you're so wonderful that I thought you *must have altered considerably.*

I'm writing about Blor in a book which is coming out about them, & as I wrack my poor old brains (bad memory as I've always had) it does take me back to the stiffened paw days.[2] If you think of any lovely typical Blorism *do* write it to me.

I've asked my bank to send you 100 dollars – will you give 50 to Donk & 25 to each boy for Xmas & say it's from their old mad aunt who loves them.

Yes the Russians are very governessy, specially the women. The chaps I feel one could twist round one's little finger, but the women give you a cold blue look out of their little pig eyes which is quite terrifying. One of them asked me if I'd like to see a workman's flat & I said no not a bit, it's the kind of thing I loathe, I want to see old silver & fine morocco bindings. I could see that she gave me up for a bad job after that.

I asked about meeting some Russian writers & she said they're all away at the Black Sea writing. She said popular novels in Russia sell about 50 million copies, goodness the lucky writers. I asked for an example, '*Cement* by the author of *Glue*' was the reply.[3]

Well Sooze, keep in close touch especially about the lovely Donk and her future. Now you have written you might as well make a resolution to do so once every 10 years.

All love, N

1 Nancy had, in fact, altered her will in 1948, leaving nothing to Constancia. This was because of Jessica's attempt to give her share of Inch Kenneth to the Communist Party.
2 When she was young, Jessica used to pick up her pet spaniel, hold it against her and squeeze its legs until its paws stood up stiffly.
3 This paragraph, which Jessica inserted into Nancy's letter when she quoted it in her 1977 memoir, *A Fine Old Conflict* (Michael Joseph, 1977, p. 190), does not appear in the original. Jessica probably took it from Nancy's letter to her previous to this one, which has not been found.

DIANA TO NANCY
10 December 1954

Hotel Russell
Dublin

Darling

I expect you've heard about Clonfert,[1] it is dreadfully sad, such a pretty old house & it had been there 300 years, and masses of things burnt which one can never get again. Oh dear. If Mrs Blake Kelly's horse hadn't neighed & woken her up they might have all been burnt except Kit, so thank heavens for that anyway. Madeleine,[2] by rushing up to the attic & having to jump into a blanket held by Kit & Alexander, prevented them saving the dining room pictures & many pretty things in there. She had been wonderful at the beginning helping to unsew the big Aubusson & then when they weren't looking she dashed up for her clothes & was cut off by the fire at once. Jean-Pierre[3] announces that he has lost £300 worth of things in *his* attic, what can they have been & how embarrassing because I know *we* shan't get anything like the replacement value, & my clothes & dressing table things which are all gone I have put at £100, and shoes alone cost almost that don't they. I had lots. The bitter thing is that these last weeks I had a lot of work done in the house; & had brought from attic that wasn't burnt lots of drawings by Tchelichew,[4] John[5] etc ready to take to France, & the whole lot went west. I haven't seen it yet because then a storm came, the worst for 100 years, & the roads were flooded. We are going to try again today. The *poor* village people, I feel so sad for them because they live near what is now a black ruin and we were their livelihood; we can rush away from it but they can't. It is too miserable the whole business.

Al is dressed in Kit's clothes, all his are burnt, I was amazed to note he is still clutching a book by Maryse Choisy, that Freudian lady, but all his other books are burnt. Not mine, except a few in my bedroom. Of my (once Muv's) four-post bed, which had just been trimmed in blue silk, all that remains is a few red hot springs.

Debo has angelically said we can have Lismore,[6] which saves our Christmas. Poor Max will mind terribly about Clonfert I fear. We shall come back to France about the 9th Jan I suppose. Kit now has such a mania about Orsay that he is going to fill the poor Temple with elaborate extinguishers (I never think one has time to use them, it's always at 2 in the morning).

Not only the sadness & the loss of all one's things (for instance *all* letters & diaries I fear) but also the boredom of dealing with the insurance, storing what's left etc is almost more than I can bear. It was *just now* really finished. *Bother.*

Do write, to Lismore I suppose we shall go on Monday or so.

All love darling, excuse wail, D

1 A beam in a chimney at Clonfert had caught fire and the house was burned to the ground.
2 The Mosleys' French cook.
3 The Mosleys' driver.
4 Pavel (Pavlik) Tchelitchew (1898–1957). Russian-born Surrealist painter and stage designer who came to Paris in 1928. Diana and her two Guinness sons were painted by him in 1934.
5 Augustus John (1878–1961). Diana sat to the British painter for her portrait in 1932.
6 Lismore Castle, Co. Waterford; the Devonshires' house in Ireland overlooking the Blackwater.

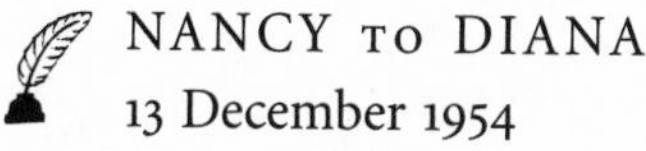

NANCY TO DIANA
13 December 1954

7 rue Monsieur, VII

Darling,

Yes, & I wrote to the Russell which I expect you've got. Only it is all much worse than I thought – Muv rather said all the nice things saved, & Jefferson[1] kept saying you can trust Kit for being over-insured. £100 for clothes – mine are insured for £1,000 to the amazement of the little agent. I'm only hoping you've left quite a lot here – big ball dress etc surely. Your tenant rang up to enquire – many people have including of course Jean[2] who, I note, now says 'aingel' etc & talks almost perfect English. I shall have a Frenchman in my next book who people only like because of the way he talks & when, by dint of being with English people, he learns, they all drop him. I can hear your *shrieks* of protest from here.

I'm off in ½ an hour to London for one night to see Farve. Noble? Actually I think less tiring than going for a week as one won't have time to get tired.

Stephen[3] is here. He says he's very poor because he has spent all his capital on statues & balustrades but they all blew down in the gales. 'But they look very pretty lying in the grass.' Yesterday he rang up – I said, 'Isn't it an awful day?' 'Dolorous – I'm going to the Ritz to cheer myself up.' He says he is trying to get taken on to strip off ermine & mink in front of a jet curtain. 'I am followed everywhere for my beauty, Nancy.'

Darling, the descriptions of the ball.[4] It seems they all came in, in £1,000 dresses, leaning forward, bottoms out, arms wildly waving. That daughter of Lady Kenmare called Pat Cameron thought her hour had come, but she fell down four times & broke several bones. Lady Kenmare furious with her. The piste was covered with diamonds where everybody had flumped.

A rat *on* my bed two days ago at 4 A.M. You'd hardly believe it could happen twice in a lifetime – so horrid & it wouldn't get off, quite tame. I fetched Minet but he only shivered in a corner & Marie had to drive it out with an umbrella.

Must get up & catch my plane – fond love & sympathy darling – oh I do think it's too hard.

N

1 Geoffrey Gilmour.
2 Count Jean de Baglion (1909–93). 'The Count' or 'County' was an interior decorator whose French accent in English enchanted Nancy and Diana. He was one of Diana's closest friends in Paris.
3 Stephen Tennant (1906–87). The exotic youngest son of the 1st Baron Glenconner was one of the models for Cedric Hampton in *Love in a Cold Climate*.
4 A charity ball organized by Daisy de Cabrol at the Palais des Glaces which was turned into a skating rink for the occasion.

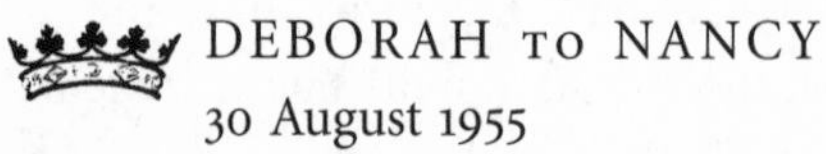

DEBORAH TO NANCY
30 August 1955

Inch Kenneth
Gribun, Oban

Get on

Oh the SAGA of all here,[1] it's a great strain on my aged 9 writing and mentality to write *any* of it let alone all. I *do* so wish you were here to study it, *and* Honks *and* my Wife.[2] Oh dear, Decca's *appear-*

ance, she has got an Eton crop & specs and wears men's trousers and smokes without stopping, it really is too sad. She doesn't seem to care in the least. Bob has grown a ½ hearted sort of moustache as a disguise to fuddle the American police.[3] He looks pretty odd anyhow, but with that he really is an old yellow peril. Dinky is wonderful looking and makes the very worst of herself by having her hair dragged to the back of her head in a horse's tail, but she is so funny & so nice, I really love her.

Dinky thinks Andrew gets money from selling slaves, I do wish we could *buy* some, I wouldn't dream of selling.

The children are all getting on fairly well, & Decca is being terribly nice & much less violent as far as one can make out without actually getting involved on some subject which means arguing which I can't do. When they go to London, two of them are going to Chesterfield St[4] & two to the Mews, I shudder to think of the result but ne'er mind. I'm afraid they'll find Chatsworth not very progressive & be bored stiff by sight seeing, all those silly pictures etc but I'll have a try with them. Progressive is a terrific word with them, it always makes me scream. Oh dear it does all seem so sad in a way but they seem happy with each other I must say.

Oh what *will* you make of these Americans, I must come & see you immediately after they've been, to hear while all is fresh. There is too much to tell, all *so* odd.

I shrieked over your article about the aristocracy.[5] The mother's hall was lovely.

Poor Andrew lost such a terrible lot of money at the Casino that he has gone back to Biarritz this weekend, I can't quite think why as he obviously won't win any back.

Much love, Debo

1 The Treuhafts were on holiday in Britain, Jessica's first visit home since 1939. They were staying with Lady Redesdale, where Deborah and her children joined them, before going on to stay with Deborah at Edensor and Nancy in Paris.

2 Lady Katherine (Kitty) Petty-Fitzmaurice (1912–95). Quiet, discreet, intelligent and witty, she was loved by Nancy, Diana and Deborah. Her nickname 'Wife' was adopted by the sisters to describe any great friend of either sex. Married 3rd Viscount Mersey in 1933.

3 Between 1952 and 1958, a prohibition banned travel abroad by Americans suspected of left-wing leanings. The Treuhafts had unexpectedly been issued passports which were revoked shortly before their departure. They nevertheless managed to elude State Department officials and board a boat for England.
4 The Devonshires' Mayfair house.
5 'The English Aristocracy', which appeared in *Encounter* magazine (September 1955), popularized the term U and non-U, for upper- and non-upper-class usage, and brought Nancy a not altogether welcome notoriety.

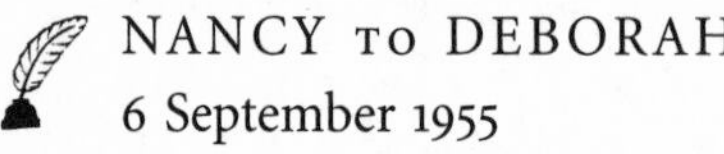

NANCY TO DEBORAH
6 September 1955

7 rue Monsieur, VII

Dear 9

I must say your letter has filled me with gloom & apprehension. TROUSERS! Well if she goes to Russia in them she'll be lynched, because no women wear them, not even those poor devils who mend the roads. When do they come here? Ay di me, as Carlyle used to say.[1]

And then Farve – sounds so pathetic. Wicked as one knows him to be I don't like to think of him really low. Do go & see. I can't move from here as they need me the whole time & will, I guess, for at least another month.[2] But I never think he really likes seeing one much.

Oh my Lanvin dress is a dream. Mme Sézille asked lovingly after you – she's a very good vendeuse I think, sees at once what's wrong.

How much did Muv enjoy the visit, that's what I do long to know. Oh I do hope so, she was dying for it for such an age. Then won't she see them again before they go back? Do write more details – I begin to see the possibility of another book. The Return of Jassy.[3]

Much love – never let the pencil out of your little fist from now on –

Nancy

1 Thomas Carlyle used, in fact, the exclamation 'Ay de mi', Spanish for 'O woe is me'. The phrase has been corrected whenever it recurs in Nancy's letters.
2 Nancy was working on the dialogue for *Marie Antoinette* (1956), a film by Jean Delannoy.
3 The character of Jassy, one of the Radlett children in Nancy's novels, was based on Jessica.

NANCY TO DIANA
8 September 1955

7 rue Monsieur, VII

Darling,

I suppose you've heard all the Decca news from Debo. Oh dear how I dread their arrival – & I have to keep hypocritically writing to say I die for them. Ay de mi. I bet they're off to Russia, hence Bob's disguising moustache. The awful thing is it won't teach them (that'll teach them) because nothing ever does teach people. But the great new smiling love between Russia & America must *bore* them rather?

Match is full of Pigmy-Peep-a-toes[1] again – SURELY we've had enough.

Much love do write, Nancy

1 Nancy's nickname for five-foot two-inch Princess Margaret (1930–2002), who wore open-toed shoes, a fashion that Nancy considered vulgar. The Princess was much in the news at the time because of her affair with Group Captain Peter Townsend.

DIANA TO NANCY
11 September 1955

Hotel Europa e Britannia
Venice

Darling

Just a bulletin from the Daisy [Fellowes] front. You know Grace R[1] & Ali Forbes[2] arrived late on Wed. to stay, & by Thurs. she was dying to be rid of *him*, well on Sat. Grace (noticing something) said, 'By the way Daisy, do tell me how long you want us to stay. Which day would it be convenient for us to leave?' There was a pause while Daisy seemed to calculate then she said, 'The 10th.' 'But today's the 10th!' says Grace. 'Oh well then, the 11th', says Daisy.

All love, D

1 Grace Kolin (1923–). Married to Prince Stanislas Radziwill 1946–58, and to the 3rd Earl of Dudley in 1961.

2 Alastair Forbes (1918–2005). Writer, journalist and reviewer who, according to his obituary, 'was frequently dismissed from lunch tables, and viewed the early train home on a Sunday morning after upsetting his hostess as an occupational hazard'. *Daily Telegraph*, 21 May 2005.

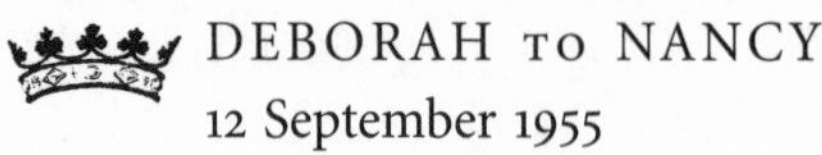

DEBORAH TO NANCY
12 September 1955

Edensor House
Bakewell

Get on

Oh dear I hope I haven't gone *too far* in my letters about the Treuhafts. *Please* don't tell anyone, it does sound so awful, but I don't know what it is about them, perhaps the *voices*, the screaming American sounds made by the children, or the fact that one feels the other two are waiting to attack one on a million things.

I really don't know what it is, perhaps it is just that there isn't one single point of contact with any of them. They come here tonight, the bitter thing is that Andrew has had to go to London & he would have been so good with them. They are only staying two nights so I shall spend hours with them at Chatsworth & see what they think & I can make them go to Haddon.[1] The children anyway. Oh dear me how difficult it all is.

I can hardly wait for news of what you think of it all.

V. few partridges, v. sad. Well I can't think of ought else, except that my Wife is still in Ireland, very tiresome without her.

I'll write again after this VISIT, oh dear.
[incomplete].

1 Haddon Hall, a fourteenth-century manor house near Chatsworth open to the public.

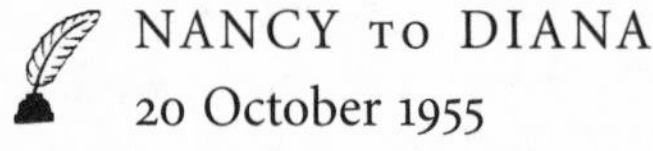

NANCY TO DIANA
20 October 1955

Edensor House
Bakewell

Dereling

Debo is out ALL day (from 8 A.M.) at a bazaar so I've a moment to write![1] I've enjoyed myself on the whole, but I see that London is too much for me. I utterly lost my voice & only really felt well again after a week on the Isle of Wid.

Evelyn is writing a piece for the U-book[2] – anti-me. Saying we must remember she only became a Hon at the age of 12, it went to her head & she's been a fearful snob ever since, & other rather cruel words. I said Evelyn do put a footnote saying you love me all the same. 'Oh that's quite evident.' Only to one with 2nd sight.

I return Sat. 29th.

Much love, N

1 In an effort to discourage Jessica from visiting Paris, Nancy had gone to England to stay with Deborah.
2 Evelyn Waugh replied to Nancy's article on the English aristocracy with a disparaging Open Letter in *Encounter.* Both pieces were reproduced in *Noblesse Oblige* (1956).

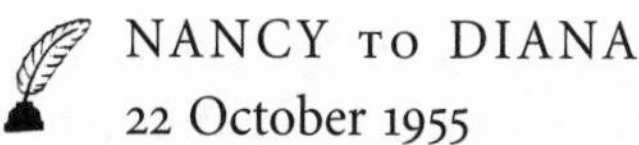

NANCY TO DIANA
22 October 1955

Edensor House
Bakewell

Oh dereling oi am in great & terrible despair. I'm almost sure, from signs too long to explain, that the Treuhafts have moved into rue Mr, & I *can't* bear it. I've written to Marie to say she must tell them *you* are both arriving on Monday for a few nights as this seems the only way to dislodge them. (I've sent them £50 for an hotel.) I rang you up but you're away & when you get back darling I beseech you to telephone to Marie & find out what's on. No good me ringing up because when I did, & got onto Decca, she merely put on that stone walling voice & I could get nothing out of her except idiotic giggles.

I nearly got into an aeroplane today, but it is enormously inconvenient to do so & Debo very much dissuaded me. I have an utter mass of things in London next week & you know how it is – & have left most of my clothes there & so on.

If you talk to Marie (were you in Paris you could make Mme Brard[1] bring her out to the motor) tell her once they've gone they're not to be allowed into the flat again – she must shut all up & pretend to be away.

I know you'll feel for me & do what you can. (And Evelyn says I am a communist agitator (the comble [limit]).

All love, N

1 The concierge at rue Monsieur.

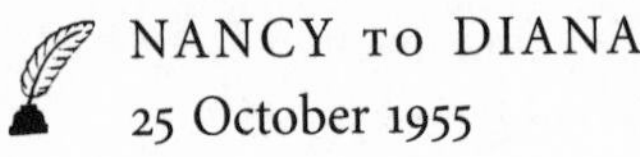

NANCY TO DIANA
25 October 1955

40 Hill Street
Berkeley Square
London W1

Darling,

Oh the relief. In fact they behaved perfectly, & I think Marie must have thought I'd quite lost my head, since Momo sent her secretary round to see what had happened! Well – I had too! I think when Decca telephoned she was a bit drunk – she'd been travelling all day & then settled down to my whisky while waiting for the call.

Anyway – she's waiting in Paris for my return, which I've put forward one day & will come back on Friday 28th. Of course Debo rather hotted me up – & Andrew says they upset her & she mustn't see them again. I can't wait to C for myself.

All news at the end of the week – love, N

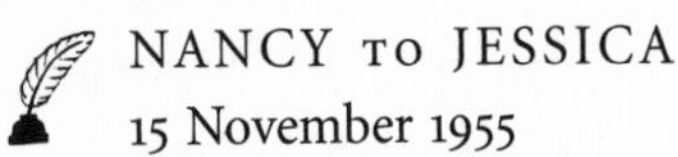

NANCY TO JESSICA
15 November 1955

7 rue Monsieur, VII

Darling Sooze

How I shrieked at your account.[1] Of course her bark is always worse than her bite – so typical telling you to come by bus & then meeting you – saying there'll be no dinner & then producing it etc. Did you note how the dangerously boiling bath water *can* only pour onto one's navel? Such a typically English arrangement somehow. You *must* have had a pow-wow! I haven't had her account yet – she said I shall *write my views*. I expect she's cooking them up.

I'm glad you're staying on. Do go & see Zella[2] – I sent you a P.C. of her address.

I'm still too busy for words with Saint-Simon[3] – but it's beginning to take shape. I've asked if I can have one more week.

Dined with Gladwyn,[4] just back from Geneva where he had gone accompanied by all the Embassy silver for a banquet we gave. He sat next to Molotov[5] who was in a very jolly mood he says. Goodness Susan what can this portend?

I also dined with some American friends & sat next a handsome & apparently powerful Mr Pulitzer.[6] He said to me 'Why do the French resist any interference in N Africa?' I said 'Well how would *you* like it if we began to interfere with your lynching arrangements?' He roared, I must say. So the world wags on.

Love to Muv & say I'll write when I've finished my essay. If she had given me any education these things wouldn't take me so long.

Love to Dinky. Mark[7] says 'as for Dinky, she *is* one'.

Much love Soo, Nancy

1 Jessica had sent Nancy a description of staying with Violet Hammersley on the Isle of Wight.

2 Vanda Séréza; the Mitfords' French governess.

3 An article for the *New Statesman and Nation* to mark the bicentenary of the French memoirist's death. 'The Great Little Duke' was reprinted in *The Water Beetle* (1962), a collection of Nancy's journalism and essays.

4 Gladwyn Jebb (1900–96). Politician and diplomat who was ambassador to Paris 1954–60, and a friend of Nancy since before the war. Married Cynthia Noble in 1929. Created Baron Gladwyn in 1960.

5 Vyacheslav Molotov (1890–1986). Stalin's loyal henchman who became Khrushchev's Foreign Minister in 1953.

6 Joseph Pulitzer III (1913–93). Grandson of the founder of the Pulitzer Prize. Editor-publisher of the *St Louis Post-Dispatch* and chairman of the Pulitzer Publishing Company from 1955 until his death.

7 Mark Ogilvie-Grant (1905–69). A great friend and confidant of Nancy since 1925 who settled in Athens after the war.

DIANA TO DEBORAH
10 May 1956

4 Chesterfield Street
London W1

Darling Debo

I went to see Midi[1] & she told me two very young men she knows went cruising with Prod, so I said, 'what did they make of him?' And she said, 'oh they thought him the most romantic man they'd ever met. They said "he could have been a marvellous writer or philosopher, but he's never bothered to do anything, just one of those marvellous people who don't bother to work."' And apparently (they said) he was once married to an incredibly famous woman, they couldn't remember who, and *that* went wrong too.

When you leave Ireland, couldn't you fit in a little visit to the Temple? Oh *DO*.

All love darling, Honks

1 Mary (Middy) O'Neill (1905–91). A friend of the Mitfords since childhood. Married Derick Gascoigne in 1934.

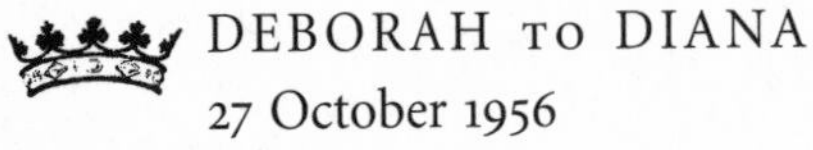

DEBORAH TO DIANA
27 October 1956

Edensor House
Bakewell

Darling Honks

I am getting all excited for you to come here.

I did not tell you before, but I'm going to have a baby.

I told the Doctor last week, & he has turned me into a prisoner as I knew he would, on account of what has happened the last two times. So what I'm *hoping* is that you really will make a little stay here, think how one longs for you, as I can't shoot,[1] drive, or even gaze much at the pigs, I am to go out just once a day, v. slowly in a car driven by someone else, stay in bed late in the morning, rest in the afternoon & go to bed early. So do be chatting companion for more than a night or two. Haven't I been strong minded not to tell before.

I told Lord[2] that I could not shoot this winter, & the reason. He looked as if the end of the world had come & then said *what*, at *this* time of year.

COME SOON, STAY AGES.

Much love, Debo

1 Deborah was considered one of the best women shots in the country.

2 Tom Lord; head keeper at Chatsworth.

NANCY TO DEBORAH
22 March 1957

7 rue Monsieur, VII

Dear 9

Nobody told me. Honks Coo[per] rang up & said 'I hear Debo has had the baby'.[1] 'No – *what*?' 'Don't know but she's said to be all right'. That's the Mitfords all over. Never mind, I'm awfully pleased & relieved because, although it all seemed all right one couldn't help remembering the Queen Mother's horse. You know how that story has haunted me ever since, the saddest thing that's happened in Lord Rosebery's lifetime & so on.[2]

Muv says it's a lovely baby so I can see she is losing her grip because she's generally sensible about babies.

Went to Lanvin. The clothes are horrid, still one must have something to wear I suppose. Those little short jackets which I *hate*. Mme Sézille more boring than ever & said would your m. in law go & see the collection & I said I was sure she wouldn't.

Much love you dear little thing.
What's IT to be called? N

1 Deborah's younger daughter was born on 18 March.
2 At the 1956 Grand National, the Queen Mother's horse was leading by ten lengths when it collapsed just short of the winning post. The racing world rallied to sympathize and Lord Rosebery declared it the saddest thing that had happened in his lifetime.

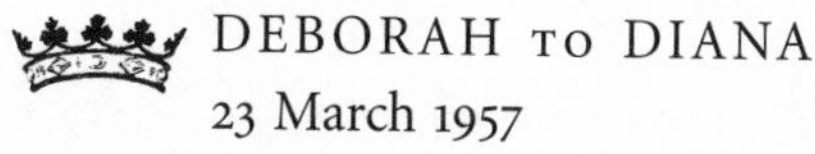

DEBORAH TO DIANA
23 March 1957

Clinic

Darling Honks

Thank you *SO* much for telegrams letters etc. You are kind and faithful to be interested.

Oh the RELIEF of everything being all right, you simply can't imagine. It took under two hours, & I heard myself saying 'is the baby all right?' about fifty-five times so that the anaesthetist got bored with the question. I got to know today that all the nurses have been screaming with laughter at the patheticness of the baby clothes, because they've never seen a baby with such old washed-out things, but of course I did it on purpose because I was so nervous. I didn't get a cot or anything, & then I sent the Wife out to buy one & she got me one which was dirty because it had been so long in the shop. Clever old Wife.

We can't think of names, can you? I am so glad it's a girl because it will be able to relieve poor Em at the deathbeds, otherwise she will have such a round to do.

Masses of love, keep on writing please, Debo

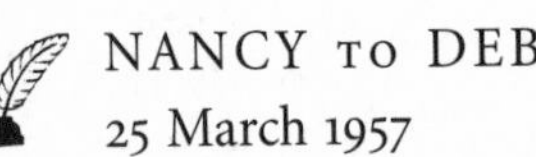

NANCY TO DEBORAH
25 March 1957

7 rue Monsieur, VII

Dear 9

Names

Zaïre, Zoraïde, Aïda, would fox the women's institute. Philadelphia (Delphi for short), Lily, Ada, Zéphire, Colombine, Eglantine, Lilac, Privet, Aïssé, Bérénice, Giroflée, Cora, Daisy, Edmée, Mirabelle, Esmeralda, Una, Esther, Natalie, Nin, Momo, Virginia, Evangeline, Ursula, Hecuba, Morgana, Susanita, Foxglove, Foxhunter. I don't know any more. What does it look like? It must suggest something (Elsa Maxwell[1] might be a nice name). What about Alice (Ali for short) or Morny? Or Douro?[2]

No news at all because of work.

Much love, N

1 Elsa Maxwell (1883–1963). The generously proportioned American hostess and gossip columnist.

2 The Marquess Douro is the courtesy title of the eldest son of the Duke of Wellington (who was annoyed when Deborah called her son Morny). The names 'Sophia Louise Sydney' were eventually chosen for Deborah's daughter and the nickname 'Sophy' later adopted.

Lord Redesdale with his dogs. Asthall, 1922.

The 'Bouds', Unity and Jessica, *c.*1920.

The 'Hens', Deborah and Jessica. Asthall, 1923.

The Mitfords with their Churchill cousins; (*back*) Diana Mitford, Diana Churchill, Lady Redesdale, Pamela, Tom; (*front*) Randolph Churchill, Deborah, Unity, Jessica, Sarah Churchill, *c.*1924.

Pamela's 'coming out' dance at Asthall, 20 November 1925. (*back*) Pamela, second from left; Nancy, fourth from left in a mantilla; Lady Redesdale, third from right. Lord Redesdale's brother Jack is sitting in the front on the far right.

Nancy, aged twenty-two, soon after her hair had been shingled. 'No one would look at you twice now', warned her mother.

Diana in 1928, the year she turned eighteen and became engaged to Bryan Guinness.

Pamela and Oliver (Togo) Watney in 1928. Their short engagement was broken off by mutual consent.

Deborah, Lady Redesdale, Lord Redesdale, Diana, Tom and Jessica at Old Mill Cottage, High Wycombe, 1930.

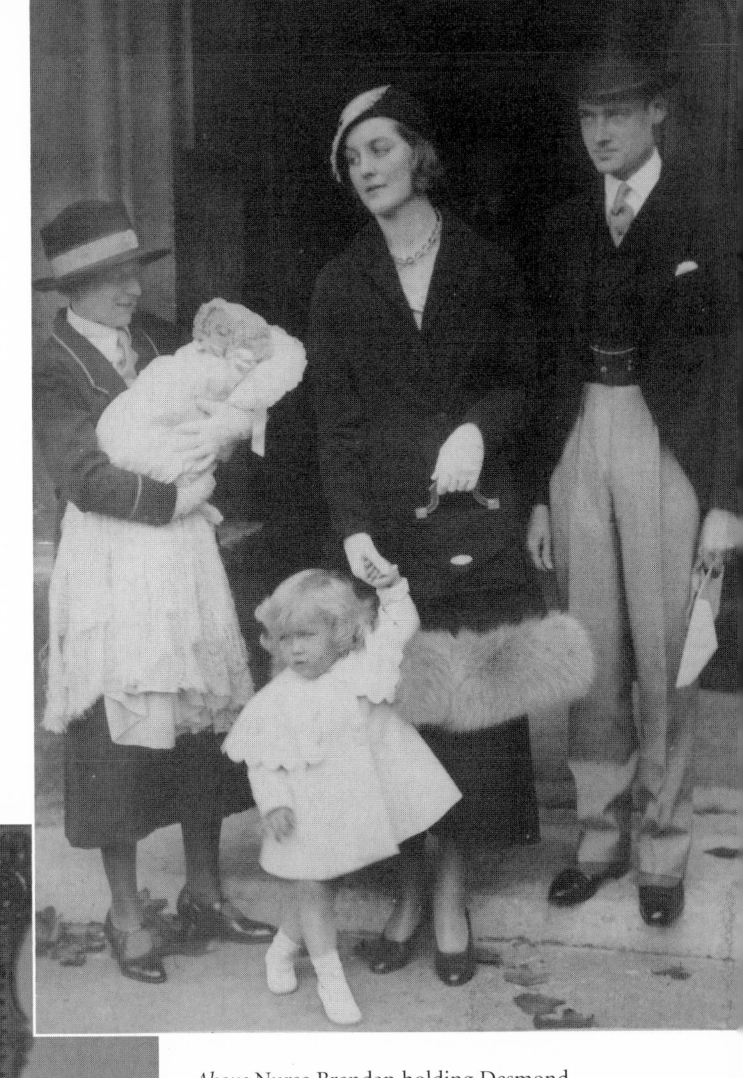

Above Nurse Brendan holding Desmond Guinness at his christening, with Diana, Jonathan and Bryan at St. Margaret's, Westminster, 1931.

Left Diana with Jonathan and Desmond at Eaton Square, under their portrait by Pavel Tchelitchew, 1935.

Above left Unity in 1932, the year before she left for Germany.

Above Pamela, 1926.

Left Sixteen-year-old Jessica with her spaniel, Tray.

Opposite Deborah, aged fourteen, collecting chickens' eggs – a lifelong enthusiasm.

Jessica, Nancy, Diana, Unity and Pamela, 1935.

Above Nancy at her wedding to Peter Rodd, 4 December 1933.

Right Nancy and Peter outside Rose Cottage, 1934; the strains in their marriage are already beginning to show.

Left Pamela and Derek on their wedding day. Caxton Hall, 29 December 1936. Unusually for a bride, Pamela wore black.

Below Derek and Pamela sailing with Putzi Hanfstaengl on the Starnberger See, 1936.

Right A keen fencer, Oswald Mosley had represented Britain in international championships.

Below Diana and Unity on their first visit to Germany, with Putzi Hanfstaengl at the Bratwurstglöcklein restaurant, Nuremberg, 1933.

Bottom Diana and Unity giving the Nazi salute.

A page from Unity's album showing her dressed for the Munich Fasching with Brian Howard, 1935.

Right Unity at the Hesselberg meeting, 23 June 1935.

Above Hitler, Unity and SA Obergruppenführer Franz von Pfeffer. Bayreuth, 1936.

Right Unity with her SS boyfriend, Erich Widmann, outside the Osteria Bavaria restaurant where she first met Hitler. Munich, 1935.

Jessica in 1936, the year before she eloped.

Esmond Romilly, navigator in an RAF bomber plane, 1941.
(*Supplied by Churchill Archives Centre, ref. CSCT 5/4/88*)

Jessica and Esmond in Bayonne, 1937.

Above Deborah, an eighteen-year-old debutante in 1938, the year she fell in love with Andrew Cavendish.

Right Deborah in a wedding dress made by Victor Stiebel. 'Masses & masses & masses of white tulle, tight bodice & sleeves, a skirt such as has never been seen before for size'. 19 April, 1941.

Top Tom Mitford, late 1930s.

Above Unity, Lady Redesdale, Jonathan and Desmond Guinness. The Mill Cottage, Swinbrook, 1940.

Left Pamela holding eighteen-month-old Alexander Mosley, with two of her adored long-haired dachshunds in the background. Rignell, 1940.

DEBORAH TO DIANA

4 Chesterfield Street, W1

10 April 1957

Darling Honks

I am so glad Sir O is better, I do hope he *feels* well.[1]

I think Wife will have a try at Bignor.[2] It is terribly nice, such beautiful country too. She has got her really dreadful black winter coat on today so I asked for it for the jumble & she looked rather sad & said could she keep it till June as it wouldn't be so much of a *wrench* then.

I hear Nancy has gone & done it again & given an interview to the *New York Herald Tribune*[3] saying how she hates & despises all Americans etc etc. I *wish* she could just keep her trap shut. I do hope everyone won't go on about it for years & years.

Much love, Debo

1 Mosley had a recurrence of phlebitis.

2 The Merseys moved back into their family home, Bignor Park, West Sussex, in 1959.

3 Art Buchwald wrote a spoof interview with Nancy in which he made her say, 'I don't like America or Americans. I'm getting old and only have a certain amount of time and I don't want to waste a day in a place where I would be miserable.' *New York Herald Tribune*, 21 April 1957.

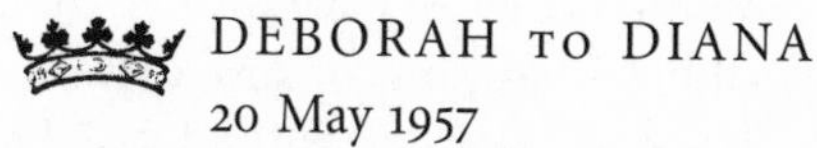

DEBORAH TO DIANA

Edensor House
Bakewell

20 May 1957

Darling Honks

I've written to Decca to try & see her[1] & I've suggested lunch or dinner on 28th, shall we try you just being there or would you rather not? I don't terribly want to see her but she has written such friendly letters that I feel I must. As for her Memoirs,[2] let's *us* do *ours* for a change. Mine would be things like '8 May 55, Dermatologists to lunch' or '15 Nov, W.I. Annual Meeting'. Yours would be '3 April, Headache', '4 April, Another Headache'.[3]

My Wife is here. I think she must be terribly bored at home, oh dear.

Em & I went to Oxford last Sat, but I think I've told you all that,

& about Em's aplomb in the interview with the Principal. I do hope she goes, I believe she would like it.

Oh Honks I am dying for you next week.

Much love, Debo

There is a Musical Festival on at Buxton this week so I went out of curiosity to hear Barbirolli[4] & the 7th Symphony, which is a tune I know. Well – I know now why old ladies queue to get in to the Albert Hall, it is the most *shocking* thing I ever saw, all that getting worked up in public, in front of the *Mayor* too. I felt quite embarrassed. Nevertheless J Barbirolli saw me & is coming to lunch on Fri with a few followers.

1 Jessica was planning another visit to England that summer.
2 Jessica had started to work on her first volume of memoirs, *Hons and Rebels.*
3 After the war, Diana began to suffer from recurrent migraines which afflicted her for many years, sometimes up to three or four times a week.
4 John Barbirolli (1899–1970). Conductor of the Manchester Hallé Orchestra 1943–58.

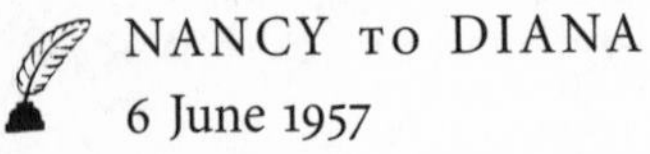

NANCY TO DIANA
6 June 1957

Lismore Castle
Co. Waterford

Darling,

Nature has stopped copying E Bowen's[1] art & we have the weather I imagine more usual, huge white clouds, lots of sun, very pretty but cold. Debo has become the sort of English duchess who doesn't feel the cold, it is the only drawback to complete pleasure. Eddy[2] had a fire all day all through the heat wave. I was with him five days, it was extremely agreeable. He had a cocktail party, Woman was there – I said to a neighbour 'When my sister comes I know I shall be glued to her because we always are' & the neighbour said 'No wonder, she's *so* amusing.' Eddy says everybody adores her & it would be madness for her to go away having made a life here. The Devonshires, par contre [on the other hand], are roundly disliked. Oh *dear* how funny somehow, what would Jean [de Baglion] say!

Raymond[3] corrected my book[4] – he is perfectly extraordinary, the eye of a needle. It has gone to the printer now.

I don't feel so depressed here as I did last time, but all is spoilt by the hanging over of the journey to Muv which is a great deal more taireeboul than I had imagined. Literal torture.

Eddy has seen a London Library book, in which Frederick's homosexual goings on are described, & in the margin is *Ay de mi* in Carlyle's writing – Shrieks! The old fraud, not one word in the *Life*.[5]

I shall be in Paris, in dust sheets, for a few days 26 June.

Much love, do write to Isle, N

1 Elizabeth Bowen (1899–1973). The Anglo-Irish novelist's most recent book, *A World of Love* (1955), was set during an uncharacteristically hot Irish summer.
2 Edward Sackville-West (1901–65). Novelist and music critic who was the inspiration for Uncle Davey in Nancy's novels. In 1957, he moved to Cooleville in Co. Tipperary.
3 Raymond Mortimer (1895–1980). Critic and literary editor of the *New Statesman and Nation* 1935–47. He became a close friend of Nancy in Paris after the war and was, with Evelyn Waugh, her chief literary mentor.
4 *Voltaire in Love* (1957).
5 Thomas Carlyle's epic life of Frederick the Great of Prussia was published between 1858 and 1865.

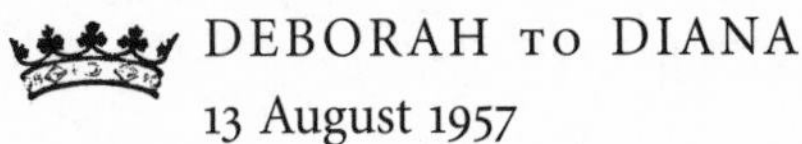

DEBORAH to DIANA
13 August 1957

Edensor House
Bakewell

Darling Honks

I would give a lot for a day or 2 of your weather, there hasn't been a glimmer of sun for 10 days.

I wonder if you've seen the papers, they are full of Hardwick & the death duty deals, I think v. satisfactory for us but sad nevertheless.[1]

Lucian Freud[2] came for the weekend, he seems very nice & not at all wicked but I'm always wrong about that kind of thing. He's mad on tennis, rather unexpected.

Evelyn Waugh came last week, on his way to Renishaw. He is a crusty old thing, he didn't actually get cross but one felt he was on the verge all the time. The Wife was here, we were talking in my room when we'd mounted [the stairs] and he kept coming in saying things like 'I hope there is Malvern Water by my bed, I hope the blinds keep the light out, may I have some lemonade to take my sleeping draught in, has Lady Mersey finished with the bathroom' & generally making one feel that things weren't quite right & that it was one's fault. I thought he had really gone for good when he came back with a look of triumph on his face, & said 'I've looked in the pedestal beside my bed and I thought I ought to tell you the POT IS FULL'. Oh Honks the humiliation, the horror. I was rooted to the bed, couldn't help in any way, left him & the Wife to deal with it, hid my head in the blankets & was properly put out. Evelyn seemed rather pleased. Oh dear, not what Nancy calls a nice character.

Betjeman[3] is in the cottage with Deacon & my m. in law, he is *sweet*, I do love him. We play tennis. The church v. the laity: him & Deacon v. Andrew & me. Keep writing.

Much frozen love, Debo

1 Hardwick Hall, which had been in the Devonshire family for fifteen generations, and nine of Chatsworth's most important works of art had been handed over to the government in lieu of death duties.
2 Lucian Freud (1922–). The artist painted six members of the Devonshire family, including a portrait of Deborah, completed in 1961.
3 John Betjeman (1906–84). The future Poet Laureate married Penelope Chetwode in 1933. When the marriage fell apart he formed an enduring relationship with Deborah's sister-in-law Elizabeth (Deacon) Cavendish.

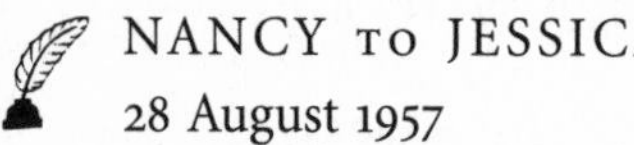

NANCY TO JESSICA *7 rue Monsieur, VII*
28 August 1957

Darling Sooze

So I weighed a letter for Mr Cass Canfield[1] my publisher yesterday & I'll put the same stamps on this & we'll see. I said is Cass short for Cassowary but no, Cass is his name. Really Americans!

Well I wasn't disloyal a bit with Aranka but she might be called *Cass*andra, I never knew such an old gloom-pot. She began about how Dinky was certain to have been killed in the earthquake[2] so I said people like us are *never killed in earthquakes* & furthermore only 29 people were, all non-U. I envy her the fun of it. Next day I got a letter from Muv saying she'd slept through it (hard cheese) so I reassured Cassandra on that point. Then there was talk about Russia

& I said, 'You must realize that to us in Europe, Russia & America seem exactly the same, two enormous countries where you can't get servants & where everything in the shops is machine-made.' She said I'd got it all wrong & her customers have gracious lives like anything.

Well that's the end of the paper I note & an extra sheet would mean a rush to the weigher. Ay de mi!

Fond love, Sooze

1 Cass Canfield Jr; editor at Harper & Row, later HarperCollins, and a director of the company for many years.
2 Sixteen-year-old Constancia was in Mexico City learning Spanish.

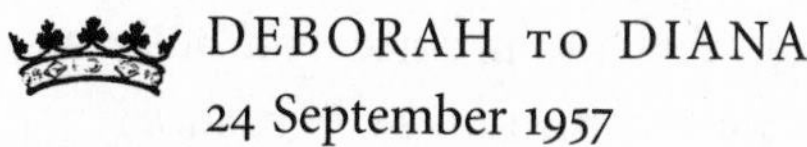

DEBORAH TO DIANA
24 September 1957

4 Chesterfield Street, W1

Darling Honks

V. glad to get yr letter with your plans. Mine are AWFUL, because we are having a sale of furniture at Chatsworth, a thing we have thought of for years but never got further with because we couldn't till the death duties were fixed. Anyway now we really are going back to the house we have got to make room & there are rooms & rooms piled with furniture which has all got to be sorted, & the sale stuff chosen and the keeping stuff chosen & you can imagine what a task that is going to be.

It is very exciting but I am rather daunted (a) by the amount of stuff & (b) whatever I do people will say is wrong. Isn't it difficult. If you could see the mountains of rubbish, maids' washstands with broken snow-shoes from Canada, a walking stick & a smashed deck chair all in one heap, and three rooms with six beds in each all piled to the ceilings with old mattresses like *The Princess & the Pea*. Three huge cupboards filled with lids only of china veg. dishes, many enamel water jugs of pantomime size, two lorry loads of cream-coloured antimacassars etc etc, as well as about 1,000 incomplete chandeliers, broken carpet sweepers, ditto oil stoves & so on. Anyway you see it's a task, but at the same time I must see you.

Wife is playing hard to get as usual, but she comes down on the sleeper Mon night so we shall have her for Tues. Please you be there too. Damn everything.

Much love, Debo

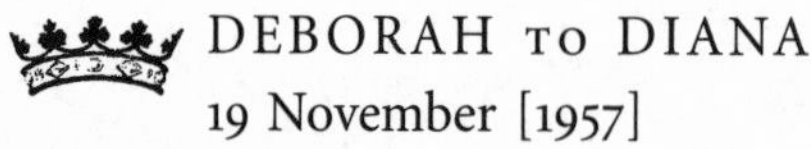

DEBORAH TO DIANA *Train*
19 November [1957]

Darling Honks

I saw Farve today, he seemed very pleased which was so touching. He certainly looks rather frightening, so thin & small, but he smiled a lot & heard what I said but he gets very muddled, for instance he said he was going to ring the bell & then picked up his lighter and tried to make it work. He hasn't been downstairs since Sept but Margaret says he can & does shuffle into the bathroom by himself. He sleeps a great deal, & drops off while one is there & then wakes up & smiles & seems pleased to find one there. He said he would like to see Muv, & I think he meant it though like everything he says it sounded vague. I saw him eat his lunch, went & had mine at the pub & went back & sat for ½ an hour.

The upshot of it all is that one feels he can't live much longer (his breathing sounds very difficult & queer) & as it obviously still gives him a little pleasure to see one it's better to go now & not leave it till he is unconscious, & so vague that he would not know who it was.

Margaret was *much* easier, & told me a lot of things about him, how he writes odd things & she looks at anything that goes in case the receiver gets a shock, she also said (which is obvious) that the doctor told her he might die at any minute.

If Muv goes she must have you or me with her don't you think so, it's bound to upset her. I'll talk to her tomorrow & see what she feels. Margaret is going away tomorrow for two nights, if only one had known that I could have taken Muv then. There is another person there (M's ladies' maid I suppose) to look after Farve.

I can't think of anything else, but I'm *so* glad I went.

Much love, Debo

DIANA TO DEBORAH
16 January 1958

Ileclash[1]
Fermoy
Co. Cork

Darling Debo

Yesterday in answer to an SOS we went over to Woman. Tullamaine is sold but the buyer doesn't want the house, it is a shop man from Cork, & he suggests Woman stays on. I strongly advised against & anyway could plainly see she really hates it there now & has far too much work to do. Giuditta[2] wants them to go near Rome & Woman pretends to agree to this but really she has her eye on Bavaria & Rudi[3] (which means throwing off Giuditta). Well *I* think she would be far happier in Germany where she speaks the language.

Please forgive saga but tell what you think & tell Muv. The atmosphere at Tullamaine is awfully sad & also rather tense – I suppose G sees herself homeless. But Woman First is the motto.

Oh Ireland, the niceness of it. We passed five cars in 95 miles driving. Tell the Wife the Min. of Finance plans to fill the valleys of Kerry with asparagus! Kit got so excited when he read this & longs to get a valley in Kerry.

All love to all, Honks

1 The house in Ireland the Mosleys bought after Clonfert burned down.
2 Giuditta Tommasi (d.1992). Daughter of a German-Swiss mother and Italian-Swiss father. An expert with horses, she moved to Ireland after the war where she became close to Pamela.
3 Rudolfine (Rudi) von Simolin (1918–79). Only daughter of a rich German industrialist and art collector. A friend of Unity in Munich, she visited her every day in hospital after her suicide attempt and packed up her Munich flat when she was sent home to England. After the war, Pamela accompanied Lady Redesdale to Germany to thank Rudi and they became lifelong friends. Married to Baron Lulu von Saint Paul in the late 1940s.

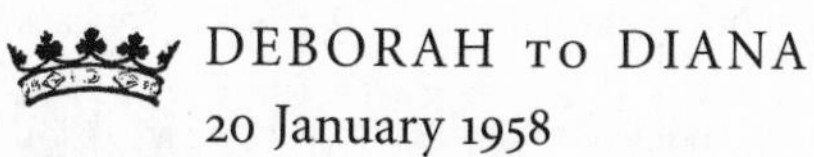

DEBORAH TO DIANA
20 January 1958

Chatsworth[1]
Bakewell

Darling Honks

I was glad to get your saga about Woman, I'm sure Bavaria and Rudi are the answer and Woman First must be the cry of course. I've written to thank her for her Xmas present and said I do long to hear what she is at, plans etc, and that I heard there was a possibility of Bavaria, *what* a good idea etc. I do hope she leaves Ireland soon, it must be so horrid living somewhere one rather hates.

I do wonder if you have got a cook to cook the asparagus from the Kerry valleys? You have been unlucky with illness & your servants.

Stoker goes back to Eton tomorrow so I am going to London with him. His reports were so good, one started 'I can honestly say no new boy has given me so much pleasure'. Do you think he will live up to that? The other bit of really good news is that Em has passed the maths of her school certificate, & now she never need do another sum which means a lot to her. She has (in July) the subjects she likes so I expect all will be well.

The review in *The Times* of Elvis' new picture[2] was rather nice didn't you think. I can hardly wait, will jolly well go this week.

Chatsworth will soon begin properly, v. exciting. We have got to sell a lot of stuff (like Woman) to pay for the move and make a fund to keep the house going, it is fearful deciding what is best to go because generations to come are sure to say 'my mad old grandfather (and grandmother) went and sold the —s. The one thing I *really* like'. So what is one to do. The very early printed books and some dreary things called the Virginia Tracts[3] seem to me to be the sort of thing, with some drawings and a picture or two, thereby not getting rid of all of any one thing.

I think that's about all for the moment, I will tell Muv the Woman Saga.

Have you had any more bad heads and how are the stays?[4] Answer please.

Much love, Debo

1 Deborah was using up old Chatsworth writing paper. The family did not move back into the house until 1959.

2 *Jailhouse Rock* (1957). Deborah's early interest in Elvis Presley developed into a passion in later life.

3 Early seventeenth-century books relating to the Devonshires' involvement in the Virginia Company.

4 As well as suffering from migraines, Diana had a bad back for which the doctor prescribed a support belt.

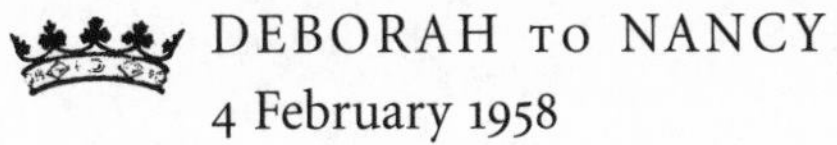

DEBORAH TO NANCY
4 February 1958

Edensor House
Bakewell

Get on

Oh I was pleased to get your letter from abroad because I have been expecting to see Famous Authoress Dead on the placards again owing to your dread silence.

Blenheim[1] – better to draw a veil. The unmitigated horror of him, the pathetic efforts of her to make a show of being alive by being sharp with people, the seriousness of the shooting & the *vileness* of him at it, shouting at beaters, his wife, guests, loaders & keepers equally loud. Oh it was an experience of nastth. The nicest thing was that the lavatory in my bathroom was called The Cavendish.

The conversation after three nights made me long for my Teds, I could scarce continue. One night at dinner Lord Cadogan turned to me & said, 'Have you ever been on a railway with 2,000 rabbits on a hot day in September?' When I admitted I hadn't, he chucked it. The whole outing was really for [Tom] Lord & then he got 'flu & couldn't come, so I did feel lonely. Anyway it was very interesting & there are some v. pretty rooms (which they are just about to change) & the park, woods, etc are beyond anything for beauty but they don't seem to notice.

It's the W.I. party tonight, I expect it will be lovely. Em is coming as my guest. Sophia does a new thing called Voluntary Nearth, when she puts her face on one's in a loving way & (special treat) gives it a lick. One has to do awful tricks to get her to do it like pretending to be dead. She goes very fast along the floor on two hands and one leg & drags the other leg like a wooden one.

I long for you.

Much love, 9

P.S. I have got God's Own Cold (Duchess of Marlborough expression).

1 Deborah had been shooting at Blenheim Palace with the 10th Duke of Marlborough.

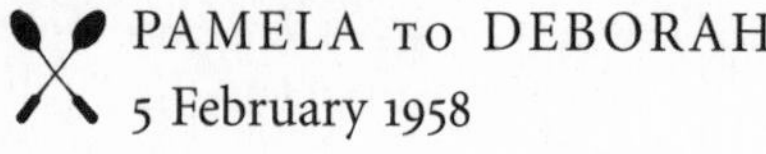

PAMELA TO DEBORAH
5 February 1958

Tullamaine Castle
Fethard
Co. Tipperary

Darling Stublow

Many thanks for your letter. Of course I will get you a cot, blankets, sheets & all. I have a *perfectly good cot*[1] that Al & Max used at Rignell. If painted would it not save a lot for you to borrow it while here? I think it may need a new mattress also a pillow. I have some *perfectly good blankets* which have a *few moth* holes; if Frau Feens[2] cut them into the right size leaving out the *eaten parts* she could put some pretty ribbon to bind them & this would again save a lot. Then what kind of sheets, linen or cotton? If linen, I have some large double bed ones which are *rather worn* but here again Frau Feens could find plenty left to make cot sheets. Let me know soon as I expect to go to Dublin perhaps the week after next. On Friday 14th is the sale here of cattle, hay & implements.

In haste,

Much love, Woman

1 Deborah, who was taking one-year-old Sophia to Lismore for the first time, underlined the words that appear in italics and forwarded this letter to Diana.
2 Miss Feeney; the seamstress at Lismore. She was taught all she knew by Ann Astaire, mother of Fred, who lived at the castle during the war with her daughter, Adele, married to Andrew Devonshire's uncle, Lord Charles Cavendish.

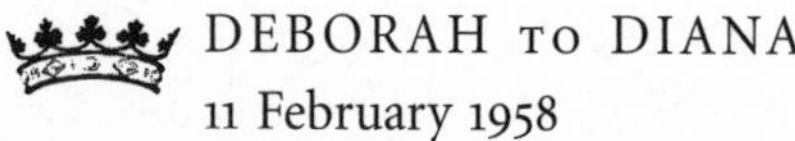

DEBORAH TO DIANA
11 February 1958

4 Chesterfield Street, W1

Darling Honks

We went to Eton on Sunday & we fetched Blor for tea, oh Honks she is *SO* old all of a sudden & her poor hands don't work so she has cut her hair off because of not being able to do it, & her eyes look red & puffy all round, she has changed very much but she was smiling & cheerful. The old sister looks quite well thank goodness. I can't imagine what would happen if *she* got ill & as she is eighty-four, it must be so hard to do all the coal & cooking & everything. I thought I would go down next week on some pretext or other & find out the name & address of the niece, to make sure someone would let us know if either of them got ill (as Blor can hardly write). I was haunted by the thought of them after we'd left. You can't imagine what a job it was winkling Muv & Blor up the stairs at the Cockpit,[1] you would have screamed if you had seen us. They left their purses about & the boys were forever going back to where we had just been to find something.

Please write.

Much love, Debo

1 A restaurant in Eton High Street, dating back to 1420; a favourite with parents visiting their sons at Eton College.

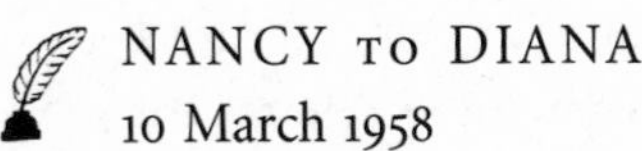

NANCY TO DIANA — *7 rue Monsieur, VII*

10 March 1958

Darling

Do you know what the English doctors did? They said old Prod had cancer of the lung & *took it out*. When pressed to tell what they found they were obliged to admit only an old pneumonia scar. But, they said, he is probably *better without it*. No Comment.

Harper's Magazine (not *Bazaar*) have asked me to write 3,000 words on why I hate the Americans. Very naughty & irresponsible of them, because how can I resist? And there'll be such trouble. I've already jotted down many a telling phrase.

I've just lunched with T Pawson[1] whose head seems to have been got at by head-hunters, it could go on a watch chain or six times into that of Castillo[2] who was also there.

Julliard is said to have found an English Sagan.[3] Violet Trefusis I guess.

Much love, N

1 Algernon (Tony) Pawson (1921–91). Ex-lover of the rich Chilean collector Arturo Lopez Wilshaw, Pawson was said to have the smallest waist in the army when he worked for British Intelligence during the war.

2 Antonio del Castillo (1908–84). Spanish dress designer who came to Paris in 1936 and worked for Paquin and Lanvin.

3 Françoise Sagan's *Bonjour Tristesse*, published by Julliard, was the bestseller of 1954.

NANCY to JESSICA *7 rue Monsieur, VII*
3 April 1958

Darling Sooze

Not off writers, but frantically busy. About 100 Farve letters to answer[1] & three jobs hanging over me.

No I don't take in clippings & love to see any thanks very much. My publisher sends a few (*Life, N. Yorker* etc) & so far they are favourable & I seem to be on the best sellers list whatever that is. Glad you liked it.[2]

I've just got back from England. Three funeral services – such tear jerkers Susan with the old hymns ('Holy Holy Holy') & the awful words, I was in *fountains each time*. Then the ashes were done up in the sort of parcel *he* used to bring back from London, rich thick brown paper & incredibly neat knots & Woman & I & Aunt Iris took it down to Burford & it was buried at Swinbrook. Alas one's life.

Lord Redesdale's funeral, Swinbrook, 1958. (*from left*) Mabel Woolvern, the Redesdales' parlourmaid; Jerry Lehane, the Mosleys' chauffeur; Diana; Lady Redesdale; Oswald Mosley.

The will is almost too mad.[3]

I'll write again very soon.

Much love & to Dinky, N

1 Lord Redesdale died on 17 March 1958, four days after his eightieth birthday. Although he and Lady Redesdale had lived apart since the War, they never divorced and had continued to write to each other regularly.

2 Nancy's biography *Voltaire in Love.*

3 Lord Redesdale, who had not seen Jessica since 1937, had cut her out of his will because of her attempt to give her share of Inch Kenneth to the Communist Party.

DIANA TO DEBORAH

Rouen

6 April 1958

Darling Debo

The last days in London were terrific, not only the usual when a move from Ireland & England to France is toward but all Kit's book[1] suddenly had to be corrected and the Mews got ready for the tenant. The packing up was terrific, drawers stuffed with everything you can think of from needlework and Birdie's SS daggers to Farve's skating boots. The miracle was that throughout I never got a single headache.

Al [Mosley] went to peer at the Commie marches of Good Friday[2] & spent five hours shouting 'No unilateral disarmament', & who should he see *marching* but Nicky [Mosley]! So they marched together chatting for a bit & then Al went back to his jeering. Oh darling doesn't this remind one of Bobo & Decca. In the same way Nicky & Al are terribly fond of each other & both certain they are right.

All love darling, Honks

1 Oswald Mosley, *Europe, Faith and Plan* (1958).

2 The first Aldermaston March against nuclear weapons.

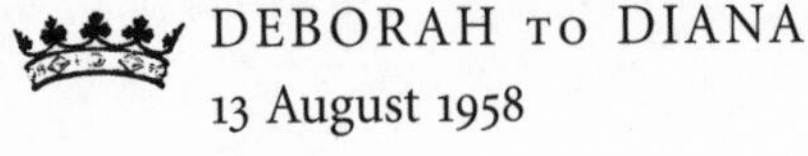

DEBORAH TO DIANA

13 August 1958

Bolton Abbey[1]
Skipton
Yorkshire

Darling Honks

Em has come back from the Urquharts,[2] saying Mrs U does all the cooking, makes all their clothes, does all the washing, all the garden *and* goes to cocktail parties. All I can say is she must be very strong.

Em makes *one* feel very small by saying Mrs U never seems to go in to the kitchen – yet a miracle dinner appears, and she goes climbing mountains & to Edinburgh & to Loch Lomond with the children and yet there is the dinner. Oh Honks I know I never could, & Wife never could & you never could, we are too weak. Here we are five or six in kitchen (can't quite make out which) and they really do seem to be in the kitchen & yet it is a struggle. I must get Mrs Urquhart to do it next year, with her bright smile. She can do all the washing too, and load in her spare time.

We went to lunch with the Sitwells on Monday. Dame Edith[3] was in a long fur coat (which she never even unbuttoned for lunch) and a feather hat & her long white hands & huge rings. She is lovely, & gone on the same people as me, viz. Cake[4] & Greta Garbo. She told us the chief things she remembered her mother saying were 'We must remember to order enough quails for the dance' and 'If only I could get your Father put into a lunatic asylum'. Poor old Osbert[5] doesn't seem much worse, but it is frightening to see him walk with that fast shuffle. He has got to go away at the end of the month because – why do you think, answer at bottom of page. So there you are.

R Kee[6] was marvellous as the question master, in *The Brains Trust*,[7] his hair style makes one feel quite funny.

Much love and I *do* hope you have a proper good holiday. Don't worry about *anything*.

Debo

He can't get a cook, so perhaps you'll send him one.

1 The Devonshires' Yorkshire estate.

2 Major-General Robert Elliott Urquhart (1901–88). The commander of the 1st Air-

borne Division at the Battle of Arnhem had become an executive in the steel industry after leaving the army. Married to Pamela Condon in 1939. Their daughters were at school with Emma Cavendish.

3 Edith Sitwell (1887–1964). The poet had been named vice-president of the Royal Society of Literature earlier in the year.

4 The Queen Mother. Deborah adopted the nickname after attending a wedding where the Queen Mother, when told that the bride and groom were about to cut the cake, exclaimed 'Oh, the *cake*!' as though she had never seen it happen before. Deborah was lastingly impressed by her enthusiasm.

5 Sir Osbert Sitwell (1892–1969). The writer was suffering from Parkinson's disease.

6 Robert Kee (1919–). The writer and broadcaster was a great friend of the Devonshires. Author of *The Impossible Shore* (1949), *A Sign of the Times* (1956) and *Ireland, A History* (1981).

7 A BBC radio programme, started in 1941 to answer listeners' queries, which became one of the most popular programmes ever broadcast.

NANCY TO DEBORAH
27 August 1958

Inch Kenneth
Gribun, Oban

Dear Miss

I had to ask for a little more to eat. The meals, which are utterly delicious, fell below the danger level & yesterday's luncheon was just nouilles [noodles] & a large jug of cream. I suppose I did it tactlessly but it's difficult to be tactful at the top of one's voice, & my words were very badly received. 'Better go back to France tomorrow if you're starving here etc'. However, corned beef was produced & for supper bacon with the eggs, although I was pointedly told that these things are reserved for workmen when they come. All is well now & she shrieks about the meals & I think sees that really they have been rather dainty.

Dialogue.

Muv 'May Courage is dead.'

N 'Oh I'm sorry.' Pause. 'What happened to the Banburys?'

Muv 'Oh THEY died in DROVES.'

The cold is quite better, but she gets tired I see.

Pelting rain today – just as well, to fill the tank. It was getting like Hydra & PAPER no longer goes down.

Goodness the rain. I leave here tomorrow week.

Much love, N

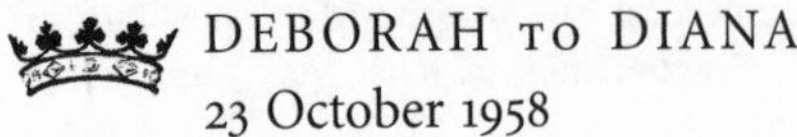

DEBORAH TO DIANA
23 October 1958

4 Chesterfield Street, W1

Darling Honks

The picture[1] is said by its author to be going very well but when I take a surreptitious look it seems to me to be a small blob of mud-coloured paint in the region of the forehead, & the vaguely drawn outline shows two *tiny* little eyes & a vast mouth. So time will show.

Yesterday I was saying how you had suggested Bérard[2] for the job & he dragged an old Frog newspaper out of a case & there was a photo of a picture he had done of him. He said Bérard was always going on about you & he sees why now.

Today I am going round Boldings etc. with our *sweet* architect for baths & things for Chatsworth.

I am quite annoyed with Mrs Ham. I asked her to *tea* on Sunday & she writes to say she must have *The Brains Trust* (4 P.M.) and dinner.

Much love, Debo

1 Lucian Freud had begun his portrait of Deborah.
2 Christian (Bébé) Bérard (1902–49). Painter and one of France's leading stage designers.

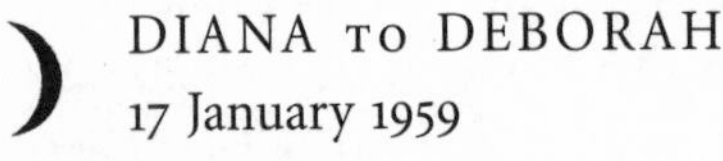

DIANA TO DEBORAH
17 January 1959

Ileclash
Co. Fermoy

Darling Debo

The Wonderfuls[1] came yesterday & told the following. Woman insisted that her landlord must put E[lectricity] S[upply]B[oard] light in Tullamaine.[2] He obeyed & a lot of workmen went to re-wire the house. She then said that she had no milk for their tea so she *must* have a cow for them. He sent a marvellous four gal. cow in a lorry from Cork (70 miles). Of course the men only used a pint a day so Woman bought four piglets which she is bringing up on the milk. Even they couldn't get through it all so she sends the rest to the creamery. While she was staying with the Ws a cheque for £10 came from the creamery. Wonderful said 'Oh yes I suppose you will send that to Mr Wood' (or whatever his name is) whereupon Woo screamed 'OH *NO*! After all MY gardener milks the cow! And but for *me* Mr Wood's workmen would have had to BUY milk in the Fethard World![3]

So she keeps the cheque *and* the pigs – and the workmen are only there because SHE insisted. I thought we should die of laughing while this story was unfolded. Isn't she WONDAIR.

All love darling, Honks

1 Lieutenant-Colonel John Silcock, the Devonshires' land agent at Lismore for many years, and his wife Juliet.

2 Pamela had sold up at Tullamaine but was staying on in the house as a tenant.

3 Pamela's local town, Fethard, was pronounced 'Feathered'. *Feathered World*, to which Pamela subscribed, was the poultry and pigeon fanciers' magazine.

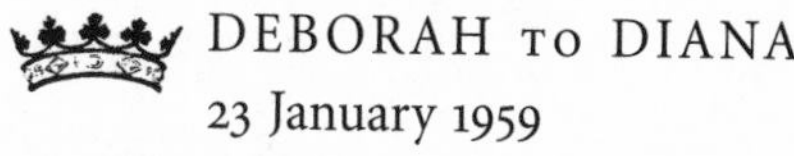

DEBORAH TO DIANA

23 January 1959

Edensor House
Bakewell

Darling Honks

Epstein's[1] fee has made my hair a) stand on end b) go white (which it was doing anyway) but I shall go on with it as Sophy is worth a mass isn't she & he is so old.

Lu [Freud] told me he (Ep) was turning over the pages of a 1926 *Tatler* the other day & after he had looked at the clothes & the adverts there was a page of Recent Portraits by Augustus John. He got very ratty and said 'it seems John is getting an awful lot of commissions nowadays'. Admit the *great* sweetness of that.

I think Muv quite likes her telly. She wants me to be the person to see about selling the Island when the time comes because of living in a handy place. Of course the only thing we must see about it is that Decca will agree with what the rest of us want. Some hope. Fancy her coming to England again. I dread it.

Much love, keep writing, Debo

1 Jacob Epstein (1880–1959). Deborah had commissioned a bust of her daughter Sophia from the sculptor. It was his penultimate work.

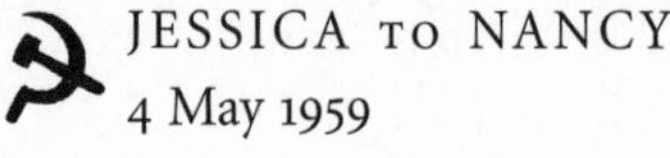

JESSICA TO NANCY
4 May 1959

c/o Mrs Rodker
71 Church Street
London w8

Darling Susan,

I'm trying to arrange things so there won't be a fearful muddle like last time.

Would your graph be notable about 7th June, in Paris?

Susan I've just had the most terrifically exciting news (it wouldn't be to you, because you are used to such things) a book I've been writing for literal ages has been accepted both here and in the U.S. It's sort of memoirs of my life with Esmond.[1] I can skeke [hardly] believe it. The awful thing is it isn't finished yet, so I've got to plough ahead like mad to finish it before Yurrup.

Yr. loving, Susan

1 Jessica's memoirs were published in England by Victor Gollancz as *Hons and Rebels* and in America by Houghton Mifflin as *Daughters and Rebels* (1960).

DIANA TO DEBORAH
14 May 1959

Temple de la Gloire
Orsay

Darling Debo

It has been real summer (80) for a whole week. Poor Kit missed the beginning by being in London, a target for oranges in Trafalgar Sq., but is now so happy in the sun. The peonies, lupins & roses have rushed into flower.

What about Decca's memoirs? A big advance from Gollancz is a bad sign I fear. I mean, if he gives money it must be because of 'frank' memoirs or whatever they are called. Kit says they can't be worse than Nancy's U & we are over the hump with that. I wonder. Nancy is loving the whole thing & never stops saying how marvellous it is to have Decca here & how good she expects the book will be. Kit took action & got Aunty Ni's awful book[1] withdrawn, well done him, a big loss for the publishers.

Would there be any chance of a bed at Chesterfield Street on the 27th for a few nights, would you be there? I literally *die* for you.

All love darling, Honks

1 *In Many Rhythms*, a volume of memoirs by Irene Ravensdale, older sister of Cynthia, Mosley's first wife, published by Weidenfeld & Nicolson, 1953. Mosley had sued to get the book withdrawn on the grounds of libel.

DEBORAH TO NANCY
27 May 1959

4 Chesterfield Street, W1

Get on

Could I have yr reaction (here) to Decca's take over bid for the Island?[1]

I can't think of anything against it, but I am going to get Andrew's lawyer to do the letter writing as we must make trebly sure that Muv won't be winkled out. Do you agree? What *can* she want it for, isn't it interesting.

Oh we had an exhausting weekend, Mrs Ham & Duncan Grant[2] punctuated by Sir John Barbirolli & the Princess Royal.[3]

On arriving at St Pancras Mrs Ham announced that our porter was 'a man of no initiative'.

Much love, 9

Saw Clarissa [Eden] last night, find her rather alarming.

1 Jessica had offered to buy out her sisters' shares in Inch Kenneth and keep the island so that Lady Redesdale could continue living there.
2 Duncan Grant (1885–1978). The Bloomsbury painter was an old friend of Violet Hammersley and a frequent guest of the Devonshires.
3 Princess Mary, Countess of Harewood (1897–1965). Only daughter of King George V. She shared Andrew and Deborah's interest in horse-racing.

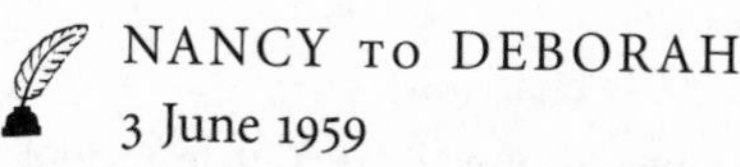

NANCY TO DEBORAH
3 June 1959

7 rue Monsieur, VII

Dear Duchess of Devonshire aged 9

Cruise – oh Miss Devon I *couldn't*. It often means getting up at seven Miss Devon. Besides in the Spring it rains in Greece (& not only in the plains in Greece) & my wife Lady Pamela[1] went & it said on the brochure there are only twenty rainy days in the year in

Greece & she was there for 17 of them. I met her in the Ritz loo on her way back & rain was still running off her neck.

I expect the Island is for a rest for Khrushchev[2] & if so McMurdo[3] will have to look a bit more snappy with the mail unless 'no letters will be forwarded'. I wonder how Khru will like living on jugs of cream?

The English pour in at this time of year & I shall be glad to leave. I go to Venice 1 July for five weeks. I've taken a flat where I could put *you* up but not anybody else. Come.

Much love, N

1 Lady Pamela Smith (1914–82). Political hostess and friend of Nancy during the 1950s. Married, in 1936, Michael Berry (created Baron Hartwell 1968), proprietor of the *Daily Telegraph*.
2 Nikita Khrushchev (1894–1971). Premier of the Soviet Union 1958–64.
3 Murdo, whose name Nancy gaelicized, was the man-of-all work at Inch Kenneth.

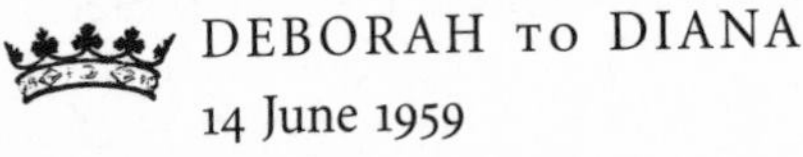

DEBORAH TO DIANA

14 June 1959

Lismore Castle
Co. Waterford

Darling Honks

Last week was very dread and a veil may have to be drawn as it was the camp of my regiment and I had to go & inspect them.[1] Oh Honks, the horror of all those women dressed as soldiers & calling each other Major Gribble & Captain Sands. I thought I was going mad among it all. As for the taking of the salute, well, there were as many photographers as at Liberace's libel[2] so I will send you one to make you scream out loud. I thought how Birdie would have loved it and I also thought how she and I got the sack when we joined the ATS[3] in 1938.

I need you for dead heading (as well as chatting).

Next week I pass to London & so does Sophy to be a little model. Diddy[4] is furious about the Epstein statue in the *D. Mail* & says if Sophy is going to be made to look like that she is going to put her fingers in the putty.

Doesn't the film of *The Blessing*[5] sound truly ghoulish.[6]

Much love, do write to London, Debo

1 Deborah was, briefly, Honorary Colonel of the 307 (Northern Command) Women's Royal Army Corps.
2 The flamboyant American pianist had brought a libel suit against the *Daily Mail* for describing him as 'an appalling man', 'the summit of sex – Masculine, Feminine and Neuter'.
3 The Auxiliary Territorial Service was the women's branch of the British Army during the Second World War.
4 Sophia's nanny.
5 Nancy's novel had been made into *Count Your Blessings* (1959), starring Maurice Chevalier.
6 An adjective often used by Pamela, who pronounced it as in 'fowl', which was taken up by all her sisters.

NANCY TO JESSICA
27 June 1959

7 rue Monsieur, VII

Darling Soo

A cold hand clutched my heart at the word 'photos' in your letter because where had I put that bit of paper?[1] A hunt far more frenzied than that for a pencil ensued, during the course of which I found two old out-of-date metro tickets, the enclosed torn by Noël Coward out of the Lausanne telephone book (look under 'Reine' and throw it away), ten dollars, a guarantee for my washing machine up to June 1956, some Italian small change, some Danish ditto & a ticket admitting me (Fancy Pogg)[2] to a Red Army Parade at Mockbar.

I then became quite hysterical, sweated, threw off my dressing gown & assumed the attitude of Le Penseur. Calm yourself Susan, I have found it. I only hope the shop isn't owned by communists – yes Susan – & the photographs won't have been browned by a hot iron. I'll go this morning & see.

Love N (Fancy Pogg)

Was the browning of the shirts in the form of a hammer & sickle by any chance?

I'm keeping Red Army Parade ticket to impress that laundry with if it ever comes into power.

F. P.

1 Jessica had been staying with Nancy in Paris and had left a receipt for photographs that were being developed.
2 Nancy's Cyrillic approximation of 'Nancy Rodd'.

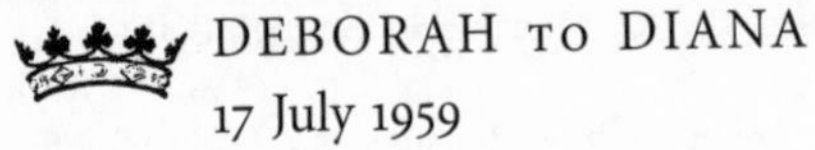

DEBORAH TO DIANA
17 July 1959

Edensor House
Bakewell

Darling Honks

I had a very terrible evening last night at the recep. at the Tate about the Romantic pictures. I had no idea it was a smart occasion – had on a cotton frock with a tie & to my horror I saw Cake advancing in crinoline & tiara & she pinned me while I talked quite wildly about goodness knows what, & she pinned me while I talked quite wildly about goodness knows what, & Sir Rothenstein[1] looked amazed at her knowing a sort of slum person when everyone else was in jewels & long dresses. It was terrible & I heard myself say, 'And the worst of it is I'm *stuck* now', & as I said it I realized how rude to complain to her about being stuck *with* her. Oh dear, I'm no good with royalties, & as I'm ¾ in love with her there is all that to contend with as well. Also my ticket had 'Lady Eden' written on it, & when Andrew saw he had 'Sir Anthony Eden'[2] he funked it and didn't come in.

Nice to be away from social traps though the weather is finished which is sad.

Much love, Debo

1 John Rothenstein (1901–92). Director of the Tate Gallery 1938–64.
2 Anthony Eden (1897–1977). The Conservative statesman had resigned as Prime Minister two years previously. He married Winston Churchill's niece, Clarissa Spencer-Churchill, in 1952.

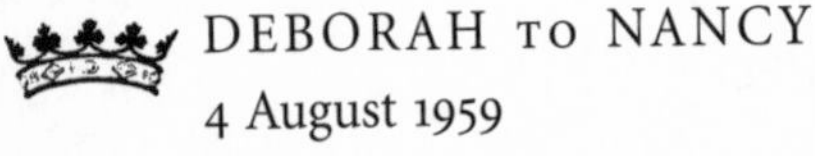

DEBORAH TO NANCY
4 August 1959

Edensor House
Bakewell

Get on

No, you can't have a suit from Hardy Amies,[1] you would have to make it yourself as well as design it & this might be beyond even your talent. Forget it.

Goodness how I would love to stay in Col's place in Rome.[2] A whole whack of *Connaissance* was devoted to it & made my mouth water. But what should I feel like in my nun's shoes, fat ankles & square thumbs,[3] a bit of a fish out of water, but I expect I could stick it. Enlarge on what would be a good time to go. Sept any good? Aug is booked by those benighted moors.[4]

Muv & Decca & Benjy came for the weekend. Muv's shaky hands[5] were so bad that I sent for Dr Evans (whom she loves & almost trusts) & he talked to her for ages & then came & told Hen & me that he had persuaded her to try one of the drugs which can help like anything. The thing about them is there are several & some of them have tiresome side effects on some people – one simply has to go on trying to see which one suits & how strong & so on. It had the most *amazing* effect, both hands were perfectly still & she was able to eat & drink at dinner without any trouble. Really it was *extraordinary. But* it made her terribly giddy & made her feet feel like ton weights. However she has promised to persevere.

Decca was much changed I thought, terribly nice & not touchy or anything. I *love* Benjy, he is so friendly & so funny.

The green silk is up in my sitting room at Chatsworth, looks quite jolly to me but I expect old French ladies like you will FIND FAULT.

Well, tweak yr ear, any chance of you coming to England? Or to Rome with

Yours truly, D Devonshire

1 Hardy Amies (1909–2003). Dressmaker to the Queen.
2 The Farnese Palace in Rome where Palewski had been French ambassador since 1957 and which he was busy restoring.
3 Nancy used to tease Deborah that she had a deformed thumb from sucking it as a child.
4 Deborah spent August shooting grouse at Bolton Abbey.
5 Lady Redesdale was suffering from Parkinson's disease.

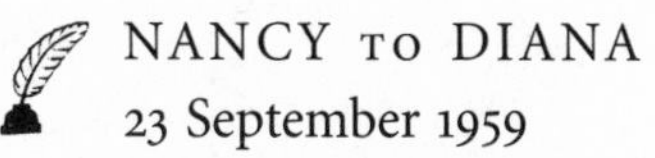

NANCY TO DIANA — *7 rue Monsieur, VII*
23 September 1959

Darling

You know the weather in Venice has been awful. Momo [Marriott] bathed only twice & they wore tweeds every day. A-Maria[1] says never has there been such a summer. So you missed nothing. She says

Daisy's face is so awful & Elizabeth [Chavchavadze] is so fat again that she (A-M) lets me off having my face lifted, as she begins to see all this monkeying about makes no difference!

The two babies in my *cour* [courtyard] – aged four & six – call each other Monsieur.

Much love, N

They say Momo ought to have her legs lifted – how can she expose herself to the cruel gaze of les gens du monde!!

1 Anna Maria Cicogna (1913–2004). A Venetian friend of Nancy with whom she often stayed during the summer months and to whom she dedicated *Don't Tell Alfred* (1960).

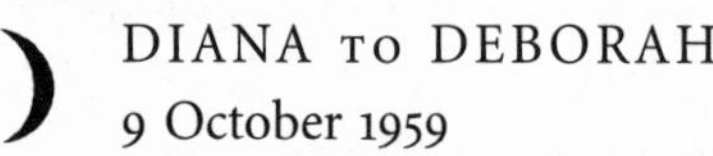

DIANA TO DEBORAH
9 October 1959

14 Cheyne Walk
London SW10

Darling Debo

We were so disappointed & *SO TAHD* last night that I didn't phone – hadn't the heart. I am glad about the big result[1] for the sake of Ingrid[2] & Wife. Our own result was fantastic, considering the canvass results. I never go by Kit's meetings because he excites his audience but that doesn't necessarily make them vote. But our canvass returns, & the fact that we drove all day round the constituency & were greeted everywhere by cheers & thumbs up & children covered in his photograph & heads out of windows smiling & waving doesn't seem like under 3,000 votes.[3] Most extraordinary. Another strange thing, in N. Kensington where there was tremendous election fever there was a lower poll than anywhere else – about 68%.

This letter is so that you shall get one when the boat comes in.

All love darling, Honks

1 The Conservatives had been returned to power in the general election with an increased majority.

2 Ingrid Wyndham (1931–). Diana's daughter-in-law. Married to Jonathan Guinness 1951–63, and to Paul Channon in 1963.

3 Mosley had estimated that he would get one-third of the votes; in the event he received just 8 per cent.

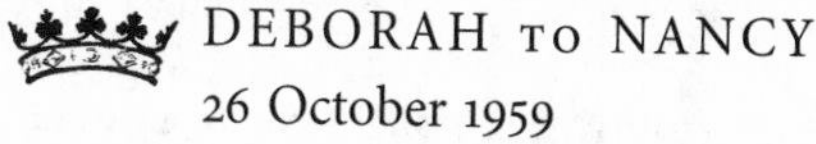

DEBORAH TO NANCY
26 October 1959

The Central Hotel
Glasgow

Get on

I am in a slight bait with Wid – she writes 'This is THE END, NO LETTER, nothing', when I've written as often as my 9 yr old hard-worked fingers allow with many a saga of various inties [intellectuals], viz. Sir William Walton[1] & E. Waugh. So I suppose nothing is forwarded as I naturally do not believe in foreign addresses, specially country ones.

E. Waugh sent me a nice present, his new book,[2] all wrapped up in bits of other books & with gold-edged leaves & all the rest. So I idly opened it feeling v. pleased, & saw 'To Darling Debo in the certainty that there is no word in this which will offend your Protestant persuasion'. I put it down having read that & got on with whatever I was doing but my Wife & daughter *being readers*, picked it up to have a further look & turned page after page with o on it till they realized it was blank pages throughout. V. kind of him wasn't it, because it's so much less trouble & so on.

I went to Uncle Harold[3] for the weekend, I simply can't begin to explain to you the change in him, it's *too* extraordinary. He sends me now. So *funny*, so quick & freely admits when one speaks up about things one doesn't know anything about. Smashing shoot, smashing food & Aunt Dorothy to boot. The only bad thing was bits of horse hair coming up through one's sheets.

I hope to see Honks for a moment tonight & then tomorrow back home as the real work has begun at Chatsworth, moving furniture &, most difficult of all, hanging pictures. It's no joke but v. v. fascinating.

Dread evening on Thurs, Princess Margaret & Gary Cooper[4] to dinner & I can't think what to have.

WILL YOU COME FOR XMAS? Please say yes.

Andrew's Grandmother is sort of dying. She woke up from a doze the other day & said 'Well it's time we left, go & order the barouche'.

Much love, 9

1 William Walton (1902–83). The composer had been taken to Chatsworth by Osbert Sitwell.
2 *The Life of the Right Reverend Ronald Knox* (1959). Evelyn Waugh's biography of the Catholic convert, scholar and writer.
3 Harold Macmillan, 1st Earl of Stockton (1894–1986). Conservative Prime Minister 1957–63. Married Lady Dorothy Cavendish, Andrew Devonshire's aunt, in 1920.
4 Gary Cooper (1901–61). The American actor appeared in four films in 1959: *The Hanging Tree, They Came to Cordura, Alias Jesse James* and *The Wreck of the Mary Deare.*

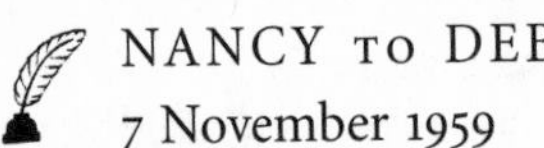

NANCY TO DEBORAH *7 rue Monsieur, VII*
7 November 1959

Dear Miss

Yes I'd love to come for Xmas. Perhaps either a few days before or on THE DAY itself, to avoid the mob? We'll see what suits. Momo wanted me to go to London, but I must get on with this book[1] & such a visit upsets the train of thought completely. But I can't go for years without seeing you & Muv & it seems to me far the best way of doing so is chez vous dans votre honorable château.

I've had Diana Week. *So* agreeable. Sir Ogre got ill in London & she has been here all alone & we've had practically every meal together. He returns today – poor old thing. Really I'm quite fond of him so it's rather horrid to go on like this – but you know what I mean! She's looking lovely so I think & hope is well.

I went to Lanvin – saw a dress, asked the price – 300. So I said out of the question. They said what about 230? I said no fear. They said 180 & I said snap. Doesn't it go to show? Honks is quite X about it, saying with truth I might have scraped up the 300. I did terribly want it I must say & of course plan to live in it for ever!! But oh *backless*, & Honks says the heating at C'worth must go slow for fear of cracking the works of virtue. Oh dear, what about cracking my back?

I shall be after Eton copy from Stoker & teenage copy from Em & dotty copy from ye.

Fond love, N

1 Nancy's last novel, *Don't Tell Alfred.*

SIX

1960–1966

6411 Regent Street
Oakland
California

March 8, 1961

Darling Susan,

Thanks so much for sending those 2 mags, I did love them. The E. Waugh article was a fair scream and not at all the sort of thing that folks in these parts do as jokes. Susan don't you really ever go out after 5 p.m? I can skeke believe it.

We've moved, which took ages, still masses of things to do (curtains etc.) But I love me new house. No point in telling you about it as I know you wouldn't displace yr.self to the point of coming to see.

Hen sent a t.gram from Washington (in response to one of mine, begging her to come here for a bit) signed Your Old Hen. The operator wrote on it "Repeat old hen, ambiguous copy." I noted her frozen face in a pic. in Life Mag, at least I think it was her, too fuzzy to really make out.

Isn't it terrific how wonderfully yr. book is selling. I see it will be out here soon. Shall I send local reviews, or do you really never bother to read them?

We're coming to England next year (1962) as Dinky will have finished her College by then, so she can come too. We have to see to the Isle.

Letter from Jessica to Nancy.

More letters have survived between the sisters from the 1960s than from all the previous thirty-five years put together. This is partly because their lives had become more settled and also because they had begun to realize the value of their correspondence and took greater care to preserve it. But the principal reason for the increase in letters was the death of Lady Redesdale in 1963. She had always been at the hub of family news, exchanging weekly letters with all her daughters, even keeping Jessica and Diana up to date on each other's lives. After her death, the sisters drew closer together and the letters they would have written to her they now wrote to one another, in particular to Deborah, the only sister always to remain on speaking terms with all the others, who took over from their mother as the centre of the family.

Lady Redesdale's death affected Nancy more deeply than her sisters. At fifty-nine, she had still not fully overcome feelings of childhood resentment and her mother continued to occupy a large place in her life. In addition to the inevitable sadness of mourning, she was overcome with melancholy, writing to Palewski, 'nothing really *nice* will ever happen again in my life, things will go from bad to worse, leading to old age and death'. Remorse was mixed with sorrow: nine months before Lady Redesdale's death, Nancy had written an essay about the sisters' nanny, Blor, in which she had painted a wounding portrait of her mother. When Lady Redesdale wrote to object, Nancy replied disingenuously, 'Oh *goodness* I thought it would make you *laugh*', but she must have known that her dagger had struck home.

The 1960s continued to be a productive decade for Nancy: she published her last novel, *Don't Tell Alfred*, and in 1966 her most successful history, *The Sun King*, a life of Louis XIV. This sold more than 250,000 copies in two years and, according to Palewski, was recommended by General de Gaulle to all his cabinet. Although the Colonel was still the focus of Nancy's existence, it was becoming increasingly difficult to keep up a pretence of happiness where he was concerned.

On his return from Rome in 1962, Palewski was made Minister for Scientific Research, a post he held for three years before being appointed head of the Constitutional Council. In addition to his work, the Colonel's romantic attachments were still keeping him busy and causing Nancy agonies of jealousy. She began to consider seriously an idea she had toyed with for many years: a move to Versailles, where there would be no danger of bumping into Palewski's mistresses and where she would miss him less than in Paris.

In 1960, Pamela left Tullamaine. She had sold the property but stayed on as a tenant while looking for another house. The sale that she held to dispose of her belongings entered the Mitford repertoire of legendary stories. Deborah remembered, 'Eggs which had been stored in brine were heard by the crowd exploding and Woman said very loudly to the assembled company Nothing Is To Leave This House Until It Is Paid For. She was delighted when glasses from Woolworth in Clonmel fetched 4 times what they had cost – & were still obtainable from down the road.' With the proceeds of the sale, Pamela bought Woodfield, a pretty Cotswold house near Cirencester. In 1962, she decided to let the house for part of the year and moved to Zurich, taking Giuditta Tommasi with her. She kept in touch with Deborah and Diana with monthly letters but wrote less frequently to Nancy and Jessica. Her letters are often about food, for which she had an extraordinary memory: she could recall in detail dishes she had eaten many years before.

In 1963, the Mosleys left Ileclash, the Irish house they had bought when Clonfert burned down, and made their permanent home at the Temple de la Gloire. Diana was sorry to leave Ireland but after five moves in twenty years, and much restless toing and froing between residences, she was thankful to be more settled. Summers were spent in Venice, winters in South Africa or the Bahamas, and they often went to London where Mosley kept a staffed office until he died. In 1966, he made a final attempt to enter Parliament and, when this failed, gave up the leadership of the Union Movement and withdrew from active politics. In the early 1960s, Diana began to sketch out memoirs but they were not published until 1977. Mosley also started work on an autobiography which Diana helped him to rewrite and edit, toning down the rhetoric and correcting the punctuation.

Diana's letters to her sisters only occasionally mention her literary and intellectual interests; she was an avid reader and many of her friends in France and England were writers. Deborah and Pamela were not readers and Nancy, the sister who shared Diana's literary tastes, was in and out of her house or at the end of a telephone. In this respect, Diana's letters to her sisters are as unrepresentative of her life as are Jessica's, who rarely wrote to her siblings about the political activities that took up most of her time and energies.

In 1960, Jessica brought out *Hons and Rebels*, the first of the sisters' memoirs to be published and the first of many books by or about the Mitfords to provoke furious reactions and divide family opinion. Unlike her privately published booklet *Lifeitselfmanship* – a swipe at communist jargon, along the lines of Nancy's U and non-U essay, which she had written under her married name – Jessica published her memoirs under her maiden name, thus revealing publicly for the first time her relationship with the sisters from whom she had spent many years trying to distance herself. Presented by the press as the true story behind Nancy's novels, it was an immediate bestseller, establishing Jessica as a witty and inventive author, and bringing her new-found respectability and financial security. Her next book, *The American Way of Death*, a coruscating attack on undertakers and their methods of preying on the bereaved, caused a national revolt against the funeral industry; and was on the American bestseller list for a year. Now in her mid-forties, Jessica began to use writing rather than direct political action to fight her causes, finding it easier to sit at a typewriter than, as she put it, having her head 'beaten in by the local police'. During the 1960s she made several visits to Europe to see her family and although relations with them were smoother than they had been at any time since the war, the tensions below the surface were ready to flare up at the slightest provocation.

The busy life that Deborah set for herself in the 1960s was a pattern that she kept up unremittingly over the following decades. Andrew was made Parliamentary Under-Secretary of State in the Commonwealth Relations Office in 1960, an appointment that he owed to the Prime Minister, Harold Macmillan, his uncle by marriage. His four years in the job involved extensive travel abroad and Deborah often went with him. After the untimely death of Andrew's sister-in-law, Kathleen

Kennedy, the Devonshires had kept up with the Kennedy family and attended the President's Inauguration in 1961. Deborah also went often to Paris where Nancy took her shopping for couture clothes and kept a critical eye on her purchases, anxious not to be outshone by her youngest sister in an area that she considered very much her own. The administration of Chatsworth fell mostly on to Deborah's shoulders; she oversaw its restoration, handled the expansion of the public area of the house, kept an eye on repairs to cottages on the estate, involved herself in local charities and functions, supervised the staff and entertained on a large scale. She shared Andrew's interest in thoroughbred racing and for some years bred Shetland ponies, or 'insects' as Nancy disparagingly called them.

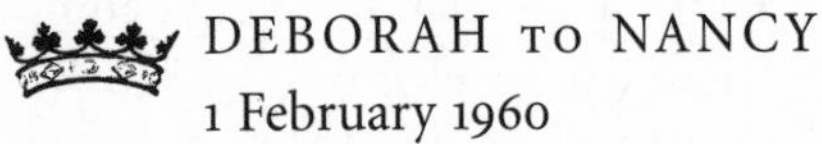

DEBORAH TO NANCY
1 February 1960

Chatsworth
Bakewell

Get on

Have you got summer clothes fixed up? Any hats for sale (or return)? Paddy Whack[1] is truly in what he calls Andrew's Damp Duchy, he has Women (Joan,[2] Janetta[3] & such like) down for the weekend & goes hunting on Sats. One day the hounds were messing about & it looked as if they were going to be ages & he noted a church which looked jolly, so he asked a girl to come with him to the gate & hold his horse while he went in to have a look, and (like I always remember out hunting) everyone followed them so he was unmasked as a sissy & an inti. He was rewarded though by finding who do you think's grave? Uncle Tom Cobley. I don't know about All, I think it was only Uncle T C. Admit.

My bedroom is done, it looks quite nice, pale blue silk & gold mouldings. COME & SEE OH DO.

Much love, 9

New slogan for Feb

A friend in tweed
Is a friend indeed.

P.S. Mrs Ham has written to say she thinks I am very hard and only interested in money so I've told her I'm never going to write again (anyhow not till she takes it back). *Say* I'm right.

1 Patrick Leigh Fermor (1915–). The writer and traveller, whose books include *A Time of Gifts* (1978) and *Between the Woods and the Water* (1986), was a close friend of the Devonshires. At the time, he was staying in the Easton Court Hotel, Chagford, Devon, an establishment expressly run to suit the needs of writers.
2 Joan Eyres Monsell (1912–2003). Photographer. Married to John Rayner 1939–47, and to Patrick Leigh Fermor in 1967.
3 Janetta Woolley (1922–). Worked on *Horizon* during the war. Married to Robert Kee 1948–50, to Derek Jackson 1951–6, and to Jaime Parladé in 1971.

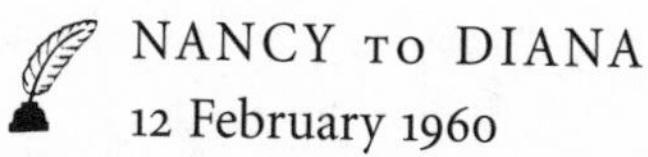

NANCY TO DIANA
12 February 1960

7 rue Monsieur, VII

Dereling,

Cora[1] has had another face lift with such appalling results she has to say it was a motor accident (Colonel's news). Violet [Trefusis] has had hers done with no results which is almost more disappointing. Anthony Chaplin's wife, who was in the London Clinic, says you should hear the nurses' views on these women – not enough hospital beds for real cases & so on & how *fearfully cowardly* they are –!

Much love – write, N

1 Cora Antinori (1896–1974). A Florentine who worked for Schiaparelli and later at the famous interior decorating shop, Jansen. Married Prince Michelangelo Caetani in 1920.

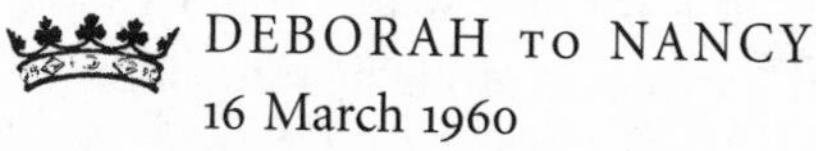

DEBORAH TO NANCY
16 March 1960

Chatsworth
Bakewell

Get along

Oh you WERE thoroughly good & kind on Monday, and I appreciated. The bit I appreciated most was the re-toiling out to go to the Invalides once more into the breach, it was noble and it obliged.

Henderson's book[1] becomes so dreadfully sad, the baby dying and Esmond too, oh she has had a tragic life, I would understand anything bitter *now*, but why *then*, before all the dreadery set in. I will never understand it.

I think Muv is prepared for all.

Much love, thanks, admiration for staying power down Main St,[2] etc etc. 9

Had lunch with who do you think yesterday? Answer upside down.

Wasn't I *lucky* – R——t K——[3]

1 *Hons and Rebels.*
2 Nancy and Deborah had been shopping in the rue du Faubourg St-Honoré, one of Paris's smartest streets.
3 Robert Kee.

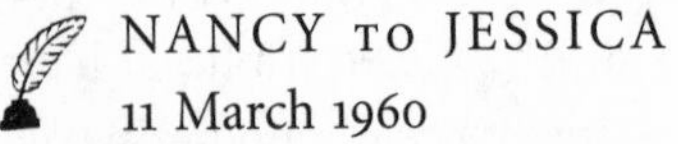

NANCY TO JESSICA *7 rue Monsieur, VII*
11 March 1960

Darling Soo

Many thanks for sending your book which I have read with great attention. I think it's *awfully good* – easy to read & very funny in parts. A slightly cold wind to the heart perhaps – you don't seem very fond of anybody, but I suppose the purpose is to make the Swinbrook world seem horrible, to explain why you ran away from it.

I loved the idea of shooting Hitler[1] – a Hon. did shoot at old Musso[2] who thought it exceedingly funny – had there been two, foreigners would indeed steer clear of the denomination!

I've no intention of having a go at Khru next week.[3] I rather long for the circus – a million Cuddums[4] are being brought from all over France (the local cleaner will probably appear in *your shirt*, yes Susan).

I long for the reviews & shall no doubt receive them as my press cutting people always send references to Mary Russell Mitford as well as to Lord Milford Haven. Heywood Hill, who always knows, says it will sell thousands.

Awful dust wrapper – silly old Gol[lancz] had much better have stuck to that Left Book Club cover (do you remember how ghastly it was the way books were *left* & piled up month after month?)

No news – I'm shut up, writing one myself.

Esmond was the original Teddy boy wasn't he, a pioneer of the modern trend & much more terrific than his followers. When does it come out in America?

Much love from Susan

1 Jessica had fantasized that she would pretend to convert to fascism, go with Unity to Germany, meet Hitler face to face and 'whip out a pistol and shoot him dead'. *Hons and Rebels*, p. 81.
2 Violet Gibson (d.1956). Daughter of a Northern Irish peer who attempted to assassinate Mussolini in 1926, wounding him in the nose.
3 Khrushchev was making an eleven-day state visit to France.
4 'Communists' in Boudledidge.

JESSICA to NANCY
28 March 1960

574 61st Street
Oakland

Susan,

For some reason I longed for, but feared, your reaction more than anyone's, even the reviewers. So I was most *awfully* glad to get your letter, although you *might* have sent it non-U mail[1] for once. I am enclosing some slightly worn postal coupons which can be exchanged for airmail stamps of any country, so do use them in future.

Sorry about the cold wind to the heart, I didn't really mean it to come out like that.

At Bob's suggestion, I have sent a short cable to the Cuddum cleaners saying 'ABOVE ALL, WHATEVER HAPPENS, KEEP MY SHIRT ON'.

The reviews have been sent on v. promptly, and I have been v. pleased. Did you note the *Graph*? March 25th, best so far I thought.[2]

Benjy, as usual, is being a hopeless tease, and when called on to read the reviews insists on reading the cooking hints and Letters to Editor etc on the other side.

No Susan, Esmond was not a pioneer Teddy Boy.

If you should chance to note any other views of me book, such as the Widow or any of the Relations, do not fail to let me know, using the Postal Coupons. Do you realize your letter was posted on 12th March and only just arrived today? But you have to take the Coupons to the P.O., they won't work if just stuck on.

Lots of love, and do write sometimes, Susan

Are you moving to Versailles? When?

1 Airmail. Nancy regarded it as 'very middle-class to be in a hurry'.
2 The Earl of Birkenhead described *Hons and Rebels* as a 'shameless but most diverting book', and Jessica and Esmond as an 'alarming couple', admirably suited, 'who were further linked together by a mutual amorality which at moments approached the sublime'. *Daily Telegraph*, 25 March 1960.

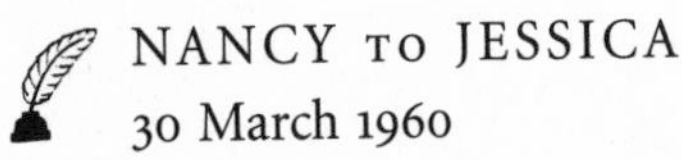

NANCY TO JESSICA — *7 rue Monsieur, VII*
30 March 1960

Darling Soo

Reactions

Muv is pleased & amused. Diana not pleased at being presented as a dumb society beauty & is really down on the book, picking too much on details & inaccuracies. We are all sorry you were horrid about Uncle Tommy,[1] always kind to us & really such a comic, original & in his way clever person. Debo really I think likes it but she had only read half when I saw her. Kept saying how sad – how sad – one didn't realize – & so on.

The Widow is to be Arbiter of All on account of knowing us from such early days, but she is gadding in London at present. I'll pass on the Arbitration.

I suppose on account of you & the Hon. Violet Gibson who shot off Mussolini's ear, I was ordered by the police here to report twice a day during Khru's visit. However I made the embassy tell them not to be so silly & all was rescinded. I saw the old fellow four times by chance quite near & waved, from you. All the cleaners were keenly there.

I sent the book to Sigrid (my maid when I first married) & she simply loved it – I sent her letter to Muv who will perhaps pass it on. I'm always pleased when simple people like one's books, it's a good sign.

Constantia Fenwick[2] says when she used to stay with us she had no idea so many pots were on the boil, everything seemed quite ordinary.

Much love, N

Versailles has fallen through – I am very sorry.

1 Bertram Mitford, 3rd Baron Redesdale (1880–1962). Jessica had written that her uncle, a Justice of the Peace, took pleasure in handing out a three-month prison sentence to a woman who had driven into a cow and enjoyed his duty of being a witness at hangings.
2 Constantia Fenwick; a neighbour at Asthall and childhood friend of Nancy.

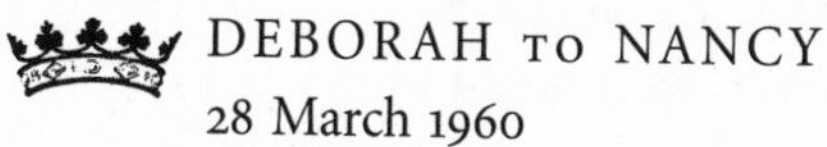

DEBORAH TO NANCY
28 March 1960

Lismore Castle
Co. Waterford

Get on

V. Good, your letter to Uncle Tommy. I was going to lunch with Honks luckily & there was Wooms so we all three signed & posted. It is *too* bad of Henderson, as though he ever did anything against her.

Ld Birkenhead's review is the only one which picked on the dishonesty (which is the theme song of the book). The other reviewers seem to applaud all that they did, from putting things down to other people's accounts, to stealing a car & so many petty thievings that they are mentioned on every page.

As for saying that Esmond was an orchid on a dungheap – well. I think Muv might have the *Observer* up for libel for saying she wasn't fit to bring up her children – defamation of the Good Body. I love the idea of regular work for Lord Redesdale.[1]

Oh dear, luckily it will soon be all over. It teaches one never to say anything in front of anyone, it is got hold of slightly altered, made serious instead of a joke & then held against one. Silly old Hen. I wonder what Mrs Ham's edict will be. I die for it.

It has been marvellous having Honks up the road, we have taken it in turns to have lunch with each other.

Much love, 9

1 In his *Observer* review, Anthony Quinton wrote, 'If they [the Redesdales] had been at the other end of the social scale they might well have been thought unfit to look after their own children, though regular work might have done something to abate Lord Redesdale's absurdities.' (27 March 1960)

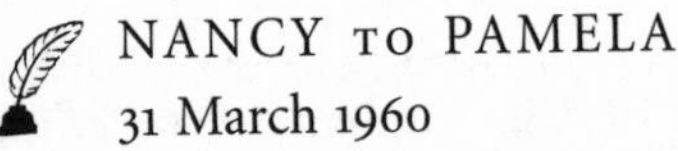

NANCY TO PAMELA *7 rue Monsieur, VII*

31 March 1960

Eet was wondair to see your rare & valuable handwriting. Aunt Iris, I'm glad to say, hasn't read & doesn't intend to read the book, so perhaps Unkel will follow suit. Much better – it wouldn't amuse them a bit. I don't think Decca really *meant* to be beastly you know – she is very insensitive. I've told her we are cross about it.

Heavenly weather here – I haven't worn a coat for ten days & winter suits are too hot. For once it's been much better than in London. Let's hope we shan't have a nipping frost to kill all.

Much love, Naunceling

They say about the Mountbatten funeral 'never can do without a splash'.[1]

1 Countess Mountbatten of Burma had been buried at sea with great pomp and wide media coverage.

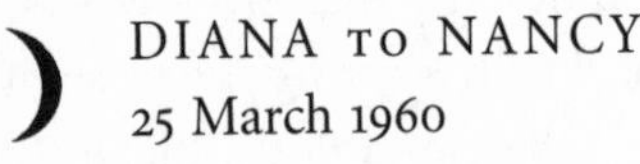

DIANA TO NANCY *Ileclash*
Fermoy

25 March 1960

Dereling

Apparently in the *D. Mail* 23rd (though not in the edition we get here) it said that you had been interviewed by the police who had mixed you up with *me*.[1] I wonder what spiteful person gave this piece of news to the paper? Surely the only person who could know this would be Jebb?[2] But he can't have told the *D. Mail*, as it must have been said (if at all) in confidence? What do you think? It is highly libellous because it sounds as if the French police never stop worrying about *me*, so untrue. It has upset me dreadfully, & I long to sue Jebb for libel or defamation.

Meanwhile about Decca's book – Muv doesn't mind *at all.* And I really don't believe she does. In which case I don't either. Debo thinks it would have been really ghoulish had it been written ten yrs ago when she went on that terrific visit. Too awful to think that in a few more years she, Decca, will be a mellow old lady. So Mrs Ham's deep thoughts, which haven't arrived because she is gadding in London, are less *urgent.*

What Ann Fleming[3] calls the Professor's Wife[4] has thrice chucked Debo & me for meals, always the same message 'Too Busy'. What do you think she's up to, writing scabrous memoirs no doubt.

All love darling, shall see you in London I HOPE, I must be there from Sunday week,

D

1 The newspaper had reported that Nancy was included in a list of people who were required to report to the police during Khrushchev's visit. The British embassy protested and it was found that the police 'had confused' Nancy with Diana. *Daily Mail*, 23 March 1960.

2 Sir Gladwyn Jebb was British ambassador to Paris at the time.

3 Ann Charteris (1913–81). Social and political hostess. Married to 3rd Baron O'Neill 1932–44, to 2nd Viscount Rothermere 1945–52, and to Ian Fleming, creator of James Bond, in 1952.

4 Pamela.

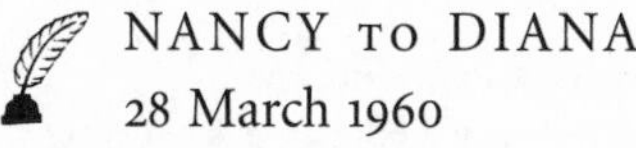

NANCY TO DIANA *7 rue Monsieur, VII*
28 March 1960

Darling,

I don't know why you think it would be Jebb – I'm quite sure it was not from the sequence of events. The only paper the embassy spoke to (not Gladwyn but Brooks Richards[1]) was the *News Chron.* The *D. Telegraph* got it (the 'story') first & when I begged them to they kept it under their hat – then the embassy rang me up two days later & said the *News Chron.* have got it & intend to publish whether you deny or not as they say they have it from a good source, so I was obliged then to tell the *D.T.* to go ahead. *D. Mail* simply copied from the others & must have invented about it being you. Of course they might have got that from Papon.[2] There's no doubt that was the reason. It's no good being an ostrich about the Fr police – they teased the concierge of a friend of ours simply because you had lunched there one day. Not on this occasion, it was some years ago now.

As my nice friend on *D.T.* said, the only way to keep it all a secret would have been to knuckle under & go twice a day, but I don't think that would have been sensible either. In fact the reason it did get out was that I went to the police station (when they first sent for me) with my American publisher whom I had been lunching with, Cass Canfield of Harpers, who insisted on coming. You may say stupid of me, but remember I'd no idea what it was all about. Then he went to London & no doubt couldn't resist telling. I'm *absolutely certain* it all had nothing to do with Gladwyn for all these reasons & knowing him as I do. Dreadful nuisance & wildly incompetent of the police I must say, considering you were there all the time. I don't mean to sound as if I were on the side of these brutes against you but I must stand up for Gladwyn whose fault it certainly was not. If you pursue extreme right-wing politics you must realize that you might be on a left-wing black list. Decca *might* have been told to report I suppose during Ike's visit.[3] You have much less reason to mind it all than I have & I don't mind one scrap.

Fond love, N

1 Brooks Richards (1918–2002). Press Counsellor at the British embassy.
2 Maurice Papon (1910–2007). Politician who was Prefect of Police in Paris 1958–67. In 1998, he was sentenced to ten years' imprisonment for his role in the deportation of Jews during the Occupation.
3 President Eisenhower had made an official visit to Paris the previous year.

NANCY TO DEBORAH *4 Chesterfield Street, W1*[1]
6 April 1960

Woman & I went to the flowers & there are camellias in my room & everything here is heavenly of course. *Can't* make out what is happening over the Mosley case.[2] Their witnesses either didn't appear or else didn't say what it was hoped they would. One man who had signed something in favour of Sir O said 'I was wild at being interrupted while watching TV – I'd have signed anything'.

There is a ghoulish article about us in *Times Lit Sup* saying how beastly poor Muv is. Mrs Ham has written up saying the reason we are all mad is hereditary & not that we were brutalized as kids.

Honks is furious with me because *D Mail* said the French mixed us up. I think she has got a little attack of persecution mania. As I am absolutely innocent – the only paper I spoke to was *D.T.* who reported it correctly & without mentioning her – I don't so much mind.

Jean [de Baglion] has got your dresses & hat. They look too lovely.

I saw Bridget[3] who is furious with everybody & everything. Really the lividry of London.

Much love, N

1 Nancy and Pamela were staying at the Devonshires' London house.
2 After his party's poor result in the general election, Mosley had asked the High Court to order an inspection of the ballot papers for evidence of fraud.
3 Lady Bridget Parsons (1907–72). Beautiful, grumpy, unmarried daughter of the 5th Earl of Rosse.

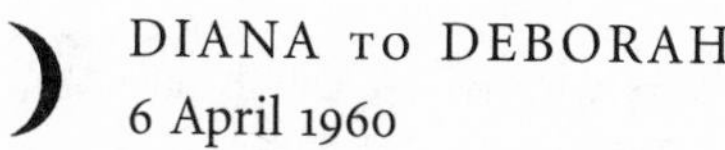

DIANA TO DEBORAH *Hyde Park Hotel*
6 April 1960 *London SW1*

Darling Debo:

A review of Decca's book in *Times Lit Sup* was a bit too much for me & I've written them a letter, they probably won't print it. The reviewer says that Muv & Farve as seen by their daughters are 'monsters of dullness & arrogance' & much more besides, but that Decca is too '*wise & loyal*' to say so. Well well.[1]

Muv is marvellous. On Monday she entertained Woman to breakfast off the Irish Mail at 7 A.M., caught a bus to Burford, was met by terrifying Uncle Jack,[2] spent the day & night with the uncles & aunts, got a train back next morning arriving in time for her lunch party, & at 3 P.M. was in Court to hear Sir O's case about the election. I was amazed to see her there, & when I took her home she chose to look at our flat on the way. Vive Dr Hensman. Nancy is about but we have a coolness about you know what. I wrote a fairly horrid letter which might make her think for one moment before she speaks to the whole world & assembled journalists next time.

Apparently Uncle Tommy was very pleased with our round robin. Last night at this O [hotel] we ran into Pat[rick] Cameron, dreadfully sweet. He said Constantia [Fenwick] had rung him up & said 'It's really too bad the way they're building Muv & Farve up into monsters when *we* know what they were really like'. Wasn't it nice of her – Pat heartily concurred. He says Farve was the most beautiful & the kindest man he ever knew, & Muv perfect.

Kit hadn't enough evidence for his case, which of course we knew & in the nature of things he couldn't have. But he spoke for hours very well, conducting the case himself against QCs very brilliantly & is pleased to have brought it. His 'opening' was truly as good as a play.

Well darling I think that's about all. I see you got a camellia prize.

I do hope you are all loving every minute, & wish we were having a game of Scrabble at Lismore. Ireland has receded into limbo already, as it does.

All love to ALL, Honks

1 Diana ended her letter, 'My sister's book was probably meant to amuse rather than be "wise", "loyal" or truthful.' *Times Literary Supplement*, 8 April 1960.

2 John (Jack, Jicksy) Mitford, 4th Baron Redesdale (1885–1963). Spent all his inheritance in one year in America and was penniless for the rest of his life. In 1914 he was married, very briefly, to Marie-Anne von Friedländer-Fuld.

JESSICA to NANCY
7 April 1960

574 61st Street
Oakland

Darling Sooze,

Thanks v. much for prompt answer, with reactions etc. Do keep it up. How about Muck,[1] for instance? (In fact, why don't you stop writing yr. book for a bit, and concentrate on getting reactions to mine?)

The *E Standard* just rang up from their New York office. They had a cable from London saying Cord said (in *Times Lit. Sup.*) that the Revereds came out 'grotesque' in the book. So, under their prodding, I told them Muv had written to say she liked it and thought it funny, but that she thought there were some inaccuracies in it. They asked what you thought of it, so I said they'd have to ask *you* that, as I didn't want to start a long thing of quoting from private letters. So I hope they don't go and make up a lot of things. The person who telephoned had not seen the *Times Lit Sup*, but had got a cable giving that one sentence. So, who knows

I fear the Wid's Arbitration will be adverse, as Muv says she is furious at not being included. A dreadful omission.

16th April. Oh dear I note I did not finish this. It was Benjy's Easter hol, and we went off to the country for a few days.

Meanwhile, I got the Arbitration, and though v. kind and complimentary for the most part, she really is cross about not being mentioned. That part of her letter is in 3rd person and starts, 'the writer of this letter', *so* Wid-like.

Do write again soon.

Love from Sooze

1 Mark Ogilvie-Grant.

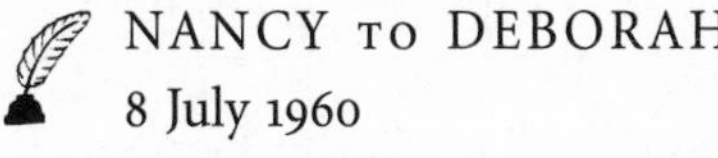

NANCY to DEBORAH
8 July 1960

S. Vio 373
Venice

Dear Miss

Old Vic [Cunard] is awfully ill & thinks he is dying. Anna Maria [Cicogna] assures me he's not. The deaths of one's friends are making an interesting study – I note that the idea of the hereafter hovering changes nothing at all. Momo goes on buying clothes, summoning up her last strength for the fittings – Victor is in a perpetual rage. I went up to Asolo where he is, three hours altogether in a hot bus, to be received by a shower of reproaches, didn't I know it is tiring to see people when you have a bad heart – oh well now you *are* here you can stay – & then all the gossip of the town larded with various grievances against me dating from about 25 years which he lies there cooking up I suppose. Ay de mi. Not a word of thanks for coming or indeed a civil word of any sort.

Do write. This address is quite serious I promise. Bad weather, no beach & I look so horrid & white beside the other women here.

Fond love, N

DIANA TO DEBORAH
21 August 1960

Temple de la Gloire
Orsay

Darling Debo:

We had a wonderful time at Bayreuth only far too short, & then Jonnycan & Ingrid [Guinness] & Max & Jean[1] went to Salzburg for two more operas, & Max & Jean got back here yesterday.

I won't bore you with Bayreuth except to tell you that Frau [Winifred] Wagner saintlily gave me her ticket for *Rheingold* & I made Max go as he'd never heard it, & he was a bit shy of going alone to the Wagners' box (none of us had a ticket although I tried last *Xmas*) so when he got back I asked if all went well & it appears he recovered enough to *kick* an American lady whose *head* he could reach with his toe through a curtain hanging in front of the box, he did this to punish her for rustling a sweet paper. He heard her whisper to her husband 'These *Germans* . . .'

Nancy was full of Venetian gossip & I was a bit shocked at the way she spoke of new people 'Yes, we all liked them' or 'We all took against them', as if she had no mind of her own but was linked to her local Jewish wife.[2] She looks very well & has ordered many a dress in Main St & agrees with me what a nice collection it is (at Bettina's)[3] so now darling *do* come in Oct, I live for it.

I rather enjoyed Peter Quennell's pretentious book,[4] & am now quite bookless, which is very horrid. We go to London for three nights on the 2nd Sept – end of next week. Can't tell you how perfect Ingrid was at Bayreuth.

All love darling, Honks

1 Diana's son Max married Jean Taylor on 9 July 1960.
2 Anna Maria Cicogna.
3 Bettina Jones (1902–93). Elegant American who worked for Schiaparelli and then Lanvin. In 1934, she married Gaston Bergery, Vichy ambassador in Russia and Turkey.
4 *The Sign of the Fish* (1960). Personal reminiscences and a discussion of literary style.

DEBORAH TO DIANA *Bolton Abbey in the Olden Days*
24 August 1960

Darling Honks

Thank you so much for your letter. So glad you liked the tunes.

It's coming to an end here. Uncle Harold [Macmillan] leaves today & everyone tomorrow & us on Friday. The second week has not been nearly so jolly as the first, one has to think before one speaks with the oldster here.

I wrote to Nancy so she may have told you, but the first night at dinner I heard Stoker say in the stentorian tones he reserves for the over 50's, 'Uncle Harold, *Old Moore* says you FALL in October year'.[1] I must say to give the old thing his due he looked solemnly at the table for a minute & said 'Yes, I should think that will be about it'. Stoker also said to me when we were alone 'if one didn't know who he was one would put him down as a vague moron'.

That's all I think. Oh for Main St, I can scarcely wait.

WRITE.

Much love, Debo

1 *Old Moore's Almanac*, an astrological magazine founded in the seventeenth century. Macmillan held office until October 1963.

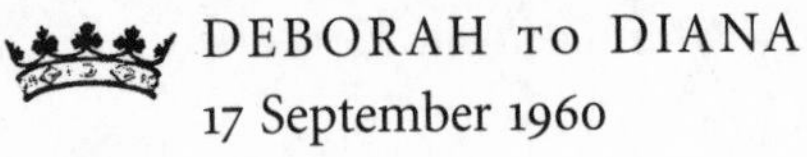

DEBORAH TO DIANA

17 September 1960

Chatsworth
Bakewell

Darling Honks

What would Nancy have done for her book if it were not for Al, Honks Cooper, Farve, Eddy Sackville-West, me & Sophy?[1] I only say that because she's not inventive, merely a very good reporter. I must say it's extraordinarily funny in bits, she's got old Al so perfectly & the Eton boys too for that matter.

Sophy said furiously this morning 'Why didn't you call me Gordon when I was a little gurl, why did you go on calling me Edward, why *did* you'.

Couldn't answer that.

Today is dread in the extreme, two ghoulish things to make a fool of myself at, then rush to Liverpool to catch the boat for old Ireland.

Haste. Write.

Much love, Debo

1 In *Don't Tell Alfred*, Nancy drew on the character of Alexander Mosley for Basil, Diana Cooper for Lady Leone, Lord Redesdale for Uncle Matthew, Edward Sackville-West for Davey Warbeck and Deborah for Northey.

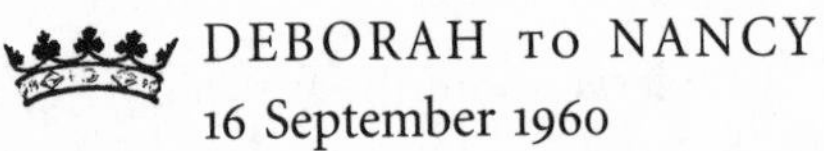

DEBORAH TO NANCY

16 September 1960

Chatsworth
Bakewell

Get on

Very well then, I've done it. The deformed thumb has turned the pages, all 248 of them. Admit the goodness of completing the task, in record time too.

I can't think how you do it, the writing I mean, it *is* so clever. I've been shrieking in the train to the livid looks of a dreary carriage full of Business Executives (which is what I long to be). Little did they know what I'd got my teeth into. I'm glad you quoted Old Sophy – she might have thought herself a bit out of it, though I note Edward isn't mentioned. Stoker says the Eton boys are exactly right which is *very* high praise from one you will admit. We will draw a veil over

Northey, & was glad to note she didn't see fit to worship anyone's body.[1]

I think people will love it, it is so funny & so clever to have brought in the brutes from the other books so people will think they are IN THE KNOW. I expect the Portfolio will benefit like mad, in which case I will give you a list of things Better Than Harpers, but have you noted how Harpers are mentioned as being bought in the Option market literally daily? That's good I can tell you. I shall hope to see you in Frogland in Oct though I note you will be with Mrs Ham & co. Lucy Freud seems to want to Hog a Week of Oct, with sittings every day & then no promise of the end. This is what it looks like now no hair, no chin, dark yellow (including whites of eyes) but I do admit very like.

So there we are & THANKS for masterpiece, 9

1 A friend of the sisters, Elizabeth Winn, inspired by the prayer-book marriage service vow, 'with my body I thee worship' was once overheard addressing her dog with the words, 'I worship your body'. 'This expression was taken on by Debo, and applied to people, animals and inanimate objects she happened to like.' *Loved Ones* (Sidgwick & Jackson, 1985), p. 50.

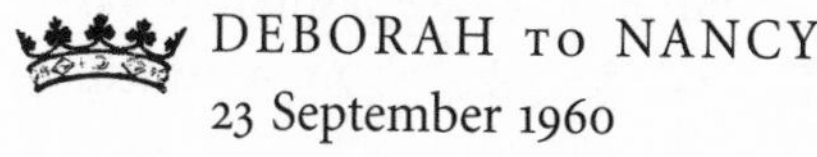

DEBORAH TO NANCY
23 September 1960

Inch Kenneth
Gribun, Oban

Get on

It's *lovely* here, but oh the journey. It's like an operation, one vaguely forgets it when it's behind one. The next bit (home) is child's play as it's all in one day (the longest day of the year, with the shortest night of the year).

The Wife isn't too well, bother it all, so we're going to try & hire a motor boat from Craignure so the start won't be quite so ghoulishly prompt. She is reading your book and screaming over it, when she's finished I'll get her to write a review to you. You *are* lucky to be so clever, it really is unfair.

Lady Redesdale seems very well, her hands aren't too bad and she's only taking one pill a day when the dr said she could have up to three. So she could be three times as well.

Station Hotel Oban is not the place for a long sojourn. I came down to brekker, found the diner full of a Granddad's tour all *smoking* (I think there ought to be a rule against it *at brekker*), stood for what seemed ages, no one showed me where to sit, so I said to a waitress 'could I have some breakfast?' She said (without looking up) 'what are you, are you a resident?' so I proudly said yes, so she plunged through the swing door into the kitchen (where she was going anyway) & yelled 'Sandy there's a resident says she wants breakfast' as though that was amazing at 9 in the morning. It all makes one very ratty, but it's *so* nice here & I think Lady Redesdale is vaguely pleased we've come. *Marvellous* food, lobster beyond anything last night.

I bought two smashing kilts in Chalmers, one is MacLaughlan tartan which I think is OK for me because we had a keeper called it.

Mr Eddy [Sackville-West] came to dinner at Lismore. There are no servants there, except some blissful dailies all aged about eighty, so everything was lying about when he arrived. Because he came so punctually, I wasn't down to tidy all up & his first words were (very trembly) '*Secateurs* on the *mantelpiece, saws* on the *hall table*'. No silver out so no candles at dinner & that ghastly chandelier for light, beating down on our poor eyes & I said 'it's the new fashion, a top light', & he really believed it, dear Mr Ed, & looked slightly pained but didn't like to say anything.

Are you coming to London for (a) your book and (b) the unveiling of the whatever it is to Farve at Swinbrook? COME & STAY. COME for XMAS.

Much love, 9

) DIANA TO DEBORAH
3 October 1960

5 Lowndes Court
London SW1

Darling Debo

You were so faithful to send the book, here it is. I adored all the bits about Uncle Matthew & Basil, fairly adored the bits about you & the Eton boys & holy David, & loathed all the part about the French. How she must make English people dislike them, most *unjust*.

Yesterday Max fetched me in the Austin Healey Sprite & drove me to Oxford where Jean had made a delicious middle day dinner. The flat is marvellous, not one ugly thing, & a view over playing fields to real country & a garden with an apple tree. ALL the wedding presents were being used – your car, Desmond's china, Emma's Derby ware, Viv's pressure cooker, Muv's pink blanket on the bed and (pièce de résistance) Wife's coffee set – also of course Freddy Bailey's[1] canteen of silver.

Oh Debo, the pathos of the young. Don't let's think.

All love darling, Honks

1 Edward (Fred) Bailey (d.2002). An East Ender who had been a keen supporter of Mosley since before the war.

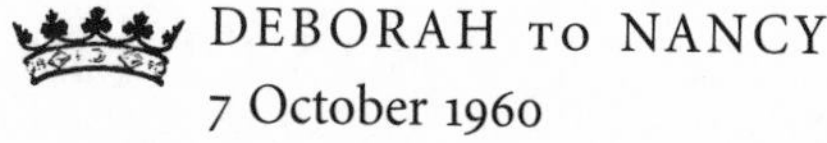

DEBORAH TO NANCY
7 October 1960

Train

Get on

It will be awfully jolly to have you in London – I will be there all week because of dear little Lucy & his picture.

I saw Honks in London. She's evidently having an awful lot of headaches. *Oh dear.*

I had two nice days' partridge shooting this week, one with that person called Bob Laycock[1] whom I've heard of all my life & never really met. The truth is that though I worship the bodies of these manly men, viz. Colonel Stirling[2] & him, I can't think of a single thing to say to them & the silences at dinner were quite worrying. I supposed it's bodies or nothing, but I do like a chat myself.

I took Em to Oxford yesterday. Her room was quite nice until she got into it. I dread to think what it's like this morning. We took a huge tea. Will it ever be washed up? I rather hope not as I was horrified to see the housekeeper at Chatsworth had sent the very best Crown Derby, oh what an idiot – I don't like to ask Em for it back so it's a gonna.

Much love, 9

1 Robert Laycock (1907–68). Distinguished soldier and Colonel Commandant of the SAS 1960–8. Married Angela Dudley Ward in 1935.
2 William Stirling (1911–83). Brother of SAS founder, David Stirling, who succeeded to the command of the 2nd SAS Regiment in 1943. Married Susan Bligh in 1940.

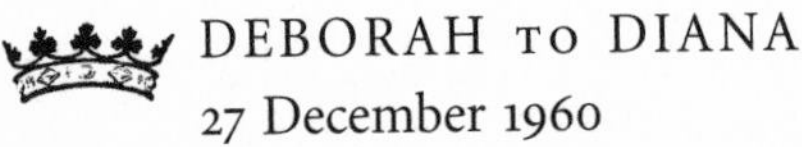

DEBORAH TO DIANA
27 December 1960

Chatsworth
Bakewell

Darling Honks

I long to hear how yours has been. Ours is breaking up – Wooms left this morning and Muv & Mrs Ham leave tomorrow.

Woman, I think, is mad. Her whole life is dedicated to those dogs. She cooks for them (*rice* of all queer things, meat of all kinds, brown bread – all the crank stuff), feeds them & takes them out. These three operations are repeated in quick succession throughout the day. Their names are fantastic & so is their behaviour. She takes them out before breakfast and their screams would waken the dead. They then come in muddy & get straight on the sofas & she makes no attempt to move them except by speaking very loud to them, which interrupts any other talk which might be going on. But they don't notice.

Honestly Honks, it's very odd. She's not *sortable*. She spent most of the weekend conjecturing as to whether there would be snow for the journey back. How I wish you & Nancy had been there, how we would have screamed at saga after saga. She was herself with knobs on.

WRITE

Much love, Debo

DIANA TO DEBORAH — 5 Lowndes Court, SW1
11 January 1961

Darling Debo:

This letter is to complain about Woman. Having bored myself dragging her pictures here & arranged to take them to the bank by having lunch early, she *phoned* to say would I take them instead to Muv's – whence I had fetched them the day before. I think it is her will-to-power at work & shall refuse to fall in with her caprices in future. We met at Muv's for tea, & guess why she'd come up. It was to look for curtain stuff at HEAL'S. Muv said 'Did you see anything pretty?' & she replied, in the holy voice used for lizard skin shoes, 'Oh yes Muv. *Wonderful*. I've chosen a simply wonderful sort of *tweedy* stuff for all the rooms.' She added Cecilia Hay[1] didn't seem to have *anything* of that sort. 'Nothing *lovely* Nard.'

She ees wondair.

Today is red letter because I have got a rendezvous with Wife. Did you miss *Panorama*, R. Kee in fine form.

Dying for you & Miss Maynard.[2]

All love, Honks

1 Deborah's childhood friend was working in a decorator's shop in Sloane Street, London.
2 A furrier who was making a sable coat for Diana, a present from Deborah.

DIANA TO DEBORAH — 5 Lowndes Court, SW1
13 January 1961

Darling Debo:

Another Womanly remark: 'Nard, would you like two absolutely *wonderful* armchairs for your flat?'

Me 'Oh Woman you are kind, but I think really we've more or less got enough now.'

Woman 'But Nard these are super armchairs. You could never afford that quality. And they've got flat arms to put a drink on. They are really *lovely*, don't you remember them at Tullamaine?'

Me 'Oh yes Woman I believe I do, lovely, you are kind.'

Woman 'It would be quite impossible to get such wonderful arm-chairs now however hard you tried.'

Me (as before).

This went on for several minutes. I know one day I shall wake up & find armchairs with drinks on each arm filling the flat. She ees wondair & really kind, but Debo those tweed chairs!

Is there any hope of a visit from the little gurl?[1] I die for her.

All love darling, Honks

1 Three-year-old Sophia Cavendish.

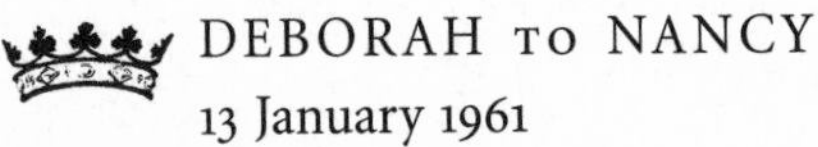

DEBORAH TO NANCY
13 January 1961

Chatsworth
Bakewell

Get on

Andrew & I have got to go to Jack Kennedy's coronation,[1] we go on Wed and come back on Sunday. I wish I'd got a decent fur coat, I believe it's bitter there. What *will* it be like.

The consul in Manchester where I had to go to prove I'm not a communist spy told me to take all my *pretties* and that I should see some wonderful *gowns & toilets*, what a strange lingo.

I'll write from America if I have a minute, if not the minute I'm back.

Much love, 9

1 John F. Kennedy's Inauguration took place on 20 January 1961.

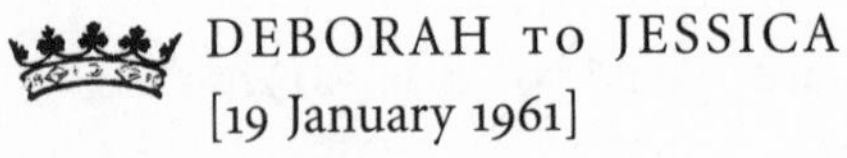

DEBORAH TO JESSICA
[19 January 1961]

British Embassy
Washington

Dearest old Hen

Alas alas we've got to go back to England on Sunday, we only knew we'd got to come here a few days ago & have got dreary but necessary fish to fry next week. *It is a shame* – twill have to be another time.

I can't imagine what this outing is going to be like but tomorrow looms so we shall see. Henderson, no one told me it is out of doors & it's not exactly stuffy outside & I haven't brought any thick knickers so if you see in the paper English Lady Frozen to Death in Main St you'll know yr old Hen has gone to the cleaners.

We've only met one American so far but I must admit we've only been here since 4.30 this morning.

We're going to a Gala with the Kennedys tonight, I think not the Frank Sinatra one which is sad & tomorrow to lunch with them after the thing. V. kind of them I do think.

Hope you're well Hen. Lady Redesdale is blooming.

Do come to the Island & be a magnate.

Tell yr plans & if you might come this year. Thanks for your telegram, it *WAS* nice of you. I wish I could have, it's partly Andrew's work which makes things difficult, there are things on all next week.

Much love, Yr Hen

DIANA TO DEBORAH — *5 Lowndes Court, SW1*
25 January 1961

Darling Debo:

In our chat last night I totally forgot to say that Miss Maynard won't be ready on Tuesday, she herself is away ill & the other lady looked askance at me & Wife & pronounced these words: '*You can't hurry sable.*' After that I hardly dared say 'oh do hurry' but I did say it, half.

A marvellous letter from Jean [de Baglion], he seems to be going to Rome, I rewarded him for his letter by a short one about the armoury. Now that the entire Kennedy bus is headed for Rome I can hardly bear it. Muv thinks you & Kennedy so like Birdie & Hitler & says, 'Yes, & Nancy & de Gaulle'. But I had to point out that de Gaulle has never jumped seven rows of seats to get to Nancy, nor has he bestowed the 20-minute stare. One must compare like with like.

All love darling & to little gurl, Honks

NANCY TO DIANA *7 rue Monsieur, VII*
5 February 1961

Dereling,

Lanvin's collection is a disaster – as awful as the last one was pretty. I sat next old Schiap[1] who said 'I only come to this one & do it for Bettina [Bergery]'s sake'. Never saw Bettina so subdued – she simply didn't dare say how lovely the dresses would be if they were entirely remade but from time to time when some even more horrible horror appeared she murmured desperately 'it's the low ceiling'. I must have a dinner dress & don't know what to do. County suggests Grès & I think I'll go & have a peep there. They say Dior appears to have bought all Momo's clothes & ironed them up – anyhow I can't sit through a Dior collection, I haven't the enthusiasm, followed by the hurly burly of the fittings.

The de Gaulles, faced by two evenings alone with *Oncle* Harold, got in a film, at Malraux'[2] advice, on Polynesia. It was absolutely feelthy. De G sees nothing – Madame says nothing – the Macmillans nearly die. One of the shots was a woman suckling a pig – her pig upon her breast. L'entourage says 'Oh well it's what the English expect, dirty pictures'.

Gladwyn is here, *adoring* H of L etc & says he wouldn't take NATO even if they offered it.[3]

Will it ever stop raining?

Much love, N

1 Elsa Schiaparelli (1890–1973). The Italian-born clothes designer had closed her Paris shop in 1954, after thirty years at the head of French fashion.

2 André Malraux (1901–76). The writer and adventurer was France's first Minister of Culture 1959–69.

3 Lord Gladwyn had retired as British ambassador to Paris and was sitting in the House of Lords as a Liberal peer.

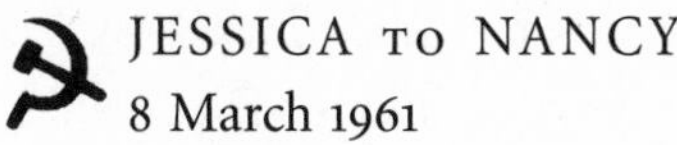

JESSICA TO NANCY
8 March 1961

6411 Regent Street
Oakland, California

Darling Susan,

We've moved, which took ages, still masses of things to do (curtains etc). But I *love* me new house. No point in telling you about it as I know you wouldn't displace yr.self to the point of coming to see.

Hen sent a t.gram from Washington (in response to one of mine, begging her to come here a bit) signed Your Old Hen. The operator wrote on it 'Repeat old hen, ambiguous copy'. I noted her frozen face in a pic. In *Life* Mag, at least I think it was her, too fuzzy to really make out.

Isn't it terrific how wonderfully yr. book is selling. I see it will be out here soon. Shall I send local reviews, or do you really never bother to read them?

Lots of love, Sooze

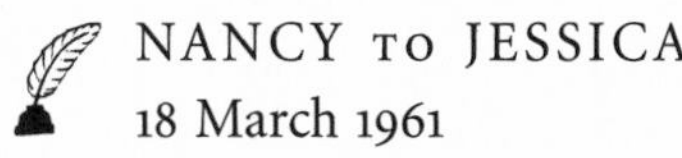

NANCY TO JESSICA
18 March 1961

Woodfield House
Caudle Green
Nr. Cheltenham
Gloucestershire

Darling Soo

This is Woman's dear little house, in the prettiest place you could see. I've been to Rome with Debo, we stayed with the Colonel (Fr Ambassador there) in the most beautiful of all the palaces & had a whizzing time. Then I came back to London with her to say goodbye to Muv, off to Island & we had three family days there, very enjoyable. Muv looks much younger & better & hardly shakes at all any more, but now Aunt Weenie has begun it. Oh *dear.*

My publisher's right hand man, Richard Brain,[1] has gone to the Congo on some do-gooder ploy – I told him it will be Brain for Breakfast[2] poor thing. It's a bore, because he really keeps them going, brainy Mr Brain, with a double first & so on. Such waste as he is quite too stringy for eating purposes, a real old boiler.

If you see an interesting review of *Alf* I'd love it. What I can't be bothered to note are those things like flags that appear, if you subscribe to press cuttings, from the North Niagara Times or the Deep South Daily – you know, places where nobody lives. When American reviews are good they are better than any because unlike European reviewers they actually read the book. (By *good* I mean well written, not favourable.)

Yes it was yr old Hen (ambiguous) in *Time*. Andrew says she's practically the 2nd lady now – the Pres. wrote himself & asked her to go back & many people think Andrew will be next ambassador.

Love, Soo

1 Nancy's editor at Hamish Hamilton.
2 A nickname given to Mark Ogilvie-Grant who, to curry favour with Lord Redesdale when staying at Swinbrook in the 1930s, had staggered down to the dining room on the dot of eight to be greeted by his host with a cheery 'Brains for breakfast!'

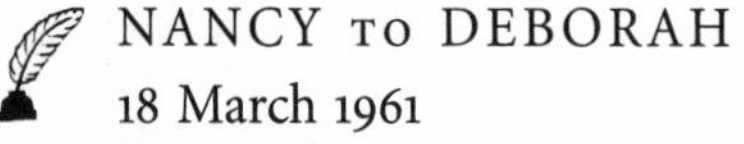

NANCY TO DEBORAH
18 March 1961

Woodfield House
Caudle Green

Dear Miss

Poor Woo, at this very minute, is having her old dog put down. Floods. I'm so sorry for her.

Oh did we not have a nice time! Oi mees u.

It really is delightful here. All seems very well & I bet you Woom will marry again soon: don't know why but I've got a strong feeling.

As we drove out of the station yard she said 'Naunceling air u toird?' I said 'oh well, only rather'. 'Because if you're *very* tired I shan't give you some really lovely wine, it wouldn't be worth it'. I let out such a bellow of rage that she nearly ran into the ditch. All was well. I got the lovely wine & I may say *wondair* dinnair of trout & a promise of a wonderful old boiler today & sugared ham tomorrow so I'm quite reassured about the grub.

I'll write again – this is just not to cut the umbilical cord.

Fond love, N

NANCY TO DEBORAH
5 April 1961

Fontaines-les-Nonnes
par Puisieux

Dear Miss

Forgotten your birthday again, I *am* a brute. Many etc. etc. I've subsided down here,[1] oh goodness it's pretty – the Spring, I'd never seen it before as it's new for Mme C[osta] to come now. April showers & boiling – no heating on & all the windows open, what a wonderful year. Roses out with the apple blossom. I dread going back to be smothered in Paris, tomorrow.

I've got a wonderful American share called Gamble which sounds like Lewis Carroll. I hadn't looked for about a month & then thought it must be a misprint it's gone up so much. As for the Chatsworth Heating Co,[2] one is obviously far too late. Next time you rebuild a house pray let me know.

I saw the chef de cabinet of Gaillard[3] who had heard all about the visit & I expect all about the great madness of English duchesses. He seemed quite giggly at the mere thought. This was at Mouchy where a real 1st April thing occurred – I thought Mouchy was a sort of Chats-Pet-Mere[4] & when Diane[5] said 'come this weekend', I thought she meant to stay. By the mercy of God my suitcase was never seen, so as soon as I twigged, which I did instantly, that I was only expected for luncheon I suborned the young man who had driven me down & it remained in the boot of his car. Because the Chats-Pet-Mere was destroyed inside by the Germans (& is anyway 19th cent. & ghastly) & they live in a house smaller than Edensor with 3 children & their pals. Oh the horror of what the embarrassment might have been! Like *The Unlucky Family.*[6]

Aïe! Here's your letter saying about adopters & birthdays. It rings indeed like a knell. My only excuse is that I always forget my own until a telegram arrives from Muv – who has more cause to remember it than I have (she had a ghastly delivery I believe, hours & hours). I can't believe that you are really 10, it seems like yesterday when the church bell tolled for you being a girl.

Harriet Hill[7] was being offered a lift by a man in the middle of the night when a police car came by. The policemen hurried her into it & brought her home. Sometimes I'm thankful to have no children – the *worry*!

Love from Lady Writer of French

1 Fontaines, a chateau near Meaux, where Nancy often stayed, sometimes for a month at a time. It was owned by her old friend Countess Costa de Beauregard (1874–1966), a childhood friend of Violet Hammersley.
2 The bills for heating Chatsworth were so enormous that Deborah wished she could buy shares in it.
3 Félix Gaillard (1919–70). The last Prime Minister of France's Fourth Republic had been staying at the French embassy in Rome at the same time as Deborah and Nancy.
4 A stately home such as Chatsworth, Petworth or Mereworth.
5 Diane de Castellane (1927–). Married the Duke of Mouchy in 1948.
6 Mrs Henry de la Pasture's 1907 novel was a comic satire of Edwardian country-house life.
7 The eighteen-year-old daughter of Heywood and Anne Hill was in Paris learning French.

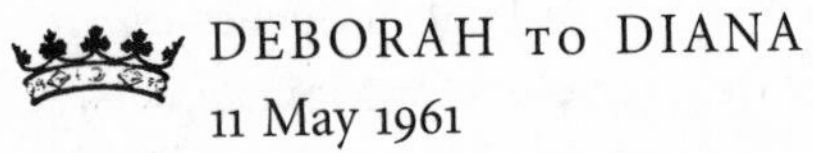

DEBORAH to DIANA
11 May 1961

Lismore Castle
Co. Waterford

Darling Honks

Well, it is too awful, I slightly got cross with Nancy yesterday when she started on about England & how she loathes London. I said I thought it was *very rude* considering she always stays at Ches St & we do our best to make her comfortable etc etc & as I got cross I expect I went too far, & heard my voice getting higher & higher. Oh dear I did feel ashamed after, but nevertheless I do think it is unnecessary to go on & on.

She is being rather needly about everything, you know how she is sometimes. She wasn't *a bit* in Rome. I suggest she goes & lives there. I do hope she'll get unprickly, it's such a waste when she can be so marvellous. THROW THIS AWAY.

Sorry for this list of complaints.

Much love, Debo

DIANA TO DEBORAH
16 May 1961

Temple de la Gloire
Orsay

Darling Debo:

Yes *maddening*, & I'm v. glad you sat on it; it's not even really genuine as she never stops rushing over.

Our tactless frog friend Jacques Brousse[1] came down on Sat. & started commiserating with me about having to be in London so much, & I said 'there are lots of things I love being there for', & so then he says 'Nancy tells me it is terrible for you because not only do you have your headaches but you are completely cut off from all friends by Kit's politics.' I replied, 'friends are friends even when they don't agree about politics', & that I also have you, Muv, two sons & three grandchildren in or about London. So he went on 'well she has told me à plusieurs reprises[2] that you see *nobody*'. To which I said 'I am now fifty & an old granny & not a debutante wondering what balls she will get invited to, people can take me or leave me & one or two even *take*'.

The inter-esting[3] thing about this conversation is that he is not an intimate friend of ours; it seems to me that that sort of broadcast is fairly spiteful – unless she really feels so sorry for one that she can't help saying it. As you know, there is truth in it, but as you also know the ONLY part about it I mind is the idea of Kit being misrepresented or unfairly condemned unheard as it were – the idea of me sitting sadly waiting for invitations which don't turn up, oh Debo can you beat it. Do you think perhaps Wife would *bring me out*?

Something for the Fr lady writer: *boiling* afternoon & we are all on lilos on the lawn. Jacques says: 'Never does one have a fine day anywhere in the Paris region without a terrific storm & buckets of rain'. He is the pessimist of all time.

Oh Debo *DO* come rain or shine.

All love, Honks

1 Jacques Brousse (d.2001). Translator of Nancy's later books into French.
2 'Several times.'
3 One of the Mitfords' governesses used to pronounce 'interesting' thus and a chant arose among the children, 'Oh how inter-esting, isn't it inter-esting'. The sisters went on using the word in this way, often to describe something less than really interesting.

) DIANA TO DEBORAH 8 July 1961

Temple de la Gloire
Orsay

Darling Debo:

Thanks for the letter you are GOOD when I know how busy you are & today is the ball.[1] Woman is here & she is being more than wondair. We had a dinner party & she sat by M. de No Eye, a cousin of Charles,[2] who is very fond of china, houses, etc & in a pause of talk I heard her giving him in halting French a very long receipt for cooking pork ending with 'Il faut le couper LÀ',[3] pointing to her own body for where the CUT should take place. Isn't she one in a million.

As to your little gurl do send her to me, I would make her my life work, I have got *four* pictures of her in *one* frame which are before my eyes. She is the child I love best of ANY I ever knew, close second comes you at one and Decca.

Last night Jean [de Baglion] came, also Martin Wilson,[4] they were too nice & took it in turns for Woman's sagas. During a silence I heard the words, 'Then you smash the potatoes in some of the best olive oil', so I think they were benefiting from her cuisine too.

Secret. She said, 'You know Nard I could stay with people all over Italy, they've begged me to come'. Me, 'Could you Woman? How lovely'. She, 'Oh yes, I mean *they've* all been to Tullamaine, for HUNTING TEAS'.

All love darling, Honks

1 A dance that Deborah was giving in London for eighteen-year-old Emma and sixteen-year-old Peregrine.
2 Viscount Charles de Noailles (1891–1981). Patron of the Surrealists and expert gardener. His cousin, Anne-Jules de Noailles (1900–79), was a connoisseur of porcelain.
3 'You must cut it HERE.'
4 Sir Matthew (Martin) Wilson (1906–91). London antiques dealer with a shop in the Portobello Road.

DEBORAH TO NANCY
21 July 1961

Chatsworth
Bakewell

Get on

Dear little Lu's likeness of me is nearly done. I think it's *marvellous*. Does D. S.[1] dismiss it just as severe, or does he think it's marvellous? Please tell. I long for others to see it & hear what people think.[2]

Lu was mixing up some paint the other day, got excited & said 'look this is *just* the colour of your hair'. I looked, & saw a cow pat with silver in it.

The London part of this week was strangely formal, dinner with Harold & Dot [Macmillan] one night, at Buckingham P another & Antonia Fraser[3] in between, a political effort of hers, very nice but it's lucky I'm old I couldn't have done those 3 nights 10 years ago. I'd never seen the rooms looking over the garden at BP in daylight before. They are wonderful, so grand. I'd no idea the garden was so huge, a literal vasty park all quiet. The roar of traffic round the rim, most telling. The D of E most affable, & he told something so fascinating – how some naturalists are working in the garden and have found things like field mice & insects which don't happen even in Hyde Park. It's an undisturbed oasis of country.

The Gov. Gen. of Nigeria (who the dinners were for) brought presents for the Queen & spread them out on a table & then stood behind it to hand them over & it looked exactly like a native bazaar. Most comical.

I'll soon be 10 if I go on like this. Also I note this letter is nothing but about me, oh how inter-esting. Sorry. Better luck next time.

Much love, 9

1 David Somerset, 11th Duke of Beaufort (1928–). Partner in Marlborough Fine Art, the gallery that represented Lucian Freud.

2 When Andrew Devonshire went to view Freud's portrait of Deborah for the first time, there was another man in the studio. 'Andrew looked long at the picture until the other man asked, "Who is that?" "It's my wife." "Well, thank God it's not mine."' *Counting My Chickens*, p. 160.

3 Lady Antonia Pakenham (1932–). The writer's career as an historical biographer was launched in 1969 with *Mary Queen of Scots*. Married to Sir Hugh Fraser, MP, 1956–77, and to the playwright Harold Pinter in 1980.

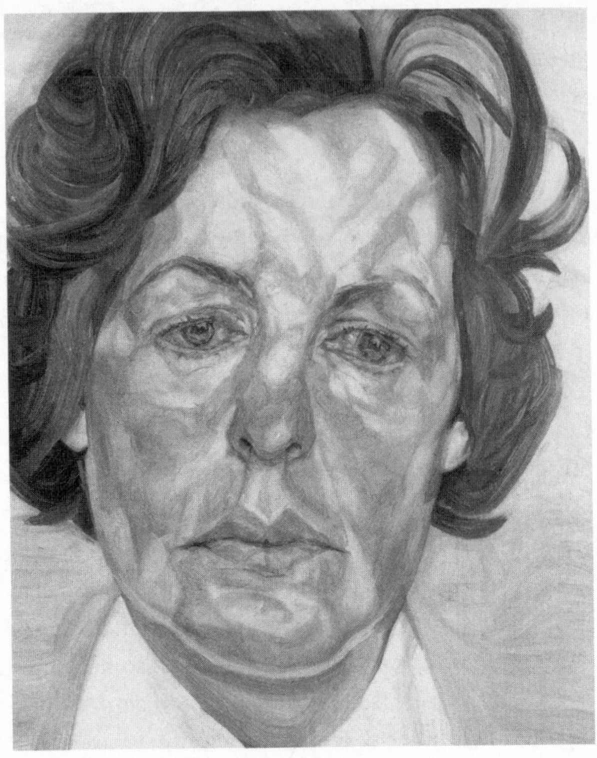

Deborah by Lucian Freud, 1961.
(© *The Devonshire Collection, reproduced by permission of the Chatsworth Settlement Trustees*)

DIANA TO DEBORAH
5 September 1961

Temple de la Gloire
Orsay

Darling Debo

Nancy came down on Sunday & we swam, she said it was BITTER. She stayed all day & yesterday I spent hours in her flat among her new & glamorous art-works. She was so nice. She talked about how she couldn't have children & that ghoulish tale of her nurse,[1] I must say it does make one's hair stand on end. Luckily she has made a very good life for herself, & is such a success.

While she was in Venice, Sir E. Cunard[2] told her, 'I've spent all day tearing up letters from you to Victor, ever since 1930'. Can you imagine. And she kept his. It was a (very spiteful I'm sure knowing him) *correspondance suivie*![3] Poor Naunceling, she rather mourns the letters.

WHEN CAN WE MEET?

All love, Honks

1 According to Nancy, the doctor who operated on her after her ectopic pregnancy asked if she had ever been in contact with syphilis. When she mentioned this to her mother, Lady Redesdale replied, rather vaguely, that Nancy's nursery-maid had been infected with it. Although it was patently not the cause of her sterility, Nancy thereafter blamed her mother for her inability to have children.
2 Sir Edward Cunard (1890–1962). Brother of Nancy's great friend and correspondent Victor Cunard who had died the previous year.
3 'Sustained correspondence.'

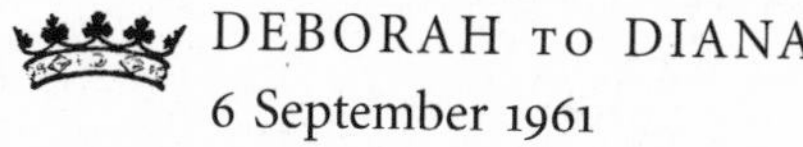

DEBORAH TO DIANA

6 September 1961 *Boat*

Darling Honks

This is m'diary.

6 A.M. Called, by various bangings all over the house.

6.30. Went down. Felt as if it was very early (which it was). Said goodbye to Muv. She really seems v. fit on the whole, & screams at the least thing.

7 A.M. Buggered,[1] in a merciful pause between thundery rainstorms.

7.15. Hired car (John McFadyen, who said the sound was cram full of traffic, meaning two boats a day) arrived Salen about 20 to 8. Boat a tiny speck in furthest distance. Sat on damp seat for ¾ of an hour. Had to ask a strange Gen. Herman to help me heave the luggage on the boat. Arms felt very odd, like broken things. Sat down for brekker, all excited. After 35 minutes something loomed, coffee with milk already in it. Sent it back. Soon wished I hadn't as to pay me out the waiter didn't bring any more for ages. Thought of Vienne, & Avignon. Longed for same.

Very cold. Thought what madness to live in the Bonny Land, what *is* Lady Redesdale aiming at? That's so far.

Yesterday 22 people sat down to a mammoth tea. I never saw so much eaten at tea, it simply disappeared. They all said yes to everything. Sweet Mrs Campbell & *sweet* Betty (sort of parlourmaid, whom I loved) did wonderfully. We couldn't think of anything to do after tea, so we didn't do anything. They sang about two songs in a very ½ hearted way & I didn't dare suggest any of our W.I. games like passing a match box from nose to nose because they didn't look as if they would like it. I felt sad leaving Muv, she seems vaguely loath to let one go, oh it is sad her being old.

We had marvellous Scrabble, when she wins she says 'that was a very good game' and when I win she says 'that game didn't seem to go very well, it was rather a *dull* one'.

How I wish you had been there.

Much love, Debo

1 An expression often used by Deborah meaning 'to leave' or 'to go'.

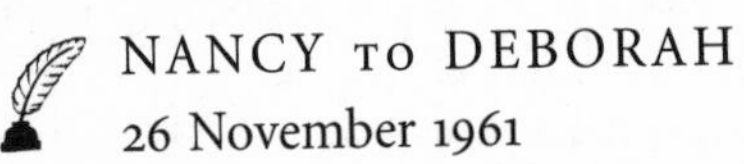

NANCY to DEBORAH
26 November 1961

The Warden's Lodgings[1]
New College, Oxford

Dear Miss

Thank you so so much for ALL – I did have a lovely time.

The dinner for Muv was delightful, no hogs, just Mr Niarchos[2] & Kensington.[3] Muv, whom I've seen such a lot this time, is sad about Honks. She said, so truly, Diana has had a disappointing life & what makes it worse in a way she can't say so or talk about it. However Hayter says the boys here & at Cambridge can't have enough of Sir O – they don't agree with him but he fascinates them.

There was a sociologist at dinner here. She said while professionally we deplore them, your books are admitted to be a very useful sidelight on the upper classes. What can sociology be? I must look it up in the dictionary. There were 12 people, the clothes ranged from beehive to deadly.

I must get up.

Love, N

1 Nancy was staying with Sir William Hayter (1906–95), Minister at Paris 1949–53, ambassador to Moscow 1953–6, and Warden of New College 1958–76. Married Iris Grey in 1938.

2 John Stuart (1925–90). Nicknamed Stavros Niarchos because his complexion was more Mediterranean than Scotch.
3 Kensington Davison, 3rd Baron Broughshane (1914–2006). Opera administrator and critic.

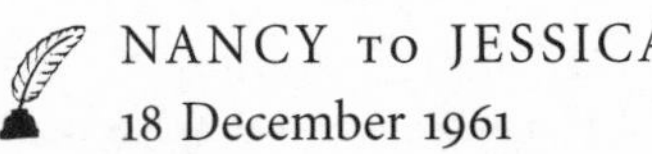

NANCY TO JESSICA *7 rue Monsieur, VII*
18 December 1961

Darling Soo

Our fast young sister went over that ocean & had long loving tête à têtes with your ruler. Andrew says Kennedy is doing for sex what Eisenhower did for golf. Well no Susan I don't feel like going.

Marie has just gone off to confess for Xmas. What ever can she have to say? As she's a saint. Somebody asked the priest at Fontaines what Mme Costa confessed (84 & as good as gold), 'C'est toujours la même chose, elle dit "j'ai été *odieuse* avec les invités." '[1] So untrue.

Much love – happy 1962, Soose

1 'It's always the same thing, "I have been odious to the guests." '

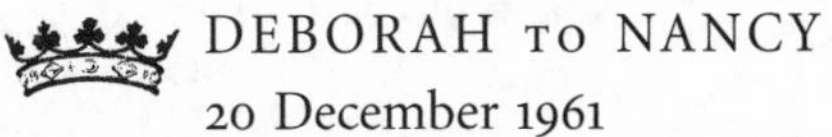

DEBORAH TO NANCY *4 Chesterfield Street, W1*
20 December 1961

Get on

I'm feeling vaguely ghoulish at not having written much, but you know how it is. I'll tell you about America when I see you (if you want to hear which I dreadly doubt) it was the very height of jolliness (which you won't believe) and the utter sweetness & great pathos of the President beats all.

Yesterday was rather fascinating as I was rung for by the Prime Minister to brief him for Bermuda (which I now note is in a muddle because of old Joe)[1] and I had ¾ of an hour alone with him &, for the first time in all the years I've known him, he vaguely listened to what I was saying. I gave him my Christmas present for the dear old President to take with him, it's got a photograph of me surrounded by Protestant clergymen & some silver footman's buttons he wanted, covered in crowns & snakes.[2] I do hope he'll like it. Anyway I was able to lay it on about the sweetness the goodness & the pathos.

Happy Xmas, do come to America with me when our drawings go next Oct,[3] I'd do ANYTHING to see you there.

Much love, 9

1 A summit meeting in Bermuda between Macmillan and Kennedy had nearly been cancelled because the President's father, Joseph Kennedy (1888–1969), had suffered a massive stroke.
2 The Devonshire family emblem is a snake.
3 A loan exhibition of 114 Old Master drawings from Chatsworth was to tour American museums, beginning at the National Gallery in Washington.

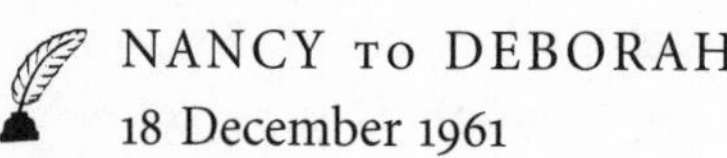

NANCY TO DEBORAH
18 December 1961

7 rue Monsieur, VII

Dear Miss

Never will I go there, not even with you. You know my hatred & loathing of those people isn't at all a joke & is now exacerbated by them sending savages into Katanga.[1] I don't suppose the English papers tell what is going on there. Why don't they do their own fighting instead of using Ethiopians & Indians? The hypocrisy makes one feel sick. There, I can't help it.

Honks looks v. ill & has headaches the whole time. I do feel worried about her.

Fond love, N

1 The United Nations had sent peace-keeping troops to the Congo in an effort to prevent a civil war. Serious allegations had been made concerning atrocities committed by UN forces.

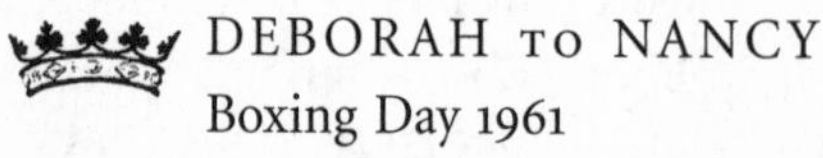

DEBORAH TO NANCY
Boxing Day 1961

Chatsworth
Bakewell

Get on

No present from the President of the United States. It is the limit, admit. Do you think he has difficulties of Xmas shopping. Well surely someone could do it. Wife refers to him as Your Fat Friend, like Prinny.[1] He's not of course. I phoned Uncle Harold the night he got back to see how the presents went, he had seen the point in Bermuda, seen the pathos & the great sweetness & enlarged for 20 minutes on this very subject, prompted & encouraged by me of course. He was fuddled by the snakes on the buttons I sent.

It's a pity you don't like the Americans. You would worship the body of the President, that's all. I told him about how people in England say it's ½ an hour with him, including shaking hands, he *was* pleased & made me say it every day for a week.

Happy New Year, keep writing

Much love, 9

1 In 1813, Beau Brummel, in a famous remark that sealed his social downfall, asked Lord Alvanley, co-host of a ball he was giving, 'Who's your fat friend?', referring to the Prince Regent ('Prinny'), the future George IV.

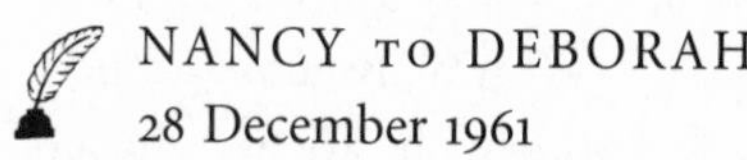

NANCY TO DEBORAH *7 rue Monsieur, VII*
28 December 1961

Dear Miss

The Fat Friend in your livery is a startling thought. Mrs Ham writes quite incoherently saying you will make history mark her words. Well if you get F.F. to be on our side you might. I would like to have the pathos & extreme sweetness enlarged on please – the worshipfulness of the BODY of course, doubtful though it must seem, one takes your word for.

Do you think Alphand[1] is loathed by F.F.? Might be worth reporting if so. Of course he's a human being & not a Peace Soldier so very likely he wouldn't go down in that land of dire hypocrisy, where, according to Maurice,[2] no birds sing, no flowers smell, no food tastes.

Muv seems to have spent Xmas in Harrods Bank, singing carols. As it's her favourite place she must have loved it.

Much love, N

1 Hervé Alphand was French ambassador to Washington 1956–65.
2 Maurice Bowra (1898–1971). Before taking up his post as Warden of Wadham College, Oxford, in 1938, the classical scholar had lectured for a year at Harvard.

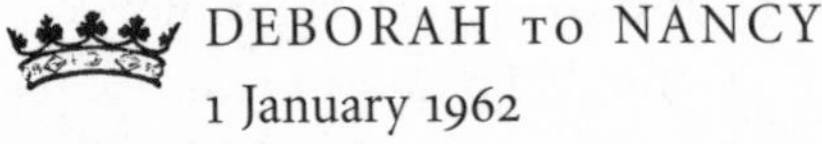

DEBORAH to NANCY
1 January 1962

Chatsworth
Bakewell

Get on

V. pleased to find a letter on my return from Yorkshire where Stoker & I had gone for a refreshing shoot with the Fevershams.

I had a *letter* from Al Mosley after he landed at Columbus Ohio.[1] Wasn't I honoured? Shall I recommend him as a White House aide (whatever that may mean but there seem to be lots of them) to F.F.?

I never said Alphand was loathed by old Pathos, but he does behave in a pretty odd way – viz. a dinner was given by some Washington host*ess* for a fellow called Adlai Stevenson[2] who is someone to do with something in the land where no birds sing.

On the way into dinner the host*ess* whispered to the Fr Ambassador, 'As this dinner is in honour of Adlai, I know you won't mind if he sits on my right & you on my left.' The said Ambassador stopped in his tracks, said to his wife 'Dear, collect your wrap, we are buggering.' Host*ess* in floods, all returned to drawing room, name places hastily changed, all returned to diner with tear-stained cheeks, sat gloomily down to eat. Well that sort of behaviour doesn't endear you will admit. He seems to have been there for years though, so nevair moind.

F.F. *IS* on our side & adores Uncle Harold. He calls him Uncle Harold now, so do all the defence people.

Well French Lady, would that you were here, and now there is a go-slow with the postal I feel I shall ne'er hear again from you.

Just had a postcard from Henderson advertising Practical Burial Footwear,[3] see why I love the Americans.

Much love, happy New Year, 9

Will enlarge on the pathos & sweetness in my next, if you promise to stop being rotten about them.

1 Alexander had enrolled at Ohio State University to read philosophy.
2 Adlai Stevenson (1900–65). Politician and diplomat. US ambassador to the UN 1961–5.
3 Jessica had begun research on *The American Way of Death* (1963), her exposé of the funeral industry.

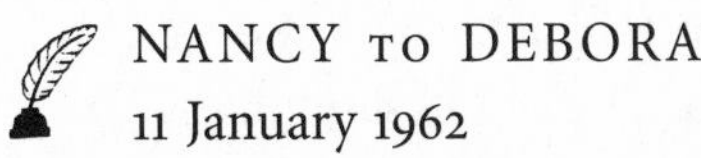

NANCY TO DEBORAH *7 rue Monsieur, VII*
11 January 1962

No, Miss. To rush hugger-mugger to one's food, wreathed in grins & snatching coconuts from fellow guests is *not* civilized. Civilized people proceed according to rule. The lowest peasant of the Danube would allow a foreign ambassador his due procedure – only monkey people would be ignorant of this fundamental usage. The ambassador, who represents his own country, not his own person, is bound to object to such an insult as you have described. When a judge sends somebody to prison for contempt of court it's not because *he* has an inferiority complex but because he represents justice; insults allowed become a dangerous precedent. Alphand was completely right to say 'Dear, we bugger'.

Your letter took three days like usual. I believe they are rather nicer to abroad letters perhaps.

I've told Wid to sell all, like in the Bible, & go to the Ritz. Otherwise she'll be murdered – it's a *murderous* name, Hotel Adria, admit.[1]

I've had a questionnaire from an American paper called *Esquire*. 'If you could have your life over again what would you like to have done?' Answer 'moon about on a huge unearned income' etc. Also there's a space for self portrait. I've spent a happy morning doing it. You wait.

I'm absolutely *whacked* as always after several weeks in a town. So I go to Fontaines on Sunday, don't know for how long – write here.

Much love – do try & be more civilized, N

1 Violet Hammersley was staying at an hotel in South Kensington which Nancy had recommended.

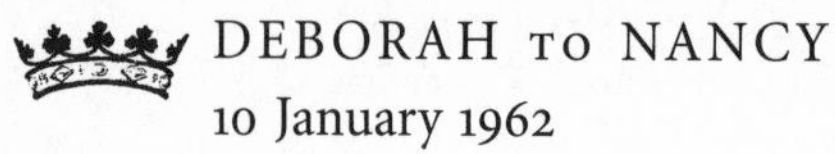

DEBORAH TO NANCY
10 January 1962

Chatsworth
Bakewell

Get on

Thanks for yrs re lecture in Washington. You see that's the *whole point*, the *sweetness* & pathos rolled into one, but I fear you'll never see it so I suppose we'd better give it up. The President (a dear old thing) is the very embodiment of the particular worshipfulness.

Oh try & see it, oh do.

I'm on my way to London to see the oldsters, it appears Mrs Ham is being really rather naughty & slaving George[1] to do all for her.

Much love, 9

1 Andrew Devonshire's secretary.

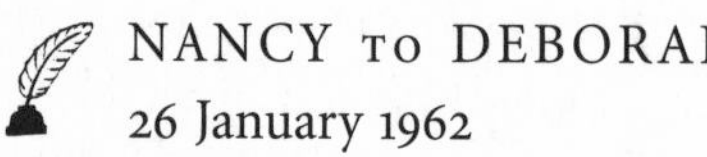

NANCY TO DEBORAH
26 January 1962

7 rue Monsieur, VII

Dear Miss

The oddity of the post. Your letter winged in a single day – I was beginning to wonder how you were. The only other English letter this week was from Wid – not a word about you or anything but her *intense* sufferings – the sinister noises & yet more sinister silence of the Hotel Adria. I replied that the noises must be rather surréalistes since we know she can't hear anything. No mention of your motor, a high pitched scream about the agony of *getting anywhere*. Wicked old bad fairy. Still, of course, if all were rosy we shouldn't love her so much.

One's not allowed to see the clothes for at least another fortnight. Come then. The *Figaro*, which is very strict, not so far enthusiastic. (They said of Oonagh's husband[1] 'he would do better to open a flower shop'.) I'm sure one can find something at Lanvin – I must have a dinner dress. Belts again it seems everywhere, oh good.

Now dear little thing do be more careful. I think your nerves are completely upset by exhaustion – if you have to take a pill in order to sleep it proves my point. Exhaustion is what makes so many women (Honks Coo[per] for ex) take to the bottle & though that's not probable I admit in your case, there may be other dangers. One's body is very fragile, no doubt, but it's the only instrument we've got – better look after it. Oh *do* listen.

Much love – tell your plans. Moroccan sunshine would be just the thing.

N

1 Oonagh Guinness's third husband, the Cuban designer Miguel Ferreras, had shown his collection in Paris.

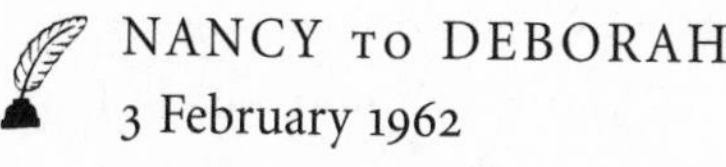

NANCY TO DEBORAH *7 rue Monsieur, VII*
3 February 1962

Dear Miss

I believe we've got a postman just for us two. Your letter saying Muv not very well was followed in three hours by one saying better.

I would put myself in an aeroplane & go & see her but there is this boring vaccination, they won't let one back without it. I have a stupid horror (Muv's fault) of being done & it's the sort of thing that always upsets me – no good arriving & falling ill in London. I evidently must have it or shall be cut off from Blighty forever. A friend of mine here has been at death's door after vaccination – oh *bother* I literally *dread* it.

Have you read *Where Angels Fear to Tread* (Forster). One screams at the first half – then it goes a bit slow. I mean it works to rule.

Wish I knew what Ici means in English. (Here it means here.) Whenever I open a paper I see Ici Row Looms.

Well I loom to Fontaines in an hour but only until Wed. morning.

All love, N

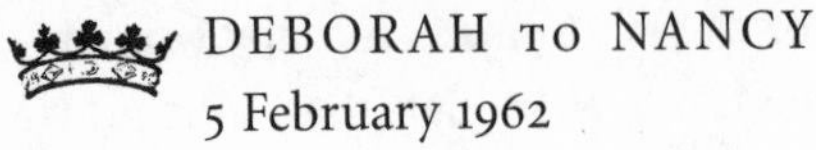

DEBORAH TO NANCY
5 February 1962

Chatsworth
Bakewell

Get on

Can I bore you with a vague triumph I had with Duncan Sandys,[1] Andrew's petrifying boss? He stayed here not long ago & old Sophy was being rather a pest in the drawing room, so I said 'Sophy don't you think you ought to mince off to Diddums?' Whereupon I heard D Sandys in a growling voice saying 'now what on earth does that mean, *mince off to Diddums*?' (As though it was rather odd.) No response of course from Sophy and about ¼ of an hour later, to my slight astonishment, I heard Sandys say 'Sophy, don't you think you'd better mince off to Diddums?'

ICI doesn't mean here here. It means a thing one's got shares in, viz. Imperial Chemical Industries. I'll tell you a few more bits of English you must try & learn. Imps don't mean little people in the garden but Imperial Tobacco. Gussies don't mean a new kind of stays but Great Universal Stores. I could go on like this for pages, but won't.

Don't be vaccinated. I believe three of the seven deaths from smallpox in this old country are from vaccination – terrifying. Haven't you got a doctor who would sort of pretend to do it & give you a card to say he has? That's the way the world goes round.

It seems Muv is much better, but it's no good thinking she'll feel anything but awful for the next week or two. I'm going to London on Wed to see her.

Much love, 9

1 Duncan Sandys (1908–87). Commonwealth Secretary of State 1960–2, and Commonwealth and Colonies Secretary 1962–4, during which period Andrew Devonshire was Parliamentary Under-Secretary for Commonwealth Relations.

JESSICA TO DEBORAH
15 February 1962

6411 Regent Street
Oakland

Dearest Henny,

Glad you liked Prac. Bur. Foot. Yes, there are some other fascinators: such as New Bra-Form, Post Mortem Form Restoration, Accomplish So Much for So Little. They cost $11 for a package of 50, Hen you must *say* that's cheap, shall I send you a few? There's also The Final Touch That Means So Much, it's mood-setting casket hardware.

Hen do you prefer a gentle Tissue-Tint in yr. arterial? It helps regain the Natural Undertones. It's made specially for those who prefer a fast Firming Action of medium-to-rigid degree.

Hen I bet you don't even know what is the best time to start embalming, so I'll tell you: Before life is quite extinct, according to the best text-book we've found on it. They have at you with a thing called a Trocar, it's a long pointed needle with a pump attached, it goes in thru the stomach and all liquids etc. are pumped out. Thence to the Arterial. I *do* wish the book was finished, it seemed to be going along well for a bit but now it's all being totally reorganized.

One thing you could do which would be a terrific help: write and describe an English funeral. That is, if you've been to any lately. Who goes to them – just the family, or what you call inties [intellectuals] too? Here, everyone goes (such as people who work in the same office etc). Anyway do try to go to one soon and write and tell all. Because I've never been to one in England.

Might you be in London in June? I *do* hope so.

Much love, Yr. Hen

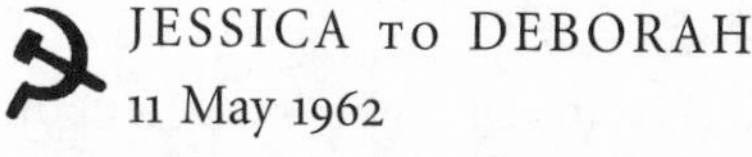

JESSICA TO DEBORAH
11 May 1962

6411 Regent Street
Oakland

Dearest Henny,

Our mournful book is coming along, but *too slowly.* I fear we shall have to take it up to the Isle to work on it. Luckily the publisher is being v. nice about *dead*lines etc.

We just got back from a longish journey; to Chicago and New

York, all on the blissful train which I love. The main point of going to Chi was that there is a thing called the National Foundation of Funeral Service there, also the headquarters of the National Selected Morticians. Among the instructions contained there about how to behave (for morticians) is one on how to shake hands. It's called *Five Points in an Effective Handshake.* Point 4 is 'Place your hand in the prospect's in such a manner that the muscle between the thumb and index finger contacts the same muscle in the prospect's hand'. So there I was, muscle to muscle with the head of the Nat'l Selected Morticians, oh it was exciting.

Lots of love, Hen

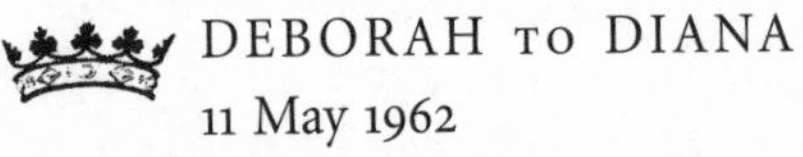

DEBORAH TO DIANA
11 May 1962

Inch Kenneth
Gribun, Oban

Darling Honks

This letter is Deathly Private & not to be relayed to the Fr Lady.

Well I sat furiously eating a banana in the Oban–Salen boat, which has as you know a lunch too vile to be eaten. After the usual endless age, Salen pier hove into sight. It hove, but nothing else, no known face, no car. The poor heart sank to the very depths. You know what it is after a 30-something-hour journey.

I think she was quite pleased to see me & the pathos was of course being her birthday & sitting alone in front of a cake.

Daffodils still out here. Oh how I loathe these late & northern climes.

Did I tell you the Lismore P.O. has excelled itself. I sent a wire to the Parker-Bowles[1] saying 'Both delighted dine 6th'. It arrived saying 'Bother. Delighted dine etc.' So Derek has sent it back saying 'if it's such a nuisance perhaps you'd rather not come'.

Muv, looking at the cliffs in a watery sun last night, 'Look Stubby, it's like the entrance to hell or something'. Too true.

Much love, Debo

IF ONLY YOU WERE HERE.

1 Derek Parker-Bowles (1915–77). Married Ann de Trafford in 1939.

DIANA TO DEBORAH *Temple de la Gloire*
23 May 1962 *Orsay*

Darling Debo:

The end of your journey! Oh Debo, a thousand times worse than even the ghoulish beginning. Of course I won't tell Nancy *that*, I mean, not more than she knows already. Just to show how she understands nothing I said yesterday, 'Really it *is* an awful place to get to', & she replied 'Yes, but don't we all know that? Why go?' And although even *she* knows the answer I said it: 'To *see* somebody'. She hasn't got much heart?

Kit went off last night & today she's coming to stay, Geoffrey [Gilmour] for lunch, & we are going to see the jools in the Louvre which are supposed to be OK but I doubt they come up to the ones in your bank.

Jonnycan is coming for the week and business, big I hope, brings him this way. As to Ingrid & her availability, I love her really more than I can say & only hope she is as happy as she looks, & after eleven years people are apt to be available aren't they.[1] So much better than flying apart after forty years like poor Muv, just when one needs the old friend. Kit & I, like the old Dutch, have been together now for thirty years & it don't seem a day too much (it's really thirty but one must tell children etc twenty-eight).

All love darling *COME*! Honks

1 Jonathan and Ingrid Guinness were divorced in 1963. Ingrid married Paul Channon, MP, a few months later and Jonathan married Suzanne Lisney the following year.

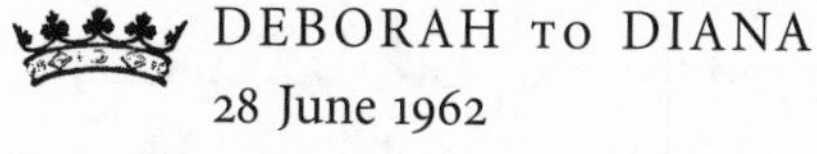

DEBORAH TO DIANA *4 Chesterfield Street, W1*
28 June 1962

Darling Honks

Well, Henderson arrived, they came to dinner last night and I must say were very nice – easy & friendly, I think they have mellowed a lot. The weekend is a bit of a hurdle. However, if they go on like they did last night, all will be v. well. Id came, & the Wife & Andrew came in after & they all seemed to get on all right.

Sir Isaac Wolfson[1] was *very* sweet the other night, he is always asking if he could sell one a washing machine on 36 easy payments.

Woman came for the day yesterday. I was *good*, in waiting, trying to find stuff for her drawing room. She is a take-off of a woman shopper, I never saw anyone so easily distracted. I suppose she hasn't the faintest idea of what she wants & doesn't really want it anyhow. We went to Liberty's & P. Jones but in between we went to Jaeger's for a coat & skirt & she said to the girl (to my great & lasting embarrassment) I WANT A FINE WOOL LIGHT GREY DEUX-PIÈCE, *TWO* PIECE in her most exaggerated slow voice. Anyway we got her a lovely one. In P Jones she wandered aimlessly about saying to everything I suggested 'No Stublow that wouldn't go at all well with my very beautiful Louis the 14th (?) Aubusson covered chairs'. So in the end we got some patterns of velveteen from the distracted assistant. I didn't dare go into Spencer's with her but I had done a day's worth I thought.

Much love, Debo

1 Isaac Wolfson (1897–1991). Businessman, philanthropist and founder of Great Universal Stores.

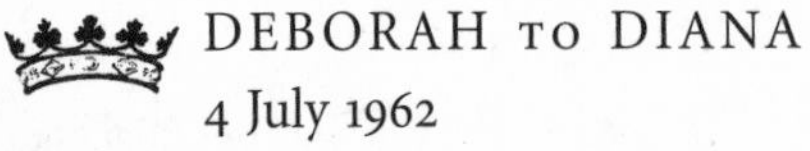

DEBORAH TO DIANA *4 Chesterfield Street, W1*
4 July 1962

Darling Honks

The Feray bros[1] were unequalled screams, I can't ever tell you how funny they were, such exclamations, such hand head claspings, such moans of agony when we went to the safe,[2] such compliments in such insincere voices. They are somehow the very opposite of Woman in shorts at Burnham-on-Crouch.

Em laughed so much I thought she was going to choke. They asked, deathly serious, whether she had been presented at court, so we screamed & said that outing had been given up years ago. So they said in unison 'Quelle déception, what, no lovely drress from Hartnell, no feathers, *oh* quelle déception', as though it truly was an 'horrible surprise'. 'Les *garden party* avec dix mille autres, ce n'est pas la même chose'[3] & they tut tutted about what a deception it was for ages & I heard them mumbling about merchants' daughters being accepted at court as they tottered upstairs to their four posters (their name for their beds). They are a killing but exhausting pair. The weekend really went on till this (Wed) morning, & so I'm done for.

Decca listened v. carefully to all yr instructions & I'm sure she will do as you say about all the things.[4] I can see she only came to England this year to see Muv, otherwise she would have waited till the children could have come too.

Keep in close touch please.

Much love, Debo

Do go to the dr about the migraine.

1 Jean Feray, Inspector of Monuments Historiques, and his younger brother, Thierry, a banker, lived in Paris in the rue Cambon and shared a passion for beautiful objects and the *Almanac de Gotha*. They died in a car crash in 1999.
2 Where the Devonshire collection of gold, silver and family jewels was kept.
3 'What a disappointment . . . Garden parties with ten thousand other people, it's just not the same.'
4 Diana had written from Inch Kenneth, where she was staying with Lady Redesdale, with suggestions for making sure that Jessica's visit to the island later in the month went smoothly.

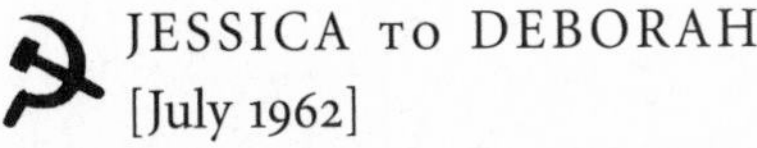

JESSICA TO DEBORAH
[July 1962]

Inch Kenneth
Gribun, Oban

Dearest Henny,

This is such a perfect place to work, I find. I am up at 5.30 (as we go to bed before 10) and have a thermos of coffee, work till 8, then work most of the day. I *really adore* it, though I don't think I should so much were it not for getting on with the book.

Yesterday Lady Congleton[1] came to tea with her bro. in law. The latter told me just about everything there is to know about how to import ponies from Iceland and train them to carry dead stags. I suppose one should be grateful to learn something new; I really think that if ever I had to import the ponies and train them, I should know exactly how to do it after yesterday. Lady C. as ever, most reminiscent of similar neighbours at Swinbrook – outstanding characteristic being absolute lack of fear of being boring, so lucky in a way.

Hen, Muv handed over the most fascinating haul of old letters, mine, from all of you in 1937 at time of Running. Yours all start with things like 'Dear Cecil Beaton, Hotcha!' Or 'Dear County Councillor, hot it up!' They describe the Chinless Horrors at yr deb dances, and how you loathed Bridget Airlie. One from Muv says, 'Had tea with Hitler, he is really most agreeable and has surprisingly good manners'. Ho hum.

The food here is marvellous, as always. I'm getting awfully fat.

Much love, Yr Hen.

Typical conversation.
Muv: 'Who's your letter from, little D?'
Me: 'Barbara Kahn, my best friend at home.'
Muv: 'Oh, Carr, must be Scotch. Deaf, is she, poor thing? I didn't know you had any *deaf* friends, little D.'

1 A neighbour on the Isle of Ulva.

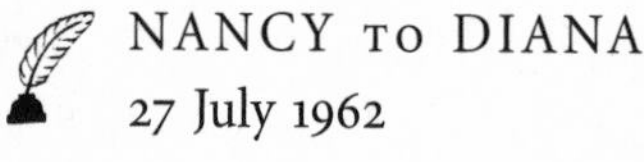

NANCY TO DIANA
27 July 1962

[23 Dorsoduro]
Venice

Dereling,

The posts! Your last letter took *one day* instead of the usual ten, I suppose they think Mosley is after them. I did worship the Man who was taken for Mosley writing a hymn of thanks giving for being still alive to *Daily Tel.*[1]

I've had to let my hair go grey (allergy to dye, & Dolly knows two people it has killed) so am now that sweet-faced old bore I've always dreaded & I see people literally fleeing. Old age – delightful &, as Voltaire used to say, this ruin is inhabited by a young person.

It's lucky we do like each other because anyhow we should have to pretend on account of Mme Ménégand.[2]

Jonnycan missed my party, I'm furious, they came one day later on account of Jasper[3] having won a prize. How too unlikely! A-M [Cicogna] has asked them to dine here today. The slice of fish etc quite good & the bill exactly (almost) half last year's, viz. £70 instead of £130. So the old adorable head waiter must have been the king of robbers I suppose. I had six real beauties & the whole thing looked divinely pretty. Twenty people.

Fond love, see you incessantly,[4] N

1 After a Union Movement meeting in Trafalgar Square ended in a fight, a man who was mistaken for Mosley wrote to the *Daily Telegraph* thanking the police for having protected him. (25 July 1962)
2 Madame (Mémé) Ménégand; an elderly dressmaker who copied expensive dresses for Nancy and Diana. She lived in the rue Villedo, above the Mosleys' Paris flat.
3 Jasper Guinness (1954–). Jonathan's eldest son.
4 A Gallicism for 'very soon'.

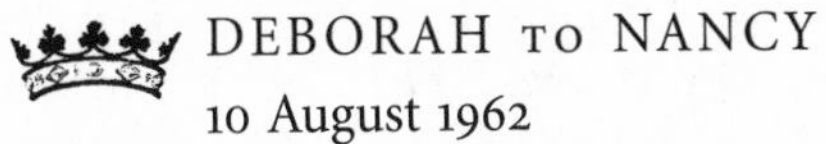

DEBORAH TO NANCY
10 August 1962

Chatsworth
Bakewell

Get on

Back here, only away a week altogether, including both journeys.[1] We came back in one of those big Boeing 707. It is extraordinary, only 3½ hours Jamaica–New York & 5½ New York–London, makes you think. It's so luxurious travelling official, how is one going to get used to being an ordinary human again? We had a private sec of great niceness who did everything from passports & tickets to seeing after the luggage.

It's nice being back after talking to Govt people of every hue. You try a few protracted dinners between the Canadian minister of Labour & the Jamaican minister of Education & it's quite a relief to be home, though I wouldn't have missed it for anything. I love a weekend in the tropics.

The US Vice President[2] is astonishing, I'm afraid *not too nice*, he spent much time & energy trying to steal the thunder of the little lady, with no success at all, partly because all worship the royal family & partly because no one knows him by sight, so his long tours round the town in a great big car were met by curious stares closely followed by disappointment when it was noted it was not P. Margaret. Rather a shame, but then he shouldn't have tried it.

There was much rain, vast drops & many of them, so the hair-styles first drooped & then became frizzy, I mean mine & Antonia [Fraser]'s, as the local ladies are pretty frizzy whatever they do.

I fell in love again, as per, this time with an ex-Governor called Sir Donald MacGillivray. I longed to ask him if he was a relation of MacGillivray[3] but didn't dare. Much & many floods over the lowering & raising of Union Jacks & Jamaican flags. Bands etc finish me. Twas very terrible.

Antonia Fraser won a prize of £10 given by Andrew for who would dance with the Vice Pres of US first. Sorry to say she won hands down & I never effected an introduction. Anno domini taking effect.

I do like Ld Snowdon,[4] he does a marvellous imitation of John Betj talking to Deacon.[5]

Interesting fact. There is a snap in this week's *Field* of one David Smith, keeper at Batsford for over 50 yrs. He *is* Farve. To prove all I put my hand over the caption, showed it to Emma, said 'who is this exactly like' & without hesitating she said 'Farve'. Aunt Weenie has always said there is a keeper there who was one of Grandfather's blessings. Must ask Andrew same question & see what he says.

Cecil Beaton spent a night here on his way to M. Duff's,[6] I showed him the orange border, upon which he shivered & said it was a retina irritant. Pathos, for me I mean, when you think what a lot of work etc etc. Thought it might appeal to you.

We might have to go to Uganda for the same purpose in early Oct, I rather hope so as I remember it being the most beautiful country ever. Also Sir D MacGillivray lives in Kenya so one might mince over. All this before America which I trust you are coming to.

Oh the Frogs in Jamaica. The head of the mission was an old gent who had been ambassador in Brazil, a dear old soul whom I danced with. He knew Colonel (my gambit – never failing – with frog diplomats) and said things like 'Your drress is a very beautiful collor' to which I replied 'so is your sash' (pale blue watered silk, don't know what it denotes). These sort of exchanges were rife for five days & now we're down to earth & deciding who is to go in which car to Bolton tomorrow. WRITE there.

I DIE for Clarys[7] at Lismore. We may have to come here for first weekend in May as Princess Margaret is going round the curse rag factory in Chesterfield[8] so we will have to put her up. That's it I think – for now I mean. WRITE.

Much love, 9

1 Deborah had accompanied Andrew to newly independent Jamaica for the first meeting of Parliament. Princess Margaret, representing the Queen, opened the session.
2 Lyndon B. Johnson (1908–73). US Vice President 1961–3. Succeeded J. F. Kennedy as President 1963–9. Married Claudia (Lady Bird) Taylor in 1934.
3 Donald MacGillivray (1906–66). Colonial secretary in Jamaica 1947–52, High Commissioner for the Federation of Malaya 1954–7. Lady Redesdale's boatman on Inch Kenneth was Neil MacGillivray.
4 Antony Armstrong-Jones, 1st Earl of Snowdon (1930–). The photographer married Princess Margaret in 1960.
5 Elizabeth Cavendish, John Betjeman's companion, was appointed Lady-in-Waiting to Princess Margaret in 1960.
6 Sir Michael Duff (1907–80). A bachelor who lived at Vaynol in North Wales.
7 Alfons (Alphy) Fürst Clary-Aldringen (1887–1978) and his wife, Ludwine (Lidi) zu Eltz (1894–1984). Prince Clary, an Austro-Hungarian nobleman of the old school and friend of the Mitfords, had fled his estates in Bohemia in 1945 and settled in Venice.
8 Robinson & Sons, manufacturers of sanitary towels, were also the inventors of the disposable nappy.

DIANA to DEBORAH

24 August 1962

Temple de la Gloire
Orsay

Darling Debo

Pam is here complete with Giuditta. As she arrived at three hours' notice it so chanced that we were dining out so they went to Nancy & saw Decca, & went to the best film I've ever seen (*Divorce Italian Style*) which I so worshipped I've seen it twice & will go a third time with you & a fourth with Kitty [Mersey] – just to show you how much one loves it. Well when we all met again at midnight to come down here, I could see they'd loathed their evening. Oh Debo what can have gone wrong.

Rather dreadful, apparently Nancy sent Muv a proof of her thing about Blor[1] Muv has written *really cross.* I can't understand why she wasn't shown the typescript when changes could have been made. It is SUCH a shame to upset her & doesn't bear thinking of. When she wrote to Nancy she was alone I think, but now Desmond & his family are up there. When she is alone everything seems enormous. I think the article is rather horrid BUT Muv didn't seem to mind Decca's vile book so one felt she'd never mind anything. O Lancaster[2] has done a cover for the book taken from that wonderful photograph of Muv & Farve & Nancy. It draws unwilling screams from one but Muv is hideous in it. *SO* untrue to life, & Farve a little dark Arab after Ramadan.

All love, Honks

1 In her essay on the Mitfords' nanny, which appeared in the *Sunday Times*, Nancy depicted Lady Redesdale as an idle, vague and neglectful mother. The piece was taken from *The Water Beetle*, a collection of Nancy's essays and journalism published later that year.

2 Osbert Lancaster (1908–86). Author, theatre designer and for forty years cartoonist on the *Daily Express*.

NANCY TO DEBORAH *7 rue Monsieur, VII*
23 August 1962

Dear Miss

Muv still fairly shirty about 'Blor' but Honks thinks she'll calm down. Fact is, I gather she had the usual slight bust up with Decca about education & very likely it (the article) seems another reminder of that vexed subject. I've written & grovelled. The fact is I can't help seeing my childhood (& the whole of my life) as a hilarious joke, whereas I think Muv feels a tiny bit sentimental about early days.

Much love, N

) DIANA TO DEBORAH
26 August 1962

Temple de la Gloire
Orsay

Darling Debo:

Before Woman went I discovered what happened at the evening they spent with Nancy & Decca, apparently at dinner Wid & her illness were spoken of & something said about Monica[1] & that she had such an unhappy miserable childhood not being liked or noticed by selfish Wid, whereupon Nancy & Decca both said, 'well, it's just exactly like *our* miserable childhoods'. In telling this Woman became scarlet & huge tears appeared in her huge eyes & she said, 'It's not TRUE'. And of course it simply *isn't*. Added to the above, not one of them threw a single word to Giuditta who, in saying so, suddenly came out with 'they were damned rude'. We smoothed them down & they went off to the Continent fairly happy I think.

I suppose today Nancy's dread article will be in *Sunday Times* & I shall have to hide it from Kit. His doings probably embarrass N just as much as her writings embarrass him, but they've been getting on quite well these hols thank goodness.

All love darling, Honks

1 Only daughter of Violet Hammersley, who favoured her sons, Christopher and David.

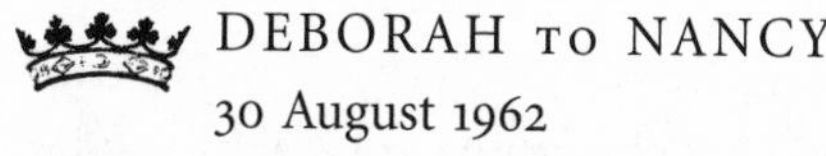

DEBORAH TO NANCY
30 August 1962

Chatsworth
Bakewell

Get on

I think, in fact I know, Muv was put out by your piece. I do think it seems a shame to harp on the vague shortcomings & never to mention the good things. Diddy said 'well I should have thought people would try to cover up any little faults they think their parents have'. You will say I am not one to speak as my childhood was very happy and when the dreaded moment came of going to that foul boarding school – which made me *ill* with misery – Muv immediately took me away, against the advice of Bridget [Airlie] etc.

I hope Decca didn't go on at her now she is old & too tired to argue the rights & wrongs of what happened forty years ago. The visit seems to have been a success so presumably she didn't. I know Woman agrees with me & I think Honks does, & Bobo got her wish of going to school & getting sacked pretty soon from all of them, so I suppose you & Decca were the unlucky ones.

Andrew is battling with the arrangements of the Commonwealth Prime Ministers' visit. He wangled an invitation to B Palace (with great difficulty, as P.M.s only are meant to go) for Nkrumah's[1] foreign sec only to see N. has bunged him into prison. That's life I guess.

I thought Uncle Harold pretty pathetic the last two weeks. Aunt Dot was lovely, she is a smasher & very indiscreet about one & all.

Sorry about the Counter Hons having a go at your President.[2] Hope no one gets mine before I mince over there.

I *think* that's all.

Much love, 9

1 Kwame Nkrumah (1909–72). First leader of independent Ghana.
2 The OAS (Secret Army Organization), a terrorist group that opposed President de Gaulle's plans to grant independence to Algeria, had attempted to assassinate him.

NANCY TO DEBORAH
1 September 1962

7 rue Monsieur, VII

Dear Miss

1. You saw the typescript & I altered everything you told me to.
2. The only tiny criticism is in the words 'of course I ought to have gone to school' – all the rest is obviously a joke.
3. She was delighted by Decca's book which is *far* more outspoken & *far* less light.
4. There is a most sympathetic real (I mean obviously not fictional) picture of her in my novels.
5. A woman said to me yesterday 'How delightful your mother sounds'. I said I wish you'd tell *her* that.

No, Decca didn't tease her but she said that Muv kept saying 'why do you work so hard at your book, it would be much better if you wrote it just as it came, out of your head'. If you'd ever done any work you would know how annoying this sort of line is. In the end she did slightly speak out. But the visit was a huge success except that the Ts having noted the weather have realized one could never live up there.

I see that autobiography is not on. Osbert Lancaster published his first in the States upon which his aunts made such a fuss that he can't do it over here. He says it was completely harmless.

Thanks for Uncle isn't he amazing![1] The clothes, the attitude – to the life. Naughty grandfather must have been as old as the hills (about my age).

I go to Woman's 22nd of this month to be for a week with Muv, to keep her amused Woman says, while Wondairful cooks. Then if you're there I could go to Chatsworth, if not I'll come back here.

Decca thought she was pregnant on the Island. 'How could I have a rabbit test, there's only one rabbit & that has got myxomatosis.' All is well however. I did love having them here – I got awfully fond of Bob – they are both much more human aren't they?

A Mrs Aykim has written to say Blor was with her & her brothers before us & they called her Nantus. I feel exactly like a husband who finds out his wife used to be married to somebody else.

Hope you're having this lovely weather.

Love, N

1 Deborah had forwarded to Nancy the photograph from *The Field* of David Smith, the Mitfords' putative uncle.

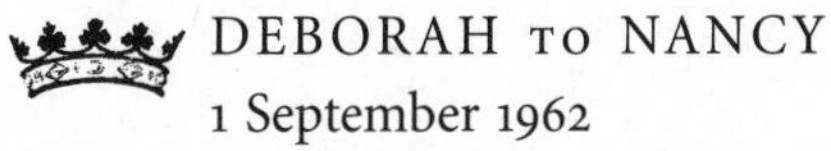

DEBORAH TO NANCY
1 September 1962

Chatsworth
Bakewell

Get on

Have been regretting the *sharpness* of the *tone* of my letter ever since I posted it and now, trembling, await your *sharp* reply.

If I was going to say all that I should have said it in the spring when you showed it to me. And I thought, since she didn't mind Decca's vile tales in her book, she wouldn't mind anything. So I have been wrong, *as usual ALL ROUND*. Sorry.

Now to lighter vein. There's a play on in New York called *Who's Afraid of Virginia Woolf.*[1] So you see why I love them.

Uncle Harold mentions the Loved One[2] in his bread & butter letter, he is coming on.

Much love COME, 9

1 Edward Albee's play opened on Broadway on 13 October 1962 after ten preview performances.
2 Deborah's nickname for President Kennedy, who had telephoned her at Thanksgiving and asked, 'Have you got all your loved ones around you?'

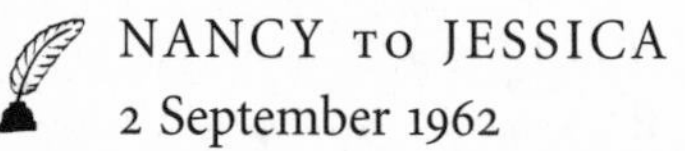

NANCY TO JESSICA
2 September 1962

7 rue Monsieur, VII

Darling Soo

You asked for a typical saying of Voltaire's. *Qui plume a guerre a*[1] is rather applying to me at present. Debo (who read the typescript of my essay) has joined the fray, accusing me of teasing Muv now that she is old & too tired to argue. As a matter of fact she loves arguing but let that pass. So I am tortured with guilt though reason tells me that this is not reasonable. I looked up the early chapters of *P of Love* & see that everything I said in the article is there. No complaints at the time. She positively enjoyed your book. So I think it's all rather unfair & exaggerated.

The marvellous weather goes on.

I dined last night with the Colonel in his ministry Place de la Concorde & we sat out on the colonnade, a new moon over the obelisk, it was really too lovely.

Come & live here oh do

Much love, N

There was a lily waver[2] on the train to Honks the other day. When I saw I couldn't help laughing upon which he furiously did them up.

1 'To hold a pen is to be at war.'
2 A flasher.

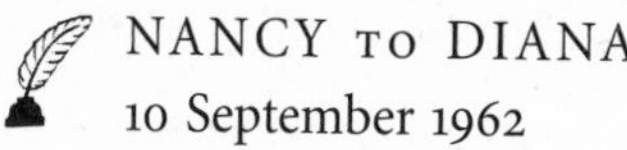

NANCY TO DIANA
10 September 1962

7 rue Monsieur, VII

Dereling

Re enclosed – I've never had this experience, have you?[1] So humiliating, I had to write & say so. What can it mean? I haven't told her I passed on her letter but no doubt if you have an observation to make she would be grateful. Her enclosures were quite lucid – I've returned them.

Oi mees you.

The French wireless said Sir Oswald's programme is to send all Jews & Niggers out of England – not a word about making Europe. Is it worth his while to contradict this? It was pretty strong, saying he ought to be in a maison d'aliénés[2] however you spell that. It was only the 3.15 or perhaps 4.15 news which I happened to turn on. Perhaps he should send them a copy of his speech for future reference or something like that. (It also said he is the only remaining adherent of the croix gammée [swastika] in Europe.) I wouldn't annoy you with this except that as you live here you might as well know it.

I gulped down *Curzon* in a day – what an awful man he was. The love letters!![3] If anybody wrote to me like that I'd be sick. Oh goodness how greatly I prefer the Colonel's respectueusement which I used to find a little chilly! I'd no idea the marriage with Grace had been such a flop.[4] Wish you were here to ask a thousand questions. Did his daughters really hate him? Half, I suppose. Then nobody was nearly as rich as I'd imagined. Two million dollars – penury! As Derek [Jackson] would say you don't have to be very rich to know how little that is!

Marie & I wandered into the Boulevard to give the General a champagne welcome & were quickly sent packing by a copper. You never saw so many policemen. He took exactly ¼ hour from Orly to Elysée & must have whizzed by five minutes after we'd been there. He must feel terribly like getting back to Swinbrook after being made much of elsewhere![5]

Much love, N

1 Following Nancy's *Sunday Times* article, a woman had written to ask her if she had ever had a feeling 'of herself as herself'.
2 'A lunatic asylum.' Mosley's Union Movement was campaigning against the influx of Commonwealth immigrants into Britain.
3 In *Curzon, The End of an Epoch* (1960), Leonard Mosley (no relation) quoted cloying letters from the Viceroy to his future wife, which were signed off, typically, 'Put up your lips to kiss and be kissed, Mary, and sway your lissom body in your lover's arms.'
4 Grace Hinds (1877–1958). The American-born widow of historical novelist Alfred Duggan became Curzon's second wife in 1917. She took little interest in Curzon's political career and was never able to give him the son and heir he longed for, which undermined their marriage and eventually led to their separation.
5 General de Gaulle had returned from a five-day official visit to Germany.

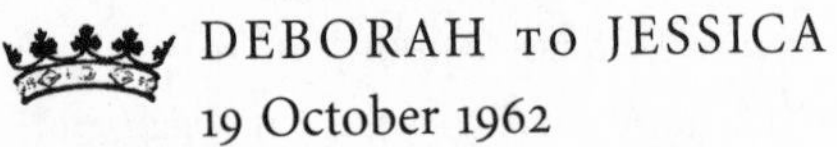

DEBORAH TO JESSICA
19 October 1962

Chatsworth
Bakewell

Hen! Your book finished! *HOW* wonderful, it was a long gestation, you must feel excited that it's literally born. Send one, Hen, when ready, because although we all know the trouble I have re reading I'll have a *real try*. I really am dying for it.

Muv is much better, herself really, though she has still got a black eye. It was awful, she was a real mess.[1] I'll see her tomorrow when I go to London.

Hen we went to Uganda to free it you'll be glad to hear. It was perfectly fascinating like Africa always is once one gets there. Kenyatta[2] was in our hotel, he is a full time ghoul in a hideous bead hat, but Mboya[3] is v. fascinating. I know someone who had a romance with him & called him Mboya Friend. The Kabaka is a marvel, so odd, & his palace v. pretty. The language is a bit of a teaser, viz. would you guess that 'Muwabutwa' means 'A well fed sorcerer easily finds a victim'? Well it does. Or that 'Mabaagira Nsega' means 'When the Kabaka kills the bodies can always feed the vultures'. It's worse than French.

Hen I'm going to Washington on Sunday because an exhibition of 120 drawings from here is going to begin on 27th & they are having a dinner to set it off to which we are going. I'll ring you up if I can get somewhere *not on my own phone* Hen. Don't know yet how long I'm

Deborah and President Kennedy at the opening of the Washington National Gallery exhibition of drawings from Chatsworth. The President's first visit to the Gallery coincided with the Cuban missile crisis and it was extraordinary that he was able to devote so much time to the evening. Washington, 27 October 1962.

staying, probably a pretty short time as things seem to be piling up here & in London.

Well that's it Hen – keep your pecker up.

Much love, Yr Hen

When will your book actually be p-bl-sh-d?

1 Lady Redesdale had been injured in a car accident.
2 Jomo Kenyatta (1889–1978). President of the Kenya African National Union 1961–3. Elected first Prime Minister of self-governing Kenya in 1963 and President in 1964.
3 Tom Mboya (1930–69). Kenyan Minister of Labour 1962–3.

DIANA TO DEBORAH
21 October 1962

Daubeuf
Bec de Mortagne
Daubeuf-Serville

Darling Debo

We went over to Fontaines last week & found Wid bearing up – just. Poor Wid, Christopher [Hammersley] had gone the day before. Nancy is being (I'm afraid) unkind to her in small ways. I don't understand their relationship – N waits to go to Fontaines until Mrs Ham looms up & then loathes her rather. Her book[1] came out, she does herself an injustice don't you think so? One would not die much for the author of that book yet in real life she *is* die-worthy.

How long are you going to be in America? I die for you.

All love darling, Honks

1 *The Water Beetle.*

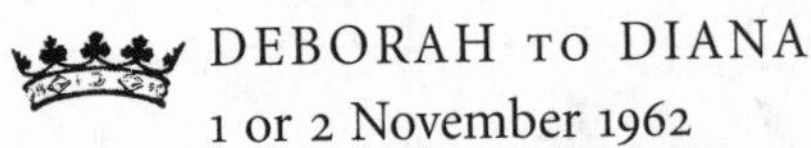
DEBORAH TO DIANA
1 or 2 November 1962

[British Embassy]
Washington

Darling Honks

I've just got back from New York where I spent 2 queer days & nights. The lingo is difficult but very funny & the kindness of the souls who live there is extreme i.e. I was lent a Bentley & a nanny of a chauffeur for two days while its owner Mrs Mellon[1] walked everywhere in the rain.

I did love Nancy's idea about the Loved One's announcement.[2] It was a shame it wasn't what you thought. He's very fit. I've got him saying mincing but sometimes he gets it wrong & says minuetting which is lovely isn't it.

Today was the biggest bit of luck – I had lunch with Cecil Beaton and how we longed for you to be there.

I'm in love again, such a bore, with a *marvellous* woman called Mrs Fell,[3] she is the pick of the bunch, beautiful & funny. The deathly secret is I'm quite fairly longing to come home, & I plan at the moment to stay here this weekend & go to Boston on Monday with the Loved One – *IF* he goes & *IF* he'll take me – to hear Teddy[4] do his eve of poll meeting & fly home on Tues. We'll see. If Boston is off, I may come sooner. Of course it's been pretty queer here but I wouldn't have missed it for anything.

I had a v. nice time in New York but it's nice to get back here to this house. Mrs Astaire is amazing, she's 84 & looks 54 & is v. spry both mentally & physically & so nice the way she fusses over one. I stayed in Adele's flat & she's in the same building.

The Loved One was on for the dinner before the opening of the drawings[5] otherwise he hasn't been too much in evidence because of no official entertaining at the White Wendy House.

Much love, Debo

1 Rachel (Bunny) Lambert Lloyd; Listerine heiress and wife of the philanthropist and art collector Paul Mellon.
2 'Nancy says when she heard the L[oved] One was to broadcast she sat up all night because she was sure he was going to announce that he was abdicating because he couldn't go on without the woman he loved by his side.' (Diana to Deborah, 28 October 1962) In fact, Deborah's visit to Washington had coincided with the Cuban missile crisis and President Kennedy's broadcast had been to announce that the USSR was dismantling its bases in Cuba.
3 A socialite friend of President Kennedy.
4 Edward Kennedy (1932–). Elected to the US Senate in 1962, filling the seat vacated by his brother when he became President.
5 Deborah had managed to persuade President Kennedy to visit the exhibition of Chatsworth drawings at the Washington National Gallery, the first time he had set foot inside the Gallery.

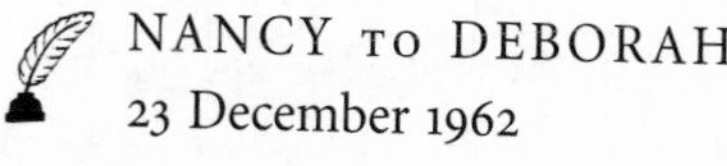

NANCY TO DEBORAH
23 December 1962

7 rue Monsieur, VII

Dear Miss

The Loved One really has surpassed himself & even I am sharked. So *rude*, letting the beastly thing off in our faces like that, do speak.[1]

Poor Honks is in despair I daresay she has told you, the puncture cure on which she had really counted doesn't seem to have worked. She looks ill & wretched oh what a worry it all is.

Daisy [Fellowes]'s funeral very beautiful (nothing but *white* flowers please note for mine) but very empty. She really had quarrelled with half Paris – there was a Stern funeral and a Murat wedding at the same time. Many regulars at rue de Lille were absent, including the Windsors, who *lived* there. They gave out that it is common to go to funerals & were photographed twisting at 5 that morning instead. (She went to Dior's however.) It seems she, Daisy, had a terrific row with Honks[2] only the day before (don't know what about) which they were to make up at luncheon instead of which she died. Grace [Dudley] came & sat with us, what a row of giantesses.

Heavenly here with one million people at winter sports & all the children gone from rue Mr. *Oh* for the fearful avalanche[3] I wouldn't mind that a bit!

Much love, Happy X, N

1 Kennedy had abruptly cancelled the Skybolt air-to-ground nuclear missile programme, which had been promised to Harold Macmillan earlier in the year, thus depriving Britain of an independent nuclear deterrent. The decision sparked a crisis that severely tested Anglo-American relations.
2 Diana Cooper.
3 'The awful avalanche' that killed the young hero of Longfellow's poem *Excelsior* (1841).

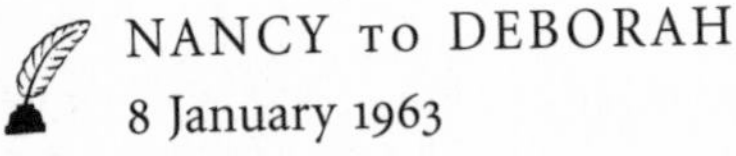

NANCY TO DEBORAH *7 rue Monsieur, VII*
8 January 1963

Dear Miss

I didn't know you were ill – you must have thought me v. hard hearted. I'll see if I can't get a private line to the White House to be kept up to date about events at Chatsworth (as well as to get off my chest what I feel about Bingo Bango Bongo).[1]

I fear these cures often work for a bit at first & then prove disappointing. You see Honks's headache is back again. The cure for *that* in my view would be to go quietly in & kill Sir Oz.

I hear that in a list of pornographic books at the Cairo museum is: 'How to Make Love in the Cold' by Miss N. M. That's the stuff. Colonel keeps saying 'Why don't you write a novel?' 'Because I haven't got a subject.' 'Why not a fascinating French politician in Paris or a fascinating French ambassador in Rome?'

Dolly is v. excited for the new collections & so am I.

That's all for now, DO be better.

Love, N

No news of Wid for a fortnight. Have you?

1 UN forces had launched a decisive attack on the secessionist Congolese province of Katanga.

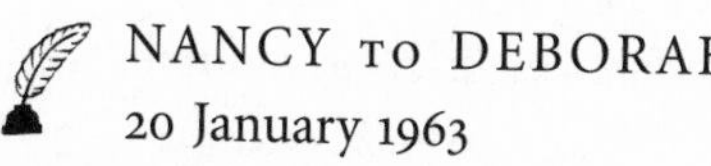

NANCY TO DEBORAH *7 rue Monsieur, VII*
20 January 1963

Dear Miss

I had a long vivid dream about Bosomy.[1] He came to rest at Chatsworth after *two* railway accidents on Br Railways. We had to explain that these are quite normal & in no way an attempt on his life. As I happened to be staying with you I made movements to go & you said, 'Stay man stay'. I said, 'But what shall I talk to him about?' You said, 'Let him talk, & laugh if he makes a joke'. He arrived & we all went to the local museum after which the dream went to pieces. Up to then it was one of those pretty, coloured dreams I'm so fond of & the *local museum*! I wish you could see it, was a sort of early Italian cloister, too lovely.
[Incomplete]

1 Nancy had once seen a photograph of President Kennedy in a bathing suit and given him this nickname.

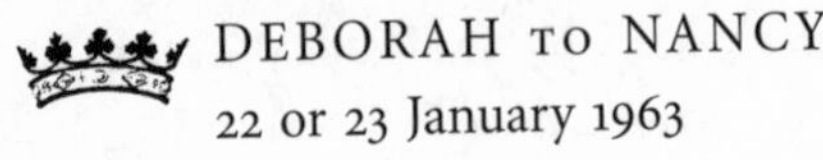

DEBORAH TO NANCY
22 or 23 January 1963

Chatsworth
Bakewell

Get on

Many thanks for the dream re Bosomy, the railway accidents & the local museum. I lived in it & was furious when it went to pieces.

I'm in such a rage with what choose to call themselves Local Authorities that I'm about to write a letter to *The Times*. Do you know that you aren't allowed, by law, to put a lavatory in a bathroom if that bathroom leads out of a bedroom & if it's the only lavatory in the house? So I found a lot of workmen putting a new lavatory in a shed in the garden of a house which already had a perfectly good bathroom. Can you imagine such madness. Poor people, think of them going outside in weather like this just because the footling Local Authority says they must. Oh the wicked stupidity. What would they have thought of the lav at Swinbrook, or in the Mews for that matter. FOOLS.

I was so angry I went scarlet & came home.

Much love, 9

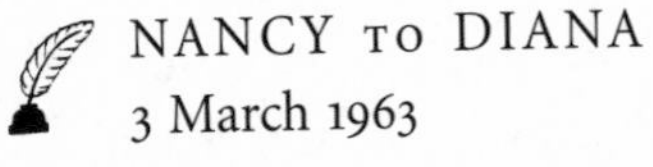

NANCY TO DIANA
3 March 1963

5 Lowndes Court, SW1

Dereling

U *aire*. The wonderful comfort – the sweetness of Emmy.[1] Oh, I am in clover!

The wedding was perfect. He[2] is really so handsome, with the long chin of Muv's mother, only he looks ill. Not a *bit* like a bumble, I never saw anybody less like one.

Woman was in a mink hat looking wondair & hissed out as I came up the aisle, 'real mink – it's insured – it belongs to the wife of an insurance agent'. I think she felt I might snatch it there & then. She stayed up for dinner & caught that 10.30 train home.[3]

Oh at the wedding, the church which is small (1868) was completely full. Muv said, 'What a lot of people, I imagined there would only be six of us!' 'Why?' 'Oh I don't know' – & then shrieked how she does.

Don't the Paris clothes look deadly.

Much love & *thank* you, N

1 Nancy was staying at the Mosleys' London flat, looked after by Emmy and her husband Jerry Lehane, an Irish couple who worked for the Mosleys as cook and driver for over forty years.

2 Lesley Prynne (1928–). Lady Redesdale's great-nephew had married Dorothy Slim.

3 Pamela was staying at Woodfield while in England.

DIANA TO DEBORAH

3 March 1963

Ileclash
Co. Fermoy

Darling Debo

The dreadery here is likely to take longer than I thought – I'm only half way through the first trunk of letters![1] Kit has b——d. He is less than no use because he pretends to sort papers & comes up after four hours in tears but having thrown away nothing. I at least have had several bonfires. Oh darling your letters! And Birdie's! The ones that make me cry most are Nanny Higgs's, 'Your two pets are very well & send a kiss, they often speak of you', etc (aged nothing & *one*).

Love darling & SO many thanks, Honks

1 Diana was clearing out Ileclash before it was sold.

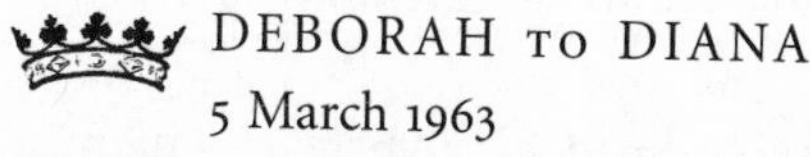

DEBORAH TO DIANA

5 March 1963

4 Chesterfield Street, W1

Darling Honks

I don't believe I *thanked* you enough for seeing Miss Cole, it was truly good of you when you had 1,000 other things to do, I *do* appreciate though.

Phone conversation between me & Ld W Beresford.

Me 'So sorry to bother you but could you tell me about a governess called Miss Cole?'

He (Throat clearing) 'Well we weren't at all impressed with her, no not at all.'

Me 'Why?'

He 'Well of course she found it very dull here, she likes the bright lights.'

Me 'What else?'

He 'Well she took the children to the cove one day and we heard afterwards she went to sleep in the sun & the children simply ran wild.'

Me 'Anything else?'

He 'Yes we heard after she left that she sometimes SLAPPED them.'

Me 'Oh.'

So I engaged her. I do hope it will be OK. I've written to say let us do a six-week trial on both sides.

DON'T throw letters away, it's madness. Just dump them at Mochuda.[1]

Much love, Debo

1 'Lios mor Mochuda', the Irish name for Lismore.

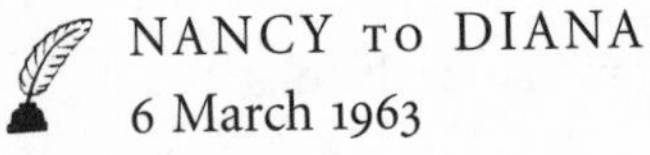

NANCY TO DIANA — *5 Lowndes Court, SW1*
6 March 1963

Dereling,

Throw nothing away. Handy[1] tells me letters from Evelyn [Waugh] for instance are worth £1 each *now* – from American universities – but a *correspondance suivie* of a whole family, so rare nowadays, would be gold for your heirs.

Thank you so so much for the *loving* time I've had here. Last night Kit asked me to dinner, how it was nice, we had champagne. But after we had to see an operation for gallstones on the telly. Well it does ruin an evening – everything is cut off & one can only go to bed after it – cold spoon in a soufflé. (Well perhaps gallstones is particularly cold!!)

I sat next Mr Profumo[2] at a luncheon he is very agreeable. I also had a long talk with David Bruce[3] – all these sort of people are much more sensible than you'd think from the papers.

The best I ever heard – from a friend: 'Did you know my sister was burnt to death in her flat?' Noises from me 'Oh well it was a nice way for her to go really!'

Before Kit came, the telephone bell rang & a foreign lady said, 'Ees thees Bel[gravia] something?' Thinking it was Debo I said, 'Oh eet ees, etc.' 'Can I speak to Sir Oswald?' Collapse of N[ancy] R[odd]. Must get up & leave London.

Love, N

1 Handasyde Buchanan (1907–84). Antiquarian bookseller who worked at Heywood Hill 1945–74.
2 John Profumo (1913–2006). Conservative Secretary of State for War 1960–63. On 2 March, a Labour MP made a speech in the House of Commons hinting at Profumo's relationship with Christine Keeler, a showgirl, who was also having an affair with a naval attaché at the Soviet embassy. Profumo denied any 'impropriety' in his relationship with Keeler but later admitted that he had lied, and resigned.
3 David Bruce (1898–1977). US ambassador to London 1961–9. Married Evangeline Bell in 1945.

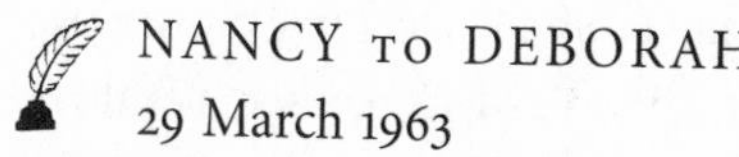

NANCY TO DEBORAH — *7 rue Monsieur, VII*
29 March 1963

Dear Miss

Quelle horrible surprise – a photograph of the Q accompanied by a *hideous Eskimo*. I imagine she is in some dread Soviet land, look again, & find that it is Princess Anne.

I've been asked to the wedding of A. O.[1] (can't say it would have occurred to me to ask him to mine but still) & think I will go, partly rather fun indeed great fun & chiefly to give an arm to Muv. Then I might as I'm half-way go on to Ireland for a very few days? As I really hadn't intended to I never ascertained your dates but if you can't have me I'll concentrate on Ed [Sackville-West].

N

1 Sir Angus Ogilvy (1928–2004). A cousin of the Mitfords. Married Princess Alexandra of Kent on 24 April 1963.

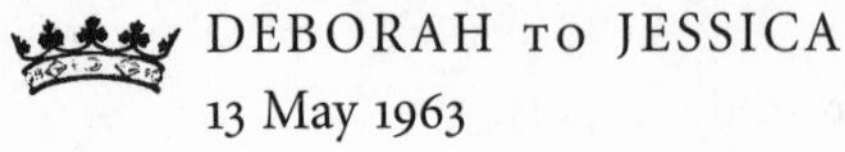

DEBORAH TO JESSICA *Inch Kenneth*
13 May 1963 *Gribun, Oban*

Dearest Hen

You will have had our telegrams and I have had yours, thanks Hen. Muv is very low, she alternates between being utterly miserable really painful to see and then sometimes she is quite cheerful and laughs about things. She can't get comfortable and is so weak she can't move herself & when she is like that she has to be changed in her position every few minutes. Her throat has more or less given out & swallowing is fearfully difficult so that she can only have a teaspoon or so at a time of whatever she fancies, milk, apple juice & sometimes a scrap of chicken jelly.

We have got two nurses now, both saintly and of course such an immense help & comfort. Even though we've got a night nurse we take it in turns to be in her room all through the night because when she wakes she is sometimes sad and likes a hand to hold.

The weather is unspeakable & no one has been able to get over today but we hope for the Dr tomorrow. Both nurses say they have had cases like this who have gone on for weeks because she's taking just enough nourishment to keep her alive. She is sleeping more now & often does not shake at all. Oh Hen it is so sad to see her like this and she longs to die, she keeps saying so & making us cry & then laugh by saying Somewhere you'll find my absurd will.

I will keep in close touch Hen – are you going to N.Y. at all or are you going to be at home?

Much love, Yr Hen

She says she wants to be buried at Swinbrook.

She makes marvellous jokes, like Woman said she was writing to Aunt Iris, 'Oh, have you told her I'm dying' Muv said.

Then she does get very miserable when she's restless.

So difficult to die, like so difficult to be born.

She sends you LOTS of love and says she thinks such a lot about you.

Early Tues A.M. Just the same. Muv says, half laughing, 'tell them I'm still here!' She is wonderful.

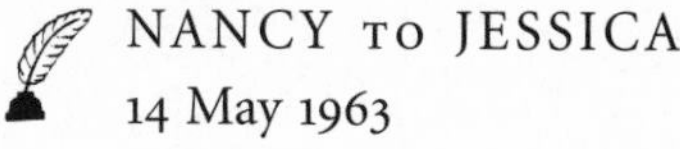

NANCY TO JESSICA
14 May 1963

Inch Kenneth
Gribun, Oban

Darling Soo

There is a little improvement & she's not so sad. There have been *dreadful* times when she has felt so ill she didn't know how to bear it. Then she has twice seemed to be going, said goodbye to everybody, said, 'Perhaps Tom & Bobo, who knows?' Messages for you & so on. She said, 'If there's anything in my will you don't like, do alter it'. I said, 'But we shld go to prison' & she laughed!! Then she rallied & for two days now has seemed stronger. We long for her to go in her sleep, but the heart is still strong & the dr says what will be final will come from the part of the brain that controls one's breathing. She has had a little stroke you see. So strange she's not a bit deaf now, not in the least. Perfectly lucid. We've got two adorable young Scotch nurses – we take it in turns at night, two hours at a time & are all rather tired. Before the night nurse came we did half the nights, two of us together, & that was exhausting.

I know Debo *much* wants instructions from you about this place, the servants & so on. *Do* let the O-Fs[1] have it, oh do!

Fond love, N

1 The Ogilvie-Forbeses; Lady Redesdale's only neighbours were interested in buying Inch Kenneth.

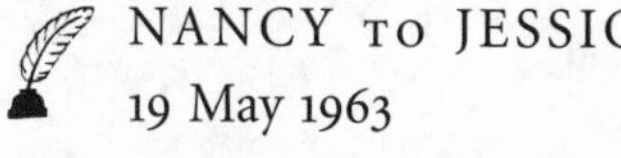

NANCY TO JESSICA
19 May 1963

Inch Kenneth
Gribun, Oban

Darling Soo

Here it goes on & poor Muv is getting so fed up. She scolds us now for 'dragging her back from the grave – what for?' But all we have done is to give her a little water when she asks which isn't exactly dragging! Three times now we have been gathered round as she seemed to be going & then she had rallied. The fact is she's fearfully *bored* & no wonder. Now Christine is coming & we think a new mug may cheer.

The wedding was most enjoyable – Muv looked smashing & we

Nancy, Pamela, Diana and Deborah together on Inch Kenneth during the last weeks of their mother's life. May 1963.

are so pleased it happened in time because she really loved it. She was got up in black velvet, lace & diamonds & was the most elegant person there by far. How she loves clothes & nice things. Even in the night she likes my dressing gown. Your nightdresses by the way are perfect for her.

My clothes are all dirty so I said to Debo 'I'm going to make Woman teach me to wash & I'll stand & look on while she does'. Well it worked like a charm & now she's going to teach me to iron.

Desmond's sweet little boy said 'Granny Muv must have been a very wealthy young lady to have everything so nice'. We asked the girl what is her favourite toy, 'I've got a fluffy dog – God, it's fluffy'. They've gone which is sad – so beautiful & *so* funny.[1]

Oh dear oh dear *Susan* it's really awful – you're lucky not to be here.

Love, Soo

1 Desmond Guinness's six-year-old son, Patrick, and five-year-old daughter, Marina.

TO JESSICA *[Telegram]*
25 May 1963

MUV DIED THIS MORNING MUCH LOVE ALL SISTERS

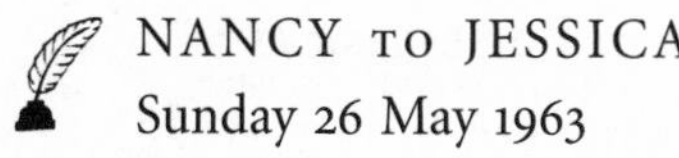

NANCY TO JESSICA *Inch Kenneth*
Sunday 26 May 1963 *Gribun, Oban*

Darling Soo

Pam, Diana & I are here to the end of Muv on the Island. The coffin arrives tomorrow at 4 then the undertakers have to be given whisky – did you ever hear anything so barbarous (with the MacGillivrays I believe), then we shall hear the hammering like David Copperfield, then we all slide after the coffin over the rocks & the neighbours will join in a procession of cars to Salen where we all spend the night. Then Lochinvar, & at Oban a motor hearse to Swinbrook where the funeral is next Thursday. Woman goes home – Diana & I to Debo in London.

Terrible sadness here you may imagine but anything is better than to see her so wretched. Debo & Woman were with her but she never came to & had been in a trance since Sunday.

Fond love Soo from Susan

JESSICA TO DEBORAH

25 May 1963

6411 Regent Street
Oakland

Dearest Hen,

That must have been a terrible, terrible fortnight. I did so agonize for you all; and it was extremely good of you to find time to write and send the t.grams as I was so longing for news, could think of naught else.

I know that you, specially, will miss Muv so dreadfully; I always thought you were easily her favourite child, she relied so much on you and when letters came from you (while we were staying there) she'd absolutely light up.

I'm *so* glad that we did go to stay with her last year. We rather thought at the time that it would be to say goodbye.

Various mothers of friends have died in the last year or so but all in beastly hospitals, sometimes in what's known as the 'intensive care' ward (the horror of it) where all they do is concentrate on prolonging life a few weeks or months – while knowing perfectly well the person can't ever really recover. Thank goodness Muv didn't have to go through that sort of thing but was at Inch K which she loved so much and with all of you there and the nice nurses instead of the Intensive Carers.

Hen this is just to send masses of love, and from Bob and Benj. Decca

Dinky is terribly sad; the only time she really knew Muv was when she was 14 that time, and we stayed at the Mews one autumn. They hit it off amazingly well (considering their difference in background as school teachers here say).

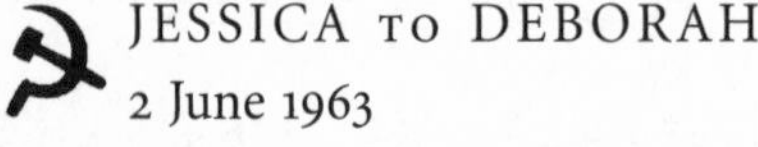

JESSICA TO DEBORAH

2 June 1963

6411 Regent Street
Oakland

Dearest Hen,

You are an angel to keep on writing. If it hadn't been for your letters (and Nancy's) I should have felt so v. lonely. Your description of the funeral in the letter that just came – talk about floods. It was absolutely as though I'd been there and tasted the pews etc.[1] Also thanks *so* much for thinking of sending flowers from me. (By the way my new book is all about the ridiculous waste of money on funeral flowers & an attack on the Florist Industry for inducing people to send flowers! But I can see, not in this case.)

Nancy wrote all about the last journey in *Puffin*, piper, flag ½ mast. Oh Hen I do wish in a way I had come, but from what you all said it could never have been in time because of the coma of last few days. I shall keep all yr. letters forever, with Muv's last one to me. It was all about the new foal etc. in extraordinarily firm typing – until one came to the end and she said Madeau [Stewart] was typing it for her. She told about the rough journey and said 'So I went to bed and stayed there until now – which is lunch time the next day'. When I read that I had a bitter premonition, because it's so unlike her to stay in bed all day.

Is there any possible chance you might come to S.F., as per my last letter? Goodness it would be marvellous. I do *so long* to see you. Got a v. sad letter from Mrs Ham (partly about her bad leg), it must have been a terrible thing for her too, because at that age, so few friends and contemporaries left.

Much love, and from Bob and Benj, Yr. Hen

1 As children, the sisters used to lick the church pews during services at Swinbrook.

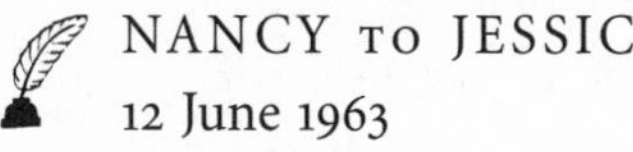

NANCY TO JESSICA *7 rue Monsieur, VII*
12 June 1963

Darling Soo

When I'm alone, & specially at night & even in dreams, those days on the Island come back – but not really sadly. I believe it's worse for you, seeing it from far off. It all seemed quite natural, something that had to happen, & when the discomfort & her own melancholy became almost unbearable she was soon unconscious & away from it all.

More cheerful news is that you seem to have had some good advance publicity for the book & I was rung up by a French publisher who thought the book was mine & is very anxious to publish it. I said 'have you got a pencil' & gave him your address & fancy, he had heard of Oakland, can you beat it! This is good as one does very well with French royalties I always find – far better than in the other countries.

Colonel has been in Washington. He says it's exactly like Nairobi. Rather liked the President however – very clever & attractive he says.

I'm already *so* tired of black clothes, so depressing in the hot weather. Never mind.

Much love, Soo.

P.S. Woman writes to say she has put fresh flowers on Muv's grave. I thought of *you*!

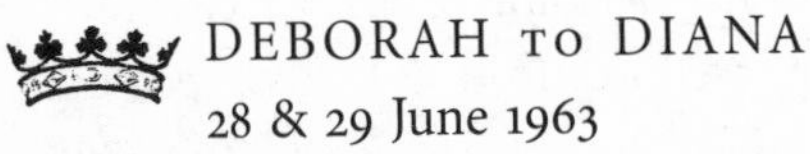

DEBORAH TO DIANA
28 & 29 June 1963

Chatsworth
Bakewell

Darling Honks

So he's coming here tomorrow, a proper mystery trip. The Foreign Office tell us it's for a quarter of an hour so we'll see. He's going to see Kick's grave.[1] Two helis arrived yesterday afternoon, I was in the meeting dept, & out tumbled ten sort of G men of super filmish variety plus a Foreign Office brigadier, bowler & stiff collar, oh my word it was comical. They spent an hour at the churchyard, looking in the ha-ha & choosing where he should land (above the church on a flat bit of park was decided on) so in one day we've got to build a bridge over the ha-ha & about twenty men have been set to work on the plot of graves, which of course was in a *terrible* state. Lots of policemen are going to be in the ha-ha & in the pathetic clump of trees which were mostly knocked down in the gale. I suppose they'll be hiding behind gravestones & all. Fire fighting things & an ambulance with blood are going to be there too.

The American secret service people said 'what sort of people live in this village?' & I said 'well, rather quiet sort of people.' At that moment Mr Thompson came out of his house on two sticks so I was able to show them the sort of people. They say he can't possibly come to this house because of the public road, also the time. It will be sad if he doesn't because you can't see the house from the village. Andrew & I are going to the military airport in Lincolnshire to meet him & come back here in the heli with him.

The Lees-Milnes[2] will be here, & Yehudi Menuhin[3] comes tomorrow night, how odd.

What about Ld Astor & Mandy Rice Davies?[4] What next.

Much love, Debo

1 President Kennedy was stopping at Edensor to visit his sister Kathleen's grave, following a state visit to Ireland and en route to talks with Harold Macmillan.
2 James Lees-Milne (1908–97). Architectural historian, diarist and biographer. An intimate of Tom Mitford since their schooldays, he fell in love with the 'celestial' beauty of Diana when she was an adolescent, became a close friend of Nancy in spite of detecting a 'vein of callousness in her which almost amounts to cruelty', and was a devoted admirer of Deborah, at whose instigation he wrote *The Bachelor Duke* (1991), a life of the 6th Duke of Devonshire. Married Alvilde Chaplin in 1951.
3 Yehudi Menuhin (1916–99). The celebrated violinist had recently opened his school for musically gifted children.
4 In the wake of the Profumo affair, Mandy Rice-Davies, a showgirl, had made lurid allegations about Lord Astor's house parties.

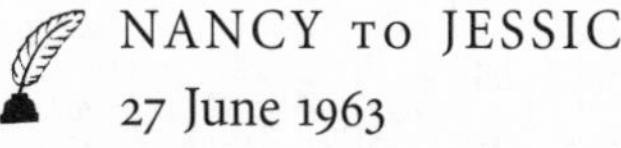

NANCY TO JESSICA *7 rue Monsieur, VII*
27 June 1963

Darling Soo

Your friends came, & telephoned, but we couldn't arrange anything because they seemed distracted, their daughter having bunked. That's life I guess – DAUGHTERS!!

Now I'm off to Venice (Dorsoduro 23) & then perhaps to Greece to stay with Mark [Ogilvie-Grant]. Hen comes to Venice for a week. Funny about the Pres going to his sister's grave – funny thing none of them have ever thought about that grave before but it makes an excellent excuse. One should have sisters' graves in every direction.

We are all loving Profumo. I met him – sat by him at a luncheon last March & thought it very odd to have a sort of rich cad in the

Govt. Do you remember Bill Astor? He was always vile. The girls are so bright & clever in the witness box it quite puts one on their side. The whole thing is pure Venice 18th century, except then Miss Keeler wld have been a nun. Much of it is strangely like the tales of Casanova. Anyway it's girls not boys which is always something!

Love, N

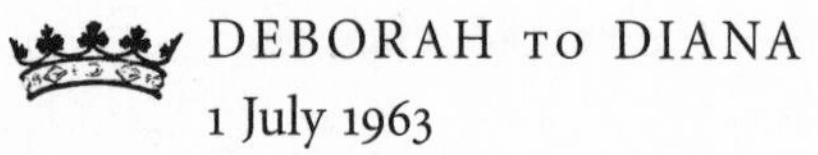

DEBORAH TO DIANA
1 July 1963

Chatsworth
Bakewell

Darling Honks

The Loved One loomed, for at least 3 minutes. We went to meet him at the air force place in Lincs & came back here in his *heeli* with him, it's really a magic carpet.

The public visiting this house got a surprise when they saw the dear old face, so did the Lees-Milnes who had come to stay. Sophy kept telling him about her little dog who has got married.

Much love, Debo

DIANA TO DEBORAH
13 September 1963

Temple de la Gloire
Orsay

Darling Debo:

It was so lovely yet so tantalizing to have a little chat yesterday – really French telephones are awful & you faded away. I boldly wrote to Emma & felt rather like Siegfried when he woke the dragon (which grumbles 'Who disturbs my sleep?'). Naunceling obviously thinks they'd die of boredom here.[1] The truth is I so adore this place & my spirits rise when I wake up in the morning & realize I'm here, but then of course I get very busy sawing up wood etc. in other words, on the *mad* side. So I can't judge. I observed to Naunceling how solemn & awe-ful it sounded to hear the vows one takes in church, & how dread to realize none of us dreams of keeping them. She said 'H'm' (in the way Mogens [Tvede] imitates so well) & I said 'After all we're all adulterers & adulteresses' – another H'm. A few

Nancy, Deborah, Pamela and Diana at the wedding of Emma Cavendish to Toby Tennant, 3 September 1963.

days later she said 'I was thinking about what you said, & it's not *quite* true, after all Debo's absolutely pure.' I said 'Yes I know, I was thinking of *our* row, you & Woman & me & Lady Dorothy'.[2]

About Colonel (who seems to have worshipped his visit) I hope my tapped telephone won't reveal to him that I said he *is* the Denning Report.[3] Anyway what I was going to tell you is that a man we know, talking at a luncheon about Le Marais, said 'C'est une maison qui a deux maîtres'[4] & when I pretended not to know what he meant he said Jimmy & Col. I do wonder.

All love darling, Honks

1 Diana had offered to lend the Temple de la Gloire to her niece, Emma Cavendish, for her honeymoon after her marriage to Toby Tennant,
2 Dorothy Macmillan's long affair with Robert Boothby began in 1930.
3 A report by Lord Denning on the Profumo affair criticized the government for not acting more quickly but concluded that there had been no breach of national security.
4 'It is a house with two masters.' Château Le Marais belonged to Violette de Talleyrand Périgord, Duchess of Sagan (1915–2003), the daughter of Anna Gould and heiress to a large American railway fortune. She was married to Count James (Jimmy) de Pourtalès and was the long-standing mistress of Gaston Palewski.

NANCY TO DEBORAH

7 rue Monsieur, VII

19 October 1963

Dear Miss

Again I say I consider that I've had so much the lion's share in Muv's furniture that I wash my hands of the rest. Why not *give* the pretty card table to Emma? I entirely leave it to you to do as you think best.

The two old ladies have shaken down – Mme Costa in sunny mood – Wid's only grievance now is that she loses at Bridge. But the fact is she plays so badly that she wouldn't win even if she had every ace & king every time. Of course I point this out: 'Bridge is a game of skill, Mrs Ham'. Deep, furious groans. I think she feels having given Little John to God the latter ought to riposte by dealing her unbeatable cards – rather like Louis XIV who when hearing of Blenheim said 'Oh God how *could* you do this to me after all I've done for you?' However she's loving Lor Ume.[1] The French wireless said 'Lor Ume n'est plus Lor Ume.' Pretty good joke if he & Hogg[2] both give up their titles to no avail! Keep writing in spite of me having no news, I beg.

Love, N

1 Alexander (Alec) Douglas-Home, 14th Earl of Home (1903–95). The Conservative MP, who was automatically disqualified from the House of Commons when he inherited his father's seat in the Lords in 1951, had renounced his peerage in order to return to the Commons and contest the party leadership. Prime Minister 1963–4.
2 Quintin Hogg, 2nd Viscount Hailsham (1907–2001). Conservative politician who, like Home, disclaimed his title for his lifetime in order to stand for party leader.

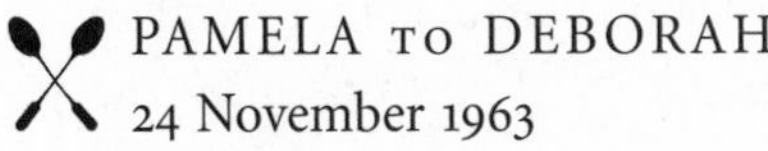

PAMELA TO DEBORAH

24 November 1963

im Chratz
Grüningen
Zurich

Darling Stublow

You will be so terribly upset at the ghastly tragedy of Mr Kennedy's death[1] and this is just to tell you how sorry I am. The whole world has had a blow & I shall never forget the shock of when I heard it yesterday in one of the shops here. For some reason we had missed the news on Friday evening. No one here speaks of anything else as all had great respect and admiration for him. He was the only person who was honestly making for world peace & was making real progress in that direction. How awful for Mrs Kennedy. Do you know Mr Johnson, will he be any good as President?

Much love from Woman

1 The President had been assassinated on 22 November.

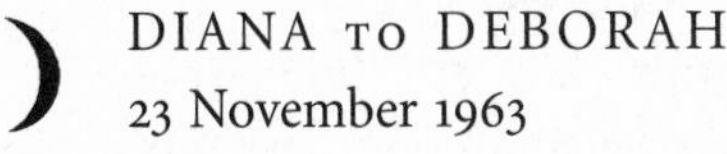

DIANA TO DEBORAH

23 November 1963

Temple de la Gloire
Orsay

Darling Debo

Don't be too sad. There is something frightful about a violent act of this kind, for everybody – except in a way the person who is killed. He had a wonderful life & a quick death. But of course it is horribly sad when friends die; dreadful & painful.

All love darling, Honks

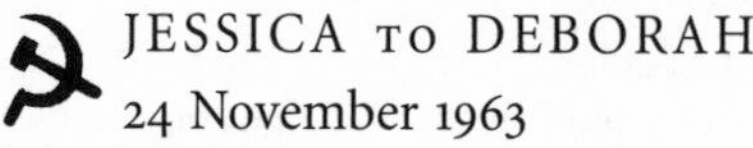

JESSICA TO DEBORAH
24 November 1963

6411 Regent Street
Oakland

Dearest Hen,

I can't describe the feeling of utter horror at what has happened. I was at home when the news came (had just got back from my long trip a few days before), and Bob telephoned from his office to say a client of his had rung up, there was an 'unconfirmed rumour' that the President had been shot at. Then I went outside and several neighbours were crying, as by that time it was known he might be dying. It was the same everywhere.

Hen thanks so much for writing while I was on the tour, and sorry I didn't answer but was *incredibly* swamped. Now of course I don't feel like writing any jolly letter.

So, this is just to send lots of love, Yr Hen

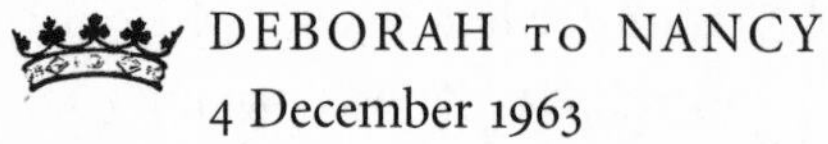

DEBORAH TO NANCY
4 December 1963

Chatsworth
Bakewell

Get on

Thanks v much for yr letter. We had such a sad time in Washington. I was more or less alright in the church till all his friends came in and then all welled & it was floods all the way. You never saw such crumpled miserable faces. I never want to see such a thing again, but anyhow one never will as whoever dies whom I know can never make such an effect on so many kinds of people.

I certainly was incredibly lucky to know him & I still can't believe he's dead, it's impossible. We had such odd journeys out & back, if it hadn't been for the great sadness of the reason for going I suppose it would have been rather fascinating, going out I had dinner with the D of Edinburgh & Mr Wilson,[1] & Andrew was with the Homes, & coming back there was only the Homes & Mr Grimond[2] & me & 150 empty seats behind. They all fetched up here because British Railways couldn't get them any sleepers. Ha ha. They slept in the sheets put on for Princess Margaret & co. Ld Home said if he crept into bed very quietly & lay still no one would know they had been used.

Haste as per.

Much love, 9

Such a sad letter from Henderson. I do wish she had known J.K. They would have so screamed at each other.

1 Harold Wilson (1916–95). The Labour MP had been elected leader of his party earlier in the year. Prime Minister 1964–70 and 1974–6.
2 Joseph (Jo) Grimond (1913–93). Leader of the Liberal Party 1956–67.

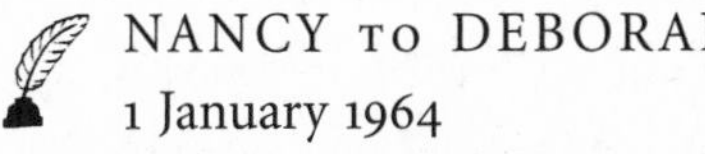

NANCY TO DEBORAH *7 rue Monsieur, VII*
1 January 1964

Dear Miss

I see you have forgotten that you've got an old sister *still alive* in Paris. One can hardly believe it but there it is. I'm told she lives in the rue Monsieur & can be seen tottering out on a fine day but none of her relations in England do much about her & her concierge tells me she very rarely receives a letter.

Oh dear another worry, Honks. The Col was so serious I thought I must hand on what he said ('let them be very careful, I might not be able to do anything another time').[1] Her poor face looked like when she has a headache. She either was, or pretended to be, utterly amazed – said Kit has never had any communication with Nasser. I then told her how Col wouldn't come that day you were here because he said it's really too bad of them to plot with Nasser. *She* says all quite, completely mad. What is one to think? Does he perhaps not tell her everything? I wish now I'd had a word with him instead because I bet she's got a headache this morning as the result, but it's not so easy, I never see him alone & if I took him aside she'd be sure to ask why so it wld all come to the same. I can't help wondering if they are not a bit double faced.

I say my furniture has come. It's transformed all. I wonder if it's not rather wicked to be as much attached as I am to objects, architecture, clothes & exterior things. Too old to change now.

1 Diana and Mosley had been planning a holiday in Egypt when Palewski warned Nancy that Mosley was suspected of being involved in a plot with Egyptian President Gamal Abdel Nasser.

DIANA TO DEBORAH
2 January 1964

Temple de la Gloire
Orsay

Darling Debo:

We are not going to Egypt, a monster disappointment. Nancy says she hears from 'unimpeachable source'! that Kit is suspected of being go between for German Atom scientists & Nasser & the plan is to drop a bomb on Israel, can you imagine such rubbish, but Kit says if that's the new libel he won't go within 1,000 miles of Egypt. He doesn't mind but *I do.* I was looking forward to it so terribly much & shall never see the Abu Simbel now. Ghoul disappointment for Emmy & Jerry [Lehane] who were *poised* for the rush to Lismore. All the same we've got to go to S. Africa. I said I would originally if we could go to Egypt as well. The whole point of the journey has gone, for me, I'm sure S. Africa is ghastly. But the Lehanes must go to Ireland & anyway I'd promised Kit to go with him so there it is. I am in the depth of depression & in fact when one hears a thing of that kind (all started & invented by the *English* secret service it appears) it makes one realize they can invent literally *anything*, & be believed by some, & that one can walk into a thousand traps – I mean if Nancy hadn't told us that, they could pretend they had heard us whispering near the pyramids heaven knows what.

All love darling, Honks

NANCY TO DEBORAH *7 rue Monsieur, VII*
7 January 1964

Dear Miss

Well Mosleys. They have chucked Egypt. Sir O came to see me & said there's not a word of truth in the tale, which is all round the Chanceries; he had no idea it was being said &, if he'd known, wild horses wouldn't have taken him near Nasser. He said (very naturally) I ought to have told them when I first heard of it. I said my excuse is one doesn't want to give Honks any more headaches – he said, 'tell me' – I said, 'yes but if I say can I have a word with you in your study, Honks will want to know what it's all about' – he said 'then send a line & I'll come & see you'. So we've left it like that. The funny thing is between you & me I got the impression he was *quite sort of pleased* it was being said – on the lines I suppose of politicians always liking to be talked about. So they are going to Verwoerdt via Portugal – in about ten days.

Well then Colonel said if Sir O says there is no truth I will stand up for him through thick & thin but they must remember I shan't always be there (in power) & they must be very careful. He was greatly relieved that Egypt is off.

So I die for you – come come –

Love, N

DIANA TO DEBORAH *5 rue Villedo*[1]
8 January 1964 *Paris I*

Darling Debo:

I asked Kit to tell about activities of the secret service in Germany against him (one assumes the story originated in Germany because, as I told you, Kit was by way of being a go-between for them – though why they should need a go-between is not clear). He says that a Major attached to the English embassy in Bonn went to German friends of ours & said everything imaginable to turn them against him. The Germans said they agreed with Kit's European ideas, & when the Major found he had not detached them he suddenly said

'Perhaps you don't realize Mosley is a Jew'. This fell flat because these particular Germans are not anti-Jew; they repeated the whole thing to Kit. (The Jew story even got into the German papers & Kit had to send photographs of reference books showing his dear old squire ancestors.) It seems this Major speaks perfect German & boasts that he escaped from a POW camp in German uniform undetected. The German friends describe him as 'a dreadful little spy'. So much for English officialdom's spite in Germany actually known to us.

A much worse thing happened in London which was that a man who said he was in 'intelligence' during the war made friends with Max & tried to persuade him to take some ammunition from the T.A.,[2] purpose not specified; this man told Max that he had been in the paras, & rather impressed him for a time with boastful stories. The suggestion about ammunition opened Max's eyes & he had no more to do with him. Imagine if Max had been stupid or gullible enough to agree. The man posed as a great friend, asked them to dinner & so on, never off the telephone. Heaven knows who he was working for. Agents provocateurs like him & fantastic stories like the one that stopped us going to Egypt should not be paid for from public funds. It is possible that the para man is not an agent (though extremely unlikely – we have got circumstantial evidence). We know the Major is, but again it is possible he did not invent the atom bomb story. On evidence of his spite, disregard for truth, and availability seems to point in his direction. Very hard to pin a rumour, or fight people who stay in the shadows – but this rumour, in order that it should be taken seriously, as it was, must surely have come from 'official' source. I only bore you with all this because you asked me to. Think no more of it. One thing is certain – there are some nasty people about. If only they could be induced to speak out loud! Kit did not go for Max's person because the T.A. officers have been very good to Max & he loves his paras – in any case it wd be his word against the man's.

All love, Honks

1 The Mosleys' Paris flat.

2 Max Mosley was training as a parachutist in the Territorial Army.

DIANA TO DEBORAH
19 January 1964

Hotel Quirinal
Hillbrow, Johannesburg

Darling Debo:

Here we are, after a ghoul journey, I slept fourteen hours & now feel perfect again. We stopped at Las Palmas (63°F) & then Brazzaville where 'twas boiling & the white people looked like characters in Graham Greene, completely done in. Here the weather is sublime, hot & quite cool at night. As we used a new surname in the aeroplane & came to this hotel on the advice of our taxi driver, nobody knows we are here & there have been no journalists so Kit is pleased with himself & his arrangements.

Johannesburg is hideous & prosperous though not (I should say) luxurious. The food so far, like Stoker's famous dictum, not good but not bad. The outskirts are a mass of bungalows nestling in roses, oleanders, hibiscus, dreadful beds of dahlias. In my room wonderful larkspurs & roses & peaches & grapes. Everything very neat. The blacks *LOOK* pleased with life but who knows – they never stop smiling; also one sees huge Cadillacs crammed with them – obviously some are very rich which I hadn't realized. The white people look like W.I. & Adria Hotel and Torquay – no better & no worse. The Brazzaville ones looked wretched & everything was untidy at the airport & masses of sorts of beggars, Kit says a change since independence. The black maids who bring breakfast have got such white clothes, dazzling.

All love darling, sorry for dullth of letter but it's just to say we are alive. Honks

Afrikaans is such a lovely language. No Smoking is Rook Verbode. By the way both Al & Max have given up Rook – isn't it good.

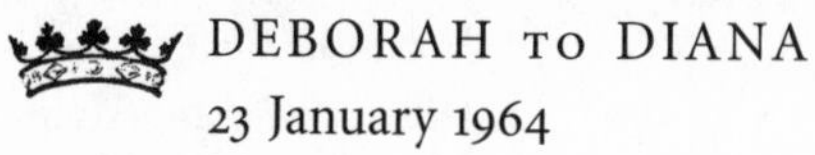

DEBORAH to DIANA
23 January 1964

Chatsworth
Bakewell

Darling Honks

A Monster Thrill, to arrive back here today & find your letter from Joburg which made me *scream* out loud during my lone lunch. I can't help being glad you're having sun & oleanders even if it does entail beds of dahlias. I believe the blacks are far better housed etc in S Africa than any of the independent dumps, I suppose the others don't admit it but it's a fact isn't it. What made me spit out my coffee laughing was the bit about No Smoking. Can't wait to know more of this language.

Antony Head[1] came to dinner in London last night, & Stavros Niarchos.[2] We had herrings, aren't they marvellous food & banned by Mrs Canning because of cheapth.

It's quite nice here, 45° which one can't complain of.

Honks. Uncle Alec[3] & Col Tattersall. Oh Heavens how it does one in, think of the endless days & nights stretching out till death. I took Aunt Weenie. We found Id there which was an unexpected treat, she knows it all so well so one meekly followed to Col Tattersall's room & oh dear the bitter pathos, almost too much. Id said you know he never has a letter or a visitor. When we entered there was a woman there whom Id seemed to know, I asked after who it was & she said 'oh it's Mary, she used to be a cleaner here & now she comes in once a week to write his letters'. Uncle Alec shares a table at meals with three others NONE OF WHOM CAN SPEAK. He said 'yes it is rather depressing'.

It seems there is a matron in command who must have a sort of power complex, forcing these *good* men to do what they don't want & refusing Uncle Alec a comfortable chair for his poor leg at meals because it makes the dining room look untidy. It seems unbelievable & the food is 'not too clever'. One can imagine what that means. They have rows with a man who contradicts & is vilely rude to all – the only one who is not deaf so he yells out against all he hears when the deaf ones have visitors. This man was accused (when asked to pass the salt) of NOT BEING A GENTLEMAN. Uncle Alec says you see he was a Sapper & well dear child of course etc etc. Surely they ought to have a man in charge, not a matron. A. Head is getting at the War Minister (no longer Profumo) about it, my goodness I do hope they make a change.

Just been to look at the big diner. There are nineteen human beings working in there, two gilders, many a carpenter, four people putting the stuff on the walls, electricians by the handful, two daily women & so on. Anyway it adds up to nineteen & I can't wait for the complete result next week.

Maud,[4] with very long face, 'They've made a terrible mistake with the new sheets'.

Me 'Oh have they Maud, what sort of mistake?'

'They've put an Earl's coronet on them. Well I've heard of people giving up their titles but I've never heard of being reduced from a duke to an earl'. She was properly affronted.

Don't learn to Rook while you're away. I'm sure we ought to buy shares in cigar makers, twill soon be all the rage. WRITE.

Much love, Debo

1 Antony, 1st Viscount Head (1906–83). Minister of Defence 1955–7, High Commander in Malaysia 1963–6. Married Lady Dorothea (Dot) Ashley-Cooper in 1935.
2 John Stuart.
3 Alexander Kearsey (1891–1967). The widowed husband of the Mitfords' Aunt Frances had had a leg amputated and was in a home for retired officers.
4 Maud Barnes; Deborah's maid.

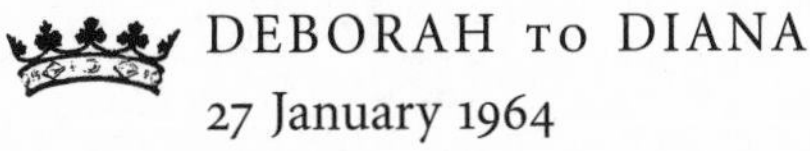

DEBORAH TO DIANA

27 January 1964

Chatsworth
Bakewell

Darling Honks

A v.v. quick line to say the sad sad news that Mrs Ham has died.

She died quite unexpectedly in the night having been quite well. The maid found her in the morning. Oh what a huge slice of our lives goes with her. Goodness won't we all miss her. I phoned Nancy, for her to tell Madame Costa as Monica was v. worried about her hearing about it.

I might go to the funeral. I'll hear what the arrangements are tonight. We are all so sad about it. I'm v. v. glad though that she came for that ten days such a short time ago & was so cheerful all the time here. Also so glad that she didn't have that awful drawn out struggle like Muv.

Great haste.

Much love, Debo

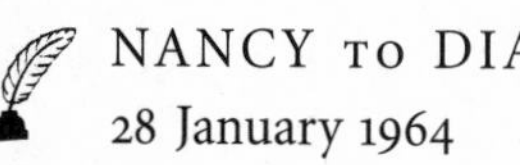

NANCY TO DIANA
28 January 1964

7 rue Monsieur, VII

Dereling

Oh Mrs Ham isn't it unbearable. All the friends here had the same reaction: *pas possible!* & it's just what one feels. I haven't told them she was found on the floor & have warned Monica not to. Mme Rödel had had a letter written the day before saying she was sick all the time – never should she have been left alone at night. No doubt she would have died anyhow, but still! Mme Costa is sort of fussing as it is & I hope to goodness she never finds out. I wonder if Monica will have any remorse or if really her heart was turned to total stone as regards her mother in early youth.

It's raining now & no doubt will do so for another 4 months.

Love, N

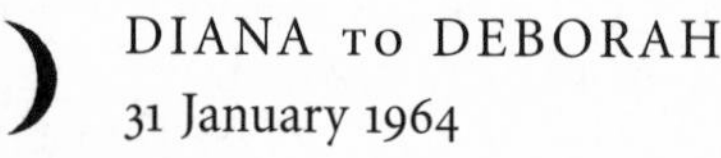

DIANA TO DEBORAH
31 January 1964

Mount Nelson Hotel
Cape Town

Darling Debo

Thank you darling so much for telling about Mrs Ham. I had a quite incomprehensible letter from Nancy, I mean it could have meant Mrs Ham had had a stroke. Then she wondered whether Monica felt remorseful – well – between you & me I think somebody else might feel a bit remorseful too.

Mrs Ham did so ADORE her visit to you, oh Debo how thankful I am you did that. You and Andrew have made simply all the difference to her for about 10 years. From my own point of view (because I enjoyed it so much) I'm glad she came to the Temple. Strangely enough I wrote to her this morning. I shall miss her terribly.

There's a hateful gale here today but heavens I do feel well. I rushed to the town looking for a few Penguins & found a few. Oh it's *too sad* about Mrs Ham. All the same, her death much less difficult than Muv's death – I see you say the same. Do send any obituaries, I'll send them back. Perhaps Julian Huxley[1] or Duncan Grant will do it?[2] If not do make Andrew.

All love, Honks

1 Julian Huxley (1887–1975). The biologist and first Director-General of UNESCO had been a friend of Violet Hammersley since his undergraduate days.
2 Raymond Mortimer wrote the appreciation of Violet Hammersley in *The Times* and compared her to one of El Greco's daughters. He described how she would float upon the Thames in a gondola, rowed by a gondolier from Venice.

) DIANA TO DEBORAH
28 January 1964

Mount Nelson Hotel
Cape Town

Darling Debo

I do feel thirty years younger at least since being here – the sun shines all day. 84° in shade but so dry that one never feels hot, or at least never sticky, a pool to swim in & all round a garden with avenues of enormous hibiscus, & jasmine scenting everything, & huge moon at night & no shawl needed. Even chatting is catered for because I saw an elderly gent examining a tree & thought if this weren't S. Africa I should think I was seeing Cyril Connolly. Well, it was. His mother lives somewhere here & he's worried about her & came down to see her. He & we almost have the sun mattresses to ourselves because the average age in the hotel is 100.

This hotel is a complete ivory tower where one is unconscious of what Kit calls question A. The servants are Indian and ideal. As far as the real world goes there is *Geen Toegang* (No Admittance). All the centenarians are English colonels & admirals, it is like Careysville[1] forty years on. They look askance at us but one or two have *spoken* to me which one rather dreads because (as Kit says) the hotel is like a liner. It is at times like these that it pays to be a pariah. I've got a truly marvellous book of vast length – the third volume of Simone de Beauvoir's memoirs,[2] which I live in.

All love darling, Honks

1 A fishing lodge on the Blackwater in Co. Cork, belonging to Andrew Devonshire.
2 *La Force des choses* (1963).

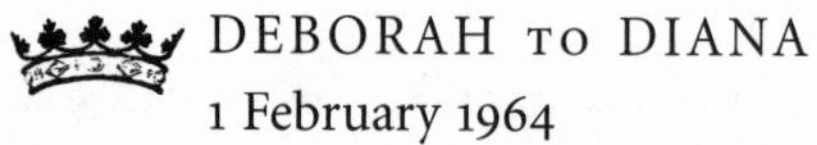

DEBORAH TO DIANA
1 February 1964

Chatsworth
Bakewell

Darling Honks

I was *so* pleased to get yr letter of 28th this morning & to hear you are feeling thirty yrs younger & I do hope you don't *look* thirty yrs younger, that would be most annoying.

Uncle Alec haunts me. I went to see him again two days ago, he is so good & so uncomplaining & oh what the days must be like there, two or three visitors a week one of whom is Pussette[1] who upbraids him throughout, otherwise no one to talk to because his three table mates *can't speak*. He could go & call on poor Col Tattersall but there is a hill in the passage & U. Alec can't do that without help & he won't ask a nurse as he says they are so busy. But it is the petty indignities foisted on them by the matron that he minds.

As luck would have it I sat next to a marvellously sweet soldier at the Australia Day (yes Honks) dinner, Field Marshal Ld Slim.[2] So I tired him with the tale & begged him to do something. Of course the important thing is it shouldn't come from U Alec or he wd be tormented (& furious with me of course) but I think I can trust Slim. Anyway I'll enlarge if anything comes of it. Sorry to go on but I really am haunted.

I keep picking up a pen to write 1,000 things to Mrs Ham. It doesn't sink in that she's no longer there, it's too sad.

Woman has gone to Zurs to get out of the fog. She took her dogs on a round of nightclubs the first night & they were 'much admired

& didn't go to bed till 2.30'. Well I do hope she hasn't gone completely mad. She is meant to be coming here this month but she is making fearfully heavy weather of it as per & 'might be able to fit in a day or two', that sort of talk.

Is Cyril C being NICE?[3]

Being a pariah has lots of advantages, as I know in Ireland.

1 Clementine Kearsey; Uncle Alec's retarded daughter.
2 William, 1st Viscount Slim (1897–1970). The Field Marshal served as Governor-General of Australia 1953–60.
3 There was a joke circulating that Cyril Connolly, who was not a handsome man, 'was not as nice as he looked'.

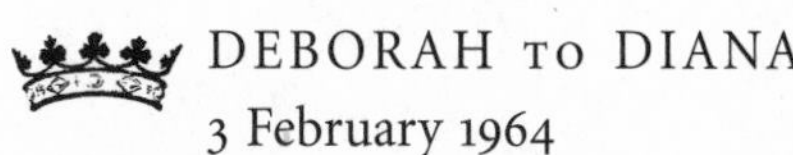

DEBORAH TO DIANA *4 Chesterfield Street, W1*
3 February 1964

Darling Honks

If you get another gold nugget in the shape of an English paper you will note the unnatural warmth in these parts. 53° yesterday at home & sun all day. Sophy & I went for a terrific walk on Calton in sun & breeze, I said '*Stop & listen* to the larks'. She said 'I know you like larks – *I* like the "Hippy Hippy Shake".'

Monica has dropped a weeny cardboard box of letters from Nancy & me to Mrs Ham. I will see if there are any from you in it & salvage same from prying eyes (including mine. I'm not going to look at Nancy's in case of little jabs one wouldn't like to see – she can have them when she looms.)

WRITE. When are you coming home?

Much love, Debo

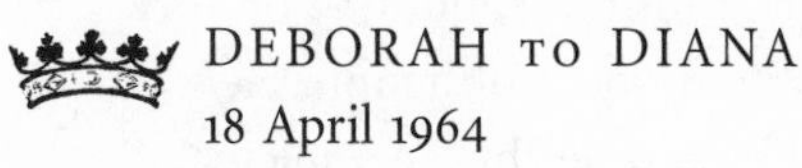

DEBORAH TO DIANA *Derreen*
18 April 1964 *Lauragh*
Killarney

Darling Honks

This is a good headline from the *Cork Examiner* isn't it, they sound so menacing.

GROWING HORDE OF UNQUALIFIED ELECTRICIANS

So nice here, bitter cold outside but my dear good Wife has made a monster effort re the inside & the drawing room is boiling.

I went to see Billy Flynn[1] in Mallow hosp. on the way here, Honks it was *too* sad, he's obviously dying & the awful thing was I couldn't hear what he was saying, he struggled to tell me something & I just nodded my head in an idiotic sort of way like one had to with Muv. He is a terrible sight, one side of his face is hugely swollen & his arms are as of a skeleton, & yet two weeks ago he was gaffing fish. I was in floods almost at once of course, so *stupid*, & the matron said we get used to it but of course it's much worse for the relations, so I suppose she thinks he is my brother. It was *so sad*, I loved him as did everyone. I hope he dies soon, he's so miserable.

Much love, Debo

1 A famous Careysville ghillie.

DIANA TO DEBORAH
17 April 1964

Temple de la Gloire
Orsay

Darling Debo:

Did I tell you the Independent telly came, ten people, spent two nights in Paris, hired cars to come down here etc, went off saying how sorry they were I should not see the programme. Well Kit went over a day earlier than he meant to, to SEE himself, & phoned after it last night to say the interviewer (a man called McGee) had telephoned ½ an hour before the programme (*This Week*) was to begin to say that 'high-ups' had seen the film & refused to allow Kit to appear. I must say I am seldom surprised but this time I WAS. He was simply answering questions about his ideas, nothing oratorical or persuasive & the questions were quite hostile, so the interview was if anything loaded against. They simply smother him completely, & yet libel him in private (i.e. the Egyptian tale) so one cannot say they entirely ignore him (!). They must have spent a lot of their horrid money I'm glad to note.

I wish you could see Jerry & Maurice & me painting the railings.

The comments of passers-by vary, we've got one fan but most of them say 'you'll never finish that'. Well, we don't mean to, we are going to do some more in the autumn. Ha ha.

Any hope of a visit?

All love darling, Honks

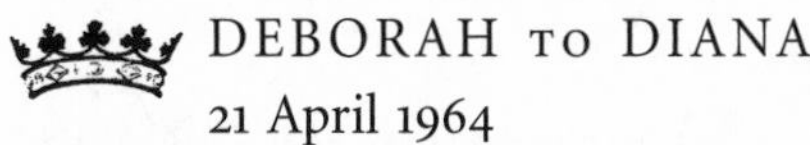

DEBORAH TO DIANA
21 April 1964

Lismore Castle
Co. Waterford

Darling Honks

Thanks for yours. The telly people & the result – it is incredibly mysterious, who are the high ups who stop all every time, it is very very odd indeed.

IF YOU REALLY MEAN IT RE A VISIT I *could* come the weekend of 10th May. Honks if you really do mean it, are you *sure*? Think on it & let me know.

Would we dare ask the Fr Lady if I could have the same dress as she got at Patou, different colour of course, but to me it seems the perfect dress. Then, if she allows, they could start it more or less as though for her & I could try it when I loom. I would order the coat as well (which she didn't). Perhaps dark brown would be nice – hers is pale brown. Then I could have a cream velvet beret from Lanvin & could dismiss clothes from my thoughts for years (well weeks anyway). Do send yr thoughts on all these conundrums.

Poor old Billy Flynn died yesterday. Can't think how he held on to life since Friday but we know how difficult it is to die.

When we were at Derreen, I banged the side of the car on a gate post & I suppose the wing just touched the wheel which I didn't realize. When we'd been going a bit Sophy said 'I hear bells & cymbals, yes bells & cymbals'. Rather a poetical description of the scraping noise, admit.

Much love, Debo

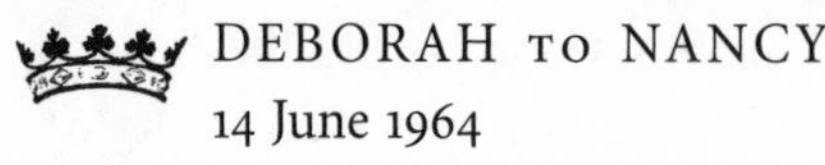

DEBORAH TO NANCY
14 June 1964

Mereworth Castle[1]
Maidstone
Kent

Get on

I wonder what you're at and in fact where you are.

Tig has got a baby thrush, she's been its mother for nigh on three weeks & it's the most fascinating object I ever saw. It worships Tig who is pale from digging up worms.

Decca seems fit. Can't remember if I've saga-ed to you or Honks re her. She's made £35,000 out of the book[2] – money from strange places like Finland is still pouring in. Ann F[leming] & I collected some left-wingers for lunch for her, R Kee, Woodrow Wyatt,[3] Tony Crosland[4] (who of course didn't come – hangover), Sir J Rothenstein (because it was at the Tate & we couldn't get a table without his help). I hope she quite enjoyed it. Woodrow asked her if she was a communist. She didn't say yes, she didn't say no, she didn't say stay, she didn't say go.[5] She muttered something about the Party being in a bad way in California. He pressed on like he does but the answers were most non-committal, isn't it inter-esting. I thought she'd given it up but I wouldn't be at all sure now. She seems to be quite enjoying it all here.

I hope you find all fit at home.

I *wish* you could see the thrush.

Much love, 9

1 Deborah was staying with her sister-in-law Anne (Tig) Tree.

2 *The American Way of Death.*

3 Woodrow Wyatt (1918–97). Labour MP and journalist who became a staunch supporter of Margaret Thatcher in the 1980s.

4 Anthony Crosland (1918–77). Hard-drinking Labour Minister of State for Economic Affairs 1964–5. Author of the influential *The Future of Socialism* (1956).

5 Lyrics from a 1930s song that Harold Macmillan had quoted when taunting the Labour Party on its indecision over Britain's bid to join the Common Market. *Private Eye* had set the words to music and released a best-selling record, 'Only MacBelieve'.

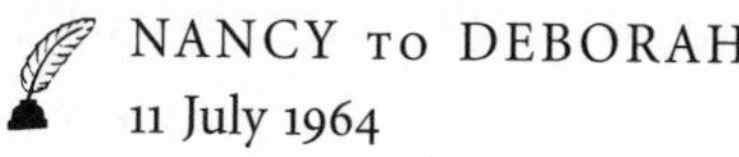

NANCY TO DEBORAH
11 July 1964

7 rue Monsieur, VII

Dear Miss

Will you ever get this? I feel most fearfully worried about Honks. I went down yesterday – she's in bed with a sort of flu – & was simply *appalled* by her appearance. I've never seen her look like that. It seems she has almost non-stop headaches & she had a temp of 102. This morning she's no better & I'm off there again. The worst of it for me is that going there means ten minutes of her – because she gets sort of over excited & I don't want to tire her – then luncheon, & till the train goes, with him. Oh dear poor old thing you know I can't like him. Naivair – that doesn't matter. I would ring you up in spite of my well known meanness plus the struggle – it's more that really. But you are in the Congo I gather or at least the jungle. Ring me up if you can when you are back – if they haven't eaten you.

Oh dear oh dear I feel in a fuss I wish you were here. He doesn't seem the least bit worried. What are these bad pains in her head? It can't be right but what really upset me was her appearance.

Fond love, N

P.S. As for *work* all I can say is HA-HA.

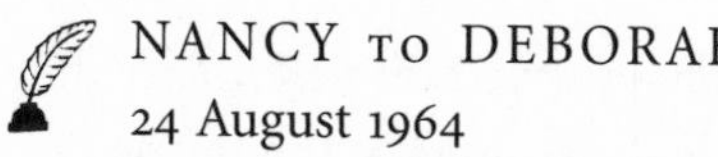

NANCY TO DEBORAH
24 August 1964

7 rue Monsieur, VII

Dear Miss

I've taught Decca about poor little Jessie *so rich*[1] – took her off to Dior &, by dint of whispering *so rich* from time to time forced her to get a v. pretty dinner outfit, plus cloqué coat, I mean a coat not a jacket to go with it. I had to prod like mad when she heard the price (under £200) but now she's awfully pleased – not sure whether she'll tell Bob the price though! It was such fun. I did wish you'd been there, as you generally are!

I've got to stay here & see a boring publisher on 1st so will go back to Fontaines 2nd, Decca leaves 3rd, so it fits in. She seems to have found quite a lot of our letters to Muv oh good. She's being *so* nice & *SO* rich.

As I see you're in the Bonny I'll finish this another time.

26th I took yr Hen to lunch with Col at the ministry. I think she enjoyed it. Bob was lunching with some Cuddums wasn't that a mercy! He's so *bor*ing I wonder if she longs to be a widow but then I always wonder that! I mean about practically everybody over forty. Xian Fouchet[2] was there, he has got a Sophy aged 7 who said to her mother when I marry I would like to marry Papa but of course it's not a very good idea to marry a divorced man. Gen de G said he could see she was going to be a real femme du monde –!

Write here, it only takes a day longer & I'm not sure when I return.

I think that's all.

Fond love, N

1 Baroness Thyssen had once said to Deborah (about the Thyssens' baby daughter), 'Pooor leeettle Cissie, she is *sooo reech*, I feeel sorry for her.'
2 Christian Fouchet (1911–74). Gaullist politician and Minister of Education in 1964.

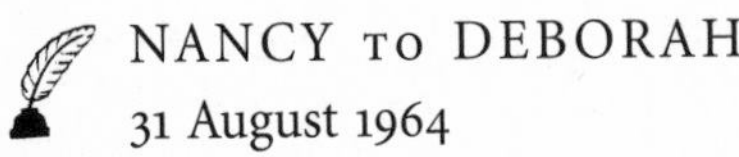

NANCY TO DEBORAH

7 rue Monsieur, VII

31 August 1964

Dear Miss

I've just got yr Xening letter.[1] Faithfully stayed on here to see the end of yr Hen who has gone to try & find her little boy in the Midi somewhere.[2] She has been so nice. Oh dear, I regard her as Muv's greatest failure, she is such a clever person & completely uneducated so that one keeps running into a wall when talking to her. It's a shame & at the root of all the troubles of course.

I took her to lunch with Col & when sitting us down he said 'the Hon here & the Rebel here' which I thought WITTY.

I gather from Honks that you will be staying *here* 28th–2nd & have booked you a room with use of bath is that right? I'll come up for the occasion, all agog.

Oh dear people are streaming back from their hols & all is much less nice. This house is divine when one's alone in it – I sit writing & baking in the courtyard.

I shall wait here for some London Library books I've sent for & go down to F[ontaines] at the end of the week I think & then I hope not to move again until you come.

Much love, N

1 Isabel Tennant, Deborah's four-month-old granddaughter, had just been christened.
2 Seventeen-year-old Benjamin Treuhaft was spending a few months at the Collège Cévenol near Lyons before going to college in the US.

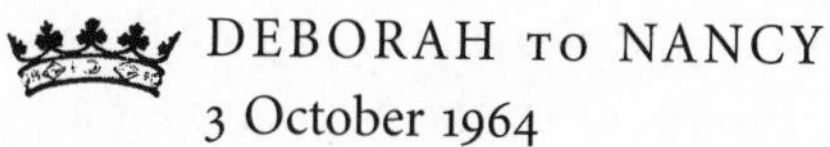

DEBORAH TO NANCY
3 October 1964

Chatsworth
Bakewell

Very well then THANK YOU for ALL the nice things, yr bed & board (soup, rec [chicken], Gloria[1] – all) yr goodness in trudging the streets day after day in the week of The Great Taxi Hunt, for not pushing Bettina [Bergery] out of the window at the 2nd fitting, & for generally making it excessively jolly. I ADORE coming to Mr Street.

Sophy & Maud seem to be fairly loving each other, I mean very. S is doing Scripture (for the first time this term) & had to draw Adam & Eve in the Garden of Eden for homework. The odd thing is both A & E are wearing pink jerseys and green skirts & when I suggested Adam might have trousers I was set upon & told *trousers weren't invented then* & hadn't I ever done Scripture? She's also doing Boadicea – says she knows what she looked like because of the pictures. It *is* unfair, I never did Boadicea,

Stoker is off to Oxford next week, he's looking forward.

I know I owe you for Stamps & Buses. Sorry.

Much love & thanks from bottom of heart, 9

1 A pâtisserie near the rue Monsieur where Nancy and Deborah used to buy cakes.

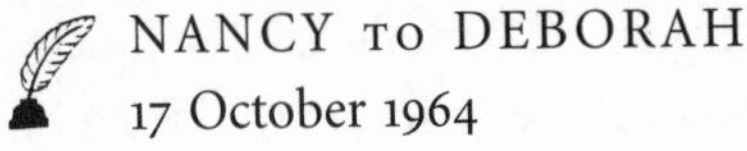

NANCY TO DEBORAH
17 October 1964

Fontaines-les-Nonnes
par Puisieux

Dear Miss

Having found this piece of rich paper I may as well use it!

I hope you're not too sad. I loathe the body of Mr W[1] but, as I said to Honks, one has to be careful, knowing what you are like about POWER & most probably he is even now moving into Chatsworth as his Midland H.Q.

Talking of power, Col was the last person to see poor old Khrushchev who said I'm just off to Moscow to greet the cosmonauts. Pathos.[2]

More cheerful subject: the owl. Thought best to leave it, hoping the mother wld come, but after two days it was quite groggy & had fallen over so I forced some raw meat down its throat & went for a walk. When I got back it had disappeared, no doubt to die in a dark corner. I searched as much as I could but the pigeonnier is full of old goat carts & bits of rubbish one can't move, so I gave up. For more than a week I had that awful guilty feeling wild animals always seem to arouse. I ought to have brought it in & kept it warm & fed it instead of leaving it to a dreadful, long cold death. I woke up in the night & grieved & of course went back many times to the pigeonnier, though I knew it must be dead ages ago. Well yesterday I went & thought I heard something & under my feet an enormous creature the size of a half grown pullet got up & scuttled away among the goat carts. Oh dear what a relief – one had done the right thing for once!

Well I've waffled on too long so goodbye.

Love, N

1 Labour had won the general election and Harold Wilson was entering his first term as Prime Minister.

2 The Russian leader had been ousted from office.

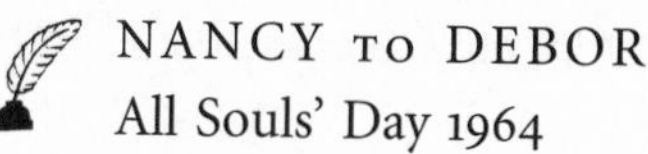

NANCY TO DEBORAH — 7 rue Monsieur, VII
All Souls' Day 1964

Dear Miss

I've been awful I know about writing but my time for letters is the morning & for some reason every day I've had to get up. One day Woman's golden head was in my bed instead & that was wondair. She brought smoked beef, well you know that leather called biltong which pioneers eat? I gave it as entrée at a luncheon party & saw the people trying to spit it out without me noticing. She said it was *so expensive.* I longed to ask for my money back.

Do you know I think you'll love the Grès – so soft & comfortable. I had a good gander at them yesterday.

Now I'm off to see our relations at Orsay.

Much love, N

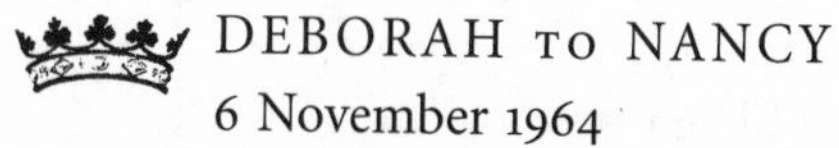

DEBORAH TO NANCY — Chatsworth, Bakewell
6 November 1964

Eureka. I've found the letters to Muv from us all, in old suitcases in Ches. St. The *relief.* I thought I'd caused them to be sold with an ancient chest of drawers from the garage. Now they'll be kept in optimum archival conditions with the rest of the rubbish here. Henderson will be relieved but no one so much as me. I thought I'd lost them.

Woman phoned this morning, she doesn't want to come here I can see, so I've sort of let her off. Why is she always in such a desperate hurry? I shall never quite understand that.

COME FOR XMAS OF COURSE WE LONG, but I thought perhaps it was too much of a bind, what Stoker calls. Have a deep think, & if Louis Louis[1] is going well throw all to the winds & loom. The room will be there, as I'm waiting to ask Wilson till he is a bit more firmly entrenched.

Much love, 9

1 Nancy was working on *The Sun King* (1966), a life of Louis XIV.

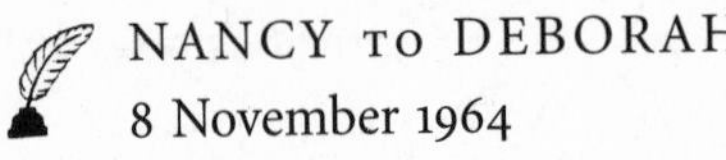

NANCY to DEBORAH
8 November 1964

Fontaines-les-Nonnes
par Puisieux

Only a scribble to feed your flame (letters) as (in order to be so rich) I'm so busy.

V. odd that the moment one buys something in Paris it turns up at Marks & Spencer & yet how many times when in London have I vainly tried to land some smashing bargain, combing Harrods Dior & Marshall's Grès in vain.

I saw yr friend Bobby K[1] & wife on T.V. They looked as if they were chewing bits of white paper – 'twas their teeth. He said 'I'm now going to quote er er the pote' (clearly had forgotten which pote) 'who said, and I quote, "We must build a better world."' Are you needled?

I'm dreadfully pleased about the letters (Muv's) just in case I ever wanted to write something about my life in France, not very likely but one never knows. I keep no diary on acc of the huge bulk of letters I write.

Keep up the correspondence as I live for your letters.

Love, N

Xmas. So I come.

1 Robert Kennedy (1925–68). The younger brother of the assassinated president had resigned as Attorney-General in order to run for the US Senate. Married Ethel Skakel in 1950.

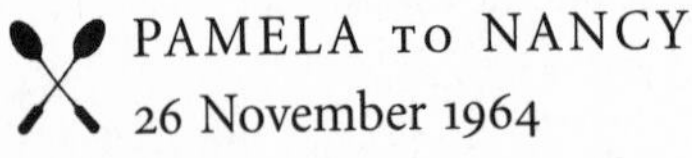

PAMELA to NANCY
26 November 1964

im Chratz
Grüningen

Derleeng,

What a horrid card showing the age! But I do wish you many happy returns of your birthday.

Do you remember forty-two years ago on my birthday[1] at Asthall when there was such a heavy frost that the wire netting of the hen pens was quite closed with frost sparkles & the sun was shining brightly. Farve gave us all enough money to take the bus to Oxford &

lunch & cinema. When we arrived we had ages to wait for lunch, so, as it was icy cold, you insisted on going to the Ashmolean Museum. We were against it as it was costing 6d each & we would not have so much lunch as we hoped. However, we agreed to go as it was the only place to keep warm till lunchtime. Then, to our joy, we met Uncle George in the Museum & he invited us all to a wonderful feast at Fullers! How wise you were to insist on going to keep warm! Yesterday was just such a day but not nearly so cold, I was able to sit out in the sun with the dogs in the garden.

I so much enjoyed my visit to France & will do it again in the spring; it is best to stay at home at this time of year.

Much love from Woman

1 Pamela's fifteenth birthday.

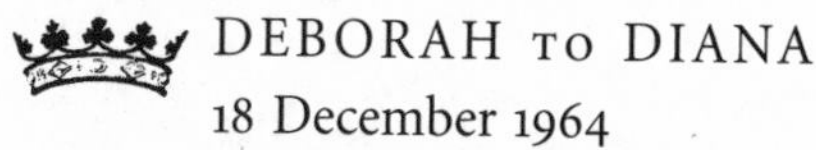

DEBORAH TO DIANA
18 December 1964

Train to Chatsworth
Bakewell

Darling Honks

Been in London since Monday & that's quite enough. It's odd how very dirty it still is although no one has fires much, I suppose it's the dreaded petrol. One's hands are never clean & in spite of sweet Mrs Winchester the house seems v. grubby, it re-looms as soon as you clean it up.

Stoker has got a friend called Lord Ancram,[1] son of Ld Lothian. He went to a party & the announcing person asked his name, he said Lord Ancram, & was announced as Norman Crumb! He is always called this now & friends send him invitations to Norman Crumb Esq. Since Lyndon B Johnson he has added B so he's Norman B Crumb now, sometimes known as Bread Crumb.

Much love, Debo

1 Earl of Ancram (1945–). Conservative MP since 1974.

) DIANA TO DEBORAH
11 December 1964

Temple de la Gloire
Orsay

Darling Debo:

We are enjoying a general strike, it began last night after dinner. We sat very peacefully by candlelight & I was just able to see enough to struggle with the crossword. We went to a memorial service for poor Charles Saint,[1] which was frightfully gloomy. Then I got your letter about Mr Thomson's dread cremation. What do you suggest exactly? A funeral first & then a cremation? But would there be a grave to throw earth in? I think I will try & get a pigeon hole at Père Lachaise, or would you prefer a plot in Orsay cemetery? What has Naunceling done about all this? I will ask her.

A long letter from Wooms, did you realize she hasn't got a fire? I can't imagine hiring a cot with no fireplace, what misery.

Naunce is getting excited about the Versailles house – she's to see it tomorrow.

All love, Honks

1 A French diplomat and old friend of the Mosleys.

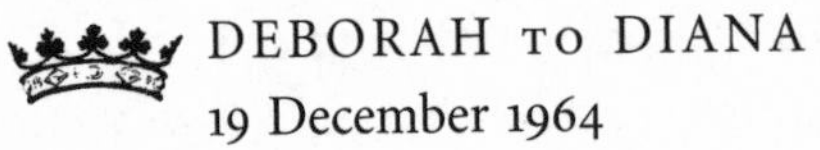

DEBORAH TO DIANA
19 December 1964

Chatsworth
Bakewell

Darling Honks

I got yours of the general strike day, what a thrill, on getting home. Shall we get up a Fire For Woman Fund, I can't bear to think of her huddled in a shawl with ne'er a glimmer & only the two gas rings to cook her one meat ball. Oh the great pathos but, one could say, all her own fault when she has Wonderful Woodfield to repair to.

I suggest NO CREMATION, just an ordinary common or garden FUNERAL, I mean you have 'All Things Bright & Beautiful' & 'Holy Holy Holy' and then the stalwarts shoulder you and heave you to the graveyard (where, side by side, lie many a long low grave) & everyone is in floods as you are lowered & a handful of earth is thrown on & the fellow says Dust to Dust and Ashes to Ashes, more floods & bowed heads & then all leave & start screaming with laughter before they're out of the churchyard. That's what I'm after.

If you've got to be planted in France I suppose you will have to be fried if it's a pigeon hole you're after, but the Orsay cemetery might fit you in whole?

Happy Christmas keep writing.

Much love, Debo

DIANA TO NANCY
22 December 1964

Temple de la Gloire
Orsay

Deerling:

Didn't we have a lovely three days, how I hope I didn't exhaust you too much. Rather lovely here – sun & a huge moon – *but* that book of S. de Beauvoir about her mother's death[1] made me terribly *cafardeuse* [gloomy] (a word I culled from it). It is brilliant & terrible, at every moment one is reminded of Muv & our time on the Island & the nurses etc but Mme de Beauvoir had a terrible cancer (though she never knew it) & was in a clinic, in a private room, & yet the utter horror of it passes belief. Even a tough & strong-willed daughter like S. de Beauvoir can do NOTHING when the doctors wish to torment a dying old woman once she is in their power. On the other hand the torments do seem to have 'done good' – up to a point – in that after them, & as a direct result of them, she felt 'better'. Which poor Muv never did, did she. Of course once *they've* got hold of one (which they would if one broke a leg) there's nothing to be done in the way of choice. Muv would have minded it all much more than Mme de Beauvoir, mentally, because she didn't *want* to prolong her life while in spite of all Mme de Beauvoir clung to it. S. de Beauvoir says that this ghastly month where she & her sister took turns at the bedside did save them from remorse, which they wd have suffered from if she'd died suddenly. So true. Apparently the old relations used to say to the mother: 'Simone est la honte de la famille'.[2] Admit.

Well, perhaps you'd better not read it. It made one think not only of Muv but of one's own future. One lars [alas]. The longer I live the more I see that 'le poteau'[3] is almost a mercy. What a dreadful Xmas letter! But my poor old mind is full of it.

All love, D

1 Simone de Beauvoir, *Une Mort très douce* (1964), published in English as *A Very Easy Death.*
2 'Simone is the disgrace of the family.'
3 'The execution post.'

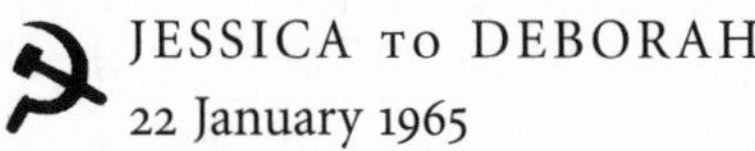

JESSICA to DEBORAH
22 January 1965

6411 Regent Street,
Oakland

Dearest Henny,

I can't tell you the swampedness of me. Not writing a book, but various articles. Mainly, one for *Esquire* Mag about Ronald Reagan,[1] an ageing film actor who is being pushed for Governor by the Calif. Goldwaterites. As I know nought of either movie stars or Republican politics, you must say it's difficult. The thing is supposed to be finished in one week from now and I'm trembling. I went to Hollywood to look into all those matters (R. Reagan, the Repubs etc) which was rather bliss; the writing part is the torture.[2]

Have you read *The Magic Christian*? By Terry Southern. It is a fair scream, v. short, do say if you want it and I'll send.

Much love, Yr Hen

1 Ronald Reagan (1911–2004). After appearing in more than fifty films, the actor was elected Governor of California in 1966 and President in 1981.
2 *Esquire* eventually turned down Jessica's article.

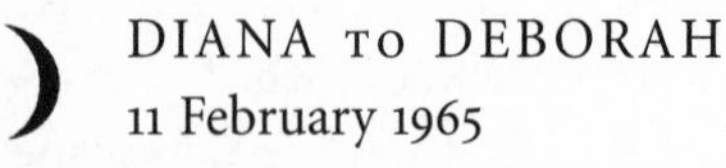

DIANA to DEBORAH
11 February 1965

Hotel Schweizerhof
Regent Road, Sea Point
South Africa

Darling Debo:

This is a ghoulish O [hotel]. One can't believe a word the agencies tell one. To be fair: we've got nice bedrooms & balconies BUT we are meant to be en pension & the dinner last night was almost Holloway work, accompanied by dread music from many a concealed loud speaker.

Last night we went down the road & saw the funeral[1] at a cinema – rather disappointing, there was only the coffin over & over again & just glimpses of private grief (which I had hoped they wd intrude into). Of course the marching sailors were perfect & one did see inside St Paul's, but I wanted more of 1,000-year-old Randolph, Sarah & Co.

It is bitter here after Durban where the water we swam in was 85°. Did I tell you about the sharks in the aquarium, well they are huge & swim about with that dreadful smile on their faces a few inches from *one's* face.

Our Catholic priest rushed in last night; he looks on the black side, just like Mrs Ham used to, is it their religion perhaps? Think what a pessimist Evelyn [Waugh] is.

Your stiletto wound at the W.I. party made my blood run cold, I think thirteen-stoners should beware of those heels. Oh Debo your letters literally do make my life.

All love darling, Honks

1 Winston Churchill died on 24 January and was buried six days after a state funeral at St Paul's Cathedral.

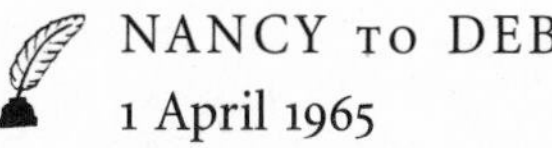

NANCY TO DEBORAH *7 rue Monsieur, VII*
1 April 1965

Dear Miss

Once again we come to the day when Fate made a Fool of Muv.[1] How well I remember the church bell tolling – the very cattle in the fields moaning & the horror with which one realized that the nursery was to have another furious occupant, shrieking like a cage of parrots. No, no!

Love, N

1 Deborah was celebrating her forty-fifth birthday. Lord and Lady Redesdale had been hoping for a boy and, according to Nancy, 'everybody cried' when Deborah was born.

DIANA TO DEBORAH

8 April 1965

Temple de la Gloire
Orsay

Darling Debo

I've had Max's friend Robert Skidelsky[1] staying & he brought an Indian economist[2] with him (a don at St John's aged 23), lovely looking in a rather Krishna-like way.

Robert is planning a book about Kit, & Macmillan has given him a big advance on it & *S. Times* & *S. Telegraph* are bidding for serial rights. Uncle Harold is supposed to have seen a sample & to have been *pleased*. Oh Debo what can it be going to be like if all these people commend it? I hope not too dread. Robert is very clever & I'm fond of his company (we chatted for 8 hours non stop yesterday) BUT I can't abide more wounds for Kit (don't tell one soul this of course – one will have to put on the usual brave face no doubt).

What about the budget, a good thing you stocked up wasn't it. We all listened in the new Citroen with the Indian – our only proper wireless. I'm afraid he was disconcerted by Nancy's & my screams (all about nothing – you know) but what matter, young people think we are mad so who cares.

All love, Honks

1 Robert Skidelsky (1939–). Historian, politician and author of *Oswald Mosley* (1975).
2 Vijay Joshi (1941–). Research Fellow at St John's in 1965 and subsequently a Fellow of Merton College, Oxford.

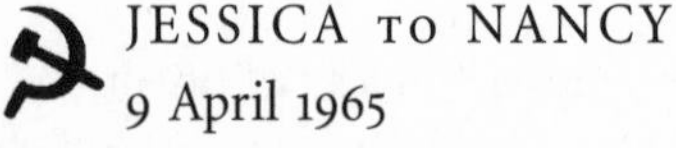

JESSICA TO NANCY

9 April 1965

Hotel Berchielli
Florence

Darling Susan,

Woman arrived here yesterday! She said she is thinking of writing a book because 1) you and I got so reech from same, and 2) she has masses of boxes of paper left over from when she was married to Derek and it seems a shame to let it go to waste. She seems in v. good fettle, I *am* glad she could come as I haven't seen her for years.

So Sue: I think we'll be in Paris on the 20th April, leave on 22nd, spend night in Le Havre and thence to our ship. *How marvellous* to see you again for a bit on the way home.

Love from Susan

DIANA TO DEBORAH
27 April 1965

Temple de la Gloire
Orsay

Darling Debo

I put a white cherry in a strategic position, very strategic, & it has just come out, late like new ones do, & it's PINK. Really French nurseries are the giddy. They are completely hopeless from beginning to end.

We went over to lunch with P. Jullian.[1] He had got *sixteen* guests waited on by a juvenile Portuguese, the food sent in from the charcuterie, bitter day, no heat except a smouldering log miles away. One had to keep one's knife & fork. ALL the frogs in chorus said what a delicious & sympathique lunch it was. I think that's the right way to treat them i.e. ROUGH.

All love darling, Honks

1 Philippe Jullian (1920–77). French painter, writer and book illustrator in the rococo style.

DIANA TO DEBORAH
5 May 1965

Temple de la Gloire
Orsay

Darling Debo

You're on the move I know (Tom used to say that Muv said 'Hm, Debo's always *rushing off* somewhere'). I am static. Kit is rushing off to yet another discussion on telly, but I've given up faith in it ever being shown.

I'm sure I begged you to read the Picasso book,[1] it is one of those books one lives in. I can see why he minds so passionately, it's partly the give away of all his magic & superstitions & partly the exposure of his methods with dealers – *so* clever the way he hots them up but of course maddening to have it all published. As to 'love' I doubt if he minds, each new lady obviously thinks she can tame him. Anyway he's 83.

Nicky [Mosley]'s novel *Accident* is very good & I believe you & Andrew wd enjoy it – much his best & one gets inter-ested in what will occur. I note it's in its second edition.

Do try & come over some time with the little gurl, I do so die for her.

All love darling, Honks

1 Françoise Gilot, *Ma vie avec Picasso* (1964).

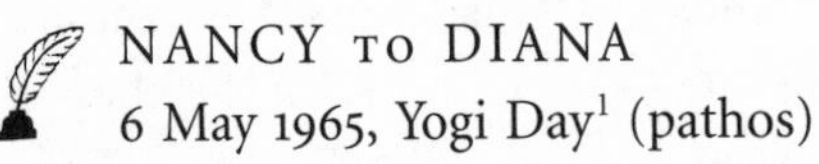

NANCY TO DIANA
6 May 1965, Yogi Day[1] (pathos)

Lismore Castle
Co. Waterford

Dereling,

Debo is looking too lovely, she sits on the lists[2] like a broody hen & the mobiles [eyes], fixed on a far horizon, show that she is only half here.

Woman is wondair. She distributes her favours among supplicating courtiers all longing for one night at least. You know, I think we have a bad effect on her. I heard her deeply discussing Goethe with Raymond [Mortimer] last night, Maltese architecture, Napoleon at Elba & many another topic. With Debo there is much talk of a sauce for trout with finely shredded ham, in fact she is Universal. We think of buying the hotel here & running it with my brains & her brawn.

I'll write v soon –

1 So designated by the Mitfords' Uncle Jack who used to pretend he was a Yogi and decreed 6 May to be 'Yogi Day', an occasion on which everyone was supposed to give him some 24-carat gold.
2 The guest lists for Peregrine's coming-of-age celebrations.

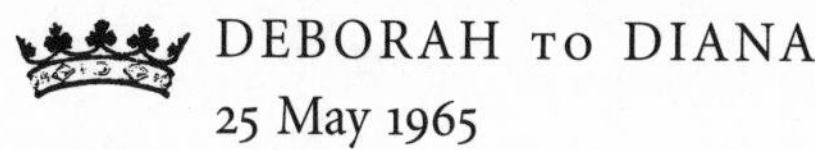

DEBOROAH TO DIANA *4 Chesterfield Street, W1*
25 May 1965

Darling Honks

I'm here, summoned yesterday by Cake to go to the Flower Show[1] with her yestreen. Her minion phoned Chatsworth at 11 A.M. for one to be at hers at 5 P.M., so a good deal of looking sharp had to be done, but I'm v. glad I did because I re fell in love with her. She really is *superb* at her own type of superbery. The P[arker]-Bowles, Salisburys & about twenty other semi drear hangers on & us assembled in the Clarence Ho drawing room & she made an entrance with one hand up saying 'Chelsea Again!' as though it was something of a surprise.

Bobbety[2] was v. fine over Boofy's[3] buggery bill, he said he was intellectually in favour but found the whole subject 'so vewwy distasteful' that he wasn't going to vote. He said the speakers boomed things out which he didn't care to think about & when a stentorian voice behind him said 'Hear hear' it made him 'vewwy nervous'.

The lilies were v fit at the show, ditto the strawberries. The giant everything was a bit too giant but the dwarf dahlias are nice & so on. I won't bore you further. I wore my pink dress & coat & rather rued the day, the evening rather, as NO FIRE at Cake's dump & you know how that dress has no back therefore no underclothes & I thought it looked a bit rude to keep the coat on.

Much love, Debo

1 The Queen Mother was a keen gardener and regular visitor to the Royal Horticultural Society's annual show held in the grounds of the Royal Hospital, Chelsea.
2 Robert (Bobbety) Cecil, 5th Marquess of Salisbury (1893–1972). Married Elizabeth Vere Cavendish, a cousin of Andrew Devonshire, in 1915.
3 Arthur (Boofy) Gore, 8th Earl of Arran (1910–83). The peer had presented a Bill in the House of Lords to legalize homosexual acts between consenting adults.

DIANA TO DEBORAH
4 June 1965

Temple de la Gloire
Orsay

Darling Debo

We had a huge (for us) dinner & Derek came with new friend & I had put names because there were two tables, & Naunceling announced that Derek & friend had been to Geneva & married each other, so I put Mrs Jackson, & Debo they're not married. Anyway, I flew down & removed her card but I'm afraid the fact that this v. circumstantial rumour is whizzing about might sort of force him into it. As Geoffrey [Gilmour] truly says he always marries when the whole thing is coming to an end, & then regrets it, & then is liable for another £5,000 a year pension. She's[1] not too bad, makes vaguely left-wing remarks & is apt to sit by herself in a corner with a mag which is disconcerting for the assembled revellers. She is early to bed (10.30 P.M.) & cooks his dinner. For a multi he lives in a dreadfully uncomfortable way.

All love darling, Honks

1 Barbara Skelton (1916–96). Writer and *femme fatale*. Married Derek Jackson in 1966 and divorced him in 1967. She had previously been married to the writer Cyril Connolly 1950–56, and to the publisher George Weidenfeld 1956–61.

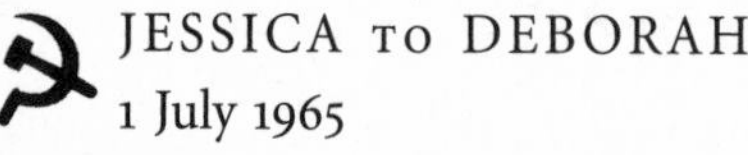

JESSICA TO DEBORAH
1 July 1965

6411 Regent Street
Oakland

Dearest Hen,

Here's a story (true) about the President, told by somebody who was there. A salary increase had been granted to the White House advisors, or staff, or whatever they're called. So one of them said to L. Johnson, 'Thanks awfully for the increase. We were wondering if it could be made retroactive to January?' Johnson answered (but you've got to imagine his voice, Hen, which you can, because you've met him, haven't you?) 'Ah am the President of the United States. Ah am the leader of the Free World. And you ask me a chicken-shit question like that.'

There is an Eliz. Arden slimming and beauty resort here where Mamie Eisenhower goes, costs $700 a week. One of the mags wants to send me there for a couple of weeks so I can do a tease on it (article) for them, so I think I shall, prob. in the autumn.[1] Isn't there a place called Tring or something in England, along the same lines? Do you know anything about it, anyone who has been there, or could you inquire? Do, Hen, it would be a help. I promise to sing 'All Things Bright And' at yr. funeral, if you do.

Love to Sophy and so on. Was she at the dance?

Yr. loving Hen

1 'Maine Chance Diary', *McCall's*, March 1966. Reprinted in *The Making of a Muckraker* (1979), a collection of Jessica's journalism.

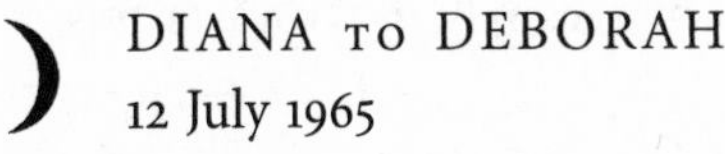

DIANA TO DEBORAH
12 July 1965

Hotel Russell
Dublin 2

Darling Debo:

I knew where I was this morning, when I said to the maid who brought my breakfast 'Can I have a newspaper?' And she said 'Indeed you can *not*, there's a strike, *and* the gravediggers are striking too.' So no lovely *Irish Times* & *Cork Examiner*, & not even a list of films to be had, & it's pelting with dread rain out there on the Green. I saw a woman in a cotton dress, white plastic mac & SUNGLASSES this morning – a real bit of Dublin.

Kit is at the Dr, & tomorrow is the operation,[1] it is really VERY weeny but I feel worried in case it hurts & in case his poor face is swollen & I do feel at his age getting better takes longer.

All love darling and to Sophy, Honks

1 Mosley was having an operation on his nose, which had been broken in a boxing match when he was young.

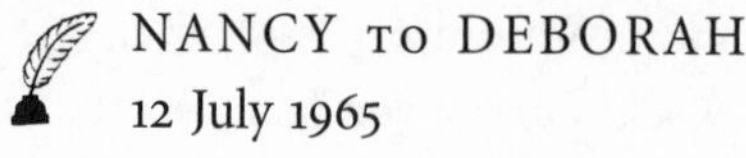

NANCY TO DEBORAH
12 July 1965

23 Dorsoduro
Venice

Dear Miss

I think I've got all your letters now – some forwarded from Mark's.[1] Still no real news of Eddy's death.[2] Raymond [Mortimer] never speaks of it. I mind dreadfully; also, though this is a minor & selfish consideration, I feel another source of fresh air has gone &, when Fontaines collapses, it will be diesel diesel diesel all the year round.[3] After what happened to T Wragg MBE[4] I shall be far too frightened to go back to the Old Land even if kindly invited. I fondly believed that the *Northern* part of the island was *Good.* Ay de mi.

I fear young men are not what they were in my day. I note that Stoker now intends to hang about the European fleshpots instead of sternly crossing deserts. (Sorry to say I am entirely in favour of this change.)

I worry about Alphy & also about Lidi [Clary] who looks quite desperate – I'm sure she thinks her Love will soon depart. Also they haven't got a servant, so, ill & unwell as he is, they must drag out twice a day to a restaurant.

No beach today as we are to lunch with Holy St Cini. No beach tomorrow because Raymond discovered I'd never been to Padua & he disloyally told Anna Maria [Cicogna] & they gave me such cruel looks I've got to go. From now on I've SEEN EVERYTHING & been everywhere – within reach at any rate. Then the weather will spoil: *We know* as Brando[5] says. It's too divine at present. Oh why aren't you here? Furious of.

About my will. I wonder if I could make a sort of trust for my indigent friends to be administered by you? I note that Mark [Ogilvie-Grant] will be far from rich if his job with Shell comes to an end. Then there's Alph if he survives one. Colonel is nice & rich now with his new post[6] which doesn't depend on a certain Govt being in power & which is permanent. You see one's friends have such ups & downs, such sudden changes of fortune.[7]

Yes I can't do Decca's caskets any more. She has certainly acquired a sort of heavy handedness from living too long among those savages. She soon sharpens up when with one, however, the dear thing.

Oh when oh when do we meet?

Fondest love, N

1 Nancy had been staying in Athens with Mark Ogilvie-Grant.
2 Edward Sackville-West had collapsed and died at his house in Ireland on 4 July.
3 Nancy stayed at Fontaines-les-Nonnes for the last time in December 1965. Her old friend Madame Costa died the following February.
4 Tom Wragg, the Chatsworth librarian, was beaten up by a gang of thugs in Bakewell, Deborah's small local town, and never fully recovered.
5 Count Brandolino Brandolini d'Adda (1918–2005). A Venetian friend of Nancy and Deborah. Married Cristiana Agnelli in 1947.
6 Palewski had been appointed head of the Constitutional Council.
7 Nancy did indeed leave her literary estate to be administered by Deborah for the benefit of needy friends and relations.

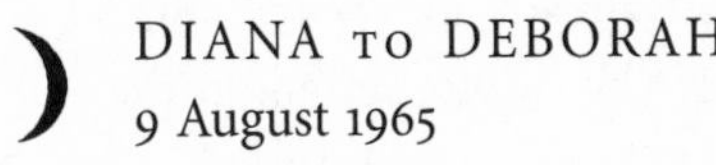

DIANA TO DEBORAH
9 August 1965

Temple de la Gloire
Orsay

Darling Debo:

Just got yours about the triumph of Easter Bonnet,[1] I do know the excitement of it as it happened to me once (with Pilgrim, my Irish wolfhound). I led him round & he got 1st in a huge class at Crystal Palace. The other leaders were in black kennel coats & I was in black velvet 'twas GHOUL. I didn't know about the proper way to dress, but in all other respects a day of days.

Apparently all the couture people are really puzzled by Courrèges[2] & why he has got workrooms but no collection, & Bettina asked [Antonio del] Castillo who thinks it's because his boyfriend has left him & he's having a crise de dépression nerveuse ('Ah oui') & went on to say when that happened to Balenciaga he was just as sad but he did make 'une collection de veuve, toute en noire'[3] – ('Ah oui') aren't they what Muv would call a *set.*

All love darling, Honks

1 Deborah's Shetland pony had taken first prize at the Bakewell Show.
2 André Courrèges (1923–). Designer who invented the 'Mod' look and opened his own fashion house in 1961.
3 'A widow's collection, all in black.'

DIANA TO DEBORAH
18 August 1965

Temple de la Gloire
Orsay

Darling Debo:

Debo, we have had a lucky escape (between you, me & d. post). Julian Slade[1] is making a musical comedy out of *The Pursuit of Love*, & Naunceling phoned many a time, & once she said I've changed some of the dialogue but of course I can't change the lyrics. Then she said U. Matthew had a song beginning 'I do want my girl to be a lady' (I *think* it was that) so I SCREAMED with horror & said 'imagine the kitchen-sink critics who are already so unfair to Slade; what a field day they will have, not only about him but about the poor old aged, decrepit Mitford "girls"'. Well, she *saw*, & she's changed lady to moron, which is funny (& true). Of course there may be dreaderies left in but I told her about Ken Tynan[2] & she said the words 'Ken Tynan' to him & he went white to the lips, so I do think I managed to frighten what Patrick Guinness calls 'the both of them'. She says it's very funny now & I'm sure it is & lovely if she made a little fortune so we can (I think) R.I.P.

The horror of Los Angeles,[3] I don't suppose you bother with telly at Bolton but it really has been awful. Rather odd they all shot at each other for 4 days & there are only 32 people killed. The really dreadful thing is that obviously having a vote isn't going to make any difference to unemployment, & the more advanced America becomes the less will the blacks be needed in industry. There was an intelligent Negro who could speak French interviewed on our telly – one felt a sort of despair because there's no solution.

Now here's another tale for you alone in fact darling please *burn* this. Marie-Zéphyre[4] has had a motor crash in S of France & Naunceling heard of it from Mme Costa & said, amid shrieks of laughter, 'They've cut her ear off & Mme Costa says "c'est tellement dommage".'[5] This gave me a sleepless night & how *can* one laugh about such a thing. Anyway it's not true, I just got a letter from Doodie[6] & she (M-Z, I mean) has had stitches in her ear & has got many a gash but nothing terribly bad. I do hope it will make her more careful. When we saw her the other day I was shocked by her sort of tough don't care attitude but I suppose her mother drives her mad.

All love darling, Honks

1 Julian Slade (1930–2006). The composer of the light-hearted musical *Salad Days* (1954), the longest-running UK show of the 1950s, was having less success in the swinging 1960s.
2 Kenneth Tynan (1927–80). The influential and often savage theatre reviewer had left the *Observer* and was working as literary manager of the National Theatre.
3 Riots had broken out in the Watts section of the city.
4 Marie-Zéphyre Costa de Beauregard (1947–). Granddaughter of Nancy's great friend Madame Costa.
5 'It's such a pity.'
6 Elizabeth (Doodie) Millar (1908–95). English-born wife of Madame Costa's son, Amedée, whom she married in 1940, and the mother of Marie-Zéphyre.

DIANA TO DEBORAH
20 August 1965

Temple de la Gloire
Orsay

Darling Debo:

We were in Paris on Wed & I went to see Naunceling & Kit came to fetch me & suggested she come down for the night & she did! And was at her VERY nicest & we had such laughs, you can imagine. She went back last night after a boiling day by the pool. I thought over her seeming heartlessness (M-Z's *ear*) & decided it's not heartlessness but a sort of reflex she has to sorrows (& which we all have, but in less degree). For example she says that one day at the Lido they were talking about motor smashes & she said 'Yes, like Ly Linlithgow' & Alphy gave a cry 'What? Not Doreen!' (or whatever Ly Linlithgow's name was) & Nancy said, 'So I began to laugh & the awful thing was *everybody* laughed, & you see poor Alphy had no idea Ly L. had been killed & in fact she was his oldest & greatest friend'. Debo, can you IMAGINE such a dread scene, in fact Dolly Costa's ear is nothing to it (& in fact thank goodness the ear is all right but for a stitch or two). Naunceling realized the beach thing with Alphy was terrible (though I don't think she realized HOW terrible!) but she simply can't help laughing.

Yesterday morning a young man came to demonstrate a new sort of vacuum cleaner, a perfect bore as we don't need one but we felt sorry for him, anyway Nancy & I became weak with laughing & so did Jerry [Lehane] and the man, it was a mad scene, in the end I said 'we MUST go' (to an imaginary rendezvous) just to put a stop to it.

I'm reading a funny book about French people 60 years or more ago. Comtesse Greffulhe was the great beauty & Montesquieu read a poem he had written to her beauty ending 'beautiful lily who looks with your black pistils' & Mme Greffulhe turned to her sister & said 'Tout à fait juste, n'est-ce pas Ghislaine?'[1]

Well darling there's *no news* so there we are.

All love, Honks

1 'Exactly right, don't you think Ghislaine?'

NANCY TO DIANA
2 September 1965

7 rue Monsieur, VII

Dereling,

I dined last night with Robert Morley[1] & six young male friends of Abby, his fat sweet daughter, who restored my faith in the Old Land. They had flowered waistcoats but short hair & were clean.

I worry about old Robert, he is so fat & looks so ill. Nobody makes me laugh like him & although wicked to work with, in private life a sort of angel. I asked about the Redl play,[2] is it really so indecent? 'Well darling, there are two scenes of men in bed together.' Do tell Alphy.

I shall now snuggle under the bedclothes to get warm enough to dress. Ay de mi.

Love, N

There's a new word, possibly crag, for men dressed as women. Robert describes arriving in Hollywood for *The Loved One*[3] & being told to go to the *costumier.*

'But I've got all the clothes I need.'

'It's for that scene where you're in crag.'

'Oh no darling, if there's any question of that I'm going home.'

'Oh but it's our best scene – you are pillion on a motor bicycle, in crag.'

'*Not me*. The idea!!'

He says the film is so revolting several people have *been* sick on seeing it. I smell the influence of Decca in all this.

1 Robert Morley (1908–92). Nancy first met the actor in 1950 when he was playing the cuckolded husband in *The Little Hut*, her adaptation of André Roussin's play *La Petite Hutte.*

2 John Osborne, *A Patriot for Me* (1965). A play about Colonel Redl, a homosexual officer in the Austro-Hungarian army.

3 Robert Morley played Sir Ambrose Abercrombie in the film of Evelyn Waugh's novel.

JESSICA TO DEBORAH
11 September 1965
(48 today, Hen, pushing 50)

6411 Regent Street
Oakland

Dearest Hen,

Benj got back and scrammed again, off to his college (here in America, this time). Thank goodness you warned me of the beard, I should have fallen out roaring otherwise. He told lots more about his time with you which he adored, and he was fascinated by Sophy. Him telling reminded me of a toy I'm getting her any day. People are always asking me to join committees against the wicked toys they've got here (like model H-bombs, etc) but I can't bear to join because I know I should have rather longed for a model H-bomb if they had been about when we were little. Anyway, the wickedest toy of all, and the one that has been written up and condemned bitterly all over the US, is a *real* guillotine (real model of, anyway) and a toy person with toy head that comes off when the knife drops, and a colouring set with red for blood etc. So be expecting it, but don't tell Sophy for fear the campaign has been successful and they've stopped selling them.

Do write,

Yr. loving Hen

DIANA TO DEBORAH

11 October 1965

Temple de la Gloire
Orsay

Darling Debo:

I must tell you my Woman saga while 'tis fresh in my mind. Well, she is absolutely monarch of ALL she surveys. She is Queen in Grüningen & receives bows & smiles from every door & window as she pounds along screaming at the Elles.[1] She showed me a cottage she craves & pointing to a door in hushed tones, 'Nard! There's a *cow* in there'. In her sitting room, a vast china stove, fed from the kitchen with wood. Ladder to bedrooms. 'I've insured myself against accidents hurrying down to answer the telephone.' In Zurich she is Empress. All her friends are multis & wherever one goes one hears the cry, 'Pamela! How vonderful to see you!' She feeds one on heavenly soup out of her head.[2] It is paradise.

All love darling, Honks

1 Pamela's dachshunds.
2 Pamela boasted that she made her soup recipes 'out of her head'.

JESSICA TO DEBORAH

1 November 1965

6411 Regent Street
Oakland

Dearest Hen,

What an *utterly sweet* grandchild, I was so glad to get the photo of her.[1] She looks to me a touch like Dinky at that age, same round cheeks and forehead.

News: there isn't much. I did go to Hawaii for a week. Honolulu is a v. square place, but I loved being with the film folk. I was staying with J. Andrews,[2] in a lovely house practically in the sea. The supposed reason was that I was to do a profile of her for an American mag. called *Redbook*. The ed. of *Red* said they were interested in the profile because Julie A. is one of the few people in Hollywood who is not a neurotic but is a sound, wholesome type with feet on ground etc. Well naturally it turns out she is in *deepest* psychoanalysis, madly unhappy – in fact what's known as neurotic. So I'm hoping they will gradually forget all about the profile.[3]

Hen did you know that Hawaii is the same place as the Sandwich Islands? Such a disappointment, as I've always dreamed of going to the Sandwich Isles.

Hen the President. Did you see that absolutely revolting picture of him showing his gall-bladder scar? One person wrote that she hoped he wouldn't be operated on for piles. He is such a fright in all ways, and those awful Birds.

Much love, Yr Hen

1 Eighteen-month-old Isabel Tennant.
2 Julie Andrews (1935–). *The Sound of Music* had been released earlier in the year.
3 Jessica's article on Julie Andrews never materialized.

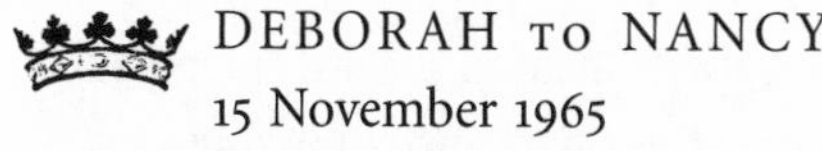

DEBORAH TO NANCY
15 November 1965

Chatsworth
Bakewell

Get on

Opening of Parliament was as beautiful (& comic mixed) as ever BUT I'm sorry to say the peeresses smelt. Can't vouch for the further ones but the duchesses were definitely high. Do you think they had rolled? Surely not, I mean where could they have found anything to roll in?

Their huge & dirty diamonds surmounted their huge & dirty dresses, & as for the Life Peeresses their wild grey hair had been specially tousled for the occasion, talk about dragged through a hedge backwards, but where did they find the hedge? All very mysterious.

I sat next to one (whose hubby is High Steward) Sally Westminster.[1] I was telling her about my m. in law & her nerves on state occasions, how she has to have a fix etc etc, so she said 'well anyway I hope she enjoys the ride here with my husband' – I screamed & said 'you don't mean to say they've put her on a horse?' but all was well, 'twas a coach she was speaking of.

Evangeline's[2] hair is like something out of *Lear* now, I'm afraid she's lost her sense of proportion. (Beautiful & nice as ever though.)

Went to dine with Ann Fleming last week & sat next to Peter Wilson[3] whom I'd never met before, I worshipped, specially when they were speaking of what made them all cry & he said fox terriers & chloroform. Well of course . . .

Much love, 9

1 Sally Perry (1911–91). Married the 4th Duke of Westminster in 1945.
2 Evangeline Bell (1915–95). Wife of US ambassador to London, David Bruce, whom she married in 1945. Author of *Napoleon and Josephine, An Improbable Marriage* (1995).
3 Peter Wilson (1913–84). Legendary head of Sotheby's 1958–80.

DIANA TO DEBORAH

11 November 1965

Temple de la Gloire
Orsay

Darling Debo:

'Twas a thrill to get your letter & the photo of you as Tiger Lady, it obviously IS you & may account for the rarity of letters one gets, I knew you were leading a double life.[1] I remarked to Naunceling that just as after a bus strike in London people get so used to walking that when the buses begin again they're empty, so your visit to S. America[2] has set up a horrid régime of *rare letters*. We suffer from it here she & I.

Last night I dined with Geoffrey [Gilmour] & rushed down here in time to hear the programme[3] about Kit. Bob B[oothby] was very praising about his gifts & said he was the greatest parliamentary speaker he ever heard except Ll George.[4] P Toynbee monstrously unfair about Olympia meeting, he did not even say (as he did in his book) that he bought a knuckle duster to go there with.[5] Masses of the reds had – & used – razors, even on women. After all the beatings-up they are supposed to have suffered they could not muster *one* doctor or hospital to say they had an injury of any kind, whereas Kit's supporters had to be sewn up galore. Oh well, who cares. The other stupid & untrue thing is to pretend that after that Kit's meetings dwindled, whereas the one at Earl's Court was much bigger & took place five years after Olympia. Also the lights turned on hecklers were not in Kit's control but belonged to independent cinema people. He wanted to go on speaking & it was a great annoyance. All the same they did admit it was a patriotic movement, & that when the war began, although he always spoke for peace, he told his followers never to do anything to hurt their country (& in point of fact they all rushed to join up & the first airmen killed over Germany were members). It is all too sad to think about. Hope you've skipped thus far.

My plans are the following: to London Thursday 9th Dec & back here Sunday 12th. *Any hope?* It is so dreadfully disappointing not to come up to you. I'll eggsplain when I see you. The fact is, while I was listening to that wireless last night I felt the unfairness to beloved Kit has been so monstrous that any little thing I can do to please (or not tease) him is worth while. You have always been wonderful to him.

All love, Honks

1 Deborah had enclosed a cutting from the *Sunday Mail* showing Madame Ho Thi Que, wife of a South Vietnamese commander, who fought beside her husband and bore a strong resemblance to Deborah.
2 Deborah had been to Argentina to visit her daughter Emma.
3 'The Threat of Fascism', part of a BBC series, *The Thirties*.
4 David Lloyd George (1863–1945). The silver-tongued 'Welsh Wizard' was Liberal Prime Minister in 1918 when Mosley entered Parliament.
5 In *Friends Apart* (1954), a memoir of Esmond Romilly and Jasper Ridley, Philip Toynbee described the 'exaltation' of trying on knuckle-dusters before the Olympia meeting and how he and his friends had thrown themselves at the Blackshirt stewards' backs.

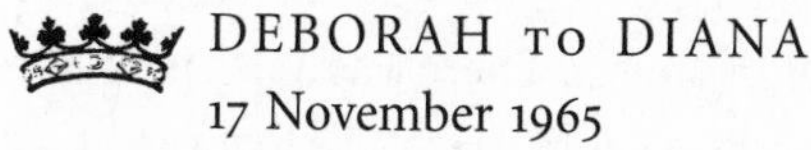

DEBORAH TO DIANA
17 November 1965

Chatsworth
Bakewell

Darling Honks

Yes I know I've been DREAD re letters. I fear you're right – it is this shooting, you see one is whacked ½ the time, fearfully over excited for a good deal more, *on the road* for the rest, plus trying vaguely to see to things here, viz. the 5 new rooms being decorated & furnished, 4 new Shetlands (not much decorated but *very* sweet) coming this A.M. from the bonny land, the W.I. annual meeting, 12 souls coming for the weekend, Mrs Canning saying she can't (or can) get herrings, the housemaid giving notice because I graciously allowed the under ditto to go to Mass (so it's ½ a day's work to get her to eat out of the hand again), plus thinking of excuses when incredibly kind & incredibly dull people ask us to dinner in London, plus seeing to Sophy all last week because Eliz doesn't come back till 22nd. Honks I know none of this Holds Water, sorry.

There is one thing I CAN'T BEAR, & that is you being in London when I'm not, oh DEAR it is so sad & *so* annoying, the days you say are impossible, shooting here 10th & 11th which means people arriving 9th. HONKS, the sands are running out & of course we shall soon be dead, all the lot of us, meanwhile we never meet while we are alive & vaguely hale. Bother bother bother.

Much love, Debo

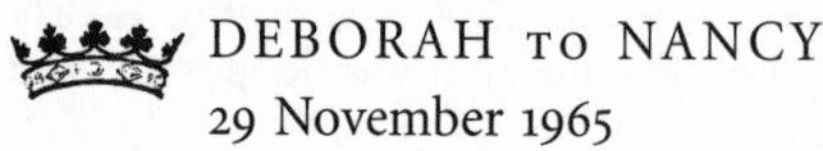

DEBORAH TO NANCY
29 November 1965

Chatsworth
Bakewell

Get on

What is this tale of the tiara & the sofa at Windsor? All I remember is Dot Head at a dance there saying as she passed a heap on the floor, 'Don't look don't look, there's been a street accident', & it was Antony [Head] who had whirled Cake round till they both fell down.

Rhodesia.[1] It's beautiful in an endless sort of way & one feels fighting fit there. My chief recollections (we stayed a week there 1,000 years ago) are being bossed about by the then Governor's wife & Andrew's fury at being made to attend a children's party. There was a recep. one night & a woman – who had driven 300 miles along tracks to loom at it – wasn't allowed in because she hadn't got white gloves.

I have no doubt that the majority of white people in Rho are vile beyond compare. Also there are some super-saints who toil away unnoticed, but I do remember being v. shocked at the attitude of the viler white people to their servants, farm workers etc, in 1947, & they've got worse since I guess. They said awful things about them in front of them etc etc. Horrid.

That's the end of that. Had I not been under the drier this saga may never have been put to paper, & I see you wouldn't have missed much.

Much love, 9

1 The country's Prime Minister, Ian Smith, had declared Unilateral Independence on 11 November 1965.

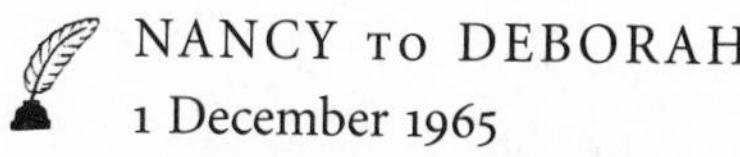

NANCY TO DEBORAH — 7 rue Monsieur, VII
1 December 1965

Dear Miss

Thanks awfully re Rhodesia – yes I see exactly. Whenever one sees anything about it on Fr. télé all seems to take place in a perpetual atmosphere of garden party. I may have made this observation to you already but you don't know how true it is. Ladies, in flowing chiffon, writing their names at Govt house & so on. The few blacks one notes *smack their lips*, according to Alphy. So they do.

Auntie [Iris], writing about my Mole,[1] says when she was young the peasants called them cunts, 'a word one never hears nowadays'. *She's* not in the Tynan set, obviously.[2]

I remember about the tiara. You came down in one (Windsor), found Cake crownless & cast yours, not upon the glassy sea, but under a sofa. Come now Miss, admit.

Somebody told me that at the coronation (Sto's)[3] P[rince]ss M[argaret] said 'Why did you ask Sir O to your party?' to which you replied 'Because he's my brother-in-law – next question please'. Any truth?

Oh my drawing room is too lovely now. *Come.*

If the Gen is not re elected, I leave France. If one's going to live in a sort of Portugal, which is what the candidates are after, entirely supported by America & voiceless & chaotic one might as well live IN Portugal & benefit by the climate.

Best love, N

I note you've taken to having your hair washed again. Keep it up.

1 Nancy's new writing paper was embossed with a golden mole, the Mitford family emblem.
2 A few weeks previously, Kenneth Tynan had been the first person to use the word 'fuck' on British television.
3 Peregrine's coming-of-age party.

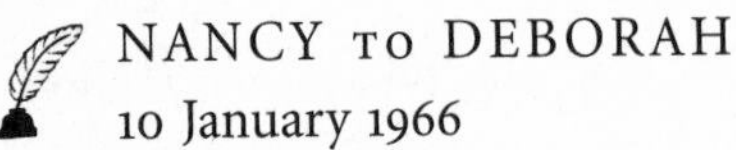

NANCY TO DEBORAH — *7 rue Monsieur, VII*
10 January 1966

Dear Miss

It's a bitter blow that I'm not allowed to walk in the procession BITTER.[1] All right. Woollen stockings beneath my long skirt, woollen vest & thick woollen shawl. Then the temp will be 80, *I know.* Heated car will make a difference, I admit, one won't arrive congealed as one used to at the dancing class. Unlike Lady D I've only got one dress, my BEST, & unlike some people we know NO SABLES. On fait ce qu'on peut.[2]

I've been feeling far from well, no symptoms, just what Grandmother used to call creechy. Can't make out whether it's the cold or the fumes. But quite suddenly, today, I'm all right again. Interes-ting.

Would you really like me to come about the 7th? I will with joy. I rather wonder if I hadn't better come back here after the orgy in case of getting ill in bitter houses. At Alvee [Lees-Milne]'s there is a draught in the bathroom which would take the horns off an ox & as for Raymond [Mortimer] the passages, unlike your motors, are unheated. I believe it would be more sensible to return & go to them another time.

About Bridge. It's only the English who get cross &, as a rule, only those who *can't play for nuts*. I play a certain amount here & never see crossness. I believe it's generally because the person is cross with herself but won't admit it. I've noticed in life there are three things *nobody* will admit they do badly: playing Bridge, talking French & driving a car. Think it over – isn't it true. Riding used to be another.

I must get up – I've got Col & Malcolm[3] for lunch & a new pudding sent by Mark [Ogilvie-Grant], operation sick-make – so reech.

Love, N

P.S. I note I'm invited to bring my wife. I suppose they know about you & think we are all the same.

1 Nancy was planning to attend Andrew Devonshire's installation as Chancellor of Manchester University, a position he held until 1986.
2 'One does what one can.'
3 Malcolm Bullock (1890–1966). MP for Lancashire (Waterloo division) 1923–50 and an old friend of Nancy.

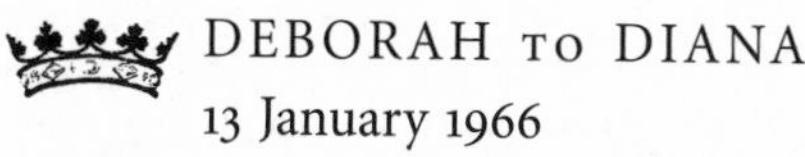

DEBORAH TO DIANA
13 January 1966

Chatsworth
Bakewell

Darling Honks

Keir[1] was terrific fun, such a wonderful shoot, over 800 in three days. Sto came which made it far more fun for me, he is just the companion I would choose. He shot *really* well, wasn't that good. Old Porchy[2] was there, he is a one man cabaret, & Archie Stirling & his beautiful wife, she was Scott of Crowood (as opposed to the Antarctic).

Old old Mrs Stirling was there, eighty-four & perfectly fascinating, she told a lovely tale of Winnie Dss of Portland in the hall at Claridge's during the war yelling at her (in front of all the porters, desk people etc) 'PEGGY, WHAT'S YOUR JOINTURE, MINE'S . . . (mentioning some vast sum) AND I FIND IT SADLY INSUFFICIENT'.

Rather a dread journey last night, the keeper & I came on the sleeper train due at Crewe at 4.10 A.M. but just before Crewe the engine failed & we sat for 2½ hours, eventually arrived here at 8 A.M. so I slept all the morning. When I woke up for lunch I found the Christie's people were still here, they've been re valuing pictures for insurance & have come out with some frightening conclusions I can tell you, i.e. the Poussin shepherds £350,000 etc. etc. What would happen if there was a fire, dread thought.

Nancy's letters about coming here & going to A's enthronement as Chancellor of Manchester are *so* funny, she might be Robinson Crusoe and/or the fellow who discovered America and Marco Polo and the whole of an Arctic expedition rolled into one. There's a desperate tone in them now, it may turn hysterical before D Day.

Much love, Debo

1 Deborah had been staying with Colonel William Stirling and his wife, Susan. Also in the house party were Colonel Stirling's mother, Margaret, his son Archie and Archie's wife, Charmian Scott, whose family had bought Crowood from the Mosleys after the war.

2 Henry Herbert, 6th Earl of Carnarvon (1898–1987). A brilliant amateur actor. Married, as his second wife, Tilly Losch, in 1939.

DEBORAH TO DIANA *Train to 4 Chesterfield Street, W1*
31 January 1966

Darling Honks

So exciting, coming to London to meet Em & co.[1]

Meanwhile I get a daily letter from the Fr Lady, clearly showing how far the Agony outweighs the Ecstasy in her impending visit. I've written to say I promise I'll never invite her again & will wait until she invites herself.

She's played such cat & mouse with Alvilde that I think A rather *minds*. After all, when she is cook & all it is quite a thing having someone for several days, & Nancy just says how vile it is sure to be etc, instead of 'oh how I long' like one would at least *say*.

I'm not going to enter in any more & will await the Final Decision as to day & time & place we are supposed to meet.

What I HOPE against hope is that you might come on 12th.

Sophy has got exams this week. She says you have to have a pencil sharpener, a clean handkerchief & 8 crayons. It sounds like voodoo to me. COME.

Much love, Debo

1 Deborah's daughter Emma and her family were returning from Argentina where Toby, her husband, had been working on a cattle ranch for two years.

) DIANA TO DEBORAH — *5 rue Villedo, I*
18 February 1966

Darling Debo:

It was so LOVELY seeing you & made my rather ghoul London visit absolutely worth while. I was rather disappointed that the papers did not report any of Kit's speech at the trial.[1] It was so damning for the BBC. You know their lawyer asked why the libel action was in respect of a letter to an individual rather than any BBC programme & Kit was able to say that over & over again he has been told he was attacked in some programme or other & his solicitors have asked the BBC for the transcript & this has been refused. So they not only attack him without giving him a chance to reply but also make it impossible to bring a libel action (as one could against a newspaper) unless somebody sits for 12 hours a day with a tape recorder just in case they decide to attack. Even *Panorama* has no detailed programme *before* it is seen.

I am also sorry the papers did not print Sachs's judgement, he was even more censorious about the BBC attacking an individual over & over again & never giving him a chance to reply. I am afraid dear Kit can't win whatever he tries, I wish to goodness he wd see it. He is really an *outlaw*.

All love darling, Honks

1 Mosley had applied to the High Court to try to get the BBC committed for contempt of court for continually attacking him and not giving him a right of reply.

NANCY TO DEBORAH — *Temple de la Gloire*
27 February 1966 — *Orsay*

Dear Miss

I was greeted by the dreadful, though not unexpected news of Mme Costa's death. This leaves me without almost my greatest friend here & a second home – I am in despair. When Dolly [Radziwill] goes I don't know what I shall do – most unwise to have these much older friends, though I must say they have survived dozens of my contemporaries.

At Chippenham the ticket collector said 'there are three porters in the porters' room but *they're not allowed to carry luggage* – one old lady's luggage has already been left behind this morning'. In the end a huge bribe fixed the matter – I couldn't have done the carrying because it's over a high bridge. Away from your sheltering wing one suffers. Tell Sto we'd better all be porters & we could have a nice game of Bridge in the porters' room. What can it mean? Oh Borah.

We went to tea at Badminton.[1] The duke as charming as I remember him when I was awfully young & used to stay at Cirencester. We talked at great length about *dry stone walls*. Jim [Lees-Milne] & I walked 6 miles (there & back) to a folly called Worcester Lodge, *so* pretty, I daresay you know it. Deacon was quite right about the cold in their house – Alvee bustles, you see, all the morning & one is left by an unlit fire. In fact she lights it too late to be any good until ¼ hour before bed time. Smashing food.

Honks is wonderful – no headache for 16 days. BUT he is standing in the election.[2] Oh Borah.

Much love, N

Woman comes, on business.

1 Cotswold home of the Duke of Beaufort.
2 Mosley stood as Union Movement candidate for the East London borough of Shoreditch and Finsbury in the 1966 general election.

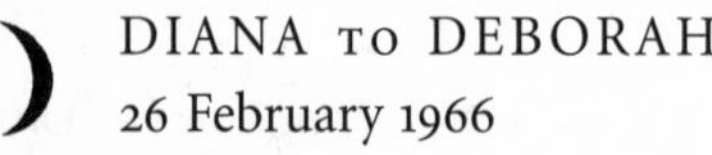

DIANA TO DEBORAH
26 February 1966

Temple de la Gloire
Orsay

Darling Debo:

No letters, there's a sort of semi demi strike going on. Went to Mme Costa's funeral, as you can imagine on the religious side it was very slap up with a bishop in a mitre, but no flowers, oh how sad, &

Naunceling, not having seen this in the paper, had sent a huge object which I suppose they'll put on the grave. Marie-Zéphyre looked truly beautiful in pitchest black, she *is* beautiful & the less makeup the more lovely which is a good sign. Naunceling came down with us so she's asleep in your room. She told many a lovely tale of Manchester & the banquets etc. Debo, do take care, I feel so worried about you feeling so sick.

Bettina [Bergery] has had her face lifted just a bit, it seems a great success if it lasts, all the sort of pouches gone if you know what I mean. The Lady & I discussed doing ditto & decided we were not vain enough to make it worthwhile. (Or perhaps SO vain that we think people will love us with our wrinkles.) I dread the election. Kit insists on standing so we shall have three sleepless weeks closely followed by a disappointment, what a delightful prospect.

We are going over to see a house for sale at Versailles just in case 'tis perfect for N. Our summer plans depend on the stupid election. We can't go to Venice in Sept if it is to happen in Oct, Kit says. So perhaps one ought to hope for it to be soon. I dread.

All love darling, Honks

DIANA TO DEBORAH
15 March 1966

Rodney House
Dolphin Square, SW1

Darling Debo:

I can never tell you the drear of Manchester.[1] Right up to within ten miles of it 'twas quite a nice day, & again when we left it, but a bitter grey pall sort of smothers it. When I said so, Kit was quite put out & said 'We owe EVERYTHING to Manchester'.[2] We saw the election workers at a room in Queen's O [hotel], the candidate is a v sweet schoolmaster. In his election address he has put 'deetained 1940' (Lancashire accent) as the high spot in a crowded life (between you & me).

Woman was wondair, in our brief 25 mins she managed to tell us every menu between Zurich & here that she had downed, not forgetting breakfast at her Ebury St O. Her price is above rubies.

The worst has occurred, finding how comf he is here compared with an O or staying with Jonnycan, Kit wishes for a permanent flat. This is deadly secret & I hope he will forget about it. You see really it is only comfortable because he's got Jerry [Lehane], & Jerry can't be everywhere at once unluckily.

We also went to Birmingham on Sunday, two different people said to me 'Boyle[3] has no stake in the country', & when I asked in what way they said 'Because he's a bachelor' – & one of them added 'Nor has Heath'.[4] Is this not a strange point of view. One of them said 'Sir E Boyle doesn't mind if the schools about here are 80 per cent black children, why should he, he's got no children of his own & no stake in the country'. Do you think people are incapable of objective reasoning; I believe most people are, & imagine everyone else is.

Well darling, Shoreditch calls. I will write again anon, meanwhile let us cling to Tuesday. By the way do you notice that since he died Bill Astor[5] has been first a worker of good works & then more or less a *saint*, I suppose we shall hear of miracles next being wrought by his remains, too marvellous I've never known a saint personally before.

All love darling, Honks

1 Mosley had been canvassing for the Union Movement candidate in the Manchester Ardwick constituency.
2 The Mosley family had been large landowners in Manchester until the mid-nineteenth century when they let out their property on 999-year leases.
3 Edward Boyle (1923–81). Unmarried MP for Handsworth, Birmingham 1950–70. Minister of Education 1962–4.
4 Edward Heath (1916–2005). Leader of the Conservative Party 1963–70, and Prime Minister 1970–74. He never married.
5 3rd Viscount Astor (1907–66). Conservative MP who had been involved in the Profumo affair.

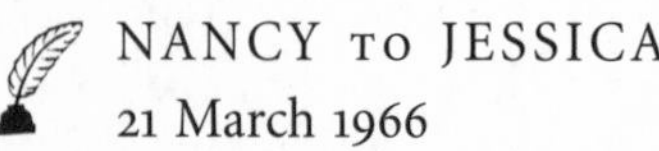

NANCY TO JESSICA *7 rue Monsieur, VII*
21 March 1966

Darling Soo

Thanks awfully for your letter.

Americans are much on my mind at present. Mr Rudkin,[1] who lives upstairs, his mother is dying of cancer, so to calm his nerves (naturally he doesn't go & *see* his mother who is dying of c at Palm Beach) he lies on a couch all day being psycho-ed. So the analyst says he must get nearer to the earth & dig & sweat so he says to me 'Nancy' (which he calls me) 'have you got a spade?' So I give him a spade & he digs & sweats & digs up all my rhododendrons. Then he says 'Nancy' (which he calls me) 'your rhododendrons are all shrivelled at the root – now I've got a friend who knows a man who will bring peat & I want to dig this peat into the roots of your rhododendrons'. 'All right.' I know I mustn't cross him or all the good of the digging & sweating & getting near the earth would be undone. So the peat arrives & he digs it in &, sweating like mad, he says it is 100 francs. Susan *30 dollars* Susan do admit – he made me pay for it. So I'm asking Gen de Gaulle to have him removed with the bases.[2]

I suppose I shall have to read Capote,[3] though I feel, from reading reviews, that I have. In some ways made for me, viz. six Americans at a blow including that sweet clean-living girl Nancy. Capote does sound a regular chacal des cimetières[4] doesn't he?

Much love, Soo

1 Mark Rudkin (1929–). American painter and landscape gardener who moved to Paris in the mid-1950s.
2 De Gaulle had given NATO forces one year to remove their bases from France.
3 *In Cold Blood* (1966). Truman Capote's classic account of the murder of a Kansas family by two drifters.
4 'Graveyard ghoul.'

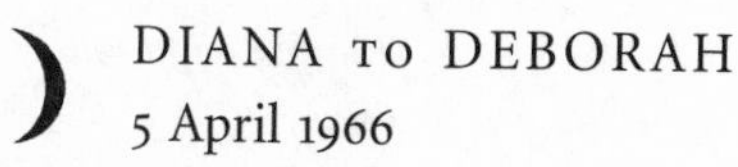

DIANA to DEBORAH *5 rue Villedo, I*
5 April 1966

Darling Debo:

Debo, you made ALL the difference to the vile four weeks, you simply can't imagine how lovely it was to think in a few days you would re-loom. We went down to Shoreditch for the booze-up & *they* aren't downhearted a *bit*.[1] Isn't it (in a way) a marvellous miracle – yes a miracle – of *faith* in, I suppose, Kit's *STAR*, because I've got faith in him as an outstandingly clever person who is about eighty per cent right in his ideas – & yet! how can one see a break through for him, ever? (*Between you, me & gate post.*)

We lunched at Jonnycan's and I saw a vast table laid in the dining room & slightly dreaded then we were ushered into a room with Catherine, Jasper, Weeny,[2] Max & Jean [Mosley], was it not lovely, my first outing for the month. Jasper is so charming now he looks like Ingrid & his eyes are huge & go round the corners of his face so that one sees them also in profile. We were forced to play Monopoly amid shouts of Hard Cheddar etc. Children of that age are so nice aren't they. As to Weeny, he's as sharp as a needle, I suppose partly he seems so clever because he looks about four while in fact he's seven. He drank apple juice & I said to him 'Do you know who used to love that?' & he said 'Who' & I said 'Granny Muv' & Debo, his whole face broke into a huge smile. They, all three, really loved her & Jasper's schoolmaster found him in tears when she died, which must be rare for a *great* granny.

Can't wait for Temple, we go there tonight. There's a letter from Mark Girouard[3] to do it for *Country Life*, of course I'm for it because of the photographs. I got Kit in sunny mood & told him, & hedged about with rules (e.g. our name not to appear). I think he will agree to it.

All love darling, Honks

1 Mosley had received just 4.5 per cent of the vote.
2 Catherine (1952–), Jasper (1954–) and Valentine (1959–): children of Diana's son Jonathan Guinness.
3 Mark Girouard (1931–). Writer and architectural historian.

DIANA TO DEBORAH
7 April 1966

Temple de la Gloire
Orsay

Darling Debo:

My lunch with David Garnett[1] was most inter-esting, it appears they were ALL in love with Carrington, viz., D. Garnett himself, Mark Gertler, Augustus John, Gerald Brenan, Ralph Partridge *and* Lytton,[2] the supremely loved one. It all came out bit by bit. You know how I loved her & how intimate we were & I never dreamed she had turned all those heads. Do ask Duncan Grant one day.

Garnett's wife (Grant's daughter) has left him & I said 'Do you mind?' & he said 'Oh yes, I feel as if I'd lost a leg'. Poor fellow. He longed to know how it was that Lytton Strachey & I became such bosom friends, so I tried to eggsplain. It was love of chat on both sides, naturally.

All love darling, Honks

1 David Garnett (1892–1981). Bloomsbury author and critic. Married, as his second wife, Angelica Bell (1918–), daughter of Virginia Woolf's sister Vanessa and the painter Duncan Grant.

2 Dora Carrington's affair with fellow Slade student Mark Gertler ended in 1917 when she took up with Ralph Partridge, whom she married in 1921. No sooner married than she started an affair with the writer Gerald Brenan. Her deepest feelings, however, were for the homosexual Lytton Strachey with whom she fell passionately in love in 1915 and after whose death in 1932 she committed suicide.

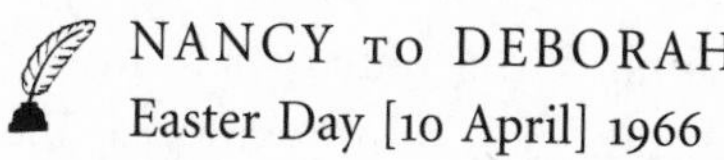

NANCY TO DEBORAH
Easter Day [10 April] 1966

7 rue Monsieur, VII

Dear Miss

Well the hot news is that Bagneux has doubled my rent (to £1,200 a year – not much by current prices but too much for me) & the very same day I've seen a house at Versailles[1] which I really think will DO.

I've been a night at Orsay. Honks is surprisingly well – he, busily analysing his vote – & all is most cheerful. She very kindly came to see the house, & approved of it. No French people will, they regard Versailles as worse than death.

I found a packet of letters written to Prod before I knew him. I'd really forgotten what a villain the dear old soul was. Every single one is a *wild* complaint, either from a mistress ('I waited for you at the Ritz for three hours') or a friend ('have you forgotten that you owe me £2.15') or his mother ('why don't you give up these people who are NO GOOD TO YOU'). I can't think why he kept them. I've also found all yours from your first little house – haven't read them yet – & the only pretty photograph ever taken of me which I'm having copied & will send.

Much love, N

1 4 rue d'Artois, which Nancy bought and moved to the following year.

DIANA to DEBORAH
10 April 1966

Temple de la Gloire
Orsay

Darling Debo:

Naunceling came & also County, but she spent the night here, anyway we all went to look at a house in Versailles & for the first time we rather loved it, at least I'm not sure Jean did so much, but one could see Naunceling in it & there's room for her things (some we've seen have been too minute) & a quite big garden, & a lovely room for YOU (you'll never come here again). NOW the question becomes terribly important – will she be lonely? Kit says NO it's so near Paris & he says ideal for a writer & such a lovely expedition for her friends & so on. I think he's right, but the only thing I slightly wonder is whether she would give up ever going out as being too much bother. No I don't think she would, she's fond of seeing people & it is a very small journey of about 15 mins (but rather far from station). Please give all this your close attention. I can hardly bear the responsibility of being the one to hand for giving advice. The arrangement of rooms, kitchen etc is not quite perfect – but she wd have a huge & lovely bedroom, a thing I should envy her very much.

The house's price is about £36,000, I feel sure they'd take less. It has got central heating (oil) & two good baths & she wd put a third. Everything here is a stupid price but Kit says it will get worse. On the other hand seventy thousand souls will leave the neighbourhood now de Gaulle is dissolving NATO, so should she wait & see a bit whether marvels come into the market? Sorry to harp. Sometimes she seems slightly helpless (who doesn't? I should be just the same faced with ghoul decision) & one must give it one's full attention.

All love darling, Honks

DIANA to DEBORAH
18 April 1966

Temple de la Gloire
Orsay

Darling Debo:

What do you think of the article on Evelyn,[1] they haven't quite hit him off have they. But then he was highly complicated.

At Woman's I was shown a mag., Swiss, rather like a sort of German *Elle*. It is doing a series of black sheep & there's an article about us called 'Six Black Sheep' or something. Anyway all the usual rot but the new twist is that Woman accorded an interview at Grüningen to the journalist. Her replies to questions will muddle the readers (if any). Things like, 'What made you settle in Grüningen?' 'Well you see my dogs are getting old & I want them to have their last few years on the Continent.' It is so completely true yet no one could believe it & 'twill take its place among aforesaid rot.

Well darling I suppose I must get up.

All love, Honks

1 Evelyn Waugh had died of a heart attack on 10 April.

DIANA TO DEBORAH *5 rue Villedo, I*
25 April 1966

Darling Debo:

Louise de Vilmorin[1] came over to Temple, she's got an old ex-husband of 80 (American) under her thumb now & has squeezed 1,000 dollars a month out of him, she says it helps a *little* bit & then tells about him 'Some people think he's all right; I *don't*' which is nice gratitude for £4,000 a year to almost strangers isn't it.

Have you been reading Lord Moran[2] in *S. Times*, rather awful of him to publish now but it is very *inter-esting* with knobs on, though one could have guessed it easily. What became of R. Kee's book about Ireland,[3] there seem to be dozens but not his.

I had a kind letter from Laura Waugh (whom I don't know, but wrote to all the same). It's so strange, you know what I told you about Evelyn's letter saying he was jealous of my other friends after Jonathan was born, well I wrote back saying I'm afraid *really* you thought I'd become a bit of a bore, & that's why you made a cruel portrait of me in *Work in Progress*. Well, really I never thought the bore in *Work in Progress* was me, but it was my turn to be humble if you see what I mean. Evelyn wrote by return to say there wasn't one single bit of me in *Work in Progress*, the only thing was the character was pregnant, as I had been during our great friendship. Then Evelyn died, & now his widow writes he was most distressed in the last days to think I could ever have imagined that the person in *Work in Progress* was in the very least me, etc. Debo! I never really did but thought I must say SOMETHING MODEST. Don't tell.

All love darling, Honks

1 Louise de Vilmorin (1902–69). French woman of letters. Married to the American Henry Leigh Hunt 1925–37, and to Count François-de-Paule Palffy 1938–43.
2 *The Struggle for Survival 1940–65* (1966). A biography of Churchill's later years by his doctor.
3 Robert Kee's history of Irish nationalism, *The Green Flag*, was published in 1972.

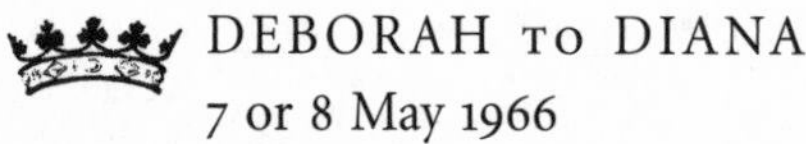

DEBORAH TO DIANA — *Lismore Castle, Co. Waterford*
7 or 8 May 1966

Darling Honks

The Lady & I went for a walk against the wintry wind on the farm and she started pulling up nettles so of course I did too. After pulling & chatting for a bit she said 'I'm afraid these aren't nearly as good as *French* nettles because you see . . .' but by then I'd said 'Dame, now you've gone too far, even the nettles aren't up to Frog standard, eet ees' etc & we both laughed so much we were in floods, luckily no one to note except a bullock.

Trust the Dame.

Please write to Chatsworth, I go there on Wed.

Much love, Debo

DIANA TO DEBORAH — *Temple de la Gloire, Orsay*
16 May 1966

Darling Debo:

The thrill of a lifetime – I saw Krishnamurti![1] Lydie[2] came down on Sat & just happened to mention she was going to his lecture next morning, so I rushed to Paris in the train (not to spoil the day off of

Jerry) & got back in time for lunch, to swim etc. with Kit. Anyway, a sort of little theatre with a kitchen chair on the stage. In comes a little rather bent Indian with hair like fine white silk, sits on the chair & talks. Of course I was *riveted* & quite tired after because I listened so carefully. I'm afraid it was all nothing! He just said one must reject all the old beliefs, dogmas, saviours, gods, which man, in his anxiety & desire to arrange everything, has accumulated during the last 5,000 years, & empty oneself. He did not once mention suffering, the evil which cannot be denied. How can a person be happy, relaxed or whatever you like to call it if he is watching a loved relation die of cancer? It is all so easy when everything goes well, as for example yesterday surrounded here by perfect beauty & sun & flowers & peace & dear Kit so content, but Krishna I'm sure is surrounded by the most maddening old ladies who worship him & long for a message & he's just telling them there *is* no message, the kingdom of heaven is within (at least, I think that's what he means). At the end there were questions & I died to ask him my question (how he fits the reality of suffering into his 'live in the moment & thus banish fear which is made of memory & anticipation' philosophy) but he answered one question & then looked at his watch & buggered.

Naunceling came, she LOVED Ireland & said 'why doesn't one live there?' & her answer is 'too many old ladies & no old gents'. Although Krishna spoke a stone's throw from rue Monsieur she didn't bother to come which shows she didn't LIVE in *Candles in the Sun*[3] & the other book like we did. Of course the audience for Krishna was very telling, lots of ladies in cloaks with straight hair cut in a fringe & idiotic smiles, but quite a number of men, some Chinese & Indian. He spoke English without any American accent, a small Indian accent, & once or twice used sort of nursery words like 'sloppy' (for emotional) which is probably why Lydie finds him assez difficile à comprendre.[4]

Oh Debo I wish you were here, isn't it dread the way you never are. The sweetness of the many families of ducklings on the pond is intense. A raven steals them & Jerry & Kit rush with guns, I hope they miss him, because don't they live 200 years?

All love darling, Honks

1 Jiddu Krishnamurti (1895–1986). The Indian spiritual teacher, darling of the Theosophists, was on a speaking tour of Europe.
2 Lydie d'Harcourt (1898–1988). Wife of the Marquess of Pomereu, whom she married in 1919. They were close friends of the Mosleys and lived at the Château de Daubeuf, Normandy.
3 Emily Lutyens, *Candles in the Sun* (1957). An account by a member of the Theosophical Society of her disenchantment with the movement.
4 'Quite difficult to understand.'

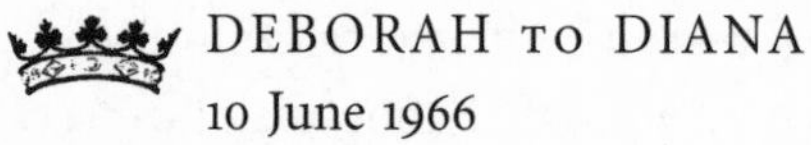

DEBORAH TO DIANA

10 June 1966

Chatsworth
Bakewell

Darling Honks

Three cygnets have hatched. Is that up-swanmanship or have you got some? The Muscovies never tried this year, very odd.

Nancy described Col's party for General & said what I'd missed. I would have loved to have viewed the fellow but have had my fill & more of Heads of State & begin to prefer the ponies.

Much love, Debo

DIANA TO NANCY

21 June 1966

Temple de la Gloire
Orsay

Dereling

I'm deep in Lord Moran, it has made my eyes ache because one can't stop reading. I can't imagine what all the fuss is about (it seems people come to blows over it). Imagine if he really had been gossipy & spilled the beans – 'Wendy'[1] at Monte Carlo, Randolph vile & making him cry, Diana[2] getting electric shocks for her hysteria, Sarah[3] in & out of the cells, etc. The doctor must have known all, with knobs on, yet there's never a hint (he does once say there was 'an uplift' in Winston's spirits when he visited the Reves at Roquebrune – it reminds me of old Beaverbrook saying to me once 'Why can't they leave him with Wendy where he's happy'). I long to know what you think of the book – much better than the extracts, as always.

We went over to the Dook[4] & there were the Alphands. M.

Alphand spoke of you & was highly interested to hear of your move. I notice intelligent people approve & fools disapprove of the move – by & large, that is. Dook said 'When I was in London after my eye operation my niece offered me Buckingham Palace garden to walk in, because I tried Regent's Park & camera men followed me around. One day I was walking in the garden & I met my niece, she was out with two of her little kids, & a camera man with a long distance lens took a picture of my niece & me from one of those new sky scrapers'. Mme Alphand: 'I can't understand why they allowed those sky scrapers to go up, near the palace'. Dook: 'You mean the crown should have bought the land? Couldn't *afford* it, that's why.'

All love, D

1 Wendy Russell (1916–2007). Texan-born ex-model, married to Emery Reves, Winston Churchill's literary agent and publisher of his war memoirs. In the late 1950s, Churchill was a frequent guest at La Pausa, the Reveses' palatial villa on the Riviera.
2 Diana Churchill (1909–63). Winston's eldest daughter suffered several nervous breakdowns before committing suicide at the age of fifty-four. Married to Duncan Sandys 1935–60.
3 Sarah Churchill (1914–82). Winston's actress daughter was an alcoholic.
4 The Duke and Duchess of Windsor were friends and neighbours of the Mosleys.

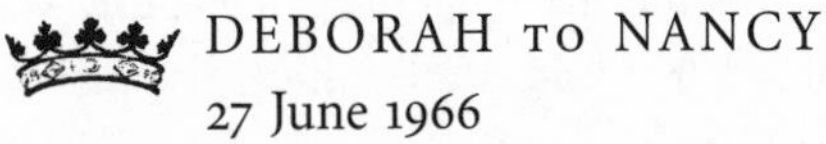

DEBORAH TO NANCY
27 June 1966

Chatsworth
Bakewell

Get on

I had to hide your letter re Wife being like Lady Labouchère[1] because she really somehow couldn't bear her & 'twould be bitter to be told she was the double. She gives an imitation of Lady L standing first on one leg & then the other, leaning slightly back, looking at Wife's Art, frowning, & waving both hands round & round windmill fashion, saying, 'Yes, there is wonderful *movement* there, *wonderful movement*'. Of course looking at pictures is a well known trap not to be fallen into lightly, & as for saying anything about them, I've learnt in 46 years NOT TO. Fatal.

D Carritt & B Sewell[2] come back tomorrow to continue valuing the drawings & prints. It's a scream watching them work, I'll keep my imitation up my sleeve & will try & perfect it tomorrow. I love them both (rather).

Much love, 9

1 'I've got a friend I love called Rachel Labouchère. She's exactly like the Wife – same dreary clothes, uninteresting appearance & swinging bag. Same heavenly sense of humour, same English ladylikeness, same thin hair, same poor health. Same slim but bad figure & long feet.' (Nancy to Deborah, 14 June 1966)

2 David Carritt (1927–82), art historian and dealer, and Brian Sewell (1931–), outspoken art critic for the *Evening Standard*, were both working for Christie's at the time.

DEBORAH TO NANCY
3 July 1966

Chatsworth
Bakewell

Get on

Tim Bailey is here for the weekend, he had a dinner in Sheffield to do with his work & remained on. He brought one David Montgomery, son of your F.M.[1] He is charming. He made one hate the wretched F.M. Do you know for five years from age eight to thirteen he never spent his hols in the same place, used to be sent to *Holiday Schools*, do admit how really cruel. His ma died when he was eight – I suppose Monty couldn't be bothered. He told it all v. nicely re his dad, but imagine how it must have been at the time.

The F.M. has got a Belgian woman as cook. The others in the house came & complained she didn't do anything to help the cleaning but just cooked & threw the dirty dishes at them. He called her in & said in his voice 'I believe you don't do the things in the house you are meant to do – have you never done any cleaning & such like?' To which she replied 'JAMAIS' [never]. He said 'the only person who says Jamais in this house is ME', & sent her back to the kitchen. Next day she said could she have some wine for the cooking – he said JAMAIS.

London & Lady Mosley tomorrow, monster thrill.

That's all for now.

Much love, 9

1 Viscount Montgomery of Alamein (1887–1976). The Field Marshal was an admirer of Nancy's novels; they exchanged Christmas cards and met occasionally. His eldest son, David (1928–), was a director of Yardley International 1963–74.

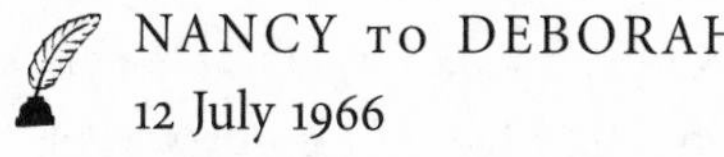

NANCY TO DEBORAH *Venice*
12 July 1966

Dear Miss

I've just got your letter about breaking your toes & falling in love. If you broke your toes as often as you fall in love you would be a sad cripple indeed. As the letter took three weeks I expect both are by now forgotten – it meandered to the Isles of Greece & on here, through two postal strikes.

Fulco[1] has been here. I miss him dreadfully as we met every afternoon for sight seeing (as well as every morning on the beach). Also his friendling who I gather is universally loathed but whom I worship for the shrieks. He & Fulco are so funny together.

I hear Sto dances like Nureyev[2] in which case our fortunes may be made as in Athens, where Nureyev had been, they were saying he has become fat & sulky & can't dance any more. (I never thought he could.) I expect they'd love to take on old Sto with his sunny nature & undoubted genius. Margot more of a whizz than ever there. Mark [Ogilvie-Grant] is in love with one of the corps de ballet – I expect I told you that – called Donald, I think that's why he has gone to the land of snow all of a sudden.

That's all I think.

Love, N

1 Fulco Santostefano della Cerda, Duke of Verdura (1898–1978). Jeweller who trained with Chanel before setting up his own company in New York in 1939.
2 Rudolf Nureyev (1938–93). The Russian-born dancer was starring in an historic production of *Romeo and Juliet* with the British prima ballerina Margot Fonteyn (1919–91).

DIANA TO NANCY
17 July 1966

Temple de la Gloire
Orsay

Dereling

We went to Paris to see the Abdys[1] they were adorable, Bertie had another 'divine hat' which made Sir O quite green, but he's only got to go to place Vendôme where Bertie's modiste lives. This one was of fine straw with a blue ribbon & he wore a tie to match.

We were talking about the burnings (Byron, Nietzsche etc) when people die & Bertie says he burnt all Emerald's private papers & put the ashes in the loo at the Dorchester until finally all the plumbing was wrecked. He says he couldn't bear for anyone to pick over all the love miseries of Emerald & then expose them to the world. I suppose Sir Thomas[2] was villain of the piece, but one feels sorry for him too because there's nothing worse than being over-loved when you can't reciprocate.

All love dereling, D

1 Sir Robert Abdy (1896–1976). Collector and art dealer. Married, as his third wife, Jane Noble in 1962.
2 Thomas Beecham (1879–1961). The British conductor and impresario was the love of Emerald Cunard's life.

DIANA TO NANCY
29 July 1966

Temple de la Gloire
Orsay

Dereling

Did you see the photo of Ld Weymouth[1] & his anti-bride, black of course, well his hair is *tied back* & he's got every sort of beard as well. Can't think why Henry doesn't feed him to the lions with the dusky anti-bride except that under or behind all the hair one sees such an exquisite Thynne face, looking the image of late Ld Bath, & according to Kit, the exact double of the Ld Weymouth whom he saw killed just near him in the first war.

Now for you: what is an anti-bride? Of course you may have SEEN in which case you don't need to be clever ('twas in the *Daily Express*).

The new dentist is IT & he has got a pretty drawing room. He was cross about me choosing a pearly tooth instead of the tomato fang which he said matched mine, & there was a lot of shoulder-shrugging & his Parthian shot was, 'I suppose you think it goes with your eyes' (i.e. bluish white).

Roy & Billa [Harrod]'s visit is in September so you'll be home thank God. Geoffrey [Gilmour] says you are escaping just in time because, with the new travel allowance, English will be on the door-step asking for francs.

All love, D

1 Viscount Weymouth (1932–). Unconventional heir of Henry, 6th Marquess of Bath, who had recently turned the grounds of his Wiltshire family seat, Longleat, into a safari park.

NANCY TO DEBORAH *7 rue Monsieur, VII*
27 August 1966

Dear Miss

Has Decca sold the Island?[1] I've got a very kind letter offering me anything I like out of it & Honks thinks it may be sold so do remind her.

I came back to 23 days' unforwarded letters, it was taireebool – some urgent, some pained, like Gerry [Wellington][2] who had ordered me to the Ritz on a certain day & there I wasn't. Monty[3] says he hopes I've sent him my book as he likes to have all my books. I suppose he's never heard of a book shop. (Actually I know my work & have put his name on the list already.)

Today I went to Galeries Lafayette which advertises English Week & Brando had told me of English (Irish?) lace for curtains etc for which I die. Well. There is masses of whiskey & a brass umbrella stand like a boot & beefeaters in plastic cases & a hundred mahogany barometers & a mass of road house furniture & *no lace*. That's life. And Beatle songs on loud speakers. All the buyers were English.

I think Kit looks *very ill*. I feel quite worried & note that I've become quite attached to him in old age. Honks hasn't said anything, probably hasn't noticed. I must get on with all these letters.

Love, N

1 Jessica had put Inch Kenneth on the market because she was too busy to spend any time there. It was eventually sold in spring 1967.
2 Gerald Wellesley, 7th Duke of Wellington (1885–1972). A friend of Nancy since the 1930s.
3 Field Marshal Montgomery.

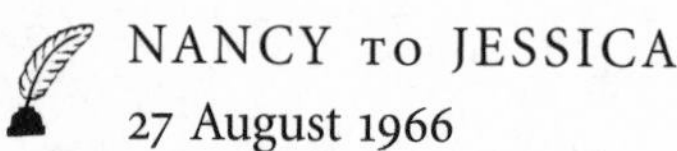

NANCY TO JESSICA
27 August 1966

7 rue Monsieur, VII

Darling Soo

I've lost so many letters that I wonder if there was one from you saying you'd sold the Island? It occurred to me that may be why you are sort of packing up there? If so & if there happened to be a chest of drawers available, that I would love to have. It would be for your room at rue d'Artois so in your own interest *in a way*. I'm also short of a bedside table for same.

I went down there yesterday, they have done marvels, & I can begin to see what it may be like in the end. I said to the foreman 'c'est une bonne petite maison.' 'Petite? Oh là là – je m'y perds.'[1]

A friend of yours called Mr Boland went to take your greetings to the Mosleys. They were amazed. He said 'I think she's warm inside'. I said sounds as if he'd been up to no good with her. He said he's descended from Anne Boleyn. Honestly Susan.[2]

I must go on with these awful letters, the horror of them. I plough away & the heap never seems to get smaller.

Much love, Soo

1 'It's a nice little house.' 'Little? Heavens – I get lost in it.'
2 Jessica denied knowing Mr Boland and accused Nancy of having invented him.

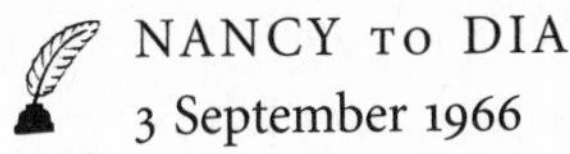

NANCY to DIANA *7 rue Monsieur, VII*
3 September 1966

Dereling,

I'm shaking all over with nerves from trying to ring up Debo. How *can* people telephone who haven't got secretaries? It took 1½ hours partly because they pretend that wretched Basloe has got a W somewhere. How can it? Bwalsoe? Bawsloe?[1] I give up. I'm crying. Anyway it was to ask if I ought to go & see dear Auntie.[2] Debo seemed to think (& I'd wondered if that might be so) that it might possibly worry her. I didn't tell Debo how ghoul it has been because she is always so sneery – how I loathe & detest the PHONE. I'd carefully written out Bertrand Anatole Sophie, & so on to please the brutes.

Another letter from Monty – he can't have enough to do – saying LBJ is mad & the General quite right about Vietnam.[3] He says he has got a team of young men working on his book about warfare. I've now written to say make them do *your table talk*. Hope it leads to something.

Love, N

1 The telephone exchange at Chatsworth was 'Baslow'.
2 Iris Mitford, the sisters' maiden aunt.
3 Neither General de Gaulle nor Field Marshal Montgomery believed that a military solution would work in Vietnam.

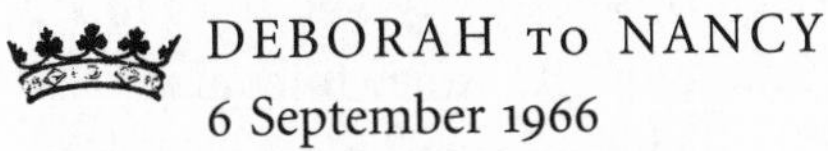

DEBORAH to NANCY *Palazzo Brandolini*
6 September 1966 *Venice*

Brando has lent me yr book.[1] CONGRATULATIONS lady. It is very beautiful & probably very clever. I've got to p.70 & I'm adoring it. Surprised? I am. Amazed.

But I see it's like the Shetland world all over again. I saw a glowing review by R Mortimer, thought that's good for the Lady, opened Louis-Louis, first thing I saw he had (a) sort of written it & (b) twas dedicated to him. Talk about nobbling the judges . . .

Alas, it's the way of the world.

Perhaps *Horse & Hound* or *Home Chat* or *Carpenter's Monthly* will give it a truly independent piece, but I doubt it, you've been round the lot I guess. Anyway Lady, you've done a grand job & we can all have a read as well as look at the pictures.

I suppose you're inundated with fan letters, do write all the same.

Much love, 9

1 *The Sun King*, an illustrated life of Louis XIV.

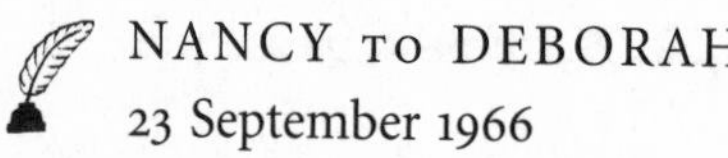

NANCY to DEBORAH
23 September 1966

Savigny Hotel
Frankfurt-am-Main

Dear Miss

I've left my pen at home – eyebrow pencil seems to work!

Goodness it's funny here.[1] They are treating me like a precious jewel. It seems (I've been told in confidence) that L[ouis]-L[ouis] is saving Hamilton's bacon because he lost thousands over Capote wh hardly sold in England.[2] He has given me a large silver bowl & Rainbird[3] a hundred (not quite) roses & I have joined the roses to the bowl. They look very pretty. LL & Uncle Harold[4] are in a photo finish – what an unlikely pair.

I dined alone with Rainbird, full of lovely tales about Monty who is writing a history of War.[5] He has found out about Nelson & Lady H & breaks off his narrative to say how shocking it was. Rbird suggested he might skip the moral judgements & Monty said 'I'll think it over but I can't give you much hope'! Young Rbird, awfully nice, came to meet me at airport – he's in the business but his father said mournfully he's got no toughness in him. I suppose publishing is a rat race nowadays. They are all running out of LL – Canfield telephoned to see if H[amish] H[amilton] could let him have 10,000 in a hurry, & HH himself is in need. But the booksellers are well stocked & they hope to have more from the printers in good time. The Capote affair made Hamilton too cautious apparently – & the squeeze also.

So that's the news from Frankfort on the Main. Funny that the Germans look so nice & are so ghoul. The Americans are equally ghoul but they don't even look nice. You should hear the news in American wh is laid on here, it makes your blood run cold – all gloating for hours over the things they are doing to those wretched little yellow people. Ay de mi.

Love, N

1 Nancy was a guest at the annual Frankfurt Book Fair.
2 In fact, *In Cold Blood* sold well in Britain and was warmly praised, except by Kenneth Tynan who attacked Capote in the *Observer*, accusing him of having done less than he could have to save the two murderers from execution.
3 George Rainbird (1905–86). Publisher and inventor of the coffee-table book, who co-produced *The Sun King*.
4 Macmillan's first volume of memoirs, *Winds of Change*, had just been published.
5 Field Marshal Viscount Montgomery, *A History of Warfare* (1968).

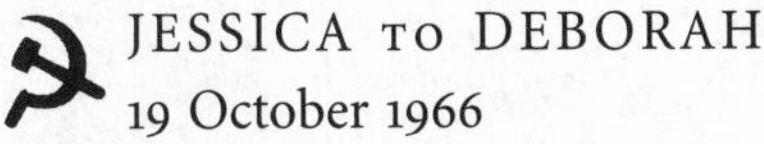

JESSICA TO DEBORAH
19 October 1966

Hôtel du Pas-de-Calais
Paris VI

Dearest Hen,

Nancy is in sunniest mood; and Woman is coming! She telephoned to say she's driving here, arriving today, so that's marvellous. We must get after her about the cookery book. I think Nancy ought to do a bit of it, though. She told about cooking a boiled egg for Farve in the war, when he had been awfully ill & had eaten naught, but one day wanted an egg when Mabel was out. 'I was quite excited at being asked, so I boiled up the water and *threw* the egg in and the most sinister things like an octopus started growing out of it.' So she threw in two more, representing the entire week's ration for three people, and the same thing happened.

Nancy seems v. pleased with huge sales of Louis. I got a letter from D. Scherman[1] (my lifeman) to say the *Life* review has closed, *Life*-ese for meaning it's definitely going to run; he says a review in *Life* automatically means at least 10,000 more sold on acct. of its huge circulation; they only do one review a week, so I'm awfully glad that worked.

Deborah and Jessica pulling 'Boudledidge' faces.
Chatsworth, 1960s.

That dress you gave me saved my life in Greece, as temp. was in the 80's. *Thanks so much*, Hen.

Oh dear it is sad to be off. Leaving here on Friday. N. is having a lunch pty for us today; I tried to get a clean suit to wear at it (as all my things are filthy by now) but no luck, all has to be made.

Much love and do write, Yr Hen

Did I tell you there's an historical note in the lobby of this hotel with an English translation that says in part, 'The famous author Chateaubriand was leaving here from 1814 to 1816'. So whenever it's time to be off, I think hopefully of Chateaubriand (I suppose he couldn't get a taxi?).

1 David Scherman; photojournalist and associate editor of *Life* magazine who had been a friend of Jessica since her arrival in America.

DIANA TO DEBORAH
8 November 1966

Temple de la Gloire
Orsay

Darling Debo:

Yesterday I went over to Naunce at Versailles. We sat on bits of *The Times* laid on aubretia on the low wall. Then this is how it goes: sweet architect shows Naunce a long bit of paper with a lot of typing & a few figures, she looks at figures & then unbelievingly at architect. '*Can* this be right?' she says 'but it's *too* wonderful, a *gift*. Only a million[1] for paint? Are you *sure*?' Turning to me, 'Only a million for all those rooms AND that cupboard & only a million & a half for the new radiators. Aren't you amazed?' Sweet architect reels & sweet carpenter turns away to hide his emotion. We go upstairs to discuss cornices. In one room there is more than ¾ of the cornice in excellent order. Me, 'Where is the rest of this cornice?' Sweet carpenter, doubtfully, 'I suppose it may be down there' indicating heaps of mouldings in the garden. He goes down & comes back, 'Can't see it'. Naunce, 'Well then, don't you think . . . ?' Me, in whisper, 'Make him mend it'. Sweet architect & ditto carpenter in chorus, 'Alors?' Naunce, 'Oh I think a new one really, isn't it simpler?' Then she says. 'Won't you have a cheque? Oh do. You must need one by now. It's ages isn't it since you last had one. When I get back? Are you *quite* sure?' Sweet arch & carp reel again. Sweet arch produces carpet patterns & estimate. Naunce, 'Only *HALF* a million for all that? Well that is a weight off my mind. Though I had a feeling *you* would find something really lovely, only I never guessed the price! I can hardly believe it.'

I think you ought to tell heirling[2] all this because he may think she's *wasting his substance*. The house is going to be TOO LOVELY.

Alvilde came. I like her so much but she is very discontented & with somebody rather low horse-power like Jim it must depress them both.

All love, Honks

1 Old francs. On 1 January 1960, the value of the French franc was divided by a hundred; 100 old francs thus equalled one new franc.
2 At the time Nancy was planning to make Deborah's son, Peregrine, her heir.

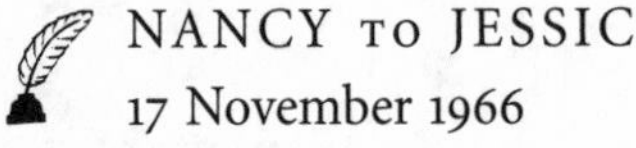

NANCY TO JESSICA — *7 rue Monsieur, VII*
17 November 1966

Darling Soo

The vileness of this paper is your fault. You are a *saint* to send that cutting – yes very favourable to sales I'd have thought. They all have to go beefing on about those wretched peasants, it's the fashion I know. Shows they haven't got a clue about either French history or the causes of the revolution wh was a middle class upheaval. Never mind.

Were it not for you I'd never have known that *Life* had reviewed the book. I get sad little letters from Canfield saying the sales are far from good, & that's all.

I've been with Henderson who had a vast house party of jolly, rich people – then to the D of Wellington, alone with him, Bettine Abingdon[1] & his librarian & that was very nice too. Came back yesterday & was told by Marie the concierge hadn't been seen for some time – I forced the landlord to ring up the police. Result: nine pompiers [firemen] & a coffin. She had been dead for days. I told Wellington – even his love of the macabre would have been satisfied (he longs to meet you & subscribes to The Casket). The scene in the courtyard by electric torches was indescribable. Poor little Mme Brard – I never liked her much but she was pitiable. They've already found about £1,000 in various parts of her lodge!

I've got a mass of letters to write, so continue in our next.

With more thanks indeed, Susan

1 Elizabeth Stuart-Wortley (1896–1978). First cousin of Peter Rodd. Married the 8th Earl of Abingdon in 1928.

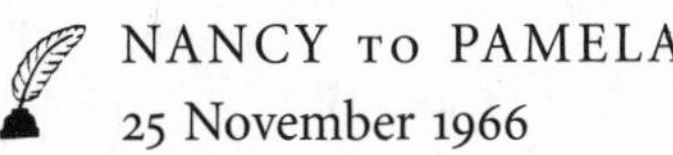

NANCY TO PAMELA *7 rue Monsieur, VII*
25 November 1966

Dereling

Many Happies – but where to send them? Oi don't know. How old we are, eet ees deesgusting – I wonder if we *smell* old like people used to. One lars [alas].

28 Nov 66 Well I left this to moulder & got yours this mg from a very improbable address but also one from Debo expecting you there.

The list![1] Diana & I are already on non-speakers over it but finally arranged for her to fetch the things (all that either you or the others don't want) & then will fight it out here. But be sure to take what you do want regardless of us. I *die specially* for the opal brooch & the Miss Mitford watch. If Debo begins to say *she* wants anything kindly direct her gaze to the Chatsworth Safe & say I said so. Take her there & shut the door on her until the things are in Forceful Lady Mosley's bag. (Though Lady M is putty in her hands I fear.)

I've got to do a thing on the Fr. wireless & must flee

Much love, Naunceling

1 A list of possessions belonging to the sisters' Aunt Iris, who had recently died.

NANCY TO DEBORAH *7 rue Monsieur, VII*
25 November 1966, Where's the Birthday Girl?

Dear Miss

I've received a cookery book[1] of unrivalled snobbishness &, idly turning its pages I was astounded by the sight of a well known hand, ah yes, that of the 9 year old. Playing at kitchens, are we? Eng. receipts are very useless to me as they are full of things like breadcrumbs which can't be got here & also I can't do ounces into French. Nevair. But I note some variations of egg mousse I'd rather like to try. Nearly all the foreign words are spelt wrong. I don't know whether to say so when I thank – perhaps not. Also the 9 year old lady writer got beaton instead of beaten, no doubt owing to a subconscious love of Kek.[2] Interesting.

I sent Alph a tiny sum of money, less than I'd meant to but it's all the foreign exchange allows without a permit. Never had such a letter of thanks. It's for his daughter's village where *all* are ruined.[3] A friend of mine who has just come from Rome says the Romans neither know nor care about the horrors in the north which she says are beyond imagination. *Italians.* The limit.

I've got a huge luncheon party now, including Andrew's friend Mary McCarthy[4] the worst part of whom is her second half – whom of course *I* shall have to sit by. Nevair.

Love, N

I see you are so busy writing out receipts that you've got no time now for ONE.

1 *Lady Maclean's Cook Book* (1965), to which Deborah had contributed a recipe for chocolate cake.

2 Cecil Beaton.

3 Torrential rain had caused terrible floods in northern Italy where Prince Clary's daughter lived.

4 Mary McCarthy (1912–89). The American novelist and critic married, in 1961 as her fourth husband, James West, a US diplomat.

SEVEN

1967–1973

16 June 1965

TEMPLE DE LA GLOIRE
ORSAY
SEINE ET OISE
TEL. 928 4211

Darling Debo We are so excited! Naunceleeng came down yesterday & I put on my dress & she said 'twould make a fairly-all-right background for all those jewels Cyril popped. She made him feel most guilty. But really we are so excited. Of course if I'd known I would have got a proper dress but who will notice one granny among so many. Nancy says it's tiaras now & poor old Cyril groans. We must cling to 'Nobody's going to look at you' — come true now. Nancy says all the grandees at the Matlock O are going to have dinner in bed so's to be in fettle for the ball, quite a good wheeze, also

Letter from Diana to Deborah.

Nancy's move to Versailles at the beginning of 1967 was a change she had been contemplating for a long time. Over the years she had viewed many houses but the one she finally settled on was a small, undistinguished town house a mile and a half from the Chateau. The front gave on to the street but at the back was a large, sunlit garden where she was able to create a wild meadow of cottage flowers – a contrast to the elegant formality of the garden at the rue Monsieur – and where she took great delight in watching the birds, field mice, hedgehogs and other wildlife that it attracted. She had barely two years of contentment in her house before being seized with severe pains in her back and legs. These were initially diagnosed as sciatica but in the spring of 1969 she was operated on for a malignant tumour on the liver. The doctors advised her sisters not to tell her that she had cancer and that they expected her to live only a few months. In the event Nancy survived for over four years, much of the time in excruciating pain. She underwent many tests and several useless operations and it was not until a few months before her death that Hodgkin's disease was at last correctly diagnosed. She did not give up hope of being cured until very shortly before her death and, despite the terrible pain and strong drugs that she took to alleviate it, she managed to finish a life of Frederick the Great of Prussia. The book did not sell as well as her previous biographies but she considered it her best work.

In 1969, Gaston Palewski married Nancy's old rival, Violette de Pourtalès. It is difficult to know how much Nancy minded. Diana believed that she had lived through the worst of the sorrow long before and was only mildly upset; certainly she made light of it to her sisters and friends and hid her feelings as carefully as ever. The announcement of the Colonel's marriage coincided with the onset of Nancy's illness, which may have lessened its impact, but it is difficult to believe that she was not distraught at the news.

Nancy's long illness dominated the sisters' letters over this period.

She was too weak to work for much of the time and letters helped to take her mind off the pain. Her sisters wrote to keep up her spirits and took it in turns to stay with her, corresponding with one another at length about the tortuous progress of her disease. In 1971, Nancy's plans to start writing her memoirs stirred up the smouldering resentment she still felt towards her mother and resulted in an exchange of letters with Jessica about their childhood that is one of the few times when the two sisters unburdened their deeper feelings.

In 1972, Pamela decided to move back to England; her dachshunds had died and she was growing bored with Switzerland. Since her Gloucestershire house was let, she moved into a flat at Chatsworth before settling at Woodfield in 1973, where she remained until the end of her life. During her illness, Pamela was the sister Nancy most wanted at her side, partly because she had no husband or family to worry about, but mainly because her calm and capable presence was the most reassuring, and her simple nature allowed Nancy to be more herself than she could with the others. When she was in pain, which was much of the time, she was often cross and took out her irritation on those around her. Pamela disliked staying at the rue d'Artois, which she found uncomfortable and claustrophobic, but nevertheless made the long journey to Versailles many times.

As the sister living closest to Nancy, Diana bore most of the daily burden of caring for her during her illness. The strain of juggling the demands of her husband and sister was greater than ever and gave her almost daily migraines and a duodenal ulcer. Nancy's illness brought Diana and Jessica together for the first time since 1937. When they first met again, in May 1969, Deborah and Pamela were also in France so there are no letters to record the estranged sisters' impressions of each other, but in her diary, Diana noted, 'Our meeting yesterday . . . seemed completely easy & natural because we were both thinking only of Naunce. Decca has kept her childlike face but her voice has changed, not the accent but the tone of voice. I felt an unexpected sympathy, even affection, for her, & was surprised.' Jessica sent her impressions of Diana to friends in America: 'She looks like a beautiful, aging bit of sculpture (is 59), . . . her hair is almost white, no make-up, marvellous figure, same large, perfect face and huge eyes. We don't, of course, talk about anything but the parsley-weeding and Nancy's illness. God it's odd.' Two weeks before Nancy's death, Diana and Jessica met a second time. 'I felt very drawn to Decca,' Diana wrote, 'I felt all my old love for her come flooding back & have quite forgotten her bitter public attacks on me, or at least quite forgiven them.' The sisters even exchanged a letter, the first in thirty-six years. Jessica's began 'Darling Cord', her childhood nickname for her sister, and Diana's 'Darling Decca'; but the temporary thaw did not last and after Nancy died they never met or spoke to each other again.

Jessica's crusading writing career flourished during the 1970s and 1980s. The success of *The American Way of Death* led *Time* magazine to dub her 'The Queen of the Muckrakers', a title she relished and lived up to with her next two books: *The Trial of Dr Spock*, an account of the US government's prosecution of Benjamin Spock, the famous childcare expert who was indicted on charges of conspiracy to aid resistance to the draft, and *Kind and Usual Punishment*, which took a critical look at American prisons. Nancy's illness drew Jessica closer to Deborah and Pamela, and fuelled their correspondence, but differences were never far below the surface. In particular they disagreed about the decision not to tell their sister that she had cancer. Jessica felt that it was wrong to withhold the truth, while the other two believed that if Nancy knew how ill she was she would lose all hope of recovery.

Deborah's role at the heart of the family was confirmed during Nancy's final years. In her will, Nancy left all her papers to her youngest sister and appointed her literary executor of her estate. Lady Redesdale's papers had already been sent to Chatsworth for safekeeping, and Deborah gradually began to build up a Mitford archive, assembling letters, photographs and other memorabilia relating to the family.

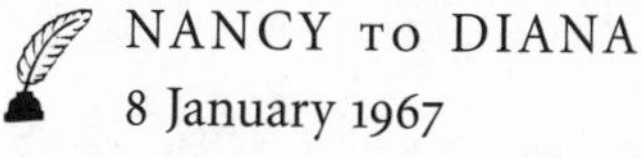

NANCY to DIANA *7 rue Monsieur, VII*
8 January 1967

Dereling,

The Lull before the Storm. It's bitter, –5, & la laitière tells Marie it's going to be much colder next week. Wireless says –16 tomorrow!

Aie! Marie goes about with her pessimistic Norman face I know so well – yesterday she had a ringing row with Marguerite, old friend of 20 years, whom she now accuses of every devilry under the sun. In short, nerves are frayed. Oh dear. As the packing doesn't begin until Wednesday I see a very testing week ahead.

I dined with Raymond [Mortimer] (or at least he with me on acc/ of the £50)[1] at Pauline's. Goodness it was cheap. I'd come armed with thousands – we had bilibi, quenelles, pineapple wine & coffee, well under 50.

Horse has got his Légion d'Honneur[2] – he saw it in the *Figaro* list. I then put my foot right in it by saying 'In England they ask you first – I well remember Evelyn refusing the OBE'[3] & of course Horse has got the OBE. I'm lunching with them now.

Later. Well, walking to the Ritz (absolutely *bitter*), crossing the foot-bridge I saw a well dressed man in a fur hat very slowly getting down some steps into the turbulent freezing river. I shouted, forcefully, 'sortez tout de suite, Monsieur',[4] which he slowly did, soaked to the waist & stood gazing at the water. So I rushed to a copper in the Tuileries but he evidently thought I was the International Gang & coldly said he was guarding the pictures at the Orangerie but I could tell my tale to his collègue – miles away. I rushed & the collègue came at once – man back in river to the waist. Collègue gently pulled him out & led him up the steps to the quai – talking very kindly & there I left them – ¼ of an hour late for lunch. Wasn't it odd? Not a person in sight except a nice girl who came to support my tale. It would have been a bore to have to go in after him. Oh yes, the first copper said he was probably débarbouilling [washing] himself – if you could see the very yellow waves!

Then I went to Village Suisse for fire irons. *Dereling* – shovel & tongs, no poker – 150 francs. I had to get them as I need them. A little wire fireguard 350 which I fained tho I also need it.

1 Under British exchange control, which was not abolished until 1979, £50 was the maximum yearly amount a person was permitted to take out of the country.

2 Derek Jackson was appointed Chevalier de la Légion d'Honneur for his work on precision measurements of isotope shifts.

3 Evelyn Waugh had refused the CBE in 1959, considering it 'very WRONG that

politicians should treat writers as second grade civil servants'. *The Letters of Nancy Mitford and Evelyn Waugh*, p. 394.
4 'Get out immediately, Monsieur.'

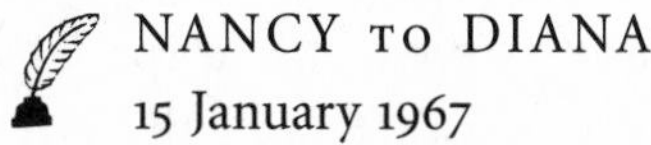

NANCY TO DIANA
15 January 1967

4 rue d'Artois
Versailles

Dereling,

Here we are. Nothing works. No telephone (I mean en dérangement).[1] Heating boils you alive for ½ an hour & then goes stone until you lean on a yellow button. When Marie lights the gas stove there is a wan flicker on one ring only – when char lights it all flames. And so on. Growing pains no doubt. The move was the greatest perfection I ever saw. Sweet cheerful careful men to whom nothing was too much trouble. Not one object either lost or so much as scratched. We all lived together for three days & I could hardly bear to part. High spot: Marie, face of doom, 'Has madam seen there is an Arab today?' 'Yes I did see him.' 'Am I to give my valise to the men?' 'Well Marie, I've given them mine.' Stage whisper '*il y a un million et demi*'.[2] So we took a taxi & I'm rather glad we did because I noted the price which was exactly 20 francs – you must say not bad & the driver says I can telephone for one just like in Paris.

The house, if you can see it for muddle, is very nice – that old Jap looks *lovely* so do the screens & all the furniture. I'm a tiny bit doubtful about so much white but that can be changed in due course & curtains will do much & pictures.

Much love, N

Lunching with Col tomorrow so I'll go & see Mémé.

1 'Out of order.'
2 '*There's a million and a half in it.*'

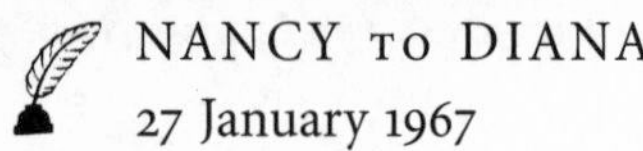

NANCY TO DIANA
27 January 1967

4 rue d'Artois
Versailles

Dereling,

A most terrible thing has happened. You know how I was going to use my old Aubusson. Well I had a raspberry moquette [carpet] put in the drawing room of which about a foot was to show all round. Yesterday they came with my carpet & the FOOLS had cut & torn off the canvas lining to which I used to sew it when torn; so that a fishnet was the result. I cried. Now I'm left with a huge expanse of raspberry *far too bright* & awful no doubt with my pink curtains. What *am* I to do? The cruel thing is the old carpet, mostly dark green, was so perfect in the room, exactly what I had hoped comme effet. I'm paralysed – couldn't sleep & nor could Faithful [Marie]. M. Gallet, the villain, said it was lucky I had the phlegm B-que[1] most of his customers would have killed him. As tears were *pelting* down my cheeks I don't quite know about the phlegm but I did keep off fisticuffs with a good deal of effort.

Hamilton is going to do *The Ladies of A[lderley]* – I'm so pleased. Goodness it's funny – I've just been reading it. Edward *is* the Col – that awful love of high society so incomprehensible to me but which is perhaps the strongest of all loves & out of which people never seem to grow.

Do tell your dates.

Much love, N

1 'British *sang froid*.'

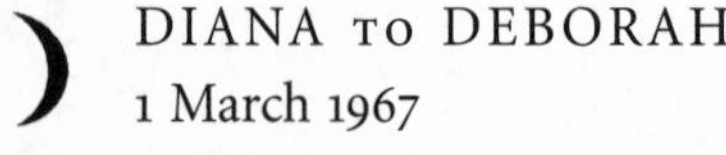

DIANA TO DEBORAH
1 March 1967

Temple de la Gloire
Orsay

Darling Debo

A killing letter from Betj[eman], it seems he's done his bit of the programme on Evelyn (Naunce & I have to do a record. Chris Sykes[1] is coming over to get it). Anyway Betj said Evelyn & he & I & May[2] used to sing hymns together, of course really May would never even stay in the dining room when the hymn-singing began & used to leave us to the under parlourmaid, even if we were 20 souls clamouring for port. She thought 'Shall we Gather at the River?' punctuated by our screams was blasphemous. Now she will go down to history as having sung with us, & Evelyn too, who hated anything in the nature of 'music'. However we must all say the same nonsense & I will play the game.

Debo, COME! It is years & years since you did & I haven't stayed at Chatsworth since Emma's wedding, it is all too bitter.

All love darling, Honks

1 Christopher Sykes (1907–86). Author, scriptwriter and biographer of Evelyn Waugh.
2 May Amende, Diana's parlourmaid when she was married to Bryan.

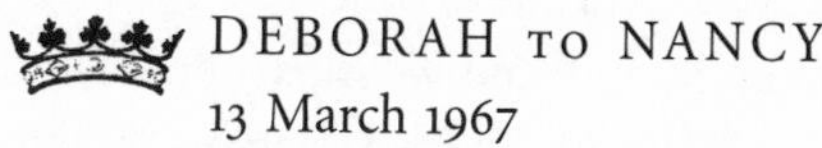

DEBORAH to NANCY
13 March 1967

Chatsworth
Bakewell

Well Lady, the inevitable has occurred, Dinky is going to have a baby by a black man.[1] I've written the saga to Honks but will do the same to you though no doubt she will have phoned with this news if hers arrived first.

Sonia Orwell[2] rang me up, she has just come back from a tour with Henderson & Bob. So she told the news & obviously one wasn't surprised as in a way it is odd it hadn't happened before, but Lady the ghoulish & so surprising part is that Bob & Decca MIND. I can't get over it, & never will, because what do they mind about it, as they have gone out of their way to bring the children up to pour boiling scorn on any old fashioned ideas of any kind, specially that one. Am I not right? I am horrified about them minding because it is such a reversal for them, & old Hen is so set in her ideas & so *proud* that to admit minding must be truly dread. I wish I knew what they mind, & I can only think it must be that they don't much like the man. He won't marry her because she is white & would be a handicap to him in his political career (he is the right-hand man of one of the leading Negro politicians from the South) & I suppose that is rather insulting, but surely Hen must know that side of politics & how very many Africans would never marry a white person, ditto v. religious Jews & Gentiles, & ditto many others who have a life which involves principles to do with such things. She is born yesterday if she wots not of such people. Anyway the object will appear in June. Dinky is longing for it so that part is alright.

I wish Henderson would appear on a magic carpet & tell all. I don't know what else she can expect as the children really were brought up to that bigoted sort of liberalism (Toby's idea) which naturally results in coffee babies & no wedding. Mrs Orwell says that Decca isn't on at all intimate terms with Dinky, which of course one knew, & no doubt that is beastly for her but it still doesn't explain why they mind. Mrs O says Bob & Decca are 'hurt' – why? Oh do explain as I don't understand. She also said Hen asked her to tell me as she didn't want to herself. Well I must say. I have a feeling Mrs O is pretty awful – but nevertheless those were Hen's orders.

I don't know how to write to her (Mrs O said we must) because I don't know what to say. Thank goodness Lady Redesdale wots not of this outcome of a liberal upbringing.

I am terribly sorry for Hen, as the bubble is sort of burst. Perhaps Mrs O exaggerated.

Much love, 9

1 The father of Constancia's child was the American civil rights leader James Forman Sr (1928–2005), whom she met when they both worked on the Student Nonviolent Coordinating Committee.
2 Sonia Brownell (1918–80). The inspiration for Julia in George Orwell's *Nineteen Eighty-Four*, who married the dying Orwell in 1949. Jessica sometimes stayed with her in London.

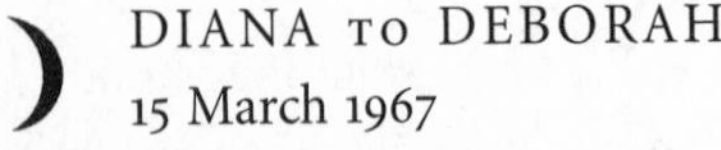

DIANA TO DEBORAH
15 March 1967

Temple de la Gloire
Orsay

Darling Debo:

Your letter about Dinky made me think for hours. The only good thing is that you say Dinky herself is pleased. So she is out of the way, as a problem. Two reasons occur to me as to Decca, & why she should mind something she has (more or less) spent a lifetime in engineering, willing, advocating. First, don't you think perhaps Madam Kliot, or whatever she's called, the mother-in-law, may mind frightfully, & through her, Bob himself? Second, I imagine that among the Civil Rights workers there are a good many prim people (like in the early Labour movement) who think the Dinkys bring the cause into disrepute, & these people may be black as well as white, & there may be a sort of atmosphere of disapproval which Decca feels. Then a third thing, possibly Decca, who seems to have been happy with Bob, thinks that Dinky will now never find a kind intelligent Jew to marry her but will end up lonely, probably with a furious son/daughter on her hands who never stops blaming her, & no loving companion? Decca has reached the age when she discovers that one's children don't always in every circumstance think one is complete perfection. All the same I agree that it seems *incredible* that Decca should either mind about it or be surprised that it happened. I'm glad Dinky held off until Muv – & even Aunt Iris – had died.

Naunce & I spoke on telephone & she gave forced shrieks (you know how she can) & when I said I was glad Muv didn't know she said '*Oh!* Do you think she'd have minded?' But all that is just her nonsense & by the forced nature of the shrieks I think she minds quite a lot herself. Do you gather it's the blackness Decca minds or the no-marriage? And are you sure Sonia Orwell has got the right end of the stick? Also did Decca depute her to tell you the glad tidings or was it her own idea? Oh Debo, I wish you were here, there are millions of things I want to ask. Here's one: do you think Sonia Orwell considers it odd of Decca to mind, or do you think really & truly all those people are just pretending most of the time & underneath the pretence are rather like *ONE*?

All love, Honks

JESSICA TO NANCY
6 April 1967

6411 Regent Street
Oakland

Darling Susan,

News from here: Susan you won't like what I'm about to tell you, except I expect you know it already (because Sonia Orwell was here for ages, Entering into our Lives): Dinky's going to have a baby in June. Beige power is my slogan, as I expect that will be its colour. I don't quite fathom why she doesn't get married (as the babe's father, Jim Foreman [*sic*], and her have been living together for ages); but she seems happy with her rum lot, so that's a comfort. I expect I shall go to NY to note it in June.

Well I do long to see yr. house, but the dear knows when. I haven't got any special plans at the moment; possibly might come in Sept or so. What I really long for is the musical of *Pursuit of*, what a marvellous idea, I do hope it comes to America.

Much love, Susan

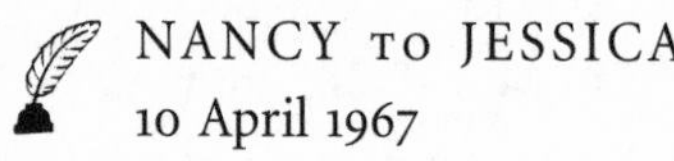

NANCY TO JESSICA
10 April 1967

4 rue d'Artois
Versailles

Darling Soo

Yes Mrs Orwell circulated a few rumours – she is a busy little thing isn't she.

Well the Ogilvys are full of black blood & then think of Alexandre Dumas & Pushkin.[1] I expect it will be awfully sweet & I shall think of Dinky, down on the plantation when the day's work is done, crooning about the old folks at home (you, Susan). Is he *the* foreman or is he called Foreman? Do you like him?

Much love Soo, N

1 Alexandre Dumas had a Haitian black slave grandmother and Pushkin an African great-grandfather.

NANCY TO DEBORAH
7 April 1967

4 rue d'Artois
Versailles

Dear Miss

My garden I liked so much has turned to dross. A perfectly harmless-looking tree has suddenly burgeoned with the most dreadful flowers I ever saw – the pink of every plastic object in the Prisunic, & all over – I mean I never saw such a mass. As it's in the foreground it completely blots out lovely pear trees & cherries hung with snow & one sees o else. By the way thanks for the radishes. Any seeds are always welcome (hint). Well then, you say, take the axe. If I did I wouldn't have a friend left. Not only do Tiresome [Marie] & her Wife the char gaze & gaze, from every angle & specially that of getting right under it, drowned in pink plastic, but the neighbours, it seems, live but for it. Oh Miss. And it goes on & on. I can't look at the garden any more. I suppose in the end the pink plastic will drop off & then there will be the kind of meadow one hopes to find in Paradise.

The washing up machine fused the lights. Tiresome, already against it, turned on me the look Monmouth turned on the headsman when his head was still on – I'm in thorough disgrace.

Woman on Wednesday. She seems to have cocktail parties every day in Paris. Wondair.

Later. Well the fuse was mended by an idiot boy & dirty plates (which she had already washed as far as I could see) were put in the machine & there was a noise like a spacecraft going off for half an hour & then, like Howard Carter waiting for Ld Carnarvon, she summoned me & we OPENED THE DOOR. My dear – washed *and* dried *and* polished. It's like a miracle & even Tiresome is now forced to admit.

This letter is pretty dull – pray forgive.

Love, N

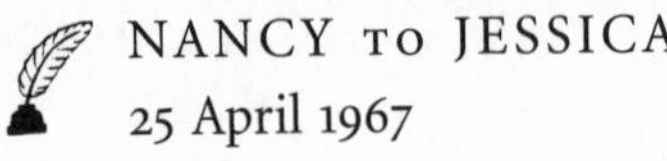

NANCY TO JESSICA
25 April 1967

4 rue d'Artois
Versailles

Darling Soo

I've just had two days in London to go over the script of *P of Love* which is coming on in Bristol next month as a musical. Thank goodness I did – error had crept in & I took out several cartloads of rubbish.

The people I saw in London with growing up children are obsessed by the drugging & that *is* awful I think because generally for life & very worrying. When I was young about three great friends drugged, David Greene,[1] Brian Howard[2] & Tony Gandarillas – all clever people who came to naught, though old Tony is still with us, stinking of opium & telling lies every time he opens his trap.

Hope all is well in the cotton fields? Mrs Orwell seemed to say you rather minded no marriage but many of our family are not cut out for that you know, of whom I am one. I expect Dinky knows best about her own nature.

Much love, Soo

1 David Plunket Greene (1904–41). A friend of Nancy's from the 1920s who drowned himself.

2 Brian Howard committed suicide, after the accidental death of his lover.

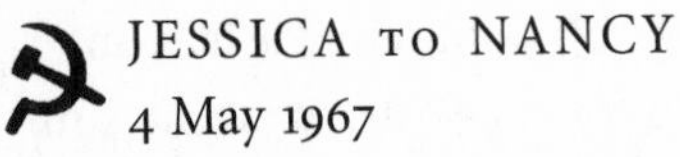

JESSICA TO NANCY
4 May 1967

6411 Regent Street
Oakland

Darling Soo,

Yes I do agree about the drugging being awful. It is spreading like mad here (LSD, which is the dangerous sort; what Muv used to call Marriage Uana is apparently not specially dangerous). And apart from the danger, the annoying thing is the people of one's age who try it. Goodness they are boring about it. They at once become pitying of one for not having some. Asked what it is *like*, they can only say, 'Indescribable!' Also it makes one love everyone, they say. For instance, a locally well-known poet called Ginsberg[1] said it made him feel very sympathetic to Lyndon Johnson. I wish they would invent a Loather's Drug.

Mrs O. slightly mis-reported me about minding no marriage. I only said that now, if someone says 'Would you want yr. daughter to marry a Negro?' I could answer, '*Rather*'. New York friends say she is v. happy, and the word radiant recurs. I shall dash there for the Birth, June 22 it is supposed to be.

Bob is in the midst of re-torturing the CIA, this time about the CIA financing of the Co-op movement. He adores that sort of thing.

Much love, Susan

1 Allen Ginsberg (1926–97). The Beat poet was a well-known advocate of marijuana.

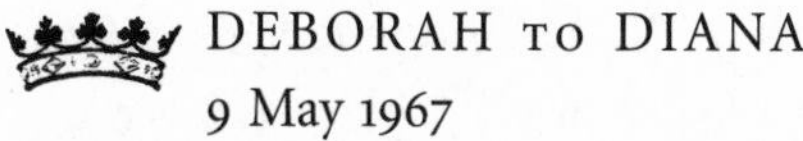

DEBORAH TO DIANA *4 Chesterfield Street, W1*
9 May 1967

Darling Honks

The Wife has taken to making coffee like I do, at table. EB[1] thinks 0 of this arrangement as it isn't formal enough. Well that's to be expected but what is unexpected is the kettle boils full tilt, & a huge funnel of steam goes STRAIGHT up to a Turner watercolour, cunningly hung to receive the brunt. If we all say nothing & go back in a few weeks there will merely be a bit of crimped paper where once there was an Old Master. When Andrew[2] saw the sketches he said 'Oh, Mother, No.'

We've had the furniture valued, & now I'm sorry to say we have all got to practise the Long Jump because there can be no more walking on the yellow drawing-room carpet & we shall have to go into meals by taking a run from the television & Alley Oop over the said carpet.

I hope Wife will perfect this new technique while she is in Ireland.

Much love, Debo

Have phoned Lauragh 3 & Wife sounded much better having done the journey in one drawing-room carpet hop.

1 Edward Bigham, 3rd Viscount Mersey (1906–79). Married the 'Wife', Lady Katherine Petty-Fitzmaurice, in 1933.
2 Andrew Bigham (1941–). The Merseys' youngest son.

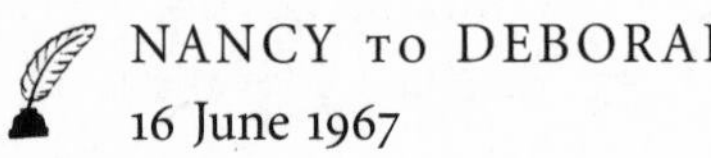

NANCY TO DEBORAH
16 June 1967

4 rue d'Artois
Versailles

Dear Miss

Your programme[1] – very naughty & silly & I don't pity you, as Blor used to say when one was *dead* after balls.

I'm really haunted by that play[2] & not on my own account for once but I mind terribly for Slade & the actors. They've been playing to more & more enthusiastic audiences, for nearly a month, in a little place like Bristol, & yet can't go to London for want of backers. Anyway the game is up, the actors are getting other jobs & it's all over but it seems unbearable, really worse than if it had been a flop in the first place. If I were Slade I should be totally discouraged & I feel deeply sorry for him.

Decca's visit was very nice & I do love her but, strictly between ourselves, I get rather tired of the harping on one's meanness & miserliness considering I gave her my share of the Island, a fact which has never been referred to since. Not that I want continual thanks etc, of course not, but I do think one could be spared such remarks as (about the bookcases, *which she offered* I never asked for them) 'Bob says, your sisters certainly know the value of things'. Nevair. I'm rather glad she's not my only sister.

Col's party yesterday was so nice. I fell in with Edwina & Leo [d'Erlanger] & we waited together to see the General arrive & see the people pushing forward with idiotic smiles to try & be introduced to him. Then the Col says 'You vanished – I wanted to introduce you'. But how *could* he expect one to push in, knowing me as he does! When the Gen had gone most of the horrors did too & left a very jolly residue of friends. Next year you must come to it. Every *single* French person started by saying you've got far the prettiest dress I've seen this year – clever Patou. The coat is ravishing too so I'll be all right I hope on the 28th.[3]

Much love, N

1 'Two runners at Newbury this evening, then London, Edward's christening tomorrow, city dinner, home at cracker Fri, 22 for the weekend, 500 to cktl pty Fri night and a dreaded fête which I had forgotten about on Sat.' (Deborah to Nancy, 14 June 1967)
2 The musical of *The Pursuit of Love*.
3 For the marriage of Deborah's son, Peregrine, to Amanda Heywood-Lonsdale.

JESSICA TO DEBORAH

28 June 1967

274 E. 10th St.
New York, NY

Dearest Hen,

Thanks awfully for yr. letter, written no doubt amidst massive weddingry. (*DO* write a full account of same, I *was sad* to miss it.)

Here's the only extant pic of me grandchild. Don't you admit fairly sweet, considering it was taken when he was but two days old?

Shade: Slightly fairer than Dinky, so far; but those who know say they usually are, at birth, & then get pitch later on.

Other notes: The birth wasn't too awful, only about five hours of labour. He's amazingly good, sleeps like mad & seems to be already on a proper feeding schedule. Dinky's in marvellous shape, and marvellous with him.

I'm getting along with my grandmotherly duties. They consist of me going to her flat in the morning, doing a terrific lot of cooking, and then there seems to be a daily cktl pty of her friends who start gathering about 6, then I scram around seeing *my* friends. I expect I'll be off home next week.

Much love and do tell about the Wedding, Yr Hen

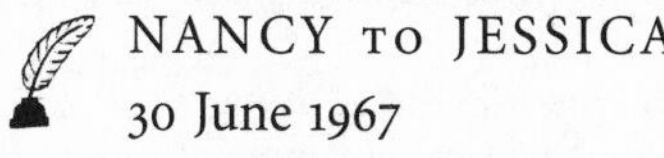

NANCY TO JESSICA

30 June 1967

Odos Aristonikou
Athens

Darling Sooze

The wedding was too lovely. Debo was a rock of diamonds as somebody once said of Pompadour. Every relation & every servant (ex. alas Mabel, too old) I have ever known was at the reception oh dear it was fun. You were fearfully missed. How maddening that it

Deborah, Nancy, Pamela, Diana and Emma Cavendish at the dance for the wedding of Deborah's son, Peregrine, to Amanda Heywood-Lonsdale. London, 28 June 1967.

had to coincide with Hugh (I think he ought to be called it on account of the hue).

Woman sat next Lord Mountbatten[1] at dinner (Stoker's). He said

'I know you are Woman'. She said, 'Yes, & may I ask who you are?' Collapse of stout party.

Much love Soozy, Susan

1 1st Earl Mountbatten of Burma (1900–79). Great-grandson of Queen Victoria. Supreme Allied Commander in Southeast Asia 1943. Viceroy and Governor-General of India 1947–8, First Sea Lord 1955, and Chief of the Defence Staff 1959–65.

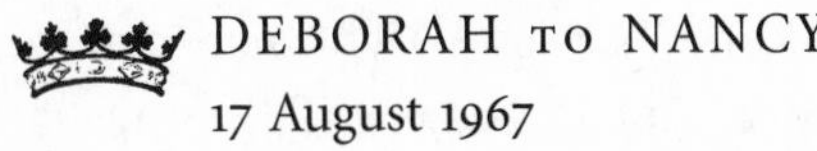

DEBORAH TO NANCY
17 August 1967

Chatsworth
Bakewell

Get on

Did you see the Duke of Bedford is having a Love-In at Woburn & a furious father of a girl who said she was going said after she'd done that, he hoped she'd go to the Marquis of Bath's for an Eat-In among his lions.

There is a nice tale told by my Berkshire friends of Penelope Betjeman. People like Nicole Hornby[1] think the smart thing to do is to have a dinner party composed of a couple of crazy old dons from Oxford, a few local grandees & some inties [intellectuals]. So my friend was there (role of grandee) & the Betjemans. After dinner when all the ghoulish women took their embroidery out of chintz bags with wooden handles P. Betj. went to her car & brought out a large plastic bag full of ancient, unwashed, unspeakable underclothes – stays, bust bodices etc – & began mending them. Do admit. Nobody actually *said* anything, but you can picture the scene.

Much love, 9

1 Nicole Ward (1907–88). Married, in 1928, Michael Hornby, vice-chairman of W. H. Smith & Son 1944–65.

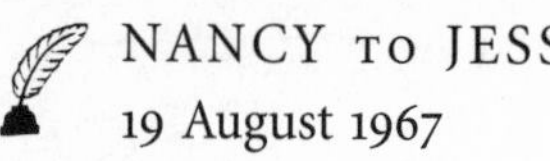

NANCY to JESSICA
19 August 1967

4 rue d'Artois
Versailles

Darling Soo

Just back from Venice & have heard about poor Giles.[1] It must have happened on your doorstep, how awful. I suppose you hurried him into a Mitford (10/–)?[2]

Andrew turned up in Venice & said the Baby (Wat Hugh) is disappointingly white after all. I also saw a friend of yours, one of those *wourm* Americans I can't care for (I only like the Wrightsman[3] type of tough brute really). She is called perhaps Lindsay or Kinloss or Graham,[4] one of those Scotch names, & says she owns *Newsweek.* She was on Charlie Wrightsman's yacht &, a man having failed, I sat next her at dinner. She loves you, but she's so wourm I guess she kinda loves the whole human race.

Do write

Much love, Soo

What is the Baby's name? Is it sweet? Is Dinky pleased with it?

1 Giles Romilly (1916–67). Esmond's older brother had committed suicide.
2 After *The American Way of Death*, a cheap coffin became known as 'a Mitford'.
3 Charles Wrightsman (1896–1986). Oil magnate, philanthropist and art collector. Married to Jayne Larkin in 1944.
4 Katherine Graham (1917–2001). The legendary owner and president of the *Washington Post* was one of the first friends Jessica had made on her arrival in America in 1939.

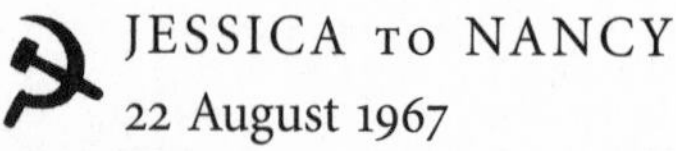

JESSICA to NANCY
22 August 1967

6411 Regent Street
Oakland

Darling Soo,

Yr. letter made me shriek, as usual; esp. Kay Graham being wourm. She is actually noted for being a *freezing terrifier* by the people who work for her; although not by me, because I knew her best when she was young and v. nice. Sorry you loathed her.

The Babe's name is James Robert, called Lumumba by some and Jamie by others. P. Toynbee said 'I bet it will look exactly like your mother only pitch black.' But on 2nd thoughts he said 'Won't you be disappointed if it's pure white?'

Much love, Susan

NANCY TO JESSICA
1 September 1967

4 rue d'Artois
Versailles

Darling Soo

That's it – keep Koko as a fugitive from justice[1] – I see him as a canine Anne Frank; he must keep a diary. I thought you had a garden – surely he need never go out again? If he must absolutely have an occasional baby one can pick them up by the hundreds outside shops where their maters leave them for hours, presumably in the hopes of getting rid of them. That is, they do here & probably there as well. Satyrs sometimes oblige & then for days there is nothing else on the wireless.

The Love-In was a huge success until somebody set fire to it – the furious father, probably. But Bedford had hired a lot of tough ex-policemen to make sure there was no promiscuity so what was the point, one asks oneself?

Heywood Hill went to a dinner where there were four couples whose children had married pitchers.[2] He says all the talk was: 'He's SO clever' 'She's SO sweet'.

Well Susan what a world.

Love from Soo

1 Jessica had written that Constancia's dog, on which she doted, was to be destroyed because it kept 'chewing up children who live in the street'.
2 i.e. 'pitch blacks'.

NANCY TO DEBORAH
15 October 1967

4 rue d'Artois
Versailles

Dear Miss

Feeling sure that I've got a dormouse in the garden (needle teeth getting at pears & apples on the tree) I looked it up in *Ency. Brit.*

'Before *retiring* it becomes very fat. Treated as a delicacy on the Continent'. I looked up in *Larousse* – alas the accent is on the word delicacy & the whole article devoted to how one can catch them. There are two ways. You can bait a trap with gingerbread, of which they are passionately fond, or (hold everything) you can make a snug little nest & catch them while asleep. Honks said Debo will never come again if you tell her that. In fact I may have to leave – but where for? Certainly not a land where they course hares. Meanwhile I'm off to buy some gingerbread as an innocent offering.

If I go to Blighty about the 17th Nov. for a fortnight, a few days in London to stock up with Pot I thought, could you have me to stay at Chatsworth? I am very much interested in Shetland ponies & would like to visit a few studs. Wife has invited me for the Sussex Shetland Club ball – will you ask her what date it is?

Do you know who comes next week? WOOMLINGS. She dos. Of course she won't say which day, oh no no, but she is giving me the treat of bringing the dogs. Wondair – oi doi.[1]

Much love, N

1 When the Mosleys were living at Crowood, one of the farm workers used to act in a mummers' play, taking the part of St George going into battle against the dragon and reciting in a strong West Country accent, 'Ba'le to ba'le with thee, oi croi / Thou upon this ground shall loi, / Clash of steel: Oi doi.'

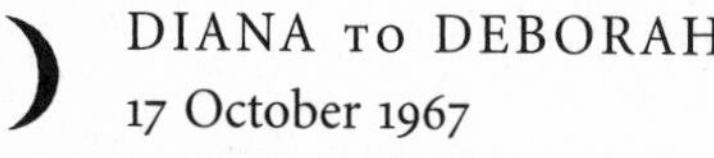

DIANA TO DEBORAH
17 October 1967

Temple de la Gloire
Orsay

Darling Debo:

We've got Robert Skidelsky here, he has come from Japan right across by trans-Siberian with stops in Moscow & Berlin, having had his hols in Hong Kong, so it's talk talk talk (like Kitty Burke).[1] Yesterday he & Naunce & I went for a vast walk in the Versailles park & Marché Commun[2] was mentioned & Naunce said 'Oh yes I hope & pray they don't get in' (the English) 'imagine if *we*' (the French) 'have to have them hanging round our necks, probably it wd mean huge new taxes'. Robert was quite at sea (!) & couldn't make out *who* had got to pay huge new taxes because it didn't dawn that it was poor old England being referred to in such an unkind & unfeeling manner, or that '*we*' meant France. All accompanied by shrieks of course (don't tell anyone). You know at Birdie's most extreme moments of Germanophilia I can't imagine her saying even in fun anything so strange. I'm not sure how much Robert took in, at that moment we reached Trianon & I made him press his nose on the window to see down the long gallery & this was a diversion.

Naunce was so *very* nice & cheerful & funny & marvellous in every other way & Robert noticed such improvement in her spirits (made by new house I'm certain) *BUT* of course that was the side that used to exasperate Wid, & no wonder. Isn't she curious to the last degree.

Max was mentioned in *S. Times* colour supplement on motor racing, it said he hoped to give up the Bar to be a professional, he is very cross because he says it damages his prospects at the Bar, he talked to his Dad for ages on the telephone, & Dad said just ask *S. Times* to deny that he's giving up the Bar. So we shall see if it does, next Sunday. He won his race day before yesterday, last of the season thank heavens.[3]

All love darling, Honks

1 The Mosleys' housekeeper when they lived in Ireland.
2 'Common Market'. Talks were taking place to decide on Britain's application for membership of the European Economic Community. General de Gaulle considered Britain insufficiently pro-European and vetoed the application.
3 Max Mosley had been driving for some years in club events. In 1968, he graduated to Formula Two before retiring in 1969 to work on the legal and business side of Formula One. In 1991, he was elected president of the Fédération Internationale de l'Automobile.

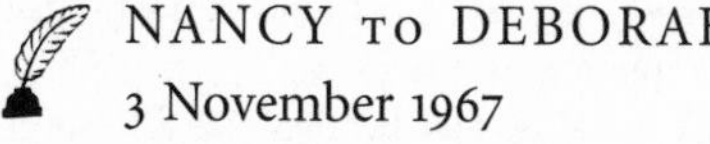

NANCY TO DEBORAH
3 November 1967

4 rue d'Artois
Versailles

Dear Miss

I say I've found the second hedgehog which I thought had been chased away. No – he's been with us all along unseen unsung, in an only fairly cosy nest in the unused green house. So I've made him more comfortable. But I'm slightly off hedgehogs since reading that their brain development is very low – only a shallow groove between the lobes. (How is Sophy's groove?) I liked to think of a brilliant genius scuttling about my garden & dreaming clever dreams all day & propounding extravagant theories as to how the milk gets to him in an apparently cow-less suburb. Nothing's ever as nice as one thinks & here I am, landed with two halfwits.

That's all. Shall I see you in London? No don't start getting cross I've got your letter somewhere & will look. I'm very old & scared you see.

N

DIANA TO DEBORAH
7 November 1967

Temple de la Gloire
Orsay

Darling Debo:

K's publisher[1] is here & we are in the throes, which threaten to go on (re-writing etc.) for months yet, it is most tahring. He told us at dinner that his father shared a room at Marlborough with Michael Bowles[2] & knew of his love for me (aged ten) & one day a mad man called Lord Redesdale burst in with a horse whip & he was hunting for Michael Bowles so Mr Mitchell asked him to wait & he rushed & found Mike & told him to HIDE, thus saving a life. Debo, I believe it is true. How amazing that this Mr Mitchell was a witness of it, he told his son & it suddenly came back to him when he heard the son was coming to stay with us. Can you imagine aged Sophy's age.

All love darling, Honks

1 James Mitchell (1939–85). Editorial director of Nelson whose decision to publish Mosley's autobiography, *My Life* (1968), was widely criticized. Co-founder of Mitchell Beazley, one of the most successful publishing companies of the 1970s.

2 Michael Bowles (1904–76). The son of Lady Redesdale's elder brother was an expert on land law and the author of *Testamentary Annuities*.

DIANA TO DEBORAH
17 November 1967

216 Rodney House
Dolphin Square, SW1

Darling Debo:

So lovely to have a chat just now & I feel I didn't nearly thank enough for asking us, it would have been *sublime* to go up next week-end. Poor old Kit is a bit up-to-the-eyes, & there is the endless struggle not to be turned into Sir Chips Mosley or Sir Oswald Chipsley.[1]

Henry Williamson[2] just phoned to say a chapter of Sir O's book he had been given to read is really marvellous, I'm so glad this happened today when all has been rather horrid for Kit (not only the telly[3] but struggles with publisher). Although Henry's own books are deadly, I think he's quite a good judge & in the past has always been very unflattering about Kit's writings. So 'tis cheering & I'm longing for Kit to wake up so that I can tell him (it's 10.10 A.M. & he's still in the land of dreams, Naunce always says he's like a débutante). As to the telly, while it was on, I couldn't stop trembling & my teeth were chattering, what an odd thing the body is & very worrying when it does things one doesn't wish it to. I was on a sofa with Max & was terrified he would notice. Don't tell anyone. Kit himself seemed quite unmoved, heavens I was glad to hear his key in the door. Robert Skidelsky telephoned immediately to say they'd all watched, at Nuffield. He said Kit gave an impression of great force & nothing to use it on.

He (Robert) hopes to get Kit on a programme about his book on the 1929 government.[4] If he succeeds, that, with the Frost ghoulery, will mean the 30-year boycott is over. Frost alone doesn't mean that & in fact I think it might hinder the Robert Ski programme more than help it. We shall see. The George Brown story was in *E. Standard* last night.[5]

All love darling, Honks

1 *Chips*, the diaries of Sir Henry 'Chips' Channon (1897–1958), the ambitious, gossip-loving American-born socialite who married a Guinness heiress and became a British MP, had just been published.

2 Henry Williamson (1895–1977). The prolific author of *Tarka the Otter* (1927) had been a member of the BUF and admirer of Nazi Germany.

3 Mosley had been interviewed for ITV by David Frost on *The Frost Programme.*
4 Robert Skidelsky, *Politicians and the Slump* (1967).
5 According to the 'Londoner's Diary', the Foreign Secretary had telephoned Frost to congratulate him on his interview with Mosley and to offer 'some useful ammunition' if Frost proposed to continue the encounter the following day. *Evening Standard*, 16 November 1967.

DIANA to DEBORAH
30 November 1967
Saint Andrew's day (I hope)

216 Rodney House
Dolphin Square, SW1

Darling Debo:

The saga of Andrew & that silly old Lady[1] is beyond all, when I was watching *Panorama* I thought about her the whole time but you see I imagined her being at Constantia [Fenwick]'s, otherwise I should have TREMBLED, but I thought at Constantia's very likely it would be engulfed by dinner. The idea of seeing it *with Andrew* didn't cross me mind. She is really awful. I told you what she said to Skidelsky. One can't understand it. I slightly wish I'd been with you all because I wd have remarked

1. the French are absolutely dreading the barriers coming down & having to compete on equal terms with Germans in heavy industry

2. the French peasants are in revolt, in Brittany, Vendée & the wine growing districts of the south

3. the franc is out of line with any other currency which is disastrous for the tourist trade

4. the civil servants teachers etc are on the verge of striking about their wages

All above only the *worst* things. I love the French & I love France but to pretend it is a marvellously run modern country is rrrubbish. The General gives it the blessing of stable government, which is *much better than nothing*, but one hears only grumbling if one lives there. Oh yes a fifth thing is the Bourse, shares very low & yields weeny.

But what amazes about Naunce is the sort of gloating attitude she adopts if something goes wrong in England. It reminds me in a way of her attitude to Muv & Farve, for ex the other day we were talking about the Mike Bowles incident & she said 'But don't you remember how really NASTY they both were?' Well, they were a bit exaggerated but NOT nasty. She must have got some sort of deep wounds inside which now make her lash out at England as she formerly did at Muv (on the Island for instance). Yet she is *so* kind & really good in so many ways, even to me, though she has got a very strange attitude to me as you know. Poor Debba, it is so really unfair that YOU should have the brunt but of course one just always does. The super unfairness is that you agree entirely with Andrew, yet you are the one he attacks. I go through just that with Kit & as you know Naunce was banned for years but luckily no more.

All love darling, Honks

1 Nancy and Andrew Devonshire had quarrelled after watching a *Panorama* programme about France during which Nancy had declared, 'The truth is that the English can't bear seeing the French do so well.'

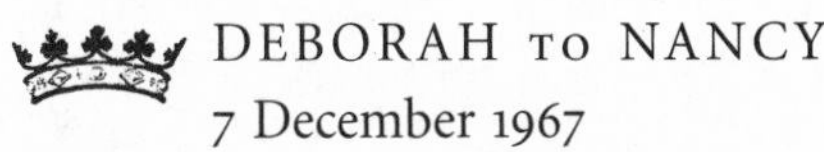

DEBORAH TO NANCY *4 Chesterfield Street, W1*
7 December 1967

Get on

Sorry about lack of letters, it is the London rush as suddenly it's time for another meal having done God knows what in between same.

Just had lunch with Geoffrey [Gilmour], Honks & the Abdys – Geoffrey's lunch – & I was Honks's husband. Twas in the Aperitif & she was wearing a Mellon Bequest[1] (the black coat with the mink) & lo & behold Paul Mellon came in. When I told her who it was, she complained all through lunch that he was eyeing her *and* her coat & she was terrified it might be snatched from her back.

Since you left the plague has broken out at three farms ON OUR BOUNDARY. Every time I come in I expect the dreaded message.

I had dinner with Ann Fleming one night, all the loved ones were there, [Robert] Kee, [Lucian] Freud, Bacon[2] & a marvellous old thing called Edward Rice.[3] There was much talk of sex & Bacon said he preferred a boiled egg – I WORSHIP that man.

The girl Andrew took a fancy to called Joanna Kilmartin[4] was there & after a bit she came up & said she had to ask someone if I was me because when we had last met she had a great impression of *colour* – blue eyes etc. etc. Then long pause 'And now . . . well I had to ask if it was you'. I said 'I know, Anno Domini does that, all faded, ah me, woe woe etc'. CHEEKY MONKEY.

Abdy is a card isn't he. Dread evening tonight, dinner dance at St Stephen's Club. Must go & get dressed for same.

Much love, 9

1 'Bunny' Mellon, who ordered from Balenciaga's couture collection three times a year, used to send a trunk full of clothes to Andrew Devonshire's mother for distribution to charity. Nancy and Diana would take first pick from what they called the 'mercy parcels' and replaced with them with some of their own old clothes.
2 Francis Bacon (1909–92). The painter's striking portrait of Isabel Rawsthorne, *Standing in a Street in Soho*, was shown in 1967.
3 Edward Rice; a barrister who was married to Marcella Duggan, Lord Curzon's stepdaughter, 1927–61, and to Nolwen de Janzé in 1962.
4 Joanna Pearce (1929–2005). Translator and writer. Married, in 1952, Terence Kilmartin, literary editor of the *Observer*.

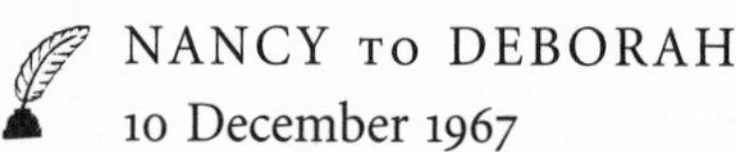

NANCY TO DEBORAH
10 December 1967

4 rue d'Artois
Versailles

Dear Miss

Oh the misery of yr adjacent foot & mouth.

Sophy's Hols I here wish to indulge in the favourite occupation of the childless: advice to young mothers. If this little girl is never allowed to be bored or given a moment for reflection, she will grow into a *great extrovert dullard*. Don't hustle her round Europe in search of pleasure – let her be – she can muse in an attic as children always have or wander with James[1] in the silent woods (screamingly funny if he kidnaps her & demands a huge ransom I must admit) or go with hot pies to old ladies in cottages. Ask Wife if she doesn't agree.

You are NOT repeat NOT faded. You look as smashing as ever when in full fig. But I think you might try a few feminine wiles like a darker fond de teint,[2] a little soupçon of hair dye & perhaps clothes of brighter hue – specially pink which blues the eyes. Eschew grey.

That pink Mellon (from good old charity times long past) was specially good I thought. Screamed at Honks being caught in the act.

Woomling came. Of course no notice – ambled in & shared my luncheon. Had I known oh what heavy loot I would have loaded on her car.[3] Nevair.

Raymond [Mortimer] got on my nerves. I don't know which is more annoying – those like Aunt Ween for whom nothing is right or the Rip van With-Its who rejoice in the idea of drugs, dirt & divorce.

That's all for now. I wish the Bonny Season was over – the posts are disrupted & I don't dare send for books to the London Library. Also some vandal has covered all the streets with fairy lights. HEEDEEOS.

Best love, N

That *disgusting* HEART[4] I can't look at the papers what would Muv have said?

1 James Penrose; son of the land agent at Chatsworth and a friend and contemporary of Sophia.
2 'Foundation cream.'
3 Pamela used to drive to England with a car full of household goods that she bought cheaply in Switzerland.
4 Dr Christiaan Barnard had carried out the first successful human heart transplant in Cape Town on 3 December.

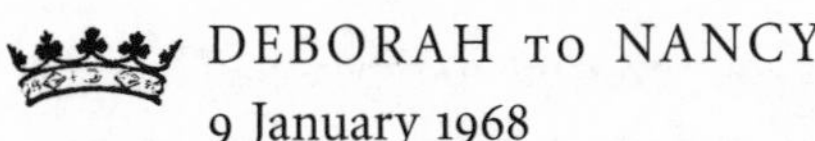

DEBORAH TO NANCY

9 January 1968

Chatsworth
Bakewell

Get on

What WOULD Wid & Lady R have said re torn out hearts. I wish the wireless would stow it.

Yes, Lady, grooms are my life and now I'm 47 I've gone back to my childhood & I know that all that sort of thing is what I like best. Sorry Lady, but it's the truth. I've done all the other things & they were very nice & now I prefer to commune with an insect[1] on a bale of hay.

Thick snow here, it's a damned nuisance.

Much love, 9

1 A Shetland pony.

Deborah driving her Shetland stallion Florestan, by the cascade at Chatsworth, 1966.

NANCY TO DEBORAH
11 January 1968

4 rue d'Artois
Versailles

Dear Miss

I say this is grievous news about you reverting to type – half one's fun in life vanishes at a blow. However I daresay it won't last, you are a rare flibbertigibbet & taker up of temporary attractions & re dropper of same. I always felt those insects were a bad egg, how right I was.

Yes I die for Wid & Muv re *hearts*. They are even a greater bore than the insects. (I'm having My Heart's in the Highlands, or better might be HEARTLESS, tattooed on my forehead in case some elderly dentist should take a fancy to it.) When I told Marie they were starting a second one she said 'I do hope *not* at dinner time', because she knows how I can't eat with the sight of those pipes leading from the nose before my eyes. Oh no no – deesgosting.

Much love, Lady

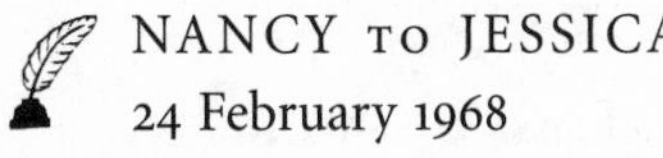

NANCY TO JESSICA
24 February 1968

4 rue d'Artois
Versailles

Darling Soo

Thanks for the young mother[1] who seems *much darker than of yore* how odd.

Susan can you get over our *Socialist* Govt? Of course one knew they wld make everything uncomfortable but could one have guessed they would egg on horrible Johnson over Viet Nam AND refuse to allow poor black people, about to be tortured to death by other black people, to take refuge in the green unpleasant land? Thank God one has left. I went over in Nov. & hardly kept my temper at a single meal. I begin to think Socialism is another word for utter wobbles & it will have to be communism or nothing. But after I am dead, I hope, because Susan it's not really made for me. Did I tell you about the Day in the Life of a Soviet Writer on télé? I won't enlarge but it was not the kind of day I like.

Our General is worried – he thinks the Americans will start chucking about the big stuff & then we shall all be made unwell by horrid rays. Do go to Mexico soon. The idea is Hanoi then San Fran & then Moscow. The Americans here are baying like hungry dogs.

I'm working away, telephone cut off & the whole organisation keyed, but don't seem to make much progress.[2] How I loathe the start of a book. In Aug. I go to Germany to look at the sites & arrange for the illustrations – mostly in your part of Germany.[3] One hopes travelling will be easier than usual with you & Bob in Mexico, if you see what I mean. Oh dear I long for you. Every time I look at the bookcases I think of you. I must give you something to produce ditto result – with disapproving shake of head.

Colonel dined with the Bentincks (Dutch Amb) & on one table was a book by me & on another was a book by you, & Col said 'C'est un festival Mitford'.

The Spring is here in all its full horror & icy bitterness. But this little house is very snug.

Much love, Sooze

1 Jessica had enclosed a photograph of Constancia and her baby.
2 Nancy was working on her last book, *Frederick the Great* (1970).
3 Nancy was planning a visit to East Germany with Pamela to do research.

NANCY TO DEBORAH
28 March 1968 MANY HAPPY RETURNS

4 rue d'Artois
Versailles

Dear Miss

I think Honks is a dreadful worry – she hardly ever looks well & those headaches, &, as you say the drug, are fearfully pulling down. It was a great mistake in my view not to go to Africa where she hardly has any headaches & comes back looking marvellous. But all now is subordinated to this book[1] – oh how I wonder what it's like. If it did well it would be a tonic no doubt to them both.

Decca says she is writing a book on Dr Spook[2] – sounds like a sort of thrilling Vampire but turns out to be some old conchie. Did you see the joke vampire film?[3] I adored it – it cleverly manages to be both funny & TERRIFYING.

Ha! A letter saying some North Vietnamiens will be in Paris on Sunday & will I be sure to go & meet them – Vanessa Redgrave[4] is flying up from Rome (you bet she is). No, I will not. You may disapprove of people being set fire to without wanting to meet them.

I hope you're having this heavenly weather.

Best love dear little thing, N

1 Mosley's autobiography, *My Life*, was published later that year.
2 *The Trial of Dr Spock*, published in 1969.
3 Roman Polanski, *The Fearless Vampire Killers* (1967).
4 Vanessa Redgrave (1937–). The actress had been protesting against America's bombing of North Vietnam.

NANCY TO DEBORAH
15 April 1968

4 rue d'Artois
Versailles

Dear Miss

Honks says you have written my article for me & *so* wittily.[1] Well I've got 'honour yr partner' 'host*ess*' & five or six others perhaps, all incorporated, & I wonder if there is more to come? *No matter* if not but I shall wait a few days to see. It's only promised for 1 May. It's quite telling I think already.

I lunched with Ann [Fleming] & Ld Goodman[2] yesterday. She looked very pretty but not well – the *very* pretty son[3] was there. Ld G, whose body I honour, is bright as a button isn't he. I did enjoy myself. Do tell her, as I know she looms, what a treat it was. He said he thought I was exactly like you which shows what a monument of tact he must be & he also said he honoured the General's body but that may have also come from a desire to please. Anyway he did please.

The rest of my news is all natural history which may bore so I'll cut it short. First of all, the water I put out for my precious birds is now taken over by bees who sit closely packed round the rim, drinking (or I'm told filling bags to take back to the hive). All right but there is one horrid bee whose function it is to chase away the birds in which it is only too successful – even the vainglorious blackbird flees & all my friends have departed.

Secondly, the hedgehogs, having spent nearly a year in different houses, have suddenly elected to co-habit. Really, I cld write a volume on those pigs & their odd ways. You don't know of a book which might throw light on their eccentricities?

That's all. If no more thoughts on lingo are to come mention it in yr next & I'll send my piece.

Love, N

1 Deborah had contributed suggestions for an article by Nancy on pronunciation and modern-day English usage in which she deplored the Americanisms creeping into the language. Reprinted in *A Talent to Annoy* edited by Charlotte Mosley (Hamish Hamilton, 1986), pp. 197–9.

2 Arnold Goodman (1913–95). Solicitor whose close friendship with Harold Wilson made him one of the most powerful, behind-the-scenes figures in Britain during the 1960s and '70s. Created life peer in 1965.

3 Caspar Fleming (1952–75). Ian and Ann Fleming's only son died of a drug overdose aged twenty three.

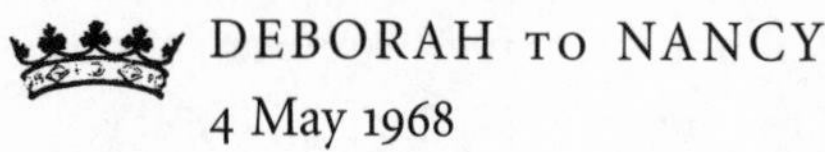

DEBORAH TO NANCY

4 May 1968

Chatsworth
Bakewell

Get on

I've had a v. good idea re Organ Transplants – which is the only thing on the news now – if they could give me YOUR brain I wouldn't be 9 any more. Do think on these things & allow me it. Confess that people would be amazed, I could speak of things like Fred the Great, & could converse in Frog, & keep my end up at Anna Maria's – Lady, I need it.

A Buff Cochin cock has arrived, he is ENORMOUS & beautiful beyond compare. What Sophy calls The Public are fascinated by those recs & no wonder.

The Queen is coming to tea on Fri. Arriving 17.07 & leaving 18.39. What shall we talk about I wonder, can't think of anything.

Lismore looked too lovely as we left, but that always happens.

Any news I might have would BORE YOU STIFF, but please enlarge on baby hedgehogs, & you will be glad to hear I saw two toads, doing bodies,[1] a sight I haven't seen for years. So *sweet* and ancient they looked.

Much love, 9 (till I've got your brain)

1 Mating.

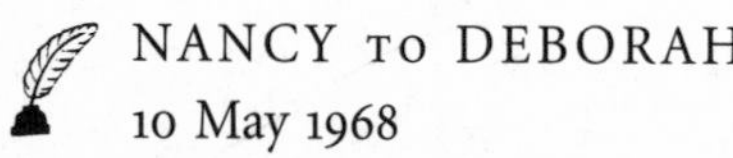

NANCY TO DEBORAH

10 May 1968

4 rue d'Artois
Versailles

Dear Miss

All right we'll *swap* brains – not like heart 'swap' which seems a very one-way affair. Shall we do it by degrees? Will you quickly put in an envelope the lobe which deals with roses? Or would it be less messy to answer my Q with the famous 9 year old fist? I've got two ramblers side by side, one bursts with health & glossy leaves & buds, the other is covered with mould. Would it be better to boldly remove mouldy & burn it? Please send relevant lobe by return – I've told Dr Dumas to be ready to operate.

Cristiana[1] telephoned, terrified by the students[2] who milled all round where she lives – said they were like furious animals. Ann [Fleming] said they looked so beautiful and good. The ones I saw on télé looked beautiful & bad.

Fleeing to Paris.

Love, N

1 Cristiana Agnelli (1928–). One of the models for Northey in *Don't Tell Alfred*. Married Count Brandolino Brandolini d'Adda in 1947.

2 The Paris uprisings of May 1968, which started as a student protest and quickly spread nationwide, had reached near-revolutionary proportions.

NANCY TO DEBORAH
8 June 1968

4 rue d'Artois
Versailles

Dear Miss

My garden looks as if 1,000 Edwardian hats had fallen into it (roses). I tore out the mouldy one & nobody else seems to have caught the mould.

I fear you will mind about R Kennedy – very sorry if so. I think Ethel looks much nicer than Madame Jacqueleen. Still she may be relieved to think no more children.[1]

Love, N

1 Robert Kennedy had been assassinated in Los Angeles on 5 June while in California campaigning for the Democratic Party's presidential nomination. He and his wife, Ethel, had eleven children.

DIANA TO DEBORAH
9 June 1968

Temple de la Gloire
Orsay

Darling Debo:

Max & Al & Jean are going back & will post this. Darling it's just to say I hope you are not sad about R Kennedy, one *must* be because it is wicked to take away his life but I mean I hope you are not extra sad.

Everything seems trivial compared with death so won't bore you with all my silly stories. I hope the post will begin to get normal now but I haven't had a letter yet.

So lovely having the three but they can only spend about 36 hrs, miserably short & is it worth it (for me yes, but for them?).

All love, Honks

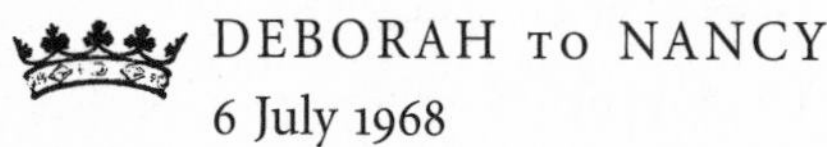

DEBORAH TO NANCY
6 July 1968

Chatsworth
Bakewell

Get on

I know I've done poorly re writing. You would *quail* & *quiver* if you knew the miles covered & the tasks engaged in during the last few weeks. So now I'll begin again.

You must be glad your Old Man did so well in his elections.[1] I only hope it won't put ideas into Uncle Harold's head. Pray, please.

I shall not recount my doings at the Royal, & Newbury,[2] as I know they BORE you. But I will say I stayed two nights with Woman & loved every moment (I was only there at night as the days were more than fully employed) & the country there looked so beautiful 'twas *painful*. Wild roses galore & every sort of other extra on the roadside where no one has touched them. She was wondair to the last. She has bought four bullocks & we watched them grazing & she said '*this property is worth a fortune*'. She said it very slowly & definitely. Then we saw a heap of sludge just outside her kitchen garden & she leant towards me & said in conspiratorial tones – 'Stublow, ALL THIS MANURE IS MINE'. She ees. She looks wondair & the food was ditto. She is bringing twelve farmers/gardeners/dailies/small holders to lunch here next week, can't wait.

Much love, 9

1 Following the May strikes and demonstrations, General de Gaulle had dissolved Parliament and held new elections which the Gaullists won by a large majority.
2 Agricultural shows.

DIANA TO DEBORAH *Hotel Cipriani*
27 July 1968 *Venice*

Darling Debo

Where are you & how are you? It is ages since I got a letter. I really die to be here with you one day. It's been such fun having Jean [de Baglion] & of course to be four would be completely perfect. He's off today. I dragged him for an immense walk & ever since then he loves me much less & in fact I've got a feeling he may not quite forgive. You see, he *said* he loved going, so on & on we went with just the odd groan from Jean & then he said he must sit so we sat at an ice place & I said, 'Jean! Haven't you enjoyed our walk?' And then I noticed his eyes were shut behind the tinted specs, it was dread, & then he said with his voice going up into a wail, 'Darlin, every *beet* of my body aches. My LEGS. My BUCK. My UNKLES'. Of course I began to laugh & couldn't stop & to make it worse I made him hop into a traghetto & by bad luck it was crammed to such a degree that it went down in the water & drops oozed over the sides & he thought his last hour had come & I heard groans all the way over the canal which was unfortunately at its widest & rather rough.

We talked about his fatness & he says he would give £20,000 to be thin but he can't face ruining his life by never eating anything he enjoys.

Ingrid says Toby [Tennant] says Jasper [Guinness] will get into the 8 if he keeps on rowing as he has this summer – how unbelievable for a descendant of *one*.

All love darling, Honks

DIANA TO DEBORAH *Temple de la Gloire*
6 August 1968 *Orsay*

Darling Debo:

We had such a storm yesterday that it *came through* in various places & it's still raining now & your letter arrived sort of sopping like they do in Ireland. What a *thrill* about the wins & somehow marvellous that P. Margaret had to see the triumph,[1] oh Debo I do wish

Muv knew, perhaps she does. It's no good pretending that winning isn't marvellous, I speak as a life-long loser.

We are really & truly rid of Kit's old book & feel like the end of a term with knobs on. I've got masses of books from H. Hill to read & couldn't because my eye-power was all used up on disgusting proofs. I couldn't get Kit to change many a thing I wd have wished to, but he often consented in the end. I'm afraid the book is too long, but his life *is* long. He insisted on putting in masses of dewdrops, to such an extent that the mad impression is now created that he is Pet number one of almost everybody. He says he *had* to because he's been so much abused.

Tomorrow Col is coming, he asked himself. I think ('twixt you & me) it is to discuss Kit's ideas about the economy. I am still very worried in that quarter (Col & Nancy) & I think all hangs on a horrid thread. If I am right it is the all-time worry. I so wonder whether *he* realizes in the least what he means to her? It's quite possible that he doesn't. He may have been so for many years, one just doesn't know. Also one doesn't know what her feelings are, but his name is forever being mentioned, opinions quoted & so on, so that he is obviously in the front of her mind, & I suppose affections. I never dreamed, when I was young, that this sort of worry went on into the sixties (yes I did though, about Emerald & Sir Thomas [Beecham] now I come to think of it, but I thought it was a unique case).

Well darling isn't it lovely that at least *I* won't fall in love any more – one worry crossed off the list eh.

All love & to Sophy, Honks

1 Deborah's Shetland pony, Easter Bonnet, bred by Lady Redesdale, was champion at a breed show. Princess Margaret handed out the winner's cup.

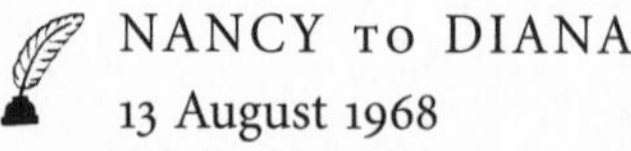

NANCY TO DIANA
13 August 1968

23 Dorsoduro
Venice

Dereling,

I suppose the Famagosta will derange the post as thunderstorms do the weather, so hasten to write.

How did Col seem – health? (It's nearly a year now since he was so ill.) He never says, in his letters.

The Italia Nostra campaign seems very well launched. One of their ideas, which I think brilliant, is to have a metro here – otherwise they say there will be roads sure as eggs is eggs.

Peter's last words were 'Oh God, I am finished – see you presently',[1] which Francis[2] thinks may mean that he was really a believer but I think more likely a typical Proddish joke of the sort one loved him for. But perhaps he was a believer & pretended not to be in order not to be roped into one of the family religions. I can't remember from old days, I don't suppose we ever mentioned the subject. So funny to think how he & Esmond & so on would all have been Cohn-Bendits[3] when they were young – really men are divided into C-Bs & non C-Bs aren't they. Let's hope the nons predominate now as they would have then.

Much love, N

1 Peter Rodd had recently died of cancer.
2 Francis Rodd, 2nd Baron Rennell (1895–1978). Peter Rodd's elder brother.
3 Daniel Cohn-Bendit (1945–). Leader of the 1968 student uprising in Paris. Member of the European Parliament since 1994.

NANCY TO JESSICA
20 September 1968

4 rue d'Artois
Versailles

Darling Soo

I've at last bought some air mail paper which I've been meaning to do for months so you're in luck. I never dare write to *you* the ordinary way though my poor publisher has to endure it & goes quietly mad.

Did Debo tell you, Aunt Weenie, walking up the hill at Asthall in pouring rain was accosted by Americans in a motor, 'Pourdon me – which is the way to the Home of the Mitfords?' They gave her a lift & after a bit of talk they said, 'Are you the ant they all hated so much?' She had to admit.

I stayed with Woman the other day & rather fell in love with her part of Switzerland, it is pretty like a Victorian watercolour – clean & really very unspoilt. Also the German-speaking Swiss are not dull like the others but exceptionally bright (I mean the ones I met with her – of course they all speak French as well).

When I was in Bayreuth I was summoned to the Presence of Frau Winifred – you realize she is Wagner's daughter-in-law? It's a real link with the past. She says Siegfried W. only had one photograph in his room, that of Grandfather.[1]

Honks & Debo & I all have a great craving for Farve so we think we'll get a medium & have a few words with him. Rosamond Lehmann,[2] who often talks to her daughter, got Mrs Ham the other day. She said, 'It's far better here than I would have expected'. She *must* have changed is all I can say. But as Honks says, we shall know at once if it's the old boy – they can't pull the wool over our heads with him.

There's really no news – here I am working away & seeing nobody. But thought I'd faire acte de présence so to speak. I suppose you are deep in Dr Bedwetter.[3] (I'm told he's taught all the Americans to do so & that's why nobody can have them to stay. Correct?)

Much love, Soo

1 Bertram Mitford, 1st Baron Redesdale (1837–1916). A great admirer of Wagner and a regular visitor to the Bayreuth Festival which was run, in the early part of the twentieth century, by Siegfried Wagner, the composer's son.
2 Rosamond Lehmann (1901–90). In her autobiography, *The Swan in the Evening* (1967), the novelist described the sudden death of her adored daughter, Sally, and her attempts to communicate with her in the spirit world.
3 In *Dr Spock's Baby and Childcare*, Benjamin Spock had addressed the problem of bed-wetting.

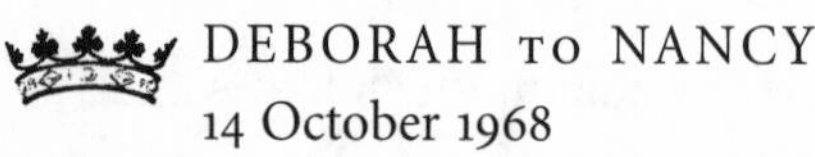

DEBORAH TO NANCY
14 October 1968

Chatsworth
Bakewell

Get on

LOOK – stamps pristine, you can use them again & thereby diddle the Frogs of several frongs. Prague Nov 4th.[1] Remember remember the 5th of November – I hope you won't get blown up in *my* coat, think of stitching it & you together again, *quelle horrible surprise.*

My hair was cut in London by what I thought was a faithful hairdresser. I was writing to you & Honks & Woman & not watching him & lo & behold I am an active Lesbian, Irma Grese,[2] a prison wardress, a Great Dane breeder, anything but an ordinary English woman. I suppose he did it to force me to buy a wig. I hope it will grow by Friday when Honks & Jean [de Baglion] loom.

I must write to my old Hen so will close.

Much love, 9

1 Nancy was planning a visit to Czechoslovakia to research *Frederick the Great.*
2 Irma Grese (1923–45). Notorious camp guard at Auschwitz and Belsen.

DIANA TO DEBORAH
23 October 1968

Moscow Road
London w2

Darling Debo:

I hope you didn't see *Panorama*[1] with a lot of semi-strangers, it was so dreadfully *sad.* Al [Mosley] said it was like a Western where the hero walks away into the sunset & the girl suddenly runs after him calling 'Come back!' but it's too late. *However,* Kit was very pleased with it & to have been given the chance to say many things he longed to say, & he got telegrams & telephone messages of congrat, & the book seems to be selling, so all is exceedingly well. Just that for anyone fond of him one wouldn't wish to watch among rather hostile strangers. The boys were delighted with it, they rushed round to the Ritz at once & we all talked about it, & then they brought me here & we talked with Wife. Jerry [Lehane]'s verdict: 'Twas *great,* but a touch sad.' (Say that in his voice & the tears will well.)

All love darling, Honks

1 Mosley had appeared on the BBC programme, interviewed by James Mossman, to coincide with the publication of his autobiography.

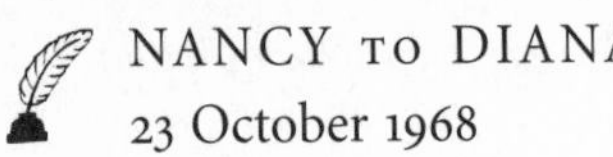

NANCY TO DIANA

23 October 1968

4 rue d'Artois
Versailles

Dereling,

Oh *keep* the reviews. I only saw Coote[1] which is what I call a good selling review viz. *longing* to be nasty but obliged to admit the merit. How was *Panorama*? When do you get back.

Col says Gen said two years ago when he saw Widow Kennedy (whom he had rather fancied) 'Au fond c'est une vedette – tout ça finira en un mariage dans un yacht de milliardaire'.[2]

Bugger I must go. I'll write again.

Love, N

1 Colin Coote (1893–1979). The former editor of the *Daily Telegraph* described *My Life* as 'the best-written volume of memoirs emanating from my generation', but said that his feelings towards Mosley, 'after admiration waned, have always been pity, possibly; and regret, certainly. Pity, because . . . so potentially great a man should have so distressingly ill led; and regret to see so many wasted talents.' *Sunday Telegraph*, 20 October 1968.

2 'Basically she's a star – it will all end in marriage on a millionaire's yacht.' Jacqueline Kennedy married Aristotle Onassis, the Greek shipowner, on 20 October; their wedding reception was held on the *Christina O*, Onassis's super-yacht.

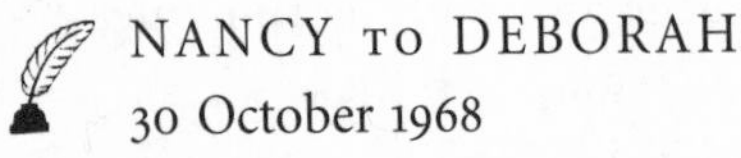

NANCY TO DEBORAH

30 October 1968

4 rue d'Artois
Versailles

Dear Miss

I went to Paris & saw the Mosleys & all is as before I read the book. The fact is they are two different people now, of course they don't realize it themselves. Very odd, because generally people hardly change at all in life. I still feel angry about Tom but nevair.[1] I wish Randolph [Churchill] was here to defend him – I wonder what Nigel [Birch], Garrett[2] & co think. There seems to have been a chorus of praise for the book & I hope it will sell but, even if not, the chorus has been gratifying.

I say *Miss* oh *Miss* do sell those 830 insects. Honks believes it is they & they alone who are driving you to the bin – where I suppose you will arrive in a padded horsebox. Be a good soul & *take the step* for everybody's sake I beg I beg. Surely you've had the insects by now? Also please have a month's holiday – while you are away the sale can take place you'd hardly know anything about it & then think how reech you will be. Reech & healthy & wise.

Love, N

1 Nancy objected to Mosley having written in his memoirs that Tom Mitford had been a paid-up member of the British Union of Fascists. *My Life*, p. 409.
2 11th Earl of Drogheda (1910–90). Chairman of Royal Opera House 1958–74.

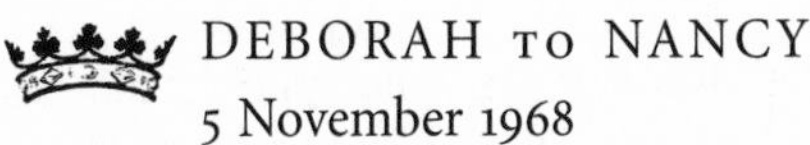

DEBORAH TO NANCY *4 Chesterfield Street, W1*
5 November 1968

Get on

I wonder where you are, did you go to Prague, wasn't it yesterday, oh I hate writing into the blue (or red).

It is v. nice of you to be concerned re me. The thing is I really prefer having slightly too much to do. The things I don't like doing (like platforms) make the things I do like doing far better by contrast. What is exhausting is wondering various things which I can't v. well write but could enlarge on when we meet & otherwise I like all the things I do except being reminded about rows between one & another, whether it is people in the house, or keeper v. forester v. farmer, or me v. the planning officer, or me ½ v. the agent about the shape of windows in a new house. But I suppose *on the whole* things go v. smoothly in that way & one of these days I'll tell you re the really tiring part.[1]

Now lady, among all that *the insects are therapy.* Most comforting, stout, staunch & square. Do say you see. And filling in pedigrees is therapy to the last, & looking up in stud books, it is relaxation like o else I swear. Sorry to go on re myself but as you kindly showed an interest I can only tell the answer.

People changing, Honks & Sir O & the book. I think people can change completely. As one can only tell exactly from one's own pathetic experience, I know it to be a fact. People didn't invent the word MELLOWING for nothing, All Passion Spent, Lady, that's what. When one is young & clever & energetic & always thinks one is right *nothing* can stand in the way (Sir Oz). When one is in love with someone one thinks is right & has been wronged or spurned or whatever you like – ditto (Honks). I absolutely know for instance that I am not the same person I was 15 or 20 years ago when I couldn't ever do anything except be in love, *such a bore* as Brando would say. Think even how one's taste changes, how one liked *completely* different houses furniture pictures colours, everything really when one was 20. Don't say you always liked the same, perhaps you did, then you must be (a) an unusually strong character & (b) impervious to noting things as time goes by.

So I'm sure both Honks & Sir O have changed enormously, & perhaps 3½ years in prison had more effect than one allows for – I wot not. That's my idea anyway.

Shall I ever see you more?

Much love, 9

You see we're all Saints now & we certainly weren't. It's quite easy to be a Saint when one's old I note.

1 Andrew Devonshire was battling with alcoholism.

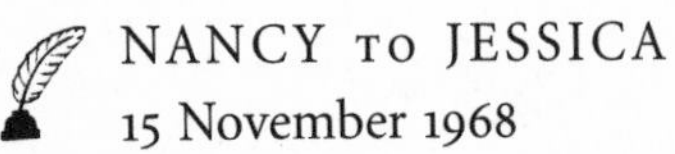

NANCY TO JESSICA
15 November 1968

4 rue d'Artois
Versailles

Darling Sooze

Prague fascinated me. It is too beautiful for words to describe & the Fr embassy, where I stayed, one of the prettiest houses I ever saw. I was shown everything of interest by a Prof. told off to lug me round. But oh dear it is sad. Russians everywhere, gazing into the shop windows – which are about on a level with Moreton in Marsh during the first war – as if they were in the rue de la Paix. Poor things, they are very small, very young & look as if they had never had a proper meal in their lives. Nobody can speak to them & my Prof, who is a Cuddum, says their officers tell them that the Czechs are lazy dogs who have been subsidized by USSR for 20 years 'Everything here belongs to you really'.

I'm exhausted, having had a young lady from *Sunday Ex*[1] for 3 solid hours interviewing me & I'm also nervous as I can't remember what I said. Interviews are the devil. I only accepted because I want to broadcast that I'm on *Frederick*, hoping to deter others. If it's funny I'll send but I expect it will only be shaming. She was an awfully nice young lady but unconscious I guess of what might embarrass ONE. The great thing they always ask is why do you live in France? You'd think they would see why, for themselves. She's pregnant. I said is it your first baby? And she said the first successful one. I longed to probe but am too polite!

Have you noted all the carry-on about Sir Oz? He says he was never anti-Semitic. Good Gracious! I quite love the old soul now but really – ! Also I'm very cross with him for saying Tud was a fascist which is untrue though of course Tud was a fearful old twister & probably was a fascist when with Diana. When with me he used to mock to any extent & he hated Sir Oz no doubt about that. If Randolph had been alive he would have sprung to his defence. I miss Randolph.

That's all for now – to work.

Much love, Soo

1 Nancy was interviewed by Jillian Page for the *Sunday Express*, 24 November 1968.

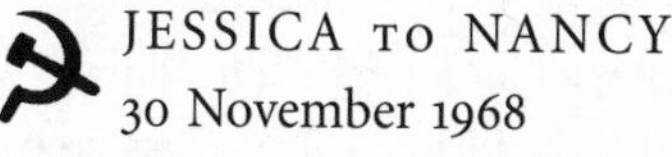

JESSICA to NANCY
30 November 1968

6411 Regent Street
Oakland

Darling Susan,

Well I noted the interview – someone sent it. Made me shriek in spots (je suis communiste – I *bet* I never said that),[1] and I also noted a slight Generation Gap between you & the interviewer? I can see you muddled her up fair.

The Sir O. hoop-la has made nary a ripple out here, but someone sent me C. Cockburn's[2] review of his book – not exactly what you'd call a *selling review*. Do tell about the book.

Tud was a pure Cuddum when he used to come to see us at Rotherhithe St. Esmond adored him. (The only one of our family he did.) And don't you remember how he used to say Diana was silly and so on? But of course he adored the Boud, in some ways I always thought she was his Favourite Sister.

Well Susan a lot of people are coming to dinner so I'd better start cooking it. Goodbye for the present.

Much love, Susan

1 Nancy had described how at a Parisian lunch party before the war Jessica, aged seventeen, when asked which party she supported had declared that she was a communist.
2 Claud Cockburn (1904–81). The author, journalist and editor of the communist newspaper, *The Week*, 1933–46, described *My Life* as 'almost unbearably tedious' and 'depressing'. *Sunday Times*, 20 October 1968.

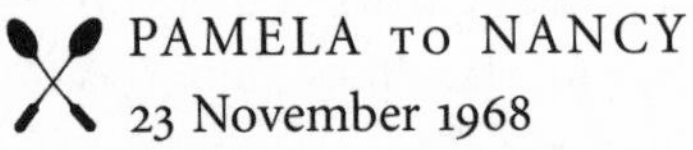

PAMELA to NANCY
23 November 1968

im Bühl
8627 Grüningen

Dereleeng

Would it be a good idea to go to you & Nard for Christmas, or would you really rather I went later on in January? I always slightly dread journeying around that time as it's just when the snow comes but of course if it looks bad I will just take a train.

Please no presents. I will arrive – if by car – laden with household goods for your store cupboard. I have bought two 5-kilo drums of soap powder for the laundry machine, they cost 20 Frs each drum, but I got them cheaper, 16.40 each. Then I could get a first-class soap powder for the washing-up machine called Dish Wasch but I have no idea if this can be had in large quantities. Bird seed & maize, of course, & would you like some packets of envelopes? They are the same as this one & are 90 rappen for 100! Just ask Marie if she wants things like floor clothes [*sic*] – which always wear out – & loo paper, the very soft, 90 rappen for two rolls. And ask your daily how many kilos of soap powder she wants.

Much love from Woman

JESSICA TO DEBORAH
30 November 1968

6411 Regent Street
Oakland

Dearest Hen,

Pity about those Conservatives, if I'd known it was for them I should have ordered up something v. different,[1] such as one of those wartime receipts I found at the Isle that say 'Soak several biscuits in water overnight, squeeze out, spread thinly with jam and bake.'

Benj went to dinner at S. Head's[2] the other night. 'What did you have?' 'The first course was cold toast, the next course was soup, and at midnight we had salmon.'

Well Hen come to think of it there are masses of people coming to dinner here, so I'd better start the cold toast, goodbye for present,

Yr loving Hen

1 Jessica had sent Deborah a recipe for fig pudding.
2 Simon Head (1944–). Writer, journalist and author of *The New Ruthless Economy* (2003).

DIANA TO DEBORAH
3 January 1969

Temple de la Gloire
Orsay

Darling Debo:

It's Tom's birthday & he would be 60 which seems completely incredible. When I thought about it I couldn't help crying. Not only do I long for him to be alive for himself but also selfishly for *me*. Kit is such a strange person when it comes to his sons & I know Tom would have been someone he would have listened to. One hasn't got a single male person to rely upon as a result of all these vile wars, so the ones who are left just do as they please which is often highly dire, eh. I have got so much to tell you that I must see you before we are much older.

All love, Honks

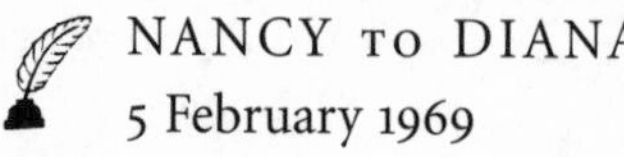

NANCY TO DIANA
5 February 1969

4 rue d'Artois
Versailles

Dereling,

I couldn't go to Mémé, I was terrassée [knocked out] with frantic pain in the leg & poached egg eye & fearful tummy upset + headache so I must be breaking up I think. This morning the leg is better, the tummy, now quite empty, is quiet, the eye must be seen to be believed & the head aches but less. But I can't go up I feel awful. What *can* it be? Come on Doctor, I had only eaten roast rec the day before so it can't be poison. I did crawl to the street to try & go but I couldn't, I feel awfully guilty. I had to put off Geoffrey too. No fever.

John [Sutro] telephoned. He had rung up the hospital & they said 'as well as possible'.[1] I suppose they always say that. Gillian [Sutro]'s brother died of it.

Love, N

1 Mark Ogilvie-Grant was in London dying of cancer of the oesophagus.

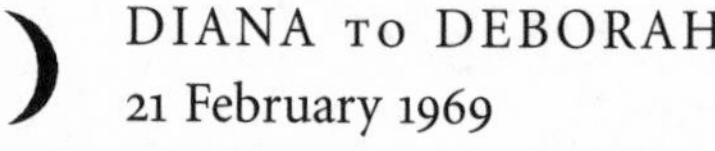

DIANA TO DEBORAH
21 February 1969

5 rue Villedo, I

Darling Debo:

I went down to Versailles yesterday & stayed three hours, & poor Naunce had had a truly dreadful morning in pain, unable to read let alone write. While I was there of course we laughed & she cheered up completely & said the pain almost went away, & she even looked different. One of the things that kills one is that she's got nobody to sort of take the Dr for example in hand, when one's ill one has no energy even to telephone. Anyway she seemed relieved when I said I would, or rather when I tentatively suggested I might, & agreed quickly. I've just got him on the telephone & he says she can take up to five aspirins a day as well as the Veophan – she didn't dare take even *one*, there's Muv for you! I do hope she will, & I think she certainly will because pain soon shows one the way.

The fact is I couldn't have been away at a worse moment with this horrible sciatica, & then Mark. She says she's had as many letters as a widow would. She dies to get her letters to him back, she says his Greek friends & Eddie G-H[1] would send them but she fears this sister (she thought all his sisters had conked) & says she sounds a real burner of letters because of 'no flowers' & so on. Poorling Naunce I felt so sad at the beginning yesterday but of course she's got terrific courage & how marvellous it is the way everything amuses her. Luckily I'd got 17 days' worth of happenings to relate. She said she could understand Dolly [Radziwill] wanting to die to be out of pain.

The next excitement is Wife's visit, Naunce is almost as excited as I am for it. Don't let her resolve weaken will you.

All love darling, Honks

1 Edward Gathorne-Hardy (1901–78). Authority on eighteenth-century antiquarian books and a keen amateur botanist.

NANCY TO DEBORAH
17 March 1969

4 rue d'Artois
Versailles

Dear Miss

I'm being *such a bore* to everybody & eating chunks of Honks's life. If I were Sir Oz I wld be fed up. I've got hardly any pain now & wld see myself nearly out of the wood exc. that a large lump has loomed in the region of my liver & lights which I suppose must be seen to. Sir O very naturally wants to ship me off to London (to have a bit more of Honks's attention) but I say no thanks, look what happened to Mark. At present lumpling doesn't seem dangerous but the London drs would soon stir it up I guess.

Much love, N

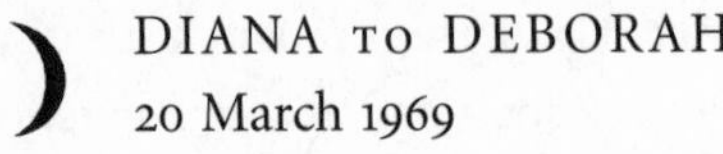

DIANA to DEBORAH
20 March 1969

Temple de la Gloire
Orsay

Darling Debo:

Wife's visit was marvellous & I *love* her sister.[1] Of course Wife & I both collapsed towards the end but Elizabeth was game to the last. I miss them dreadfully, needless to say. We lunched with the Count [de Baglion] on their last day so Elizabeth saw four queer dwellings (counting Ferays[2] as two). Is this worth putting in Guinness book of records?

Jean won't let us near his dungeon[3] when we do our tour next month. It's only because the covers aren't made for the chairs. But one can't talk him into it bother him.

All love darling, Honks

P.S. Just spoken to Naunce & Col has told her he's going to marry Violette[4] & she (Naunce) really doesn't *seem* to mind in the least. As I knew this was looming (or thought I knew) it was one of the things I most dreaded, but it has come so late in the day (Col is almost seventy) that she has got over the annoyance years ago, evidently, & now just thinks it rather a bore for *him* & also (which is true) rather silly to give up one's freedom. Well darling it is a huge relief she's taken it like this. How strange life is.

1 Lady Elizabeth Fitzmaurice (1927–). Married Major Charles Lambton in 1950.
2 The brothers Jean and Thierry Feray.
3 Jean de Baglion's house in the country was called 'Le Donjon'.
4 Violette de Talleyrand-Périgord had been Nancy's rival for Palewski's affections for many years.

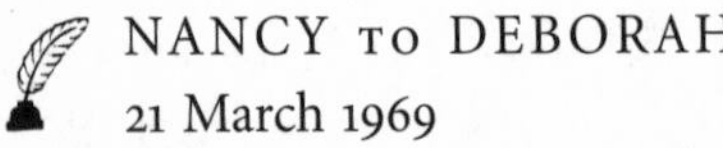

NANCY to DEBORAH
21 March 1969

4 rue d'Artois
Versailles

Dear Miss

I've been *felled* by disappointment. Did you read about a 1933 penny fetching thousands? Well you know how I've never spent a penny since you once told me their immense value, so reading about the 1933 one I rushed to huge heavy bagling where I keep them – was not at all surprised but highly gratified soon to see the magic figures on a particularly fresh new penny. So I was dialling Honks when I noted that it was a ½ d. DON'T! ADMIT! EET EES.

Well the tortoise. Marie & Mme Guimont[1] (10/- an hour) dug her out of her igloo in MY time, *destroyed the igloo* scientifically designed by Y[ours] T[ruly] & woke her up by putting her in the warm kitchen. I was *really* good & controlled my feelings but explained to M that she must put a box full of hay on its side in the garden so that the tortoise can go in & out as she likes. That worked very well & she went to sleep again. Then, when we had 4 degrees of frost, the cats fought over the box, the hay was all over the place & the tortoise had vanished. I thought she must be dead & made such a fuss that the ladies said 'after all a tortoise is not a baby'. However as soon as the sun came out again there she was galloping down the path. So I've chucked it & left her out now. She is evidently rather tougher than I thought.

My progress continues though I rather dread next week's tests. Naivair. I am most exceedingly feeble. Well, 3 weeks motionless!

Kay Clark's effort is printed every week.[2] Utterly brilliant. I don't know when one can hear it. It'll surely be a book.

The East German Govt considers me & Wooms as their guests. Good egg. Oh how I pray I shall be all right.

A letter from Monty: 'I give Frederick full marks (for the Thirty Years War)'.[3] The dear soul says he's not very well: 'father & mother of a cold'. Shades of Farve!

Yrs to hand. When I see you appearing I shall *know* that I've had it so pray keep away – though I rather long for those wildly swivelling blue eyes I must confess.

Oh dear this letter is TOO LONG.

Love

1 Nancy's cleaner.

2 Kenneth Clark's thirteen-part television series, *Civilisation*, was being serialized in *The Listener*.

3 Field Marshal Montgomery had confused the Thirty Years War (1618–48) with the Seven Years War (1756–63), which was won by Prussia and England, largely thanks to Frederick the Great's military skills.

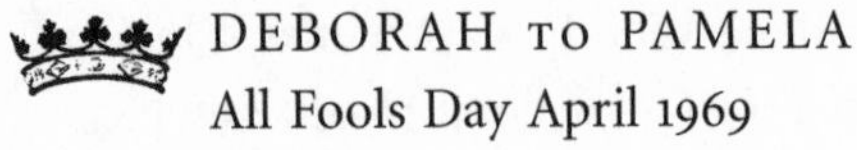

DEBORAH TO PAMELA
All Fools Day April 1969

Chatsworth
Bakewell

Darling Woman

I am so sorry about the thief & your things, what a foul thing to happen. Honks tells me you have successfully wormed £400 out of poor Mr Budd for them, you must rush to Patou with it.

As for Nancy, she is the all-time worry isn't she. The result of the tests has come through but she has not yet heard of the reaction of the specialist to them. There is something there, in her stomach, but *what* they don't know, as liver & kidney are quite OK. I dread them opening up to see, better leave it if it isn't annoying her, or do you think it could be what is causing the pain, I do wonder. Anyway it is all beastly, & she sounds very brave but low, at the same time, and no wonder.

Then, to crown everything, that wretched Colonel has had to choose that week to get married to that person he has been more or less with for ages. One simply does not know how much she minds, as she is such a private person & so desperately reserved one perhaps never will know. It must be miserable for her. I believe you are going to see her soon, that's *very* good, and I am going for the weekend of 25th April, for chatting.

We are in turmoil here as the house opens tomorrow & they have *just* finished putting a steel rod to support the main landing on top of the stairs where crowds congregate & it might have collapsed, imagine how *awful* if that had happened.

Do ring up from Nancy's, I long to hear the latest.

Much love, Stublow

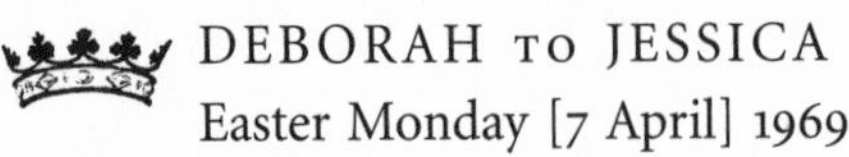

DEBORAH TO JESSICA
Easter Monday [7 April] 1969

Chatsworth
Bakewell

Dearest Hen

Nancy – Well, she has got a slipped disc AND a lump in her stomach. The slipped disc dr says he can't & won't do anything re his kind of cure till a Big Lump Man has seen the B.L. So, on Good Friday the B.L. man loomed. Luckily she re-fell in love (having already fallen for the Disc Man). He looked at Everything and was mystified because the tests of last week showed the blood to be in v. good order and he says she *looks* so well that he can't understand what it can be. She insists it's her twin & calls it Lord Redesdale. She pictures it small, grey haired, in a beret & a *very* good cook. She told the specialist all this so he must fear for her sanity, eh.

Anyway in spite of all this AND that Col marrying she sounds v. cheerful on the phone. Honks says she gets very low, well who wouldn't, but the minute she – Honks – goes, screaming with laughter sets in. It's a question of 'Silly this morning aren't we miss?' like the shop assistant said in Elliston & Cavell 1,000 years ago.

Well Hen, keep in etc. We are deep in the Hols here, horses horses all the way with Sophy.

Much love, Yr Hen

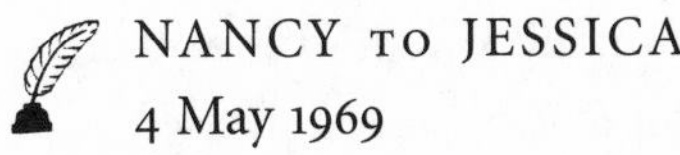

NANCY TO JESSICA
4 May 1969

Clinique rue Georges Bizet
Home on Tuesday

Darling Soo

I was deeply gratified to hear that you phoned (on your own phone) all the way from California for news of me. I call it faithful in the extreme.

I'm very well. They sawed me in half like a martyr & sewed me together again with raffia & the ghastly pain in my back has gone for good.

This is such a heavenly place. Except for two rather nasty days I've had a blissful time here – rivers of uninterrupted chat with yr Hen & your other sister – v. rare as far as Hen is concerned. Looked after by a nun we are all in love with – huge sunny room, marvellous food. In spite of the sawing I felt o unless I laughed which was agony non pareil. Even Muv wld have had to admit they've been marvellous with me.

That's all. When do you come.

Much love, Soo

DIANA TO DEBORAH
10 May 1969 Muv's birthday

Temple de la Gloire
Orsay

Darling Debo:

Thank you darling for letter, & Decca, & much phoning. Dr Dumas has got the analysis at last & of course it *is* cancer, but he repeats, not *necessarily* going at all quickly. He says they were obliged to leave a good deal behind though they did remove some of the liver. He says she ought to have ray treatment. Here is the frightful dilemma – he wd like her to go to Curie Foundation, but naturally the name of Curie *may* tell her everything in a flash.

After long discussion this is what we decided: I am to telephone Dr Dubrugeaud (the Versailles stomach specialist) & ask him if he knows of a good radiotherapy person in Versailles. I dread constant journeys to Paris for her, when sometimes I might not be able to take her. If he does know one Dr Dumas says we should tell her that as she still has some pain in the spine she must have heat treatment. I think that sounds plausible don't you.

Oh Debo yesterday one sort of died of it all, I went over & there they were, she & Woo, she had been to coiffeur & was so pleased with clean hair but had really suffered there, & she was so brave & really looked so ill in the bright sun, yet interested in everything & laughing over Woman's 1926 diary etc. I came away done for, it is so completely sad & frightful & I can't bear pain for her. *Poorling* Naunce the unfairness of it all is too much.

All love, Honks

Wooms is being so truly wondair. I will go over every other day.

DIANA TO DEBORAH
10 May 1969

Temple de la Gloire
Orsay

Darling Debo:

I've sent a letter, but this can go tomorrow. I forgot to say *of course* (but you knew it) I would be friends with Decca, naturally. Poor Decca I can so imagine how she's feeling, so far off. I think June wd be better than Sept in every way, if she can manage it, because of Naunce's book. Now I've had an awful idea. Do you think Naunce might blame us terribly for keeping her in the dark if finally she can't finish her book? Do you think she might say if only she'd known she wd have (perhaps) given up Venice in order to finish it? I know she thinks it will be her best. There was a huge article in a German mag about Fred the Great & she asked me to translate it & I forced myself to do it & she rang up to say how much she was interested & how she looked forward to demolishing the silly man who wrote it (she LOVES Fred & can't bear him to be denigrated). On the other hand it obviously is intensely frightening & preoccupying to know one's got such an illness. What do you think?

Kit says radiotherapy is something they do do for rheumatism etc so that will be easily explained.

All love darling, Honks

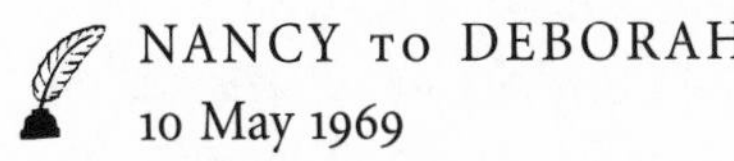

NANCY TO DEBORAH
10 May 1969

4 rue d'Artois
Versailles

Dear Miss

A *slight* blow has fallen – yr Hen so very very kindly suggests coming when Woman goes. I can't possibly say no & in many ways I shall love to see her but I had counted on a good month of hard work before Venice. I'm desperately behind, you see. Also it means divorce from Honks. Also I can't help wondering for how long? If she comes on purpose, as she almost says she will, it won't be only for a few days. All these thoughts go round in my head, I can't impart to any but you. It's the work that worries me – I'm incapable of it with somebody there, I truly can't. Oh dear oh dear. Nevair.

Woman is so perfect. When from time to time I wish to cry (it's always over something quite silly) she puts the thing right in a minute. She took me to the dresser – I nearly died but goodness I feel better. All that grey hair (yes Miss please note) so depressing.

Last night Marie & I but not Woman were woken up by terrific screams in the garden, *not* a cat. It must be the hedge pigs worshipping each other – can't think of anything else. Marie thought in her chaste & virginal way that they were murdering the tortoises – couldn't make out if it was supposed to be the tortys screaming or the murdering pigs. Tortys pristine this morning – hand in glove.

I've ordered a chair like mine for Honks as a slight reward for all her g & l kindness for months. She talked of getting one but I can see she won't.

I've started properly sleeping again at last – thought I'd lost the art. It was the only disagreeable thing that I never truly slept well. (Inter)

Much love, N

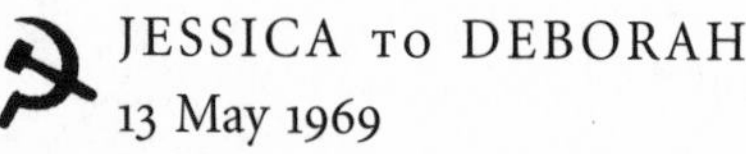

JESSICA TO DEBORAH
13 May 1969

6411 Regent Street
Oakland

Dearest Hen,

Oh dear things are getting *madly* out of hand, plan-wise. Got yours of 9 May today and *three* from Nancy which more or less go as follows: 9 May, she says do come any time before end of June. 10 May, she fears it will be so dull for me because she simply must get back to work. 11 May, she says *don't* come, because Marie is too tired & there's no point in offering to help as she won't allow.

These crossed mine to her, saying I'm arriving on 20 May & should like to put up in a hotel in Versailles. *Alas*, Hen, so by now she'll have got that and I'll have fussed her up no end.

Behind it all, she prob. thinks that what a bore having to work out the oubliettes for me & Honks, or some such. On the other hand if Honks & I turned up at same time & all was OK, & normal, it would seem like Mrs Ham's dreamed-of death-bed scene, don't you agree? But if I cld. stay in a hotel (& scram there quite a lot) this cld. be avoided.

I rang up Bob at work, & read out all the letters, to see what he thought shld. be done. Apart from saying with some acerbity 'your family is v. difficult to fathom', he thought I shld. go anyway. So, am. The pt. being, that we've already put off our trip to the South etc., and I've put in train massive arrangements in NY, or made Dinky do so; but mainly, I do awfully want to see Nancy.

Later. HEN! You just rang up, so this is an ongoing conversation.

I couldn't quite make out all you said re the medical facts except that it's obviously very bad; yet somehow, in back of mind, I always thought it would be in spite of all the seeming improvement that you and she told of in letters. So all I want to do is a) come, b) do anything possible to help, c) not be in any way a bother – and I can see from N's letters that this will be the most difficult of all. And in this regard, Hen, I do implore you to make clear to Honks how I long to avoid all friction etc etc, as I think I did say in another letter.

One thing has puzzled me a good deal: why have you so firmly decided *not* to tell her anything at all about what's wrong with her? That is, I can quite see one would have to exercise a good deal of judgement about that (no point in giving gloomy reports right after the operation when a person is at lowest ebb, etc) but I must say I think I should far *prefer* to know, for masses of reasons. Which would range all the way from the thing you said about her book (wanting to get all done possible on it) to the horrid disappointment of getting iller & iller without knowing why.

Oh Hen. It's all so very sad & bad and unbelievable, such a nightmare & those drs. sound so awful, never getting in touch with you for all that time.

Am so longing to see you, Yr Hen

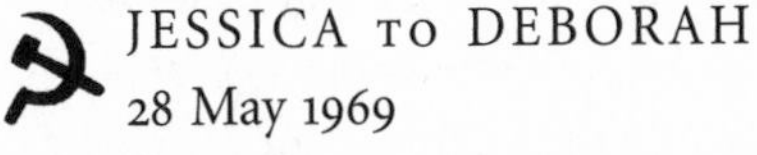

JESSICA TO DEBORAH
28 May 1969

4 rue d'Artois
Versailles

Dearest Hen,

N. continues to improve just exactly like any ordinary convalescence; still has a bit of pain in morning, but not bad at all, she says, the last few days. Otherwise beginning to look and *be* utterly her old self.

Tomorrow, my friend from Dallas called Frances Mossiker[1] comes; she's going to pick me up here, tour the chateau, we'll have lunch in the town & come back to tea. While Nancy *says* she's a great fan of Mossiker's books (she wrote a v. smashing one called *The Queen's Necklace*, another of the letters of Buonaparte & Josephine) I can see she's actually planning to loathe her. 'Sounds awfully bossy on the telephone. Let's see: if *she* died and *Bob* died and you married her husband, you'd be called Jessica Mossiker' etc. (You can see she's getting *much* better, Hen.) So I'm longing to see how these two lady Fr historians hit it off. Fri, I'm going to Paris & the Col. lunches here. Hen I was allowed to get the things for tomorrow's lunch *and* the Col's lunch *today*! There was a bit of groaning about how they'd have gone bad by lunch time, but do admit a bit of lamb, put in fridge, should last 24 hours?

Diana left as planned this A.M. Nancy v. put out: 'Fancy you *leaving*, when I'm ill'. Oh she is a rum one.

Yr loving Hen

1 Frances Mossiker (1906–85). Author whose *The Affair of the Poisons, Louis XIV, Madame de Montespan and One of History's Great Unsolved Mysteries* was first published in 1969.

DIANA TO DEBORAH

5 June 1969

Temple de la Gloire
Orsay

Darling Debo:

All continues gloomy here, Decca will have told you what the doctor said. Naunce hates the idea of more & more pain killers, & naturally the reason she hates them is because they destroy one's intelligence & even one's personality; the question (I begin to wonder) is whether, if she knew the truth, one couldn't spare her a lot of pain, because then she (possibly) wouldn't hesitate to take whatever was offered? It is all so difficult & ghastly. Decca thinks she ought to be told, the doctors all agree that she mustn't be, & I just don't know. Sometimes I feel it would be the end, if she were told, because she would just give up.

Jean & I went yesterday for Decca's departure & stayed till nearly lunch time, she had an awful pain & I got her to take her drug & it went away while we were there. I've got to lunch in Paris today so I shall go to Naunce fairly early & again in afternoon & I shall offer Jean for the middle of the day *if* she'd rather not be alone.

You just telephoned. It is such a comfort to have a chat. Kit is *very* kind but it's not you.

All love, Honks

NANCY TO DEBORAH
10 June 1969

4 rue d'Artois
Versailles

Dear Miss

I am very dopey but everybody tells me I am better. Perhaps.

Sitting in the garden I was startled by clash of steel, you never heard such a noise. Well: it was the torties making love. They charge head on at full gallop about 4 or 5 times & then horrors, Stublow, they turn tail & DO ALL, coming so far out of their shells you'd think they'd never get back. It went on for about ½ an hour. Neither Woo nor Dec here to see – what waste – & old Marie frankly shocked. Now they are about as far apart as they can be, I do hope that's not it for the summer.

Mogens [Tvede] wishes to marry Woman. I said to Marie the trouble is his flat is too small so M says he must buy another. He must. He saw at a glance she is the PICK of the Bunch, clever old Dane.

My garden is dazzling, would you could see it. Roses & daisies, & a huge bush of wild roses, my favourite flower, is performing.

Oh Miss the departure of Marie.[1] Nevair.

Much love, N

1 Nancy's cook was retiring after twenty-two years.

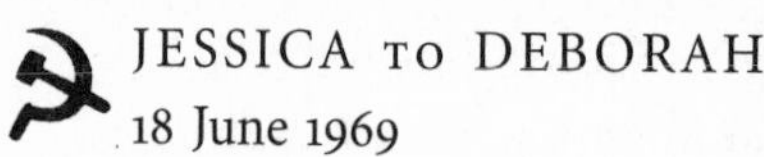

JESSICA TO DEBORAH

18 June 1969

6411 Regent Street
Oakland

Dearest Hen,

I'm amazed, and profoundly gratified, that my visit there seems to have met with such favour. Because do you see how one was on a slight tightrope – between going up to her room too much, with the attendant danger of either tiring her or boring her (or both, as judges always say – $5,000 fine, 2 years in jail *or both*), and not going up enough, danger of seeming to neglect? As for me, I can't say how glad I am that I went, & really it is thanks to you that I did, because I couldn't have, after her letter, if you hadn't smoothed the way.

I adored being there. 'What did you do in Europe?' people ask. 'Shopping, weeding and chatting.' I miss it all v. much.

I got a marvellously dotty letter from Woman all about how she couldn't come on June 4 because the weather was too cold to leave her door open, so the dogs couldn't get out, & she had to be there to let them out.

Much love, & from Bob, Decca

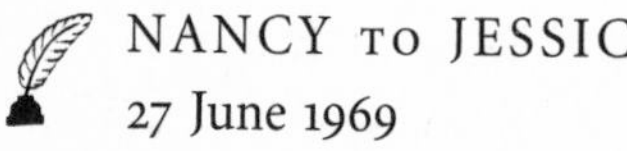

NANCY TO JESSICA

27 June 1969

4 rue d'Artois
Versailles

Darling Sooze

I go on improving – it's wonderful you would hardly know me.

I'm missing Marie more terribly than words can say. The New is so nice, so efficient & a bore. Not one scrap of sense of humour. I have to hear by the hour how poor old Marie, whom I physically crave, hadn't got a single reserve of food in the house. The frigidaire I note is crammed with ghastly old bits of things & the greatest crime in my eyes, she *sprays flies*! Oh Susan those flies, to begin with, suffer horribly & then they go off & get eaten by some bird & it dies! She wants to spray an ant heap I was cherishing but I was in time to stop that. Susan Susan –!

Best love, Susan

P.S. Of course I long to put the Fly Sprayer in a book but never can as it would wound I fear. I'm alone with the F.S., all sisters having buggered.

JESSICA TO DEBORAH
17 July 1969

6411 Regent Street
Oakland

Dearest Hen,

Thanks awfully for yr. v. informative letter of 13 July from Versailles.

I do feel most terrifically strongly, and must stress this point Hen very much, that it is now verging on wicked not to tell Nancy, in view of Dr Evans' report.[1] Because don't you see, it's awful enough to get such news when one is feeling fairly OK & strong; but if it is delivered very late in the thing, when one was completely weak anyway and in much pain, so much harder to bear, *I* should think. Now might be the time. Bob suggested that it be put in terms of new information from Dr Evans, newly discovered, or some such. To me, it seems a sort of awful betrayal not to tell the truth, & I must say it caused me many a horrid moment when there.

Well: I think I said all this before, so no more of it.

Much love, Yr Hen

1 'He says the thing they took out was "highly malignant" . . . and the blood is full of "bunches" of dreadery, so that it is sort of universal and being continually circulated so it might fix itself anywhere in the body at any time OR it might go on like this for some time.' (Deborah to Jessica, 13 July 1969)

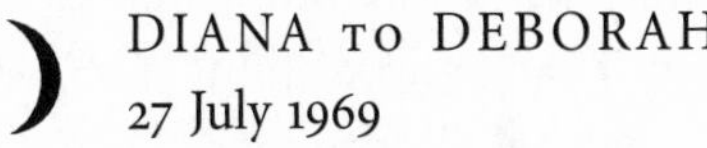

DIANA TO DEBORAH
27 July 1969

Hotel Cipriani
Venice

Darling Debo:

I got your last from Artois, *thank* you darling for writing often, I got such a picture of it all. Can't help feeling optimistic in the extreme! The cancer might take years & years, & if the mysterious pain is better what does the other matter? Or am I just stupid? You never said what Dr Evans thought of the analysis. Decca's letters have got such a horrid undertone, it is all of a piece with her communism, a sort of attitude of 'You won't like this & it will ruin your life & make you miserable but it is right for you to know & therefore it would be immoral of ME not to tell you that, contrary to what you are blind enough to imagine, you are very ill indeed'. Preserve us from such. By the way Col completely agrees with us about not telling her, & Alphy [Clary] is certain it's best not to. Both he & I have had *v* cheerful letters from her.

I had a frightful nightmare, the first for ages, which I connect with Decca's cold letters, they sent a shudder eh. When she's there she is much much better than one would suppose from her writings (letters & books), don't you think so.

All love & to Wife, Honks

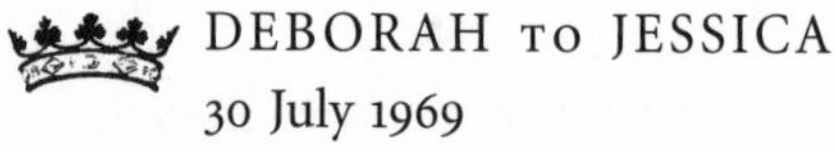

DEBORAH TO JESSICA
30 July 1969

Bignor Park
Pulborough
Sussex

Dearest Hen

Thanks so much for your latest. I note you're still for telling, but I also note you note I'm not. And I'm still not, because of destruction of HOPE, death sentence when not feeling too bad, it seems to me better by far not to have to think about it all the time which is exactly what anyone would do and search for lumps & symptoms, wouldn't one Hen?

I left last week & all seemed well & much work was toward, she read us the first 3 or 4 chapters, it's BRILL, so well written, like a sharp negative, no extra words or woolliness, and very funny quite often. She says 3 months will finish it but it can't appear till 1971 because of the sloth of everything to do with the illustrations.

Honks returns to Temple from Italy tomorrow so she'll have a regular caller again.

Great haste, home on 1 Aug, this is just to thank for yours & to say things are really quite well, very cheerful in Artois Road.

Much love from Yr Hen

DIANA TO DEBORAH
6 August 1969

Temple de la Gloire
Orsay

Darling Debo:

As I told you yesterday Naunce had a wretched day on Monday & asked me to go over yesterday & then she telephoned to say don't come because it had been so bad that she took two stronglings, & would be sure to sleep all the afternoon. So I didn't go, & felt miserable. At 8.30 I telephoned & she answered & was feeling better, but here is the rather ghoul bit. Newling,[1] who knew she was specially bad, had gone out to see her mother off, *in Paris*, & was only expected back late. She had left some soup for Naunce (*water* with a potato floating, she said). Naunce is totally alone now when that happens because Mme Guimont is holidaying & so are the chemists. I suppose really & truly she put me off because she thought she wouldn't hear the bell, if she was sleepy.

I said 'I'm coming straight over now', but Naunce just laughed & said 'Oh no she'll be back soon & I'm quite all right & reading a marvellous book'. Then Kit & I sat down to dinner & the soup was a sort of vichyssoise & I thought of the water & potato & could hardly swallow. And then I thought if Newling, having been told to make almost nothing, did what Emmy would if one was ill & sent in a soupçon more & something we hadn't ordered, & Naunce chanced not to want it, poor old New would be in the doghouse for extravagance. Isn't it *all awful*. The only real answer is Woman.

You know we are going away this weekend, all the pleasure has gone & it is just a mad worry. Kit can't go without me because when we get there I am driver, also he wouldn't go, & he has been looking forward for ages. I am at wits end. Giuditta is on her hol so Woo can't come for a week or so anyhow. I will continue this dreadful letter anon when I've phoned.

Poorling Naunce refuses point blank to see the Dr & says 'what's the use?' Then, as you know, she often has several good days in a row & really likes to be left to work. But of course when the pain is bad I know she must need somebody. I need Kit when I'm ill, just to hold his hand, & she's got *no hand.* When I think of her I can't stop crying.

All love darling, Honks

Naunce says you & I are for fair weather only, & I said no, for foul too, & she says no, only Woo for foul.

1 Nancy's new housekeeper who had replaced Marie.

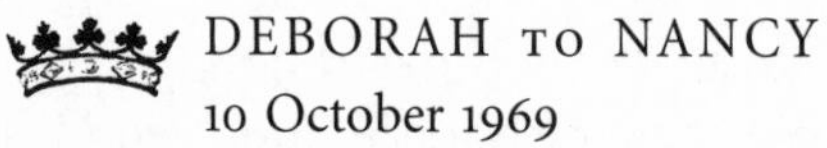

DEBORAH to NANCY
10 October 1969

Chatsworth
Bakewell

Yes, Lady Writer, I am glad that AT LAST you begin to see the point.[1] You've taken a long time about it. I've been staying with Ld Sefton[2] (whom I ADORE) shooting grouse (admit how brave). The Duke of Roxburgh (who is an unpleasant animal dressed as a sort of human) said, re the Arc, 'I don't suppose Andrew said it but I would have said "YOU BUGGER" to Piggott when he got off'. Well, Andrew didn't say it. What a surprise.

The owner of the winner had a father, McGrath senior, who won the Derby not long back. He was summoned to Brenda's[3] box, which is the way of owner of winner of Derby. He said 'this is the second time I have received hospitality from your family'. 'Oh' said the Queen, '& when was the first?' 'When I was in prison madam' came the answer.

Honks tough? Are you mad? The slightest thing sends her into floods, she wakes up screaming when anything goes wrong with any of us, she takes things to heart in the way none of the rest of us can. Oh Lady, admit.

Much love, 9

1 Nancy had written to Deborah to commiserate after Andrew Devonshire's mare Park Top was beaten by ¾ length in the Prix de l'Arc de Triomphe at Longchamp. Her jockey, Lester Piggott, told the racing commentator Peter O'Sullevan that he blamed himself for her defeat.

2 7th Earl of Sefton (1898–1972). Deborah was a frequent guest at Abbeystead, Lord Sefton's Lancashire estate. She wrote of her host, 'He was a curiosity, stranded in the 20th century, sort of touching in ridiculous grandness and *so funny.* People were terrified of him but I happened not to be.' (Deborah in a letter to the editor)

3 *Private Eye*'s nickname for the Queen. After the BBC documentary 'The Royal Family' was shown in June 1969, the satirical magazine gave each member of the family a working-class nickname, as though they were characters out of *Coronation Street*, Britain's longest-running soap opera. Prince Charles was 'Brian', the Duke of Edinburgh, 'Keith', and Princess Margaret, 'Yvonne'.

NANCY TO DEBORAH
31 October 1969

4 rue d'Artois
Versailles

Dear Miss

The journey was a total success,[1] we all adored it & Woman was the heroine. I shall never go away without her again – though I expect you heard there was a nasty moment at Orly when she was bagless.

I can now count myself as cured – you can't imagine what a lot I did, on my pins for hours in the galleries. I don't say it wasn't sometimes v. painful esp. at the end when my back got out again – still, I did it & Mlle pushed the back in when I got home & I've not been so well for nearly a year as I am now. We saw marvels & the wonderful thing was being so much looked after by three jolly policemen. It had its slightly sinister side – we were never left alone for a moment with anybody & an English friend of Decca's who came to see us gave us the creeps he looked so pathetic – in fact I should think he's for committing it. Perhaps I've told you all this though.

Woman's sagas went down like one o'clock. I see that they are like modern art & literature; pointless & plotless, but it is the manner – she ees weeth eet, clevair. She went to see Marie on her way here, so good of her, & found her on top of the world surrounded by friends.

Yes I wish all Commies could be forced behind the curtain. You can't know until you've seen the curious sinistry of it. And that is in spite of the oiling – oil-less it must be fearful.

You say airily that we meet soon. Is England's Darling coming back for some hurdle races?

Josephine says what can she go as to Redé(sdale)'s ball (Oriental) to be different? I said go as Joan Ali Khan that will be *quite* different.[2]

Love from Lady (busy)

1 Nancy had returned from her trip to East Germany.
2 Josephine Loewenstein went to Alexis de Redé's Oriental ball dressed not as Joan Yarde Buller, the Aga Khan's mother, but as an odalisque.

JESSICA to DEBORAH
17 February 1970

BOAC
Flying between London and NY

Dearest Hen,

Oh dear I *didn't* go to Nancy's after all. Was to go today for 2 nights, but she *rang up* (fancy!) this morning at Sonia [Orwell]'s to say that Woman's got a v. bad stiff neck, can really hardly move; & also they are snowed in, so not to come. I'm so sad about it Hen, but what could I do? So changed all plans, & left for America instead. Diana rang up yesterday & we had a long chat about Nancy, but it was all about what I was to look out for etc, so all has come to naught. I am in near floods about it all.

Meanwhile Dinky's baby was born last week, a bouncing 8lb 8oz boy.[1] Hen I was *SO NERVOUS* until I heard, isn't it stupid because *she* wasn't, but you know how it is. Bad dreams about her falling down stairs etc. His name: you'll shriek, a string of names like a royal baby: Chaka (I *think*, couldn't quite make out, after a Zulu hero of last century) Esmond (after you know who) Fanon (of *The Earth*[2] & other works) – P. Toynbee calls him Bongo-Esmond, refusing to remember Chaka. So I'm on my way back to that scene – longing to see all of them, yet bitterly sad not to have seen Nancy. You know: wondering if I ever shall again? Diana said she's *so* thin in spite of eating heartily. Hassan[3] sounds marvellous, he must be terrifically rich to afford all that food, as Woman & I can attest to.

One other good thing: the English publisher is going to re-issue *BOADILLA*[4] with foreword by Hugh Thomas![5] Proceeds to Bongo-Esmond.

Hen, this letter is naught but a wail, so sorry.

Yr loving Hen

1 Constancia's and James Forman's younger son, Chaka, became an actor.
2 Frantz Fanon's anti-colonial classic, *The Wretched of the Earth*, was published in 1961.

3 A young Moroccan who succeeded the unsatisfactory 'Newling' and who was nicknamed 'Beamish' because of his cheerful presence.

4 Esmond Romilly's account of the Spanish Civil War was first published in 1937 when he was eighteen.

5 Hugh Thomas (1931–). Historian, author of *The Spanish Civil War* (1961), whom Nancy had known since he was a student in Paris.

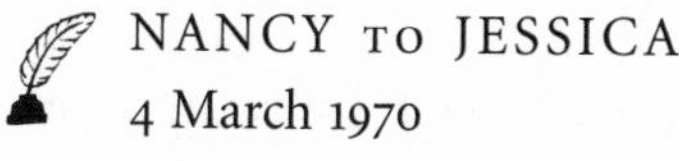

NANCY TO JESSICA
4 March 1970

4 rue d'Artois
Versailles

Darling Sooze

Yes Susan, I am not a Cuddum & I need *much gold* with wh to feed Hassan who eats like a wolf. All I think of now is how to keep what Woman & I call H for Happiness because having once tasted such bliss how shall I ever manage without it? You know, bar chaff, a proper servant properly trained in things like opening the door & a real cordon bleu. There's not a restaurant in Paris, said one of my guests, where you wld get such a meal.

Woman is still here – she has been awfully ill but has come to now. I wish to goodness she would settle in for our old ages but don't like to suggest it. Her company suits me exactly – but people must have their own lives I know, furniture, pictures & so on (worst of all, dogs).

Your publicity has been stunning[1] & must do good & do me good too as I always feel it's a family build-up. My agent saw you on TV & praised the performance.

I can imagine those black babies with huge blue eyes must be irresistible – what Queen Victoria called strong dark blood & longed for it in the Royal Family.

Fondest I mean warmest love, N

1 For *The Trial of Dr Spock*.

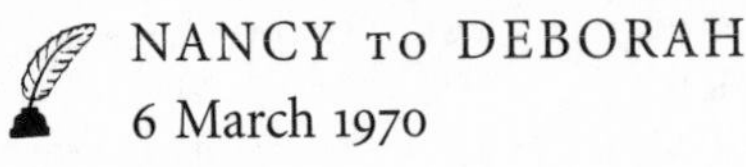

NANCY TO DEBORAH
6 March 1970

4 rue d'Artois
Versailles

Dear Miss

A spate of letters from you from *all over the shop*, viz. several different continents, for which many thanks. I see about the animals, they do sound fascinating though I am quite contented myself with Mrs Tiggy Winkle.

Fancy you looking at *The Water Beetle*. I often think it's the best of a poor lot in spite of the strictures of Marghanita Laski who said it was embarrassingly bad.[1]

Woman was rung up by an old admirer whom she hasn't seen for 35 years. He asked her to lunch – she wrote down the place, Plaza Artemis. When I had put her right[2] she retired to her room & presently: 'Naunceling it's the most expensive restaurant in Paris'*. So she is flinging her bonnet over the windmill & planning to take a taxi from the Gare St Lazare. Now the question arises, how will they know each other? She can only remember that he is very tall. She had her hair done yesterday & looks smashing again from having looked very ill for an age. One can see the eyes from the other end of the passage.

Best love, N

*Naturally she's got a book of European restaurants.

1 Laski had panned *The Water Beetle*: 'Despite some illustrations on nice grey paper by Mr Osbert Lancaster, this collection of mostly reprinted trivia hardly adds up to more than a non-book.' *Observer*, 21 October 1962.
2 Pamela meant the Plaza Athenée.

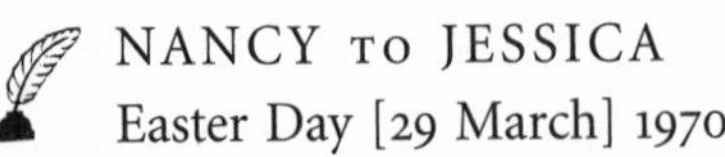

NANCY TO JESSICA
Easter Day [29 March] 1970

4 rue d'Artois
Versailles

Darling Soo

Exchange between your two wicked sisters.

N: 'Do you think that, as an English lady, it's my duty to teach Hassan to read & write?'

Honks: 'Like little Eva? Do be careful or he will escape over the ice-floe.'

Perhaps I needn't. He will never be Président du Sénat, he's just a nice cheerful extrovert. Loves the télé. I suppose very soon nobody will read or write, they'll just love the télé. So I needn't be Miss Eva.

Is it Pryce-Jones[1] who has taken your house? He's coming to interview me. Do describe.

There's a marvellous book I'm plunged in about Dickens. He thought all crime was caused by unhappy childhood, just like we think it is caused by happy childhood. It *is* rather odd that the richer & happier people are the worse are their crimes. So we have to come back to Satan I suppose.

I've just had self-cooked lunch (Hassan is on his weekly ice-floe). Scrambled eggs with a strong taste of marmalade smiling through (couldn't be bothered to wash the plate after brekker). Oh I *loathe* it all so terribly.

Madeau [Stewart] is coming to interview me for BBC. One of the questions: Some historians say your history books are really a description of the Mitford family? Answer: Very true. History is always subjective & the books we yawn over are often the descriptions of the home life of some dreary old professors.

I believe you have organised some sort of postal strike so you may never receive this.

Best love, Soo

1 David Pryce-Jones (1936–). Journalist, novelist and biographer who had exchanged houses with Jessica for the summer. He interviewed Nancy for a profile in the *Daily Telegraph* and subsequently wrote a biography of Unity.

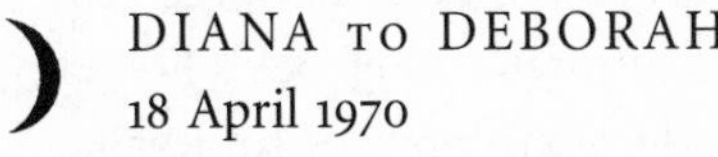

DIANA TO DEBORAH
18 April 1970

Temple de la Gloire
Orsay

Darling Debo:

I have got a new preoccupation, not to say worry, which is that Kit is beginning (only beginning mind you, but one sees the trend) to say we must normalize (awful word) everything now we know it's not cancer.[1] This only means that I mustn't rush over every day. Poor old Kit, I know well he has been very very good, but of course whatever name you call it by changes nothing much, Naunce is still by any standards a very ill person – a desperately ill person – & a desperately lonely one.

The transparent efforts of for example Colonel to find a new 'subject' for another book make her quite cross & yesterday the poor man got a good snubbing (also he fetched himself a garden chair & planted it on the scyllas, there were stifled screams from poor Lady & I made him move it, but it touched a daisy, & then he sort of fingered a narcissus while chatting & she was in utter agony – I mean garden agony not pain). Of course while she can sit out & watch Hassan put in radish seeds all is well, but this weather won't last.

All love darling, Honks

1 In one of many misdiagnoses, the doctors had ruled out Nancy as having cancer.

NANCY to DEBORAH
16 May 1970

4 rue d'Artois
Versailles

Dear Miss

I've spent two whole days with David P[ryce]-J[ones], doped to the eyes. I hope I didn't seem too stupid but my recollection is that he did most of the talking & he did tell some fascinating facts of modern life. He remembers staying (?) at Lismore when he was 12 & being made to play intellectual games à la manière de Racine & so on. I said oh they've chucked all that & they dress up as horses now & have steeple chases over the Berlin china. Roughly correct? He bitterly regrets that Alan[1] didn't marry Eliz. [Cavendish] I'd forgotten that they courted. He says the Dss[2] is a disaster in anybody's life. He says his little girls aged 6 & 7 loathe & despise hippies & so do all their mates. How SWEET. I greatly enjoyed the ole thing – the interview will appear about when the book does. There was quite a friendly one in *D. Exp.* with me looking the image of Aunt Iris.

I'm retaking the only pill that suits me but which stopped working – it works again oh the bliss. If ever I do get better I shall be SO happy nothing will ever matter again.

Much love, Lady

1 Alan Pryce-Jones (1908–2000). David's father was a journalist and editor of the *Times Literary Supplement* 1948–59. Married Thérèse Fould-Springer in 1934.
2 Mary (Mollie) Lascelles (1900–93). Cousin and companion of Alan Pryce-Jones. Married 8th Duke of Buccleuch in 1921.

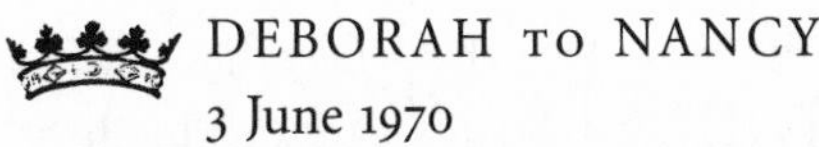

DEBORAH TO NANCY *4 Chesterfield Street, W1*
3 June 1970

Get on

Now, Lady, to be serious. I've heard through beastly London grape vine that D Pryce-Jones is going round saying that you said all sorts of things about Birdie & SS Men & Hitler in your interview.[1] No doubt you did not, but if it is said you did that's enough to make an intensely interesting story, so for the sake of all I implore you to get a copy of what he proposes to say at once, & if he has invented anything, & if you said something ½ joking & not meaning it to be down in black & white, you can scrub it all out.

It would be so awful for everyone, & specially Honks, if a lot of stuff was written all wrong & all beastly about poor old Birdie who can't answer. I'm all for saying anything in an interview about oneself if one feels like it but for someone like Pryce-Jones to get hold of the wrong end of the stick about Birdie is too much you'll agree.

How I *loathe* journalists for their utter unreliability, they always seem as if they won't do & say anything rotten & then do exactly the opposite. *Do report on this*, what can it all be? Or perhaps you've seen what he's going to publish already & I've been given an exaggerated account? Anyway I thought I'd write at once to warn you what's being said.

Much love, 9

1 According to the rumour, Nancy had told Pryce-Jones that Hitler had wanted to marry Unity but would not because she had been promiscuous with so many SS men.

NANCY TO DEBORAH
22 June 1970

4 rue d'Artois
Versailles

BOAST OF THE YEAR

Dear Miss

A French Lady Horse has been named after me NANCY MITFORD & has won her first race.

I can't help noting that no racehorse has been called Deborah Mitford, 9, de Horsey, Hen, Elle or Bakewell Hannah.

It's the old story of the Tortoise & the Hare or Cinderella. Under my air of quiet indifference the discerning French owner, the Duke of Blackears or some such name, has perceived a true heart steadily beating for the cause of equine encouragement. He has acted.

That's all for now. Enough?

Love, Nancy Mitford

(Lester Piggott keep out)

NANCY TO DEBORAH
23 June 1970

4 rue d'Artois
Versailles

Dear Miss

Hope you got the Boast of the Year.

The editor of the (I don't quite understand, is it *D*[aily] *T*[elegraph] magazine? – a Sunday supplement or something – we don't get it here) says there's nothing deleterious in the article, which he thinks very good, & nothing which could possibly be regarded as a scoop. He is sending a proof. You know one mustn't have one skin too few, as you say Jews have, on acc/ of being a Mitford. I read Decca's book & – exc for what she said about Uncle T, unpardonable – I couldn't see much wrong with it & as everybody has read it I can't think quoting from it could matter. What I would object to is misquotations of me. I always think you & Honks never really *read* the book. Probably the best thing would be not to read P-J, a course I warmly recommend to you.

I'm in complete torment. I lie & watch the swallows & remember how I watched them last year in complete torment the same. I think physical pain is the worst infliction, though perhaps having no money would be even worse. Fancy if every day was like Sunday with Woman not about. Have you ever tried to wash up a saucepan? I wash it & then I smell & it smells of grease so I wash it again & it goes on smelling of grease. Tairebool. If I leave it for the Hassan to do the kitchen smells. One lars [alas].

Best love, de Horsey-Mitford

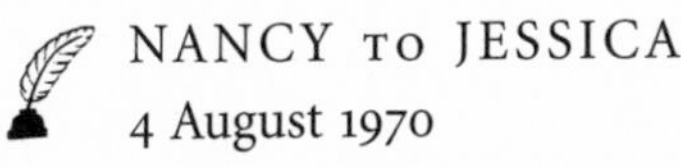

NANCY TO JESSICA
4 August 1970

Dorsoduro 23
Venice

Darling Soo

I don't know how long I'll stay here. I've got a dr in whom I feel confidence & if he seems to do me good I'll stay as long as he says. But I'm sure to be back before you leave & it would be a great joy to see you if not too much trouble.

Susan the Americans on the beach. Per cent Dow Jones. I can't think why the beatniks haven't performed ritual killings on them, no jury would convict. If I wasn't such a cripple I would do something myself in the way of drowning. I'm sure they are very weak. I can swim much better than I can walk & the dr encourages it but the water is too cold for me.

I screamed about the criminals & their sibling troubles, well what about us? I'm sure all they really want is a free hand to do each other in, which incidentally would solve the problem of over crowding.[1]

Of course Honks has got a good line on prison & how one *longs* for solitary confinement. Then your m in law saying to the German Commandant 'there are two things I always insist on in prison, one is *bread* & the other is *water*'. Duff [Cooper] always used to say Nellie [Romilly] was the funniest person he had ever known & he used to begin to giggle at the mere thought of her. But I think she had lost it by the time we knew her.

Well Soo you won't have time to read all this drivel so I'll close.

Best love, Soo

I'm not too bad, it depends on the day, but I've always *got* a pain how I would love to be cured!

1 Jessica was writing an article for *Atlantic Monthly* about the Californian prison system, which she later developed into a book, *Kind and Usual Punishment, The American Prison Business* (1973).

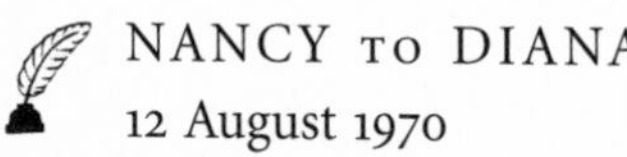

NANCY TO DIANA
12 August 1970

Dorsoduro 23
Venice

Dereling,

Cecil [Beaton] came back for a night. He is fearfully worried about a tiny wrinkle on his cheek. People gaze in the glass & don't realize that the *general effect* is 100. I saw the old soul from my balcony – didn't know he was coming – & wondered who the *old* gent was until I heard the voice. Nothing to do with the tiny wrinkle.

You know my thing about grey hair. Lidi [Clary] was telling of some friend aged ninety who dyes her hair, saying men hate grey hair. With Lidi's before my eyes I couldn't say, but I know exactly what she means, I hate it too. (I don't mean yours which is silver gilt.) If I wasn't allergic to dye I would have it boot black like a French housemaid.

The fact is I fear old people are boring as I once told Evelyn (when he said 'your odious letter arrived on my birthday'). Until I realized the old gent was Kek I felt bored. What a horrid look out.

I've often said this before but I believe I'm better. Will enlarge in my next.

Much love, N

I'm reading a book about the Tsars. Oh God what people. Stalin was infinitely less awful.

Right Gaston Palewski, the 'Colonel', the love of Nancy's life, in his flat in the rue Bonaparte, Paris, *c*.1945.

Below Nancy in Christian Dior, on the steps of rue Monsieur, 1952.

Pamela, Deborah and Derek Jackson. Rignell, *c.*1946.

Pamela with her companion, Giuditta Tommasi, and Jessica, 1950s.

Right Lady Redesdale aboard *Puffin*, Inch Kenneth, 1947. The grief at losing her only son and the strain of caring for brain-damaged Unity is etched on her face. (*Photograph by Julia Budworth*)

Below Diana, after her release from prison.

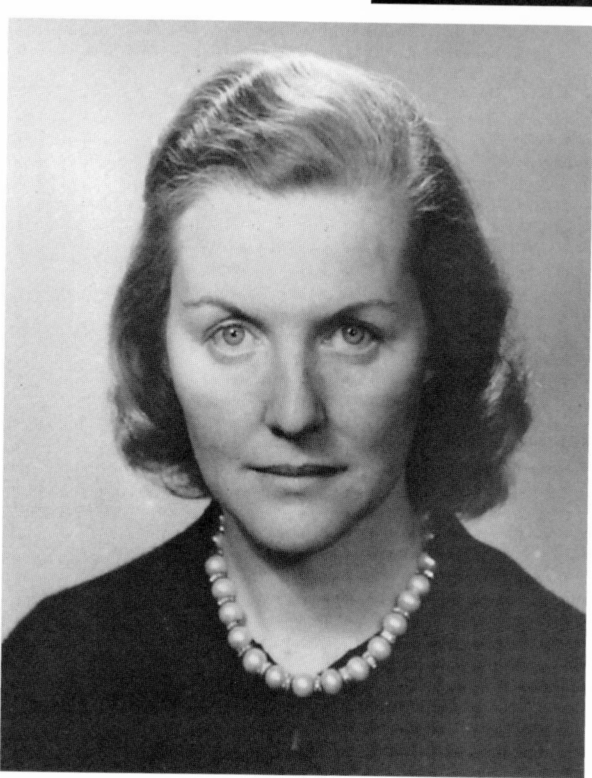

Above Alexander, Oswald, Diana and Max Mosley, reunited at Crowood after wartime separation.

Below Diana on the Lido, Venice, 1955.

Right Temple de la Gloire, Orsay, the Mosleys' house near Paris.

Above Jessica with Benjamin, Nicholas and Constancia, 1948.

Right (*back*) Evelyn Louise Crawford, Constancia Romilly, Emma Cavendish, Peregrine Hartington; (*front*) Lady Redesdale, Robert Treuhaft, Jessica. Inch Kenneth, 1955.

Above Deborah painted by Mogens Tvede. Edensor House, 1949.

Left Deborah at the Beistegui Ball, in a dress copied from a John Downman watercolour of Georgiana, wife of the 5th Duke of Devonshire. Venice, 1951.

Right Deborah in coronation robes with nine-year-old Peregrine, who was page to Mary, Duchess of Devonshire, Mistress of the Robes to the Queen, 1953.

Below Deborah parading at the Royal Show, Britain's largest agricultural fair, with 'the Wife', her great friend Lady Mersey, 1950s.

Above left Deborah's elder sister-in-law, Anne Cavendish (Tig), at her wedding to Michael Tree, 1949.

Left Deborah's sister-in-law Elizabeth Cavendish (Deacon) with her companion, the future poet laureate John Betjeman, at Lismore Castle, 1958.

Above Deborah's daughter Sophia, aged three.

Left Violet Hammersley, 'the Widow'. Chatsworth, 1960.

Below left President Kennedy leaving Edensor churchyard after visiting his sister Kathleen's grave, June 1963.

Below right Eunice and Edward Kennedy at Edensor, May 1965.

Bottom Deborah between Robert and Ethel Kennedy at Edensor churchyard, 1963.

Left Oswald Mosley and Nancy at the Temple de la Gloire, 1965. Nancy disliked all her brothers-in-law and they her.

Below Nancy at rue d'Artois, 1972.

Above Pamela and Diana. Orsay, 1965.

Right Pamela at Woodfield, 1980. (*Photograph by Brian Donay*)

Below Diana, 1990s.

Five generations: Diana in 2002 with her son Desmond Guinness, grandson Patrick Guinness, great-granddaughter Jasmine Rainey and great-great grandson Elwood Rainey. (*Photograph by Christopher Simon Sykes*)

Right Jessica and Duncan Grant in the dining room at Chatsworth, 1960s.

Below Jessica with her son-in-law, Terry Weber, Robert Treuhaft and Constancia, August 1986.

Bottom Robert Treuhaft and Jessica playing Boggle with Maya Angelou, 1980s.

Right Deborah and Harold Macmillan by the River Blackwater, Co Cork, in 1964, the year after his resignation as Prime Minister.

Below Andrew and Deborah (*right*). Chatsworth, 1985.

Opposite Andrew and Deborah, 1977.

Pamela and Deborah. Lismore, 1979.

JESSICA TO DEBORAH
22 October 1970

6411 Regent Street
Oakland

Dearest Hen,

Harrods: Last time I was there I noted on the board of departments: Funeral Arrangements, 4th floor. So I scrammed to the 4th fl, where the Funeral Arrangements door was closed. There was a note on it saying: 'If shut, apply to Adjustments Dept.' So there you are, she was Adjusted. Am amending me will to be shipped to Harrods & adjusted – will you come & view? One of the Toynbee children, when little, thought the name was Herrod's like Wicked King H. I must say they're getting more Herrodish all the time.

I've finished my prisons thing, oh you'll never know the relief: 6 months of work it was, although it's only an article of about 6,000 words (28 pages of typing). I'm afraid it would only bore you, so shan't send, but to me it was my entire life for ages and ages.

Much love, Yr Hen

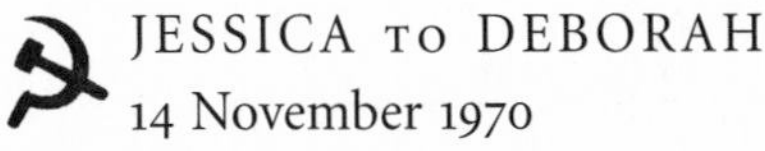

JESSICA TO DEBORAH
14 November 1970

6411 Regent Street
Oakland

Dearest Hen,

Thanks SO much for your marvellous and detailed reports, they sustain me. The dreams: odd, she gets whiter & whiter in mine too but no spurting tooth thank God. More or less twisted visage of agony, all of a sudden, after being quite ordinary. Va. Durr[1] sent me the most smashing photo (colour) from *Sun. Times* of Nancy in her gdn, and ones of the house.

I wonder if you've found Woman? Do you remember how Muv, when we thought Woman might have been kidnapped for ransom (as she had disappeared in her car for about a week) saying 'Mmmm. In that case, *Debo* would have to *plunge*.'[2]

Do give lots of love to Woman if you find her, & report on a) Her Glos. Ghast-House if she's having it, b) Her book.

Much love, Yr Hen

1 Virginia Foster (1903–99). Southern belle who became a leader of the civil rights movement. Married Alabama attorney Clifford Durr in 1926. The couple were among Jessica's closest friends in America.
2 In 1959, Jessica described this incident in a letter to her husband: 'Muv began laughing the inner laugh of one who has thought of something frightfully funny. I said what's the joke, she said "I was just wondering if Woman has been kidnapped for ransom on her way to London." I suggested we should start making pledges in that case, and offered 10 pounds for a start; Muv said "I'll double that." "We should make Debo cough up, don't you think?" I suggested. Midst gales of laughter, Muv said, "*Debo* will have to *plunge*."' *Decca, p. 225.*

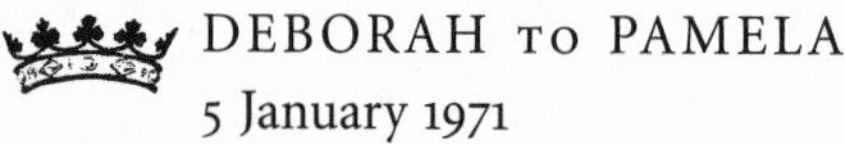

DEBORAH TO PAMELA

5 January 1971

Chatsworth
Bakewell

Darling Woman

I feel so worried about Honks now – you'll have heard she's got an ulcer & that Dr Dumas has given her a pill which stops the pain & she's on a strict diet.

If one had stopped to think one would have guessed she'd get something like that as she's been on the receiving end of all the worry of Nancy, & Sir O had an op. this time last year & one way & another she's had a pretty foul time. I suppose she'll have to rest a lot & all that now.

Much love, Stublow

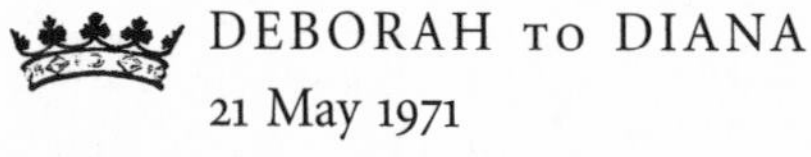

DEBORAH TO DIANA

21 May 1971

Chatsworth
Bakewell

Darling Honks

Now Honks I enclose something very touching from Hen.[1] I've *sort of* told the Lady that she'd come if pressed & I'm sure she won't press. I couldn't bear it if Hen made all that huge & expensive effort & then was not too welcome. Do tell what you think. Return letter some time. It shows what a heart that old Hen has got, still, under all the fury & bitterness. (Which I think she's nigh on shed, a lot of it anyway.)

We've had a summit here re the farm. The dotty-seeming answer may be to have parties to see the cows milked, school children & such like. Most of them have never seen anything of that kind & of course the first person who starts it will benefit like mad. It sounds wild doesn't it, but I suppose it might be quite a good plan all round. One could make it rather jolly, with refreshing drinks of milk just milked etc. (No one's tasted that sort of milk for YEARS.)[2]

I must stop, & write to Hen. What a great mistake for the Lady to refuse to see people, she hasn't told me that. How much weight has she lost? Enlarge please (in pounds).

Did you hear Heathy[3] on the wireless speaking French? It was rather like I would have sounded. Park Top has been tested in foal. Good.

Much love, Debo

1 Jessica had written to say that although very busy she would rush to be with Nancy if she was wanted and relied on Deborah to let her know whether to come.
2 The Chatsworth children's farmyard opened in 1973. 'One little boy from the middle of Sheffield said, "It's the most disgustin' thing I've ever seen in me life. I'm never going to drink milk again."' Deborah Devonshire, *Round About Chatsworth* (Frances Lincoln, 2005), p. 46.
3 Edward Heath.

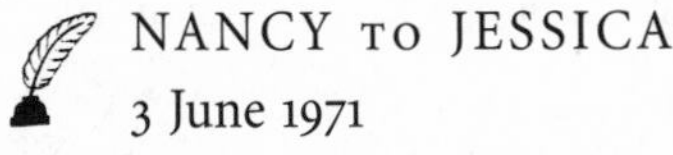

NANCY TO JESSICA
3 June 1971

4 rue d'Artois
Versailles

Darling Soo

Useless to pretend I wouldn't adore to see you but honestly it's not worth it. I spend half the time doped & stupid & the other half crying on my bed or really unable to chat. By 7.30 I'm done in, it's so tiring all this pain. Let's wait until this crisis is over. Some think it comes from the cobalt rays. In any case I'm never going to have any more treatment, everything so far has made me worse. Very luckily the last dr has lost my radio photographs, so no new one would take me on without them. I've seen 22 drs since it all began & that's going to be it.

Woman came, she was so nice. Makes me laugh with her projects.

The latest is to buy a house in Scotland of all places. One listens with half an ear.

I see Mary McCarthy has written another disobliging book[1] about the French, I do wonder why she lives here. But she always says she doesn't know any Frogs. What a funny person.

Fondest love, Soo

1 *Birds of America* (1971).

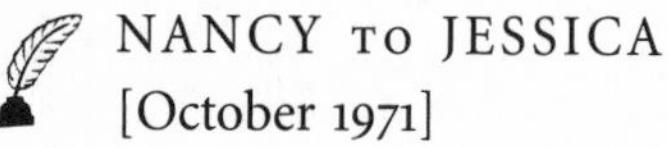

NANCY TO JESSICA
[October 1971]

4 rue d'Artois
Versailles

Darling Soo

Thanks for your letter, you needn't answer this but you might like to know that I go on having prac. no pain & it still feels heavenly because I have enough to remind me what it was like. The only drawback is great giddiness – I am talking to an old ambassador (here, I can't go out) when hey presto there I am on all fours as if about to kiss his toe. I'm, naturally, weak, I weigh now less than 6½ stone (the putting on stopped but I've not lost it again) & I'm giddy, so shopping which I so long for is out of the question. I can't begin my memoirs but I think about them. I've got the advantage over you of the drelders being dead.

I shall say about Muv: I had the greatest possible respect for her; I liked her company; but I never loved her, for the evident reason that she never loved me – I was never hugged & kissed by her as a small child – indeed I saw very little of her . . . I don't believe this really applies to you & Debo? Certainly Debo loved her & Diana did in old age but not when we just grew up. She was very cold & sarky with me. I don't reproach her for it, people have a perfect right to dislike their children but it is a fact I think I must mention. If you write memoirs at all they must throw some light on the personality of the writer, if, as in my case, nothing ever happens. They only begin when I am 40 & came here but of course there will be flashbacks.

Did you read Mary Mc's book? (Susan do write one like that

about the Americans! I said to Honks oh why doesn't she? & Honks said because she is a Crusader.) Did you scream at it? It had awful reviews here & I believe in America too – the reviewers are honestly too dim nowadays. Then she got on the wireless to explain a bit & the interviewer had never read the book so they never spoke of it at all. I daresay the public will be faithful, but it wants a bit of a lead, at first.

We shall know in three weeks whether the TV will do the Mitford saga & then I'll put them in touch with you if they do it. The trouble is me having sold *P of L* to films for a pittance 100 years ago. The owner is making trouble. Unfortunately *P of L* is the key book.

Lovely autumn weather, a great help to me. I'm out of doors all day.

Much love Soosie, N

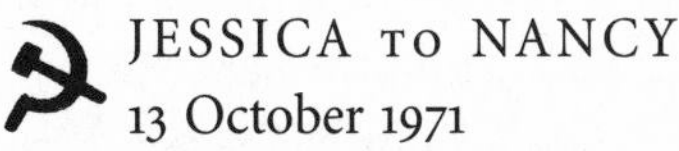

JESSICA TO NANCY
13 October 1971

6411 Regent Street
Oakland

Darling Soo,

The few things you said about Muv in yr. letter opened up a perfect *flood* of thoughts in that direction, so I must just impart them.

The fact is that unlike you I actively loathed her when I was a child (esp. an older child, after age 15), and did not respect her, on the contrary thought she was extremely schoopid and narrow-minded – that is, sort of limited-minded with hard & fast bounds on her mind. But then, after re-getting to know her after 1955, I became immensely fond of her, really rather adored her. Therefore in my memory she turns into 2 people; I'm sure she didn't change much, because people don't except for a certain mellowing with onset of old age.

The thing that *absolutely burned into my soul* was the business of not being allowed to go to school. So much so that when she came here, when Dinky was 7, the subject came up and I found myself literally fighting back tears of rage. Do admit it was maddening. One thing I specially remember: when I was about 11, I wanted to be a scientist (natch I didn't tell *you* about it, Susan, because whenever one told you one's deepest ambitions it was only to be TEASED UNMERCIFULLY and laughed off face of earth), because I had just read *The Stars in their Courses* by Sir James Jeans. So, noting I should have to go to college in that case, I biked to Burford and rather shudderingly went to see the headmaster of the grammar school. He said I could be admitted to the grammar school (which had a scientific laboratory, that's why I wanted to go) if I could pass a fairly easy exam, which I cld. learn to do by reading a list of books he gave me.[1] I was v. excited over this, rushed home to ask Muv if I could get the books, take the exam, and bike to school each day. A cold NO was the only answer, no reason given. After that lessons with the gov. seemed totally pointless, although I admit I could have learned far more than I did.

She must have been fairly horrid when young, too. For instance when she was about 30 living in Dieppe, Nellie Romilly (not yet married) aged 20 came to her in deep despair to say she had lost 10 pnds. in gambling, owed it as a debt, and could Muv lend it to her? Muv went straight to Aunt Natty and told all, I expect poor Nellie was bitterly punished. Muv herself told me this, but simply couldn't see what a vile thing it was to have done. I guess it's that awful disapproving quality that I always hated about her.

Another thing I remember – but perhaps you've forgotten, or perhaps I dreamed it: when you were about 29, we were going for one of those long, wet Swinbrook walks when the rain seemed like one's inner tears of bitterness because of boredom & general futility of that life. You told how Muv had given you a terrific dressing down for not being married, having just turned down yet another proposal of marriage, & that you would be an old maid if you pursued this hopeless route. Something like that. *Did* it happen?[2]

I know it must have, I can almost hear squelch of one's gumboots as you imparted this odd bit of information. And the certain conviction, in my mind, that one had to get away from that dread place at all costs.

As for the Hen, I don't think she was much of a noter of anything until much older – and, by then, was fairly free of the Revereds. I mean she never specially wanted to *do* anything except what was there to be done, rather adored the daily life at Swinbrook. When things came up such as fainting dead away on the flagstones on acct. of Woman's engagement to Derek, that was more or less from outside causes (such as being in love with D) rather than from inner, don't you think?

After the Revereds became Nazis, Swinbrook life became even more intolerable; but by then, you had more or less left. Again, no effect on the Hen; don't you remember Mrs Phelps[3] saying she was perfectly happy picking fleas off Jacob? Or ticks out of? Which is quite an oversimplification of that complex Hen's character, but nevertheless a telling observation, in its way.

When one thinks of all the things Muv told about *her* extraorder childhood, being in charge of Grandfather's household & political campaigns etc, one can dimly see how her naturally bossy nature got more so, given that unnaturally free rein from age 14.

Oh dear I *still* haven't read M. McCarthy's novel, in spite of the fact it's the only new book I crave to read. The fact is I don't read anything any more except PRISON stuff, on acct. of me being a CRUSADER. Yes, Susan.

I am *cheering* for your continued recovery,

Much love Susan

1 The accuracy of Jessica's memory of this incident, which she described in greater detail in *A Fine Old Conflict*, is open to question. James Jean's book on astronomy was published in 1931, the year Jessica turned 14. Burford Grammar School, which was founded in 1571 for the sons of farmers, did not admit girls until the early 1960s.

2 'I think I was telling lies if I said Muv wanted to marry me off. I think I was probably in a blind temper about something else & talked wildly.' (Nancy to Jessica, 18 October 1971.)

3 An American who rented the Mill Cottage at Swinbrook before the war.

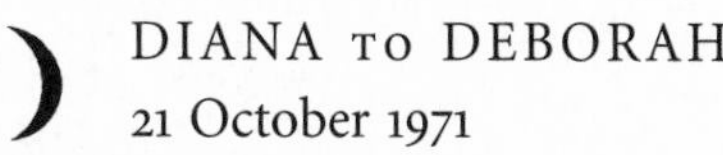

DIANA TO DEBORAH
21 October 1971

49 Shawfield Street
London SW3

Darling Debo:

Naunce wants enclosed back – but gave me the option of showing it to you. Please send it to Naunce.

I had a talk with her about Muv before I left & I suppose she then wrote to Decca & got this letter back. She (Naunce) was speaking of a proposed autobiography which was by way of starting in 1945, & then I imagine she saw there wasn't enough to fill a book (descrips of silly old Dolly etc & none of the inwardness of her relations with Colonel, naturally) so she harks back to Muv & her supposed wickednesses. It is all a great bore. Decca & Naunce are a couple of bitter old creatures who can't forgive life for being so cruel & look for a scapegoat & find it in – Muv! Really rather rubbish. When I was 16, I begged to be allowed to learn German & was furiously refused permission. But I learnt it later on & it has been one of my *greatest* joys. I don't 'resent' not having learnt it sooner. Of course to be a scientist one wd have to begin as a child I suppose with mathematics – though if Decca had really wanted to be a scientist she could have 'gone on' at Muv & I bet you finally she wd have got her way. It all sounds so romantic & 'clever' but when one looks back it simply wasn't like that.

I had such a strange talk with Naunce, about Mrs Ham & her sons. I said Mrs Ham worried so dreadfully over them being poor, & that really what wrecked their lives was that both married such dud wives, so Naunce 'Yes, but it was because they were poor they made bad marriages' (*bad* is so meaningless, they chose hopeless *people*) & I said 'But what about us? We were poor, but some of us married rich & some poor people' & that partly silenced her clamour. It's like Decca's mother-in-law saying one must know rich people in order to meet other rich people. Naunce is NOT a vulgar half-wit but she sometimes pretends to be one.

It is rather telling that when considering writing about Muv she should turn to Decca. Bother everything.

Well darling it was RICH seeing you & knowing you are in the same country.

All love, Honks

DEBORAH TO NANCY *4 Chesterfield Street, W1*
26 October 1971

Lady

Tea. If you give Wife Earl Grey large tears will fall into it. It wd be like giving water to a whisky drinker. She likes thickest Indian, army style.

Now Lady, yr memories of the Oldsters & Henderson. Remember how incredibly uncivilised teen aged girls are, that's one thing. To go on with, I was *as one* with me old Hen until she turned bloody minded – really till she buggered I suppose. I wouldn't be at all surprised if she had conjured up something in her imagination re Burford Grammar School, like Muv being X with you for not marrying. I'm *quite sure* I should have known if she'd done that, she couldn't not have told me at that stage of our lives.

Swinbrook was sold when I was 15 and it broke my heart. I can *absolutely remember* the last rides through the woods, and the dread sorrow of it all. Nothing has ever taken its place & nothing ever will. The other terrible thing that happened when I was a child was the two nights in that school at Oxford. Muv saw that, & took me away thank God. I don't know what I should have done if I had been left there.

Those two things were worse than anything that has happened since, the loss of three babies, my four greatest friends being killed in the war – nothing has saddened me like the going from Swinbrook. So the poor parents seem to have messed things up all along the line.

Hen seems to have forgotten the lengths Muv went to to try & cheer her up when she turned so sour, she's perhaps forgotten the terrific thing of the round the world journey she & Muv & me & the Brett girl[1] were about to embark on when she left us all in the lurch without a word. Poor Muv, she had Farve to contend with as well – it's a wonder she survived.

I note Hen says she was bossy. That's odd – it's not my idea of her at all – cold, possibly, distant, vague, but not *bossy*, that's how I would have described Bridget Airlie & many others, but not Muv.

Is Hen crusading for letting all murderers out of prison? I do wonder.

Tomorrow is Duncan Grant & Honks. Ann Fleming is coming as Adjudicator.

Last night Jakie[2] took me to a Reading of Yeats, all by one man. He never stopped talking for 2½ hours. Give me the W. I. where the actors say Pardon? to the prompter.

Much love, 9

1 Virginia Brett (1916–90). Daughter of 3rd Viscount Esher.
2 John Jacob Astor (1918–2000). Conservative MP 1951–9 and successful racehorse owner and breeder.

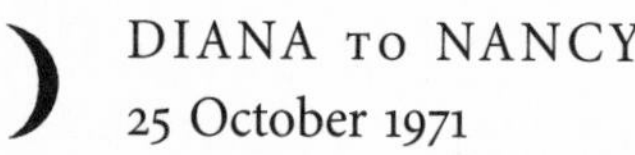

DIANA TO NANCY
25 October 1971

49 Shawfield Street, SW3

Dereling

We went to the motor races yesterday, with Micky,[1] it was a boiling day. Max raced in a sort of semi-joke race but I could hardly bear to watch. Then we had a picnic & then there was the big race & the roar is unbelievably loud. All of a sudden, from out of sight beyond a lovely golden wood, one saw a plume of black smoke, & then silence. The race had been stopped. All the cars were invisible to us, other side of the hill. No announcement made for ages; finally the man said an accident, & the race not to be finished. Then Max came & told us Siffert[2] was dead. It was so dreadful, & unbearable. Huge crowd on pleasure bent, perfect day, & this horrible death. Max very sad because he knew him well. We just went away, couldn't think of the other silly races. We were to dine at the [Edward] Rices & as we were very early went to see Canterbury cathedral.

The Rices said 'The old ladies of Eastry are coming to dinner' & who should appear but Patricia Russell[3] & a Hungarian lady she lives with. You can just imagine how amusing, her impressions of Asthall, she said 'I've known you for *50* years'. About Uncle Jack she said 'Didn't I have a lucky escape?' Then we talked of Bobo & Tom & you, she sent you best love. She told me one interesting thing: Bobo told her & Jimmy Erdödy that she wd kill herself if Germany & England went to war. They said 'What with?' & she produced her little pistol.

Jimmy, who knew all about firearms, said: It won't kill you. And proceeded to tell her what she must do (I couldn't ask what it was – there were such a lot of people moving about & so our talk was semi-overheard). They didn't try to dissuade her, which wd have been useless, but tried to make her do it more efficiently.

Altogether yesterday was battering & harrowing – yet I was pleased to see Pat Russell. She says I *am* Farve to look at – can't quite see it myself.

All love dereling, D

1 Michael Mosley (1932–). Oswald Mosley's younger son from his first marriage.
2 Jo Siffert (1936–71). Swiss racing driver who won the British Grand Prix in 1968 at Brand's Hatch, the circuit on which he died three years later.
3 Lady Patricia Blackwood (1902–83). One-time fiancée of Lord Redesdale's younger brother Jack. Married to Henry Russell 1926–37.

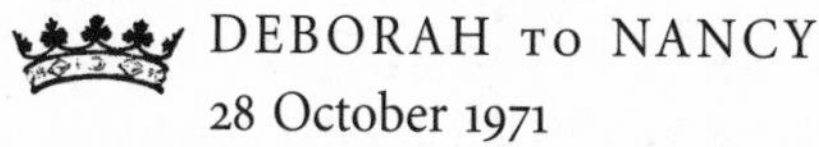

DEBORAH TO NANCY
28 October 1971

Chatsworth
Bakewell

Get on

Your Memoirs From '45. I suppose it will be Got Up, Dressed, Went Out, Came In, Had Lunch – I can't see you enlarging on your Love Life and so what *will* you say. Can't wait . . .

Much love, 9

I'm afraid Duncan Grant has got a bit old all of a sudden (88). He faithfully came to lunch & he & Honks had quite a good jaw. He says he's plagued by American students asking about all his erstwhile mates who have become so fashionable. He is the absolute nicest man in the world I think.

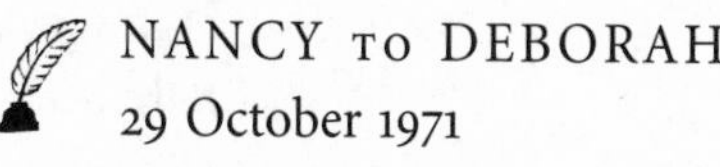

NANCY TO DEBORAH
29 October 1971

4 rue d'Artois
Versailles

Dear Miss

I see I'm on the verge of being scolded (holier than thou is beginning to raise its hackles). I repeat & can't repeat too often that all sisters will receive copies of the book & will have the right of veto. If one writes an autobiography it's not enough, as so many people seem to suppose, to tell how many housemaids one's father employed – one must UNMASK oneself. Roughly speaking I shall say what an unsatisfactory relationship I had with Muv, to explain my love for old ladies: Aunt Vi[1] (Peter's), Mrs H[ammersley], Mme Costa, & others. I would like vaguely to try & find out if this relationship, shared with Decca & Honks, but not with you & Tom, was one's fault or hers. The others loved her in old age: I deeply respected her & liked her company & jokes but never loved her. Owing to your *right of veto* I shan't mind asking questions & shan't leave things out for fear of annoying, which might not annoy at all. That was Decca's great mistake in my view. I might make each of you write a review of Decca's book. Incidentally my book will begin in 1945 when I came here with flashbacks at the death of Boud, Muv & Farve. I won't bore the public again with our childhood to the extent of more than a few pages. Never thought of Muv as bossy far too vague.

Now pack up your Church Army uniform & keep in close touch.

Fond love, N

Wooms is here but for such a short time but it's *so* dull I can't urge her to stay a few days.

Do you realize that *envelopes* are soon to be very valuable, you should keep a few as a dowry for Celina.[2]

1 Violet Guthrie (d.1953). Peter Rodd's maternal aunt. Married Major-General Edward Stuart-Wortley in 1891. Nancy wrote an introduction to her memoirs, *Grow Old Along With Me* (1952), in which she described the months staying with her at Highcliffe Castle as 'among the truly happy times of my life'.

2 Lady Celina Cavendish (1971–). Elder daughter of Deborah's son, Peregrine.

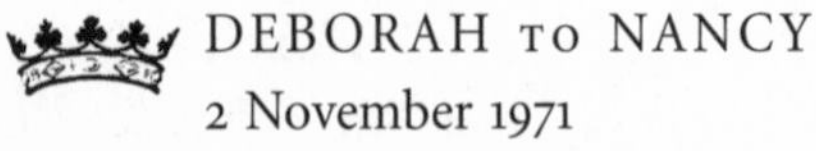

DEBORAH TO NANCY
2 November 1971

Chatsworth
Bakewell

Get on

I CAN'T WAIT for LADY UNMASKED. All what I've never dared ask you – and it's the ONLY thing people are interested in, love-life to the last. Are we going to get POSITIONS, & will Lord Longford[1] like what's coming? Oh Dame, the thrill of it. I may take off my Church Army uniform for a quick read of it behind locked doors.

I've written something. A brill piece for The British Goat Society's Year Book. Do be impressed.

I usually keep Valuable Envelopes if the letters are two page affairs, like yours of yesterday with the unmasking news. Otherwise I'd pity the monkey's orphan* who would have to put the thing together.

If Woman really takes up residence here from Xmas shall I let her have all Muv's letters etc to ponder over, & do you think there might be some things which might make her sad, I mean refs to her, one never knows. There's a lot of stuff.

Well lady get on with the Dance of the 7 Veils, the thrill of the Century.

Much love, 9

*Brill person of about the year 2000 who will make a thrilling, silly book on the Last Correspondence Between People using Pen & Paper.

1 7th Earl of Longford (1905–2001). The unconventional peer had set up a private study group to investigate the 'incipient menace' of pornography in Britain. Published as the Longford Report in 1972, it earned him the sobriquet 'Lord Porn'.

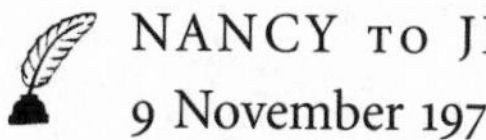

NANCY TO JESSICA
9 November 1971 posted 12th

4 rue d'Artois
Versailles

Darling Soo

How lovely it would be if you came but I shall send a list of strikes I mind – viz. I hate a postal strike & snap my fingers at a plastic bag one (scented for sanitary towels).

I've got two doctors I comfortably believe in so the awful struggle against drs is over. The English pen pal & a French one here in Versailles. They write to each other because the English one knows French. Froggie's new pills are labelled very large *contre sénilité* & I've even forgiven that. He is such a dear. He clasped his hands yesterday & said '*Comme* je voudrais vous aider'[1] which I have never felt was true before. He has written to the Eng. surgeon to ask why he operated – I said for £200 I imagine & doc (dark) was shocked (sharked). He thinks that may be the clue to all. Meanwhile I take 6 pills at every meal, what would Muv say? I've become reckless. And I'm bound to say the pain doesn't compare with what I've had but I'm as senile as can be, no hope of beginning souvenirs. I'm going to make the others review your book for it & *you* can review *it* if you like but, as it's '45 onwards, you hardly come in alas. Woman is grumbling already at the hard work entailed. It ought to give your *Hons* a boost. I can't wait to start, I'm already sharpening up in every direction.

Yr letter about Muv. As Honks said it is probably we who changed & not her, there's nothing so awful as teen aged girls. We none of us, Debo, Honks, me, see her as bossy – too vague. Didn't know about scientific interests – yours – one thought of them as literary. Susan you might have invented the Bomb what a wild tease – still there's always the Mitford[2] to help poor suffering mankind.

People don't know much about Arabs I've discovered since living (!) with Hassan. His adorable qualities & very harmless faults are all aristocratic, one can't imagine that such as he could ever succeed in an industrial complex. Frightfully stupid exc. at his work – as much unlike old Marie as chalk from.

That's all – keep in close touch N

1 '*How* I wish I could help you.'
2 A cheap cardboard coffin.

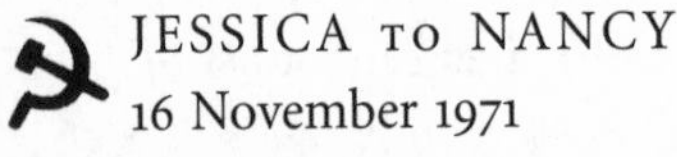

JESSICA TO NANCY *[Oakland]*
16 November 1971

Darling Susan,

Well I shrieked about the counter-senility pills, I wish I cld. lay hands on a few, just what I need about now. Otherwise the *medical* news sounds so incomparably better, with two trusted Drs. in the act, and pain receding.

I agree bossy isn't the word: more, implacably *disapproving* and thus arbitrarily disallowing anything one craved to do. (I mean she didn't make one do things, which was too often the fate of other wretched children in those days – being forced to eat food one loathed, or Susan in the case of one I know having one's BOWEL MOVEMENTS EXAMINED by the gov. each morn.) While the Hen may not have noted this I bet Diana did, having been on receiving end of said disapprovingness from at least age 14 to 18 & then again when the Divorce Courts were nigh! said Annie to Pam.

Alas, I agree with Diana that *she* prob. didn't change, as people don't, much, esp. after middle age; more likely we did. Or at least – and in my view this is more like it – the balance of power changed once one had fled the coop. So one met on totally different terms. I was much struck by this when she came to Oakland that time, about 1947 or 48 after what then seemed like aeons of time since I'd seen her. I was in a state of near terror about her visit. And then she tottered forth from the aeroplane (it was a v. rough trip, she was quite done for by it) and at once it became apparent she had come to make friends at all costs. Same thing when we went to Inch K. in 1955 etc. And I could see what an incredibly thin time *she* had had, on the whole, in life.

Do you remember the letter that Jim Lees-Milne wrote to *The Times* after she died?[1] I thought it was marvellous (although it took me to task for falsifying), and if you haven't got it I'll send, if of any use, as I have kept it somewhere & cld. easily find it. All about how she had the soul of a mariner. All very well for J. Lees-Milne, thought I, but who wants to be brought up by a mariner? And, at that, a fairly ancient mariner by the time I came along. I think one trouble is that people sometimes get militantly nasty in middle age (oh dear, my age) and that's the time of her life when I was growing up.

Of course I long for the sisterly reviews, but suppose I shan't get same. So far, from those quarters I have received: 1) your letter when *Hons & Rebs.* came out, which I was extremely pleased & reassured to get but you sent it by Surface Mail and it didn't come for six weeks, 2) total silence from the Hen, 3) a letter from Woman saying I was beastly about Uncle Tommy, 4) a furious letter from Diana in *Times*

Lit. Supplement, also one in some issue of said *Supplement* from Mrs Ham. Susan, DO send the sisterly reviews. But I suppose Xerox has never been heard of in Versailles. (A Xerox strike is the one I shall never organize, as I depend on this amazing thing for all my PRISONS research.) Couldn't that nice typist make a copy for me?

Another thing: I've kept an awful lot of *your* letters, & could sort out and have XEROXED if that would be any help? In terms of remembering times and things, I mean. Prob. not too much in '45, as I don't think we were writing much then. But if you want what I can find, do say.

1 James Lees-Milne described Lady Redesdale as 'acutely perceptive, well read, fastidious, yet surprised by nothing and amused by practically everything . . . Nothing, however, is further from the truth than the popular conception of her gleaned from *Hons and Rebels*, as a philistine mother with hide-bound social standards'. *The Times*, 28 May 1963.

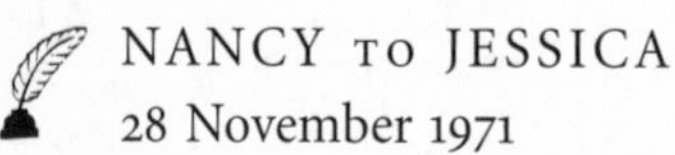

NANCY TO JESSICA
28 November 1971

4 rue d'Artois
Versailles

Darling Sooze

How kind you are to say you will look out some letters – such a boring task. Later I'll surely be grateful. I'm not well enough to start work as yet & in any case my scheme is to write down what I remember & then pad out or fill in from letters – or correct the most violent errors (unless they are funnier than the truth – oh *I hope* I shall be honest). The idea is to put what the others think of your book into mine, me as umpire. Yes disapproving is right, bossy wrong: Honky says the 10 years dividing us brought many a change for the worse. Tom & his clever friends, I & my pretty ones, were dispersed. There was no longer a library where one could sit quite alone & read away from the Revereds, one sat under the nose of the male Revered. Perhaps you weren't allowed to have people to stay? Our friends were certainly a great help specially all the Oxford ones.

What *could* Xerox be? A sort of anti-senility?

Oh dear I think people get nicer with age – I hope I have. But perhaps they need a stiff dose of Xerox. Must stop or weighage must take place such a bore for poor old Hassan.

Fond love, N

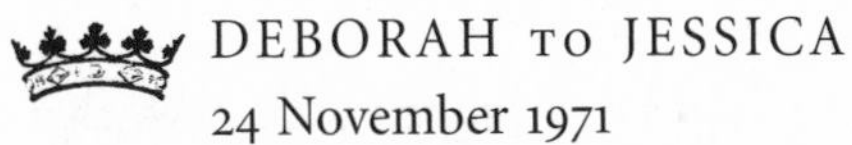
DEBOROAH TO JESSICA *Chatsworth*
24 November 1971 *Bakewell*

Dearest Hen

Many thanks for yours. Sorry I haven't written for such ages – the usual wild rush & being first in one place & then another. The Lady is certainly a CASE. As you know she has been much better lately because Duckie[1] has found a pill which has more or less dealt with the pain. It has side effects – dizziness, & dopiness by early evening – a nuisance but *nothing* compared with that foul pain.

I slightly dread the memoirs, but of course I'm all for her having something to do which amuses her. She promises any of us can veto anything we don't like. I suppose if she goes for Muv & I say how foul she is she'll start on the Holier Than Thou again. Oh well, time will show. She says she's going to unmask herself. Hen the thrill of that, shall we be explained her love life at last, all what we've never dared ask, I can't wait.

Well Hen I must close now. All the grandchildren are coming for Christmas, what a study it will be.

Much love, Yr Hen

1 Dr Stephen Blaikie; so called because, to Nancy's annoyance, he used to address her thus.

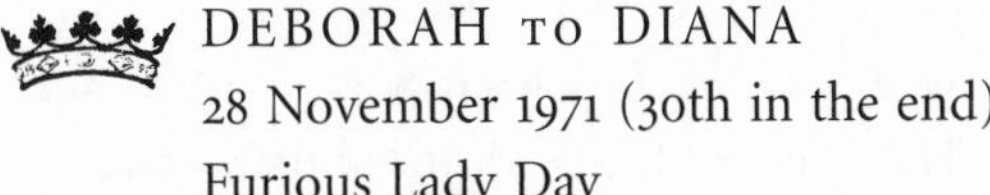
DEBORAH TO DIANA *Chatsworth*
28 November 1971 (30th in the end) *Bakewell*
Furious Lady Day

Darling Honks

Woman & I went to a concert (one man singer/entertainer) for the hosp. for dying folk I told you about in Sheffield. She was wondair & wore her thickest tweed coat throughout & held the Master Cutler enthralled in the interval. She thought we were in Leicester, but it didn't matter.

We rang up the Lady & buried various hatchets on her birthday – I don't think she noticed mind you but it didn't matter. I suppose we're all raving now – but *are we*?

I went to shoot with Ian Walker[1] today – all foggy & foul which ruined the shoot, but Ld Scarsdale[2] was there, well, talk about mad. He & I arrived at the meet before the host & for some minutes there was brilliant blue sky & a huge aeroplane went over miles high up. Ld Scarsdale looked up & said 'Russian. They often come. Damned cheek.' Then the fog came down, so we didn't get any more thrilling bits of inf of that sort.

In Train (30 Nov) to London.

Another FURIOUS letter from Nancy more or less saying she doesn't want any of us. How awful to be so proud, & I freely admit I long for ALL sisters ALL the time. Oh well it's easier if we aren't wanted isn't it.

Much love, Debo

1 Sir Ian Walker-Okeover (1902–82). Lord Lieutenant of Derbyshire 1951–77.
2 2nd Viscount Scarsdale (1898–1977). A nephew of Lord Curzon.

DIANA TO DEBORAH

12 December 1971

Temple de la Gloire
Orsay

Darling Debo:

We had such a day of it yesterday. We were eleven for lunch & then Max asked to come with Ronnie Peterson,[1] so that was 13, so I roped in the Count, & we were 14. Also Jerry went *twice* to Orly, *and* over to Naunce to take the Harrods. All this with more than good humour because of the thrill of seeing Ronnie Peterson! Mogens was here & he murmured a word of Swedish which drew an unwilling smile. He has been made 'driver of the year' by the press. What made the lunch party quite testing was that we'd got a very serious French economist to meet Roy [Harrod], so the two different sorts of people were so utterly unalike that there was hardly a bridge. I had a table of really boring talk about the dollar & its vagaries. The Frenchman started: 'Sir Roy Arrod, I very much admire *you*'. Roy then proceeded very very slowly to tell him that I was the only person of female gender to be beloved by Lytton Strachey. I don't think Frenchie understood one word of this declaration except that somebody, long ago, had been in love with me. It was very complicated.

Max was lovely & he blew in & had dinner, wearing a dinner jacket because there had been some prize-giving ceremony in Paris for which they had to dress. Then he rushed to aeroplane & I think got home to Jean soon after eleven English time – rather marvellous. They had come for the prize-giving, but also for a demo of a fire safety device at Montlhéry & they all came, Jackie Stewart[2] included, so Jerry saw the lot at Orly. And John[3] got an autograph.

I must describe R. Peterson. He is very tall & slender, with long palest gold hair (like Sophy's remarkable hair when she was 4) & blue eyes, & tiny perfect hands & weeny feet, & his skin is so fine I should think he never had to shave. One can't BEAR the thought of the risks he takes.

All love darling, Honks

1 Ronnie Peterson (1944–78). The Swedish Grand Prix driver made his debut in 1970 with March, the racing team that Max Mosley had started in 1969. He died after an accident at the Italian Grand Prix.
2 Jackie Stewart (1939–). The British driver won the World Championship in 1971.
3 Emmy and Jerry Lehane's eleven-year-old son.

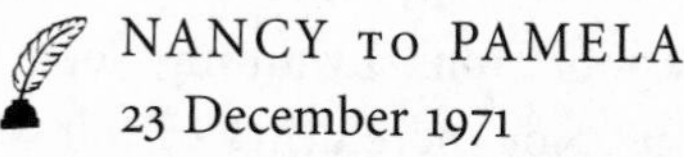

NANCY TO PAMELA
23 December 1971

4 rue d'Artois
Versailles

To wish you a Happy Xmas & 1972 & to thank you for all the trouble you have taken with me this year. I don't know what I would have done without you especially in the hospital. Wondair. Since you ask (linen bag) I'd rather have the flowers.

Much love, N

DIANA TO DEBORAH 5 rue Villedo, I
7 January 1972

Darling Debo:

Sure enough yours came & 'twas worth waiting for. What would one do without your letters, it would be a grey waste.

Naunce had a bad day & I went down & think she felt better because we began to laugh about something & couldn't stop. She is in the very best mood. She said something I never thought to hear from her lips, viz., 'Isn't it extraordinary to think that a civilized country like England could put a man in prison for years, who's done nothing? I always thought he was in a plot, everyone did.' (This was evoked by the Cabinet papers which have at last been revealed,[1] & Robert wrote about the bit about Kit in *S. Telegraph*.) Well well.

I have GOT to get a bathing gown for Bahamas, I've gone on with my old ones only fit for a beautiful teenage person because I can't abide the sort of solid kind with falsies attached. Well yesterday I found a fairly pretty one, & it's nearly £40. *Must* I? The answer I suppose is yes.

All love darling, Honks

1 Cabinet papers had been released concerning Mosley's arrest and internment in 1940.

NANCY TO DEBORAH *4 rue d'Artois*
21 January 1972 *Versailles*

Dear Miss

I was so frantic I sent for the dr but, as I said to him, I know you can't do anything but I must talk to somebody about myself. I do try & not depress others (exc. sisters & esp. poor Honks) with my woes. He is such a sweet man. He has given me some more drugs so will see. The pain is no worse than it has been from the start but much more constant. I never get a let up in the day & have to take things at night now but I do sleep thank goodness.

I had Hamish [St Clair-Erskine] for two nights, it was a worry really as I was so unwell. He has got £90,000 from a broken trust –

very bitter about having been penniless until over 60. He said 'We would have been married now for 30 years'. Help!! He is very dull & might have been more difficult to get rid of than poor Prod was. I don't like being married. I suppose too selfish. Anyway it would have been far worse for me this illness with some wretched old husband hanging about & either telling one one hasn't got anything or else forcing one into ever more hospitals.

Lovely sunny morning. I've got three roses out, I mean from last year. They are quite different from when young but very pretty!

Much love, N

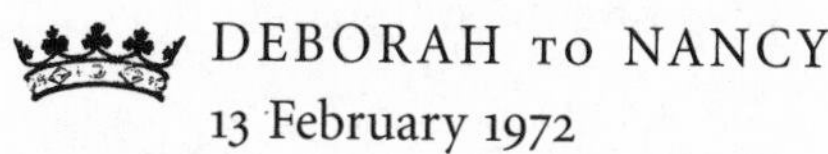

DEBORAH TO NANCY

13 February 1972

Chatsworth
Bakewell

Get on

It's quite incredibly pleasant having Honks. When Wife was here too we were a sort of *full house*, & I wish you'd been as well to make a flush (with Woman).

Yesterday the Portlands[1] came to lunch. We were in the Stag Parlour because when the electric cuts[2] are on the lift won't work, & the five of us were sitting happily at a tea table, just finished a rec pie, & were looking at the blackcurrant fool, spoons poised, when the phone rang wildly and the v. nice girl who works it said in an odd sort of voice 'I've just had a call to say a bomb will go off in the house in an hour'. Well that was rather a funny thing to say in the middle of lunch you'll freely admit. So everyone was told to go out of the house, Nanny said she couldn't because she hadn't fed the baby, so I had to say 'Can't help that, please go out of the house'. So we all gathered in the hall & Sonny [Portland] put on a coat of mine & we went to the lodge to wait for the police. They took 20 minutes to come which I thought was a bit off. The Inspector said 'Would you like me to search the house?' I said 'Do but it will take you a bit longer than the ½ hour we've got left before we go up'. He said we could look for boxes. I said 'You'll find plenty'. Meanwhile Woman flew off to put her *new car* out of the way of flying glass (never mind the Velazquez) and Nanny had legged it towards Baslow with a pramful of two objects. Maud & Miss Feeney appeared and many a gardener, odd man, carpenter, agent etc etc.

When the hour was nearly up & we were getting dreadfully cold & bored an old man said to Woman 'When they said an hour in the first war it was nearly always an hour and five minutes so I should wait a little longer'. I said to Sonny 'I'm so sorry this should happen when you come to lunch' and he said 'Oh my dear it's *most amusing*'. Giving it 10 minutes over we went back & finished our pudding. So that's our news really. *Most amusing*. I'm so glad the man didn't say three hours, we should have been even colder.

The electric cuts have produced a rash of very good silver candlesticks all over the house. But as they tell one when it's going to be off there is no thrilling element of surprise.

Last night Honks & I had dinner with Woman. It was SUPREMO. Head Soup (out of) & Scotch Collops. No pouding. Huge coal fire. Bottle of wine she had smuggled from France. Would that you had been there.

Going wooding now.

Much love, 9

1 William Cavendish Bentinck, 7th Duke of Portland (1893–1977). Married Ivy Gordon-Lennox in 1915.
2 A miners' strike had caused power cuts throughout Britain.

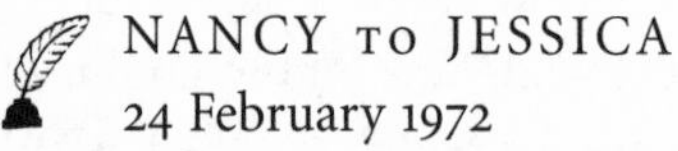

NANCY TO JESSICA
24 February 1972

4 rue d'Artois
Versailles

Darling Soo

Somebody rang up & said they liked what you & I had written in the *Observer*. What did we write? Do tell. The *Ob* rang up when I was very bad & God knows what I may have told them. I never see it.[1]

Did you see the Mosleys on American TV?[2] They seem to have been made a great fuss of – next they'll be off to China no doubt. One interviewer said 'What did your father *do*?' 'Nothing.' '*Nothing?*' I remember being asked the same except that I said English people made such huge amounts from the slave trade they've never had to work since. Sir Oz was cross with Honky & said she ought to have answered 'he was in agriculture' but, as she says, that would have been a plain lie.[3]

Do ante up a spot of news

Love, Susan

1 In an interview with Penelope Leach about sisters, Nancy had said that she pitied children with few siblings because there was nobody 'to stand between them and life's cruel circumstances'. To this Jessica had retorted that as a child her sisters *were* the cruel circumstances, 'particularly Nancy, who was immensely clever and sharp'. *Observer*, 20 February 1972.

2 Mosley was in America promoting his autobiography.

3 This exchange took place over dinner (and not during a TV interview) between Diana and a friend of Mosley's editor at Arlington House, his US publisher.

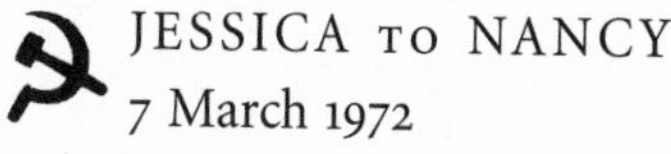

JESSICA TO NANCY
7 March 1972

6411 Regent Street
Oakland

Darling Sukie,

Thanks awfully for yours of 24 Feb – I've been away, so only just got it.

The *Obs* – well I've never seen it, although the brute of a lade who rang up promised to send. But I think you said that sisters are a shield against cruel adversity, and I said I thought you *were* the cruel adversity, or something like that. Oh how *beastly* of me, but do admit you were, a bit?

I didn't see the Mosleys on telly, how maddening, never even knew they were on telly until someone told me they'd seen Sir O. on the *Today Show*. Fancy that, I suppose it was Cord's first time in the US?

I'm *so* sorry that horrible pain keeps up. The Hen says the excellent Bristol Dr will be going to see you in April? Oh I do hope he'll do some good.

My book's coming along all too slowly. The hope is to finish it by end of summer & then scram to Europe.

Much love, Susan

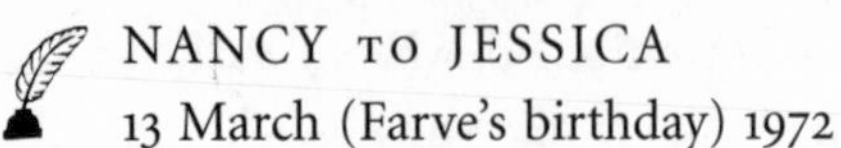

NANCY TO JESSICA
13 March (Farve's birthday) 1972

4 rue d'Artois
Versailles

Darling Sooze

You are dreadful. The only thing is, if one is such a Beast of the Apocalypse, I can't think why one keeps up relations – let alone come here & shake one's pillow. Anyway, I'm being well paid out for a spot of teasing I can tell you.

There was an article on prisons here. Most of them are medieval buildings, & treatment more or less the same. But there is one which makes every Fr. tax payer see red*: it's like a businessman's hotel with bed sitters & running music & so on. But the man who wrote the article said if given the choice he would rather be in one of the old ones (& I bet so would I).

I'm reading *Les Misérables* & so should you. That & *Monte Cristo*[1] wonderfully describe the hopeless feeling that prison must give & the awful situation after one has been let out. (Not in the case of MC who immediately became the richest man on earth!)

I wonder if you'll see old Don Harrod, his white beard stained with, I fear, whisky. I gave yr address but it's probably 1,000 miles from where he is. Billa, now Lady Harrod because the old Don is a Sir, came for 10 days & was so kind. I was rather bad at the time. It's funny how people differ & some are so wonderful if one is in pain – the best of *all* is Mme Guimont my femme de ménage – all sisters are perfect.

Best love Soozy Woo, N

*Fr. tax payers still believe in punishments you see.

1 Victor Hugo's *Les Misérables* was published in 1862 and Alexandre Dumas' *The Count of Monte Cristo* in 1844–5.

JESSICA TO NANCY *6411 Regent Street*
19 March 1972 *Oakland*

Susan, now don't be like that, after all it is but the Teaser Teased, wouldn't you say? But you sounded BITTER, saying I don't know why you bother to keep up relations etc. Anyway I still don't know what the *Observer* said, as nobody sent it & I haven't seen it. Do send, if you've got it. And also do stop being cross; it makes me v. sad as *I* thought you'd be AMUSED. (That is, assuming they did not misquote.)

Thanks for info. about the Fr. businessmen's club prisons. Mine's going to be about how the supposed to be *kind* prisons are far crueller than the known to be vile ones – my dear Susan how would you like to be forced to go to GROUP THERAPY as a condition of being let out on parole?

We are vaguely hoping to come to England etc in Sept, hoping the book will be finished by then. Can I still come & see you, in spite of all?

Much love, Susan

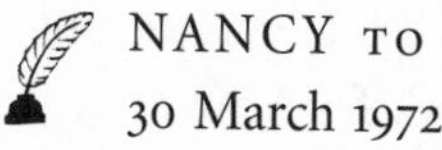

NANCY TO PAMELA *4 rue d'Artois*
30 March 1972 *Versailles*

Only a word to say I've got the Legion of Honour – you may imagine I'm terribly pleased. Gilly [Madame Guimont] for some reason *simply furious* – Hassan pleased. Gil sniffed just like Blor would have & said she wondered if it was true – I showed her the medal after which she sniffed & said no more.

I wish you were here to go & buy me the little red buttonhole I don't dare ask Gil! Do be pleased!

Love, N

I'm also a bit better thank goodness. U wair so *good*.

NANCY TO JESSICA
Easter Monday [3 April] 1972

4 rue d'Artois
Versailles

Darling Soo

You are kind but don't send prison books I'll read yours. Everybody seems to agree that the kind prisons are worse than the old sort. In the Venetian lagoon there is an island looney bin, marvellously beautiful, 18th cent. A looney dr friend of mine went to see it with a letter for the Governor who said I suppose you've come to see the chapel & was amazed when it was the loons. My friend said they are treated the same as in the 12th cent but it makes no odds, all lunatics are miserable & in many ways *we* make them more so.

I've got the Legion of Honour (for my *œuvre historique*) – busy sewing it into all my clothes. Susan I fear you will sneer but all the *workers* of my acquaintance are pleased but I suppose they are all Uncle Toms.

Teresa's *Hons & Rebels*[1] has even fascinated Honks so perhaps I'll send it to you? Say yes or no – you are prob. too busy. There's a fearfully funny account of her barging into a luncheon party & making a speech to Enoch Powell,[2] oh how brave.

I'm very bad but clever Woo has found a lady to bring my brekker on the days (Sundays & Bank Hols) when Uncle Hassan prefers to lie in the arms of his Spanish mistress. I can't fend for myself at all, the pain is too bad & that's partly why I so much dread your & Teresa's revolution. The nerve specialist said, what I seem to have noticed, that it must be very painful & there is no cure. Rather a mercy, no more horrible & expensive treatments. But for the moment I am in euphoria, you can't think what heaven after all these horrible months. The pill has a slight disad. I tumble about like a Russian doll, fearfully giddy. The servants hate it although I explain it's not the least dangerous – for one thing I have warning: everything goes black & white like an old photograph. I admit it's a bore. Hassan is having his holiday. He writes 'votre fidèle serviteur'[3] – when he left I was in the depths & he was so good & kind. I do hope for his sake I shall pick up as it must be lowering for him.

Mary McCarthy's book[4] is quite dazzling, you will – or will have

– adored it. But isn't it touching that the Americans still go on seeing themselves as simple good & honest compared with the twisty Europeans!! The rest of the world regards their cold cruelty with terror. You must be having a field day, almost too much copy, with your prisons. When?

Send a little word.

Love, Soo

1 Teresa Hayter, *Hayter of the Bourgeoisie* (1971). Nancy described the book written by the left-wing daughter of her diplomat friend Sir William Hayter as 'a better written more educated less funny *Hons & Rebels*'. *Love From Nancy* (Hodder & Stoughton, 1993), p. 515.
2 Enoch Powell (1912–98). Conservative MP who campaigned against Commonwealth immigration to Britain.
3 'Your faithful servant.'
4 *Birds of America.*

NANCY TO DEBORAH
9 April 1972

4 rue d'Artois
Versailles

Dear Miss

It was so good of you to come I'm afraid I was very depressing. I know what a nuisance I am to Honky. I know I ought to bugger off into a nursing home & be heard of no more but it would be prison for life; if I did it it would *only* be for her sake. But knowing her & our relationship, in the end it might be yet more of a nuisance. You know she only comes here about twice a week & in a way the *worry* is that I've got a pain. In a nursing home I'd be utterly wretched as well, miserably unhappy & pointless. You must see that the present crisis is slowly calming down, it has been very bad. In future I won't tell Honks that I'm having one, she must be protected. I can see Sir Oz is fed up & I don't wonder. Oh what an affliction to fall on one. This is the fourth summer & though at the start I was much better in myself the pain was the same – I remember old Marie crying when she saw me. What's so extra horrid is feeling so ill, no doubt from the drugs. Nevair.

So Miss don't force me into a hospital. Admit I goodly spent

3 months in one last year really only to please you & did all the vile things, lumbar puncture & so on, for nothing. Admit oh do.

Love, N

DIANA to DEBORAH

5 rue Villedo, I

2 May 1972

Darling Debo:

Naunce has got a CBE!! She said on (very faint) telephone 'I've got CBE'. I was horrified & said 'Got *what*?' (thinking 'twas a new illness). Well it has cheered her up & made her feel better, is it not perfect. Between you me & doorpost she was telling me (after d'Honneur) that nothing would induce her to accept an idiotic English equivalent. I believe people often *say* that but seldom *do* same. (I know Uncle Harold is an exception, & in a small way so was Evie Waugh).[1] About Naunce I am so pleased because all these things really & truly do help her. She said something very disarming: 'What I love about my CBE is thinking of all the people it will annoy'.

All love darling, Honks

1 Harold Macmillan refused a peerage after his resignation in 1964 but accepted the title of the Earl of Stockton twenty years later. Evelyn Waugh refused the CBE in 1959 and later regretted it.

DIANA to DEBORAH

5 rue Villedo, I

25 April 1972

Darling Debo

Something I've been meaning to tell you for ages, of terrible all round pathos. Last time Wooms was here we spoke of Rignell & the war & she suddenly said 'I'm afraid I wasn't always kind to Nanny & the boys'. I quickly said 'Oh Wooms you were, it was wondair of you to harbour them'.

But of course it's true, & one of my great (past) sorrows is that not only did I miss all those years of them, but they had no love from any one except Nanny [Higgs], who was marvellous but definitely *not* like our Nanny. It is not only a waste, but I'm sure was very bad for them. It just couldn't be helped. Even Nancy would have been MUCH better I'm certain. Woo just couldn't help it. She doesn't like children, & then she'd also got none & probably half wanted some. Muv would have been good, & you ideal, but it wasn't possible. Very unlucky, in such a big family, that they went to the only one who really hates children, wasn't it. I never thought Woo wd ever say it, poor Woo, not her fault in the least.

P.S. Very lovely about Garrett's garter[1] is it not. I must say of all our friends he & Frank [Longford] would have seemed (in those days) the least likely to be given it. I don't know the moral of that. (No, Brian Howard the LEAST likely, but nevertheless very *un*likely.) He deserves it & so does Frank.

To go back to the war, when Al & Max came to Holloway Al used to say over & over again 'I don't live at Swinbrook,[2] I've got a *HOME*, I go there every night. It's in Russia. I'm Mr Russian.' It was so sad the emphasis on home, it killed one. Then aged 12 he was torn from Crowood. It doesn't bear thinking of. '*You* think I'm asleep, but you see really I'm at my *home*.' Oh Debo.

1 Lord Drogheda had been made a Knight of the Garter.
2 In 1942, Alexander and Max had been paying guests at the Mackinnons', who had bought Swinbrook from Lord Redesdale.

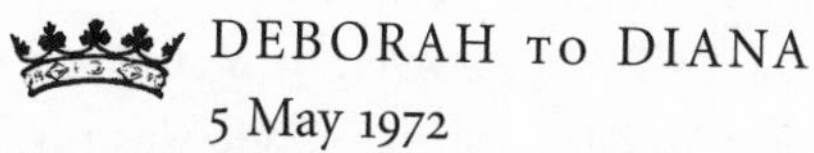

DEBORAH TO DIANA
5 May 1972

Lismore Castle
Co. Waterford

Darling Honks

Now Honks, the war & the boys. It doesn't bear thinking of. It was odd, looking back, that Muv didn't get a bigger house & have them, but of course Birdie was nigh on a full time job with the bed-wetting & everything else. Of course I was too stupid & too young. The Mackinnon interlude was an odd one, I can't remember how long it lasted. It's honest of Woman to admit to not liking children.

The other thing is that everyone has something untoward which happens in childhood (or thinks they have in later life, viz. Em & her lack of education, Nancy ditto etc etc. I must admit I've got no complaints, I adored my life till Swinbrook went & even after that. I never ceased to be grateful that I was taken away from that awful school) but of course their experience was specially odd & beastly. What *you* must have suffered, as you were such a specially maternal sort of bloke, doesn't bear thinking of but perhaps that's what's turned you into a saint. Yes, Honks, quite likely.

Much love, Debo

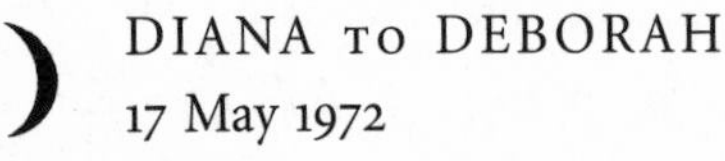

DIANA TO DEBORAH
17 May 1972

Temple de la Gloire
Orsay

Darling Debo:

To go back to an old letter & subject, Al & Max in the war, of course I absolutely agree that everyone has traumas in childhood, & *a fortiori* in wartime, when one thinks of whole cities wiped out & the few pathetic children left, & so on. I don't a bit imagine Al & Max had a very bad time. It was just that it was rather unlucky they went to Woo, & that Woman Mackinnon & her sister also rather loathed children. That's why I worship Miss Lowry-Corry,[1] who used to be so kind & friendly to them & to dear old Nanny. In a way what I regret is the *waste of sweetness* but probably not many people wd mind that.

My own childhood was fairly happy, & I was in the ideal position in the family, utterly un-noticed & sandwiched between so many. I preferred Farve to Muv then, & Nanny to either of them. She was my all-in-all. As I got older my all-in-alls were you & Decca. You were like Stella & Willie Whitelaw[2] rolled into one, & Decca was lovely too. Well, there we are. We are lucky to be alive, well, with all those grandchildren. I got a letter from Jasper [Guinness]'s Eton tutor saying he will always be grateful to Jasper for making the house such a happy place (!!). Do kindly admit.

All love darling, Honks

1 Patricia Lowry-Corry (1905–2003). A cousin of Pamela Mackinnon and a frequent visitor to Swinbrook.
2 Two of Deborah's grandchildren, Stella Tennant (1970–), the future fashion model, and William Burlington (1969–), the future photographer.

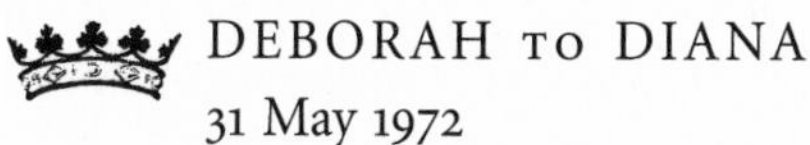

DEBORAH TO DIANA
31 May 1972

Chatsworth
Bakewell

Darling Honks

All the programmes about the Dook[1] have been tragic in the extreme. Last night we had nearly the whole of the interview with Harris.[2] The charm came over anew, & all the more poignant now. The interview with that FOUL Taylor,[3] *IDOL*,[4] [Bob] Boothby & that other grey haired effort called something like Coon, no [Colin] Coote, was v. interesting. Coote and Idol were the best, Idol simply said it was *no good* marrying someone with 2 living husbands & of course that was the beginning & end of it. Earlier in the day Boothby had said what a pity he hadn't been Viceroy of India – well of course they wouldn't have had him, just think of the old-fashionedness of the Dominions in 1936 which is another age anyway.

I said to Andrew but the Honest Injuns all had masses of wives each & he said the English there wouldn't have had it, & anyway the Indians were so different that one couldn't compare – it was she who had had the husbands not he wives.

Do you suppose she has got any friends, real sort of *Wives*? And I wonder how her illness is? Oh do enlarge.

Much love, Debo

1 The Duke of Windsor had died on 28 May.
2 The Duke and Duchess of Windsor were interviewed by Kenneth Harris for the BBC in 1970.
3 A. J. P. Taylor (1906–90). Controversial left-wing historian.
4 Bridget Hore-Ruthven (1896–1982). Married, in 1947, Sir Walter Monckton, the Duke of Windsor's legal adviser during the Abdication crisis.

DIANA TO DEBORAH
5 June 1972

Temple de la Gloire
Orsay

Darling Debo

Dook. Here are my deep thoughts. His marvellousness was wasted, but what could one have done differently? Viceroy of India wd have been hopeless, out of the question. If he'd lived in England *with nothing to do* they wd probably have been in English café society (have rushed to Aspinalls[1] etc) which wd have been much worse in every way than doing it here, or in Florida. He would never have made a 'country gentleman' any more than she could have been a farmer's wife. The whole thing was hateful & tragic yet I can't see what else could have happened really than what did. It might have been far worse, for example if they'd been poor. They lived in terrific luxury thank goodness.

I think her choice of Wife for the funeral was perfect; Grace [Dudley] not being English, & Dudley having been a great friend. I am very glad so many people struggled down to Windsor for his lying in state. I think one thing that should have been cancelled (if one was going to pretend to be in mourning) was Pcess Margaret going to a ball at Quaglinos (!!) Trooping the Colour was perfect, & having 'The Flowers of the Forest'. You know how much I loved him & I can't think of him without the tears welling up yet, despite all, I think he was rather happy & generally amused & busy, & he really did love & adore her, that was completely obvious the more one saw them. I think the royal family could have been more generous, & probably the theory of their contemporaries that Cake was rather in love with him (as a girl) & took second best, may account for much.

As to her not being royal highness I think it perfectly absurd & petty & probably quite untrue – I mean I daresay one should have had an Act of Parliament to proclaim that she was only a morganatic wife. Because if she was his wife she was also HRH, as laid down by Q. Victoria, since he was the son of a sovereign. I don't believe there is any 'right' to withhold it. (Walter Monckton's opinion.) Well darling enough of all that & now he is at this minute being buried at

Frogmore. On the whole I think all those arrangements have been decent & right, & shining by his niceness is Prince Charles, who seems to have made things so much easier for the Duchess. I rather dread the future. She is ill, that's certain. I am glad he died first, he wd have been in total despair without her.

I have had millions of headaches. I only tell you this in case you find me looking ill. I pin faith on the sun & heat & if it goes on when good weather comes I will try something ('something must be done'[2] ha-ha, easier to say than to find a remedy eh).

All love darling, Honks

1 A London gambling club.
2 The phrase used by the Duke of Windsor in 1936 (when he was King) when he saw the suffering caused by mass unemployment in Wales.

DIANA TO NANCY
11 September 1972
Decca's birthday

Temple de la Gloire
Orsay

Oh Derel,

I feel so sad over you, it really is despairing & unbearable. I shall hear details from Debo tomorrow. (*Hear* is the operative word because when the line's bad like just now I can't.)

We've got the whole of Robert Skidelsky's book[1] now & I rushed through it. Sir Oz hardly allows me to comment because he doesn't wish it to be considered 'authorized'. Enough to say that as far as *I* go the two sources are Decca & Auntie Ni [Ravensdale] (do you remember Auntie Ni's book[2] which you chose for your desert island). The awful thing is, as one grows older one minds less & less & lets everything pass, & as you so truly say, what is between hard covers is considered the truth, later on, but tant pis.[3]

Something I mind much more is that the World Service has completely disappeared from its old wavelength, I suppose one must write to the tahsome BBC. When you think how they go on & on boring one with wavelengths & metre bands & mega hertz or whatever they're called, yet from one day to next there's nothing but a sort of drum doing the first bar of the V Symphony. Maddening.

All love derel, D

1 The manuscript of *Oswald Mosley*, published in 1975.
2 Irene Ravensdale, *In Many Rhythms*.
3 'Too bad.'

DIANA TO DEBORAH
28 November 1972

Temple de la Gloire
Orsay

Darling Debo:

I got your long letter written in the train on paper given by a gent, & it may be the last for a bit because I see in the vile paper that the tiresome post here is striking again but please go on writing just the same. Last time I telephoned there was a hint of a *laugh* from Naunce, the first for weeks. It was about Duckie II asking her whether she wants to live or die, & that she had answered 'die, of course'. But it's no laughing matter if she's really got to live with the pain plus the awful weakness. *Poor* Naunce. Birthday today. I note you are at Chatsworth & darling I do hope they don't disturb you, for once.

Yes isn't J. Thorpe perfect when he 'does' Uncle Harold,[1] once in Venice it made me weak with laughing, it was at midnight & passers-by must have thought we were all drunk. He is so clever as a clown & so clownish as a politician, always on the wrong side (except for Common Market that is).

Kit took me for his favourite daily walk in the wood, oh Debo how you would have laughed. There are enough old stoves thrown away in brambles to furnish a block of flats not to mention tins & reams of paper. He simply doesn't see all this & says, 'Percher,[2] look at the tops of the birches in the wind, aren't they beautiful, & look at this glade' (with a burnt-out car in it) 'isn't it like a glade at Wootton, how I hope they won't spoil it, look at the stream' (choked with rubbish) 'sometimes it rushes along, isn't the sound of it beautiful' etc etc, one could hug him but I can't make out whether he just ignores or literally doesn't *see* the horrors, I think it's the latter.

All love darling, Honks

1 Deborah had sat next to the Liberal Party leader, Jeremy Thorpe (1929–), who did 'a perfect imitation' of Harold Macmillan and the Archbishop of Canterbury.
2 Mosley's nickname for Diana was 'Percheron'.

DIANA TO DEBORAH
4 December 1972

Temple de la Gloire
Orsay

Darling Debo

Yesterday we lunched with the Duchess of W[indsor], pathos personified, about nine people including a nurse (in a green silk dress) & she (Duchess) tried to set the ball rolling by saying nowadays people are only inter-ested in SEX, well as we were all well on the way to the grave the ball refused to roll. However it was all very jolly, & the food to dream of, she is a genius for food.

We dined with Mona [Bismarck] & the dinner was really foul, money *can't* buy good food can it. We also dined with Mogens, he has got a dread talent for finding really dull people & we got 3 total strangers, it's ages since I felt dinner taking quite so long. If Kit hadn't been there 'twould have been better, because one suffered for him, & he tried so hard (because he's fond of Mogens), he is good in those ways. It probably comes from having been deadly bored in politics in constituencies – don't.

I can't tell you what the stores are like here this year, the hideous drear of what they sell, I'm sure Moscow couldn't be worse. No wonder people go to London for the shopping. Unless one can afford the grandees there is literally nothing on the clothes front.

Well darling a dull letter I fear but just to prove I'm still alive.

All love, Honks

I sat next a man yesterday who told me that Louise de V said the reason teeth are so important is that they are the only part of the skeleton to show. Rather a bold remark when one remembers *her* teeth eh.[1]

1 Louise de Vilmorin had the teeth of an aged nanny goat.

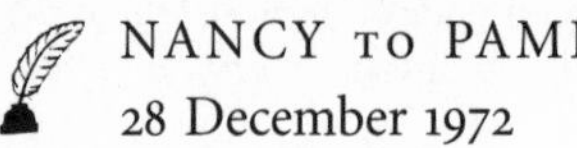

NANCY TO PAMELA
28 December 1972

Fitzroy Nuffield Hospital
London W1[1]

Derel

I wish you were here I can't find anything!!!

I'm rather low with a very bad pain. They say everything is all right now – no more cancer or anaemia or sweating, in short I'm absolutely well but I've had a murdering pain all all day. It's true I have it less than formerly & not every day but I can't lead an ordinary life when it may descend at any time. This morning it was the crying sort. Oh Woman! & the thousands of pounds I pour out. The drs say I would have died in about three weeks if I'd gone on like in the summer. I rather wish I had. But I suppose one's hold on life is very strong & the will to live.

Have you read a fascinating book called *Lark Rise*?[2] If not oi send.

Oh do give my love to all those kind friends & even strangers who send me theirs. Giuditta must have been pleased to see you.

My Xmas dinner was Joy's[3] left-overs. I can never tell the deliciosity. She has got a genius for sauce. Ending with gooseberry fool. She is really good to me.

Keep in touch.

Love from Naunce

Pitch dark here the sun never seems to rise.

1 Nancy spent six months in hospital in London where she was eventually diagnosed and treated for Hodgkin's disease, a cancer of the lymph cells which in her case was rooted in the spine.

2 Flora Thompson, *Lark Rise to Candleford* (1945), a memoir of rural life at the turn of the twentieth century.

3 Joy Spira (1927–). Picture researcher for *Madame de Pompadour, The Sun King* and *Frederick the Great*. Married Richard Law in 1955.

DIANA TO NANCY — 5 rue Villedo, I
15 January 1973

Derel,

Constant's[1] uncle, aged 91, died & he feared it would be un coup dur[2] for the old father who is 94. Jean said no it wouldn't & that when his aunt died aged 88 his mother, who was ninety, only said 'Elle a toujours été *fragile*'[3] & didn't care a bit. After 85 one only thinks & minds about oneself. Another way in which extreme age joins up with the first months of life, babies only think of themselves, eh.

I'm reading the last vol of Simone de Beauvoir's autobiography,[4] it is rather good but more bitty than the *Force de l'age* & the *Force des choses*. It seems too strange that this woman living in the same town as us, & just our age, & loving many of the same things we do (for instance she adored the Orieux *Talleyrand*,[5] loves Rome, Piazza Navona & all the places one loves, thinks Champ de Bataille the most beautiful château of all, & so on) & yet in her opinions about people is so unlike *one*. All the friends she describes go practically mad in one way or another & are more than pestilential. Then one thinks of Sartre at the tomb of Chateaubriand.[6] What a crew.

All love darling, D

1 Constant Plantin; a close friend of Jean de Baglion.
2 'A heavy blow.'
3 'She was always *delicate*.'
4 *Tout compte fait* (1972).
5 Jean Orieux, *Talleyrand ou Le Sphinx incompris* (1970).
6 The philosopher Jean-Paul Sartre (1905–80) had urinated on the tomb of the illustrious nineteenth-century author to demonstrate his contempt for the notion of 'a great writer'.

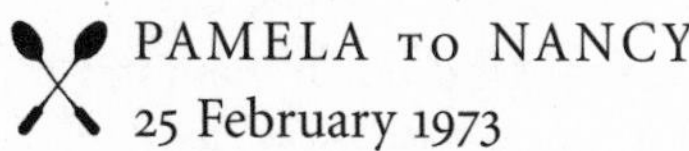

PAMELA TO NANCY — Woodfield House, Caudle Green
25 February 1973

Dereling,

This is just to announce that I am now back here at Woodfield. It all seems so nice & I am going to get the inside tidied up a bit & some of the rooms re-decorated. It is badly needed after 12 years!

Derel, I do hope you will be better by the time you get this, I gather from Nard & Cynthia [Gladwyn] that you were very bad this last week, I am *so* sorry. If you need help you must let me know.

Much love from Woman

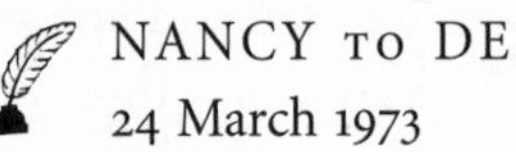

NANCY TO DEBORAH
24 March 1973

4 rue d'Artois
Versailles

Dear Miss

Woman with her own little house she must long for is doing filthy things for me like bedpans without anything but smiles, how *can* she be so noble? What can I do for her? You must think & tell me.

I am in horrid pain from the leg perhaps the very worst ever though one can't say that & I imagine it is really the same old pain I've always had.

Such beautiful P.C.s from Joy [Law] in Peking – no wonder our grandfather was utterly bowled over by what he saw there.[1]

I'm very unhappy, so so grateful to Woo, I feel I'm a burden to all, it is part of the horror.

Best love, Lady

1 The 1st Baron Redesdale had been sent by the Foreign Office to China in 1865.

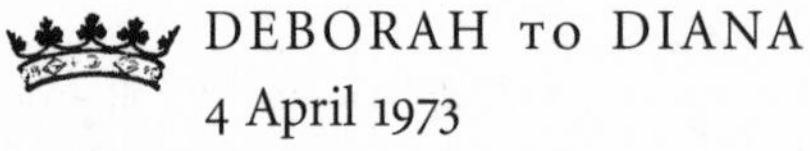

DEBORAH TO DIANA
4 April 1973

Chatsworth
Bakewell

Darling Honks

I had such a nice letter from Decca, saying she'd drop everything & come to Versailles if it wd be any help to Nancy or to us. I've written & tried to explain to her that it is v. v. kind but it wouldn't really be worth the terrific effort (because I absolutely know she would only get a luke-warm welcome & that in itself wd be so depressing wouldn't it).

So it is just a question of waiting & I quite realize, & said so to Hen, that it may be ages. I feel it is all putting an awful lot on you.

This last week must have been a monster effort – I do hope your voice is back & that you aren't whacked to the last, but I know you must be. Oh *Honks* it is ghoul.

You would think the Palfium would have sort of poisoned her by now. Henderson says why on earth not heroin in your own home. Think of addicts – quite true. Anyway we just know nothing is possible until *she* demands something more & different.

Well Honks I am so sorry for all you've got on hand.

Much love, Debo

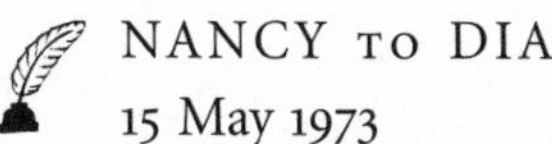

NANCY TO DIANA
15 May 1973

4 rue d'Artois
Versailles

Derel,

When next you come you must tell the old woman I am not as tough as I look. I can't bear to be shouted at & last night I wept sadly thinking what it would be like to have somebody like Marie at one's deathbed. She roars into the room & always has something to scold me about. I don't always even know what it is & in my weak state haven't got any comeback. I'm very miserable though I know with all the advantages we must CLING. But if she could be a little politer like she was in the beginning & fear of you might do the trick!

Mrs Hadfield I am told died quietly in the night why can't I. Quite unexpectedly, you couldn't say that of me.

Love, N

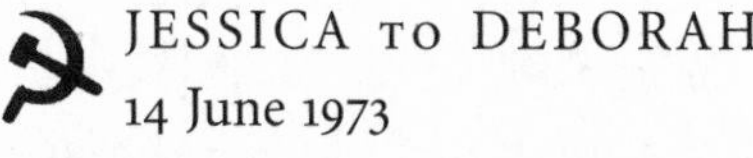

JESSICA TO DEBORAH
14 June 1973

'Mon Impasse'
Versailles

Dearest Hen,

I'm not at all sure how well *I* am doing as Sis-in-residence. I feel always either too-little-and-too-late, or too-much-too-early. Two examples (& remember this is my first day on the job, always fraught with awkwardness in my experience): Hassan brought in massive vases of roses soon after I came, whisking away the old ones.

Suddenly, her eyes filled with tears & she said, 'everyone says there are masses of roses in the garden, *why* doesn't anyone bring them up here?' So I said I'll dash & get some, which I did. As you may have noted, it does take a few minutes to get them, & I raced back with 3 more vases. So N., in cuttingest tones: 'I see your life does not contain much art and grace.' Too true, but *Hen*! So I got lots more & put 'em round. Nancy: 'I can't think why you didn't get them earlier, you haven't got anything else to do'. In other words, I think she's rather taken against me. Yet I can't make out whether *me* sitting in her room & reading or writing letters as distinct from *you*, Woman or Diana doing ditto pleases or annoys.

Diana rang up & I told her all the part about the roses, saying I long for advice & instructions; turns out one was automatically *supposed* to do the roses each day, so now I shall, but one can't exactly guess these things. Of course Diana pointed out, which I absolutely do see, that she's not herself etc, so one must just get on with it – which I am totally willing and longing to do, Hen.

Goodnight, Henny. Think of me sometimes in these foreign parts,

Yr loving Hen

) DIANA to DEBORAH

15 June 1973

5 rue Villedo, I

Darling Debo

We are only here one night. This is just to tell you Naunce has been so foul to Decca, don't let Decca know that I said, but it is really so dreadful when she came so far, it made me cry & still does when I think about it. You see I telephoned last night (as she'd been so bad in the morning when you were with me) & asked for the nurse & Decca came & apparently Liliane de Rothschild[1] was visiting (after a lot of on & off & finally on from Naunce) & in the morning, no doubt on that silly account, Naunce said, 'Why can't I have any roses in here?' & Decca went & picked them & put them in vases & Naunce said, 'Anyone can see you've never had anything gracious in your life' (those were the words Decca told me), & Decca said to me 'So you can imagine how useless I felt'.

Well darling I can't get over this piece of horridness. How could one say that to someone of whom it's vaguely true, it literally gave me a (physical) pain in my heart. Decca is so wonderful & tough that possibly it isn't as bad as one thinks. I kept on saying, 'One must just remember that it's not her any more', & Decca, 'Of course I know it isn't, it's only that I want to find out what to do, for instance does she like one to sit quietly in the room or does she prefer to be alone?' I said, 'I think she rather likes to open her eyes & see a person sitting there.'

The fact that Decca told me the saga may show she didn't mind too much but I think she did mind – not about not being an expert rose-arranger but the unkind tone of her voice & real rudeness after that endless journey, not to say expense & so forth. Oh Debo, it has upset me so much, it's the sort of thing one can't bear. How well I understand your feeling for your Hen. I said to her can you stick a week & she said she could.

All love darling, Honks

1 Liliane Fould-Springer (1916–2003). Art collector and philanthropist. Married Baron Elie de Rothschild, by proxy, in 1942.

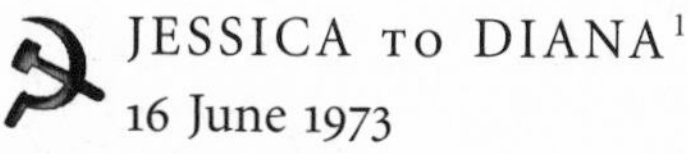

JESSICA to DIANA[1]
16 June 1973

6 Impasse Clagny
Versailles

Darling Cord

Just a word to say today was (after you left) foam rubber day, as distinct from la visite de Mme la Baronne de Rothschild day or Electric Toothbrush Day, all of which merge in one's mind anyhow. Language barrier both sides Pacific/Atlantic came straight to the fore when Ann[2] said she wanted a rubber sponge. 'Eponge en caoutchou', I was wondering? Having long since forgotten most Fr. words for things. Turns out she meant to say the stuff used in pillows, mattresses etc which she calls rubber sponge & we call foam rubber. I set out to find out what the Fr. call it: la mousse! One wouldn't want that for pudding, don't you agree, although I've often had it. Not obtainable on our shopping rue, so forward to Prisunic, which had it in ample supply. Ann had fashioned a v. clever border of it around the bedpan to ease the agony of sitting. In my view, a v. good invention bound to find far more favour than the elec. t.brush etc.

So, coming back to the Impasse & dying for a *Herald Tribune* (sold out everywhere, I've looked all day) I stumbled on a Gare [station]. All shut (newsstands etc) except for a photo place, 1 fr, three mins, which invites you to record yr 'mood of the moment'. Here it is.

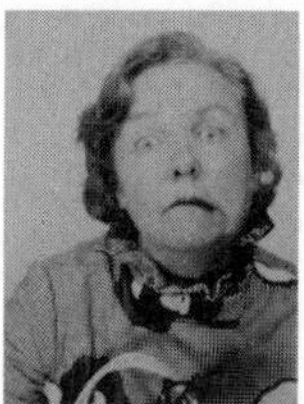

Much love, Dec

No change in her general condition after you left, although she was pleased to see La Mousse trekked in (fearing the while it was unsanitary etc, yet I believe she'll like it once tried).

Tomorrow, the Wars of the Roses – pray for me, as there aren't too many good ones left, they often fall to bits as one picks them . . .

1 This is the only post-war letter from Jessica to Diana.
2 A New Zealand nurse who was looking after Nancy.

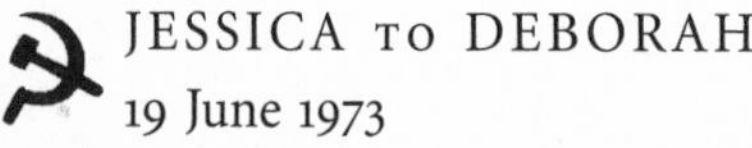

JESSICA TO DEBORAH *Versailles*
19 June 1973

Dearest Hen,

Just a word to say I do think the events of yesterday, Dr visit & ordering 4 double morphine injections daily, have made a huge difference.

All this makes me not so much mind abt. leaving tomorrow (and feeling that when I do I'll probably never see her again). I'm afraid I haven't been much help, too little & too late, also it was so awful having to stir poor Diana out; yet N. looked so very near death & so much worse than any time since I've been here (this was all before the Dr came & the double injection) that I thought I simply must ring D; and of course she said that was perfectly right.

I do hope you had a jolly horse show. Sorry this writing's so illegible, I was doing it under the dryer at the local h. dresser.

Much love, Yr Hen

P.S. I'd written all the aforesaid before returning here – so must just say a word abt. the saying goodbye which was pretty ghastly. After supper I got my things together (such as they are, you know, bag, basket, coat but dawdled over) & then went to have a word with Hassan. I said that in every single letter my sister has written ever since you came here she has spoken of you & can't say enough abt. how good you are to her (etc etc) & he responded, 'I look on her as a mother' (!!!) so I said I am your aunt, in that case, & we both fell to sobbing, Hen. So I mounted to N's room, full of resolve to say briskly 'well goodbye for the present' but sensing I was losing control just said 'goodbye Soo' & fled in floods. Ann said [Nancy] gazed at my retreating back & noted the floods & started crying like mad but *long* before I actually left was sound [asleep], so all that part's OK. As you've perhaps noted in life, to me she's a) a hurler of slings & arrows as in last few days re roses etc (yet starting when I was 5, in my recollection) & b) stellar attraction, sort of alternating between these. And now she won't be there to alternate.

Hen sorry for this dreary wail, any blood on this paper is *pure* flea blood the brutes.

Yr Loving Hen

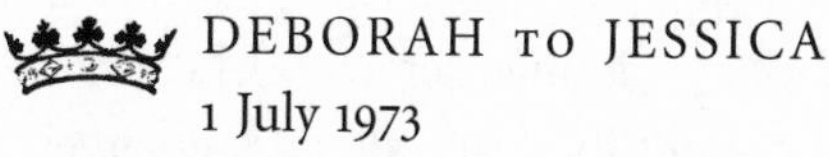

DEBORAH TO JESSICA
1 July 1973

Woodfield House
Caudle Green

Dearest Hen

Nancy died in her sleep at 1.30 P.M. yesterday.

The Colonel had been to see her in the morning & *thought* she recognised him.

Thank goodness it is over, she really had the most awful time any one can ever have had.

It was so marvellous of you to do that awful journey the other day. Thank goodness we didn't put you off till July, which we so nearly did. And thank goodness she died at home & not in some foul hosp. She is going to be cremated in France on Tues or Wed and Honks & Sir O will bring the dreaded casket back on Thurs and 'twill be buried at Swinbrook on Sat 7th. Everyone thinks that is the best, and friends who want to come to the funeral can, instead of.

Apparently one awful complication about bringing ashes to England from abroad is that it is the usual approved way for drug people to move their wares about, so it just makes it more difficult and complicated.

Oh Hen how odd life is. And death. Terrific haste, this is just to tell you the plans.

Much love, Yr Hen

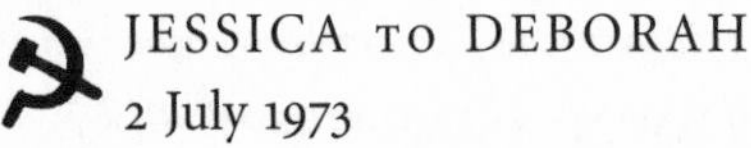

JESSICA to DEBORAH
2 July 1973

6411 Regent Street
Oakland

Hen, you can imagine how *immensely* glad I am that I went to Versailles – very much Bob's doing, he flogged me on & said I shld. regret it if I didn't go, very right. Also having actually been there, & seeing, is perhaps the only way one could really grasp the fact of wishing it was all over for her, and thus not minding so terribly when it was. Oh Hen wasn't it all too vile for words. In yr. gram you said 'peacefully', & I do so hope that meant the last few days were a bit less foul for her.

So many things come flooding to mind about her, such as Muv saying 'Nancy is a very curious character', too true. The great regret being that she hadn't got the strength to do the Memoirs, where said curiosity of character wld. have come out full force, don't you agree? But she did leave far more behind than most people, such as her smashing books & the general memorableness of her. Some of which even comes through in the obit. in the *S.F. Chronicle*, though dimly, & through the puzzled eyes of the obit. writer.

You must be absolutely swamped with the thousand horrid details that crowd in after deaths, so don't bother to answer. I'm mainly writing to say thanks awfully for the telegram; by a quirk of time etc. I didn't get it until I'd seen in the paper, 'Author Nancy Mitford Dies', a chill yet blank message since the actual mourning for her has been going on so long.

Much love, & to the others, Yr Hen

DIANA TO JESSICA[1]

8 July 1973

Temple de la Gloire
Orsay

Darling Decca

I'm staying with Woman really. (Not as above.) We had Naunce's funeral yesterday. Swinbrook was looking wonderful, green & summery & blue sky. There were many friends & none of the ghastly people who crowd into memorial services.

All the French part was what Woman wd call ghoulish, this was because of various things like boiling hot brazen days, & the fact that she was cremated. We are having a service later on in the church one saw out of her window. Debo is sending the obituary from *The Times* which was the only good one (Raymond Mortimer). Her grave is next to Boud's.

Well darling that's it. You were more than wonderful to have come, & I'm so thankful we settled for June, since July would have been too late.

I enclose what Col & I put in *Figaro*, & a letter to make you laugh (throw of course).

All love, Cord

1 Jessica noted at the top of Diana's letter, 'I stayed with N in June & a few days later she died. After the funeral I got an incredibly nice letter from my sister Diana.' Diana wrote one other letter to Jessica, in 1996, when she learnt that Jessica was dying but the letter has not been found.

DEBORAH TO JESSICA
8 July 1973

Woodfield House
Caudle Green

Dearest Hen

Well it's all over, and one feels an incredible *LIGHTNESS OF SPIRIT* to think that awful pain is done.

I really think she had a FOUL life – not only the last bit which was like being tortured for 4½ years, but all of it. I know she had success as a writer but what is that compared to things like proper husbands & lovers & children – think of the loneliness of all these years, so *sad*.

There was many a drama over getting the Mitford casket to Swinbrook, it was a question of will she won't she till the last minute. Poor Honks had the most awful week in sweltering temps arranging it all with the delightful strikes going on all round & five hours delay every time one wanted to phone, which was all the time.

The actual funeral was so unreal (like they always are) that one could scarce believe one was at it. A devilish photographer from the *Observer* was lurking behind every wool merchant's gravestone, & the

'Three witches', Diana, Pamela and Deborah at Nancy's funeral. Swinbrook, 7 July 1973.

result is enclosed, of three witches, to make you scream. I got wreaths from home from all of us & we put Andrew & 9, Nard & Kit, Woman & Decca on them.

I guess it will save poor old Honks in the nick of time, not having to worry about N any more. She looks grey & thin & worn out. They have gone off to Italy for 2 weeks.

I do hope my telegram landed in Bob's office, the person said we can't send death messages over the phone & I said oh please do & they said alright if it was expected we will.

The flowers were marvellous and still are today.

Well Hen.

Much love, Yr Hen

DIANA TO PAMELA
10 July 1973

Monte San Michele
Capri

Darling Woo

You were so truly wondair the way you welcomed Kit & me, I was just about finished, & staying at Woodfield made just ALL the difference. As to the funeral, I felt sad & then not sad. How lovely for her to rest *there*, with no more vile pain & suffering. Poorling Naunce. I thought the Sunday papers were much more sympathetic to Naunce than the dailies (except *The Times*) had been.

Looking back, Naunce's long illness seems like a terrible nightmare. You had a lot of the worst part, & she LOVED it when you were there in the draughty visitor's room. Oh Woo, *poor* Naunce. Thank heaven it's over. It has made me dislike & despise doctors more than ever. Always *pretending*.

All love Woo, come soon to Temple,
& THANK you, Nard

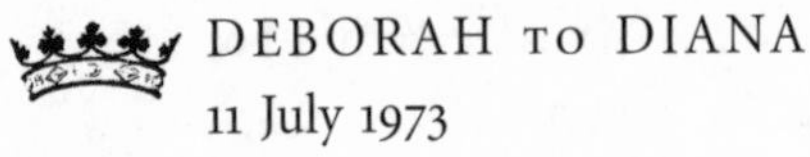

DEBORAH to DIANA
11 July 1973

Chatsworth
Bakewell

Darling Honks

I am thinking of you in the sea. I do hope I'm right? Oh Honks what a time you've had. No one except me will EVER KNOW what it's been like. But when you do eventually get back to Temple it will be a haven won't it . . .

I've had 160 letters. You'll have the same no doubt. I haven't started on them yet, they are daunting. Nothing from Anna Maria [Cicogna]!

Now Honks, 12 of the most eminent cancer researchers came to lunch yesterday to do with the Campaign which A[ndrew] is head of. We were talking about Food. One said smoked things have a very high content of something dangerous which can start cancer. Two off him sat the man who is the last word on that & he said 'oh no that is not so at all'. So you see even at that level they simply DONT KNOW. They were utterly charming of course & one was undone by their niceness & cleverness, but . . .

The Shetland Show was lovely, only one first prize, good for the soul.

Much love, Debo

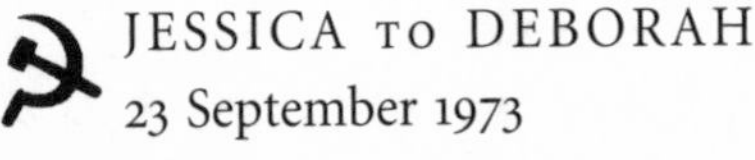

JESSICA to DEBORAH
23 September 1973

6411 Regent Street
Oakland

Dearest Hen,

It's been such ages since I heard from you, & I do hope all is OK – I was away for a v. long time, first on hol in East Hampton & Cape Cod & other delightful spots, then on a GRUELLING tour of me book[1] (telly interviews etc). Am only here for a breather as tomorrow I go down to San José to live there for 3 days a week on dread Distinguished Prof. caper.[2]

Have you sort of recovered from Nancy's death? I must say I haven't, quite – that is sometimes I can't quite take in the fact she's really gone. Those terrible days in Versailles are still awfully vivid, more so come to think of it than everything that's happened since such as our hol., soon faded, Hen. Of course, you had so much more of it during all those frightful 4½ years.

Much love, Yr Hen

1 *Kind and Usual Punishment.*

2 Jessica was teaching a semester at California State University.

EIGHT

1974–1994

Woodfield House Caudle Green Cheltenham Gloucestershire
Miserden (0285 82) 300

Darling Stublow. 30 July 1985.

Thanks for two letter & the Sheep Book, I so agree about the ridiculous dialect. The photographs are good.

Tim arrived yesterday & is better than I expected. He is delighted with his new "second" hand Rover & is busy studying the Manual all about it. Tomorrow the Budheim arrives and for lunch we have Tim's old friend Barbara Shackerly

What good news about the Grouse! When do you set forth for the Abbey? The lunch on Sunday with Jim & the Corteis's was a great success, they

Letter from Pamela to Deborah

The rapprochement between Jessica and her sisters that followed Nancy's death was soon tested by a biography of Unity by David Pryce-Jones. The project was opposed from the outset by Pamela, Diana and Deborah, who were angered by what they saw as Jessica's cooperation with an unsympathetic author and by her refusal to condemn the book when it appeared. In the climate of mistrust created by Jessica's perceived disloyalty, a further row erupted over a missing scrapbook that threatened to sever relations completely. Jessica described the incident as a nightmare, 'one of the worst things that's happened (in a long life of awful things)'.

Over the ensuing two decades, books, articles, documentaries, a television series and even a musical about the Mitfords all served to resurrect old rivalries, and many of the sisters' letters were taken up with managing the runaway family image and mediating old resentments that were revived as a result. The established pattern was that of Diana and Deborah seeing eye-to-eye, Pamela following their lead, and Jessica disputing their version of family events. Because Diana and Jessica never communicated, and Pamela and Jessica wrote only occasionally, most of the disagreements were expressed in angry letters between Jessica and Deborah. Jessica dreaded being cut off from Deborah completely, but resented Deborah appointing herself arbiter of all that went on in the family, especially since, as she wrote to a friend, 'I am 3 years older than she is.'

Pamela settled into a contented old age at Woodfield with her black Labrador for company. She introduced a rare breed of hen, the Apenzeller Spitzhauben, into Britain from Switzerland and became an expert on the rearing and breeding of poultry. During the late 1980s, until the lameness that was a consequence of her childhood polio made it impossible, she accompanied Diana to South Africa to escape the cold European winters.

As Mosley reached old age and began to suffer from Parkinson's disease, he cut back on the restless travelling that had characterized his life since the war and this gave Diana the time to finish her memoirs. *A Life of Contrasts* was published in 1977 and was fiercely attacked for its unrepentant portrait of Hitler. Three years later, Diana wrote a biography of her friend the Duchess of Windsor, an attempt to rehabilitate an unpopular figure whom she felt had been unfairly treated. *Loved Ones*, which appeared in 1985, was a collection of pen portraits of family and friends. In all her books and in reviews for *Books & Bookmen*, the *Evening Standard* and other publications for which she wrote regularly, Diana seized every opportunity to defend Mosley and to advance her own unpopular point of view. Her hostility towards those she held responsible for destroying his career did not lessen with age.

Jessica was now a famous, respected author and personality in America. Her second volume of autobiography, *A Fine Old Conflict*, was published in 1977, at the same time as Diana's memoirs. Over this period, she also produced *The Making of a Muckraker*, a collection of her journalism, *The American Way of Birth*, and two books about English subjects: *Faces of Philip*, a memoir of her old friend Philip Toynbee, and *Grace Had an English Heart*, the story of the Victorian heroine Grace Darling. They sold less well than her previous books but she was still much in demand for her tough investigative articles and as a guest speaker on the lecture circuit, where her funny and subversive talks were greatly admired.

Deborah's book *The House: A Portrait of Chatsworth*, published in 1982 when she was sixty-two, was the first of eight books about the house and the estate that she was to write over the next decades. They were a success and showed that she had the same gift of direct, lively and witty prose as her sisters. Writing gave her and Jessica a shared interest other than family matters for the first time since they were children. They seized on this opportunity to correspond about a non-contentious subject, and this helped to heal the rift caused by their disagreements.

The survival of Chatsworth continued to be the Devonshires' main preoccupation, at a time when rising costs and taxation made the maintenance of large houses in England increasingly difficult. In 1981, Andrew set up a charitable trust, endowed with proceeds of the sale of the *Holy Family* by Nicolas Poussin (which fetched £1.65 million) and seventy Old Master drawings, which helped to meet the huge cost of running the house. Deborah opened a shop in the Chatsworth orangery, selling gifts that reflected the Devonshire art collection, and a farm shop in a nearby village which sold the best of local and British produce. She also opened a restaurant in the converted carriage house in the stables to feed the 500,000 annual visitors to Chatsworth, and this proved as important as the shops in providing funds to support the house and garden.

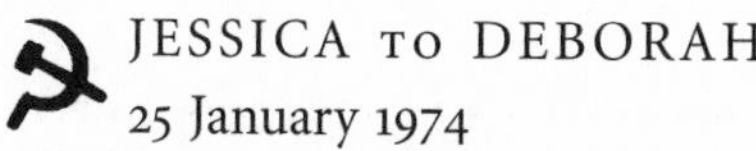

JESSICA TO DEBORAH
25 January 1974

6411 Regent Street
Oakland

Dearest Hen,

We are *practically* on our way, it does seem so unbelievable & exciting – that is, we actually get to London on 2nd March.

You may/may not know about D. Pryce-Jones' plan to do a biography of the Boud.[1] Anyway, a publisher just rang up to say David told him he's doing it 'with your cooperation' (meaning *my* coop). As it's not quite like that, I'll put you in the picture re my position.

David got after me re this some time ago, last time we were in England for a longish while. He said someone is bound to do such a book eventually, so why not him? In my view, if anyone does do it D. would be the best person as a) I think he's a very good writer (I've read some of his books, & like the interview with Nancy – did you? I can't remember), b) he seems to have a strange sort of sympathy, or affinity with the actual Boud, c) I don't think he'd do the sort of sensational horror-tale that others might.

So I told him that while *I* am not averse to his having a go at it, the other sisters might be; and that I thought it would be hopeless to try to do it in the face of family opposition. After that I forgot about it until now, when it seems to be hotting up again.

So that's it, Hen. I like David v. much, & think he could write a good & fascinating book. (For one thing he is evidently stuck on the idea, having been on about it for all this time, which is a prerequisite for writing anything worthwhile as any practitioner of that dread trade will affirm).

1 David Pryce-Jones' biography, *Unity Mitford, A Quest*, was published in 1976.

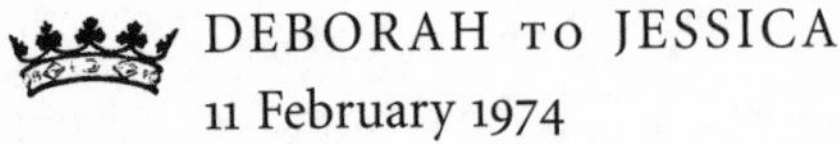

DEBORAH TO JESSICA *4 Chesterfield Street, W1*
11 February 1974

Dearest Hen

How marvellous that the Year of the Hen is at hand, it's such a good prospect because of no hurry attached, you're usually going instead of coming and staying.

I had a letter from D Pryce-Jones about doing a book on Birdie – I thought and thought & I thought about your letter, & I thought again & then I honestly believe it's too soon – not only do I think that but I also think anyone who didn't know her intimately simply couldn't possibly get the hang of the amazing contradictions of her character, nor her great funniness, nor all her oddness, therefore it could only miss the point & it would just be Nazis all the way.

It's so much easier to say yes than no to anything like that, but I feel it would lead to many an agony. So I wrote what I hope was a sort of fairly nice letter, saying exactly what I've said to you.

Oh bother it all, I do wish people would stop writing books.

Much love, see you in three weeks, Yr Hen

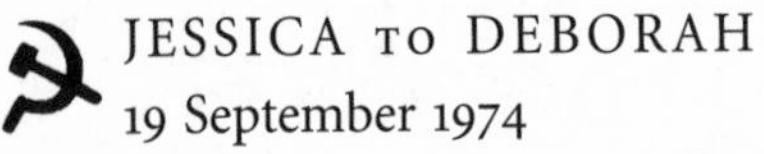

JESSICA TO DEBORAH *8 Rumbold Road*
19 September 1974 *London SW6*

Dearest Hen,

I *did* adore staying with you & thanks so very much for everything.

Oh those letters were overwhelming – I still feel o'erwhelmed a day later. Also, in a way, by our conversation; I never quite knew all you said, before this time, I mean the way you took all that. Oh Hen.[1]

Re Diana:[2] it's not exactly politics now (except for the feeling one must draw the line somewhere & you know all that part), it's more that having really adored her all through childhood, it makes it 10 times more difficult to have just casual meetings. That's why even our meetings over N's illness (in which Diana was marvellous) were rather agony. Do you dimly note the form of that?

Again, Hen, Millions of thanks, much love to Sophy and all, Yr Hen

1 Jessica and Deborah had been looking through old family letters at Chatsworth and had discussed Jessica's elopement and the effect it had had on the family.
2 Deborah had asked Jessica if she would agree to lunch with Diana.

) DIANA TO DEBORAH *5 rue Villedo, I*
3 January 1975 Tom's birthday

Darling Debo:

Oh Debo I'm so sorry for all your worries, there's nothing so awful as being responsible for people's livelihood. Who is to go & who to stay.

Thinking about it I've been tormented with wondering about one's heedless behaviour in youth. For example, what happened to Annsk?[1] She was at Biddesden. Did anyone give her a pension? Perhaps Wooms might know. I got a Xmas card from dear Mrs Healey (Crowood) & it said, 'this is written by my niebour (sic) because I have lost the use of my hands'. Of course I rushed to answer & hope to hear more. The nice old Ramsbury Dr (who dug the pellets out of Mogens's leg when Desmond Forbes-Adam peppered him) has retired I think. Really it was the war which cut me off from masses of those old people because one wasn't able to write from prison & one was so taken up with various worries to do with the boys etc. But how could I have lost touch with Annsk, it is wicked of me.

All love, Honks

1 Anne Aldridge; a housemaid with the Redesdales for many years who went to work for Diana after her marriage to Bryan.

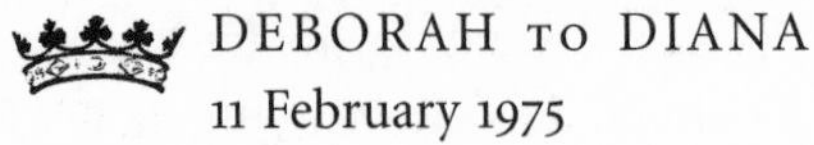

DEBORAH TO DIANA
11 February 1975

La Pietra
Florence

Darling Honks

I am so sorry & worried re your headaches, it seems too queer for words the way they come & go & usually come. I'm all for telling that osteopath man, it's just possible he might fiddle about with whatever works them.

This dump is quite amazing.[1] I imagine not a thing has been changed for 50 years, it is pitch dark of course & heaped & piled with THINGS, real man traps, I mean if you pick something up off a table at least two covers come as well, ancient lace & under that brocade & under that velvet which looks like a dog with mange. The objects are all shapes & sizes & from all quarters of the globe, lots of wooden looking virgins on gold backgrounds. My bedroom is the size of the diner at home with enormous bits of positively papal furniture covered in the said brocade & velvet. The lamps (what there are of them) wd make you die because of the shades, they are like little fitted caps of tiny beads sewn together & sitting *on* the bulbs & shaded in colours of green & brown so no glimmer comes through, plus the killingness of the object themselves.

Harold says he can't get them any more, well what a surprise. They wd fetch fortunes in the King's Rd. He is kindness itself & the manners are such that one doesn't know when one ought to appear. We have sitting up talks from 5 till after dinner (bedtime really) with ne'er a break but he doesn't seem to mind. I must say it has been a major rest cure, he obviously doesn't want to go to the town & I was dead when I arrived so I've just sat & read, in a way it is a treat because it's what I never do.

Yesterday we went for what H called a country walk, it was about 100 yards of paths up to his fascinating little farm, everything in miniature. He takes off his hat to farm man & gardeners & generally spreads his marvellous manners all around. The dump is an oasis, & almost in the town. It has got lots of other houses which belong to it but are let to Olivetti typewriters & students of new techniques belonging to them, all with ancient gardens of shapes of green. The driver is so bad & truly terrifying that I dreaded going to Pisa (1½ hours) but spoke about going PIANO although he didn't seem to take the slightest notice. I suppose it wd have been even more frightening if I hadn't. It's a marvellous thing about being old, one doesn't mind SPEAKING.

As for the BOOK,[2] I could enlarge for hours but won't bother you with what you know far better than I. I simply couldn't help saying something about Jerry.[3] He had added a weeny sentence. No one knows your part in the 4 years of illness except me & Woman. Oh well. It has fired me to get *all* the letters put in order at home. It will be a long & terrific work but I think it must be done, perhaps I'll get a stoodent in the summer hols because if people are going to be interested in this book (and I think they will) they had better know the real story one day. H has put 'Colonel' for the Colonel instead of the GP rubbish.[4] Much better, eh. He's written to the old soul enlarging on this. N's last journey back to France is so typically described 'I went on the night ferry etc etc' without a single word re stretcher, me, nurse, injections in the night, you at station in Paris etc etc. A sort of FANTASY. And if you remember the airy plane was out because they were frightened she'd die on it & upset the passengers. OH HONKS, what a travesty. I got him to put in how the old Hen had come all the way from Calif to do a stint, because she DID. But of course the brunt was borne by you & no-one else. I do so wonder what the publishers will make of it all, & I relish the thought of Duckie [Dr Blaikie] etc reading it, Duckie & his egg cup of choice flowers. What a hash they made of her.

H is planning a trip to Norway (well to anywhere really) in August to escape another possible visit from Princess Margaret. He really is too old to be subjected to that. In the heat of last summer he pined for fjords. Pathos.

He has told wonderful descriptions of Eton, & of China & of life here before the flood. He showed me a freezing ballroom where there were thés dansants [tea dances], & he described people gliding over the floor, tangos, foxtrots & all.

I have been entrusted with the top copy of this book, what a responsibility. He knows that N's life was all in fantasy world, but I don't know that it comes through, quite. He told me he was really upset when he saw rue d'Artois, thought it so terribly sad & all. You told me that at the time but I don't think I took it in. He was expecting something so different.

Well Honks thanks again for my rich night. So dying to see you when you come to London, so please enlarge on date & time.

Much love, Debo

Thinking of dear old Harold arriving back at his house after hair-raising drive – my word he must be pleased I've gone.

1 Deborah was staying with Harold Acton at his magnificent fifteenth-century Florentine villa.
2 Harold Acton, *Nancy Mitford, A Memoir* (1975).
3 The Mosleys' driver and butler, Jerry Lehane, had been a tireless help during Nancy's illness.
4 In the draft of his memoir, Acton had referred to Gaston Palewski by his initials.

DIANA to DEBORAH
31 March 1975
Your birthday

Ritz Hotel
Piccadilly
London w1

Darling Debo:

This is to tell you the boring tale of my headaches because I know you are kind enough to be interested (not inter-ested) & because I can't bear to do it on the telephone.

The first two visits to Dr Sherwood he gave my head a pull. I had a good deal of 'discomfort' specially at for example the theatre (having to sit still) & two headaches. I then asked him not to pull, & he didn't. I improved quite a lot, went back to five-day intervals between headaches, heard a bit better & *felt* better. Then the Wednesday before the last treatment he wanted to pull my head & I let him (because he seemed to be doing good & he thinks it v. important). I got a headache that night. The Friday was the last treatment before we left & he did it again & again. I got the headache that night. Ever since I have had a bad feeling in my neck (the seat of all the trouble one thinks) & a headache every 48 hours. I have had seven in fourteen days no, in *eleven*. Even Kit is a weeny bit discouraged & I am totally so. I've got an appointment with Dr S & shall quietly tell him what's happened. I'm sure the good body will get it right – or fairly right, I mean 'normal' – after a while. I am not at all ill, often very cheerful, I have great fun at the Temple doing odd jobs in the garden & I'm not in the least worried. I tell you all that because there's, I promise, no need to feel sad about me.

All love darling Honks

P.S. I don't suppose you saw Kit on telly the other day (Thames) anyway Robert Ski[delsky] wrote him a letter saying that it gave an impression of someone with megalomania. The letter made me SCREAM & Kit said 'Did *you* think I seemed like a megalomaniac?' and I said 'Well I'm so used to you being one that I simply don't notice it any more'. But I do hope he won't seem quite crazy on telly this week. You see he really & truly believes he could have done this & that & prevented England running down hill in the way it has done & is doing. His solutions are all down on the printed page year after year & they do seem now to have been very wise. (An example: in 1950 he said 'hold Europe, leave Asia'. Which wd have prevented the Vietnam horrors & the terrible consequent loss of self-confidence in America.)

He says: 'Is the pointing out of such things a sign of megalomania? Or should one modestly pretend one never did suggest the right road?'

I am so curious to see what the reception of Robert's book will be. It contains plenty of abuse of Kit which can be picked out by reviewers.

P.P.S. Do look at top right-hand corner of today's (31st) *Times* (it makes the blood run cold) page 3.[1]

1 The page featured an article about a fire at the Alabama Browns Ferry nuclear power station that was started by an employee using a candle flame to check for air leaks. The fire burned out of control for seven and a half hours and almost triggered a catastrophe.

) DIANA to DEBORAH
4 June 1975

Temple de la Gloire
Orsay

Darling Debo:

Your classic about Woman & Rudi being Professors of Past Menus made me SCREAM, of course they should get some public recognition. Shall we get a steaming pie carved on Woo's tomb (what a horrid idea – forget it. She will out-live us all luckily).

We've had the Skidelskys here. I won't bore you with his worries, suffice it to say that his vehement condemnation of Kit for anti-Semitism in the thirties, which I think very unfair, isn't nearly enough for the Jews who are stopping him from getting a university appointment. One eminent person, Lord Kahn,[1] says he has put himself beyond the pale simply by writing objectively (or fairly so) about Kit & that no decent person wd wish to have anything to do with him. As Robert himself has got a good bit of Jewish blood isn't all this *incredible*? He says historians now are intimidated & one must not mention certain things. His great crime is that having ferreted out police reports of the thirties he found that most of the violence was Jews attacking Kit's people in dark lanes etc. Sorry darling I won't go on I promise. I feel really upset over Robert because one can't live by writing & he must get some sort of job. He has got a wife & child to support.

We are sad to be missing telly these last days of the campaign. Do you not think Benn[2] looks like Uncle Geoff? Some of the lunacy too.

I suppose you are at the Derby, you are lucky.

Love darling, must rush, Honks

1 Richard Kahn (1905–89). Professor of Economics at Cambridge University 1951–72. Created life peer in 1965.

2 Tony Benn (1925–). The left-wing politician was campaigning against Britain's membership of the European Economic Community.

DIANA TO DEBORAH
11 August 1975

Temple de la Gloire
Orsay

Darling Debo:

Harold's book came, have you got one? Al thinks the cover rather awful, she looks like a pert sort of governess on it. He says 'twould have been so much better to have Mogens's picture.[1] True, & once again shows that the camera is the biggest liar out. As to the text, I noted that Al couldn't stop reading it. The bits I read made me think once again how ghastly all Mitfords *sound*, though of course in real life ha-ha they are ideal.

I still think the best bit is where she describes (to Muv needless to say) the marvellous delicious feasts & warm luxury of Paris after bitter starving London, & then her hostess Alvilde gives the game away by her descrip of hunting for carrots & potatoes, & savage electricity cuts.

Alphy [Clary] sounds much better & his friends in Switz are sending a motor to Venice to bring him & Lidi to their mountain top. It reminds me of when Andrew offered Mrs Ham to send a car for her, 'where to?' & she answered, 'Isle of Wight'.[2]

Debo, have you ever read *The Way We Live Now*, Trollope, if not I *charge* you to. How Naunce would have revelled in it. I can't bear to think this gem existed & one didn't give it to her when her need was great, poorling Naunce.

All love darling HOW I wish you were here,
Honks

1 The photograph on the cover of Acton's memoir of Nancy showed her sitting primly at her desk in the rue Monsieur. The portrait by Mogens Tvede shows her wearing Dior's 'New Look' in the flat on the quai Malaquais where she lived in 1947.
2 The journey between Violet Hammersley's home on the Isle of Wight and Chatsworth involved a sea crossing and 230-mile drive.

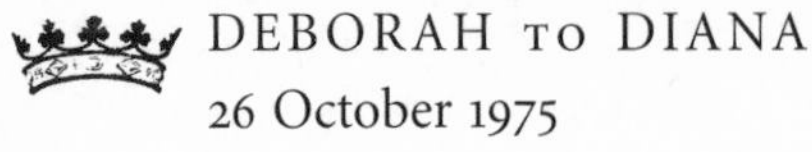

DEBORAH TO DIANA
26 October 1975

Chatsworth
Bakewell

Darling Honks

YES, come on Mon 24th CAN'T WAIT. Woman is coming, for her birthday. We'll pretend it's the W.I. dinner.

Your Memoirs.[1] Yes Honks, let's have them. Let's US have them, no excuse, sit down NOW & begin with Once upon a Time an Old Lady was a Young Lady. I thought you had a *sort of* diary?[2] I believe you have, you're hiding it under a bushel. Come on Honks, get a move on. Needn't be published, just gloated over by me & the Wife.

Much Scrabble here, we got X one night according to Wife. I didn't notice it myself, hide like rhinoceros. Wife says her bed here is a fright. She has also discovered complete rotting of webbing of armchair in her room, broken lampshade & probably many other items missed by me. Pity.

Much love, Debo

1 Published as *A Life of Contrasts* in 1977.
2 Diana kept a diary from 1968 until shortly before she died.

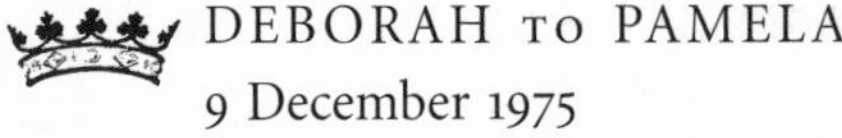

DEBORAH TO PAMELA
9 December 1975

4 Chesterfield Street, W1

Darling Woman

Thanks so much for your letter. I wish you had come to Smithfield,[1] it was lovely, & a lot more people than last year at much higher entry fee – so they were pleased.

We had Mr Peart,[2] Mrs Thatcher,[3] the Queen & Prince Philip, & the Lord Mayor of London for notables. I sat next to Peart at lunch, the biggest old fraud you ever met & no more Socialist than you are – all on the side of tied cottages, against capital transfer tax & wealth tax etc (or so he said!). I said it must be difficult for you in the Cabinet if you disagree with them on these fundamental things, he said several of them agreed with him. I expect he just said it all to make lunch more jolly!

Mrs Thatcher said How-do-you-do to me three times! Each time as if she'd never seen me before. As I was the only woman in the party I thought it a little bit dim of her. Once at the entrance, second time in the main ring, third time among the sheep. Oh well.

The Queen was marvellous & truly interested in the animals but we had to spend most of the time in the machinery.

The last day was a tear-jerker, my three years are over. To my horror I was presented with a terrific jewel to mark the end of my term. I really was dumbstruck. It is very pretty – I long to know who chose it.

Much love, Stublow

1 Deborah was president of the Royal Smithfield Show, a livestock and farm machinery exhibition, 1972–4, and president of the Royal Smithfield Club in 1975.

2 Frederick Peart (1914–88). Labour Minister of Agriculture and Fisheries 1964–8 and 1974–6.

3 Margaret Thatcher (1925–). Chosen as Conservative Party leader at the beginning of 1975, she was elected Britain's first woman Prime Minister four years later.

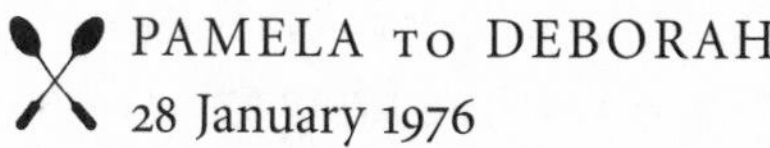

PAMELA TO DEBORAH
28 January 1976

Woodfield House
Caudle Green

Darling Stublow

Mr Hine[1] telephoned to say that Muv & Farve's headstone had snapped off in one of those high gales & should he get it fixed up again, so I said yes please. I hope to go to Church there next Sunday & also call to see Mrs Stobie.

Mark & Anne[2] were in such good form on Sunday & it was a real joy having them for lunch. I gave them Pot au Feu, & must admit it was delicious & *all* the guests had a second helping. I might give it to you & Andrew when you come.

Nard says her Memoirs are getting on fast. She says that *FOOD* comes into it too often. No doubt if I started my Memories it would be nearly all Food!!!

Much love from Woman

1 The clergyman at Swinbrook.

2 Mark Wyndham (1921–). Married to Anne Winn in 1947.

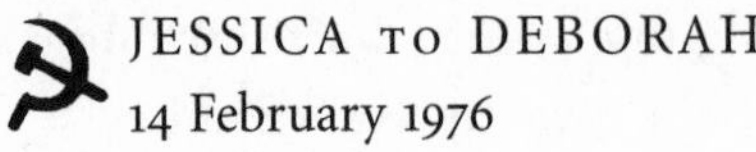

JESSICA TO DEBORAH

14 February 1976

Yale College
New Haven

Dearest Hen,

I am adoring it here.[1] The architecture is an utter lark, all copied from the Dreaming Spires of Oxford in the 30's but with notable differences, mainly an *extraorder* heating system so that I got a heat rash the 1st few days here (temp. outside was below zero). I've got a lovely huge flat in the college with *three* sitting rooms, some with extra couches or beds for the Oys[2] when they come.

Am loving the students. The first few days were pure torture as I had to choose 18 students (max. size of class) out of 200 applicants, goodness it was difficult. They'd all had to write on a card why they wanted to take the course. Mostly I rather followed instructions of higher-ups (deans etc.) & chose illustrious-sounding people with Rhodes Scholarships. But one boy aged 17 wrote on his card 'I believe I have the qualifications for a journalist as I am tall enough to look over walls & thin enough to hide behind trees', so I could see I would worship him, & let him in. A girl wrote 'There comes a time in every person's life when he or she must burst into some new form of action'. She's an athlete, so I let her in mainly because I long to see her burst into some new form of action.

Well Hen shall close with love
hoping you might try writing. Henderson

1 Jessica was teaching a semester at Yale.
2 Jessica's two grandsons, James and Chaka Forman.

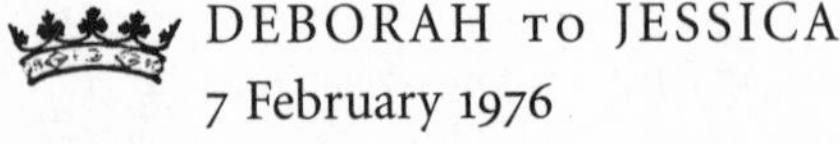

DEBORAH TO JESSICA

7 February 1976

Woodfield House
Caudle Green

Dearest Hen LECHEROUS LECTURER[1] in REAL LIFE

How really awful that I haven't written before to your Collegiate address.

The braveness of you, being an old lady professor, I can't get over it & wd do a good deal to hear you telling the brutes their lessons.

What do you tell them? All sorts of ways to bomb people I suppose, oh Hen, how rash.

Wretched objects, how I loathe *students* & all their works, they always think there's been nothing like them before, but my word there has. People between 18 & 22 ought to be put away, well I suppose in a way they are put away into Yale & your TENDER CARE. Well done Hen. (Or are they all 30 & much married with children on their backs – oh no, marriage is out, just children on the backs? Do ENLARGE, I love hearing at long range, it's just I don't like having to look at them.)

I'm here for one night, Woman is blooming, it's a rest cure.

Honks is in London for three weeks – he is going to debate in the Oxford Union some time. Otherwise there is no real news, it's all of the country variety of farms & houses & all the multifarious things I do which wd bore you STIFF – like Nancy. (Are you bored? Answer was always STIFF.)

Honks is doing memoirs, absolutely BRILL of course, I had a reading the other night & *screamed*, then cried, all emotions battered. I believe Pryce-Jones' book looms, how I dread it. He still puts about that we are *all* for it, how eccentric. Oh Hen.

Much love, Yr Hen

1 The nickname given by the Radletts to Boy Dougdale in *Love in a Cold Climate* after he had addressed the Women's Institute. 'The lecture, it seemed . . . had been very dull, but the things the lecturer did afterwards to Linda and Jassy were not dull at all.'

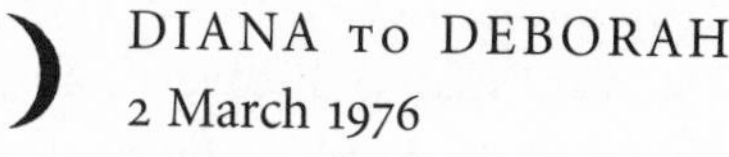

DIANA TO DEBORAH
2 March 1976

Temple de la Gloire
Orsay

Darling Debo:

Darling, could you write a short account of when you & Muv fetched Boud from Switz? Or would you prefer to keep it for your own memoirs? I only want (as it were) a shorthand synopsis.

Nicky [Mosley] says however awful P-Jones's book is, Boud will one day be a heroine, I mean a tragic heroine. I expect it's true. It was her love of *two countries* which went to war which made her resolve to die. A tragic dilemma which she faced with extraordinary courage.

I had a near-quarrel with Nicky about Rhodesia. I feel so terribly strongly about it that it makes me almost ill. It's years since I felt anything so much. The point of view of people like Nicky is so typically Christian & foul.[1] Sometimes I think the Church of England is the fount of all evil. When I said that to Muv she used to say 'Oh no, Dana; as Tap[2] always said, no religion is wholly bad'.

All love darling, Honks

1 Pressure was being put on the Rhodesian government by the US and Britain to introduce black majority rule. Nicholas Mosley, who had been a committed Christian as a young man, supported black rule while Diana, who was an atheist and contemptuous of Christianity, was strongly against it.
2 Lady Redesdale's father, Thomas Gibson Bowles.

DIANA TO DEBORAH
21 March 1976

Temple de la Gloire
Orsay

Darling Debo:

Your account of meeting poor Bird is *genius*. I must tone it down, but I also remember being so shocked by the vacant smile & orange teeth . . . How cruel it was, really, to bring her back to life. As to the sheet hanging on the line, it reminds me how *good* Nanny Higgs & Mrs Healey & everyone were when she stayed with us. A real nightmare.

Now darling two questions & RSVP. 1. Should I call Muv & Farve that, or my parents, my father etc? 2. Could you please discover from Wife whether she would prefer to be out or in? I shan't be a bit hurt if she says out, but she has been such a big part of my life for such ages I would love just a page or two. When I ask her she evades (you know).

Oh Debo, Nicky's book about Lady Desborough[1] one lives in it, I've almost finished & can hardly bear the thought. Made for Wife too & for Andrew. It will be out 15th April but 'twas sent me for review.

THANK you more than I can say for Bird; poor Bird, it kills one. She was so marvellous. About Wife: what I mean is she might prefer not to be in the pillory for having befriended such a wrong-minded person. You are all right because it's not 'voluntary' being a sister! Anyway I can't do without you.

All love, Honks

1 Nicholas Mosley, *Julian Grenfell, His Life and the Times of his Death* (1976). A biography of the First World War soldier-poet, the son of Ettie Desborough, siren of her generation and a leading member of the mainly aristocratic group of friends, The Souls.

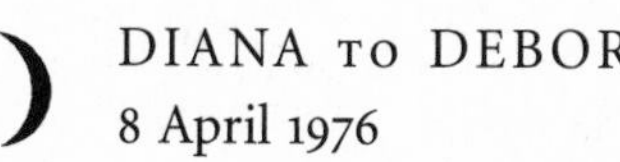

DIANA TO DEBORAH
8 April 1976

Temple de la Gloire
Orsay

Darling Debo:

Nicky writes that he & Verity want to give a party for Kit's 80th birthday – I'm amazed they realize it will *be* his 80th. All the family. Kit is less than enchanted but I've accepted with joy.

I'm afraid N won't like my review of the Grenfells. He's written to say Julian wasn't a bully – it's nonsense, he is convicted out of his own mouth or at least in letters to Lady Desborough. He did things, setting on people several against one, that I couldn't imagine in a thousand years Kit ever doing & it makes me so cross that Julian is supposed to be a perfect knight & Kit a low thug. Truth! Where *is* it. Deeper than the bottom of the well.

I'm trying to get Muv down on paper, she's very difficult. It makes me miss her all over again.

All love darling, Honks

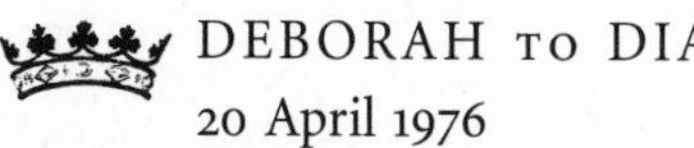

DEBORAH TO DIANA
20 April 1976

4 Chesterfield Street, W1

Darling Honks

I'm thinking of you writing about Muv – impossible. Like you I miss her much more now. There are a lot of things I should like to ask her & as she was almost the only really truthful person I know, the answer would be likely to be *interesting*, or any way real.

Didn't she have an awful time in the way of Farve always selling & moving. I should have really resented that. Do you think she liked Asthall best of the houses? She never had what she really wanted, a sort of Wilbury,[1] always those overgrown cottages.

The photograph book at Chatsworth with all the bits about you & Sir O leaving prison etc etc has completely disappeared. Very odd & *very* annoying as it had many a classic in it. Too big to steal surely, & anyway who would want it? Pryce-Jones I suppose.

Much love, Debo

1 An early eighteenth-century house in Wiltshire which had been Lady Redesdale's home for much of her late childhood and adolescence.

DEBORAH TO DIANA

28 April 1976 (Sto was 32 yesterday, how *old*.)

Lismore Castle
Co. Waterford

Darling Honks

Tales of Woman. In the days of cooks, she came with a worried (& cross) face & '*Stublow, ordering with Mrs B is a nightmare*'. Then the Game Soup saga – 'You know, Stublow, isn't GS the loveliest & richest soup you ever *laid hands on*? WELL, a *milky affair* came up.' She remembers meals 40, 50 years ago, even on the boat going to Canada.

Well Honks . . . more soon.

Much love, Debo

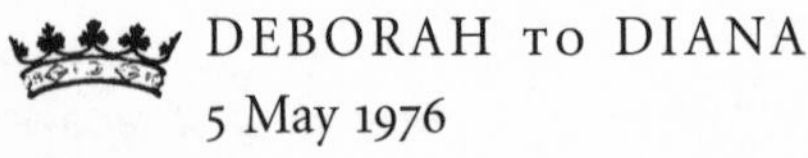

DEBORAH TO DIANA

5 May 1976

Lismore Castle
Co. Waterford

Darling Honks

I'd have given anything for you to have been here last night. Woman got out all the papers re standing for the Parish Council of Caudle Green (Brimpsfield really) from her Unscratchable[1] and

Derek P[arker] B[owles] made us all literally die. She is truly *wondair.* She isn't going to be there for Polling Day neither has she canvassed a soul. Nevertheless she is now referred to as Councillor and her opinion is keenly sought re everything from drains to foreign policy. The answer usually ends up 'so I wrote a furious letter . . .'

She adores being teased by someone like that.

Well Honks, this is only an Interim Report. Longer & better will follow.

Much love, Debo

1 An attaché case of fine leather which Pamela would allow no one to touch in case it got scratched. It travelled in a cloth bag of its own so as not to be damaged.

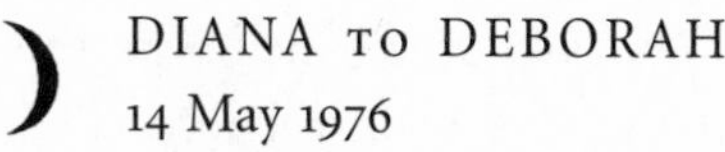

DIANA TO DEBORAH
14 May 1976

Temple de la Gloire
Orsay

Darling Debo:

I *screamed* about Councillor Jackson & could picture the scene. Do let me know the dénouement, was she elected?

My silly book is almost finished. I'll show you the bits about you of course. Debo, the game soup is *wondair* but can you think of a Woom story which isn't funny. I can't put the bagless cow[1] & the game soup & then just leave her at that. Of course I've said she was noble (& so she was) about our release. I've drawn a veil over her quickly putting down poor Grousy & Edna May[2] – she probably had to but it was so sad just hearing about it in prison.

I *dread* Pryce-Jones's book.

I've got a long bit about Lady Evelyn[3] in me book, do you think it's awful of me not to ask Bryan first? She is very attractive in it but naturally very eccentric too. I couldn't bear to be made to drop it. It's all so long ago, nearly half a century*.

All love darling, Honks

*It's the only fairly non-dull bit in the book.

1 When Pamela was farm manager at Biddesden, she bid for an expensive cow at a

local sale. It was not until she got home that she discovered, to her outrage, that 'the brute was bagless' and useless therefore as a milking cow.

2 Diana's spaniel and mare.

3 Lady Evelyn Erskine (1883–1939). Diana's fey and unconventional first mother-in-law. Married Walter Guinness in 1903.

DIANA TO DEBORAH
21 May 1976

Temple de la Gloire
Orsay

Darling Debo:

I wrote to Deacon asking her to tell the contents of her pouch[1] about the Duchess of Windsor dying all alone & (according to Anne-Marie von Bismarck) rather hoping for a sign from her in-laws that they do realize how she *is* dying. I admit it's a strange desire on her part but thought I should pass it on. I got such a wonderful letter back with the time-worn tale that the Windsors are blamed because his abdication in 1936 made George VI die in 1953 (or whenever it was) & that being K & Q not only killed him but half killed Cake. So out of loyalty Deacon thinks her pouch contents may not wish to send a flower or whatever it is. Well, if Cake hated her spell as Q I'll eat my hat & coat, & then how about all the Christianity & chat about widows, the dying, & forgiveness of sins, & loving one's enemy etc. Isn't it richly hypocritical (BURN please & don't tell Andrew). I never can get over Christians, their unkindness is so much deeper than ours. What could it all matter, we shall soon be dust & turned to clay.

We got some rain, overjoyed. We went to see Sauguet presented with his sword,[2] you know he's a composer, well they've made the hilt this shape (like a treble clef, can't draw it) don't you think a clever idea. It was such fun all the loved ones including the Count, seldom seen now because of his big Bridges.[3]

Such a marvellous letter from Woo whose village shop has conked & she's bought the entire contents for a song.

Oh darling when shall we ever meet again, Kit shows no sign of wishing to move.

All love, Honks

1 Deborah used to say that when Elizabeth Cavendish was Lady-in-Waiting to Princess Margaret she carried the tiny princess in her pouch and produced her when asked.
2 Henri Sauguet had been made a member of the Académie des Beaux-Arts.
3 Jean de Baglion was a fanatical bridge player who warned Diana that she was in for a sad old age because she did not know the game.

DIANA TO DEBORAH
16 June 1976

Temple de la Gloire
Orsay

Darling Debo:

I've got the [Pryce-]Jones book, a proof copy. It is very nasty. Yet fairly difficult to attack in a review, because most, or at least many, of the foul things purport to have been said to Jones by 'Old friends' of Birdie, therefore unless one goes for the said friends! The nastiest, well one of the nastiest, is Mr Float, Woman's intended.[1] He (apparently) told such an obviously false story of Bird saying, in connection with the abdication, that Cake was like a shop girl. It is so particularly offensive & silly &, as we all know, Birdie had strong *race* feelings but not so much as a soupçon of *class* feeling & thus it's just something she couldn't have said.

Johnny de Lucinge is rather horrid, he apologized to me for having had any truck with Jones. So silly of him. Paulette[2] quite nasty, also a few sort of Hungarians I never knew. The most surprising is Mary Gore,[3] extremely voluble & quite horrid. What a contrast to Pempie![4] I thought Mary was really fond of Bobo & it gave me a shock. However one must say this: obviously with anyone who would talk he would go on & on with questions for two or three hours. Then no doubt he boiled down the result to a page or so of just the disagreeable remarks. What made me angriest was Mabel [Woolvern] (fancy listening to someone *over ninety*) who said Farve had said 'Mabel, I can never lift up my head again' (when Bird came home). Can you remotely imagine him saying such a thing to *anyone* let alone to Mabel. Jones is the worm of worms. Of course *all* the emphasis is on Streicher,[5] that was Birdie's fault, I admit, for her statement saying 'I want everyone to know that I hate all Jews'. Jones obviously tried & tried to get people (e.g. the Streicher son) to say Bobo had had an affair with him. Of course such an idea is completely mad & luckily they all say so. He was about two feet high & wildly unattractive. Oh Debo it all makes me long for poor Bird & to defend her with tooth & claw but it's not easy.

Hamiltons (the publishers) have just gone. He came to read my twaddle. Rather marvellous after thirty years hard publishing to be so keen to read a typescript. There he was hour after hour hard at it. I've got a bit more to do – a difficult bit. He was v. nice & flattering but I'm afraid really it's quite boring. I'd give *anything* for you to be here this minute & for us to go through Jones together.

All love darling, Honks

1 The Reverend Float was vicar of All Saints' Church, High Wycombe. One day, his mother went to tea with Lady Redesdale and said to Pamela, 'Has Wilfred *asked* you?' The question was referring to whether Pamela would have a stall at the village bazaar.
2 Paulette Helleu (1904–). Daughter of the painter Paul-César Helleu and a friend of the sisters since before the war. Married Rear-Admiral Clarence Howard-Johnston in 1955.
3 Mary Ormsby-Gore (1914–2006). A debutante at the same time as Unity. Married to Robin Campbell 1936–46 and to Alexander Lees Mayall in 1947.
4 Penelope Dudley Ward (1914–82). Beautiful daughter of Freda Dudley Ward, mistress of Edward VIII. Like Unity, she had lodged with Baroness Laroche in Munich in the 1930s. Married the film director Carol Reed in 1948.
5 Julius Streicher (1885–1946). Virulent anti-Semite who founded and edited the inflammatory newspaper *Der Stürmer* ('Hotspur').

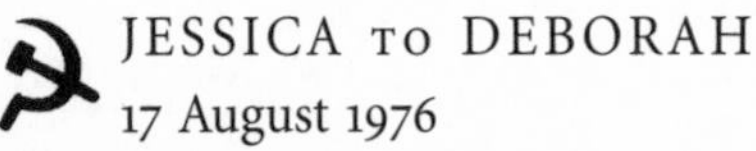

JESSICA TO DEBORAH
17 August 1976

6411 Regent Street
Oakland

Dearest Hen,

The book: Yes I have seen it (draft manuscript, not the published version). I suppose it's mainly a tour de force of research, as he went to Germany & saw many who knew her there then, also various hitherto secret documents & papers. There's lot in it I didn't know about, but then I wouldn't as I never saw her after 1937. But her real character doesn't come through. I expect it would have been far better if you'd agreed to talk to him, & taken him up on his offer to let you make changes in the MS. I asked him to quote the bit I had about her in *Hons and Rebels*,[1] so he did, & I was glad of that as it

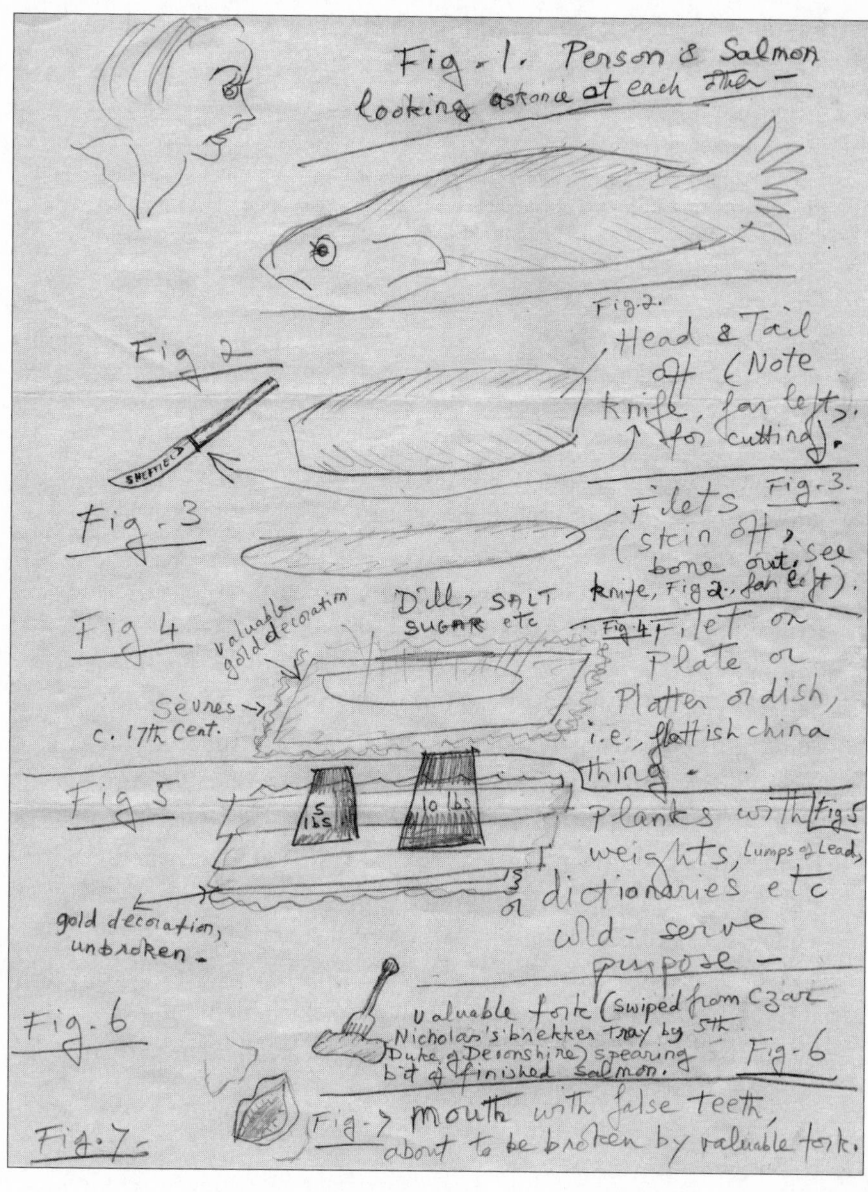

Jessica's recipe for salmon, sent to Deborah, 18 August 1976.

was the best way I could find of describing her in the end; although actually the inner Boud is almost impossible to describe. Once he was determined to go ahead with it, I thought it would be best to put him in touch with people who really knew her.

Much love, Yr Hen

1 'I still loved Boud for her huge, glittering personality, for her rare brand of eccentricity, for a kind of loyalty to me which she preserved in spite of our now very real differences of outlook.' *Hons and Rebels*, p. 63.

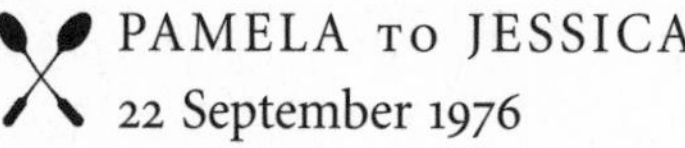

PAMELA TO JESSICA
22 September 1976

As from Woodfield House
Caudle Green

Darling Steake,

Thanks for your letter of 3 Sept. The worm's book will not be published yet which is a relief. I don't agree that it was a mistake not to discuss Bobo with him. We couldn't have given him any idea of what Bobo was really like because as I see now his only wish was to write a book to make a sensation & that is why he has made it so pornographic, in other words to sell to that kind of public. If you had also refused to help he would no doubt then have given up. Some of the photographs were in Muv's album so I suppose you gave them to him. You could have asked us first if we wished them to be published. The album full of newspaper cuttings & photographs that Debo always had in her drawing room can't be found anywhere. Did you borrow it perhaps as I believe you are writing your life. If so we would all like to have it back.

The grandsons must be sweet now, just the age which I like almost best. I am hopeless with babies & small children.

I am off for a short holiday to Switzerland, back home early in October.

Love from Woman

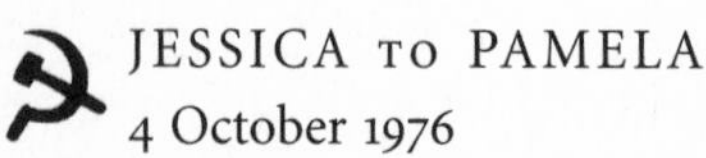

JESSICA TO PAMELA
4 October 1976

c/o Mrs. Cadden
59 East 73rd Street
New York, NY 10021

Woman:

I was absolutely enraged by your *foul* letter, implying that I've stolen one of Debo's scrapbooks & given P-J photos from one of Muv's scrapbooks.[1] As you well know, Muv left all hers to Jonathan Guinness so why don't you get after him. I have practically no photos of Bobo, & have given none to P-J. There are, obviously, huge amounts to be had in newspaper offices & I suppose that is how he got them.

Once & for all, the sequence of the P-J book:

1) As I told Debo at the time, I advised him *not* to go ahead without access to Bobo's papers, left to J. Guinness by Muv.

2) He went & saw Diana, who apparently whetted his appetite & told him all sorts of things that I for one didn't know about Bobo.

3) Ditto, his interview with Nancy published a few years ago in *D. Telegraph.*

4) Seeing he was determined to proceed, & had in fact gone to Germany to see various decaying old Nazis such as Putzi Hanfstaengel or however he spells his hideous name, I thought best to put P-J in touch with people who could give a more sympathetic view of Boud than he would otherwise get from her – so to speak – public life: Rud, Timmo, Clementine etc.

5) You say he'd never have gone ahead if I hadn't helped; totally untrue. Mine was v. *minimal,* as you'll see if you ever read the book. I knew naught about the St Margaret's Bushey Herts part, naught about the German part. In fact I never saw Boud again after early 1937. My thoughts about that strange character were set down in *Hons & Rebs,* which you probably haven't read; anyway, I asked P-J to quote what I'd said & he did. He would have done the same for all of you.

Am sending a carbon copy of this to Debo, with assurances that I did not pinch her scrapbook.

Decca

1 While her sisters' immediate assumption that Jessica had taken the scrapbook seems gratuitously unfair, and while they were no doubt ready to seize on any pretext to try to prove that she had closely cooperated with Pryce-Jones, Jessica's somewhat casual approach to other people's property gave them reason to believe that she could have taken it. In 1959, when Mosley was standing for Parliament, Jessica had written to a friend regretting that she could find no photographs of Mosley with Hitler or Mussolini,

in order 'just to remind people', and added, only half-jokingly, 'I guess that leaves it up to us to steam some out of Muv's scrapbooks at the Island; I *do* hope she won't notice.' *Decca*, p. 207.

JESSICA TO DEBORAH
26 October 1976

6411 Regent Street
Oakland

Hen:

I don't know where we stand, having no word from you since I sent you a carbon copy of my letter to Woman. I was in a blind rage when I wrote it, & I bet you'd have been, too, had you been the target of those snidely-phrased accusations.

All incredibly infuriating & I can't help thinking you and/or Diana may have put her up to it.

I shan't say any more about my part in it as I've said it all a thousand times before. I do think that the sisterly efforts to suppress it (led by Sir O. Mosley, as I gather from the newspapers) were most ill-advised, a rotten thing to do & from your point of view disastrous as it gave the book enormous prepublication publicity.

I'm mainly *terrifically sad* to think that perhaps this all means it's curtains for us, that we shan't be seeing each other any more or writing. If so, that's absolutely up to you, I mean if you don't answer this obviously I shan't have another try. So as this is prob. my last letter, it may be rather long (sorry Hen, I know how you loathe reading long things but here goes).

There were obviously deep things to be said, dating from more or less childhood, that I was really unaware of until *1974*, thirty-seven years after the event, when you said that my running-away without telling was the worst thing in your life. I was v. astounded, and I honestly think you've revised all that, somehow, in yr. mind; as I remember us in those days, we weren't all that adoring. That is, we weren't interested in the same things and I was probably v. jealous of you for being so much prettier; it was far more Boud & me, strangely enough. Then you also admitted (in 1974, when we went over all this) that if I had told about running you'd have told Muv & Farve, so do admit my instinct *not* to tell was right.

That whole year in England (1974) was a bit strained, as far as you & I were concerned. I suppose the P-J book was already a cloud, no bigger than a man's hand. But also, I noted that you excluded me completely from anything to do with H. Acton's book.[1] I asked you if you'd like to have any letters from Nancy to me, & you said no you'd got tons of letters, mine were not wanted. Then H. Acton asked if he could quote from *Hons & Rebs* & I said of course, & he did, extensively, but only to contradict everything I'd said. You & Woman were closeted with him about the book, but not me.

I admit that at that point a certain stubbornness set in; I mean, why should you be the final arbiter of everything about the family? It was a bit maddening, so when you issued the Directive to the cousins etc *not* to talk to P-J I did not feel bound by this, on the contrary. In fact, they were the only ones who brought out a bit of the true Boud we knew.

To chuck in a reminder about a couple of other things: Not only didn't I steal your photo album, I sent you all the Muv letters from the Isle for max[imim] arch[ival] conditioning. Ditto, I sent anything else any of you asked for from the Isle, such as Nancy's bookcases she wanted, yr. writing table, Woman's table. As Bob remarked at the time, 'your sisters know the price of everything and the value of everything'. (A paraphrase, Hen, in case you hadn't noted. See Oscar Wilde.)

Needless to say I've been asked to review the P-J book by mags & newspapers from hither to yon; so far I've said non, non, non. But I may yet do it, haven't seen the finished vol. If I do, though, it will prob. be more about the drear efforts to squash the book than a review of the actual book. Haven't decided, but thought I should say this so as not to be accused (once more) of duplicity.

Well Hen I'll be coming to England in December, as BBC propose to do a sort of documentary of me forthcoming memoir,[2] a sequel to *Hons & Rebs* but mostly about Calif., with a few English bits as I gather with P. Toynbee, C. Cockburn & others of that ilk; not many still alive, alas. BBC already did a killing bit about Forest Lawn,[3] with me being the Tour Leader at said cemetery. My book's all finished, out here next August, don't know about England.

I don't know if Abyssinia,[4] am anyway in floods of tears re-reading this last letter, so will close with love,

Henderson

Dink, Oys, Benj all in fine fettle.

1 Harold Acton's memoir of Nancy was dedicated to 'Diana, Debo and Pam, with love and gratitude'.
2 *A Fine Old Conflict*.
3 The Los Angeles Forest Lawn Memorial Park that inspired Evelyn Waugh's novel *The Loved One*.
4 'I'll be seein' yer'.

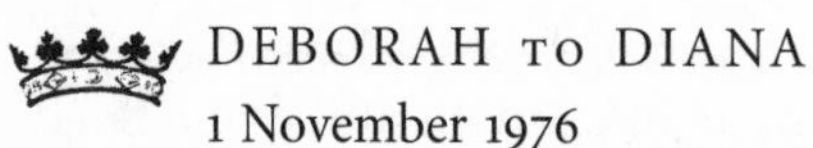

DEBORAH TO DIANA
1 November 1976

Chatsworth
Bakewell

Darling Honks

Oh dear, the enclosed. I can't make a break with her. The whole thing makes me so SAD, & the odd thing is it does her too.

I will think v. carefully before answering. I do hate the little pin pricks she can't resist. No doubt there will be much irritation with her BBC interview. Oh dear.

Much love, Debo

DIANA TO DEBORAH
5 November 1976

5 rue Villedo, I

Darling Debo:

I've seldom been more depressed by anything than by Decca's letter to you. It is so dreadfully sad. Despite her digs at me I can't help (half) feelings of fondness for her & I'm sure you must have them much more than I do. Then one really hates & despises things like the horrid little husband's remark about the furniture at Inch Kenneth, which is made even worse by her rude & silly assumption that you won't recognize its extreme wittiness. She is SO *ghastly* in those ways & then the pathos comes uppermost & one forgets about it.

I am very surprised at her reactions to Harold's book. When you write do please point out that he didn't put (or ask for) one single letter from Naunce to me – or to you, did he? Anyway I know there were none to me. The idea that you & Woo sat over him telling him what to put in or leave out is pure fantasy. Can't she SEE that *Hons & Rebels* is ninety per cent lies & rubbish & that any would-be biographer wd have to reject most of it? She is just so obtuse.

One thing that worries me rather, if you go on seeing her as before, is whether it's a bit unfair on Woo who has been so loyal & steadfast throughout, while hardly (probably) much minding *herself* as it were, do you see what I mean. But there again, she doesn't seem to mind a bit about (for example) Decca's nasty letter to her. To tell you the truth I am torn in every direction & I think perhaps on balance you *should* see Decca because she probably can't help being spiteful & obtuse & underneath everything there is *Decca*, somebody one loves. I felt that so strongly when Naunce was so unkind to her, when poor Naunce was dying & Decca would have done *anything* to please her or help her.

Oh Debo my heart is like lead thinking about it all darling.

All love, Honks

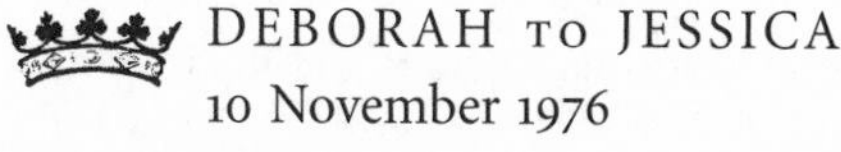

DEBORAH TO JESSICA
10 November 1976

Chatsworth
Bakewell

Dearest Hen

Thanks v. much for yours. For goodness sake don't let's quarrel. It would be *too sad*, & here we are getting OLD & really I couldn't bear it, severing ancient ties is no good, I think we'd both mind very much indeed, probably more than we think.

I suppose what we must do is face the fact that we are deeply divided in thoughts about many things and that underneath the ties are v. strong. So perhaps the best thing is to admit that, & continue from there, if you see what I mean.

I must tell you what I think about the book about Bird, & then I shan't mention it again. Have you read it? It leaves a v. nasty taste in the mouth & completely misses Bird, is insulting in an insufferably condescending way re Muv & Farve & other perfectly good relations. Far the best bit (the only good bit) is the quote from *Hons & Rebels.*

Her qualities didn't exist according to the author & I guess it's because he wots not of them himself, her huge bold truthfulness, funniness, generosity, honesty, courage – never heard of such things, or anyway doesn't mention them. He never once describes anything nice about her, the sneering style comes through every sentence, none of her friends are reported as saying they loved her etc etc till one is left wondering why on earth those friends saw so much of her, as presumably they needn't have done. He uses a despicable form of writing which unfortunately is within the law, viz. putting in quotes things meant to have been said by people who are dead.

I am more than glad I did not see P-J because nothing I could have said would have changed his attitude to Bobo, sneering & hateful on every page. When it comes to her attempted suicide he is unable to understand it or deal with it except like something out of *Woman's Own.*

Luckily the book is very bad. I see he teaches English in America. I pity his pupils as he can't write. He also falls into the fashionable trap of giving deep psychological reasons for the smallest things, some of them perfectly ridiculous, like the reason for her becoming a Nazi was the move from Asthall to Swinbrook – what of soldiers' children, or diplomats', if every move of house is to turn a child to politics of extreme views.

Now Hen that's me answer to your points. I loathe the book about Bobo because of the final unfairness of her & the parents & all the dead people not being able to answer the foul & inaccurate way they are described. But I do not want to break our friendship over it and for my part, having written all this, I will not mention it again.

So Hen there we are.

When we meet there are heaps of other things I long to (a) ask & (b) answer about childhood, lovings & loathings & all.

Anyway do let's remain in touch – when are you coming, & where?

Much love, Yr Hen

JESSICA TO DEBORAH
19 November 1976

6411 Regent Street
Oakland

Hen of course I want to be friends, that was the whole point of writing as I did. I can't begin to say how pleased I was to note yr. envelope, having been passionately looking through my post for it day after day. I absolutely agree that we'd mind terribly if we cut off – I know I would, in fact I've been incredibly upset because when you didn't answer for such a long time I thought you'd decided on this dread course. Bob & everybody here noted I was deeply miserable & v. shaken; but you know how difficult it is to explain to anyone outside the family so it was SUFFERING IN SILENCE.

To answer: As for being deeply divided in thoughts about many things, that is v. true. I sometimes have felt a trifle hurt that you are totally uninterested in things I write etc, but on the other hand I admit I'm not much of a hand at farming or horse shows! So I suppose we're about even on that score. But I also agree about the ancient ties being far stronger than the fact we happen to have completely different interests & viewpoints.

I don't think the P-J book itself should divide us, but I do fear your attitude to me re it might. You seem to think I'm in some way responsible for it, although I've told you dozens of times exactly what I did & why – I was glad, at least, that you thought the quotation from *Hons and Rebels* was good. I agree with much you say about the book, also with what P. Toynbee said in his review which you've obviously seen, but I enclose with the bits I agree with underlined. However I also thought the efforts to suppress it very wrong, so to me the shortcomings of the book faded before that.

The way it came across to us here, from the newspaper accounts, was that Sir O. Mosley was leading the pack for suppression largely because the book would undermine his recent efforts to rehabilitate himself via his self-serving autobiog. in which he never was really all that anti-Semitic (am pleased his t.gram to Streicher was in P-J's book and also got mentioned in reviews), ditto the Skidelsky book.[1] So obviously you can see how *that* struck *me*. Of course I realize *your* motives (suppression-wise) were v. different, as you said in yr. letter.

Anyway, that is why I came to the defence of the book when the *Sunday Times* man rang up. In fact if I had reviewed it (which I'm not going to) that is what I shld. have stressed, the Mosley effort to suppress, not the book *qua* book.

In your letter you go very lightly over the main divider, viz. Woman's *really vile* accusation of scrapbook thievery, & that I gave P-J photos out of Muv's albums (which as you very well know I haven't got, & never did). You say you 'didn't try to stop her' writing that, so I assume she did discuss it with you? Also you say 'we must all be allowed a point of view'. Well I don't call implying I'd stolen your scrapbook a 'point of view'.

Woman's written too, saying let's forget it all but she also says not one word about her letter re the scrapbooks. So while I'd love to forget it, I can't bring myself to write to her pretending all is OK when it isn't at all, with me. In fact I think she bloody well ought to apologize and you might tell her this.

There's another thing, this BBC film. Essentially it's about Calif (Civil Rights Congress in 1950's, funerals, prisons, other aspects of Calif life). But also there'll be some brief background out of *Hons and Rebels*, & of course Boud will come into that. What I intend to do is to say all you said (I might even crib your very words – 'huge bold truthfulness, funniness, generosity courage') and particularly to say how much we all adored that amazing character. After she died, which was just after Muv came to stay here, I wrote to Muv saying that in a way I had mourned her as dead when politics first parted us. Muv wrote back, 'Yes, I suppose Bobo also mourned you in that sense, she knew you would probably never meet again, but her love for you was quite unchanged. When I gave her your love when she came back, she knew it was with one part of you, I could see by her face. I think you both understand each other. I remember saying to you, I am so glad you sent a message, after all we shall all be dead soon. But how little did I think she would so soon go away, I thought I would be the first.' Hen I wrote all this out from Muv's letter because that is the sort of idea I should like to get across in the film (although v. briefly as the film isn't about that).

I'm putting all this down (afraid the letter's getting monstrous long – are you still reading, Henny?) in aid of for once, trying to set forth some inner feelings about us and specially what I think are the *dividing* things. Because otherwise although I, for one, am v. much in favour of The Reconciliation on *any* terms, I also think it would mean v. much more if some of these murkier areas of our relationship could somehow be cleared up, & at least a mutual respect for each other's opinion arrived at. Viz., you thought it was RIGHT to try & suppress that book & I thought it was WRONG, but I can sympathize with your reasons (although *not* with those of Sir O).

As you said, there really are heaps of things to discuss from childhood on, & I should love to try, although I suppose neither of us is specially good at introspection. But we might be getting better at it now we're getting OLD? (*60* next year for me.)

Yr. long-winded, Hen

1 In May 1935, Mosley had sent a telegram to Streicher's newspaper *Der Stürmer* saying, 'The power of Jewish corruption must be destroyed in all countries before peace and justice can be successfully achieved in Europe.' Robert Skidelsky had not included the letter in his biography of Mosley.

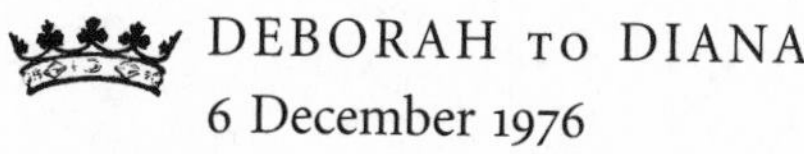

DEBORAH to DIANA — *4 Chesterfield Street, W1*
6 December 1976

Darling Honks

Henderson is in London, we are having dinner tonight, I pray it won't lead to anything untoward, I will not waver or quaver from certain PRINCIPLES but am very anxious not to put up barriers which wd, or might, never come down till we're dead.

Woman & she are meeting, dinner in Burford!! Hen suggested Shipton (perhaps she's staying there, don't know) & Woman said it was too far, I should have thought three more miles wouldn't have made much difference but Woman works in a mysterious way. I don't know if this meeting has happened or is still to happen, will find out all tonight.

Much love, Debo

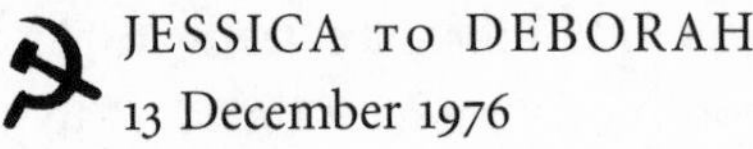

JESSICA TO DEBORAH
13 December 1976

53 Gloucester Road
London SW7

Dearest Hen,

I *can't say* how pleased I was with our meeting (also THANKS for smashing dinner) – I do so hope we have more time in May when I'll be back for the next episode in the Mitford Industry as the *E. Standard* calls it.

Am writing in a terrific rush as my time here is almost up & 1 million things still to do.

Am off to NY from here to meet up with Bob, we'll be there until 27 December then home. The main thing I'm doing at the mo. is translating my book for the English edition: sidewalk = pavement, clippings = cuttings etc. I'm sure I'll get it all wrong, unaccustomed as I am to yr quaint tongue.

The filming was INCREDIBLY gruelling, they make one do every word about 3 or 4 times. Woman came to dinner in Burford, we were rather surrounded by Toynbees & Michael Barnes[1] & Co. She & Sally T.[2] hit it off like anything. All were in stitches most of the time as Woman explained her forthcoming book of country sayings, & how cows need a change of view etc.

Much love, Yr Hen

1 Producer of *The Honourable Rebel*, the BBC documentary about Jessica.
2 Frances (Sally) Smith; American-born wife of Philip Toynbee whom she married in 1950.

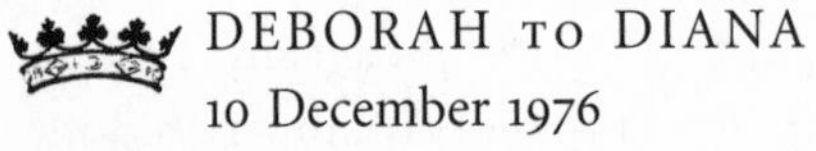

DEBORAH TO DIANA
10 December 1976

Chatsworth
Bakewell

Darling Honks

Well. I had dinner with Decca & I think we cleared up many things & parted ½ tight & in floods at 12.30 having started at 8. I will tell you when I see you, better so I think. She & Woman had dinner last night in Burford, I WISH I had been at that one. Woman said 'Philip Toynbee was awfully nice, a dear old man', OH HONKS do admit & of course he *looks* a human wreck, teeth & hair no how, & always had a specially revolting skin.

She also said (attractive) Mr Hine had put on a purple robe to be on the telly round the churchyard with Hen – 'very *sweet* of him'. What will be the outcome of these strange interviews. She is going to say how she adored Bird & how we all did & is going to say it again & again GOOD. If she does that nothing else matters except I *think* that she's going to say about Muv turning Nancy out of the car on Mull when the war began & she hurried to London. The tale is that N said Hitler was something or other upon which Muv is meant to have said 'if you say that again you can get out & walk'.[1] Now then I was on the Island when the war began & *I don't remember* N being there but alas I can't trust my memory.

I quite understand you aren't interested in yr book any more. I feel just the same when I've made a gargantuan effort re something like the Farmyard here, & now I'm on to the butcher's shop, yoghurt, etc at the Jersey farm in Pilsley & all one's pathetic self goes into the damned thing & when it's set up & running someone else can do it, eh. It's just like a book & I suppose a painting or having a baby & doing up a house. *Must go.*

Much love, Debo

1 See Nancy to Jessica, 21 September 1939, p. 151.

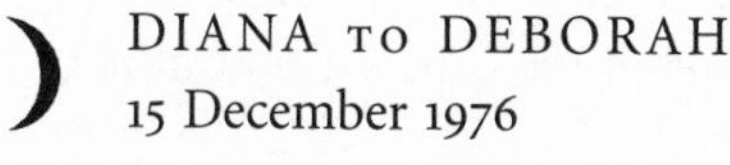

DIANA TO DEBORAH
15 December 1976

5 rue Villedo, I

Darling Debo:

I was so interested in your letter about Decca & longing to hear what transpired, viz., what *does* she think of that book? She told you once she thought Rud had got Unity about right, that's to say the Jones version of poor Rud. Does she take that back? & what about Muv?

The private Decca is Decca, but the public Decca is somebody unforgivably callous & hard. Of course you are in a different position from me, because I can never forget that she gave interviews to the papers when we were released saying that Kit must be imprisoned at once. He was so ill. Of course one may say it doesn't matter as nobody wd pay any attention to Decca, but in my wildest nightmares I cannot imagine myself doing that about either of her husbands. It was so brutal as well as so stupidly unnecessary to intervene, when one's a near relation.

Well then you say she's going to say that Muv made Nancy walk to the station because of something she said about Hitler. Whether the story is true (& we all know how Nancy could distort) it makes Muv appear a bit mad, to anyone who doesn't realize what Nancy could be like to her, needling for days on end, trailing her coat, being as nasty as she possibly could. No. For the public, Nancy is the delightful writer of funny books. Muv is unknown, & therefore anything against her will be readily believed. And Nancy comes out of the story as a sinned-against right-minded liberal & patriot. I do think this is monstrous, even if Decca does say on television that she loved Unity. If you are friends again please make her take that out. Nobody who hadn't seen Nancy & Muv together could ever realize how vile Nancy could be. I'm sure she often longed to be vile to me, but she relied on me & just managed not to be (!). I remember how years & years later when Muv was old how she unkindly complained about the (delicious) island food, just being nasty for nastiness's sake so to speak, & upset Muv.

I hate unfairness. Muv was so much more marvellous than Nancy, & now that they are both dead to recite Nancy's version of a dispute to an audience of millions seems to me simply frightful in its hard disloyalty.

All love, Honks

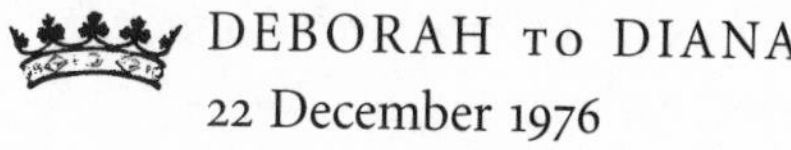

DEBORAH to DIANA
22 December 1976

Chatsworth
Bakewell

Darling Honks

I've just got yours of 15th, not bad for strikes & Xmas mixed. Glad to think you're installed in the nice warm flat, don't DO TOO MUCH, will you have to struggle out on Xmas night, I hope NOT.

As for Hen & what you write, it is perfectly right. *I think* her sojourn in W. America (which I believe is much nastier than E. ditto) has given her some blind spots & she just does not see that it's nasty (the book, for a start) & *nothing* seems to touch part of her. Yet she is as soft as soft in places.

One can't understand it, or her. She is a mystery & a complete muddle as well. As for the sayings about you in 1943 they beggar all, & THEY are what is lost in that lost book. Yet when I asked her to come to lunch that day ages ago in London when you were coming she wouldn't because she *had* loved you so much years ago, she pretty well said that. What can you make of it? I don't know. Hard & soft. Some of the old invented stories she must know to be invented but she sort of believes them now. OH DEAR.

Well Honks HOW I wish you were here, but you aren't.

Much love, Debo

Doesn't the wireless go soppy at this time of year, such a bore.

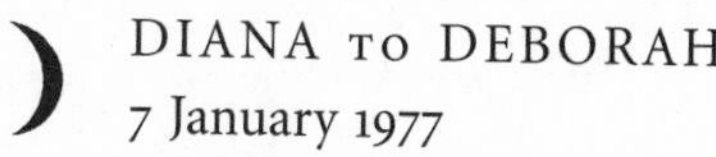

DIANA to DEBORAH
7 January 1977

5 rue Villedo, I

Darling Debo

Don't breathe one word about Kit even to Wifey or Andrew. I'm just as worried since the Dr came, and it is worth anything to be able to tell you. Of course all may yet be well, but Dumas offered no explanation. He has given several medicines which I will rush for today. I just don't feel very hopeful of *medicine*. It was Tuesday eve that the temperature shot up. It's all been very quick & a very short time, but it weighs upon me so that I feel months have gone by. He was (has been) so cheerful & so well & has loved all we've done in the last three weeks. He doesn't seem nearly as depressed about himself as one would imagine. He eats, not much but quite likes it. I pretend everything is quite normal & ordinary & speak of flu, chill & all those silly words which mean nothing.

Well darling 'tis the limit to inflict all this on YOU, but you understand. I love him so much & sometimes can't, literally *can't* bear the thought that he's eighty. Oh Debo. I'm so glad we've had these happy cheerful weeks.

All love darling, Honks

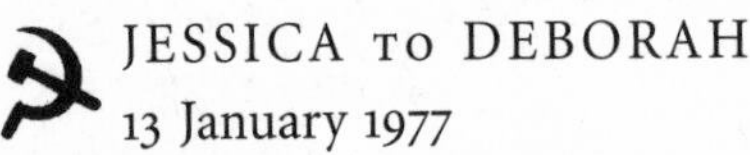

JESSICA TO DEBORAH
13 January 1977

6411 Regent Street
Oakland

Dearest Hen,

Your Xmas sounds marvellous, so was ours, Bob came to NY & we stayed there for a wickertoo, doing massive Oy work, such as *poor* Bob took them to an 11 A.M. showing of *King Kong*.

I note from Rud's letter that Aunt Joan[1] died. Muv & I went down there once, & on the way in the train Muv was saying the last time she'd seen Aunt J. they'd had a terrible row. 'Goodness, what about?' I asked. 'Mmmmm, it was about Queen Victoria.'

Much love, Henderson

1 Joan Mitford (1887–1977). Lord Redesdale's younger sister. Married Denis Farrer in 1907.

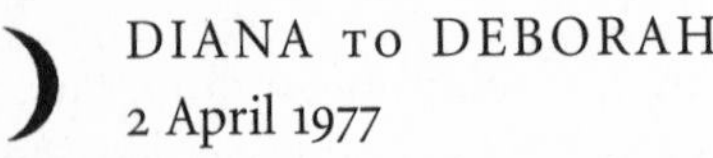

DIANA TO DEBORAH
2 April 1977

Sloane Court East
London SW3

Darling Debo

It was so kind of Tony[1] to occupy the (empty) slot & *so* kind to say he liked my interview.[2] How I wish you & I could have watched it together, I think you *might* have died of laughing. It was my appearance & my *voice*, one couldn't imagine anything so ghastly & ladylike.

I shall have to have elocution lessons like Mrs Thatcher, to change it. Of course it gave *me* a shock but Jonathan said to Kit 'Of course it didn't worry us because we've always known it, haven't we?' Well I haven't, & 'twas a shock. Russell Harty had cleverly put a working-class actor dressed in leather & home-spun just before me, for an interview, & this man said 'the trouble with England is class, it's rotten with it', & he said it was usually the fault of people like his own relations who often come home & say they've met a real lady on a bus, which drives him completely mad with rage. Then for good measure Harty showed a bit of a film this person had acted in, where Jews are being herded into a train. I knew none of this, naturally, at the time; I suppose the interview was done really on another day. I wished I hadn't done what they told me to about wearing evening dress.

However Tony & two or three other kind people found us in our lair at Dolphin [Square] & telephoned that they'd liked my interview, which consoled me. You would have been helpless with laughter that's all.

Well darling I think you are all very good to put up with someone with a voice like mine.

All love, Honks

1 Viscount Lambton (1922–2007). Conservative MP, Parliamentary Under-Secretary for Defence 1970–73. He resigned after being involved in a call-girl scandal.
2 To tie in with the publication of *A Life of Contrasts*, Diana had been interviewed on *The Russell Harty Show*. Deborah was unable to watch the interview because it was broadcast in London only, but Lord Lambton saw it and telephoned her afterwards.

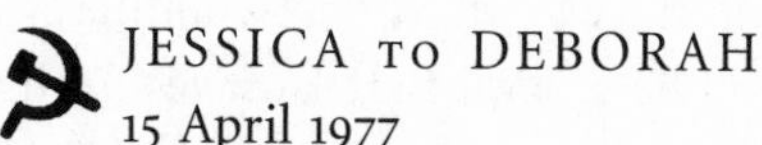

JESSICA TO DEBORAH
15 April 1977

6411 Regent Street
Oakland

Hen, oh good I note you'll be in London a bit of the time when I am. Letters crossed as usual.

As for the beige book,[1] a proper one should be arriving any day now as they are ready, & I asked them to send. Well Hen I doubt if you'll like it much; by the way, the Introduction is a fearful re-hash of old stuff but I more or less had to, to put the reader in the picture. *But* (see page 25, para 2) I did put in, as I said I would, practically yr. exact words about the Boud, that is, cribbed from you as my views. Which they are.[2]

There's an index in the finished book – I rather fought against it as far too pompous for this sort of book (none in the American edition), besides lots of the names are fictitious (see last para. of Acknowledgements – Hen, I keep telling you what to look for so you won't have to plough through the whole thing, well I know you won't anyway).

So, index story this end: Do you wot of 2 American writers called Gore Vidal and Norman Mailer?[3] G. Vidal wrote his memoirs, sent a copy to N. Mailer who was rather surprised that there was no inscription in front. Instead, G. Vidal had written, 'Hi, Norm!' next N. Mailer's name in the index. Do admit that's rich, I mean people always turn first to Index to see if they're in.

Yr loving Henderson

1 *A Fine Old Conflict.*
2 Jessica wrote of Unity, 'She was immensely bold, generous and funny in a sort of *sui generis* way that is very difficult to describe to anybody who didn't know her in those days,' p. 25.
3 The two writers had been sparring partners for many years.

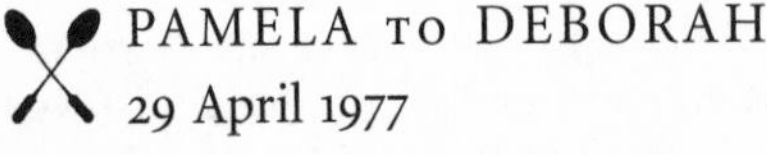

PAMELA TO DEBORAH
29 April 1977

*[Woodfield House
Caudle Green]*

Darling Stublow

We are deep in our Jubilee Party arrangements.[1] Just only the people of Caudle Green & it will be on the Monday because all the other parties are on the Tuesday. It will be a Barbecue, Sausages from the Monks, rolls from the Nudist Colony!!! a real Cheddar cheese in its own skin, a *barrel* of jolly beer, some of the Appenzeller eggs pickled in vinegar as one sees them in the Pubs. There will be a bonfire and games, three-legged & sack races etc etc. And the room with the great west window[2] is to be tidied up for the occasion – it's exactly what we need with light & water laid on!

How worrying about there being so few visitors to Chatsworth. Don't you think it is partly due to this very bitter weather? When it gets warmer people feel more like going out for a jaunt.

Much love from Woman

1 The Queen's Silver Jubilee, which marked the twenty-fifth anniversary of her accession to the throne, was celebrated with parties and parades throughout Britain.
2 The barn where Pamela kept her chickens.

DEBORAH to DIANA
6 May 1977
Yogi Day

Lismore Castle
Co. Waterford

Darling Honks

Two odd things about Henderson's book – she doesn't mention two of the most *searing* things in her life – the death of her first baby which surely was the reason they went to America, nor the death of Nicky Treuhaft. The other thing is, and I shall ask her why she did it, why if she is so ashamed of & so hates all to do with her childhood & first youth did she write her first book under the name of Mitford. I'm only asking. It seems so odd.

Have you had Woman's descrip of Caudle Green Jubilee celebrations? It's going to be held in her *Chicken House*!!!! Oh Honks, would that we could all be there.

Much love, Debo

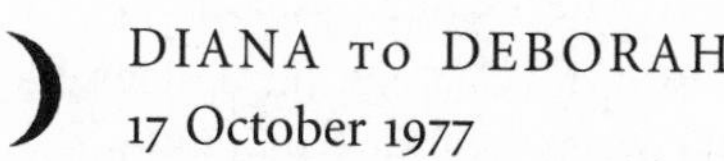

DIANA to DEBORAH
17 October 1977

Temple de la Gloire
Orsay

Darling Debo

Wooms is being wondair. Yesterday I got the whole descrip of her Jubilee party, I couldn't stop laughing, it went like this, 'The farmer on the hill said no he wouldn't come & he was sure his sons had a party already, well *one* day before, he *cave*d in, & of course they all *loved* it, I knew they would. Most people said yes at once when they heard it was in my cowshed, but some said no, but in the end they all *cav*ed in. I just got hold of the monks & the nudists for more sausages, we hung up tea towels everywhere, it was just like the little dog herself,[1] & of course everyone *loved* it, & we lit our bonfire when the Queen lit hers. One man who said no came in the end with two guests, he just *cav*ed in at the last moment, I knew he would, I said to Mr Mills they are sure to want to come & of course they did. They just *cav*ed in.' Oh Debo why weren't we there.

At dinner last night we had half a dozen menus, one of them was 'Nard, do you remember the *liver* we used to have at Asthall?' 'No Wooms, I don't think I do.' 'Oh *yes* Nard, that liver. You see, Kit, we had it at *least* twice a week, it was made with a thick, brown sauce, oh ghoul, don't you *remember*?'

All love darling, Honks

Wooms showed me *Country Life* with all your lovely shop things[2] – I'm sure people will fly to the shop from far & wide. A *marvellous* advertisement.

1 A phrase used by Pamela to describe anything good, derived from her affection for her long-haired dachshund.
2 Deborah had opened a farm shop at Chatsworth.

DIANA to DEBORAH

25 October 1977

Temple de la Gloire
Orsay

Darling Debo

I wrote yesterday but in such a hurry & never had a second to put how thrilled I am to think of your BOOK[1] darling, Jamie Hamilton will be out of his mind with excitement. It will be a raging best-seller until kingdom come because it will never grow old as we who are left grow old. You must give it chief priority over everything even Haflingers[2] & cows. When you get a bit depressed just picture it in the SHOP & you will cheer up & go on with the grind.

We are going to Ireland next week. Please write Leixlip Castle, Co. Kildare. I haven't been to Desmond for about fifteen years.[3] Kit was asked to stand as Rector (yes) of Glasgow University & he accepted. He says he will get two votes (proposer & seconder). He doesn't have to go up there, it seems the candidates never speak on their own behalf. Hearing this is what decided him to say yes. A Scotchman wearing a kilt appeared at the Temple while I was in Switz, in connection with this outing. The people in the metro must have loved it, you know how frogs feel about tartan.

We came back from Paris via Versailles yesterday. I never go there now, it makes me frightfully depressed. I saw the top cupola of St Symphorien – Naunce's church. Every house & street there is full of the most horrible sad memories for me, not to speak of the drive home through Jouy. Of course Kit noticed nothing except the fall tints but then he didn't really take part, did he, in those awful years.

Hope everyone has now got the same date for our three-day event, 'tis Wednesday 23rd November eh?[4] I *can't wait*. We must discuss the menu one of these days. Of course we don't know numbers yet do we. Wooms recited her lovers – all dead. She didn't say they were lovers but they were ha ha.

All love darling, Honks

1 Deborah planned to reprint the handbook to Chatsworth compiled by the 6th Duke of Devonshire (1790–1858) and supplement it with notes and photographs of the work that she and Andrew had done to the house. It was published in 1982 as *The House: A Portrait of Chatsworth*.

2 Deborah was breeding Haflingers, small, sturdy horses imported from the South Tyrol.

3 Diana's son Desmond Guinness had lived in Ireland since his marriage in 1954. Although they had often seen each other in France or England, Diana had not visited Desmond since the sale of Ileclash in 1963.

4 Celebrations for Pamela's seventieth birthday.

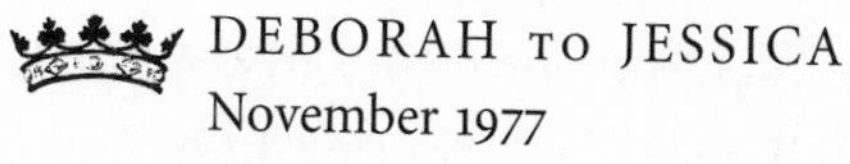

DEBORAH TO JESSICA *Telegram*
November 1977

EUREKA PHOTOGRAPH BOOK HAS TURNED UP.
HENDERSON

JESSICA TO DEBORAH
23 November 1977

6411 Regent Street
Oakland

Hen, *your telegram*. I was amazed, as had expected it to be found 100 years hence mouldering in a trunk like the Bride at Minster Lovell.

Obviously I'm *incredibly pleased*. Yet there is, it seems to me, a certain amount of Unfinished Business (an expression from agendas, Hen – but I expect you know that from the Royal Bantam Club etc). I suppose what I really want to know now is whether, from your point of view, true friendship is still possible – as perhaps in your mind the scrapbook thing was only a small part, the major point being that you loathed my book & the BBC film? I've no way of knowing if this is so, so please say.

As for me, 18 May (date of that horrible evening at 4 Chesterfield St)[1] marked the beginning of what seemed like an interminable & incurable illness, or a sort of non-stop condition of mourning. At least with the scrapbook find, convalescence is now setting in.

I'm going on a dig, in Egypt! Next March, a place called the Temple of Mut (Luxor-Thebes, I'd no idea where these were until I looked them up on a v. inefficient map). I *do hope* that Mut doesn't turn out to be an early version of Mitford, hence yet more Mit-industry. No, Hen, I don't think so judging by pix of Mut, a goddess with v. slanting eyes.

But the major archeological find of recent years was, to me, the one at the Temple of Henderson.

Not much news otherwise.

Yr loving Hen

P.S. I should love to have details of the Find, if possible set forth in proper Archeological fashion including use of such up-to-date data as X-ray technology used by the diggers. In any event, The Great House of Henderson Shall Suffer Wrong No More, don't you agree?

But actually Hen, I *can't say* how delighted I was to get the 'gram. And to think it might be the prelude to Peace Talks.

1 Jessica had dined with the Devonshires and felt that she had been invited in order to produce 'absolute proof' that she had stolen the scrapbook.

DEBORAH TO JESSICA
29 November 1977

Chatsworth
Bakewell

Dearest Hen

I was more than delighted & relieved to get your letter.

Convalescence is definitely ON. THANK GOODNESS.

The bloody thing was suddenly there, in its place. I shall never know (archaeologically speaking) when or why it turned up. The drawing room is, as you know, crowded with many a book, photograph & otherwise, & I'd got so used to it not being there, having searched high & low again & again that I stopped a detailed study of the pile. And then, when we had some young folk of Sophy's who were looking at those albums, my eye suddenly lit on it. I could hardly believe it. Anyway, there it was, just as if it had never been away, the most extraorder thing, complete, and its old self. So I rushed to send the gram, & now yr letter has come & it is a GREAT LIFTING OF WEIGHT I promise you. Oh Hen how odd life is. One thing which makes it odder or less odd is that a tiny silver thing, about two inches long, with weeny ivory numbers in it to do with shooting (birds not people) disappeared from its accustomed place just inside the safe in the pantry. It was mourned by Andrew, who for some reason was very fond of it, everyone did the high & the low search, to no avail, & lo & behold this curious little object was back in its place last week – no explanation of any sort, it had been missing for nearly a year.

Is this a Poltergeist? If so, it's MORE than a BORE. I wish I could explain the success of the Mut dig. The Data is meaningless, the X ray (my eyes) ditto, anyway all's well that starts Peace Talks & that's what it's done. Thank goodness.

Did you realize Woman was 70 last Fri? Unbelievable. She looks younger than me I'm afraid. Honks & I had a few folk in a hired flat (v. nice but v. small) in Rutland Gate, it was like a Jubilee Street Party, squashed up like sardines. I think she rather loved it. Derek Jackson came all the way from Paris for the night, insisted on sitting next to her, huge bunch of red roses & VAST cheque as presents, & he took her back to Claridge's where they quaffed champagne till one in the morning. Do you think he'll marry her again?

She's bought Mrs Stobe's cot in Swinbrook to retire into when she can't cope with her palace-ette any more, egged on by us. I shall be opposite in Mill Cottage & Honks promises to go to Winnie Crooks'[1] but I said only if she swears to sell acid drops in twists of paper & 2d bars. So will you be a grand lady at the Lodge?[2] I fear your loathing of Swinbrook would win, oh dear.

Well Hen bottoms up, keep in touch.

Much love, Yr Hen

1 The cottage once lived in by the Swinbrook postmistress and keeper of the village shop.
2 The Lodge was the largest house in Swinbrook village.

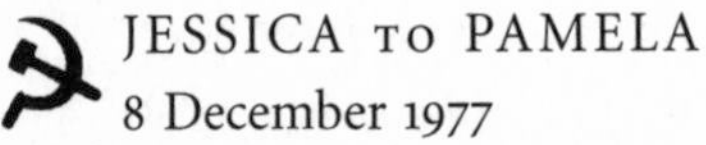

JESSICA TO PAMELA
8 December 1977

6411 Regent Street
Oakland

Darling Woman,

Yes Debo told me about the photograph book being found; apparently it was there all along. *Very* strange.

Of course now that obstacle has been removed (or rather found!) I'd love to see you again. But you must realize that it is pretty impossible to rub out of one's mind your original accusation, and all that followed from it. All that business about *borrowing* – once & for all, to borrow something means to take it with permission of the owner with promise to return. Doesn't at all apply to swiping a huge scrapbook, size of a table as I remember it, smuggling it past everybody at Chatsworth, and using photos out of it, which I was accused of doing.

I'll be coming to London in March for a couple of nights. Perhaps we could meet on neutral ground?

Much love, Steake

DEBORAH TO JESSICA
13 February 1978

Chatsworth
Bakewell

Dearest Hen

V. many thanks for yours.

Now Hen. You say you wonder if I didn't notice that awful evening last May.

Notice it I did. I couldn't sleep that night nor for many a night after, it made me miserable and still haunts after 9 months. I LOATHE a row of any sort, probably much more than you do because I note whenever you give an interview it ends with 'I love a scrap' or something like, but I know those scraps are matters of principle or theory or political something and not inter-family – still you are more of a row-er than me I guess.

Anyway a row of that proportion between sisters who love each other in the depths is foul beyond anything.

I could write down the things I minded in yr book & yr television programme if you really want to know, but it seems utterly pointless & will get us nowhere except probably a further quarrel since we are diametrically opposed on many things chiefly your strange view of the past and chronicling thereof. If you press for enlargement on this I will tell you but again I just think it will make a bother & do no good.

I wrote to you once before to say something of this sort, as we are all getting OLD & will soon be quietly dead so I guess it's better not to delve into row-making subjects.

It's up to you Hen. I would LOVE to see you & would rush to London, specially 8th lunch if it suits you?

Much love, Yr Hen

Nothing I can say wd change your view of things & ditto the other way round if you see what I mean.

I absolutely admit that the episode of the photograph book was very odd indeed but I think I did tell you of other strange losings & findings in this house & that it must have been like them. I am very sorry indeed if you still think I wrongfully accused you (which I did not) it was all so odd.

PAMELA TO JESSICA
19 February 1978

Woodfield House
Caudle Green

Darling Steake

At last, this winter, I have had plenty of time to settle down to some reading which is impossible in the summer as I am usually out till it's dark. I have read your book[1] & so much enjoyed it. There are so many things you tell about which I had almost forgotten & many people also! And I hardly knew about your life after you had gone to America, except for the short while when Derek & I were in New York in 1939 & we saw a good deal of you & Esmond then. Do you remember the boiling hot August day when we lunched with you in your flat in Greenwich Village? You asked me to carve the chicken & even that slight effort got me into a muck sweat by the time I had finished. You kept all your money in books in the bookshelf & I was always worried that you might have left a lot behind when you moved! There are a few inaccuracies such as you say I broke a leg at the canteen on the main road. So far, luckily, I have never broken a leg although I may well do so one day as I fall about like a ninepin.

You say you couldn't return to England after Esmond's death because all the family were pro-Nazi. This was a sad figment of your imagination, what about Nancy, rabid anti-Nazi & always announced she was a socialist, Debo, Andrew, Tom, Derek & myself? We had all very much hoped you would return & I thought it was probably because of the very hazardous journey that you decided not to do so. I had to skip a great deal of the American political part as I couldn't really understand it all, but everything else I enjoyed & you do explain all the incidents so well.

Much love from Woman

1 *A Fine Old Conflict.*

DIANA to DEBORAH

5 rue Villedo, I

20 January 1978

Darling Debo

The publisher I did the translation for telephoned & he seems so pleased, wasn't it nice.[1] Really quite a struggle because Kit was so anti & quite put out if I went to my room ever, to work. He likes 100% attention & really he does get it because I only translated during the night, mostly, when he was in land of nod. Kay Gaudin[2] typed & we are now both so inter-ested in Lauda. I feel I know him so well. Of course nobody but fans will read the book, like all those sport books no doubt. Al's book about Roger Dean[3] – the only picture I've seen absolutely sends me. He is a sort of fairy story illustrator. (Al publishes it.)

Love darling, Honks

P.S. Ages ago you asked whether Gladys Marlborough[4] was fascinating, yes, she was, though (when I knew her) mad. Now did you see, last week, she left a quarter of a million pounds? What *can* this mean? Either she was an incredible miser, or else she had about tuppence & it was all invested in IBM or something; Daph[5] said she was miserably poor in the loony place & delighted with a new woolly coat, or an orange, brought by Daphne, & I think D told me the nephew was paying for her to have a room, though a very measly one, to herself.

1 Diana had translated racing driver Niki Lauda's autobiography, *For the Record*, published by William Kimber.

2 A friend of Nancy and Diana who typed several of their books.

3 Roger Dean (1944–). Artist celebrated for his record-album covers and futuristic designs. *Views*, a compilation of his work, was published by Dragon's Dream in 1975.

4 Gladys Deacon (1881–1977). American beauty who married the 9th Duke of Marlborough in 1921. After her death, a sale at Christie's of her jewellery and works of art fetched nearly £800,000.

5 Daphne Vivian (1904–97). Married to Viscount Weymouth (later 6th Marquess of Bath) 1927–53 and to Alexander (Xan) Fielding 1953–78.

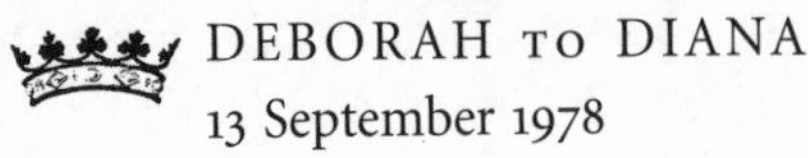

DEBORAH TO DIANA
13 September 1978

Chatsworth
Bakewell

Darling Honks

The International Sheep-dog Trials have been & gone & left me drained of all emotion.

No good starting on about it, but just picture those sheep men (Wales, Scotland, Ireland, England, that's what International means, FOOL) in their stiff new suits, stiffer new boots, dogs of all shapes & sizes (no standards of make & shape, the only criterion is performance), the tension is worse & more tense than in any competition I have ever seen of any sort. The packed stands (thanks to television chiefly) were silent as grave while the dog was working, & a great cheer went up when it finally penned its sheep.

The prize-giving has completely finished me. The supreme winner was a small farmer from Ayrshire, white as a sheet, unable even to say thank you for the cups & trophies which were loaded on him, supreme dog of nondescript appearance on huge heavy rusty chain loathing the crowds & only wanting to be left alone.

The chief of the Scotch team was an ancient of terrific charm & eye, he held on for ages, hugging, repeating 'this is the GRREATEST Day of M'Life, Ooooh, the grrreatest day'.

I've been interviewing cooks till I'm blue in the face, all seem so nice competent young clean smart *but* how does one tell if they can cook? The very young ones speak of hygiene. No thanks. I suppose that's all they've learnt, washing the taste out of everything.

Uncle Harold says he had a typed letter from Bristol saying 'We note you are now a Senior Citizen'. Twenty years late I guess & going on to enlarge on pension etc. He wrote back & said 'I am not a *citizen* but a *subject* of the Queen'. No good, the computer had sent the first one so it just comes shooting back every month.

I asked him to send a copy to the Queen as it might tickle her.

Much love, Debo

DIANA TO DEBORAH
23 October 1978

Temple de la Gloire
Orsay

Darling Debo

It was so rich having a chat yesterday.

I don't think I told you a very odd thing about Colonel. We were alone & he suddenly said he'd been terribly hurt because Naunce didn't mention him in her testament. So I said 'But her will was just one line leaving everything to Debo', & he said 'Oui, je sais, mais elle aurait pu quand même dire un mot de moi'.[1]

Well, can you imagine, isn't that wanting everything all at once? He married, & yet expects that! I feel certain he simply wants it for his biographers, if any. He was almost in tears. When I told him about the telly thing[2] he cheered up & wanted to know who is to act *him* in it. I'm afraid vanity is strong. He must be very put out by the Pope dying[3] because he knew him from Venice & loved saying so.

Well darling I must fly. I know I'm not to expect a letter & in any case a strike looms.

All love, Honks

1 'Yes, I know, but she could still have just mentioned me.'

2 An eight-part ITV adaptation by Simon Raven of *The Pursuit of Love* and *Love in a Cold Climate*.

3 Pope John Paul I had died on 28 September 1978.

DIANA TO DEBORAH
16 December 1978

Temple de la Gloire
Orsay

Darling Debo

Such a dreadfully sad thing has happened, Eric[1] has been killed. He was on his way to work, on a motorbike, vile motor road, & a car touched the bike & it turned head over heels & he was killed. All going too fast & probably half asleep (8 A.M., dark). They telephoned at 8.30 & I flew to dress & tell Maurice before the police came & I went down & said something to Jerry & Maurice rushed into the dining room, he was in the kitchen, & I hugged him & told him &

I shall never forget, his poor head just sank down in such a gesture of despair. Everyone loved Eric, he was such a dear charming boy. Then his mother had to be fetched from work & then the granny & we had a terrible visit in the cottage all in floods. Emmy's John is in despair – they were really like brothers as you can imagine. We go to Paris today, all very deep-laid, the Lehanes are off on Monday. I shall come down by train for the funeral. What a horrible waste that it isn't one of us old people killed. Oh darling I'm so sorry to inflict all this on you.

I set myself a task in order not to sit & think & I cleared up Kit's papers. Made four monster bonfires. Al always says when I do that thousands of pounds worth of archives go up in smoke.

All love darling, Honks

1 The son of Diana's gardener, Maurice Pasquier.

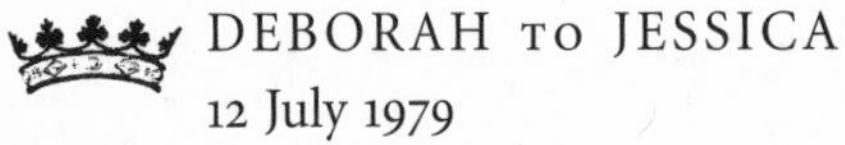

DEBORAH TO JESSICA
12 July 1979

Chatsworth
Bakewell

Dearest Hen

Well, *what d'you know* (as I heard one American say to another & it made me laugh all day) your friend Billy Abrahams[1] came to lunch on Monday. Odd enough you'll say, but WHAT *DO* YOU KNOW, Benj [Treuhaft] telephoned that evening & now I've got a letter from you, so it's Hen Week.

I'll start with B Abrahams. I LOVED him, so quick & funny. He glided in & out, much too fast, not the gliding but the time he spent here, arrived on a train just in time to swallow lunch & bugger off again. I know he's got heaps to do & I was honoured by being given a few minutes of his time but it did seem a bit dotty. I guess he's more interested in people than things so perhaps he didn't want an endless Rembrandt-ish tour. Anyway the upshot is I see his point & he certainly sees yours.

The idea is (don't laugh, I can hear a CACKLE) Macmillan's want me to do a book so I suppose he wanted to have a decko from the American angle. I keep thinking how Nancy would have laughed at this wild idea. I've told them I can't read let alone write but nothing daunted they phone away like mad & speak of contracts. Mr Billy says you love contracts, not as much as I will I bet. Does he always glide? RSVP.

The other excitement (as I know you won't want a chronicle of the Royal Show, or talks with Manners re Farm Buildings, or discoveries of ghoulish heaps of FILTHY sheets in the linen cupboard here on retirement of ancient & dotty housemaid, plus things like Christmas Cake of three cooks ago, grapefruit skins with thick fur coats of green stuff, FOUL) was a glimpse of the filming of *Love in a C C* at Swinbrook church. The idea was it would be the wedding scene (Louisa was it, years since I read the book) & therefore the whole cast would be there. But, needless to say, the electricians were on strike so they could only film outside the church. It was a boiling hot day & Swinbrook looked incredibly beautiful.

So ODD to see all the followers of filmers, trailers of picnic food, people everywhere who seemed to have nothing to do with it but perhaps they did & *us* Hen, acted by three girls who may turn out to be very good but somehow didn't remind me of us.

They did a rotten thing, clipped in a bit of talk which was NOT in Simon Raven's script & I'm sure he would not have written, one of us (you I think) coming out of the church in a great hurry dying for the lav, someone else comes out & says 'what's the matter with Jassy – she's Gone to the Bathroom on Uncle Matthew'. Well, Hen the *Bathroom*. How hopeless. Otherwise it was quite alright.

Much love, Yr Hen

1 William Abrahams (1919–98). The former poet and novelist was a friend of Jessica and her editor for *The American Way of Birth* (1992).

DIANA TO DEBORAH
13 September 1979

Temple de la Gloire
Orsay

Darling Debo

It is so sad (for me) but I think I must refuse the wedding[1] alas, you see I can't leave Kit. I long to come. I have loved Sophy so much, never will forget her aged two to eight, the intense sweetness. I will get her present next week, there's a list at P[eter] J[ones] isn't there.

I got a letter from E. Winn with snaps of you in Yorkshire. She said Collie is Norman Scott to Beetle.[2]

We are still swimming, so good for Kit. The garden is full of flowers but rather hideous. Maurice isn't up to hoeing, badly needed.

I feel very sorry for Decca about her son, it must be a constant worry.[3] There is something about Decca which sort of kills one, even me, I can well imagine your feelings. Of course mine are *mixed* but there is something. One feels she is *acting* most of the time & wd prefer to be quite different.

All love darling, Honks

1 Deborah's younger daughter, Sophia, was marrying Anthony Murphy, who starred in the 1971 television series *Tom Brown's Schooldays.*
2 Collie and Beetle were Deborah and Pamela's dogs. In June 1979, the former leader of the Liberal Party, Jeremy Thorpe, had been acquitted of attempting to murder Norman Scott with whom he was alleged to have had a homosexual affair.
3 Benjamin Treuhaft had been diagnosed with bipolar disorder.

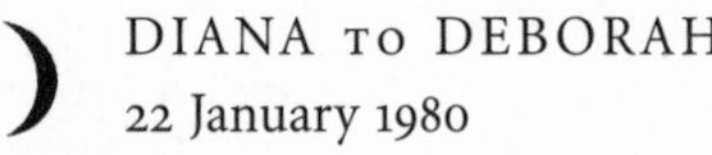

DIANA TO DEBORAH
22 January 1980

5 rue Villedo, I

Darling Debo

When you say Tig is having an awful time finding a school for her expelled daughter it takes me right back to when my boys were always being expelled, Desmond & Max once each & Al twice. One feels total despair, who will take them on. Schools are so feeble the way when anyone is the least bit difficult they make no attempt at reform but just expel. How I hate them ALL.

Did you see Diana Cooper in some mag saying 'Of course we

were not allowed to go to school, the idea was if one did one would come back wearing bangles'. Now if Naunce had said that it would have made headlines. Why is it that anything we say or do is always supposed to be so inter-esting, I wonder.

Now darling is your book extremely serious or can you have an absurd joke, just remembered a marvellous description by Mrs Hwfa Williams in her memoirs.[1] She & Mr Hwfa always spent Xmas at Chatsworth & the side splitting joke was to give the Duke a gift-wrapped present & it was a box & out jumped a jack in the box & they all died laughing.

I am so sad about Cecil,[2] had just re-found him after so many years.

All love, I die for you, Honks

1 *It Was Such Fun* (1935).
2 Cecil Beaton had died on 17 January.

DIANA TO DEBORAH
4 February 1980

Temple de la Gloire
Orsay

Darling Debo:

Our conversation of last night. Here are my thoughts. I don't think it is fair for Decca to use this rather frivolous programme for her tiresome political spite.[1] It is all so easy to answer but naturally one isn't given the chance to do so. The idea that Tom, a clever man & very deliberate in his actions always, should need poor drunken Randolph to 'defend' him is really almost too mad, even for Naunce, yet as we know she wd say anything. Rather awful of her not to mention all this to me, as we saw one another non-stop. I expect this particular letter of hers to Decca was in response to some sort of furious outburst of Decca's. Who knows & who cares. But I don't wish to be branded a liar in that programme (I said in my memoirs about the attack on Tom by the gutter press for giving a fascist salute at Kit's Earls Ct meeting July 1939).

I haven't discussed the thing with Kit though I may have to. He will take ages to understand who wrote to whom etc (!) & then he will harp until kingdom come. One of the things I most dread is conversations about Decca, he asks questions I can't answer, I really know so little about her since 43 years ago. He never thinks about her unless prompted by someone & then my heart rather sinks.

All love, Honks

1 Jessica had made it a condition of participating in *Nancy Mitford, A Portrait by her Sisters*, a TV documentary by Julian Jebb, that she be allowed to read out Nancy's letter to her of 15 November 1968 (see p. 521), in which Nancy objected to Mosley saying that Tom Mitford had been a fascist and in which she claimed that Tom had hated Mosley.

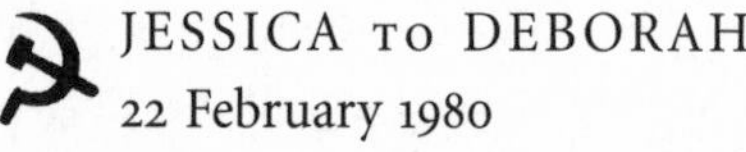

JESSICA TO DEBORAH
22 February 1980

6411 Regent Street
Oakland

Dearest Hen,

Good J. Jebb telephoned to say the filming (viewing of) had all gone off well, I AM GLAD. Should love a blow-by-blow of it, so do write all. The sad thing is I suppose we'll never see it, although JJ did promise to send a sort of video cassette, in which case I'm sure we can get some kindly telly studio to run it through.

Funeral plans: There's an embalmer's aid called the Natural Expression Former, it's a sort of half-moon-shaped bit of plastic, rather like dentures without the false teeth if you see what I mean, that they put into the deceased mouth after Rig-Mo (as we call it in the trade) has set in. Then they can make a seraphic smile. So you can guess what *my* natural expression will be (the Impasse, or Boudledidge face). Am making Benj promise to see to it.

Your book: I long to know more about it. Will it be the room-by-room organization that you once described? Do you do it every day? Obviously it *isn't* boring, or they wouldn't have forked over dough. How long do you reckon it will be? Title? Etc etc, do enlarge.

Much love, Henderson

Did you ever hear the sad tale of Mitty's[1] honeymoon? Muv had asked them to Inch K. for it, so they went. She took them up to see their rooms, saying, 'Mmmmm, Jean, this is your room, and mmmm, Mitty, here is yours' – which turned out to be miles down a corridor. So never having noted form of a dressing room, poor Mitty thought he was supposed to stay in it at all times – and *did*. Not much of an h. moon.

1 Bertram, 2nd Baron Denham (1927–). The Mitfords' first cousin married Jean McCorquodale in 1956.

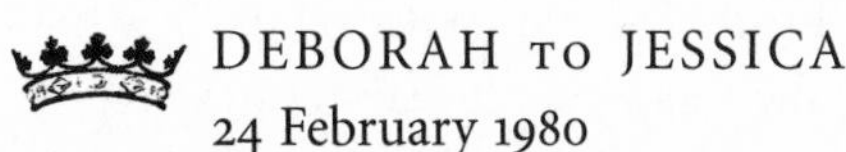

DEBORAH TO JESSICA
24 February 1980

Chatsworth
Bakewell

Dearest Hen

Honks & Sir O & Woman & I went to see the film of us re Nancy last week, also Jonathan & Middy [Gascoigne]. We squeezed into a tiny room in a basement in Soho among Porn, Hard & Soft (whatever that may mean), & saw the uncut version.

You will SCREAM – Woman's the star, absolutely at ease & saying things like '*Of course it was most unusual for* ANYONE *to travel 3rd class in those days*' (describing the journey when Brownie wasn't allowed in the guard's van so Farve put him in a carriage with the rest).[1] I love the idea of masses of 3rd class carriages thundering empty through the length and breadth of England. And feeding her recs & talking to them, 'Woman in conversation with a chicken', she is brill, & reading about the Chubb Fuddler on a tree stump by the Windrush.

Diana & I are v. boringly discreet, I look like a headmistress about to retire & sit absolutely still, don't move in front of the camera, you know. Honks looks 1,000, which she doesn't in real life. Her house looks beautiful, which it does in real life. You are practised in the art, the only one of us (except Honks, once) who has done it before, oh how unfair. The view from your typewriter is distinctly limited, oh Hen fancy staring into a wall when between words, how can you think what to put. The Colonel is fearfully good. He makes one killing mistake in English & says she was a 'spiritualist'.[2]

Jonathan too is good. Julian says there is much alteration to do, viz. he has left out all re Mitford voice & awfulness thereof but he's going to put that in.

When the thing really comes to life is at the very end & he records the last bit of N & Madeau's interview on the wireless fairly ages ago & N's voice is proper, not shy like all of us (except you) earlier in the film, & 'The Lost Chord' mixed with a nightingale comes thundering out. Marvellous. And she says how she's looking forward to heaven. Really funny & good.

As for yr letter which you want in. Of course we could all have found letters being beastly about brothers-in-law, what is plain is that they none of them liked her, nor she them, & one doesn't have to look far without finding such a one about Andrew, Bob, Derek or Sir O. She was a great hunter with hare and hounds & often dashed off what wd please at the other end, like everyone does to a certain extent, but her more than most. What struck me was it is a shame for someone v. old, but v. much still alive, to hear that Tom 'hated him' forty years after, when I believe Tom stayed at Wootton a terrific lot in the late 30's & they were all great friends. Tom was *against Honks' divorce* I don't doubt so I expect it may have telescoped time in Nancy's mind, because they certainly were friends later & it was Nancy who didn't go & see Honks at that time, not Tud.

Anyway I believe Honks will answer, so there we are re that.

The television film showers, JJ plus two mates, were astonished when they heard that neither Sir O nor Andrew (nor Derek I guess) have read one word of N's writings. V. comical, somehow, & I suppose people wouldn't believe it. Has Bob, I wonder.

Much love, Yr Hen

1 Brownie, a very small pony bought by Lord Redesdale in 1908, travelled in the train carriage while the infant Pamela was placed in a luggage rack.

2 Palewski meant to say that Nancy was witty, 'spirituel' in French.

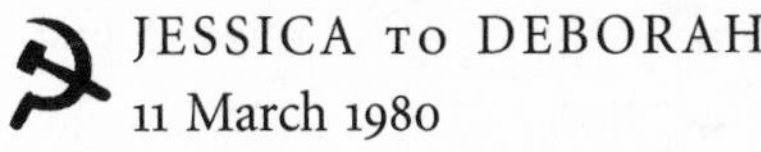

JESSICA to DEBORAH
11 March 1980

6411 Regent Street
Oakland

Dearest Hen,

The filming sounds marvellous, & I can see J. Jebb thinks so too. Last I heard from him he had unearthed a hitherto-lost telly interview she did, & may be using some of that. Apparently BBC has absolutely no system for keeping track of old programmes, & often simply destroys them for lack of storage space.

The letter re Sir O. Mosley: I quite agree about N. & the bros-in-law in general (although I thought she rather liked Derek? Used to see him a lot in Paris) but Hen that *wasn't the point.* Perhaps it's useless trying to explain, but I'll have one more go. All the memoirs etc. are now saying Tud was a fascist, which I for one never believed. Neither, apparently, did Nancy, so I wanted to be sure to get that in, which is why I made it a condition of being in the film at all. She said 'Randolph would have come to his defence if he was alive'; Randolph isn't alive but I am, so included N's letter for what it's worth. The reason I got so FORMAL about it (making J. Jebb sign that paper, which he did with screams of anguish) is that I was told that you & Diana would have final say as to what went in the film, after seeing the rough cut. Speaking of FORMAL: I have sent, as you asked, written permission to J. Jebb to use any photos he wants, & hereby reaffirm same in writing to you. Oh dear. Shall we ever get back on ordinary Honnish terms? I do wish we could.

Much love, Henderson

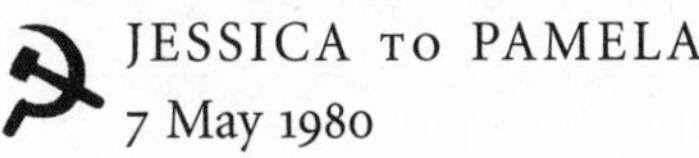

JESSICA to PAMELA
7 May 1980

6411 Regent Street
Oakland

Darling Woman,

Sorry not to have written for ages. The fact is (as I'm sure you may have realized) that I was fair boiling with rage over the scrapbook theft accusation; that has now receded into a low simmer, & perhaps should be turned off altogether.

We are indeed extremely pleased about the Dink's forthcoming nuptials,[1] to which we shall nip (Atlanta) in June. We like her bloke no end, a distinct cut above others in her past.

Longing to know when the film looms, ditto J. Jebb's article on the subject.

Much love, Steake

1 Constancia married Terry Weber later in the month.

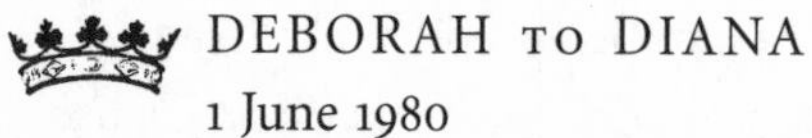

DEBORAH TO DIANA
1 June 1980

Chatsworth
Bakewell

Darling Honks

I've got your book![1] That nice M. Willes[2] sent it, not bound, you know how it is when they're in bits. I read a long bit out to Andrew, he was completely fascinated & thinks it *terribly good* (I left out the bit about Evelyn Devonshire).[3] He is v. critical, so it was proper praise.

You are truly clever, because it runs along most wonderfully & isn't at all gossipy, it's Discretion Please all the way. Oh well done Honks. How *did* you do it with people coming & going all the time & Sir O wanting this & that. Goodness knows. I long for it in real book style. Not long to wait, & then another flood of reviews.

The film seems to have been well received on the whole. A retired carpenter came up to me at Edensor & said without any preamble 'I always liked Mrs Jackson best'.

Tomorrow I go unwillingly to London for the Derby & two dinners which I would be happier without, except one is Annenberg[4] whose sister (Mrs Neck, of New York) told me her furniture was so Louis it was Louis Louis. Who knows, she might be there, & then 'twill be an evening well spent.

I'm looking at F Ashton Beatrix Potter film which is so completely wonderful beautiful & sad that if I've written more twaddle than usual that's the reason.

Honks *well done* re yr book. It's lovely to think its reviews will soon be with us.

Much love, Debo

1 *The Duchess of Windsor* (1980).
2 Margaret Willes; editor at Sidgwick & Jackson.
3 Andrew Devonshire's grandmother, who was Queen Mary's Mistress of the Robes, used to pass on information to her about the future Duke of Windsor's visits to nightclubs when he was a young man.
4 Walter Annenberg (1908–2002). Publishing billionaire. US ambassador to London 1969–74.

DIANA TO PAMELA *5 rue Villedo, I*
31 May 1980

Darling Wooms

Two things I object to in Jebb's *Sunday Times* effusion: the fact that he says the picture of Bobo in Nazi uniform was taken out by us, thus drawing attention to it far more than if he had flashed it on the screen. 'Off the record' is supposed to be sacred to journalists. Of course she wasn't in Nazi uniform which was forbidden to foreigners, so he is doubly at fault. The other thing isn't his fault, but Decca's story about Farve's will is a complete lie. Inch Kenneth came to us by mistake when Tom was killed, & Decca asked for her part to be sold & given to the communist party funds. That was why Farve much later cut her out of his will; he didn't want his money to go to communist funds. Of course she couldn't sell her bit of Inch Kenneth because we refused to sell ours. By changing the dates round she has a dig at Farve.[1]

I've written to Jebb about Bobo. Only got the *S. Times* on Thursday, we don't get the colour part here.

Yesterday I ran into Colonel in the street. He wants to see what the papers say about the film but I must censor them because some are rather horrid about him. He & Violette are invited to the Elysée to meet the Pope. I said *do* take Emmy & Jerry [Lehane] with you.

All love, Nard

1 In Julian Jebb's article, Jessica was quoted as saying that she had tried to give her share of Inch Kenneth to the Communist Party in 1958 after discovering that she had been cut out of her father's will. In fact, she had unsuccessfully tried to give it to the Party after Tom's death in 1946.

DEBORAH TO DIANA

Chatsworth
Bakewell

4 June 1980 In train to London

Darling Honks

Yours came this A.M. with yours to J Jebb. I should think it will make him shrivel into the very ground. I would love to see the answer, if any. Please remember. I am still composing mine, having had a euphoric one from him saying he's never had so much praise, from colleagues & strangers alike.

I've had lots of letters, including Holiday[1] & the Prince of Wales.

Ann Fleming, who always has an original point of view, hated Snowdon's snaps. I thought the one of me was in such a good place all that ivy, & somewhere no-one had chosen before, the old Dutch peasant was lovely,[2] Woman & Decca not so good. Ann says Woman does not 'throttle herself in white bandages' like you & I do.[3] She says we use them as beauty deterrents.

J says they are going to repeat it 'very soon', three months probably. Apparently, this is proof of much praise (or is it that they are broke, who knows). Anyway people seemed to have enjoyed it. Most of my letters have said 'don't worry about your voice dear it's very nice'. Several have said 'anyway you all pronounce things so the words can be heard'.

So there we are. Woman ought to have her own Chicken Chat Show, eh.

Much love, Debo

1 A nurse who looked after Nancy in the Nuffield Hospital.
2 Snowdon's close-up portrait of Diana.
3 Diana and Deborah were photographed wearing white, high-necked blouses.

DEBORAH TO DIANA

Chatsworth
Bakewell

3 August 1980

Darling Honks

Congrats on yr book being reprinted. That really is wonderful.

Sidgwick has sent (I asked for) a HUGE photo of you, looking

101 & in dire need of a bust bodice, to go up behind the heap of said book in the shop here. People will be terrified & think it's written by a corpse. The one I've got now is truly beautiful & the marvellous person who does the shops has taken terrific trouble making a notice which says, inevitably, Lady Diana Mosley.[1]

Maud has gone on her hols. Collie won't let Mrs Carr[2] make my bed, so Henry[3] has to come & hold his head while she does it. And he won't let her open any drawers, he is v. eccentric & possessive. So I must see he doesn't leave me. (He rather likes slinking off to bed on his own.)

Much love, Debo

1 As the wife of a baronet, Diana's correct title was 'Lady Mosley'.
2 The housekeeper at Chatsworth.
3 Henry Coleman; the butler at Chatsworth.

DIANA to DEBORAH
9 August 1980

Temple de la Gloire
Orsay

Darling Debo:

How good you were to write among the busy-ness. I was so touched to think of the display of my book at your shop & screamed to hear of the corpse needing a bust bodice, it sounds almost too disgusting, well of course it *is*. Put one (a photo I mean) of Dooky,[1] much nicer. I never look in a glass now as I don't like what I see.

In the *Economist* it says Inch Kenneth will sell for £250,000. It's Rutland Gate over again, I mean such a quick & vertiginous rise.

Jim [Lees-Milne] loving me, you know it's very strange. I was devoted to him (as a 'brother') & the other day I asked him why, when he was apparently in London & I was at Buckingham St,[2] he never came to see me. He says it's because he was so poor. But he couldn't have been poorer than for example John Betj & others who came the whole time. I can hardly bear it because one could have fed him. Also I loved being with him. He says he saw Tom. Isn't it a mystery really. Then I was cross with him because he was rude about Kit in a book, but needless to say Kit neither minds nor holds it against him, so now we can all see each other with one foot in the grave. Alvilde must be thrilled by the success of her garden book.

I am thrilled by the Treasures going to the Academy.[3] Isn't treasure a lovely word. Colonel calls Violette 'mon trésor'. He wrote me a very clever & perceptive letter about my Windsor book. When I compare what he said with A. Forbes's outpourings[4] it made me rather *value* old Colonel. If Forbes were funny as well as spiteful – but he isn't.

A French illustrated mag seems to be going to buy two chapters, Al says they pay well. A Swedish one has given £1,500 (but I get v. little, most goes to Sidgwick I think). An American mag called *W* is sending down a reporter. He sent me six copies of the mag, it's one of those full of society hags meant to make ordinary people feel out of it & jealous. Now darling don't get too tahd. Give my love to Jean-Pierre.[5]

ALL love, Honks

1 The Duke of Windsor.
2 Diana's London home when she was first married to Bryan Guinness.
3 The 'Treasures of Chatsworth' exhibition opened at the Royal Academy in October 1980.
4 In the *Spectator*, Alastair Forbes had compared the Duchess of Windsor unfavourably with the Queen Mother. (2 August 1980)
5 Jean-Pierre Béraud (1956–96). A young Parisian chef, found by Diana, who had gone to work at Chatsworth.

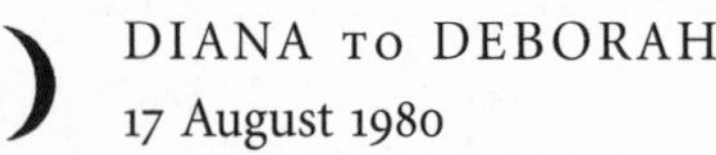

DIANA TO DEBORAH
17 August 1980

Temple de la Gloire
Orsay

Darling Debo

About the Nancy book, I don't think I could ever edit her letters. There are two things about them I abominate, one is the falseness (e.g. the letter Decca read out on the television thing) that one could be seeing her all the time, 'smarmy as be damned' as Dooky wd say, & then she'd creep off & write like that, & the other is the sort of snobbish boasting she indulged in to Muv & others partly meant to annoy & partly to impress. I couldn't say this to anyone but you. I think I knew her just a bit too well & someone like Selina[1] would sail on without really seeing it. Of course we know it was all part of her unhappy life & I don't blame *at all* only I don't want to be immersed in it. So you can cross me off the list. I think Selina wd be good in many ways. I also think a vol of letters will have to wait until everyone's dead, don't you, because of hurt feelings?

All love darling, Honks

1 Lady Selina Hastings (1945–). Journalist and biographer whose life of Nancy was published in 1985.

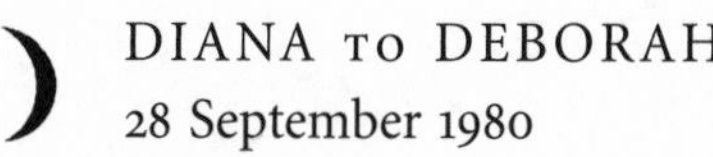

DIANA TO DEBORAH
28 September 1980

Temple de la Gloire
Orsay

Darling Debo:

I gritted my teeth & dialled your number with the firm intention of spending £10 or so in a mammoth chat only to be told you are in Ireland, which if I'd thought for a moment I would have known.

Ian Curteis[1] came with ½ the dreaded script & we spent seven hours doing it. He was very good & took out most of the worst most embarrassing & inaccurate bits. An example: he'd got an elaborate funeral of Decca's poor little baby with all of us there together. He imagined it as the last occasion on which we all met. Anyway he was extremely nice & did almost all I asked. I don't think it's too bad & I *do* think it wd have been ghoul with knobs on had I refused to help. But I think it's rather dull & probably will never reach the screen. Also of course so much depends on the way the actors say things & it may well become far more awful in the end.

Oh Debo I got such a nice letter from Sally Emerson, the editor of *Books & B.* You know I was so worried lest the attack on me in *N.S.*, in which Philip Dossé was mentioned in a nasty way, might have precipitated his suicide.[2] Sally E says she was with him all the last days & she is sure he never read any papers let alone *N.S.* She was devoted to Dossé & scarcely knew me so I do believe her & don't think she says it to comfort me.

As to Evelyn's letters[3] there's a gem on every page & I am miserable to have finished the lovely great book. Far the best letters are to Naunce & Ann Fleming. The ones to Maimie[4] aren't a bit amusing or even clever. Isn't it amazing how the person one's writing to influences one. *Poor* Evie at the end, deaf, toothless, bored & *boring* (unbelievable) at 63, it's too sad for any words & he must have welcomed death as few do. He dreaded twenty more years getting worse & worse. I am dreading poor old Dig reading things about her & Henry [Yorke] & I'm afraid Jamie Hamilton's feelings will be lacerated. Both so easily hurt.

I wish you were here. These golden days it's paradise on earth. Kit v. well. He reverted to whisky but has given it up again.

All love darling, Honks

1 Ian Curteis (1935–). Television writer who was planning to make a film about the Mitfords. The project never materialized.
2 Diana was attacked by Christopher Hitchens in the *New Statesman* for saying in a *Books & Bookmen* review that Dr Goebbels was 'clever and witty' and his wife 'charming and beautiful'. The publisher of *Books & Bookmen*, Philip Dossé (1926–80), had committed suicide because his company was bankrupt.
3 *The Letters of Evelyn Waugh*, edited by Mark Amory (1980).
4 Lady Mary (Maimie) Lygon (1910–82). A friend of Waugh since 1931 and a lifelong correspondent.

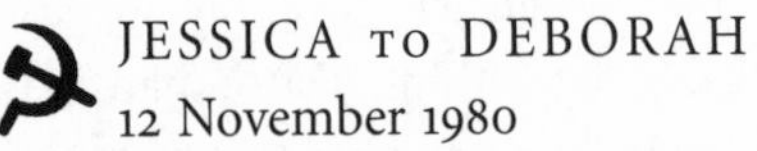

JESSICA TO DEBORAH
12 November 1980

6411 Regent Street
Oakland

Dearest Hen:

Main thing: FINALLY Bob & I saw the Julian Jebb film. We found someone who had the right equipment (for English television) & nipped there yesterday. Well I must say I agree with Jay Allen[1] (see my last letter) that you were easily the best, a needed breath of sanity. I was so amazed at Nancy's interview – I'd never seen it, & there she was large as life & twice as unnatural. One could absolutely get the form of how she was loathing doing it, & was coming off far more affected than ever she was in real life. But yet was awfully good, fielding the questions. The whole thing was (to me) so sad yet funny. All extremely old hat to you, but new hat as of yesterday to me. Wasn't she marvellous about Heaven? Makes me long to be a Believer, the thought of all meeting up there one day. I shouldn't think St Peter will be best pleased at that moment.

How is your BOOK coming along? The Glider[2] longs.

Much love, Henderson

1 Jay Presson Allen (1922–2006). Playwright and Hollywood producer who was planning to make a film of *Hons and Rebels* and who told Jessica that she thought Deborah had 'introduced a welcome note of sanity in the general welter of eccentricity' into Jebb's documentary. (Jessica to Deborah, 7 November 1980).

2 William Abrahams.

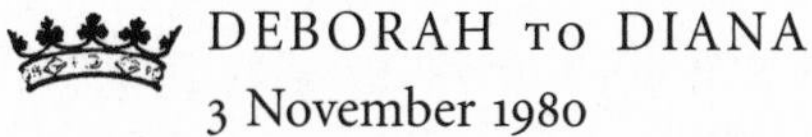

DEBORAH TO DIANA

3 November 1980

Bignor Park
Pulborough

Darling Honks,

Love in a CC was TOO AWFUL. *Hideous* children, most fearfully bad actors, couldn't hear one word but in a way it was a good thing because what one did hear was embarrassing beyond all. The ugliness of the whole outfit was too sad, what would Nancy have said, she'd have minded terribly. Surely there must be some decent looking children somewhere who can speak. And the Hons' Cupboard with no linen was bleak beyond words.

J Jebb rang up, he's hoping they'll put his film on again immediately after *Love in a CC*. He hopes for BBC1. He wants to change the name to The Real Mitfords. Has he got mixed up with *The Real Charlotte*?[1] I said why not The Mitfords Now as we're SO old & depressing & it wd be sad if people thought that's what we used to be like, eh. Or leave it like it is. Or just not put it on.

And he, JJ, has been to see Ned Sherrin[2] & heard the tunes for the high kicking show. Says they're marvellous, well of course tunes of 20's & 30's ARE marvellous, you can't go wrong there. I am supposed to go on 20th to see & hear what has been done so far. The burning question is whether to end it at the beginning of the war. I said YES as loud as I could, & said you must because all the *gaiety* wd go out of it if you start on the sad or controversial stuff. Can you imagine a musical with the things that happened then. I must say I wish they'd leave us alone, people are going to get v. fed up, headed by Andrew.

Much love, Debo

1 The novel by Edith Somerville and Martin Ross was first published in 1894.
2 Ned Sherrin (1931–). The writer and producer was working with Caryl Brahms on *The Mitford Girls*, a musical which opened at the Chichester Festival Theatre in 1981.

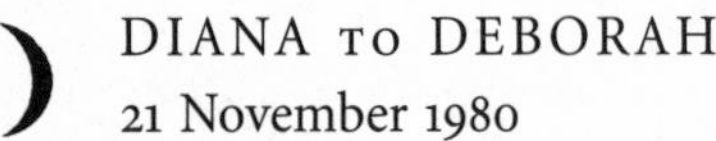

DIANA TO DEBORAH
21 November 1980

Temple de la Gloire
Orsay

Darling Debo:

I hurried a letter to you yesterday, really in order to rid myself of Decca's[1] & Sherrin's letters, so now I must finish what I have to say. Over the years, since 1943 when Decca 'demonstrated' in an attempt to get Kit & me put back in prison when he was very ill (that no one paid any attention to her is neither here nor there) I have never reacted in any way to her pin-pricks. Nobody has felt the pathos of Decca more than I have. I really suffered in 1973 when Naunce was dying & was *so* unkind to her. I don't mind in the least what people's politics are, I am old enough to realize that if nobody can 'convert' me it's not very likely that I could 'convert' anyone else. Between friends, & sisters, it just doesn't matter. But what happened with Jebb's silly film shows the depth of seething hatred Decca feels for us. It is much more painful to hate than to be hated, & I am well aware that her life is in many ways rather awful, but not quite awful enough to excuse her behaviour. As far as I go, I put her out of my mind. If someone behaved to you or Woman as she has to me all these years, I should not wish to have friendship with that person. I know you try to be friends with all & sundry & I quite understand why, but for me it wd be absurd, & certainly not what Decca hopes for. I shall never attack her publicly as she attacks us. I always say (when asked) that I know so little that my comment wouldn't be worth having. I didn't mention her in my book, except as the dear little child she once was.

If you think Sherrin is all right I won't object. I suppose it will be silly, & in so far as Decca has a hand in it, spiteful. The whole point of my being involved in the television film they plan to do is to try & make it vaguely truthful.

All love, Honks

1 Jessica had written to Deborah expressing concern about Ian Curteis's film and annoyance that she had not been consulted.

DIANA TO DEBORAH
2 December 1980

Temple de la Gloire
Orsay

Darling Debo:

Despite our mammoth chat there's more to say. I just peeped at Kit & he is peacefully asleep poor darling.

Fancy meeting Bernie.[1] Did Max produce him from his pouch like you used to say Deacon did Princess Margaret, & then he failed to perform? You never told the *menu*.

I *wish* I could have been fly on wall while you & Bernie boasted of leaving school at twelve years of age. Robert [Skidelsky] must have relished it. He says he's to be 'the Lord Clark of *the Slump*',[2] a series of telly programmes about 1930–31 of which he is compère & I think he says we shall see them next Feb. I am DEVOTED to him.

Oh Debo I wonder whether I shall get to London next week, I think it's most improbable, but I suppose Kit will do his utmost. Think of those stairs in Rosie [Macindoe]'s flat, my heart will be in my mouth.

County & Lydie [de Pomereu] never stop telephoning, they are such good friends, nobody else knows about Kit being ill.

Well darling THANK you for being recipient of all my sorrows.

All love, Honks

1 Bernie Ecclestone (1930–). Formula One racing supremo.
2 The thirteen part TV series *Civilisation*, broadcast in 1969, had made Kenneth Clark a household name.

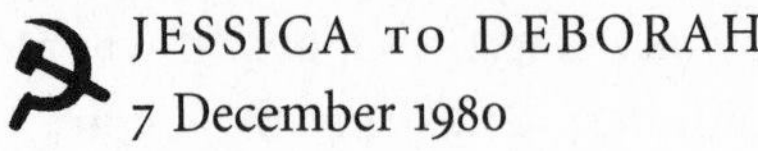

JESSICA TO DEBORAH
7 December 1980

6411 Regent Street
Oakland

Dearest Hen,

En route from Los Angeles to Arkansas I read in L.A. paper that Sir O. Mosley died. Diana must be so incredibly sad & lonely. For obvious reasons I shan't be writing, but if inclined do transmit message of sympathy.

Much love, Henderson

Oh dear what a v. odd & awkward letter. But you know how it is, Hen.

DIANA TO DEBORAH
11 March 1981

Temple de la Gloire
Orsay

Darling Debo

I can't deny that I have felt very very sad since I got home. Luckily the weather became warm suddenly & everything burst out (hedges etc) & I have been working in the garden, at least transplanting yews, all my silly fads, so I get tired & sleep better. But I can't get him out of my mind for more than a few minutes *ever*, even when I'm laughing & chatting the thoughts & sad visions come, I can't explain. I'm *afraid* TIME won't really help much, it is all too much part of me, like losing legs or arms, no not quite that either. People here are very kind they really are. Then what I have to do in the clearing-up line seems endless (despite the smallness of the house) & desperately sad, so full of him in every way.

Woo telephoned about that vile thing in the *D. Mail*[1] that I also sent to you. She was *so* lovely on the telephone saying 'What with the *Daily Mail AND* the Budget!' She says she can't afford to leave the house because of petrol so I said 'Woo come & live *here*', quite forgetting that petrol here is an even more ghoulish price.

All love darling, Honks

1 A Miss Perkin, who purported to have been the Mitfords' governess, claimed that eleven-year-old Unity had 'made her life a lasting misery'.

DIANA TO DEBORAH — Temple de la Gloire
24 June 1981 — Orsay

Darling Debo

Selina went to interview Colonel after meeting him here & she had to FIGHT for her honour, it was Cristiana with knobs on,[1] she says he's terribly strong. I must say I hand it to him aged eighty & after three operations. In one way it is wonderful because she sees what he's like but isn't it mad of him when he knows she is going to write. I mean he couldn't hope for 'success' so it makes him a bit absurd, doesn't it? What a funny person to be in love with all one's life, or at least 30 years or something. Apparently there was no attempt at compliments & seductive words, just a wild rush.

Selina lent me a proof copy of the book about Diana Cooper[2] & I know Colonel will rush for it & he's referred to as 'my grinning spotty friend', awful. Duff is quoted as calling Kit 'a snivelling bolshevist' – I think those were the words – in the twenties. But then Kit was having a wild affair with her so I don't suppose he was v. popular with Duff & of course about the war they took opposite points of view. John Julius was sent pronto to America whereas Kit, from prison, opposed the same thing being done with Micky [Mosley]. The Coopers sound much more ghoul in this book than they were in real life I think.

All love darling, Honks

1 Selina Hastings had asked Gaston Palewski why he thought Nancy's handwriting had changed after meeting him. 'Shall I show you?' he replied, making a pass at her. On another occasion, he had asked Cristiana Brandolini to hold up a painting and had then pounced.

2 A biography by Philip Ziegler (1981).

DIANA TO DEBORAH — Temple de la Gloire
17 August 1981 — Orsay

Darling Debo

I don't think I've *ever* been so pleased to get home as I was yesterday.[1] Various things made me really long for the Temple. Max & Jean were *so* kind & so were Al & Cha,[2] & the little boys[3] were incredibly nice, *but* I don't know quite why (between you & me) I was frightfully sad & almost in tears (nobody knew it) nearly the whole time. Even every signpost one saw brought back so many memories, it was *awful.*

Then the first evening in the dark I fell over a kerb onto a very rough pavement & grazed my knees deeply (what Kit wd have said 'knocked the noughts off'). The knees hurt very much & seemed to get worse all the time, it is strange how many things touch them, one's skirt, bedclothes (only a sheet it was so hot) & then without thinking one sort of pushes a door with a knee, anything of that sort agony, very hard to get in or out of bath, really dozens of annoyances. I seemed to have lost all sense of balance & had to look carefully at a chair in case I sat on the floor & not on it. Anyway all is well now but it made me feel a hundred years old.[4]

It is so lovely here just right. Emmy & Jerry have done something really wonderful, they've washed all the festooned blinds which having been beige, or really *brown*, are now snow white. I wish you could see the difference it makes to sitting rooms & drawing room, oh how inter-esting.

All love, Honks

1 Diana had been staying with Max and Jean Mosley in the South of France.
2 Charlotte Marten (1952–). The editor of these letters married Alexander Mosley in 1975.
3 Max and Jean's sons, Alexander (1970–) and Patrick (1972–).
4 These were the first symptoms of a brain tumour, initially diagnosed as a stroke. Diana was operated on and made a complete recovery.

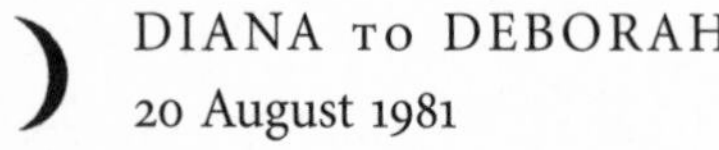

DIANA TO DEBORAH
20 August 1981

Temple de la Gloire
Orsay

Darling Debo

It's *SO* good of you to bother about me. I am afraid I just *can't* see a Dr at the moment. I can't even do up my hair, or dress, or anything. I promise to stay in bed & not risk falling down. PLEASE DON'T COME. I am fit for nothing. Al & Cha are coming to dinner but I'm going to ask them not to visit me, in my room I mean. Emmy looks after me PERFECTLY.

Now the telephone is broken again, I hear the person but nobody hears ME. It happened before. I will send Jerry to complain.

PLEASE don't worry I shall be all right I KNOW I shall.

Love darling & so many thanks for worrying but *don't* worry. There's nothing anyone can do, I only want Kit & he can't come.

Honks

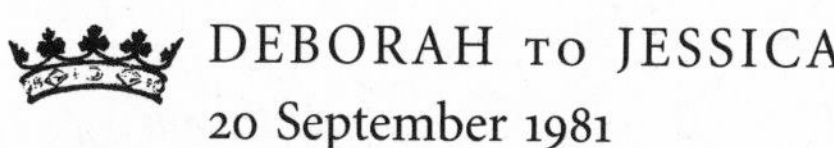

DEBORAH to JESSICA *4 Chesterfield Street, W1*

20 September 1981

Dearest Hen

After many alarums & excursions they've brought Honks to London – she's in the London Hosp in Whitechapel, under a great Dr (one of those professors called Mr who make lesser drs & nurses shudder, you know the kind) who Max knows because he's the head of the team of drs who look after the motor racing drivers.[1]

While I was staying with her in France she had a relapse & is paralysed down the left side, that arm & leg don't work. It was AWFUL & happened gradually, I always imagined quite the opposite. Anyway her *mind* & her *face* are perfectly OK but she is very thin & weak, can't turn over in bed & all that. Now she's being properly nursed she *looks* much better & is v. brave of course, laughing about some of the worst things & the dr (who I haven't seen yet) says he's hopeful of getting her to walk again but guesses he can't do much with her left hand. This is all depending on her staying the same, viz. not having another stroke. No one can tell if that will happen. So all the drama (ambulance-plane etc) is over & it will be a long haul of slowly getting better I HOPE. Old John Betj has made great progress. He is older than she is, and already had Parkinson's quite badly. OH DEAR. *BODIES*.

Much love, Yr Hen

1 Sidney Watkins (1923–). Professor of neurosurgery and medical adviser to Formula One 1978–2004.

JESSICA TO DEBORAH
22 September 1981

6411 Regent Street
Oakland

Dearest Hen,

What absolutely foul news, Diana's stroke. In fact you've had such a beastly time altogether re illnesses of various kinds. I am sorry & can't say how much I sympathize. Can only say they (illards) are jolly lucky to have you to help.

Much love, Yr Hen

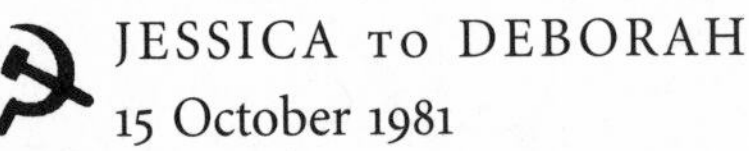

JESSICA TO DEBORAH
15 October 1981

6411 Regent Street
Oakland

Dearest Hen,

Have you ever read the *Book of Job*? A jolly good read, might even cheer you up in the circs. Anyway do keep up the medical bulletins. A friend of ours had the sort of operation Diana's sounds like from yr. letter, & *he got completely OK*; the drs. had been in dire doubt about it, as anything to do with the head can be so awful. I wonder if that was why she had those headaches? If so, the op. might cure them.

I DO so hope your next will bring better news of the invalids; can only say how immensely LUCKY they are to have ye on board at this point of time.

Well Hen *much* love –
longing to see you in December. Henderson

Hen just after I wrote the above a BURGLAR was here. *Quelle horrible surprise* as Nancy (or you) wld say. I'd gone out for a bit, came back, heard a bit of a bang on me back porch – sort of a terrace, with glass doors – & there he was, trying to break in. So I called out a cheery 'Hello, there!' & he was gone in a trice. Agile fellow, means climbing up a fairly steep thing to the windows. He called out a cheery 'Goodbye', thank goodness. So be looking for 'Elderly Oakland Woman Bludgeoned to Death' (we don't say *old* in this country, thought impolite). Anyway it was rather shaking; I was SO relieved when he scrammed away, also thought it far preferable to aforementioned b. to d. In other words I was quite filled with gratitude to him for buggering off. However I did do one awful thing: rang up police, who came pronto. I DO hope they don't catch him, in the circs, as he did no harm. If they do catch him, I may well refuse to testify against him because of the total hell that awaits him should he be sent to prison.

DIANA TO DEBORAH
? October 1981
Friday (I think)

London Hospital
London E1

Oh darling Debo I'm so horrified to think of the bundle of useless helpless old bones that will be dumped on your doorstep.[1] I shouldn't allow it. Am fit for nothing & can't see light at end of tunnel.

All love darling, Honks

1 Diana was going at Chatsworth to convalesce after her operation.

DIANA TO DEBORAH
26 November 1981

4 Chesterfield Street, W1

Darling Debo

You must have thought me so strange when you got back from the shoot last night. You see I was feeling SO sad at leaving that I couldn't even get courage to go to the kitchen & say good bye except with terrific effort, I felt like going to sleep (eternal rest).

In the hospital I several times had doubts as to whether it wouldn't have been better just to let me fade away. I've lost my darling, & lived to see all my children doing what they seem to love doing & more or less successfully. Then of course I was saved & went up to you, & what with YOU, Chatsworth & its denizens, the beauty, the kindness, the laughter with friends & acquaintances & so on, a will to live came back as I got stronger. Isn't it all so strange & hard to explain. Also I felt (& feel) that with my *Times* letter I can still defend Kit as no one else really is in a position to do, & *possibly* (not certainly) influence Nicky in his Memoir[1] a bit. (One has to remember that fond as we are of each other we do NOT see eye to eye politically.) Well then the sweetness of Max & Al & Cha & Jean & Jonathan all those things somehow have made me feel life is worth while for a few more years. But the big thing was YOU darling & all your loving care, medications galore, *everything* thought of without having to be asked for, & bed arranged to look over that heavenly park, & Nijni Novgorod[2] drawn back by me before dawn so that I could see the light coming. You can never never know what you have done to make me want to live. Not that it matters whether I do or not but here I am perfectly well & it is your doing.

When I've seen Sid [Watkins] & Mike[3] I will write again though really I mustn't become too egotistical & absurd.

Jerry drove so smoothly I slept all the way up. I was tired with the sorrow of leaving. Then I slept most of last night as well. Oh how interesting.

Debo how can I ever tell what you have been to me.

Love darling, Honks

1 Diana's stepson, Nicholas Mosley, was working on the first volume of his biography *Rules of the Game: Sir Oswald and Lady Cynthia Mosley 1896–1933* (1982).
2 The curtains in Diana's bedroom at Chatsworth were made of Chinese silk, bought in Moscow and smuggled through the market of Nijni Novgorod for the 6th Duke of Devonshire.
3 Michael Swash; professor of neurosurgery at the Royal London Hospital where Diana was operated on.

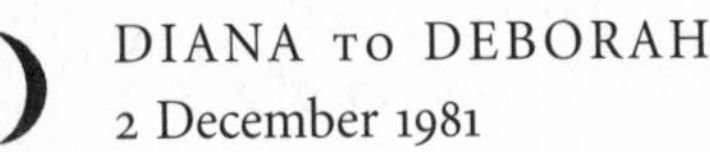

DIANA to DEBORAH
2 December 1981

Temple de la Gloire
Orsay

Darling Debo

So good of you to telephone & it cheered me up no end. You see these three nights are the anniversary of those terrible nights last year – I know it's really the 3rd he died, that is early tomorrow, but in my mind it was last night because it was between Monday & Wednesday that he was so restless & early Wednesday (today) he died & I live through it all over & over again. I *don't* believe in anniversaries, quite meaningless, but one just can't help one's thoughts. I had a good cry & only hope I recover for County & Lydie [de Pomereu], I shall I'm sure. Being so near to death myself has made me see it all in a new light, we all have to die & once you have become either very ill or very helpless life has absolutely no meaning & is simply a burden, as it was becoming – *had* become – for him. *Perhaps* he knew he was dying because each time I rushed for his bell he said such wonderful things, as if he wanted to be sure I knew all that he felt. I was so *stupid* it never occurred to me & I can't forgive myself for not being with him at that terrific moment. Oh darling I shouldn't burden you with these memories & thoughts but there's only you one could say them to.

We have got lovely sun & I have been wooding, yes, & feeling perfectly well. A bit worried about my hair which has bald bits. Oh Debo you have been SO wonderful.

All love, Honks

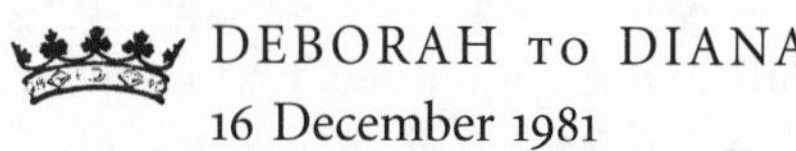

DEBORAH TO DIANA
16 December 1981

Chatsworth
Bakewell

Darling Honks

I have been too awful about writing. There hasn't been a single day without some major something, usually combined with some ghoul journey, all those wasted hours in a car are v. tiresome but will go on till the hotel[1] is finished. Now Richard Garnett[2] is here & today & tomorrow we struggle with those long bits of paper plus 115 photographs. He is so *good*, he is going to do the index *himself.*

Now then. I knew you would have an AWFUL week over the first days of Dec, I dreaded it because I knew you would re-live the whole thing day by day & did I ring up or do anything, NO. AWFUL of me.

Do stop saying no point you being alive, one of the *great* points is being receiver & reader of a letter like this, what would I do if you weren't there. And what would all those others do, children & grandchildren, Emmy & Jerry, Woman & all. RSVP. So Honks brace up please & get on with the wooding.

But don't think I don't realize what those days were like.

Much love & VERY SORRY for not being in touch over your awful week from Debo

1 Deborah was redecorating the Devonshire Arms at Bolton Abbey, a two-hour drive from Chatsworth.
2 Deborah's editor at Macmillan.

DIANA TO DEBORAH
13 December 1981

Temple de la Gloire
Orsay

Darling Debo

Debo, my hair. Don't laugh. It's not only a shaving brush, but like so many shaving brushes it's partly *black*. Now what can this mean? I've never had a single black hair. I was so hoping for gleaming white like Aunt Iris & Farve. Well, pepper, salt, & black. Do be sorry. Also it is literally made of wire.

I am not reading the mountain of letters[1] but I did read one from General Fuller[2] who says of Churchill 'What a mountebank the man was'. I also found a P.C. from the laureate from Ireland signed Sean O'Betjeman. How is he by the way?

All love darling, Honks

1 Diana had sold a writing desk and found a pile of old letters in one of its drawers.
2 J. F. C. (Boney) Fuller (1878–1966). Military strategist and historian.

DIANA TO DEBORAH
18 December 1981

Temple de la Gloire
Orsay

Darling Debo:

Yesterday I had an evening outing, going to *Carmen* with Cha & her friends in an old theatre in the slums where one sat on wooden benches.[1] I loved it but was terribly tahd after (though Jerry whizzed me home in twenty minutes, empty roads) so shall not go out again, but before the opera, at Cha's, SID [Watkins] came, Debo he is so marvellous. We had pink champagne & a deep talk. Apparently he was called in to poor Naunce, too late to avoid the useless operation on her back (spine). It was too amazing the way he remembered every detail of her case. I asked whether, had it existed then, the scanner could have diagnosed what was the matter with her, & he thinks it could have. *Poor* Naunce.

On a more frivolous note, I mentioned my piebald hair. He didn't ask to see it but just said airily 'Yes, you never know what sort of hair will grow'. So there we are. I suppose one might dye that bit. Cha loves Sid just as much as I do.

The clear-up continues. I have to *force* myself to do it.

All love darling, Honks

1 Bizet, *La Tragédie de Carmen*, directed by Peter Brook at the Théâtre des Bouffes du Nord, Paris.

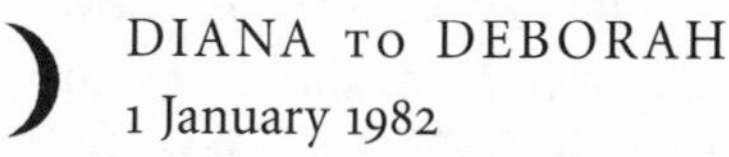

DIANA to DEBORAH
1 January 1982

Temple de la Gloire
Orsay

Darling Debo

I have been terribly sad about Kit. To tell the truth I always am & probably always will be. Laughing etc means nothing. He is at the back of my mind & no 5 minutes goes by without sad thoughts & (however illogical) I blame myself all the time. I don't think the awful sorting of papers has got any thing to do with it. He wrote so little that wasn't political. What courage he had never to let frustration make any difference. I hope Nicky will bring that out. (Heaven knows what his book will be like.)

Such a strange thing, Max has found Grandfather's Peking diary, a private diary, with dread SEX mentioned & not mealy mouthed like the published books.[1] Of course it must have been among the books Uncle Tommy sold at Newcastle, & I bought, like your diary.[2] What luck it turned up before J's book[3] rather than after.

All love, Honks

1 The 1st Baron Redesdale published an expurgated record of his posting in China, *The Attaché in Peking*, in 1900.
2 In 1972, Deborah bought from a dealer two volumes of a diary she had kept in 1938. The books had been forgotten in a crate in the Mosleys' London house after they left.
3 Jonathan and Catherine Guinness's biography, *The House of Mitford*, was published in 1984.

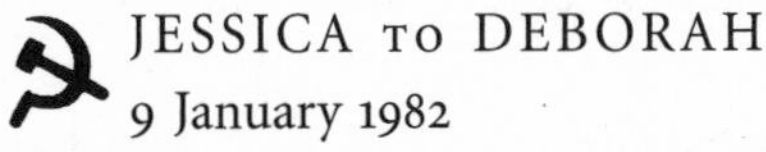

JESSICA TO DEBORAH
9 January 1982

6411 Regent Street
Oakland

Dearest Hen,

Your article in *The Dial.*[1] These days, all US mags have a thing called Checkers. Checker's job is to ring up the author & verify sources, spellings etc. For instance if you've spelt MacDonald two different ways (Mac & Mc) which is right? If you have quoted from a book, where can checker find said book to verify quotation? A huge lot of nonsense, & fairly new, but they all do it now.

So the other day I was sitting about thinking no harm when a call came from checker at *The Dial.* 'Sorry to trouble you' (said she) 'but did your father refer to people he didn't like as "a meaningless piece of meat?"' And lots more along that line. I was shrieking with laughter, & saying 'Yes, yes, yes' – finally, asked her what it was all about. 'We have an article scheduled about your sister Nancy's TV programme.' 'Who wrote it', I asked? 'Not at liberty to say, but a close relation of yours.' HEN!!! Of course I twigged straight away that it was ye. Longing to see finished product; checker promised to send same. I'm doing one for *TV Guide* (to coincide with N's telly series of her books, due here in March); as I more or less shot my bolt in the Foreword for the books, am hard put to it.

Much love, Henderson

1 Deborah had written an article in the Los Angeles monthly TV guide to coincide with the American broadcast of Julian Jebb's documentary on Nancy.

JESSICA TO DEBORAH
22 January 1982

6411 Regent Street
Oakland

Dearest Hen

Letters X-ing like mad, sorry. I just wrote when yours came. But with me it's always NOW or NEVER: I've got a huge file called *Letters to be Answered*. In a year or two, these go into a far huger file called *Letters Never Answered*. (Would never happen to yours, Hen. If no answer after a year you'll know she's dead, she's expired, she's so neriogely[1] put out her tongue.)

There was SUCH a killing thing on telly last night – I was watching the non-news, a sort of early bit before the actual news. Re a book[2] in England that proves the Devonshires are descended from J.C., & a v. short thing of Andrew saying 'Preposterous! This will annoy a lot of people' or words to that effect.

Well – I suppose it IS annoying, Hen, but do admit a bit of a shriek to come on it all unexpectedly?

And fancy Sophy being a descendant of. Do give her lots of love when you write & ask her to intercede for this lost soul with her great-great (to the Nth decimal point) grandpapa.

Much love, Henderson

1 'Horribly' in Honnish.
2 Michael Baigent et al., *The Holy Blood and the Holy Grail* (1983). The book claimed that Jesus married Mary Magdalene, fathered a child and staged his own crucifixion.

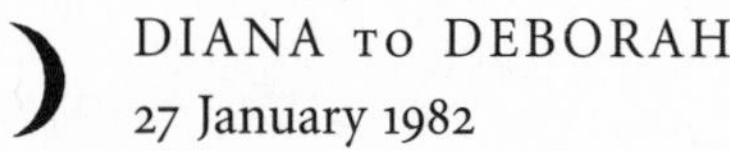

DIANA TO DEBORAH
27 January 1982

Temple de la Gloire
Orsay

Darling Debo

I have been reading old letters. I've got dozens of pre-war ones from Mrs Ham. A very very kind one from Farve after Birdie's funeral. None calculated to cheer one up.*

The sun came out yesterday, a rarity. Do you know I believe that thing on my brain was nature's way of saying life is over, & that the wonderful cleverness of the way it was removed & life saved was most likely a great mistake. A few years ago I suppose I should have died. But perhaps not, I might have been a vegetable annoying you all. I asked Sid but he says they don't quite know.

I am so dying to see you & it's so good of you to have Rosie [Macindoe]. She is a perfect guest, just sitting & knitting.

I cry for *nothing*, even seeing the bulbs coming up set me off. I hope to be better before I see you. I miss Kit more, not less.

All love darling, Honks

*Do you want them for your collection?

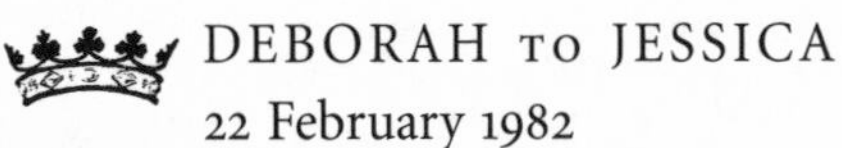

DEBORAH TO JESSICA
22 February 1982

Chatsworth
Bakewell

Dearest Hen

A v. sad thing, Derek Jackson died yesterday. He had had an awful time, had a leg off a few months ago & they were threatening the other one so I suppose he was spared longer torture.

Woman & I were poised to go to the funeral (Switz) but we noted from her phone call last night that the wife wd rather we went to a memorial in Paris later. Honks minds terribly. He was a staunchly loyal friend all through the war & after, never cared a hang what anyone else thought & lent his house when they came out of prison. She minds things far more than most people, & has got another dying person in poor old Geoffrey Gilmour, he is a bit of yellow skin stretched over a skeleton, cancer, *oh dear*.

Much love, Yr Hen

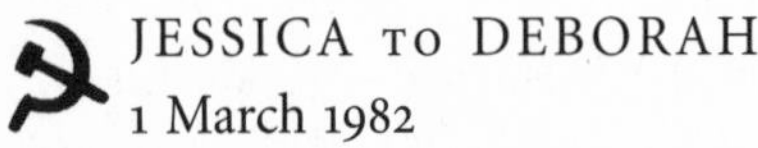

JESSICA TO DEBORAH
1 March 1982

30 East 9th Street
New York

Dearest Hen,

Writing in a huge rush to say *The Dial* arrived with yr. article & I must immediately have my say re same (am off in 30 mins, not yet packed but writing na'therless).

Well I thought it was *marvellous*, oh you were so good re Farve & Nancy. I so adored them being a pair of comedians & all that bit; ditto, all the last several paragraphs about Nancy & above all 'comic & indom. spirit . . .' the whole last paragraph.

Forward to bones to pick: YOU never had a new dress? The Wendy frocks – yours *was* new (being the smaller & hence, I suppose, cheaper size) & it was *mine* that was copied by Gladys. Have you still got yours? Mine disappeared somehow, in various moves.

Main bone: Education produces people as alike as peas in a pod? All I can say is it would have to be an enormous & v. distorted pod, not like any pods I've seen. Leaving out the boys, just mentioning a few girls that we both know: Emmas, Good & Bad;[1] Polly Toynbee;[2] Selina Hastings; Marina Warner[3] (not sure you know that one). As unlike as any peas I can visualize, all educated chapesses. Really Hen be rethinking, or I shall ring up the Checker to say you've got the facts off.

Must be off; otherwise shall miss aeroplane. DO drop a line to above address if inclined (put To Await Arrival). Longing for your review of my review of your *Dial* article.

Much love, Henderson

1 Emma Tennant, Deborah's daughter, and her sister-in-law, the novelist Emma Tennant (1937–).
2 Polly Toynbee (1946–). Columnist on the *Guardian* and broadcaster.
3 Marina Warner (1946–). Novelist and cultural historian.

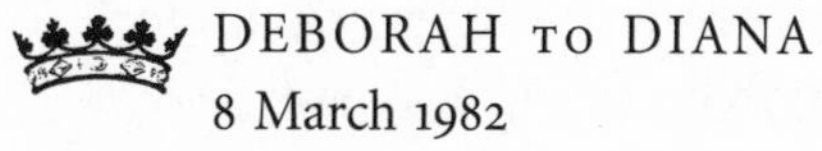

DEBORAH TO DIANA
8 March 1982

Chatsworth
Bakewell

Darling Honks

I'm afraid you've had a truly awful fortnight, it's so odd those two dying within days of each other.[1]

How wonderful that J Belmore[2] exists, I mean he, Geoffrey, might so easily have been quite alone except for you. There is something so sad about people who haven't got anyone, & I can think of quite a lot.

Honks don't think that about Sir O, death is so seldom like Geoffrey's, it nearly always has something horrible attached & the wonderful thing about Sir O's was the lack of that for him. One can't arrange that fading out way, you know what I mean. It was wonderful for him when you think what might have been – hospitals, indignities, pain & all that misery. Oh Honks, whatever it had been it would have been awful for you, but I keep thinking it could have been so much more awful for him.

Much love, Debo

1 Derek Jackson and Geoffrey Gilmour.
2 8th Earl of Belmore (1951–). Cousin and heir of Geoffrey Gilmour.

DIANA TO DEBORAH
16 March 1982

Temple de la Gloire
Orsay

Darling Debo

I will write you the full horror of Nicky's book[1] when I've got a moment. Such *wonderful* Woo news. I die to mention but of course I won't. She is being so wondair. A moment ago I said something about the by-election in Glasgow & she said 'I suppose *Andrew* will be in *full flower*'.[2]

I think Al is so horrified by the book that he's going to London to see Nicky. But there's no tinkering to be done. The whole tone is VILE. And Nicky went on & on emphasizing how he thought it would give people a new insight into Kit. Even this last visit he kept telling me. I needn't tell you I don't mind a bit for myself, it's for *him*. Al can't get over the way everything of the most nasty is carefully selected, & everything else passed over in silence. Far the worst part is to publish one's parents' poor little loving or silly or cross letters to the world. It is frightful. I completely trusted him.

Love darling, Honks

P.S. Woman has just said she 'had to sign something in Switz for Derek to do with America'. Horrors! *What?*

1 Diana was reading the proofs of the first volume of Nicholas Mosley's biography of his father, *Rules of the Game.*
2 Andrew Devonshire had joined the Social Democratic Party, an offshoot of the Labour Party founded in 1981. The by-election at Glasgow Hillhead was won by Roy Jenkins, one of the founders of the SDP.

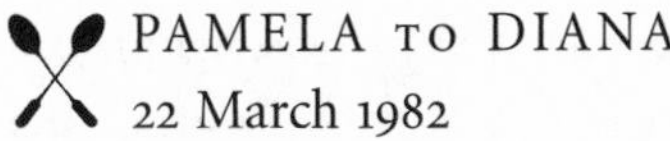

PAMELA TO DIANA
22 March 1982

Woodfield House
Caudle Green

Darling Nard

I can't get over Derek's will of the American money, I shall be so well off & won't know myself. What is terribly sad is the fact that I will never be able to thank him, it quite haunts me.

For me, one *great* worry has been taken away – Mr Machell[1] says the cooking book would be no good. I am deeply relieved & can now really relax, it was such a hideous effort & I had to struggle to find time to do it. He quite rightly says that there are already too many cookery books on the market & unless it was something completely out of the ordinary it would not sell. It was E. Winn Esq[2] who suggested it to Jamie [Hamilton] who had already twice asked me to write a book & I had declined each time. It's not like me to burst into print & your book on our childhood is so perfect & so there is no need to do another.

Again millions of thanks & much love from
Woman

1 Roger Machell (1908–84). Editor at Hamish Hamilton.
2 Elizabeth Winn used to receive letters addressed thus.

DIANA TO DEBORAH
27 March 1982

Temple de la Gloire
Orsay

Darling Debo

Many happy returns darling of your birthday. Heaven knows when I shall see you but how lovely to be at Lismore. Viv & Micky [Mosley] came, their reaction to Nicky's book is that they are 'outraged' by it. I can't tell you the incredible tastelessness of it. I feel I have failed Kit in not having read his private 'papers' but I trusted Nicky in a way that one naturally would never have trusted an ordinary biographer. Also I felt (& still feel) that letters between Kit & his first wife belong absolutely to their children & not to me. I suppose with hindsight I should have given them to all three, & then Viv & Micky could have overruled Nicky & refused to allow these agonizingly private outpourings to be published.

The utterly unfair & biased view of Kit is painful but I feel, although he's not here, he can take care of himself. He was such a strangely unique figure & will always interest people. Al disagrees; he says this is ultimately true, but that Nicky has destroyed him as a serious political figure for a generation. (Al also says that later on he will recover from the attack, because he was intrinsically of great interest despite his failure.) Nicky's mother would mind so much, isn't it odd that a soi-disant [so-called] 'sensitive' man should behave in such a way. I still can hardly believe it. A French writer I'm very fond of told me months ago that he was really touched by Nicky's attitude to his father (it was Michel Mohrt,[1] he & his wife, devoted to Kit). Well, so was I. He went on even last January when he was here, saying he had tried to depict idealists who hoped & believed they could 'change the world'.

Another thing, he has got Auntie Ni's diary, & he said he couldn't use it because it was so histrionic and crazy. He knows & I know that she was usually drunk, but the 'public' doesn't know it, & contrary to what he told me he has constantly quoted from it & always to Kit's discredit. Ordinary people (who, for example, didn't read her memoirs, an *incredibly* absurd book) will think 'there now, even his sister-in-law', etc.

As to me, I truly don't mind for myself. I suppose I shall come out badly in the next vol (pretty awful in this one). I mind for Kit & for Cimmie & the whole family, & for Nicky himself because he will seem such a shit to anyone not blinded by hate for me & Kit. I trusted Nicky absolutely. I haven't spoken to Max who is only just back from Brazil, but I think he will say that although the letters belong to me, I gave them to Nicky knowing he was writing a book.

I didn't read them, that was my awful mistake. Sorry darling to go on. Viv & Micky were very good.

All love, Honks (Haste for post)

1 Michel Mohrt (1914–). Novelist, critic and member of the Académie Française.

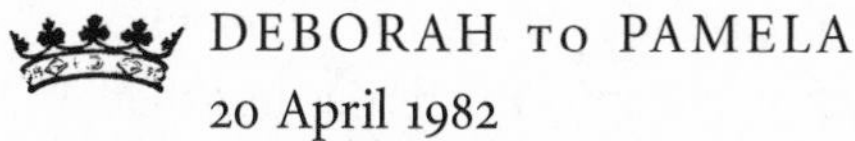

DEBORAH TO PAMELA

20 April 1982

Lismore Castle
Co. Waterford

Darling Woman

I should like to hear your screams at the prices of things here. They are FIERCE.

Conversation between Rothwell[1] & me re shepherd's ancient cottage. Me 'Has it got a bath?' Rothwell 'Well you could say it has a kinda bath'. Me 'What kind of bath?' Rothwell 'Well it's a type of a *half dry* kinda bath . . . & you have to climb under the roof to get at it.'

And Betty[2] in our diner: Betty, 'What kind of china is this?' Me: 'Belleek'. Betty: 'Ow, I love Belleek but this is HIDEOUS'.

Such astonishing weather here, really hot in the day out of the wind & v. cool at night. Not a drop of rain since we arrived, getting very dry.

WONDERFUL VEG.

Much love, Stublow

1 The Devonshires' farm manager at Lismore.
2 Elizabeth Farquhar; an outspoken neighbour of the Devonshires.

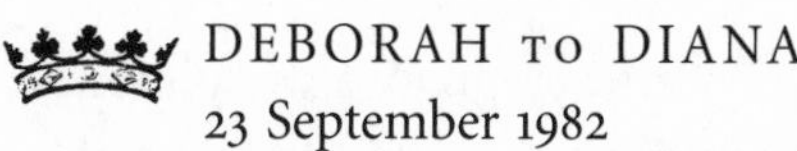

DEBORAH TO DIANA

23 September 1982

Chatsworth
Bakewell

Darling Honks

Never fear, that book of Nicky's will infuriate &, I think, SHOCK everyone, not just you & Al & Max.

Even nowadays, when all is revealed by all about all, people have a sort of standard of not dragging nearest & dearest through the mud. All the remaining Curzon side will hate it, poor old Bar Bar,[1] her children, & anyone else mentioned but of course specially her & them will be enraged by Nicky's totally unnecessary way of doing it. This may not be any comfort to you but it ought to be because it just shows he's gone berserk and people will turn it on to him & won't like it. If he's trying to squeeze out of himself his own unhappy childhood he has done it at the expense of all the others & no one will love him for it, at best they will pity him for being so pathetic as having to publish it to rid himself of unhappy memories but that jolly well isn't good enough & I'm sure even the most anti-Sir O will think it pretty squalid. It will be fascinating to see the reviews. But the point of writing all this is to say how you are only one of the sufferers-to-be through his awfulness in doing it. What a strange muddled up man he is, so charming to meet & then throws up something as squalid & LOW as this. Idiotic as well as unpleasant.

Much love, Debo

1 Lady Alexandra (Baba) Curzon (1904–95). Nicholas Mosley's aunt was the Viceroy Curzon's youngest daughter and had been Mosley's mistress before the war. Married Edward (Fruity) Metcalfe in 1925.

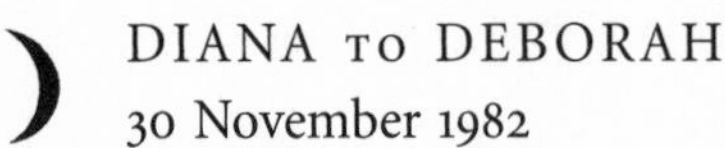

DIANA TO DEBORAH
30 November 1982

Temple de la Gloire
Orsay

Darling Debo:

I am desperately sad these days, much worse than last year, I think it's because last year I was still half ill myself. It's the *days*, not the *dates*, that one suffers from & I'm in the middle of them & luckily alone.

I've finished Mrs Ham,[1] wish you were here to give an opinion. Don't know who to be at now. I'm longing for my visit to Woman but also *terrified* because she suggests we cook each every other day. First of all I can't, & second, imagine how I'd do every single thing WRONG, wrong times, wrong ingredients, wrong casseroles (the latter bound to be ruined if I cook in them). Oh Debo do you think she wd take me to Marks & Sparks & I could secretly buy all? You see

I'd love to 'make the dust' but there again I'm so bad at it, can't manage Hoover except by knocking over every bit of furniture & dainty china going west. Actual dusting a dead loss when I do it, it looks worse after I've finished. You see I did cook for Kit at Villedo but he loved whatever one produced, not at all critical. Can't you picture Woman & Beetle back from walk & Woman saying 'I smell burning' or 'Nard, you should have put the potatoes on *long* ago'. Do you think she wd allow what she calls 'a pub lunch' on my day? Probably not as we shall be snowed in. It really will be the agony *&* the ecstasy because I love Woodfield & Woman & all but am not house trained. I am a drone & no mistake.

All love darling, Honks

There's such a *disgusting* article by Penelope Betj about killing a hen it made me feel *sick*.

1 Diana's chapter on Violet Hammersley in *Loved Ones.*

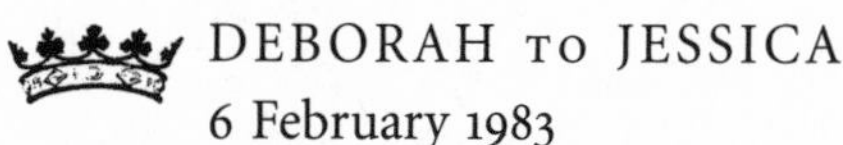

DEBORAH TO JESSICA
6 February 1983

Chatsworth
Bakewell

Dearest Hen

Now then Hen. Things are bad here, in that poor Andrew is really ill, that is to say the real cause of all his troubles, which I guess you guessed ages ago, is drink & it has really taken him over.

It was the cause of his falls which dislocated the hip, & so on & on, it is just much worse than it has ever been partly because of the awful hazard of the hip, as you can picture. So we (me & the children) have consulted all sorts of drs & they all agree that covering up, acting that all is well etc, not only doesn't help but hinders, & that we must all make a stand and say we love him & long for him to get better but that until he decides to get what they call 'help' we will disappear & leave him to it.

I can tell you this decision wasn't come to lightly, it has taken *AGES* & endless meetings & telephonings & all that, but there was a ghoulish crisis last weekend when he fell downstairs & that decided us all that we must act on the advice of all. So we've said that we're not going to be around when he gets back from Ireland. You can imagine the agony of it. I've told the people here, & exactly why & all that.

I'm not sure where I'll go, have to see what happens. The good Wife says I can go to her for a bit, Heck Knight[1] ditto, & Sto has a cottage at Bolton which would be good. It is altogether FOUL as ½ of one feels such a rat going off when he's in such a bad way but they all say I'll get ill if it just goes on & on as it has for years so there we are. The great hope is that he *will* go for treatment as he did once before, then all will be as ever.

Sorry to weary you with all this Hen, but it's better to out with it.

Meanwhile much love, Yr Hen

1 Hester (Heck) Loyd (1920–2001). Married Major Guy Knight in 1944.

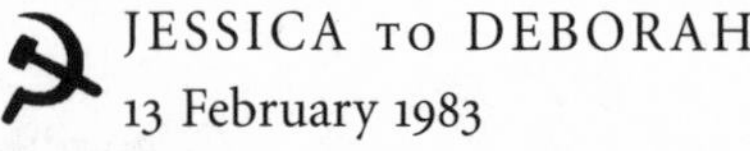

JESSICA TO DEBORAH
13 February 1983

*[6411 Regent Street
Oakland]*

Dearest Hen,

What a thoroughly despairing & beastly situation for all of you – Oh I'm so v v sad about it. I suppose the ray of hope is that he *might* agree to try a cure, given the drasticness of you & children's decision – also, he must himself be so very miserable. Oh Hen. I do think you did the right thing; from all you say, that sort of JOLT might be *the* best help you can give.

Do send every word as to outcome – that is, when you've got time; I imagine that all the implementing of everything will be the time-consumer of all time. Anyway I really long to know what happens next. Far from being ½ a rat, I thought what you decided was bold as a lion & exactly right.

Much love, Henderson

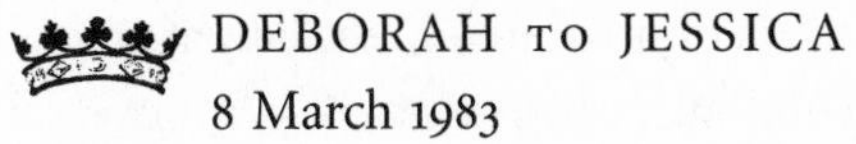

DEBORAH TO JESSICA
8 March 1983

Chatsworth
Bakewell

Dearest Hen

Now Hen things are *much much better* here, a sort of miracle after crises one after another & each one more horrid, depressing & foul heaping itself on an already awful situation. Anyway, the fact is that no drink has been taken for 2 weeks and health seems to be coming back gradually, spirits not too brill, but not too bad except sometimes. Walking better (the poor new hip got a terrible hammering with so many falls) & so everything is definitely looking up. Still it's all supremely delicate as you can imagine. He hasn't agreed to see & talk to any of the people who kindly offer themselves. But he may come to it, hasn't turned it down completely, just says he hates talking & wants to do it on his own. But that is what they one & all say is nigh on impossible.[1]

Much love from Yr Hen

1 After lasting two weeks of a six-week cure in a clinic, Andrew Devonshire gave up drinking and never touched alcohol again. He concluded a short chapter entitled 'Drink' in his autobiography with, 'To anyone reading these pages and suffering a similar problem I can tell them that alcoholism can only be defeated by determination.' *Accidents of Fortune* (Michael Russell, 2004), p. 103.

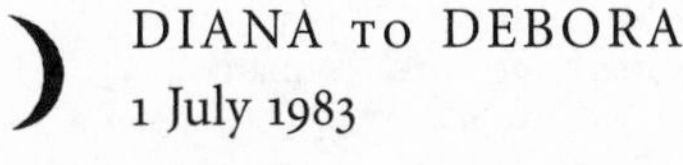

DIANA TO DEBORAH
1 July 1983

Sloane Court East, SW3

Darling Debo:

I go to Wifey today, longing for the country, & her. I can hear on bedroom telephone but not downstairs I've discovered.[1] So sorry about the other evening.

Yesterday I lunched with Frank [Longford]; at H of Lords because he had to rush to a committee. He asked me to be early & I was & sat in an armchair to wait & a very very old man tottered in dressed in corduroys. He hung a filthy mac & a plastic bag on a hook, & something made me say very quietly 'Bryan?' He rushed over & kissed me & said 'Which of you is it?' At that juncture Frank loomed

& I said 'Look who's here & he doesn't know me!' Great laughter of course. I *hope* he thought I was you, our only peeress, if so it takes ten years off, but you see I had my back to the light.[2]

He came & stood by our table for ages at luncheon. Oh Debo! Then he said 'See you on the great day' (Catherine's wedding)[3] & I feel sure he's no idea of the scrum it will be, & all night too. He said 'I've no idea who's coming'. Just as well, like not knowing beforehand how painful an operation is going to be.

This is really to say that Margaret [Willes] is very remorseful about Soph[4] but she's got a book OUT by Carol Thatcher[5] which is a record, about the election, & it entailed Margaret working day & night. She is *v* pleased with Soph. She says the reason Frank was late at H of Lords was that he changed into a suit from the cleaners & couldn't make the zip work & she said 'Give it to me' & he said 'Promise not to look' & handed the trousers round the door & of course it worked. This happened TWICE. Somehow so typical of Frank. All at Sidgwick office. She told me later.

I die for you.

All love darling, Honks

1 Diana's deafness grew increasingly severe with age until in the last years of her life she had only ten per cent hearing left in one ear.
2 James Lees-Milne recorded in his diaries that after this meeting, Bryan Guinness told Selina Hastings, 'Do you know, that was the first time I have met Diana in fifty years that I have not wept.' *Holy Dread: Diaries, 1982–1984* (John Murray, 2001), p. 109.
3 Diana's granddaughter Catherine Guinness was marrying Lord Neidpath.
4 Deborah's daughter was preparing a book of photographs, *The Mitford Family Album* (1985), and was annoyed by her publishers' lackadaisical attitude.
5 *Diary of an Election, With Margaret Thatcher on the Campaign Trail* (1983).

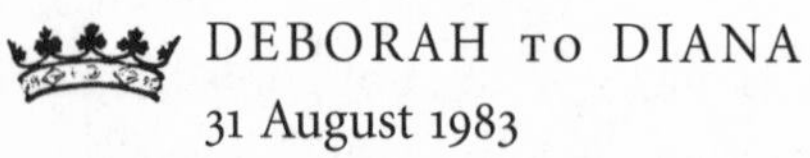

DEBORAH TO DIANA
31 August 1983

Bolton Abbey
Skipton

Darling Honks

50 years.[1] It is AMAZING that you were grown up & on the go such an age ago. It's the suddenness of getting old that has surprised me, looking in the glass one day & the face being *sort of* alright & the

next it's as old as the hills & as full of ups & downs & brown patches & beards & all sorts of odd & horrible things that were never there before. And reading in the paper of An Elderly Woman Aged 63 being knocked down, murdered, standing up to armed robbers in her Sub Post Office, all the things which seem to happen to Elderly Woman in the papers. And realizing . . .

We've had a marvellous time here, I suppose it was the weather that made it, day after day of boiling calm, as rare as rare in these parts. The atmosphere in the house has been lovely, perhaps because there were so many servitors of every description it was a question of coffee in the pantry for hours for most of them as there can't have been anything else to do. (Not Henry of course, he is for ever working.) When they lined up to say goodbye to Prince Philip I was really embarrassed by the number & the fact that I couldn't remember the names of ½ the dailies, oh Honks how awful.

On Bank Hol Monday I judged the Shetlands at Keswick Show in the Lake District. I started at 6.30, as I feared bumper to bumper, but there wasn't a car in sight even when I left the M6 for the lakes & I shall never forget the stunning beauty of the country all the way with the early morning sun behind me and the certainty of a brilliant day.

Honks *the people* there, the ones which belonged to the animals (Herdwick Sheep like pink guinea pigs, sheep dogs on binder-twine leads which have to walk along a door laid on the grass to show their paces, indecent looking long legged terriers brown & tan, Lakelands I think, Fell ponies, as well as the really bad lot of Shetlands I judged), were v. easily sorted out from the Bank Holiday-ites.

The lunch in the tent looked so disgusting I bought some goat yoghurt & plums, delicious.

There was a tent called INDUSTRIAL which turned out to be jam, cakes, knitting, arts & crafts etc. I've never thought of Crab Apple Jelly being Heavy Industry but that just shows how wrong I was. The man on the loudspeaker said please no worms in the Pet Class. Last year someone dug up & entered 3. The best of it was the astonishing country & mountains & the women in cotton frocks which surely they can hardly ever wear & all looking so happy in the sun. And for me the rare luxury of not knowing one single human being.

Much love, Debo

1 Diana had written to Deborah (24 August 1983), 'It's fifty years since I went to stay with Gerald for a month in Rome. How can one be so *old*?'

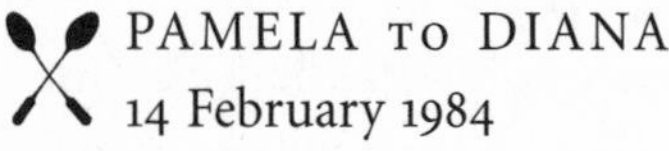

PAMELA TO DIANA
14 February 1984

4 Chesterfield Street, W1

Darling Nard

Alas, we will never see the Chicken programme because it was shown *only* to London viewers – *so* unkind – and it was late Monday night, 11.50 P.M. Never mind; I was only talking for 2 minutes, one of many others & the thing only lasted 15 minutes. The others were *so* funny, 6 ladies from the Liberace Club, which of course I had never heard of before, a couple from near Manchester who were Railway enthusiasts & have beautiful model Railways all over their garden, a Canadian who now lives in Sussex & also a Railway enthusiast but his railway is indoors & very small. He had some beautiful models in plastic cases, one was a Canadian Pacific engine just like the ones I remember. There was a peculiar seedy looking man dressed in a pink satin suit all embroidered with jewels & very open in the front to show a tattoo on his chest 'King Elvis'!!! A girl with hideous crinkled hair that looks greasy & never combed out, she was in a black suit the jacket of which was very open in front so that she looked as though she had nothing underneath. When it was her turn to talk she stepped down & took off the suit & a very bronzed figure stood there in a tight-fitting swimsuit & then she figured about & showed the muscles in her arms & stanced about – she certainly had a beautiful figure. She belonged to the Health & Beauty people. When it was my turn I was questioned about chickens & how I had become 'obsessed' with them. I said that as a child it was just my hobby & that we had all kept chickens or ducks. Then I told about the hen that Nancy had in the rue Monsieur. It was all so funny, I wish you had been there.

Much love from Woman

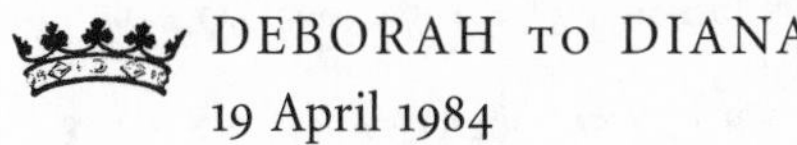

DEBORAH TO DIANA
19 April 1984
(43rd anniv. of wedding, MY WORD how queer.)

Lismore Castle
Co. Waterford

Darling Honks

So now we're here. Didn't come last year if you remember so it's two years since I saw it & NOTHING has changed, most reassuring. Wife is here thank God, & Woman.

Jonathan [Guinness] sent his bit re me, have you seen it, it's v. nice. I wrote & said so but also said (the only suggestion I made except for correcting a few factual mistakes – he'd put I'm Managing Director of Tarmac,[1] oh Honks for a banker that's a bit out isn't it, imagine what the Tarmac-ites wd think if that had been printed) about having had three babies who conked because it looks sort of so bland, unalloyed luck, pleasure etc etc. Perhaps not completely accurate but, as one can't put why, one may as well say the other nasty thing in my life, viz. only rearing ½ my children – like a 3rd world woman. Perhaps he won't put it, twas only an idea.

Woman thinks she hasn't had his piece on her but I'm sure I remember you altering a few things before she saw it & then her OK-ing it? Yes? No? RSVP.

Last night she told about her childhood & when she was first grown up, I hadn't realized quite how awful Nancy was to her. I asked what happened to the Chicken's Mess[2] & she said Birdie craved it so she gave it to her & Bird gave it to Hitler & this made us laugh so much that we completely collapsed, it was the way she said it as if it was the most ordinary thing in the world. Isn't it odd the way the others saw more *personal* bits ought to be in yr Sir O chapter,[3] I suppose I thought so underneath, but I have no critical thing, I can only see what's there* & couldn't make suggestions & thought it perfect. Now I agree with them entirely, it's the humanising we're after so Carry On Honks.

I bet you loved having Jonathan. When shall we see his book?

Much love, Debo

*Like I never can imagine anyone else in a theatrical part except the person I've seen. Dim, I'm afraid.

1 Deborah was a non-executive director of Tarmac plc 1984–92. Jonathan Guinness had sent her a proof of *The House of Mitford*.
2 The replica of King Alfred's jewel given to Pamela by Oliver Watney. (See Nancy to Diana, 7 January 1946, p. 223, n2.)
3 Diana's chapter on her husband, to be included in *Loved Ones*.

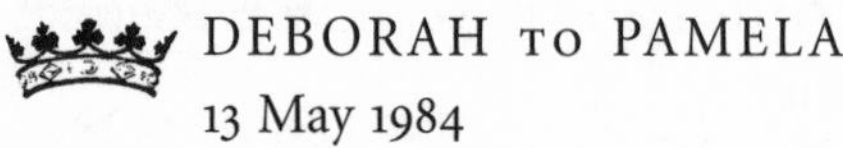

DEBORAH TO PAMELA
13 May 1984

Chatsworth
Bakewell

Darling Woman

Uncle Harold[1] is being *very* good, what Nanny would have called No Trouble. Sometimes he gets up & sometimes he doesn't. When he stays in his room he has bread & butter for breakfast lunch tea & dinner. Yesterday he got up & had 2 helpings of curry at lunch & 2 pancakes after lots of other stuff at dinner. I can't imagine what his stomach must make of such contrasts.

Longing to see you next week, let me know if I'm to bring anything else.

Much love, Stublow

1 After Harold Macmillan was widowed in 1966, he often stayed at Chatsworth, sometimes for weeks at a time.

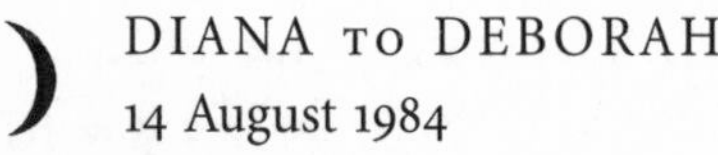

DIANA TO DEBORAH
14 August 1984

Temple de la Gloire
Orsay

Darling Debo

I *loved* having the baby,[1] he is so incredibly sweet now. The fly in the ointment is his keeper. Though *very* nice it's rather like having for example Isabel[2] as tidier up. The dreaded plastic toys are simply *everywhere* – drawing room, both sitting-rooms, porch, garden, even orchard. His & her shoes here & there. Pram of course (*hideous*). Cushions awry. The whole place a slum. One daren't look in her room (your room) awash with clothes & unmade bed. Bathroom with plastic toys to the ceiling. It's just bad luck, people of her generation are born untidy. His *books* are so terrible with pictures of squinting moronic children supposed (probably) to be amusing. Cha came back & Al came & the joy of the baby was wonderful. But it made me sad because it confirms what I always suspected, that Al *did* miss us terribly in 1940 when he was just the age Louis is now. And one can't explain anything even when it's good news 'They're coming back!' which it wouldn't have been.

Wife comes tomorrow, I will report.

All love darling, Honks

1 Louis Mosley; Alexander and Charlotte's eighteen-month-old son.
2 Isabel Tennant; Deborah's 21-year-old granddaughter.

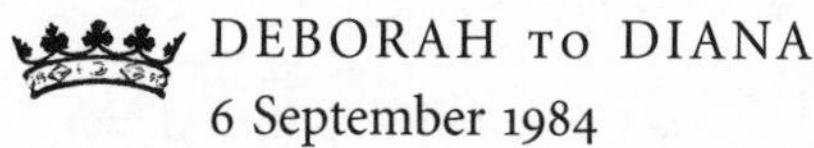

DEBORAH TO DIANA
6 September 1984

Chatsworth
Bakewell

Darling Honks

Oh the Col,[1] he had a sumptuous obit. in *The Times*. I've kept it in case you didn't get it. No mention of NM. Good.

Do you think THEY are busy in the many mansions now. It's all so odd, one can't help thinking there's something at the end of all this. But I don't think you do, in which case you won't notice if I go to tea in another mansion. So THERE.

Much love, Debo

1 Gaston Palewski died on 3 September, aged eighty-three.

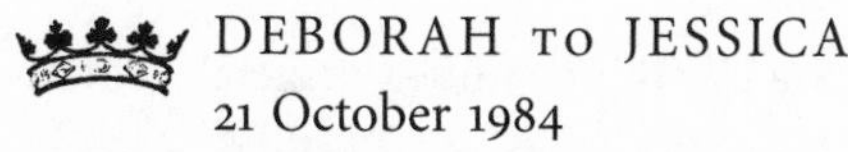

DEBORAH TO JESSICA
21 October 1984

Chatsworth
Bakewell

Dearest Hen

Just back from a v. sentimental journey to Asthall, Swinbrook, Batsford. Woman took me & Sophy (so she could vaguely see, she's never really been to any of those places). We were allowed into Asthall, more than allowed, got a v. kind welcome from Tony Hardcastle (oh I do hope he's called Tony, that's what I've written to him) engineered by a young Mrs Walker wife of, I suppose, a grandson of the old farmer of yesteryear.

I don't think I've been in that house, except possibly once, since we left. I can't tell you what an odd feeling I had when we went into the nursery. There is still a proper nursery fender there & the shape of the room & the sort of *feel* of it made me think so much of Blor & what a saint she was. Too odd. It all seemed weeny of course, specially the drawing room. Oh dear. It must have been much odder for Woman as she was properly grown up when it was sold.

Then we did Batsford. What a bugger that house is, no redeeming feature of any kind, cruel proportions, frightfully cold because of being so huge & impossible to heat, ghoul in the extreme. The Dulvertons (he really is called Tony, right this time) were v. kind & again showed all we asked to see.

They produced a picture of the house Grandfather pulled down, how *could* he have squandered a fortune on such a rotten exchange.

Woman is marvellous, 77 next month, how can she be so old. She doesn't seem to get tired, it is wonderful.

We didn't do Swinbrook House, only the Mill Cot & the good Miss Buckland. I still find it sad to go back there, but fascinating as well.

Much love, Yr Hen

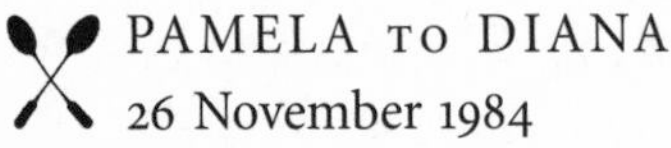

PAMELA TO DIANA
26 November 1984

Woodfield House
Caudle Green

Darling Nard

Thank you for the Telephone Call & the beautiful bracelet. It was lovely to hear your voice. I shared my Birthday with Beetle & we had two lovely walks in sunshine. The two days before it was impossible to go far as it poured all day so we were pleased to get out for a good stomp.

Tomorrow Catherine, Jamie, Dick,[1] Rosemary [Bailey] & Madeau [Stewart] are all coming for lunch, so exciting.

I am deep in Jonathan's book & am loving it. I rather wish he hadn't said the Gnomes clicked their heels & kissed the hand; that's French, German & Austrian behaviour, but the Swiss are far too reserved & heavy to do such things! They are always tied up in ghoul complexies & have to be treated by Sechiatrises (can't spell the beastly word!). I am at the Hairdressers so have no dictionary with me! The Old Dog has been taken for a walk by the Mythical Figure,[2] so much nicer for him than waiting in the car.

The menu tomorrow is Roast leg of Lamb (from Chatsworth), chicory & red chicory salad & one other vege, Aura Potatoes & then Apple Charlotte & various cheeses & I am already in a worry that it won't be ready in time! Catherine is such a good cook. I *wish* you were here.

Much love from Woman

1 Diana's granddaughter Catherine, her husband, James Neidpath, and their infant son, Richard. They were neighbours of Pamela at Stanway.
2 Mrs Clements, a neighbour who was so thin that Pamela used to say that it was difficult to tell whether she really existed.

) DIANA TO DEBORAH

13 May 1985

Temple de la Gloire
Orsay

These are Tony [Lambton]'s words: 'What I find so irritating is the way the critics treat you. I honestly believe that ½ the people who read all about the Mitfords are motivated to do so by a kind of fierce jealousy which drives them where they do not want to go. But that when they write about you, or rather have their chance of venting their spleen, they turn on what they cannot resist & on those whom they would like to resemble. I think your television experience bears all this out.'[1]

(Of course he didn't see the telly which was really rather *kind* to me but he means the nonsense about my friends living in big houses – Mrs Ham's bungalow, Lytton Strachey's sort of vicarage, Rignell which was sub-stockbroker, the Clary's attic etc.)

I must admit 'the Mitfords' would madden *ME* if I didn't chance to be one.

1 Diana was promoting *Loved Ones*, which had just been published.

) DIANA TO PAMELA

15 May 1985

Temple de la Gloire
Orsay

Darling Woo

I read Selina's book[1] all through again & cried all over again, & I think if she will point out – as people are so dense – that Naunce was *never* truthful in letters, above all about Muv, it really is a very good book, as well as a very sad one.

I only wish Naunce's descriptions of Paris weather *were* true! They used to make me & Geoffrey [Gilmour] laugh, one heard her saying to English people 'Oh, it's been lovely & hot here', when really it had been bitter & cold. This year has beaten all records for cold, for May.

All love Woo, Nard

1 *Nancy Mitford: A Biography.*

) DIANA TO DEBORAH

6 June 1985

Temple de la Gloire
Orsay

Darling Debo

Yours with Decca's came. I do so agree with Decca about Selina not using her manifold interviews with friends, plus press notices of Naunce's books etc.[1] Of course one gathers much from the many letters, & I *hope* one will gather more if she incorporates some of our observations. But it really boils down to a book about a very successful writer with talent for being extremely comic, who has two desperately unhappy love affairs. All of which could have been done by anyone who had the letters even if they'd seen nobody. Selina was so wonderful at not leaving stones unturned & then makes nothing much of it.

Where I don't agree with Decca is about Colonel being horrid. One can't pretend to be in love. If one is in love I suppose by superhuman effort one might quell it, for reasons of morality or something of that sort, & thereby achieve a sort of miserable saintly resignation. This is the theme of many French novels. But I don't think the opposite is possible. That is, to feign love one doesn't feel.

He never for one moment pretended he did. The result is tragic but I for one can't blame him. I think he too suffered from it. He & Kit & I spent days in each other's pockets when she died & one felt that he minded. He was a kind old object. He didn't lead her on, ever.

Oh Debo, I went to see 'my *friend*, Mme *Rödel*' as Mrs Ham always called her. Greatest pathos. The (huge) flat getting very shabby, Jeanne in the usual purple clothes, ditto. Still talking about Fontaines & Mme Costa. Don't let's live to be too old, it's no fun. I'm sad that I shan't see Louis grown up. He is such a pet.

All love darling, Honks

1 Jessica felt that Selina Hastings' life of Nancy was poorly written and relied too heavily on previously published books, but she acknowledged that its account of Nancy's illness and death had moved her to tears.

DIANA to DEBORAH

18 July 1985

Temple de la Gloire
Orsay

Darling Debo

I really *loved* Woo's visit & we had such luck with boiling weather, she had a final swim at 4 P.M. the day she left, & yesterday I got her on the telephone – safely arrived. The *calm* is so marvellous. She quite gave up menus after the first two days – Cha thinks they are due to nerves. She is a proper saint.

Hugo's *Cecil*[1] is a gossip column. It amuses me but, of course, except the actors & actresses, I knew the characters. It is sumptuous & worth its dread price for the photograph from *My Royal Past*, please study F Ashton[2] in that. But you've got the *Royal Past* I expect – mine went west years ago.

Re-reading Selina (proof) I do think the second part extremely good, it is completely true to Naunce. The mental & physical suffering are too terrible. It's not quite true that she *never* confided, I got bits of confidence. But it's almost true. Of course what makes the first part dull is that one knows it all.

I am *so so* sorry about Decca. It sounds very bad, poor Decca.[3] Somebody sent a mag from S. Francisco, a sort of *Derbyshire Life* type, with a long interview. Not too bad, but the usual lie about me, that I asked to see her & she refused. I never did because of Kit. The exact opposite is the truth, *she* asked if I would see *her*, at Naunce's death bed, & I naturally said yes. No matter, but it's strange how untruthful both she & Naunce were. I will send the mag if you like, if not I'll throw.

All love darling, Honks

1 Hugo Vickers, *Cecil Beaton* (1985).
2 Frederick Ashton (1904–88). The principal choreographer to the Royal Ballet, 1933–70, featured as 'the Baroness' in Beaton's spoof royal memoirs published in 1939.
3 Jessica was deeply upset by an affair her husband was having with a long-time friend of the family.

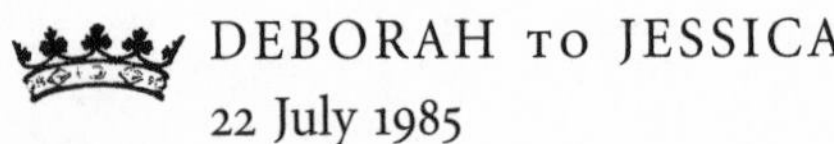

DEBORAH TO JESSICA
22 July 1985

Chatsworth
Bakewell

Dearest Hen

I hope you loved your S. of France week. I bet you did. There is something about it there which is conducive to loving it, if you see what I mean.

Bob told me I didn't apologise to you about the photos.[1]

I do now, unreservedly.

I am very sorry.

Much love, Yr Hen

1 The missing scrapbook.

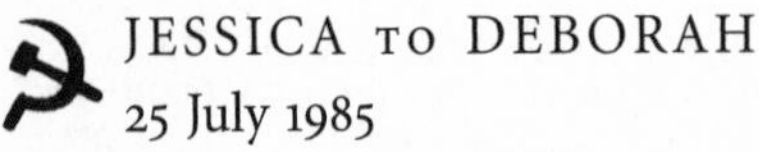

JESSICA TO DEBORAH
25 July 1985

6 Dunollie Rd
London NW5

Dearest Hen,

That was really most good of you. It's put a FINAL end to that perennially nagging business – or such it was to me. Thanks, Hen.

We scram to Calif on 30 July; rather sad, yet longing to get home.

Much love, Yr Hen

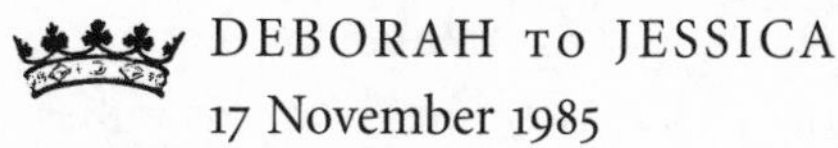
DEBORAH TO JESSICA
17 November 1985

Chatsworth
Bakewell

Dearest Hen

The party for Selina's book was wholly predictable. Full, noisy representatives from the Olden Days (Ly Dashwood, Lees-Milnes, Gladwyns etc etc), from H. Hamilton, friends & family of authoress (one sister is chief psychiatrist to the Army, do picture), Sophy (looking v. good I must say in sheath dress & short hair), various young secs. etc wanting to know what Nancy was *really like*, not too easy to know what anyone is really like, specially Nancy & specially when an *Evening Standard* person is hovering. So that was the party.

As for the American outing it was amazing. Started at Dallas for Tarmac – took 19 hours to get there for various boring aeroplane reasons. Poured with rain without ceasing for the three days. Not at all like the film weather. So low was the cloud that we didn't go a planned journey in a small plane to the south, a v. great relief when the mist was about a sky scraper height, & we spent a fruitful morning in Neiman Marcus instead.

Good Lady Bird Johnson came all the way from Austin to have dinner. I do love her. There was a lively discussion about her age after she left. Can you give the answer? She ordered Fee Lay of Sole & the waiter understood, brill eh. And a nasty wind is called a Her Cane in those parts. Like V[irginia] Durr speaking I suppose, I do love it but am sometimes in need of an interpreter.

Thence to Washington. Hen that exhib,[1] it's faultless. Not often you can say that about anything but it jolly well is. The trouble taken, the attention to detail, & the things themselves, 'tis breathtaking. I went round 4 times & could happily have gone 4 more.

We were royally entertained, dinner after dinner, lunch upon lunch, smashing food. The waiters (who they say go round & round to Washington things) are dangerously handsome & are supposed to be out of work actors. They act being waiters very well. Sophy came & adored it. I sat next to a fellow called Shultz one night who turned out to be the Foreign Secretary.[2] I said 'What shall we talk about, I know, YOU', so we did & he told about some incredible club he belongs to in California & they meet under the trees & loll about. As it seemed he was sort of on his way to Russia I thought it was rather sporting of him to come & what's more he didn't look at his watch, I didn't catch him at it anyway.

Stayed 2 nights with Governor Harriman[3] & Pam who I last saw when we were about 18. He's 94 blind & v. deaf but absolutely on the spot when one can get through to him, tales of yesteryear galore.

Saw Charlottesville. No one prepared me for the beauty there, I was dumbstruck by the university buildings, have you ever seen them? And Monticello. IT to my mind.

Then New York. Hen isn't it ghoul beyond compare, how can anyone like it. I stayed in the Waldorf Astoria, 1,800 rooms, queued for 35 mins to book in & had the strong feeling that if I had died in my room someone would have turfed my body out of the window and made the bed for the next unfortunate.

The biggest certainty of the whole outing was the clothes & jewels worn by the rich ladies at the Washington festivities. At one dinner I sat next to Mr Zipkin,[4] a sort of minister of information who knew which shops the c's & j's came from, how much & who was in them. Riveting.

Well that's about it I think. I bet you haven't got as far as this but if you have congrats on reading power.

Much love, Yr Hen

1 *Treasure Houses of Britain: Five Hundred Years of Private Patronage and Art Collecting* at the National Gallery, Washington. Chatsworth had lent twenty-nine exhibits.

2 George Shultz (1920–). US Secretary of State 1982–9, and a member of the Bohemian Club, made up of America's political and business elite, which meets once a year in Sonoma County.

3 William Averell Harriman (1891–1986). Presidential adviser. US ambassador to the Soviet Union 1943–6, Governor of New York 1954–8. Married Pamela Digby, former wife of Randolph Churchill, in 1971.

4 Jerome (Jerry) Zipkin (1915–95). Escort of fashionable women for whom the term 'walker' was coined.

JESSICA TO DEBORAH
2 January 1986

6411 Regent Street
Oakland

Dearest Hen,

Thanks ever so for yr pre-Xmas letter found on return from Dinky's & other points.

BOOK OPENERS.[1] I agree that 'THE' isn't much cop. But 'And so . . .' seems to present problems, because 'And so' – what? Unless you are planning a super-sexy novel in which the 'and so' becomes apparent in the very next sentence. 'WELL', ditto. Anyway I've started mine & the first words are 'Who was . . .' followed, as you may have guessed, with 'Grace Darling?'[2] Then, don't you see, I go on to say that nobody in America has ever heard of her but in England, la-di-da etc.

Your idea of looking to see how other people's books started is good, yet might be a trifle time-consuming. Actually I've just found two fairly good ones: the *Bible*, 'In the beginning . . .' & *Pilgrim's Progress*, 'As I walked through the wilderness of this world . . .' Any good, Hen? If yours is, as I gathered, hist. of Derbyshire countryside, either of these cld be made to order. 'In the beginning, only old shepherds & their flocks roamed . . .' Or: 'As I walked through the wilderness of factories & waste-lands, I thought back to the time when . . .'

Over to you, Hen. Let me know the outcome.

Much love, Yr Hen

P.S. We saw ye on telly (Stately Homes series) & so did lots of our friends. All thought you were marvellous.

1 Deborah was writing a piece for the *Spectator* 'Diary' about the difficulty of choosing the opening words of a book. She had begun work on *The Estate: A View of Chatsworth* (1990).

2 Jessica's biography of the Victorian heroine, *Grace Had an English Heart*, was published in 1988.

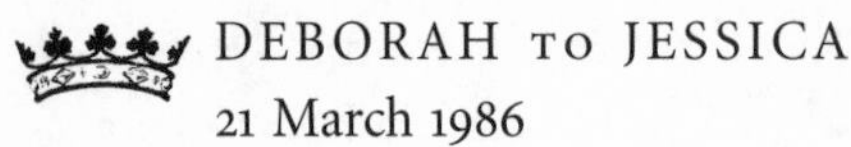

DEBORAH to JESSICA
21 March 1986

Chatsworth
Bakewell

Dearest Hen

Here is F Partridge.[1] She seems to have been in love with Robert AND Janetta.[2] What do you think?

It's a good read. I note she thinks it awful for anyone to have what is now called Help in the house but was in quite a bait with her person when she got home from a journey & found only spuds in cold water as a welcome. Oh well. Mixed Farming & Muddled Thinking.

Much love, Yr Hen

1 Frances Partridge (1900–2004), *Everything to Lose, Diaries 1945–60* (1986).
2 Robert Kee and Janetta Woolley were married 1948–50.

DIANA to DEBORAH
7 April 1986

Temple de la Gloire
Orsay

Darling Debo

Yes it's so strange that Woo doesn't realize about leaving the garden saddening one.[1] Oddly enough at the moment it's more what the locals call 'le parc', where there are primroses & violets, hyacinths in the grass which has *at last* become green, & where bushes & shrubs show signs of life.

You can't imagine what it was like in prison. Much as one died for letters (only two a week) I used to dread opening hers. She had no notion of the agony it was not to have the babies, & even boasted of things like making Al walk through a field with thistles, his poor little legs, he was twenty months old. It's not her fault, she doesn't like babies. Well then in one letter she'd had Grousy put down, such a dear dog, & in another Edna May, that pretty little mare we got from you. Of course I knew they were killing bloodstock in order to plough for potatoes & it was inevitable Edna May should go I suppose, but she failed to realize it would upset one. On another level, she wrote to say all our clothes in trunks had been eaten by moths in her attic so she'd burnt the lot. As you remember one rather needed old clothes then. But of course none of it mattered compared with the babies. She never thought I'm sure of just how foul the prison was, how one never stopped dreading the lavatory & so on. *No* imagination. I mustn't dwell on these things, long forgotten. It would have been better *not* to tell me about the animals. If 'they' had given me house arrest I think all would have been very well at Rignell, I could have had the little boys with me & not annoyed her with them. As you know, we were all packed up to go there on a Monday, but they arrested me two days before, on Saturday. What *devils*. Looking back, wasn't Nanny Higgs good really. *Her* letters were *supreme* by the way.

Love darling, Honks

1 Diana was letting the Temple de la Gloire for a few weeks while she went to stay in a cottage at Swinbrook.

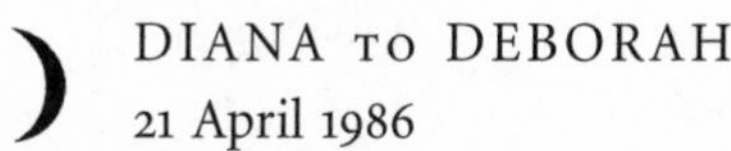

DIANA TO DEBORAH
21 April 1986

Riverview Cottage
Swinbrook, Burford

Darling Debo

My daily letter. Max [Mosley] & Co came yesterday, both boys dead white faces but Max says it's make-up. The food was *disgusting*. Woom was *wonderful*. We went up to Asthall. It looked charming & of course one can see nearly everything from the church yard. 'The Barn' looks just as old as the house, well of course it is except for the rather grandiose east window, but even that looked nice I thought. Oh how mad to have done all that & then sold it at a loss to build Swinbrook. Farve must have had a strong & obstinate character & paid no heed to Muv.

On the front of today's *Times* there's a picture of the Queen in one of those bowler hats women wear in the Andes. I hope she'll treat you to a crown today or at least something slightly less Andean.

Woman is off to the surgery for her dog bite. A man is coming to work on the Rayburn, not sure why, I shan't hear him I'm sure. Also the electric cooker has gone mad. The awful thing is I *can't* listen to

Woo's wise words about all this. But one realizes the heating has gone off & it's *bitter.*

Max *loved* Asthall. Oh Debo what a pity. Farve should have built one room & two lavatories up at South Lawn where he could retire away from us, our friends, & our super-boring governesses. He loved lavatories.[1] Asthall was so perfect because the library & big piano were far from the house *ideal* for a big family. He could have hung on if he hadn't built Swinbrook. 'Poor darling Dowdy, always so unlucky' as Grandmother used to say.

Love darling, Honks

1 Lord Redesdale was chairman of the House of Lords' Drains Committee and, according to Nancy, had opposed the bill to allow peeresses in their own right to sit in the upper house because he objected to the idea of them using the only lavatory close to the chamber.

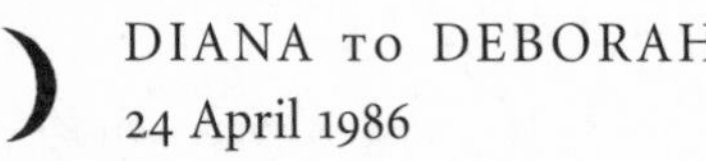

DIANA TO DEBORAH
24 April 1986

Riverview Cottage
Swinbrook

Darling Debo

I've done a whole week. It's very snug now that Woo has gone because I just watch the rain from my bed, putting the electric blanket on & off according to how boiling I get. There's ground frost & snow on the hills so not much point in getting up, though I do at about 3 to walk to the POST.

Don't laugh but the terribly important, in fact vital, list I made for the last-chance-in-Burford-with-Woman got so rained on that it was unreadable & as a result ½ the things never got bought. Monday, when Coote[1] & Robert come, Daph [Fielding]'s last *MEAL* is coming cooked.

I've finished Strindberg's *To Damascus.*[2] I do wonder what you'd make of it. I should so love to talk it over. The subject is the sex war & the overcoming of lust & how lust destroys love & turns it to hate. Of course true for poor Strindberg but not for everyone. The horror of the 'happy marriages' which turn quickly to boredom & hatred is appalling, & *there* there's a sort of awful truth, or half truth, practically universal I imagine. The hatred turns back to love, then boredom begins again, & finally hatred, it's a roundabout, never static. Jealousy hanging around all the time. Well well.

All love darling, Honks

1 Lady Dorothy (Coote) Lygon (1912–2001). The youngest of the Lygon sisters whose family inspired the Flytes in Evelyn Waugh's *Brideshead Revisited.* Married Robert Heber-Percy in 1985.

2 The Swedish dramatist's trilogy, *The Road to Damascus*, was published 1898–1904.

DEBORAH TO DIANA

25 April 1986

Lismore Castle
Co. Waterford

Darling Honks

Well the Dss of Windsor. What a mercy. As for the poor old thing spending her last years gathering inf. which wd rock the royal family I guess not. I wonder what actually finished her. You will be thankful she can't be tortured by the drs any more. Now I suppose old Maître Blum[1] dare die, I bet she was keeping alive till the coast was clear.

I am struggling with that stoopid *Spectator* diary, mad to say I'd do it, I'm sure they want heavy stuff like Russia & Libya but they're going to get road signs in Ireland.[2] Do think of some subjects.

Asthall, oh yes I think of all that every time I lean on the churchyard wall. I am really longing to see it all at close quarters again, do let's see if we dare ask if we could walk in Hensgrove.[3]

Much love, Debo

Yr letter about years ago & Ali & Max & prison. OH HONKS. Don't think I don't see. There is more than one blind spot in their hostess, there is an animal shutting-off & un-understanding of *lots* of things & of course children are the first to be completely discounted for obvious reasons. Bother it all. I'm glad you wrote it.

1 Suzanne Blum (1898–1994). French lawyer to the Duke and Duchess of Windsor whose interests she defended ferociously.

2 Reprinted in *Counting My Chickens*, p. 58.

3 An oak wood on the Swinbrook estate.

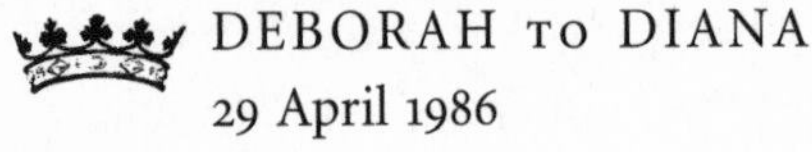

DEBORAH TO DIANA
29 April 1986

Chatsworth
Bakewell

Darling Honks

I'm glad you're going to that funeral[1] & long to hear all. As for the papers saying the royal family will be hidden behind a screen, what TOSH, they always go in the sort of choir place & are invisible there because of THE screen, they were for the service the other day, nothing odd in that. And what wd be the point of HRH-ing her now she's dead, I really think the papers are too awful for words at times like these. I freely admit there is a mountain of hypocrisy too, but that's England & its ways.

Much love, Debo

1 The Duchess of Windsor's funeral service was being held that day at St George's Chapel, Windsor.

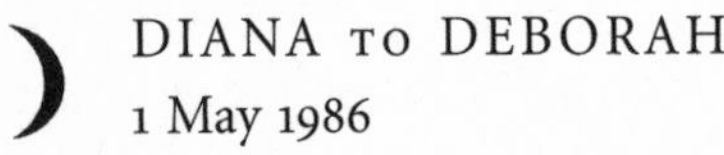

DIANA TO DEBORAH
1 May 1986

Riverview Cottage
Swinbrook

Darling Debo:

Yes, as you say, the papers excelled themselves in spite & vileness. Nothing could have been more perfect & dignified than the funeral. Of course if one had been in the nave one wouldn't have seen much but that's the way the chapel is built. The idea that the royal family hid is such absurd rubbish. The choir (which sang too beautifully & so quietly) & the Knights of Windsor or whatever they're called in their splendid scarlet, & the Welsh Guards, & the archbishop, & the entire royal family – what more could have been done to give the poor little person an honourable funeral. The Queen in her clever way gave the best seats to Georges & Ofélia.[1]

I was so glad I asked if Catherine [Neidpath] could come with me (she was perfectly willing to wait in the car) because the whole thing was so interesting. We were opposite the Garter stall of Emperor Hirohito. I thought what on earth is that strange device of a sun, & the banner had just one huge chrysanthemum, & of course it was the dear little Jap. Mostly Paris friends, Anne-Marie Bismarck came from Hamburg, Hubert[2] had one of the grand places! & climbed across knees to hug me to (I think) the general surprise. Next to us was Laura Marlborough[3] & the other side of her the present Duke. You know how they abominate each other so of course she whispered non stop to me. I told Catherine to be sure I gathered up what she said & it was 'When I told Diana Cooper I'd hired a car to come, she said "Oh *do* take me", but I said "Sorry mate no way, I can't carry you up the steps"'.

About two seats away from me were the Hendersons,[4] he busied himself with Tarmac papers while he waited for the Queen. Opposite was Gladwyn also reading – a whodunit. The ladies were very smart, mostly French. I went back to Stanway & described all to Jamie [Neidpath]. In my room at Stanway there was a roaring fire & I went to sleep with that lovely flickering on the ceiling one never sees now.

All love darling, Honks

1 Georges and Ofélia Sanègre; the Duchess of Windsor's French butler and his wife.
2 Hubert de Givenchy (1927–). Couturier to the Duchess of Windsor.
3 Laura Charteris (1915–90). Married the 10th Duke of Marlborough in 1972, a few weeks before he died; he was her fourth husband and she his second wife.
4 Nicholas Henderson (1919–). Deborah had become friends with the ex-diplomat when they were both on the board of Tarmac. Ambassador to Washington 1979–82. Married Mary Cawadias in 1951.

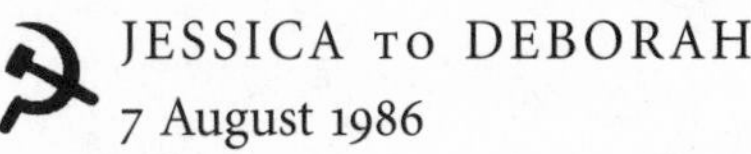

JESSICA TO DEBORAH
7 August 1986

14 Falkland Road
London NW5

Dearest Hen,

I got a v. sweet P.C. from Sophy & she asked for 'good suggestions for reading matter'!![1] So here they are, please relay: 1) Get a supply of books you had always meant to read, but never had time, such as *Plutarch's Lives, War & Peace*, Bacon's *Essays* etc. You'll find your attention unaccountably wandering – you seem to have read the same paragraph several times & still can't quite get its import. Put the books on a chair to be read some time later. 2) Next, fetch up some novels that you know one ought to have read in childhood but never did – Hardy, Conrad, the lesser-known works of Dickens. Same, alas, as in 1) above. 3) Find some books that you know you like, as you've read them before – *Catch 22*? *Catcher in the Rye*? *Pride & Prejudice*? (but you'll have to fill in the titles of your own favorites). This is far easier going, far more pleasurable. 4) Try some collections of short stories, the shorter the better. Also, *Grimm's Fairy Tales* – that sort of thing. That way the constant interruptions – meals, pills, baths etc – don't specially matter. 5) Above all – lay in a huge supply of mags, the more trivial the better, & leaf through them languidly while waiting for your cup of tea. That, anyway, is what I usually do when a) ill, b) travelling, c) on holiday; in the precise order as given above.

Well Hen DO come to London one day. Bob's gone home (left today) so I'm all alone by the telephone. Longing to hear from you.

S. of France most enjoyable except there seemed to be all sorts of subterranean undercurrents of rows between Tony Richardson & Grizelda.[2] A bonus was Natasha Richardson (Tony/V[anessa] Redgrave product) who we'd seen here last year in *The Seagull.* She's a smashing actress – an incredibly good cook, she did all the meals à la Emma, & extremely nice unlike most good actresses & cooks.

Much love, yr Hen

1 Sophia was convalescing in hospital after an operation.
2 Tony Richardson (1928–91). The film director's partner during the last twenty years of his life was Grizelda Grimond (1942–), daughter of the former Liberal Party leader, Jo Grimond.

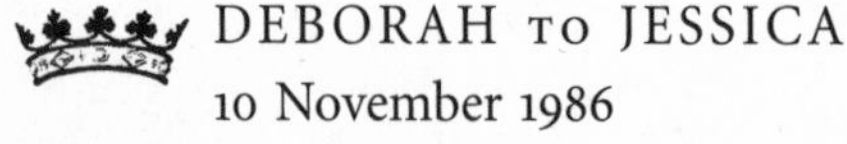

DEBORAH TO JESSICA
10 November 1986

Chatsworth
Bakewell

Dearest Hen

America was amazing. It always is. The mixture of formal & informal catches me out every time. I always get it wrong by miles. Killed by kindness of course, specially in New Orleans (the voices Hen aren't they wonderful). We were taken from house to house, new people every time, except for the saintly fellow who took us (architect by the wondrous name of Grover Mou*ton*)[1] & saw many a marvel.

Aren't they clever the way tall buildings are only allowed in one part of the town so the rest is real.

H Wakefield[2] (my leader, nanny, lady in waiting, the person who is behind the incredibly good fake furniture which was the point of the trip) went out late one night to listen to the jazz (I'd gone to bed hours before of course, stupidly), felt sorry for a fellow who was playing a trumpet outside a café, gave him some money, he played some more, H.W. gave him more money, they started talking & he was a sort of old Etonian, spoke like you or me, do admit the surprise. We stayed in a new hotel of undreamed luxury, I had a ridiculous suite, 5 rooms including one with a piano, & a kitchen. Hen do explain the point of that, I mean not likely one wd stay in a hotel at thousands of dollars a night & immediately start cooking.

The graveyards are wonderful, little real buildings for the ghosts. V. good having an architect to show us everything, I loved that.

Then Chicago. Another vastly grand suite on the top of an O which looked over the lake. Lapping waves, sandy shore. Was told all was concrete & the sand is brought every year. The oddness Hen.

The dinner where your Bergs[3] were was 24 souls in room with v. low ceiling & the noise was deafening. I sat next to some grand old ancient head of everything to do with operas. These rather lost on me as I've only been to one in my life & loathed it. Do you like those fat screamers? Anyway I had a short go with Bergs but much too short as I could see he was full of point & I'm a sucker for an architect do you know. I saw some of Berg's wavy buildings, not too sure but I'm so out of tune with all new building I'm no judge. She doesn't look like a social-ite, more 'ist' I thought, but take your word for it. As you say those sort of evenings are most unsatisfactory, they leave you exhausted on the one hand & longing for more on the other. It's practically royal the way those people go on, tons of waiters in white gloves handing unwanted this & that & standing about making one feel rather uncomfortable. But all v. kind & well meant.

The best person in the whole outing (after dear G. Mou*ton*) was a 78 yr old Jewess called Mrs Mottahedeh[4] (yes Hen, Hedda Gabler to me) who has a business which copies china. Impeccable taste, not an ugly thing in her catalogue, & v. beautifully made. Even things like

Ludwig's Dresden swan service. I longed to be closeted with her for hours, no hope of course, whisked away to talk to more socialites with hidden claws & not too polite to their drivers.

The evening in Marshall Field's was an eye opener, 1,000 people paid fortunes to come to the party to see the furniture & Hedda Gabler's china & some v. pretty & wildly expensive stuffs by the yard copied from here & elsewhere. Americans do that sort of thing so brilliantly, seriously good food all looking so pretty, flowers ditto, far better than the best here.

Baker Knapp & Tubbs, the furniture makers, have been bought by a maker of baths & lavs called Kohler.[5] He sent his plane for me to go & see his dump in Wisconsin because he is also a farmer & has 150 Morgan horses. You simply can't imagine how funny his lav. showroom is, lav. upon lav. are hung on a wall in the 'design centre' & he gives a great shout when showing you round 'And there, there is the Great Wall of China'!

On that note I'll end this interim report.

Much love, Yr Hen

1 Grover E. Mouton III; director of the Urban Design Center at Tulane University, New Orleans.
2 Sir Humphry Wakefield (1936–). Founder of the Stately Homes Collection of Antique Furniture and Objects of Art.
3 Bertrand Goldberg (1913–97). American architect, trained at the Bauhaus, who designed the 'corncob' towers at Marina City, Chicago. Married to Nancy Florsheim.
4 Mildred Root (1908–2000). Renowned collector and producer of fine porcelain reproductions. Married Rafi Mottahedeh in 1929.
5 Herbert Kohler Jr (1939–). CEO of the Kohler Company.

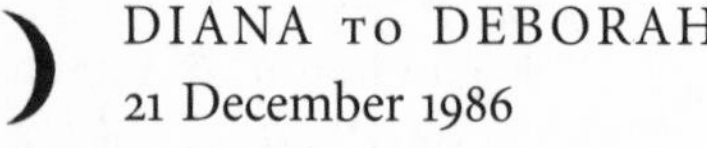

DIANA TO DEBORAH
21 December 1986

Temple de la Gloire
Orsay

Darling Debo

How inter-esting that the mad postcode might speed letters, here it's essential, but is the same all over what Woo calls the Continent, only England *so* difficile – anyway I'll try though this time not quite fair. Your letter was among 15 Xmas cards.

About Derek Hart's[1] bleak funeral, I'm afraid such funerals are bleak. It's just like being married in a registry office. Although I *can't* (try as I will) believe three impossible things before breakfast, you can give me a religious funeral if you like, I don't mind in the least, much as I loathe the C of E & although I do find Christians more hypocritical, cruel & offensive than dear old pagans. But services are just for survivors, when one's dead what difference can it make? I couldn't arrange a service myself but as one's gone it's quite immaterial. So you have got carte blanche eh, or noire.

Merry New Year!

All love darling, Honks

1 Derek Hart (1925–86). Broadcaster, film-maker and founder member of the *Tonight* programme, transmitted on weekday evenings 1957–65.

DIANA TO DEBORAH
8 January 1987

Temple de la Gloire
Orsay

Darling Debo

What a terrifying sermon at Macmillan's funeral[1] saying on the resurrection morning we shall all see him again. If *that* comes true it will give me a turn I don't mind saying. It was on the wireless & sounded like a threat. I'd rather see Lady Dorothy but don't want Bob [Boothby] at all.

Love darling, Honks

1 Harold Macmillan had died on 29 December, aged ninety-two.

DEBORAH TO PAMELA
23 January 1987

Chatsworth
Bakewell

Darling Woman

I am longing for you to see & taste the FOOD.[1]

We had 38 'distributors' (commercial travellers really) here on Wed, lunch for all, a tour in the freezing cold of the State Rooms etc, to try & show the fellows what we have to look after here, warmed them up with lunch, then we went to the Stag Parlour set up with chairs like a school room & THE PRODUCT was unveiled, along with various pots & tins from rival firms to show how much better ours are! I long to know what *you*, specially, will think of them. We had a tasting lot but they were so full of lunch they didn't do enough of that!

I think it was all v. well received, they seemed enthusiastic. Of course it depends enormously on the distributors, they have to push the things into the shops. Then we took them to the Farm Shop which of course will be a leading seller, along with the Orangery.

Then the poor things (who had bravely come from as far as Darlington, Isle of Man, Newmarket, Devon etc) disappeared into the fog.

The next excitement is on Mon when we have the editors of some of the trade mags, *The Grocer* etc, to tea at Ches. St. to show them & hope they will write nicely about it.

Then the Birmingham Gift Fair which opens 1 Feb then the Olympia Food Fair from 5 Feb. So you see the excitement is INTENSE.

It would be wonderful if it becomes as big a thing as we hope. All the profits will go to the house.

I'll try & telephone over the wkend.

Much love, Stublow

Do PRAY for THE PRODUCT (22 different things, or is it 25, I'll count).

1 Deborah had started a 'Duchess of Devonshire' line of groceries to be sold in the Chatsworth shops and other outlets.

DIANA TO PAMELA *Temple de la Gloire*
3 July 1987 *Orsay*

Darling Woo

I can so imagine how you miss *sweet* Beetle. But I'm sure his life had become a burden to him as well as to you. I only wish when that happens to *one*, one could 'send for the vet'. So wonderfully easy.

Such a pity you're not here! 29° day after day & the pool is 74° Fahrenheit.

All love, Nard

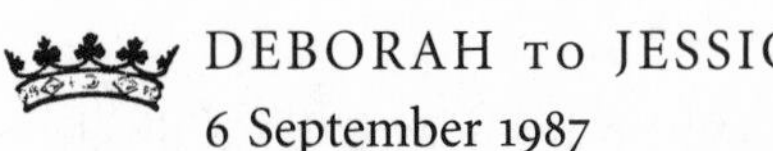

DEBORAH TO JESSICA *Chatsworth*
6 September 1987 *Bakewell*

Can you really be 70 on 11th? *Impossible.*

Dearest Hen

What about this truly ghoulish thing which ½ the population of England will be sending you this very moment.[1] When I think what beautiful china used to come out of Stoke on Trent. I've been round the Doulton factory & it makes you despair of anything approaching TASTE, all gone out of the window. Poor Grace.

Stella Tennant thinks I talk very funny & says 'Granny do say my specs have *simply GORN*.' She doubles up with laughter. She says 'eye level' instead of A level & 'foive' for five. She is a wonder.

Books. The thing is not to do it, writing I mean. ANYTHING to put off beginning: telephone, take the dogs out, read yet another ridiculous mag, & then when one has begun it's lovely & v. difficult to stop. Do you find that? I can't do anything unless I've got all the things to do it with just right, paper & soft B pencils *sharpened* which they soon aren't because of the softth. I wish I could type, one could see what it looks like instead of waiting on someone else to do it a little bit wrong.

I bought a hugely expensive typewriter thinking I'd try but somehow haven't. There have been so many distractions lately that I've done 0, well nearly 0. Hopeless.

Now I'm going to Pittsburgh for a moment or two, 3 days actually, with an exhib. of drawings from here. Can't think why I said I'd go, must have been mad & ought to be in bed with pencils & paper. But there we are Hen, blinded by flattery as usual. I mean if flattered am blinded.

Much love, Yr Hen

1 A Royal Doulton 'Grace Darling' figurine.

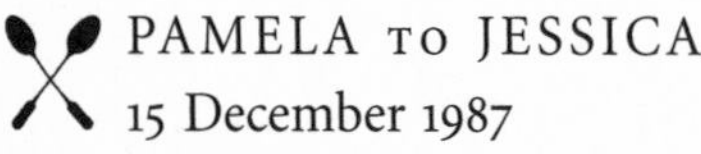

PAMELA TO JESSICA
15 December 1987

Woodfield House
Caudle Green

Darling Steake

It was good of you to remember my old Birthday & I was thrilled to get the telegram from you & Bob, it was there, waiting my arrival at Brooks's Club & I was amazed. It was sad that you couldn't have been there as you would have found many old friends such as Jim Lees-Milne, Derek Hill, Middy Gascoigne & lots of cousins, Madeau [Stewart] in great form with her camera, taking lots of photographs. We were 43 altogether I think. It was all a great success, lovely company, delicious food & marvellous wine & in a most beautiful room. Those houses in St James's Street are so lovely inside. The dinner was Borsch Soup, Saddle of Lamb, Profiteroles with hot chocolate sauce. Champagne before dinner, a lovely Meursault & then Léoville Barton, & Champagne again with the coffee. Everyone seemed to be enjoying themselves & were in top form. It was so good of Andrew [Devonshire] to give such a party, I had expected to be here, quietly. Oddly enough I feel just as I did *before* I was 80 – somehow I had expected some magical change to take place but all is as usual!

I hope you plan to come over here in 1988. I go to South Africa for 6 weeks to avoid the worst of the winter here & will be back on February 26th.

Very much love to you all from Woman

) DIANA TO DEBORAH
30 March 1988

Temple de la Gloire
Orsay

Darling Debo

Fancy you phoning about the telly,[1] I never dreamed you'd look at it let alone *react*. THANK you. Can't remember anything about it, years ago. Sorry about the old skirt, ought one to dress up for them, I suppose one ought.

County sounds a little bit happier, he's back at the dungeon. Thyra[2] persuaded him to go to church & he has for a year, 'no result so far' he says (like me he can't 'believe', I only wish I could).

Well darling I shall telephone tomorrow though I don't care for the way we all grow old as we who are left grow old.

Tonnes of love, Honks

How goes the book? I die for more bits.

P.S. Jim says Woo told them: 'I *never* allow my daily to clean the bath because she wastes *so* much water. And another thing I strongly urge is, if you must run the hot water tap waiting for the water to get hot, *always* run it into a bucket or two, to be kept handy. Then you can *take* the buckets of tepid water downstairs & out into the vegetable garden, where it will always be welcome.'

'How we laughed. Isn't she a scream about money?' (That's Jim, but what I want to know is, why *water*? It's as though she lived in Greece & dreaded the well giving out. She ees wondair. She was the last word in generosity in S. Africa wanting to pay more than her share.)

1 Diana had been interviewed for *Russell Harty's Grand Tour.*
2 Thyra de Zayas d'Harcourt; married François, duc d'Harcourt in 1961.

DIANA TO DEBORAH
10 May 1988 (Muv)

Temple de la Gloire
Orsay

Darling Debo

I think the long & short of aidy is: not very pleasant for *one* but a relief for everyone else, so I'm delighted. I do know how wonderful you've all been shouting away for years. And I do remember how tiring it was being with Muv. But aidy is tiring too in its horrid little way & now I've got two whole days when I can leave it & its mate in their boxes & live in the delightful silent world that I love, when every prospect pleases as it does at this time of year.

I've been asked to be on telly for the Hitler centenary next year & refused. If I were an old spinster I would rush to voice my uniquely unpopular views but it's not fair to my many descendants. Not that I would ever condone the crimes but I should have to describe the charm & the brilliant intelligence. So now nobody need worry. Perhaps it's cowardly but I don't think one has got any right to be 'brave' at other people's expense.

All love, Honks

DIANA TO DEBORAH
28 July 1988

Temple de la Gloire
Orsay

Darling Debo

Did you see a review in *S. Times* about Betj,[1] it made me so cross I *wrote*, but much too late I'm afraid so not much point. It said he was vindictive, snobbish & disloyal. A more loyal friend never breathed, & as to *vindictive* I think it's because of mild teases of the old Chetwodes,[2] *far* less than they deserved. Betj was my friend from 1929, or even 1928, so it's sixty years. Can't remember which year he died. The review was vile so I imagine the book must be. What *are* we coming to, the world is upside down. The more wonderful you are the more you are attacked when you die seems to be the new rule.

Love darling, Honks

1 A review by John Carey of Bevis Hillier's *Young Betjeman* (1988).
2 John Betjeman's parents-in-law.

JESSICA to DEBORAH
25 August 1988

30 Grafton Terrace
London NW5

Hen –

Here's one for *Believe it or Not* (I *do* believe it having found the teller of it to be fairly truthful & reliable over the years): Friends of ours, Sophy Bernal aged 25 (dau. of Martin[1] & Judy who I think you've met) got married so I promised them a BOGGLE SET[2] – not to be had in this neighbourhood. Bob swore he'd find one. He was strolling past Hamley's, thought of going in but it was v. crowded so he didn't. Suddenly an OBJECT fell at his feet – a Boggle set. He looked up at the shop windows, three storeys of them, none were open & provenance of Bog. was unknowable. He picked it up – it is, by the way, dented on one corner which he claims is proof, though I doiter [doubt] a jury wld think so. A passer-by said 'Why don't you stay here, you cld do all yr Christmas shopping the same way'. Our acquaintance is divided about equally between believers & non-believers. What say you???

1 Martin Bernal (1937–). The British-born Sinologist's controversial book *Black Athena: The Afroasiatic Roots of Classical Civilization* was published in 1987.
2 The word game.

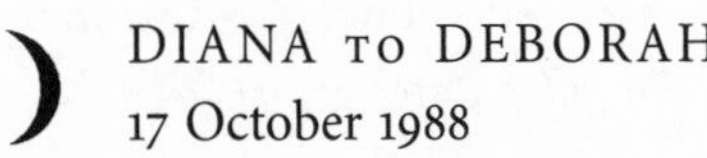

DIANA to DEBORAH
17 October 1988

Temple de la Gloire
Orsay

Darling Debo

Do you remember our three mallard drakes, one of whom had his foot hanging by a thread, & I told Jerry to wring his neck but he couldn't catch him? Well, all was perfect, his good body mended it. I was quite fond of them because of their Chinese blue & green heads. About a month ago they disappeared & Jerry said 'they'll be back'. Back they are, & they've brought eleven friends, fourteen in all, both sexes. Horrors! This sort of nature note is more for Woo than for you. She sits on that stone seat for hours & has improbable tales of doings on the pond.

I got a classic from Woo about how they collected rubbish too weighty for the usual collection. Enormous list, ending up 'ancient old metal feeding troughs, rusted and holy'.

Sorry no news but as a post strike is threatened I thought I'd better nip in.

Love darling, Honks

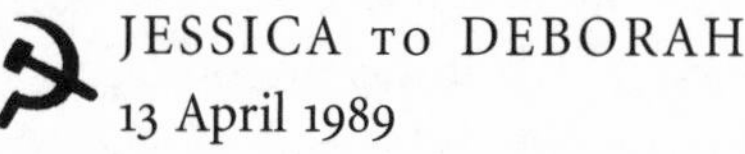

JESSICA TO DEBORAH
13 April 1989

6411 Regent Street
Oakland

Hen

I'm starting on a new book, motivated largely I must confess by HUGE advance, more than 10 times what I've ever got before (which was max. about $35,000). $500,000 or half a million, said to be closer to $1 mill. with paperback. I suppose you get twice that for the Devonshire chutney sales, but to me it's an amazing FORTUNE. Can't wait to take YOU to the White Tower of blissful memory next time in London.

Book is the *American Way of Birth*. Point of it, the cruelty & avarice of drs. here – 25 per cent of all births are caesarean, for convenience & profit of drs. Counterpoint is growing vogue for home birth attended by midwives (who, I hasten to add, do shove the patient to hosp. at any sign of real trouble). So obviously mine's pro-midwife – but oh Hen the awful drivel one has to choke down from that sisterly group. Titles like *Spiritual Midwifery*, and *Hearts and Hands*. These go into orbit describing the ineffable pleasure & glorious feeling of last stages of labour. Muv, asked by Nancy what it feels like, answered 'like an orange being stuffed up yr nostril' – more like it? Anyway, I'm madly at it.

Am off to Dink's in Atlanta for the Southern way of birth; being a nurse, she's utterly au fait of what happens when/why/under what circs. Back here 27 April.

Much love, Henderson

DIANA TO DEBORAH
17 June 1989

Temple de la Gloire
Orsay

Darling Debo

The *D.I. Disc*[1] research girl came, so nice. Just a try-out, I've asked if I might do it in Paris. If I must go to London I shall go by train. Every aeroplane now gets hours of delay & I hate that so much. Of course the *D.I. Discs* girl went on about the Mitford girls, 'It must have been quite something when you were all together'. I pointed out that when you were three Naunce was eighteen. All such nonsense as though we were the same age. The difference between a grown up & a child, really. I also said the whole phenomenon was invented by the newspapers. Of course Birdie really *was* original to the last degree but the rest of us weren't a bit.

I never thought I'd live to be eighty! Well perhaps I won't.

All the Tories (the few I see or hear from) are saying Mrs Thatcher ought to go. She's done a wonderful job etc but the time has come. I bet she won't. It will be like old Winston over again, she'll cling like a limpet.[2]

Love darling, Honks

1 Diana had been invited to appear on *Desert Island Discs*, interviewed by Sue Lawley.
2 Margaret Thatcher resigned as Prime Minister on 22 November 1990.

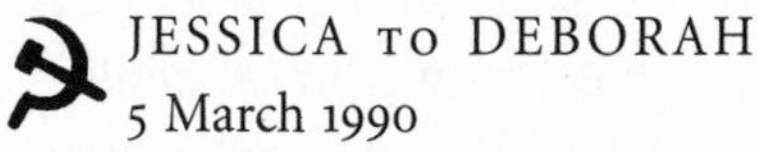

JESSICA TO DEBORAH
5 March 1990

6411 Regent Street
Oakland

Dearest Hen,

Copy eds. are mostly an awful bane although once in a very blue moon you get a good one. A friend of mine just sent me the following: She had written 'By 1971, Consumer Affairs was one of the few city agencies in the black'. Copy ed: 'This term has unfoertunate connotations'. ('Unfoertunate' was her spelling.)

Words in my book: You won't be finding 'birthing' or 'parenting' or above all 'bonding', means mother must BOND with newborn if they are going to be fond of each other in later life. You've NO IDEA the amount of bosh one has to sort through. Oh dear.

Accdg to Mabel, you never bonded or were bonded: 'His Lordship's face was like thunder. I don't think anyone looked at Miss Debo for the first three months, but she came up trumps in the end, didn't she.'

Tup up, Henny.

Love, Henderson

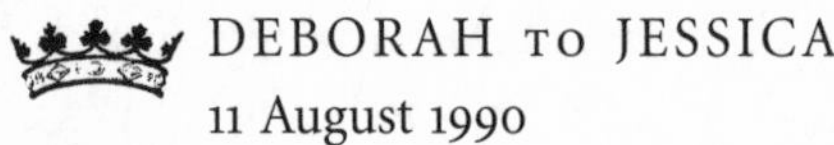

DEBORAH TO JESSICA

11 August 1990

Chatsworth
Bakewell

Dearest Hen

What have I been doing since our hop[1] – not writing to you is the answer. Sorry. Well . . . I WISH you'd been here. *They* (the flower lady, the caterer – Searcy's of yester year do you remember the name? & the tent & lighting man) turned this place into fairyland. Can't think how they did it, but it happened.

The courtyard was tented in for dancing & a vast tent covered the two flights of steps from the drawing room into the garden, more sprang up either side of the main one till you didn't know where the house ended & the tents began. It was a major feat in itself because the ups & downs & measurements were so peculiar, all had to be specially made. Then the lining of the tents was black roof & little lights like stars, there were endless swags & garlands of box with lilies & a chandelier made of moss & lilies, all huge because of the ghoulish scale of this place. The main tent sticking out over the lawn was for dinner & breakfast & that had rocks (Paxton-like[2] but I'm sorry to say made of plastic – what yr countrymen call *feather rocks*, do admit) foxgloves, white delphiniums & more lilies so the smell was o'erwhelming. The other tents were games, things like a dread machine called a bucking bronco, a 'simulator' which made you think you were on the Cresta Run, a crashing aeroplane & the like, NOT for the ancients. The Prince of Wales lent us an Arab tent, given him by one of those who are being a nuisance just now, & the inevitable disco. The outside flood lighting was done by a magician & the whole thing was a wave of wand type miracle.

It was agony re who to ask, we all had a list, William (grandson, whose 21st birthday it was for) had the lion's share & the other five grandchildren had their friends, Em, Sto & Sophy a list each, & then some for us, so 1,000 people were asked. Dinner for 250 in the flowery tent, breakfast for all later. In the middle I consciously longed for everyone I like in the world to be there, just for the spectacle, it was extraordinary. Our drawing rooms were lined with lilies, nothing else in the flower line.

Amazingly, the grandchildren said white tie or black tie & heaps of the young people did white tie. I thought it had gone out with the flood & only happened at v. old fashioned civic & City things, wrong as usual, it's creeping back. Too odd.

We were promised that people would be drunk, sick, drugged, thieves & that our beds would have piles of humans in them. Not at all, the behaviour all night, till 7.30 A.M. when it finally stopped, was impeccable. Why? I wish I knew. The women wore everything that shone. Those amazing jewels, which come out every 10 years or so & look so cheerful, amazed the Frogs present who don't seem to have anything of that kind. I wore that big crown of a tiara & felt like Mrs Toad of Toad Hall. Only about 10 bathing-gown dresses on the v. young, the sort that JUST cover the telling bits of body & show vast thighs, as if anyone wants to see them. They made a big effort, most of them, & wore long dresses.

We had buses coming from London with dinner on & the hotels round here were bunged to the gills & the stoodents' rooms in Sheffield University too. All very jolly. I think William loved it. He is v. nice indeed, his hair is Strewwelpeter style, or a tiny bit shorter, dead straight straw-coloured stuff but clean. I'll send some snaps when we've sorted them, to give the flavour. Bother you not being there, & Dink & Benj.

Lots of old folk, Billa Harrod, Coote Lygon; Paddy [Leigh Fermor] faithfully came from Greece; the only gate crasher was one Jerry Hall,[3] a nice Texan whom I was pleased to see because she is a sort of beautiful, goat-like, tall creature.

The fireworks were over the canal & were made miraculous by Beethoven's 5th symphony belted out as loud as you can belt music in the open air in time to the rockets. Quite extraordinary. Made you cry. I can say it was all wonderful because I had nothing whatever to do with it, Searcy's thought of & arranged the lot, we just weakly said yes to all their ideas.

The day before we had 2,400 people to a sort of evening garden party, FREEZING cold, but no one seemed to notice. And the day after was a huge charity day when all the things A & I have been to do with for 40 years had stalls in the tents. So it was a three-day-event. So sad to see the fairyland dismantled. All signs gone now.

Much love, Yr Hen

1 A ball given for twenty-first birthday of Deborah's grandson, Lord Burlington.
2 Joseph Paxton (1801–65). The architect of the Crystal Palace was head gardener to the 6th Duke of Devonshire and designed the rock garden at Chatsworth.
3 Jerry Hall (1956–). Actress, fashion model and ex-wife of Mick Jagger.

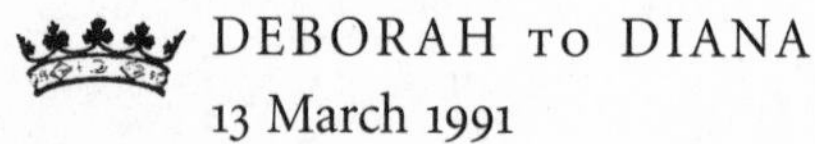

DEBORAH TO DIANA
13 March 1991

Chatsworth
Bakewell

(would Farve have been 111? something like that.)

Darling Honks

Isn't it odd, re N's letter about Sir O, Farve & Ld Moyne,[1] that she & Decca were (& are) equally *economical with truth* or whatever the expression for malicious imaginings is. She liked to think he had knuckle-dusters & there they were.

Equally odd that Muv & Farve, the 2 most honest people ever born, could have produced 2 such fancifiers.

N & D as good as believe what they say, I think. Anyway it's what they decided to believe, even if in the very depths they know it's not true, a monster lie in fact. Very odd indeed. Of course it's also done to impress.

I've only done 2,000 (very poor) words of the 10,000 I'm supposed to have finished by the end of this month for the intro to the Constable picture book of THINGS from here.[2] *Oh Honks* & the last

10 days of this month is wireless etc for my rotten *Farm Animals* book.

So I must get back to grindstone.

Much love, Debo

1 Diana and Deborah were reading the manuscript of Nancy's collected letters. In 1932, in a letter to Hamish Erskine, Nancy had written that Lord Redesdale and Diana's father-in-law had been to see Mosley to ask him to give up Diana and found him 'dead white & armed with knuckle dusters' (*Love from Nancy*, p. 53).

2 *Treasures of Chatsworth, A Private View* (1991).

DIANA TO PAMELA

19 May 1991

Temple de la Gloire
Orsay

Darling Woo

Just this second heard the exciting news about your operation. I know it's terrifying & you are *wonderful* with your courage & bravery, but one hears such amazing stories about knees now. Last night I dined with Margaret Hudson[1] & she asked about you & when I told her of the lameness she said she had a friend who has had *both* knees done & he is completely a new person. I was going to write & tell you this when Debo telephoned. Oh how I hope & pray that it will go well! And like with my operation, it's so lovely that you've got Chatsworth to go to & get strong again. Chatsworth cured me as nothing else could have done, the pure air & the kindness of everyone, and above all Debo.

All love Woo, Nard

1 Margaret Oulpé (1918–). A friend of the Mosleys who long after Diana's incarceration became chairman of Holloway Prison. Married James Hudson in 1946.

DIANA TO DEBORAH

16 May 1991

Temple de la Gloire
Orsay

Darling Debo

Such a bumper post from you today including your small grumble which has made me feel I might inflict some of my (compared I mean) miniature grumbles which last week loomed so large I got nearly ill with them. One was a letter from Naunce to you saying I didn't *love* Birdie but was just *jealous* of her.[1] Knowing Naunce I do see it's mad to mind, & I don't, for example, her hates against Kit plus extravagant lies, because I expect she'd have loved to plant a dart in him & never had the pleasure of that, because she knew the riposte would be painful as he was much cleverer than she & if he was attacked in private life even wouldn't hesitate with a riposte. All the same, my feelings & love & sympathy for Bobo were probably one of the things in my life about which (I thought) there could never be any question. We *loved* each other & there was never any hint of jealousy though I often wished (before the bullet) she could marry & have children as she so loved children. Anyway I've put N's wild lie behind me now & simply won't allow my life to be ruined (what's left of it) by her absurdities and cruelties. She had a thin time, & hoped everyone else did too.

The other grumbles are hardly worth telling: 4 b & b letters including snaps so that one's got to write back. The ceiling of your room here pouring with leaks & the plumber coming & simply making it WORSE; none of my beans bothering to germinate, Jerry thinks it's the cold but after all they're hardly orchids; painful twinges in a knee so that I could hardly get in the bath (this has *completely* disappeared oh how inter-esting).

We've got a woman P.M.[2] Jerry says in the shops the men are all outraged. I think France is very sexist, is that the right word. In fact the President is dictator & it doesn't matter who is P.M. so all great nonsense.

Love darling, Honks

1 The paragraph in which Nancy suggested that Diana was jealous of Unity was cut from *Love from Nancy*, the only excision that Diana requested be made from the letters.
2 Edith Cresson (1934–). France's newly appointed Prime Minister resigned in April the following year.

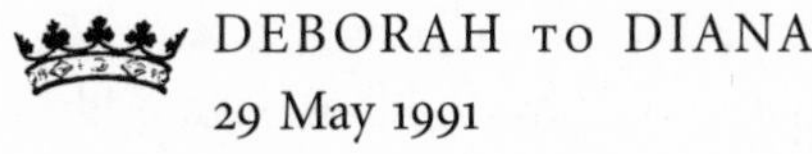

DEBORAH TO DIANA

29 May 1991

Chatsworth
Bakewell

Darling Honks

N's letters. Nothing more revealing. The one you mention *is* her sad character, always wanting to be what she wasn't, like lots of people I suppose. An unhappy *nature* plus a lot of real unhappiness, much of it self-inflicted via the unhappy nature, I reckon. Isn't it strange to think how 99 out a 100 probably envied her, v. pretty, an immensely successful writer, wonderful clothes, flat in Paris, beautiful unchanging figure – what more could you ask. Yet very few things went right, only the books I suppose & that is hollow compared to the real stuff.

What I find hard to stomach is the double facery. And when I look back on the extreme difficulty you had in the almost daily drive to Versailles with Sir O not too keen & so on & on. Very *wearing* it was. I suppose she had no idea.

You being jealous of Birdie is THE strangest notion yet. I wonder what else is to come.

Woman. She's being so good. I will be able to take her to the hosp. perhaps with Ce,[1] perhaps without. She has to be there at mid-day on 6th. Rather long, all that P.M. & all the next day to wait.

Much love, Debo

1 Celia Knight (1949–). The daughter of Deborah's friends Guy and Heck Knight was a registered nurse. Married 3rd Baron Vestey in 1981.

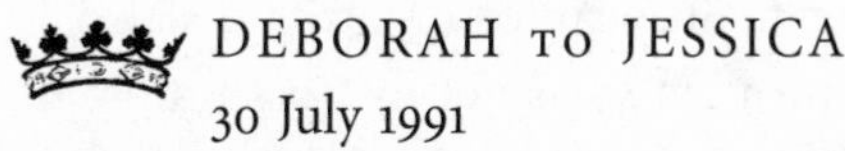

DEBORAH TO JESSICA

30 July 1991

Chatsworth
Bakewell

Dearest Hen

So glad to get yr letter of 19 July to say Bob had come out of the op OK.[1] DO ENLARGE on how he is now?

Hen, something lovely. I was in the garden talking to a friend (too loud I expect, in what Ann Fleming used to call Confident Upper Class Accent) when a man stopped me & said 'I've *read* about a 1930s voice but I've never *heard* one, do go on talking'. So go on I did & trotted out the things that make my grandchildren scream like *lost & gone*[2] forever. He was doubled up, so was I of course. In the end he said 'well I'll say this for you, you haven't got a stiff upper lip'. Do admit.

This is interim, haste as always. I'm meant to do a piece for the *Independent* about a villain (they've had too many heroes). Can't think of one. Do help.

Love to Bob and DO WRITE re progress. I suppose Dink has *gorn* – not lost & gorn forever I hope.

Much love, Yr Hen

1 Robert Treuhaft had been operated on for a knee replacement.
2 Pronounced 'lawst and gorn' by Deborah.

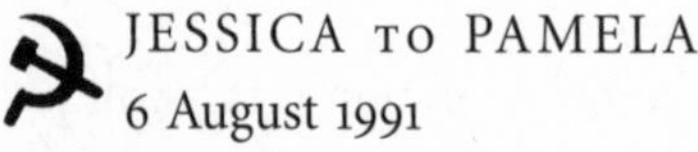

JESSICA TO PAMELA
6 August 1991

6411 Regent Street
Oakland

Darling Woman,

Thanks for excellent report of 31 July – I see that both you & Bob have done wonders. His op. was 3 weeks ago (17 July) and he's now not only totally up & about but drives to his office every day, plus does all the shopping & cooking.

Rud's electric chair (as I'm sure you know, the term 'Electric Chair' has a slightly different & more sinister meaning in the USA): At one point, Muv was contemplating getting a motorized wheelchair called by Timmo Bailey the Racing Bath Chair, as Muv thought the max. speed shld be approx. 40 m.p.h. She wanted one with a side seat for José,[1] and it should only turn left so as not to cross traffic. It would only go to Harrods & back from the Mews. Unfortunately it never materialized – can't you see her whizzing down Brompton Rd?

Much love, Steake

1 Lady Redesdale's dachshund.

DEBORAH to DIANA
7 April 1992

Chatsworth
Bakewell

Darling Honks

Yesterday came a woman whose ambition was to nurse a piglet.* You simply can't imagine what a comic scene it was, her & me sitting in the straw with first one & then another of a litter of nine Glos Old Spots, eight days old. She looked like the Alice in Wonderland person, & you never heard such a noise as the squeals of the unlucky piglets whose ambition was not to be nursed. The dau. of the woman had kept it a secret as she said her mother would have been so excited she might have given up coming. As it was, when I asked her if she had enjoyed her birthday treat she said in broadest Derbyshire 'I'M STILL SHAKING'. 'What are we to do for your next birthday' I said. 'Well my other ambition is to go on a fire engine when it's on the way to a fire'.

Much love, Debo

*Her dau. wrote to me to make the plan – secret.

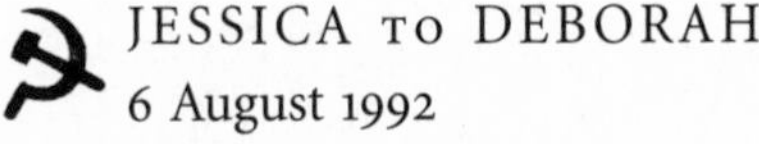

JESSICA to DEBORAH
6 August 1992

6411 Regent Street
Oakland

Dearest Hen,

Sickness & Health Notes: Woman will outlive us all, from yr account. In America, one is constantly reading in the pop. press about the Heart Attack Prone Personality, means lots of worrying & striving for high achievement & all such bosh. So Woman takes all in stride, including amazing quick death of her erstwhile wife[1] & not worrying at all about it. 'Wonderfully unmoved', as you wrote.

This end: Bob's replaced knee is working fine, but now the OTHER knee is giving trouble. So forward to that, but he is actually amazingly OK such as going for a hiking/fishing trip in the Sierra mts. the other day, & springs out to his office daily to ply his trade. My slogan: NO NEW KNEE UNTIL THE NEW YEAR, as he's coming on all travel NY–London.

I'm also annoyingly crippled (I think I was last time we met when Woman got me a really smashing walking stick in local PO, Bamburgh, Grace Darling territory) so now I've got a physiotherapist student who comes & walks me, as 'twere a footman with his employer's dog, three times a week. Goal is for me to spring about Hampstead Heath like a mountain goat when in London, v. doubtful of achievement, but am hoping for the best. She also makes me do strengthening exercises when she comes. I fear that the real trouble is laziness on my part – not minding as much as some might not walking spryly. I am trying.

The next treat in store will be Alzheimer's Disease (known by Pele[2] as Old Timers' Disease) which has struck many friends my age AND YOUNGER. Horrors. I can see it coming – loss of memory, already here. Am expecting to forestall main symptoms until after our London trip.

Lastly, sickness/health-wise, just yesterday I got some false teeth – not the whole lot, things on a sort of metal holder to replace a few lost ones. As King Lear said, Sans eyes, sans teeth, sans everything.[3] That's yr Hen in advanced years.

Well Hen – so much for a cheerful account – never mind. See you VV SOON.

Yr Hen

1 Giuditta Tommasi, Pamela's long-time companion, had died.
2 Pele de Lappe Murdock (1916–). American artist, member of the San Francisco Graphic Arts Workshop and a close friend of Jessica.
3 'Sans teeth, sans eyes, sans taste, sans everything', from Jaques' soliloquy in *As You Like It*.

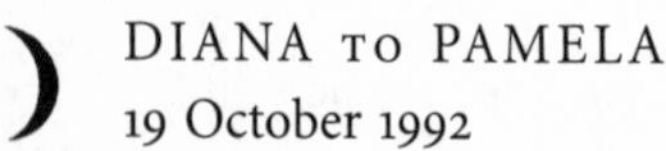

DIANA TO PAMELA
19 October 1992

Temple de la Gloire
Orsay

Darling Woo

All the news from England is just too sad I can hardly bear to listen.[1] How can it *ever* get better? I expect it (England) will leave Europe, just as well as everyone is so anti. It won't affect Europe but it will make things harder for England. I sometimes think England would love to have another war, luckily it *can't* so there's no danger. Germany & France so hated, can't imagine quite *why*. Can you explain.

It's so beautiful here, I wish you were here. Lovely sun. Quite hard frost.

They sent a book about the Profumo affair for me to review, I thought how mad & then remembered it's nearly 30 years ago! So young people have probably never heard of it.

All love Woo, Nard

1 Britain was debating ratification of the Maastricht Treaty on European Union and Euro-scepticism was at a peak.

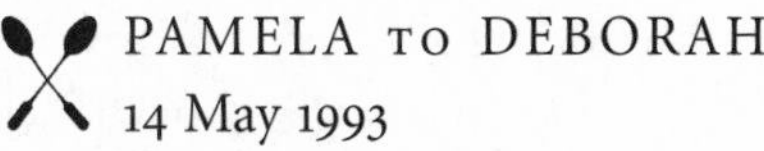

PAMELA TO DEBORAH
14 May 1993

Temple de la Gloire
Orsay

Darling Stublow

I wish you could have seen us two travelling & in Zurich. As Nard says we make one person: she can't hear but can walk, I can hear but can't walk. The result is that she rushes ahead & I can't call her if anything important happens. Our compartment on the train was ¼ mile up the platform – she was there before I was ½ way! She carried the bags as I can't carry a thing with two sticks, only my bag slung round my Kneck.

Much love from Woman

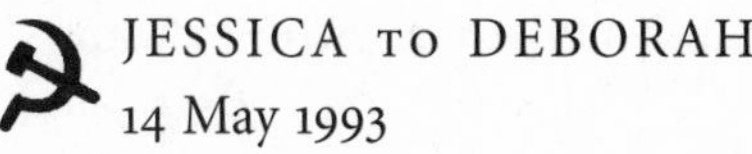

JESSICA TO DEBORAH
14 May 1993

6411 Regent Street
Oakland

Dearest Hen,

V.v. glad to have yrs of 8 May. My corrections minuscule.[1] Point is, though, that reading the letters memories came flooding back – more like ghosts in fact.

Comments on yr comments: Fully agree abt *snobbishness*, already noted by Bob who'd read the whole thing before yr letter came. I wasn't too surprised, always thought she veered in that direction. But it comes in undistilled double dosage via the letters.

Nancy & money: Did you note how it's a wild see-saw ride, even after she became 'so *riche*' (her to me in the Dior boutique – 'poor little Sissie, she's so *riche*') she's either absolutely awash with dough or sunk in poverty. Thinking back to childhood, & watching her all through engagement to Hamish & how she loathed Swinbrook & longed to be free of Muv etc – *her* fate, to be stuck in that life because she hadn't got any way of escape being without money even after she started writing, was a huge influence on me, then and forever. That is, the rather obvious fact that one can't be independent of others (whether parents or husbands) unless one can earn one's own living.

Dink/Terry are coming here from June 11 to 21, I'm so excited for their visit. She/Benj are planning a 50th wedding anniversary for Bob/me on 20 June – you'll be getting an invite. It's to be at what Benj calls the 'FUCK', i.e. First Unitarian Church, Kensington. No Hen not a real church like Swinbrook, more a hall with kitchen food.

Yr loving Henderson

1 Jessica was reading a proof copy of *Love from Nancy.*

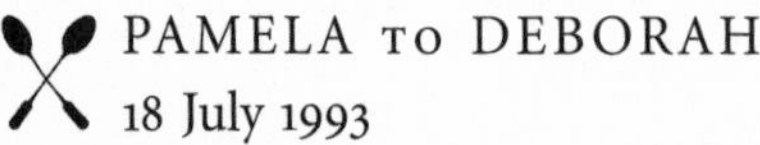

PAMELA TO DEBORAH
18 July 1993

Woodfield House
Caudle Green

Darling Stublow

I wish Sophy had a nicer name for the baby, it sounds like something out of arithmetic or out of Latin. Isn't there a lesson in Latin – declining?[1]

Much love from Woman

1 Deborah's daughter Sophia, who married Alastair Morrison in 1988, had named her son Declan James.

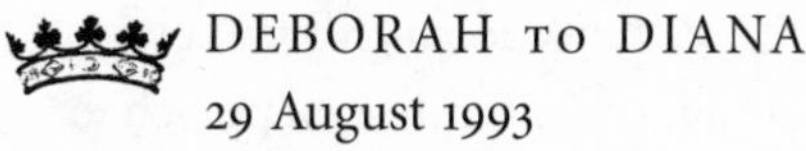

DEBORAH TO DIANA
29 August 1993

Chatsworth
Bakewell

Darling Honks

The *D Tel* ed., whom I've never seen but am rather keen on over the telephone, rang up at the 11th hour after I'd sent him last week's effort, obviously embarrassed. It took him ages to get it out, 'what's wrong?' I said after his humming & hawing. 'Well, although you've done the right number of words you've used such short ones that I'm afraid I want 50 more to fill the space.' Honks do admit. When I send the last go on Tues I shall put in the covering Fax letter that I promise I'll learn some longer ones & that I did warn Max Hastings[1] that I can't even do proper joined up writing . . . let alone use long words.

Much love, Debo

1 Max Hastings (1945–). Editor of the *Daily Telegraph* 1986–96.

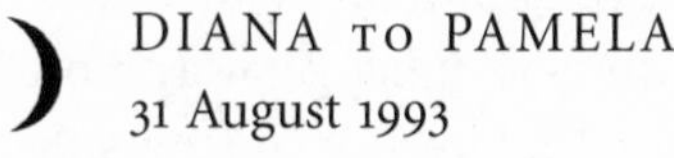

DIANA TO PAMELA
31 August 1993

Temple de la Gloire
Orsay

Darling Woo

I quite agree N's letters do make one feel sad. Nearly all adolescents are in revolt, but almost always some childhood love of parents remains. In Nancy's case she really sounds as if she *hated* Muv & Farve. I was very unpopular with Muv & Farve when they strongly objected to my leaving Bryan, but I always realized *they* thought I was ruining my life, & only wanted the best for me. We quite soon made it up & as you know Muv loved Kit & he positively adored *her*. Years later Farve came here & was wonderful with Kit, but that was in 1952 I think. As to Tom, N's letter to Decca[1] is not just rubbish but so spiteful. I don't mind, it's all so long ago, & poor Naunce suffered most from her own spite because the result was she never knew a happy love. The *Evening Standard* asked me to review the book but I *couldn't*. There are some very funny letters, the best are to Heywood, but I do agree it's sad, & somehow hurtful to Muv & Farve. The awful dinner when Farve was so rude to Jim was *not* typical, everyone lost their tempers! But I at any rate look back to a happy childhood though I wished we could have stayed at Asthall, I suppose we all did. Don't we all sound horrible in the book! Except you. Perhaps we are, but we do at least all love each other. I shan't go to the party[2] as it would spoil it for Decca if I was there.

All love Woo, Nard

1 Nancy's letter to Jessica of 15 November 1968, in which she had said that Tom Mitford had hated Mosley (see p. 521).
2 The launch party for *Love from Nancy.*

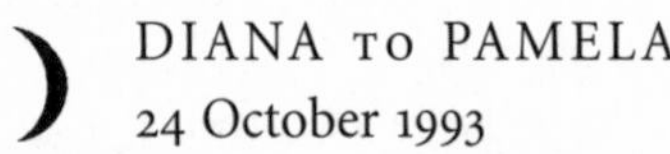

DIANA TO PAMELA
24 October 1993

Temple de la Gloire
Orsay

Darling Woo

I'm reading the Naunce letters properly, not dodging about. What a *miserable* time the Hamish time was. No money. Not getting on with Muv & Farve. Yet no possibility of leaving Swinbrook or O.M. Cottage. A real nightmare. I can't think why she didn't go away more for visits. I'm sure lots of people asked her. Perhaps *the* worst was the pennilessness, it must have made her feel trapped. Oh dear I would a thousand times rather be very old like now than so miserably unhappy & yet young. She ought to have had a lovely time. I *loved* my life but of course I never had an unhappy love affair & I always had a little money – enough to go & stay with Gerald at Rome for example. You had your Stork[1] & rushed about all over Europe. Why was she so utterly stuck, poor Naunce. She *always* had her room at Eaton Square I'm glad to say.

All love, Nard

1 The 'Stork' was a grey Morris Minor with red painted wheels, hence the name.

DIANA TO DEBOROAH
8 November 1993

Temple de la Gloire
Orsay

Darling Debo

I'm afraid you're right, I *am* often lonely & bored. The few of my Paris friends who are still alive I don't really want because I'm *too deaf* & a pest to one & all. When I've got a fascinating book it's all right, & when it's summer I go in the garden & amuse myself. At this time of year what I want is what I can never have again, Kit. It's the worst of a happy marriage, you go on missing it for ever I suppose.

Now there's my grumble but I must tell you I'm *much* better & almost back to really well. So you see I've *no* cause to grumble & feel v. ashamed of it when I think of various nightmares one hears of.

Love darling, Honks

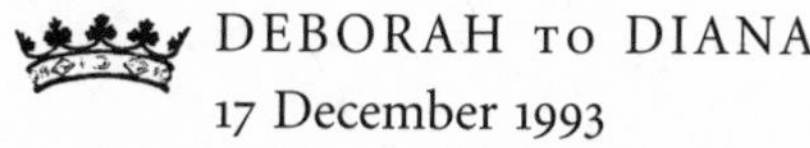

DEBORAH TO DIANA
17 December 1993

Chatsworth
Bakewell

Darling Honks

Did I tell you the Aunt K[1] saga. Stop reading if so.

She went to the opening of parliament, ermine & velvet & all. Tripped, fell, broke her hip. Was taken by ambulance to the new hosp. in the King's Road where Isabel had Rosa.[2] Black Rod,[3] only interested in his own, telephoned. Got a black nurse. Rod to Nurse (both black) 'you've got a patient there in peeress's robes, they are worth £10,000 & I want them back at once'. Nurse already thought Aunt K was a crazy old woman in fancy dress, confirmed in that by B.R. asking for the fancy dress back.

History doesn't relate what happened to them, pushed down the sluice do you think? But history does relate what happened to Aunt K. She was on a life support thing, the drs thought it was time to switch it off & let her die, which it looked as if she was going to do anyway. Switched it off. She not only didn't die but started to get better, so much so that she went in an ambulance from London to HAWICK,[4] please picture that. She's in the hosp.

there, asking for books. I've sent her *Parnell*, I do wonder if she's up to the weight.

SO GLAD you'll come in Feb.

Much love, Debo

Woman met more glittering grandees c/o Ldy M Keene, her new friend, including Mr? Sir? Lord? Richardson, ex gov. of Bank. I expect she gave him some sound financial advice.

1 Katherine Tennant (1903–94). A great-aunt of Deborah's son-in-law Toby Tennant. In 1958 she was one of the first women to be created a life peeress. Married the politician Walter Elliot in 1934.
2 Deborah's great-granddaughter Rosa Tennant.
3 Admiral Sir Richard Thomas held the parliamentary position of Gentleman Usher of the Black Rod 1992–5.
4 Approximately 350 miles.

DIANA TO DEBORAH

1 March 1994

Temple de la Gloire
Orsay

Darling Debo:

Dear old Harold [Acton] has died. What a character he was, right from Eton days. I wish he hadn't written such silly fiction, his genius was in his conversation & personality. How we laughed in the old days. He *made* any party.

About Abe Bailey,[1] he did a wicked thing to me. I met him at Chartwell when I was about 15 & he discovered I loved ostrich feathers, they were the fashion & beyond our means. He said 'Oh I'll send you a trunk full of ostrich feathers'. I went home & boasted & the sisters said 'he won't really, he'll forget'. Well, they were right. I was *so* disappointed I made a vow never to promise a child something & then fail to keep the promise, & I hope I never have. Diana C[hurchill] married his boring son John but it didn't last. He was an old buccaneer & doubtless one of Winston's many rich benefactors. The story about the strike is garbled. The Gen. Strike called to support the miners collapsed in a few days. The miners went on striking for many months & were starved into submission by the mine owners. It horrified people & is I think the reason why to this day the miners are treasured by the public. I was 16 & it made me violently anti-Tory.

Love darling, Honks

1 Deborah had sent Diana an article about Sir Abe Bailey (1864–1940), the South African mining magnate and financier.

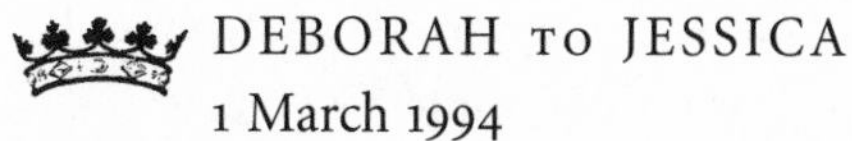

DEBORAH TO JESSICA
1 March 1994

Chatsworth
Bakewell

Dearest Hen

Since I wrote about American pronunciation[1] people have sent me some pearls, viz. someone from Virginia told a friend of mine she was coming to England for the honey. Hunting, Hen. And when Ld Antrim went to Texas to raise money for the Nat. Trust he was introduced as rustic royalty & then there was a right muddle about earl and oil.

Births Marriages & *Deaths*. Harold Acton. He was pushing 90. I shall never forget the terror of when he took a log out into the snow at Biddesden & pretended it was a baby & murdered it. I suppose I was 10 & it haunts me still. He came to stay here once & his manners made going in & out of a room impossible, already old he struggled to get out of a deep sofa every time. M de Givenchy did the same when he came, makes the English look v. off hand. (I know H Acton *was* English but didn't carry on like one.) His obit. said he started a mag at school called *The Eton Candle* which was immediately changed to *The Eton Scandal*.

Inspired by Declan & Rosa I've started sticking in photos (there is a sort of coffin with 8 years worth waiting, ghoulish prospect), of course I've started with the latest & am on your golden wedding, & the invite to Bob's 80th birthday & yr 75th. V. comical. How HAVE WE HUNG ON IN THERE so long? Goodness knows.

Much love, Yr Hen

1 Reprinted in *Counting My Chickens*, p. 50.

PAMELA TO JESSICA
7 March 1994

Woodfield House
Caudle Green

Darling Steake

What splendid news of your grandson James.[1] He has started so well & you must be very proud of him. How old is he now? I well remember him not only when you were all staying here a long time ago but also lunching one day in London on another occasion.

I rather doubt being able to go out to you because I am getting very wobbly, not as agile as when you were here in the Autumn & I do fall very easily. It would be awful if I broke something when in America. Also I dread long air flights & there really is no other way to get to you. So I do hope you will be over again in the Autumn. I feel very feeble saying that I am not able to accept your lovely invitation & I know I would love to see America again but honestly the old legs are beyond it now alas. Of course you were miles & miles from the earthquake, I always forget that it took us four days in a rubberneck coach to get from Los Angeles to San Francisco, staying in lovely places on the way up. We did spend two nights in the Yosemite.

Much love to you all from Woman

1 Twenty-six-year-old James Forman had finished law school and was clerking for a Supreme Court Justice before joining the Public Defender Service in Washington.

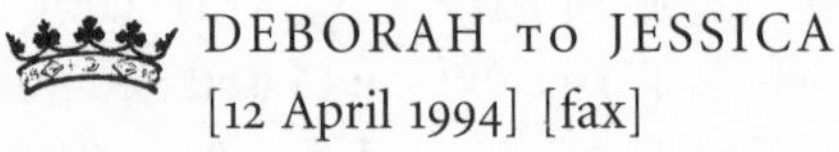

DEBORAH TO JESSICA
[12 April 1994] [fax]

Chatsworth
Bakewell

Dearest Hen

Well there we are.[1] It is the shock, I suppose, & the FINALITY, which make one cry so much & all the little things which went with her. There'll never be any one remotely like her, will there?

To put you a bit in the picture. She was staying with Margaret Budd[2] for a jolly London wk-end, they'd done shops, dinner with E. Winn, more shops & then went for a drink with a next door friend, fell down steep stairs & broke both bones in the right (weak) leg below the knee.

Ambulance men perfect & very quick ('we've got an English *lady* here' they said – rare bird, true enough), hospital at once – wonderful in every way, new, off Fulham Road. Spent a dopy night & next A.M. was operated on to put plate in the usual way. All went well & on waking she asked what won the Grand National. I spoke to her (asked for the nurse & got her) THAT EVENING, still a bit sleepy but quite OK. That was Sat. Sun & Mon never better, seen by E. Winn who said she looked v. pretty in bed & was in fine form & very funny. Tues A.M., A & I went to London from Cork, punctual, drove to Margaret's where we found her outside her door saying quick quick, they've just telephoned to say come at once. So we dashed. Found curtains round the bed, I said I'm her sister I must see her & the Sister said talk to the dr. He took us to a little room which I suppose ought to have been a sign of the seriousness, he said all the technical things which had happened in her poor body & I said so what's her future & he said she died 10 minutes ago. Hen. Please picture. After a bit we went to see her, so odd, just a bod with no one there.

I will keep you in touch about everything & will do flowers of course. Mon at Swinbrook 2 P.M.

Much love, Yr Hen

1 Pamela had died that morning, aged eighty-five.
2 Margaret Cross (1917–). A friend of Pamela whose husband, George Budd, was in Squadron 604 RAF with Derek Jackson during the war.

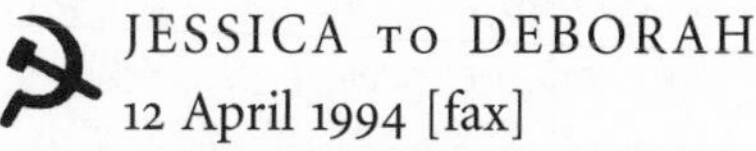

JESSICA TO DEBORAH
12 April 1994 [fax]

6411 Regent Street
Oakland

Hen – after we rang off one idea did occur, viz. obits in the newspapers. Obviously there'll be the usual canned obits (always at the ready in the newspaper files, ready to spring when the Grim Reaper does) but I was wondering if some cld be organized as in case of Sally Belfrage[1] from friends who knew her? E.g., Jim Lees Milne, whose letter about Muv all those years ago in *The Times* or more likely *Telegraph*, was so strikingly good – he'd be a prime choice to write about Woman. You cld doubtless think of others. This would have to be organized p.d.q. because of newspaper deadlines.

I DID love being allergic to kidneys. Reminded me of a few other Woman-isms; when Nancy got another tortoise to mate with the one she had, Woman rushing in from the gdn to say 'Those tortoises are hand in glove!' And even when we were children & Super Cinema opened in Oxford, Woman saying 'Oh good, I see we can get supper there'.

Funeral on Sunday; Hen do send flowers from Decca & Debo. I loved what you said on last floral tribute occasion (Rud) that Decca and Debo was a long-ago leftover from childhood.

Much love, yr Hen

1 Sally Belfrage (1936–94). Human rights activist, journalist and friend of Jessica's whose last book, *Un-American Activities, A Memoir of the Fifties*, was published posthumously in 1994.

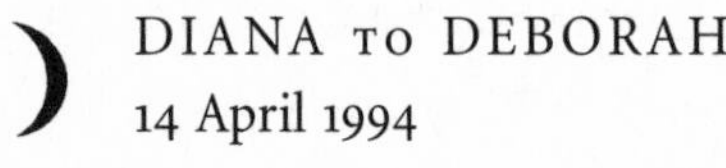

DIANA TO DEBORAH
14 April 1994

Temple de la Gloire
Orsay

Darling Debo

I made everything worse for you by being so frightfully upset. I know it seems impossible but it was the very last thing I had envisaged and in each message they all seemed so 'pleased' with her, but of course common sense should tell one that any operation at her age just is dangerous. I'm so sorry but it was the terrible shock and I was in physical pain for ages, you know that French expression 'le cœur gros', well my heart seemed to have become huge and pressed on everything. Being alone it went down again & now I'm just very sad for *me*, and *you* but not really for *her*. Not much of a life if it had been a wheelchair. So lovely that she'd had such fun with Margaret and had seen nearly everyone, wasn't it. Also a peaceful death, how lucky that is.

Oh Debo the hymns I'm afraid they will set us off again, can't be helped. Al, Max, Desmond everyone such a help & so good, also of course Jerry. My misery is that I haven't been able to help in any way & just hindered with my tears.

I feel worse than useless.

Love darling, Honks

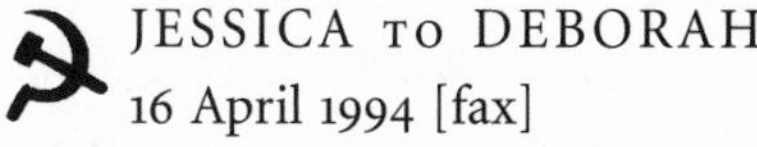

JESSICA TO DEBORAH
16 April 1994 [fax]

6411 Regent Street
Oakland

Dearest Hen,

How v. excellent that Emma [Tennant] is to have the house & contents. I know she adored Tante Femme as she called Woman. Ages ago, Em told me how at age 14 she was for the 1st time together with all the sisters (except me: Nancy, Pam, Diana & you), & how appalled she was at how all of you teased Woman – worse ragging than any seen since school, she said! So in a way, I think Em saw herself as a Woman champion or protectress. Actually, Woman rather thrived on all that teasing, don't you agree? Anyhow, as I saw it from afar there was a marked change after Nancy died & Woman had been such an utter trooper looking after her. Somehow it looked to me as though she really came into her own re appreciation of her efforts, & rare qualities.

As for me – there was a fairly long estrangement following her missing scrapbook accusation (which you may have forgotten, but I haven't) but of recent yrs we became great friends, Bob & I adored going there, she used to come to parties in London – last one, at S. Belfrage's where she & I sat side by side as a sort of inappropriate Receiving Line. All my friends loved meeting her & vice-versa, I think.

Well Hen, I long for all reports of funeral etc.

Much love, Yr Hen

DIANA TO DEBORAH
20 April 1994

Temple de la Gloire
Orsay

Darling Debo:

You must be just so tired. Sorrow makes one tired & then all the myriad arrangements fall upon you and I feel hopelessly inadequate, just an extra burden hearing nothing or very little. You have been fantastically *wonderful*. I can't tell you how much I feel it & how grateful. Of course you know as well as I do that you *MADE* Woo's life in EVERY way. Just as you do *mine*. You are a genius of true sympathy and what that means is you are pure gold. But we batten too much and I implore you to REST if you possibly can. Oh darling how I wish we were together this minute.

I want to explain something you may not know, about the hymn 'Eternal Father, Strong to Save'. When we were at Batsford Uncle Tommy came once on leave, about the time of Jutland.[1] We all went to church of course & Uncle Tommy was outraged that there was no prayer for sailors, only soldiers, & from then on the parson Mr Spencer Jones was told every Sunday there must be 'Eternal Father, Strong to Save'. It was always the last hymn & one longed for it because it meant the end of durance vile. Woman loved Batsford & that hymn must have simply meant Batsford to her.

When I think of happy childhood it's of Batsford I think. Whenever Farve came he was in high spirits & we had such fun but also we had much more freedom than after the war when (for example) we weren't allowed to play with the village boys. Farve made many *rules*. The first year at Asthall was lovely but I missed Tom when he went to school, & after that except the holidays I wasn't very happy, at least only on & off. I think after the building at Asthall & the disastrous farming Farve was eaten up with worry about money. He made a few quite wild investments all egged on by Uncle Geoffrey. Muv could have kept everything all right but he would do it without her. We did have lovely times but his miseries made an atmosphere of worry & there were too many of us, Muv must have so hated it, successions of dull governesses at all times, really agony *I* should find it. Leaving Asthall was the last straw for us. The time Woo & I were completely happy was until I was ten or eleven & she twelve or thirteen, but we never again had the heavenly freedom & fun of Batsford with the Normans.[2] You may know all this but you may not. At Asthall her joy was the animals, & my joy was you & Decca. I literally worshipped you both and Nanny. It is lovely to be alone & I'm thinking about her, and you.

Love darling, Honks

1 The Mitfords' uncle, Bertram, had served in the Royal Navy during the First World War.
2 Neighbours of the Mitfords.

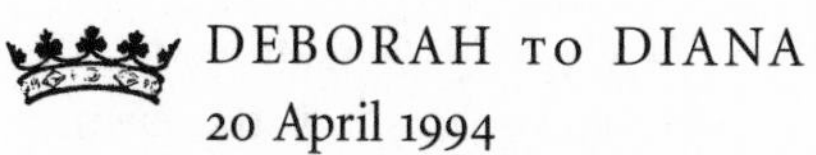

DEBOROAH TO DIANA
20 April 1994

Woodfield House
Caudle Green

Darling Honks

In some ways (selfishly) I wish you'd stayed & in lots of ways I'm thankful you didn't. Arriving here was awful. When I started my task I felt like a burglar & still do, rather. It's odd beyond anything not to find her here. I've faithfully been round the garden plant by plant & am glad she can't see the precious new tree peony (expensive) which has been struck by a frost & the new growth hangs in that horrid way. I'm also glad she can't see the way we treat the water & the electric light, wickedly extravagant.

Keith, Stella's husband,[1] has been through the larder & thrown away some items, the *earliest* should have been eaten in 1977. Lots left. Heck Knight came & was a great help in that I suddenly saw it isn't necessary to empty every drawer, so now anything of use remains.

Derek's letters are so boring, just plans or a little list of things, all the sadness which goes with divorce. Really that was so horrid for her, one is apt to forget because she became so serene later on but must have suffered terribly at the time. Very few letters (so far) from anyone else but there is a little cache of Muv's in one cupboard which we will come to today. I'll report.

Much love, Debo

I hope you're alright?

1 Keith Mellors was houseman at Chatsworth; his wife, Stella, was housekeeper of the private side of the house.

DIANA TO DEBORAH
27 April 1994

Temple de la Gloire
Orsay

Darling Debo

Me yet again. Don't be too sad about 1951. I think the 2 or 3 years when she realized the Irish adventure wasn't going to do were very horrid, but Derek after the war thought he would be so happy hunting & racing & of course he quickly got bored because he wasn't working, & he got cross no doubt. But, probably luckily, 1951 was when we left Crowood. It was deathly for me because Al minded so terribly, & I hated leaving the people who had worked on the farm, but we filled Tullamaine. I don't suppose she much cared for having the boys & tutor, & me rushing every day to Clonfert, but she wasn't alone. Rudi came, & she (Woo) often came to Clonfert where she met Giuditta, & G. settled into Tullamaine. She may have been a mixed blessing but at that stage she *was* a blessing & when they went to live in Switzerland Woo really loved it at first. She was Queen there for ages with devoted friends. She often drove here with the Elles,[1] I remember them being sick & that she was terrified of rabies.

I often stayed in Switz, in one cottage & then in the other. Of course Woodfield suited her much better in the end but at first she did love Switz & constant visits to Rudi. I went with her to her divorce, I think he'd been so horrid & cross she was quite glad to be rid of him. Then all that stopped & he remained her friend. I do think Switz filled the gap. She went all over the place but on the Island had to leave the Elles. Taking them to Switz was a terrific decision. The divorce was naturally horrid but also a relief I believe, & her new life very much what she liked ('the Continent'). When Naunce died she said 'Nard, let's face it, she's ruined four years of our lives'. Poor Woo how she *hated* Versailles & I expect Naunce blew hot & cold, in fact I know she did. Oh Debo! Her best & happiest years were Biddesden cot, Rignell & above all Chatsworth, Woodfield & YOU.

Dear good darling Woo I want her here this minute.

Love darling, Honks

1 Pamela's dachshunds.

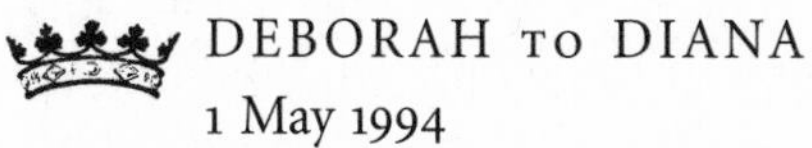

DEBORAH TO DIANA
1 May 1994

Chatsworth
Bakewell

Darling Honks

I'd really forgotten about the happy Swiss years, that's true & a comforting thought. I know she knew Derek was mad, well not like others, & perhaps it made it easier to bear. I wonder, looking back, that she didn't marry again. I suppose Giuditta really put a stop to it & then it was too late.

One thing (very tiny, but something) I'm glad about, is that I wrote & told her the kitchen garden here was entirely her doing, it was too. She inspired it and I'm so pleased it's there & that she got the richly deserved credit.

Gone back to yr letter & I had QUITE forgotten that you all lived at Tullamaine while Clonfert was readying itself, just shows. I suppose I was completely taken up with SELF (I know I was, I remember). N's poor illness certainly did take up 4 years for you & Woman & I remember her hating Versailles & you juggling Sir O & Nancy like a Three Card Trick. Impossibly exhausting, how did you manage it. She took you completely for granted & wrote all those horrid things but if she had been without you please picture. All too strange for any words.

Much love, Debo

JESSICA to DEBORAH
14 May 1994

6411 Regent Street
Oakland

Dearest Hen,

I WAS glad to get yrs of 11 May – anyway, I thought it was me delinquent re writing as I've been thinking so much about you & longing to be in touch. You/Dink must have same genes or whatever it is that makes you plunge ahead & simply do what must be done, such as arduousness of all the planning of Woman's funeral plus aftermath. Dink was so impressed by yr v. smashing letter to her, which she read out to me by t.phone; and so was I, in view of obviously thousands to answer. (But Hen, someone wrote & said you'd forbidden the clergyman to do a sermon – *well done*, although you must admit it was rather cheeky of you, and SO like Farve with his stopwatch set for 10 mins. for sermons in Swinbrook Church.)

After Woman died (12 April, right? so just about a month ago) I kept thinking of all the dead people I've known beginning, obviously with people like Nanny, Muv and my own dead children. Also Hen do you remember as children: 'She's dead. She's expired. She's too neriogely [horribly] put out her tongue, she's (etc). I must make her alive again. How shall I do that? I must prod, I must poke.' I don't think I've remembered that for 60 years. But it doesn't work, alas, in real life.

Anyway, for you the loss of Woman must be incredibly awful. For me – obviously far less so, as we so seldom saw each other & also barely wrote letters to & fro. I did get v. fond of her in late years, but absolutely nothing like your v. long-standing & v. close symbiotic relationship – in which she was a familiar in your house & you in hers. I did come across a few Womanly letters of last year – but as usual, mostly about hoping to meet etc. & naught of stunning interest. I barely knew her as a child, and only fleetingly in the last many decades; but I did (even dimly) note her amazing qualities, which Emma described so vividly.[1]

Yr loving Hen

1 Emma Tennant's obituary of Pamela concluded, 'In old age [she] radiated serenity

and goodness. Her huge blue eyes were as innocent as a child's. Indeed, innocence along with courage, honesty and cheerfulness was one of her remarkable qualities.' *Independent*, 16 April 1994.

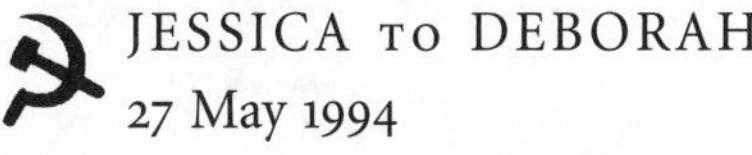

JESSICA TO DEBORAH
27 May 1994

6411 Regent Street
Oakland

Dearest Hen,

Funeral arrangements. Do FAX or LAX me a copy of yours when you've got them in order. So far, I've only thought of one idea for mine, arising out of the long-ago funeral of Sonia Orwell. It was a memorial mtg à la Belfrage & many others we've been to. David Plante[1] – do you wot of him? A controversial writer, I rather like him – took it upon himself to arrange the whole thing & he sent for Mary McCarthy to come from Paris for the event. Sonia & Mary had been absolute bosom best friends for years, but had had a complete falling-out after McC. wrote a catty review of G. Orwell,[2] total non-spkrs for ages, although they'd made friends again before S. died – anyway so M. McC gave the main eulogy, something like this: 'of course we all loved Sonia, but she was a terrific snob – not just a social snob, but an intellectual snob . . . Poor Sonia had absolutely no sense of style, her clothes were atrocious . . .' & more along same lines. This, it seems from many reports I had from various friends who went, set the tone for the post-funeral drink-up where all gathered to chat. It went like this: 'I was SO fond of dear Sonia, *but* . . .' then came the complaints against her. So my plan is to have my Estate pay the fare for my students from Yale etc to come to my funeral, with one proviso: if they hear the word BUT, surround the But-sayer & eject him forthwith. But perhaps I'll take yr advice & settle for C of E service, less complicated. By the way – did you note that they had 'For Those in Peril on the Sea' for J. Onassis?[3] Was that because of the Onassis yacht?

Much love, Henderson

1 David Plante (1940–). Novelist and author of *Difficult Women, A Memoir of Three* (1983), portraits of Jean Rhys, Germaine Greer and Sonia Orwell.

2 A review of *The Collected Essays, Journalism and Letters of George Orwell*, edited by Sonia Orwell, in the *New York Review of Books*, 30 January 1969.
3 Jacqueline Onassis had died of cancer on 19 May 1994.

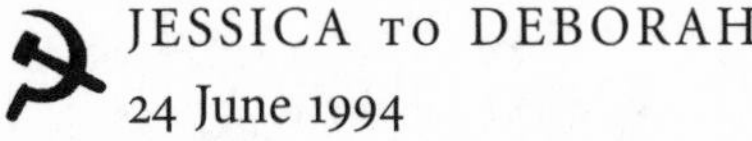

JESSICA TO DEBORAH
24 June 1994

6411 Regent Street
Oakland

Dearest Hen,

Thanks awfully for the Toby reading.[1] Actually Verse 13 was v. apt – 'that every man should eat & drink, and enjoy the good of all his labour' what with all the obits saying about Woman's noting of all menus at all meals.

I've often wondered about Woman not having any children. Was there any reason that you know of? I suppose she'd have made a super mum, esp. in view of the reviews of Emma & others of that generation, how they adored her when they were little. Conversely, Nancy – although she was said to long for children, I rather pity their fate if she'd had any.

I do so sympathize with your point – things reminding you of her, & suddenly realizing that there she isn't. The exact same thought kept occurring to me when P. Toynbee died, ditto more recently S. Belfrage. It really takes ages for the fact they are dead to sink in properly.

Thinking it over, in my case it's the letters that I miss mostly – which, obviously, comes from living so far away from most dead people I really adored. (Oh for the writing on the env!)

Much love, Henderson

1 Toby Tennant had read from Ecclesiastes, Chapter 3, at Pamela's funeral.

NINE

1995—2003

Chatsworth,
Bakewell,
Derbyshire,
DE4 1PP
Baslow 2204

15 Oct 02

called Stephen Fry

Darling Honks

An actor (funny, I believe very, but needless to say I don't think I've ever seen him) is making a fillum of Vile Bodies. He wants help with How They Talked etc etc. Well I'll talk to him & his actors in our voice which I suppose is sort of 20s.

He wd value answers to questions from you. He is a gt friend of Friend & others I know & sounds a kindred spirit on the telephone. I said I thought you MIGHT do some written answers.

They (him plus actors) are all coming to Ches. St. the next time I'm in London to learn how to say lorst and gorn.

Aunt Elsie used to say the test ~~was~~ is Shooting Boots, no young person can manage that without ~~putt~~ saying ew instead of oo.

So we'll see.

We had a shoot & the usual 14 guests, ½ William's ½ Eddie's. The Peregrine

Letter from Deborah to Diana

As she approached her nineties, Diana found the upkeep of the Temple de la Gloire too much to manage and at the end of 1998 moved to a flat in Paris where it was easier for her friends and many descendants to visit her. Except for her almost complete deafness, she was in good health and had the upright carriage of a young woman. She still read omnivorously, contributed the occasional article to the English newspapers and took a keen and opinionated interest in politics. But increasingly, she found life a burden and longed, as she put it, to 'fall asleep and never wake up'.

Jessica was the only one among the sisters who had smoked and she drank heavily for much of her life, habits she had taken up during her marriage to Esmond. She suffered a stroke in 1984 and when she broke her ankle in a fall at the end of 1994, she decided to give up alcohol completely. She wrote to Deborah that it was the realization of the trouble that her alcoholism was causing her family, rather than the damage it was doing to her health, that had made her give up. At nearly eighty, she was still asked to give lectures including, to her astonishment, at a funeral service seminar – which she compared to Ralph Nader, the crusading attorney and terror of the auto industry, being invited to speak by General Motors. When Jessica died in 1996, Deborah could not turn to Diana to express her grief – the estranged sisters had been distanced for too long for Diana to feel any great emotion – and, unlike the outpouring of sorrow that followed Pamela's death, the interchange was perforce brief and unemotional.

At seventy-five, Deborah had the energy of someone half her age. Chatsworth was now one of the most visited houses in Britain and the commercial activities that she had started and built up over forty years led to her being voted '2000 Rural Businessperson of the Year'. Her letters recount her gruelling schedule of writing, travelling, lecturing, entertaining and overseeing the hundreds of staff working on the Chatsworth estate. She wrote especially to Diana, the sister to whom she had grown closest in old age and who was now too deaf to hear on the telephone. They exchanged letters or faxes almost every day of the week.

DIANA to DEBORAH
7 January 1995

Temple de la Gloire
Orsay

Darling Debo

Phillip Whitehead[1] is doing a 3-part Churchill for telly: Lord Randolph, Winston & Randolph. I'm to be filmed next week. I objected my nose[2] but he makes o of it. My value is my vast age, very few left who remember the first years of Chartwell. He says Mrs Harriman[3] has been v. nice about Randolph. Also they've seen Lord Randolph's medical reports & he was *told* (poor man) he was sure to die of G.P.I.[4] which explains much, the wild hurry for example.

Phillip says the spite of the Press against Brussels is unbelievable, of course really against Europe. He is an MEP. He says England cannot now stop the advance & can't afford to opt out. How I wish some voice could be raised to say that the making of Europe is the ONLY way to stop another war, this time finally destructive of all that makes life worth living, including all our grandsons & all your marvels. I can feel the hate building up in England just like last time. But old Winston has made us so weak that perhaps there's not much we can do this time in the way of harm. A dead nettle. How wretched to have to hope for that. Phillip thinks the Tories will ditch Major[5] before the next election, & that it will be very close. He used to be on the Left, I wonder now; was Pres: of the Oxford Union, a friend of Max's.

Love darling, Honks

1 Phillip Whitehead (1937–2005). Journalist, author and Labour MEP. He was president of the Oxford Union in 1961.

2 Diana had recently been operated on for skin cancer.

3 Pamela Digby (1920–97). The legendary Washington hostess and Egeria of the Democrats was married to Winston Churchill's son, Randolph 1939–46, to the film producer Leland Hayward 1960–71, and to the millionaire W. Averell Harriman 1971–86. In 1993, she was appointed American ambassador to Paris.

4 Winston Churchill's father, Lord Randolph, was believed to have died of general Paralysis of the Insane brought on by advanced syphilis.
5 John Major, Prime Minister since 1990, resigned as party leader in 1995 but was re-elected. In 1997 he resigned after the Conservative defeat in the general election.

☭ JESSICA to DEBORAH

8 March 1995

6411 Regent Street
Oakland

Dearest Hen,

Enclosed: a killing article by Xopher Hitchens in *Vanity Fair*,[1] at least I loved it. Did you catch the telly programme about Mother Teresa? I always thought she was just a boring old saint, hadn't realized she's a disgusting old fascist. Xopher is v. good value – will be a high point of our Washington trip (we are off there on 21 April, mainly to see Oy #1[2] at his work, thence to NY to stay with Dink & Co. for a few days).

Also on the lit. front, have you read Selina Hastings's book about E. Waugh? To my annoyance I note that it's had marvellous reviews, just when I was thinking what a hopeless idea – yet another book on well-worn subject.

Well Hen not much news here – we're going to Los Angeles for a few days, but you don't know the people there so what's the use.

So, as you can see, I'm v much up & about. Nary a drop to drink & so it goes. Re giving up: a year or two ago I decided to try, method being to taper off, starting with a ration of 3 of those wee aeroplane bottles of vodka a day. But once I had them I craved more, so the tapering didn't work at all. Oddly, the total giving up is actually working OK. I suppose everyone is different in that line?

Much love, Henderson

1 The article by Christopher Hitchens described Mother Teresa as 'the ghoul of Calcutta' and a self-serving egotist. *Vanity Fair*, February 1995.
2 Jessica's grandson James had joined the Public Defender Service in Washington.

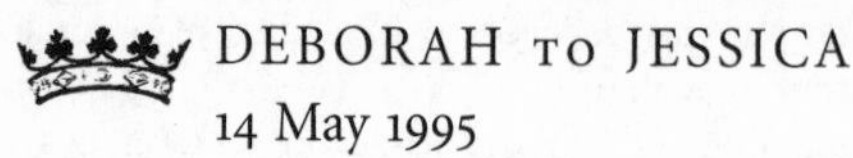

DEBORAH TO JESSICA

14 May 1995

Chatsworth
Bakewell

Dearest Hen

I forgot the best bit of the Hattersley[1]–Rich People lunch.

Andrew has had ghoulish dentistry of late involving (as the wireless says with emphasis on the O) 6 or 7 new top front teeth sort of hooked on to some remaining back ones, you know the kind of thing they do. It cost A FORTUNE & he spent many an unpleasant hour in the chair. All done, they said, for years – or probably forever, seeing as how old he is. Alright then. In the middle of lunch the whole lot slowly descended, very slowly but very surely. He couldn't talk because he wasn't sure what was happening. He couldn't eat for obvious reasons.

Desperate, he somehow got my attention from t'other end of the table & I saw he had turned into a wolf, those frightful teeth sort of took over the whole face & yet they didn't come out entirely, still just fixed to the real ones but hanging. Oh Hen please picture. Of course it was incredibly funny but the complete strangers in our midst were discomforted to say the least.

So that was the entertainment provided by mistake.

Much love, Yr Hen

1 Roy Hattersley (1932–). The former Deputy Leader of the Labour Party was a neighbour of the Devonshires at Great Longstone, Derbyshire.

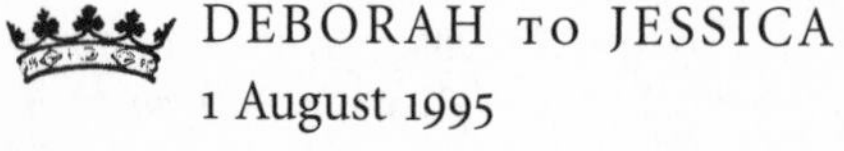

DEBORAH TO JESSICA

1 August 1995

Chatsworth
Bakewell

Dearest Hen

Daphne Fielding, 92 & often as odd as odd, sometimes hits the nail on the head. Jim [Lees-Milne] was talking to her last week.

Jim: Isn't Paddy [Leigh Fermor] the best octogenarian any of us knows by far?

Daph: Yes he ought to be squashed up & made into pills for the rest of us.

Too true. HASTE.

Much love, Yr Hen

DIANA TO DEBORAH
27 September 1995

Temple de la Gloire
Orsay

Darling Debo:

Did you find hundreds of little mistakes (typing) in EW/NM?[1] When you were here I thought I noted you scribbling away. I ask, because I found very few, which may be rather worrying & the beginning of senile dementia, I used to be rather good at proof reading.

The letters end so sadly somehow. Evelyn was miserable for years & his books lost all their wonderful hilariousness. I read *Love Among the Ruins* & it is boring & disgusting (the heroine's beard). Poor Naunce no more Colonel, no more hero in other words, but her books got better & better. I think after the wretched U-book[2] the friendship was never again the least bit loving. I think she felt he'd made a fool of her. There's a lot that is rather painful but I don't think anyone would see it much who didn't know them both. I'm longing to hear your impressions.

Helleu[3] was always just going to take me to see Boldini[4] but never did, I think he didn't want him to see me. I was allowed to meet Sem.[5] No wonder they hated the modes of the twenties, it must have seemed such drear fashion. Like punk is to us.

I can't see that it matters the IRA having guns as long as they don't shoot people with them. They'll never honestly give them up. Isn't it rather mad to make everything depend on an impossibility?

Love darling, sorry for dullth, Honks

1 Diana and Deborah were reading the manuscript of *The Letters of Nancy Mitford and Evelyn Waugh.*

2 *Noblesse Oblige.*

3 Paul-César Helleu (1859–1927). The fashionable French artist, a friend of the sisters'

grandfather, had painted and drawn several members of the family and had been an admirer of Diana when she was in Paris aged seventeen.
4 Giovanni Boldini (1842–1931). Fashionable Italian portrait painter who settled in Paris in 1872.
5 Georges Goursat (1863–1934). French caricaturist of the Belle Époque who worked under the pseudonym 'Sem'.

DIANA TO DEBORAH
29 October 1995

Temple de la Gloire
Orsay

Darling Debo

Yette[1] came down. She says you are SO beautiful, so I says yes *and* good and VERY CLEVER. Yes Debo.

Now we have spoken.[2] I'm not sure I can write about Lytton [Strachey] & Carrington. I think I did what I could in *Loved Ones.* I think looking back what he loved was my extreme youth. When I met him (with Emerald) at Russian Opera we flew together like iron filings & magnet, I suppose my admiration shone out & perhaps pleased him. I was 18. He often dined at Buckingham Street. Biddesden began when I was 21 & by then I'd stayed at Ham Spray & become instant friends with the adorable Carrington who never hesitated a *direct* compliment, she too loved the fact I was young, by then 21. Lytton liked to teach & I was avid to learn after a sketchy education. During my two terms in Paris I had read much Racine & other favourites of Lytton's & seen them on the stage at matinées classiques. All of us elder children went three or four times a year from Asthall to Stratford so we had seen more Shakespeare than most I suppose. Anyway he always spoke as if one knew, like a well-read grown up, though I was callow. My enthusiasm was probably what he liked. I had read all his books before I knew him. They (he & Carrington) were amused by me being rich (!) & in the two years I was at Biddesden there were Boris Anrep's[3] mosaics, gazebo by G. Kennedy,[4] & the wonderful lead nude woman statue in the walled garden by Stephen Tomlin.[5] I got most of the furniture in Venice & had my bed made. It was *so* pretty, 65 years ago but I still think it perfect. Lytton & Carrington constantly came over & I made a great fuss of them & they of me. There's a lovely letter of Carrington's about Muv, Bobo, you & Decca, she adored you. It seems so unbelievable that I was only 21½ when both died.

Peter Quennell says in *The Marble Foot* that he was a bit in love with me, something I never dreamed of at the time.[6] He used to come & chat at Cheyne Walk, & later on at Eaton Square. He was one of my little circle. Evelyn [Waugh] was Buckingham Street. I think I was very obtuse & never realized when people were a bit in love, *only* thinking of my own feelings. I suppose Gerald [Berners] was, in his mysterious way. I twice stayed a month in Rome with him & frequently at Faringdon, & at Eaton Square he came all the time & I went to Halkin Street. He, like Lytton, taught me almost all I know. I could never have had my Gerald life married to Bryan.

Another bosom friend when I was at Eaton Sq was Henry Yorke. I was great friends with Dig but he often took me to cinemas & dinners. He amused me with his paradoxes. After the war they came to stay at Crowood but by then he was getting rather mad. But when he was a hermit I always went when in England, mostly for Dig's sake as he'd become disagreeable.

Another bosom friend at Eaton Square was Peter Watson (he not the *least* in love of course) & with him & Edward James I saw many Paris friends like Tchelichew, Dali, Sauguet, Marie-Laure [de Noailles], & Kurt Weill & Lotte Lenya[7] from Berlin.

Looking back, perhaps Kit wanted me at Wootton miles away from all inties [intellectuals] of different nationalities. I loved him so much that I look back on Wootton as a dream of happiness. What luck we had. The *food* there was sans pareil [matchless]. Fancy remembering that, but I do, & the pretty garden which I left entirely to the two gardeners, not interfering in any way, & it was heavenly with a thrilling kitchen garden full of tiny peas & new potatoes.

You won't have got as far as this. I could also be lyrical about Birdie & Munich & the fun & excitement we had. I was terribly sad to be deprived of you and Decca by Muv but she was so splendid later & so fond of Kit that I've purposely forgotten her cruelty, & you & I have made up for it since haven't we. As to Naunce I did my best, she had her room at Eaton Sq but after that there was so much spite & disloyalty that I couldn't really love her, though often amused.

Love darling, Honks

A constant companion throughout was of course Tom.

E. James asked me to marry him, but, like Max [Mosley] when Rudi invited him to stay, I said 'No fear'.

1 Henriette Mabille de Poncheville (1926–). A friend of Diana. Married Leonard Byng in 1961.
2 Deborah was encouraging Diana to write another book about the people she had known.
3 Boris Anrep (1883–1969). Russian artist best known for his floor mosaics in the London National Gallery in which he portrayed Diana as Polyhymnia, muse of sacred music and oratory.
4 George Kennedy (1884–1954). The well-known architect had designed the swimming pool and gazebo at Biddesden.
5 Stephen Tomlin (1901–37). Bloomsbury sculptor.
6 Peter Quennell (1908–93). The author wrote in the first volume of his memoirs that he had formed 'a romantic devotion' to Diana when she was married to Bryan.
7 Diana met the composer Kurt Weill (1900–50) and his wife, Lotte Lenya (1898–1981), in the early 1930s, soon after they were driven out of Germany by a Nazi-orchestrated campaign.

DIANA TO DEBORAH

5 February 1996

Temple de la Gloire
Orsay

Darling Debo

I've got an awful feeling the new editor of *E. Standard* has banned me,[1] I'm not surprised, was much more surprised that I was wished for.

Andrew Wilson[2] telephoned but I couldn't hear what he said. What I earned was so wonderful, it paid for all presents for 18 great grandchildren & a few young grandchildren, and more. Anyway Xmas is now o'er for a minute or two, & birthdays on the whole I skip.

My eyes are awful, red & watering & I have to ration my reading. The Dr gave drops but they seem useless. I'm *so* deaf that I really dread people, but it may improve, I mean it comes & goes. I can hardly hear my wireless even pressed on my ear. Isn't it tahsome.

My diary is terribly sad in parts, all our friends dying, very few left, & of course *terrible* poor Naunce's illness, I lived through it all over again. What a ghastly thing it was & even now I'm not sure what caused the pain. Several doctors said long before she died 'If it had been cancer (the pain) it would have killed her by now. It's a *nerve pain*.' But isn't all pain nerve pain? It sounds quite meaningless to me. I do think Kit was good, he didn't like her & for years put up with my rushing to see her, often from Paris in the train & then coming back with agonizing migraine. He *always* managed to be so sympathetic about my wretched headaches.

As to you, you were perfect. All the same we do seem to have had lovely golden days & jokes. The diary tells all. Not a bit interesting except to us. *Poor* Naunce.

Love darling, Honks

My misshapen nose has turned bright red.

1 When Max Hastings took over as editor of the *Evening Standard*, Diana was indeed dropped as a regular reviewer.
2 A. N. Wilson (1950–). The novelist, biographer and literary editor at the *Evening Standard* had become a friend and correspondent of Diana.

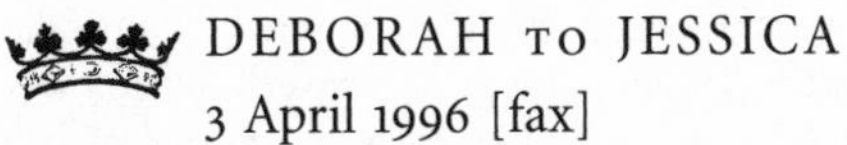

DEBORAH TO JESSICA
3 April 1996 [fax]

Chatsworth
Bakewell

Dearest Hen

Thanks for the kind fax for birthday. What I can't believe is that I'm nearer 80 than 70. Did you think that at 76?

Cows. Yes, MAD.[1] Everyone is, it wd take too long to explain now but it's dread if you happen to like cows, sane or mad. Did you see the wonderful cartoon in the *Spec*[*tator*] of a cow at the piano singing 'Mad About the Boy'? Oh it is lovely.

Haste, packing for Lismore.

V. much love from Yr 1000 yr old Mad Hen
(Diseased)

1 Britain was in the grip of a BSE 'mad cow disease' epidemic. Jessica had written to ask whether it was not mad to kill cattle when nobody knew which cows were infected.

DIANA TO DEBORAH
10 April 1996

Temple de la Gloire
Orsay

Darling Debo

I think on Friday it's two years since Woo died & I miss her more than ever. The other two I think of every day are Wife and County.[1] It's far the worst part of old age, having to do without the very ones you long for. I've been reading such depressing accounts of old age, the worst the Kennedys (Joe & Rose). He unable to speak for years after his stroke when he was *longing* to & still all there & wanting to say a thousand things about all his businesses etc, such a brain full of executive ideas it must have been torture. And she living to 104 poor thing.

Then I've been reading about Mary Berenson,[2] long illness, pain, longed to die & couldn't. Very depressing.

Mitterrand[3] a perfect subject for R. Kee – the most curious man ever born. Al has lent me so many books about him I know it by heart but R. Kee will come up with something marvellous I'm sure.

Love darling, Honks

1 Lady Mersey died in 1995 and Jean de Baglion in 1993.
2 Mary Smith (1864–1945). Married the art critic Bernard Berenson in 1900. She underwent an operation in 1931 from which she never properly recovered. Diana was reading *A Self Portrait from her Letters and Diaries*, edited by Barbara Strachey (1983).
3 François Mitterrand (1916–96). The French President had died at the beginning of the year.

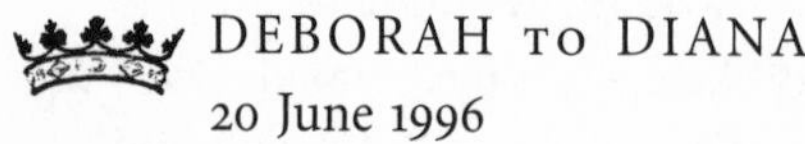

DEBORAH TO DIANA
20 June 1996

Chatsworth
Bakewell

Darling Honks

FREEDOM has set in – I've sent my last piece to the *Sun. Tel.* You can't think how marvellous it is not to have to think of *NEXT WEEK*. How does Auberon W.[1] or any of his peers, go on day after day, week after week. Can't imagine.

The Garter day was amazing.[2] Like a medieval play, clothes, language & background. We left London at 9 A.M., had the usual wait in a lane, went into the castle at 10.30 & from then on it was Disney with Knobs On. Much waiting about while Andrew & his mate Sir Timothy Colman, of mustard fame & Lord Lt of Norfolk, rehearsed & generally fiddled about out of sight of the hen pheasants who were the women.

Only 2 female Knights now Lavinia[3] is dead, Pss Anne & Mrs Thatcher, so Denis [Thatcher] was among the spouses and what do you think: he LIT UP & smoked incessantly in those hallowed rooms. It was so comical & so like him, I was delighted that he broke the rules – not that there are any rules but sort of unspoken, you know.

Anyway eventually it was the actual giving of the thing by the Queen. That was done in a long narrow room with 50s brocade & curtains, not the real room because that is still being restored after the fire. Only the Knights & spouses go in (I asked the Queen's private sec. after about some detail & he said 'oh I don't know, I've never seen it'). There is something very touching about the ancients hardly able to waddle, like Leverhulme[4] & Hailsham, all dressed to kill. Longford looked quite spry compared to them. Cake is *weeny* but was her usual amazing self. Andrew & T Colman were presented one by one. They get dangerously close to the Queen who does something with a 'collar' & something else with a sort of dressing gown cord. She is highly practical, quick & neat & of course the 'presenters' are not and fumble with the cord etc etc till she grabs it herself to get on with the job. The language is thrilling, ancient & rather frightening, nothing but battling with things & people. All v. moving, partly because it has happened since Edward 3rd & partly because of the slowness of each movement, like a slow-motion film.

Then a long wait for disrobing. All of us round the walls while the Queen says how-d'you-do to everyone, followed by Prince Philip, Friend,[5] Cake & Pss Anne. Another long wait & drinks & cigs for Denis then lunch in the Waterloo Chamber. I drew husband & son, & Andrew 2 queens. I had exactly the same Nature Notes talk to Prince P that we had done 2 months ago when I last sat next to him. I wonder if he noted it, *not* I suppose or he'd have thought of something else. Friend sweet as always. I don't know why I love him but I do.

Then, after fairly ages, the wives & Denis went out into the brilliant sun to walk down to St George's Chapel between the crowds of people who had tickets to be on the walking route. Henry & Joan, Roger & Sue Wardle, & John & Mrs Oliver[6] were our guests & by a miracle I spotted the first four. Saw the real procession, again incredibly beautiful, old men dressed as cards & even older ones called the Knights of Windsor. Then into the dark, cool chapel, up the choir stalls so one can't see the congregation.

¾ of an hour & one of those anthems which might never stop, you know how they go back again & again & Amen can go on pretty well for ever.

Processed down the aisle & glimpsed Heck [Knight], whose grandson William Vestey is a page to the Queen, & Sto & Amanda but not the others – Soph & Al, Em & Toby – they were very much there but didn't spot them. Out in the boiling sun again, cars this time, back to the Waterloo Chamber (all the Lawrences have been cleaned & have the miracle new picture lights) for tea. This time all the royals disappear so there was a great feeling of hats off, hair down & general relaxation.

Dear me what an extraordinary day. Next day was Ascot, very jolly. Sto will take over in the autumn next year, secret, but I don't suppose you will shout it from house tops. He will be HM Representative.[7]

Well that's enough for now you won't have got this far.

Much love, Debo

1 Auberon Waugh (1939–2001). Son of Evelyn Waugh and prolific author who contributed his decided opinions to many publications including the *Daily Telegraph*, *Private Eye*, *Spectator*, *Books & Bookmen*, *Evening Standard* and *Literary Review*.

2 Andrew Devonshire had been installed as a Knight of the Garter in a ceremony at Windsor Castle.

3 Lavinia Strutt (1916–95). Married the 16th Duke of Norfolk in 1937.

4 Philip Lever, 3rd Viscount Leverhulme (1915–2000). Lieutenant of Cheshire 1949–90. Steward of the Jockey Club 1973–6.

5 Deborah's nickname for the Prince of Wales who was a regular guest at Chatsworth.

6 The Chatsworth butler, land agent, comptroller and their wives.

7 Deborah's son, who had been chairman of the British Horseracing Board since 1993, was appointed Her Majesty's Representative at Ascot in 1998.

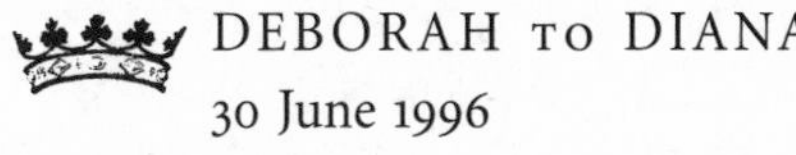

DEBORAH TO DIANA

30 June 1996

Chatsworth
Bakewell

Darling Honks

Decca is not well. Dinky faxed me to ring her (Dink). I did, last night. Decca has two worrying things, spitting blood & a v. swollen leg & ankle. I'll keep you in touch. They've 'looked at' her lungs, all clear except a corner which the camera didn't reach so they won't say it isn't cancer. It is not tuberculosis. So what is it? Leg painful, lungs not. Lots of slaves looking after them. D hates admitting illness. Bother. Bob better.

Much love, Debo

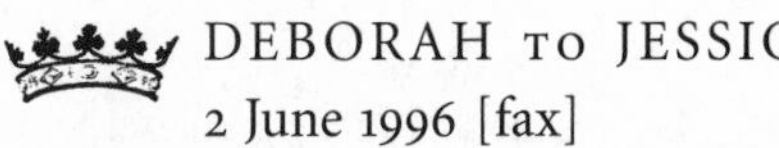

DEBORAH TO JESSICA

2 June 1996 [fax]

Chatsworth
Bakewell

Dearest Hen

THANKS for reassuring message and my word I am glad that Dink is with you, she will give confidence and SEE TO the doctors[1] and anyway Bob will be so cheered by the sight of her.

Go on faxing, please.

Much love, Yr Hen

1 Constancia was a qualified nurse.

DEBORAH TO DIANA

2 July 1996

Chatsworth
Bakewell

Darling Honks

In the most crowded week I've had of years we went to dinner with Jayne Wrightsman.[1] Rothschilds,[2] D[avid] Beaufort, Kay Graham (of *Washington Post*) & many more including the de la Rentas[3] who had been to stay here the weekend brought by Jayne, all assembled when in blew the Pss of Wales, 7 feet high on tottering heels dressed in black jodhpurs with a black tunic on a hot summer night. The Kissingers were there – he had come for the FOOTBALL,[4] do admit, Mrs K & the Princess are doubles, they could do an act together, same hair & same height.

Anyway Andrew sat next to her & hasn't been very forthcoming but they talked about old times & he got the impression she is sad. Well I expect she is. The trouble is she's mad. But she is a brilliant actress/manipulator and can twist & turn people with her little finger.

The *Antiques Roadshow* was THE best fun in the world. They asked me to choose something of this house to talk about so I took the hawk[5] because it is such a surprise – first the date, 1697, then opening it to find the cup. Did that the day before. 3,500 people came up the west drive & down the steps to the w. garden where there was a huge tent but it was the perfect June day so all the EXPERTS set themselves up under garden umbrellas dotted about. People queued for 3 hours to take their objects, all quite content in the sun & seeing a garden which the regulars don't see. I took Evie's *Ronald Knox* with its blank pages[6] (price? that stumped them) & the drawing of Elvis I got through the Las Vegas auction. The drawings lady (from Sotheby's) said hold on to that it will increase in value – as if I'd ever sell it. One excitement was a little landscape belonging to Mrs Dean,[7] alas not well enough to bring it herself so one of the Farm Shop ladies took it for her. Bought for 2/- in an open-air junk market in Sheffield 20 years ago 'twas £5,000. By Lord Leighton. I thought it might have been more, high fashion & all that. A good buy all the same. Your fan, whose name I never can remember who writes for *Derbyshire Life*, brought a clock which he'd paid £50 for years ago – £10,000. All very jolly indeed. The first people started queuing at 7.15 & it ended at 7 P.M.

I spoke to Decca. She is unwilling to talk about herself but Dink tells me she has 5 drs, 2 for the leg, one for tuberculous lung, one GP or whatever they're called in America, & one for lung cancer. She was to be scanned yesterday. I'll get news from Dink as I had the distinct impression Decca would prefer that. Last invasion of the summer tonight, trustees. Meeting tomorrow, they leave after lunch then NOTHING for a bit. Well not nothing but much less.

Much love, Debo

1 Jayne Larkin (1919–). Trustee and munificent benefactor of New York's Metropolitan Museum. Married Standard Oil mogul Charles Wrightsman in 1944.
2 Jacob, 4th Baron Rothschild (1936–). Chairman of the National Heritage Memorial Fund 1992–8. Married Serena Dunn in 1961.
3 Oscar de la Renta (1932–). Fashion designer from the Dominican Republic. Married Annette Reid in 1989.
4 Henry Kissinger (1923–). The former US Secretary of State was a well-known soccer enthusiast. Married Nancy Maginnes in 1974.
5 The Kniphausen 'Hawk'; a late-17th-century gem-encrusted goblet in the shape of an eagle.
6 See Deborah to Nancy, 26 October 1959, p. 319.
7 Dorothy Dean; housekeeper of the public side of Chatsworth.

DEBORAH TO DIANA
6 July 1996

Chatsworth
Bakewell

Darling Honks

The enclosed[1] explains all re Decca. The extraordinary thing is she had no idea there was anything wrong anywhere till she coughed up blood & went to the Dr. The only pain she has is in the hip & as you see they thought that was because she put all the weight on that leg because the other ankle was broken a year or 2 ago. Even now they don't know re the hip. But the rest is indeed a shock. The Dr says the lung may have started a year ago, the brain probably 3 weeks ago. *Probably* you will note.

I talked to her yesterday, she is amazingly cheerful & they have given her 'mood uppers' which must be working. Oh my word how odd cancer is. Of course she was a chain smoker but that wouldn't be responsible for kidney, liver or brain, would it? She is determined to go to Cape Cod, 7–14 Aug. And to finish her book.[2] The Dr says she has 6–9 months to live. We know they don't know that. I mean if the brain cancer only started 3 weeks ago it must have grown fast to be spotted so why shouldn't the kidney & liver do ditto, & they can't treat it all. She has had 2 radiations, 3 more next week. But as I say she sounds cheerful & is pleased to have been told the whole story. Dear me.

Dink is there, she is the all-time support of course. I keep finding things about funerals in England, seems a bit *macabre*, near the knuckle etc now. But she doesn't think so.

Much love, Debo

1 A letter from Constancia.
2 *The American Way of Death Revisited*, a revision of her 1963 bestseller, was completed by Jessica's husband and published after her death.

JESSICA TO DEBORAH
6 July 1996 [fax]

6411 Regent Street
Oakland

Hen – you are a marvel & thanks SO, SO much.

Boring medical news just to keep you in the picture. Turns out cancer is also in bones (bad hip) as well as brain, so it's radiation in all those places daily until 24 July. Doesn't hurt at all plus I get marvellous pain pills and blue cheerup pills – Dink's in charge. So I'm feeling v. well at the moment.

FUTURE PLANS: Am much hoping to get to England, possibly late autumn or even Xmas so don't come here. But DO come to me funeral, about 9 months or a year off accdg to the Dr. I thought I'd make SCI give a free one with all the best?[1] I'll let you know as plans progress.

That's about it for now. Point of brain radiation is to spruce it up a bit so one can get on with the book etc. Time will tell. All hair will fall out I'm told, so various ones are making wigs.

Yr loving and GRATEFUL old Hen

1 Service Corporation International, the largest funeral services company in America. In the event, Jessica's cremation was simple and inexpensive.

DIANA TO DEBORAH
9 July 1996

Temple de la Gloire
Orsay

Darling Debo

I feel miserable about Decca & her poor husband not well himself, it doesn't bear thinking of. So glad she's got the marvellous daughter. Oh Debo.

Love darling, Honks

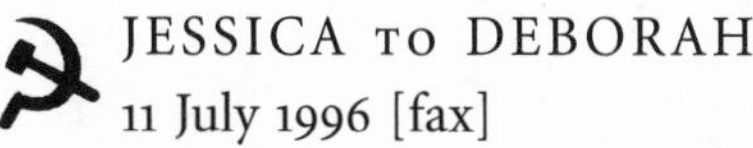

JESSICA TO DEBORAH
11 July 1996 [fax]

6411 Regent Street
Oakland

Dearest Hen,

I note you are in London but this will doubtless catch up.

So what happened – as you have it, pretty much. Coughing blood, X-ray – first no cancer cells – other procedures – cancer of lung & other places incl. thigh. I asked how long the cancer had been there – can't say for sure, about a year they thought.

Not only no malaise whatsoever, no headache which one wld be absolutely expecting don't you agree with c. of the *brain*, hardly any pain except in thigh & that's under control with marvellous medicine for same. Daily radiation at hosp. But here's the point Hen: SO much better than just being hit by a car or in plane wreck. At least one can plan a few things – also feeling absolutely OK, life is v.v. pleasurable with people coming to chat plus work on bk. It all really is quite extraorder, do admit.

Needless to say I'm taking *full* advantage, everyone's bringing meals on wheels, delicious things for me & all marvellous helpers who are absolutely smoothing every path here, so it's sort of a non-stop party, all my favourite people flocking by. So why worry? Also doing all sorts of things such as helping Benj with his Cuba pianos,[1] everyone now in mood to give him dough for same because of their affection for his old Mum. Did I tell that when I went to register at hosp name of Jessica Treuhaft the social worker said 'Are you by chance related to the piano tuner?' oh I was pleased. Dink's coming to live here with us after C. Cod, isn't she a trooper.

July 12, about 5 A.M. in Calif. Yrs of 09.54 from Chatsworth just rec'd, so I've answered most of it. Are you getting envious of my extremely comfortable situation? One day I'll describe the helpers, but will get this off now. Did I tell you about deadline (mot juste). First they said (Drs) about 6 to 9 months but for some reason have upped it to more like 3 months which is rather a drag as was hoping to get to London. Meeting with them in a few days – it's so almost unbelievable, and I suppose they might be all wrong – in which case helpers etc might get livid, boy who cried wolf. By the way Dink thinks v.v. highly of the whole cancer team – she's in constant touch with them FAX/t.phone.

Yr loving Henderson

1 Benjamin Treuhaft had set up 'Send a Piana to Havana', a project for exporting pianos to schools in Cuba in defiance of US trade sanctions.

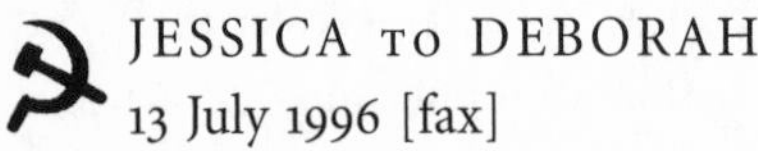

JESSICA TO DEBORAH
13 July 1996 [fax]

6411 Regent Street
Oakland

Hen,

Of course I'd adore to see you, but when, how? Aunt Weenie: 'Geoff, George is dead and now Sydney's gone, don't you think we shld meet?' Uncle Geoff – long pause: 'But we *have* met.'

If you do, that wld just be extra bonus as I do so hope to come for proper visit to England for a proper Honnish chat. Be thinking on't.[1]

Yr loving Hen

1 Jessica died ten days later, before Deborah was able to go to America to see her.

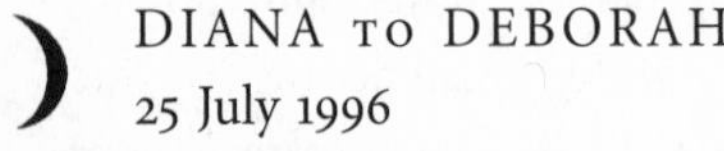

DIANA TO DEBORAH
25 July 1996

Temple de la Gloire
Orsay

Darling Debo

I'm so thankful you didn't go to America, no point whatever. She knew you loved her & the great thing was to be in constant communication, which you were. I feel dreadfully sorry for the little husband, not well etc.

Love darling, Honks

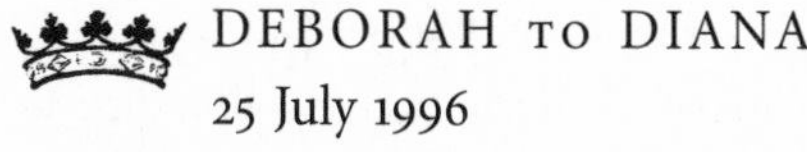

DEBORAH TO DIANA
25 July 1996

Chatsworth
Bakewell

Darling Honks

The speed of Decca's illness is so extraordinary & the way 'they' look after such a thing now is totally different from the ghoul way of Nancy's long agony. According to Em, doctors can't tell relations anything they haven't told the patient. Perhaps it is better. I'm sure it is. But Dink, with her long experience of nursing, was surprised by the way it went so fast. Even after the brain thing swelled & gave her the equal of a stroke, paralysed one side, the Drs thought she would be OK & get to the famous Cape Cod holiday next month. No suffering, except the horrible indignities of pipes through nose etc but she stopped that herself & said no more of feeding through tubes.

I talked to Dink last night. She said the telephone had been 'busy' all day. I bet it had. Two people rang here from America, Teddy Kennedy & Kay Graham of *Washington Post*. They do that it seems, & English people rather dread it. Even so it never stopped here.

I asked Dink re funeral, cremation she said, & a 'Memorial Service' on Mon. What form does that take? All friends go to some public sort of room, I mean one you hire, & get up & do a talk or sing something in praise of the departed. A poem? I asked. Hadn't thought of that she said so I'm faxing E. A. Poe's *Annabel Lee* which she used to spout endlessly. I can't tell you what a BOON the fax has been. If the hours are as muddlingly different (8) you can send it any time without annoying & they get it when they wake up & you don't feel you're bothering anyone. A miracle. They will have another 'Service' – (funny word?) in New York in Sept or Oct & most likely one in London.

I talked to Hen the night before she died. *To* was the key, she mumbled things I couldn't hear but she knew it was me.

Much love, Debo

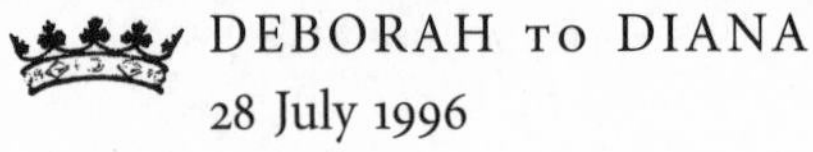

DEBORAH TO DIANA
28 July 1996

Chatsworth
Bakewell

Darling Honks

I've had some strange letters, dug out of the past. One from a woman who was in a Paris family with Decca in 1934 including a photo of her with quite a fat round face and Id, really beautiful. I had forgotten that Id was with her when she was learning French (?!!) The writer of the letter says she only has jolly memories, Hen was not cross or sad then.

The obits. were unbelievably inaccurate. To be expected I suppose. Not one got it right (facts I mean).

This is a luxury week, NOTHING written down & no one coming to stay. Very rare. So I feel like you, mooning round the garden. But I'm even luckier because I haven't got to cook what I pick.

The *F.T.* has asked me to do 800 words on *tourists.*[1] I will, with a will. I've asked all & sundry for quotes & await the harvest from the wardens who stand about. The best so far is from the (v. nice) girl in the Information place. Someone asked if I had been an air hostess? Another said 'I saw the duchess in the garden. She looked quite normal.' I'll send when it's done.

Much love, Debo

1 Reprinted in *Counting My Chickens*, pp. 97–9.

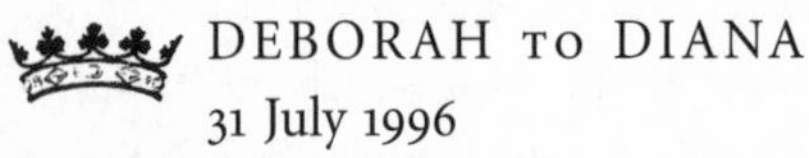

DEBORAH TO DIANA
31 July 1996

Chatsworth
Bakewell

Darling Honks

Reading the obits. of Decca, the Mitford Girls are described, variously, as Famous Notorious Talented Glamorous Turbulent Unpredictable Celebrated Infamous Rebellious Colourful & Idiosyncratic. So, take your choice. The *D Express* has a long article about us called 'Sex & Power'. I suppose anyone who is married, & most who aren't, have what is now called Had Sex* at some point in their lives. As for Power I don't quite see how that comes in to it. So why are we different from anyone else?

Much love, Debo

*Look at the people walking down Oxford St, all products of Having Sex.

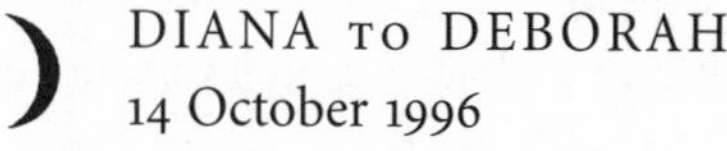

DIANA TO DEBORAH
14 October 1996

Temple de la Gloire
Orsay

Oh Debo it's simply *TOO* sad.[1] Please get a wreath with enclosed & please do not tear up the cheque. Will the funeral be at Edensor or is there a Catholic church?

Love darling, Honks

I was in such floods but even with Jerry's help *failed* to get Bolton but will speak to you tonight I hope.

1 Jean-Pierre Béraud, the chef at Chatsworth, had been killed in a car accident.

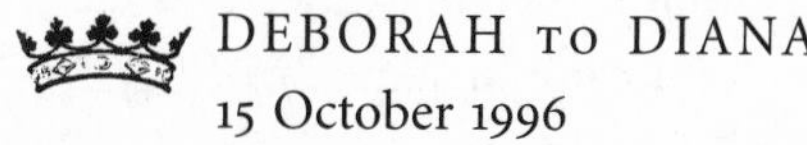

DEBORAH TO DIANA
15 October 1996

Chatsworth
Bakewell

Darling Honks

As you know I went to Bolton yesterday, encouraged by Andrew not to sit about & mope. I got back to find this place stunned, numbed, everyone quiet, so strange & so unlike usual.

It was all because of you that Jean-Pierre appeared. Jerry played a huge part. I'll write to him. It was 17 years ago. The ripples caused by his death don't surprise me but they have gone far & wide. Andrew has chucked New York of course. He is wonderful beyond words at such times. Went up to the restaurant yesterday morning to encourage them all on, something I just could not have done.

He said the response was touching in the extreme, they are determined to go on 'as he would have wanted' but oh the loss is deep. He was one of the best friends I have ever had. When he was younger he had a temper & an impatience which could be awful, I suppose it was the genius in him, he could hardly bear to be thwarted or to put a brake on & even at 40 that streak was still there & it was that which killed him.

One of the children said he was like a sparkler here, so true.

I can't imagine the place without him but I shall have to. So many little things keep cropping up, all to do with him. He was on the crest of the wave, his wonderful birthday party, then Diane's[1] when he took her to London last week & they had 2 dinners in the best restaurants in London & he brought back the menus & we went through what they'd eaten mouthful by mouthful. He had loved that. The day before he died he got a letter confirming a television programme for him, cooking everything produced here, thereby different from the usual cooking programmes. This had been on the go for 18 months & he began to think it wouldn't come off & OH he was pleased about it.

What an extraordinary man.

They are closing the restaurant on the funeral day & we'll put notices on the gates . . .

Oh Honks what a tragedy. We had such plans for this winter, the new bar, new cooking class place, a room for lectures, meetings etc.

Last night they did a dinner for 200 I can't imagine how.

Much love, Debo

1 Diane Peach married Jean-Pierre Béraud in 1983.

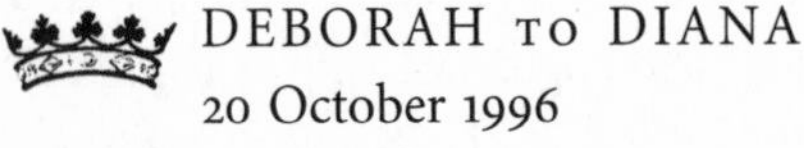

DEBORAH TO DIANA
20 October 1996

Chatsworth
Bakewell

Darling Honks

We are in limbo waiting for the funeral. Poor Christine & husband[1] came back from their hols, knowing nothing, to the sombre atmosphere, they can't believe it.

People have written as though he was my son, it is really quite strange.

Friend[2] has sent Diane [Béraud] most of Moyses Stevens[3] *and* he's written to her – that is why I love him.

Much love, Debo

I've suddenly thought are Jean-Pierre & Woman cooking for each other in heaven? And is she telling him he's doing it all wrong?

1 Christine Thompson was head of the sewing room at Chatsworth and her husband, John, was in charge of clocks and carpets.
2 Prince Charles.
3 A London florist.

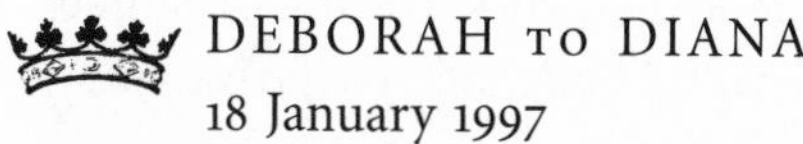

DEBORAH TO DIANA
18 January 1997

The Carlyle
New York

Darling Honks

Oh Graceland.[1] 2¼ hr flight in an incredibly grand private airy, delicious lunch given by v. nice crew. The excitement was intense, please picture. The party was Jayne [Wrightsman], Annette de la Renta, Ashton Hawkins (the v nice lawyer of the Met), Mrs Blackwell,[2] & Warren Davis[3] of the Nat. Trust.

Met by one of those clever vans which holds 7 people. The first sight of the Mansion was a thrill & the gates with the music notes on. Drive round to back door. Very few 'public', a dead time of year I suppose. Went in through the kitchen where we picked up the audio things for the tour. A sweet but hopeless black girl in a woolly hat was our guide but the audios made her not necessary. They were perfect, Priscilla Presley talking, & sometimes Elvis plus music, allowed one the right amount of time in each room. The furniture was too lovely, white 'custom made' sofas all along a wall, down 3 steps & a white piano on a shag carpet so deep it went ½ way up its legs.

The Jungle Room had outsize chairs whose arms were carved crocodiles' heads, enormous, & a vast round one which no one could sit in because of its depth. Green carpet 2 inches long, (thick) & *the same on the ceiling*. Do admit. Alas no upstairs (like Blenheim),[4] stairs carpeted & ceilinged. The dining room was very gracious & we were told on the audio that they all made jokes there & Elvis used to eat with one eye on the television. Another games room or 2 then out via the kitchen.

One portrait, not very like, quite a nice lot of photos.

Out of doors, bitter cold bright sun, to see some horses in a paddock which, a notice said, wore plastic eye shades to protect from injury, what could that mean? Then a fives court, a shooting range, out again into the Meditation Garden, weeny & made when he was interested in various eastern cults. Alas it is now the family graveyard, the mother, father & HIM, huge granite slabs with a lot of writing on & hung about with teddy bears & flower offerings of every shape & colour, so many that they continued along the fence past the garden & a permanent flame like the Unknown Warrior. Our guide, who unbelievably was called Morticia, told us that they arrive every day & when the anniversary of his death comes round there are so many they go all along the street.

I forgot: the museum, long dark passages with show cases of his clothes, including the army uniform & sequins galore. Sadly, the Sincerely Elvis museum of *intimate* things was shut for refurbishment.

The gold discs were arranged along long walls in patterns just like swords in a Scotch castle.

Then across the (very main) road to see his aeroplane – enormous, with a huge bed in it. By then we were about whacked & only got to one shop & the idiotic Morticia never told us there were 2 more so we missed the sequin tee shirts & such like, maddening.

Much love, Debo

1 Deborah had visited her idol Elvis Presley's Memphis home for the first time.
2 Blanche Lindo (1912–). The Jamaican-born friend of Deborah and Diana was a close friend of Ian Fleming during his last years. Married to Joseph Blackwell 1936–45.
3 Warren Davis (1937–). Head of Communications at the National Trust.
4 The upstairs rooms at Graceland were not open to the public.

DEBORAH TO DIANA
16 March 1997

Chatsworth
Bakewell

Darling Honks

I looked at *Birthdays* in the paper. Saw Lord Moyne. Thought surely Bryan must be a bit older than that? And it's JONATHAN.[1] Impossible to believe, he is a private school boy to me.

Sophy is 40 on Tues! Al[astair]'s dog, Jack, bit Nancy[2] on the face (not badly) so he's been put down. 'JACK'S DEAD' Declan said, oh aren't children of three funny. I remember Sto coming into my room after I had a baby which died in 1947, so he was three, saying gleefully '*our baby's buried*'.

Did I tell you re Swinbrook or did that day fade into the busyness of last week? I made a dash for the day to Highgrove for a Royal Collection's meeting.[3] So I came back by Swinbrook to see the new people at The Swan. It was 70°, everything shimmering & green starting, I can't tell you how lovely. I walked from there to the churchyard & was in sort of floods all the way. Woman's grave has got some crocuses & two sawn off lavenders put by Madeau [Stewart] I think. Birdie & Nancy have *vases* of daffs – who *could* have done that? The church as magic as ever, the Fettiplaces[4] are just it, aren't they. So, floods. I'm so glad you will land there, resurrection of the ashes.

Much love, Debo

1 Diana's eldest son was sixty-seven.
2 Nancy Morrison (1995–). Deborah's youngest granddaughter.
3 Deborah was a Trustee of the Royal Collection 1993–9.
4 Seventeenth-century tombs of the Fettiplace family, Lords of the Manor of Swinbrook.

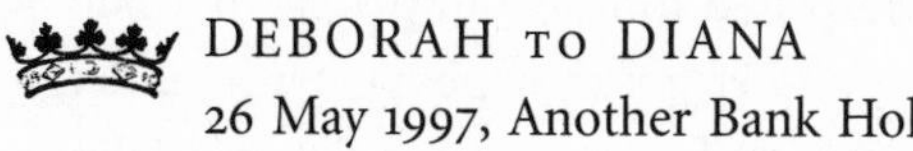

DEBORAH TO DIANA
26 May 1997, Another Bank Hol

Chatsworth
Bakewell

Darling Honks

Jim's diaries[1] have taken me back 25 years, which they are meant to do. He is in despair over various mistakes in notes etc. I must say I have spotted a few which you will too, & omissions in the index which always seems to happen now. There is a marvellous descrip. of Dow Ly Lytton writing to her twin Ly Loch every day of her life & when she went mad . . . well you'll read it, p. 132. Us, to the life.

Andrew went to the Royal Academy dinner & wore the Garter & white tie for the first time. He walked there from Ches. St & no one took any notice or threw what Americans call rocks. I know people are very oddly dressed now but he must have looked a bit of an apparition.

We've put a notice by the fountains (because when there was nearly no water they could only be on for a couple of hours) & now it says The Fountains Will Play 11.30–5.30. A woman standing by it, when going like Billy O, looked at her watch, which said midday, 'Oh, we've missed 11.30 & we can't stay till 5.30. What a pity. Now we won't know *what* they play.'

The ash trees are still like winter. What does it mean.

Much love, Debo

1 James Lees-Milne, *Ancient as the Hills: Diaries, 1973–1974* (1997).

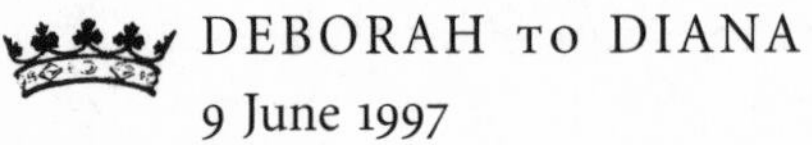

DEBORAH TO DIANA
9 June 1997

Chatsworth
Bakewell

Darling Honks

The Irish elections are very Irish, how can they take two days to count about ten votes. Andrew is glued to every news, the European money glues him. You are lucky to be invested in it.

Last week was what is called action packed. I had dinner with Jean [Lloyd] on the way to London and we had a marvellous talk NOT about Europe you'll be surprised to hear but people, her family mostly. The next evening was a dinner given by people with Garters for the Queen & Prince P's golden wedding. It was at Spencer House. All the royal family there. Cake had to ask for a cushion, she has become so TINY her chin was on the table.

Mrs Thatcher looked 18, I wonder if she's had her face lifted, really incredible. I said 'oh you do look wonderful' & she said 'it's

America, I like them & they like me & that is never the case in Europe'. Denis kissed everyone's hand. I said 'how did you do it all those years?' & he said 'love and loyalty my dear'.

Tomorrow I'm going to the school in a weeny village who said I was the nearest famous person. I'm afraid they'll be bitterly disappointed. They expect a tiara & a train & long white gloves.

Much love, Debo

DIANA TO DEBORAH
22 June 1997

Temple de la Gloire
Orsay

Darling Debo

You ask what it's like to be 87. It is *awful*. I am so well, better than for ages, very few aches & pains, a bit wobbly but walk normally, easily for example to the coiffeur & back, do a very little gardening but get tired quickly, do the flowers for the house & have to lie down after.

BUT I am almost stone deaf, so that people tire me *terribly*, I am so blind that I dread winter as then it's all I have to do (reading). I dread inviting people or accepting invitations. Of course no question of plays, concerts or opera for many years past, telly irritates & exhausts me (eyes & ears). I see things outside that need doing but can't do them, there's a constant feeling of frustration.

The beauty of my surroundings is a perpetual joy & when I go to Paris I love its beauty more than ever. But it's not enough to make a life. I could live to be 100 like Aunt Daphne, but imagine 13 more years getting more hopeless all the time. I love being alone but of course only if I can read, which I still just can but not quite easily. Sometimes when I'm alone I worry about all of you worrying and really long for the end, but see faint hope as there's nothing wrong. I dread an accident, hospital, wild expense just for the fun of being tortured. I love warmth but the sun hurts my eyes & I have to stay indoors. I had a swim when it was hot but probably shouldn't do it. My blessings are you, Al, Cha, all my sons, almost all my grandchildren, my joy are your & their letters (which I *can* read much more easily than print). I must not grumble. I am so lucky but wish I could see the end. It might be such a wild bore for you all.

Love darling, Honks

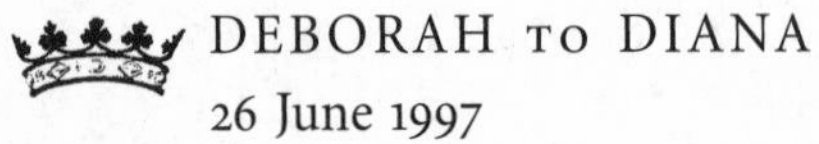

DEBORAH TO DIANA
26 June 1997

Chatsworth
Bakewell

Darling Honks

Your letter re being old is sad. Of course it is, when the time comes for eyes & ears to wear out, what's left?

Blessing counting gets ever more difficult and aching voids of boredom which haven't happened since very young must come back.

The mere idea of not being able to read doesn't bear thinking of. When I think of the vols you consume for pleasure and then to be denied the one thing which makes being alone almost better than having loved companions it is just a bit too ghoul. People don't realize the effort of trying to hear, either.

Frustration at not being able to garden etc added. I can't get over you walking to the hairdresser etc that is something you have not lost at all.

Thank goodness for the beauty of your house & garden though I know it is the other things which really matter, eyes & ears.

Wishing to die is not at all surprising and wondering about alternatives.

The trouble is the uncertainty and of course you think about it, so does Jim [Lees-Milne], I know, and no doubt everyone of your age and mine who has any imagination, it could not be otherwise. Thank goodness for your children, grandchildren & greats – something Woman never had, and the thing which made Nancy so waspish.

Dear me, I keep looking at your letter and wondering. I won't forget, that's one thing.

Oh Honks how odd life (and death) are.

Much love, Debo

DIANA TO DEBORAH
2 September 1997

Temple de la Gloire
Orsay

Darling Debo

We all felt terribly sad about the princess, what a fearful tragedy.[1] I wish she could see the incredible explosion of love & sympathy.

I can't tell you how kind & sweet Live & Die[2] & Jean [Lloyd] were, they have been the best visitors ever, we only longed for you to make it perfect.

Now I am alone again I can't help feeling sad, she was so brave and beautiful wasn't she. I never saw her or knew her at all so I suppose what I feel is just the same as what the whole world, the crowds, feel.

Louis [Mosley] goes back to school tomorrow, imagine the poor little prince, I wonder when he will. So terribly pathetic.

Love darling, Honks

1 Princess Diana had died in a car crash on 31 August.
2 Peter Maitland (1937–). Director and chief executive of the London antique dealers Mallett & Son 1978–97. He often signed off his letters to Diana (Mosley): 'I live and die to see you.'

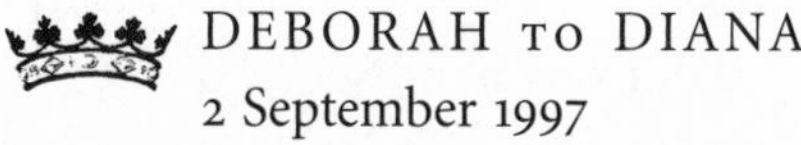

DEBORAH TO DIANA
2 September 1997

Bolton Abbey
Skipton

Darling Honks

How strange it is, this adoration & beatification of the princess. If only they knew. It just shows how humans must have an icon and there she was, beautiful, elegant *and* charming & quite extraordinary with ill or old people – I've seen her at work & it was a case of touching the hem, almost unbelievable. BUT 'they' have no idea of the other side. She was mad of course.

As for our papers they have gone far too far. When you think of her lover[1] & who & what he was, & all the things which aren't allowed by the papers who have never been able to bear the idea of anyone, let alone a public figure, enjoying themselves – dinner at the Ritz after the 3rd 'holiday' in a month with the son of a man who has been refused citizenship & whose mother was a sister of Koshogi (spelling) who should have been a kind of devil according to the papers but was excused everything because she is now a saint. It is so ODD that I give up.

Much love, Debo

1 Emad (Dodi) Fayed (1955–97). Egyptian-born film producer who was killed in the car crash with Princess Diana. He was the son of Mohamed al Fayed, the owner of Harrods, whose application for British citizenship was rejected on the grounds that he was not of good character, and Samira Khashoggi, sister of Adnan Khashoggi (1935–), the Saudi international arms dealer who was repeatedly involved in allegations of stock manipulation and fraud.

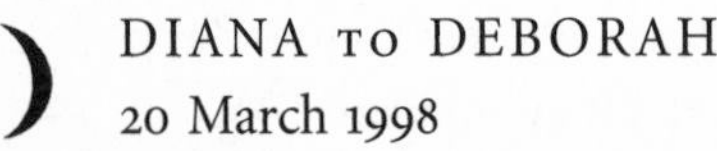

DIANA TO DEBORAH *Temple de la Gloire*
20 March 1998 *Orsay*

Darling Debo

Thank you for the Berners reviews. My little effort was not in *The Times* yesterday so they've most likely lost it, anyway I don't mind now because there've been raves which I wanted partly for Gerald & also partly for Mark who struggled so long & is amply rewarded.[1]

About Proust, it had to be so short what I wrote that it was impossible really & I suppose I ought to have said no.[2] I'm not nearly as clever as you are & I terribly regret your one blind spot, you would *LOVE* not just Proust, but Flaubert, Henry James, George Eliot, Goethe's novels, Tolstoy, Dostoevsky, Turgenev, Chekhov, all these brilliant treasures & many more. I think possibly it comes from impatience, you want to be up & doing, well you *are* & think of the wonderful achievements! You have got the patience to plant trees, hedges, you know they take ages but once they're in they grow & you can be *doing* again, something else. You don't want to sit ruminating over a book, you want quick action. I do regret it, I can't help it, thinking how you would laugh at Proust's jokes or be terrified by Conrad's descrip of the slow fire in a cargo of coal ready to turn & drown them all if the wind changes. It's true my world is peopled by characters in books, & it's a mystery how you, so interested in human nature, can do without it seen through eyes of genius. But perhaps it's clever nature at work which gave you a task far more important than just loving to read. Your fund of wonderful human sympathy is much more unselfish, in fact reading *is* selfish & would probably waste your time which you spend making life bearable for one & all. So in the end I applaud your choice. It is much cleverer to *do* than just to *think*.

Love darling, Honks

1 Diana's review of Mark Amory, *Lord Berners, The Last Eccentric*, appeared in *The Times*, 27 March 1998.
2 Diana had chosen *A la Recherche du temps perdu* as her book for 'On the Shelf', *Sunday Times*, 15 March 1998.

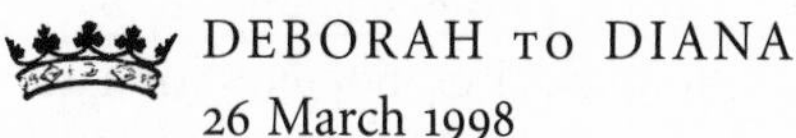

DEBORAH TO DIANA
26 March 1998

Chatsworth
Bakewell

Darling Honks

Thanks so much for your incredibly nice letter. I am only TOO AWARE that not having read the books by all the people you mention is MY LOSS. Like no operas, an immense hole which can't be filled by anything else so remains a black emptiness.

Impatience is indeed a reason and also what the papers call a *short attendance span* – that's why I like lists, reference books & such like, just little bits of inf. which I quickly forget. It may come from having too much to do.

Ages ago, when Andrew couldn't do much (and certainly nothing detailed) to do with this old dump and its surroundings, because he was a minister and therefore in London or travelling, I took to trying to keep abreast of what was happening & trying to stop the then agent from pulling down (his favourite occupation) & various other sorrows which would undoubtedly have happened. It was not easy & every now & again I was accused of interfering, which, of course, was right. I was interfering. It was a bit of a tightrope. Then I started things like the Farm Shop & the children's educational Farm Yard. Both were a battle, specially the shop. Derrick Penrose[1] was dead against it saying we had no experience of such things; the estate was tenant farms with a mineral interest, woods (which lost £300,000 a year) & it would make a lot of work, we weren't shopkeepers etc etc. I don't know why I drag all this up, but added to the house & garden & Lismore & Bolton Abbey & the shoots, both here & at BA, it was more than most women do and entirely brought on by myself simply because I couldn't bear to watch what was happening &, almost more difficult, what wasn't happening, when I knew it could be a help to the old dump.

Of course these things aren't excuses because if I had been interested I would either have read all night like you do or not done the other things. The truth is I couldn't live here & not do the other things when what was needed stuck out a mile. So it was pretty well a 24-hour a day job & made more complicated by having to weave around & not be seen to be doing it. I got in the habit of it & couldn't stop.

Oh Proust, shall I try now or is it too late? I do hope it's too late.

And then you remember what you've read, that's what's so amazing. Not in one eye & out the other while the page remains unturned & the print becomes meaningless. Oh Honks – it's *hopeless* Granny.[2] If we ever leave here not in a coffin then I really will. And we ought to of course.

Your *sentiments* in your KIND letter much appreciated.

Much love, Debo

1 The land agent at Chatsworth.

2 What Deborah's grandson William had said to her when trying to explain a game she could not understand.

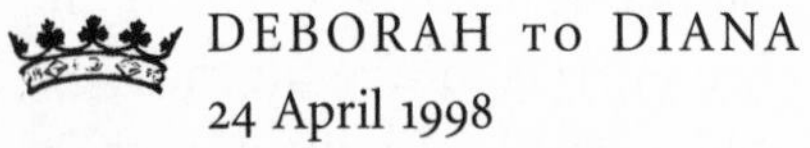

DEBORAH TO DIANA
24 April 1998

Chatsworth
Bakewell

Darling Honks

It was lovely to see you & to be at the Temple on that staggeringly beautiful day. Wasn't it luck, squeezed between winter before & after (it is here anyway).

I was v. relieved to find you *well*. I absolutely understand the domestic worries & I wd give anything to get them resolved.

The more I think about it the more I feel you ought not to move. The lesser of the 2 evils, to my mind, is new people. A total upheaval, from a 50 year HOME would be worse than anything I can imagine.

The D of York's helicopter looms so I suppose I must stop. I had a nightmare that I'd gone ON VACATION with Fergie[1] & woke in a sweat.

I'll tell you how it goes. THANKS for my visit, car, food, chats & everything else.

Much love, Debo

Look after yourself please.

1 Sarah Ferguson was married to Prince Andrew, Duke of York, 1986–96.

DIANA TO DEBORAH
3 May 1998 [fax]

Temple de la Gloire
Orsay

Darling Debo

Thank you *so* much for understanding. In a way, Andrew Wilson put his finger on it, by writing he wished he could come & chat for an hour instead of having to burden me with a night's visit – well, of course it's not a burden & yet it *is*. Arrangements have to be made, meeting agreed, often involving the dreaded telephone, as well as depending on Jerry or someone else. Whereas in a flat you just open the door! *Everything* here is in greater or lesser degree like that and, even with reliable people, has to be, up to a point, tiresome, not to speak of those who get out at the wrong station etc. Also being so deaf short visits are so much more welcome.

Philip Ziegler sent his life of Osbert [Sitwell] & I couldn't put it down. I do wonder what the critics will say. Osbert's (ridiculous) snobbery, *and* his attitude to the war & other things will press every button loathed by not just the Left but all the politically correct people. Which has become nearly everybody! He (Ziegler) praises Osbert's autobiography, it's fifty years since I read it. Of course Sir George is wonderful, & the valet. But on the whole I don't think Ziegler gives credit for Osbert's funniness, he was such fun to be with

& the jokes perfect. The quarrel with Sachie is terribly sad when you think how much they adored each other. I must re-read the autobiography. The last years *terrible.*

Love darling, Honks

DIANA TO DEBORAH
Yogi plus 2 [8 May] 1998 [fax]

Temple de la Gloire
Orsay

Darling Debo

Blazing sun, & again this morning, and warmth. Tony [Lambton] approves my plans which I told him not to speak of.[1] It's such a business coming here for chat, Jerry made a sort of *House and Garden* dinner à la Emmy.

Tony says Harold left 65 millions. He left Mrs Acton's jewellery to the nice young man who was so good to him. It's worth 2 million. Very nice.

Talking of language difficulty Tony says Selwyn Lloyd[2] introduced him to Khrushchev saying 'He's the best shot in England', & the translator said 'Lord Lambton is to be shot tomorrow'. Khrushchev thought it quite normal but patted him on the shoulder kindly.

Well darling that's it.

All love, Honks

1 Diana had finally decided to move to a flat in Paris.
2 John Selwyn Lloyd (1904–78). British Foreign Secretary 1955–60.

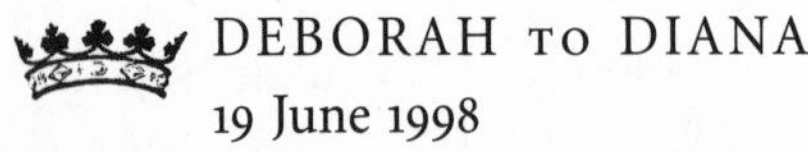

DEBORAH TO DIANA
19 June 1998

Chatsworth
Bakewell

Darling Honks

I think you'll have to speak to Ld Longford about his Garter get up: soup, egg & just London dirt all over, a bit much & the poor Queen had to eat her lunch next to him. I was next to Ly Longford in church, she whispered stage-like 'HOW IS DIANA?' but that was all we could do, we were overtaken by anthems after that.

My word that ceremony is beautiful. Ld Longford comes in a London taxi, they say he goes into the street, shouts TAXI, gives the driver the parking thing & says 'Windsor Castle'. Quite sensible, it's far easier for a 93-yr-old to get out of than a car but it does look very funny between the Bentleys.

Ld Callaghan[1] is the next oldest-looking & Ly C's feet are a series of knobbles, poor her. I drew one Lord Bramall[2] at lunch. As we went in to the huge newly done room I said 'sorry I didn't look at the plan' & he said 'oh I did, we go this way'. Well it was the wrong way so as we turned to go back I said 'how did we win the war with generals like you?' to which he replied 'I'm not a general I'm a Field Marshal'. He is *sweet* & grows peas & beans & has a Gurkha on the box, lucky thing.[3] Ld Leverhulme just sits with his mouth open these days & Quentin [Hailsham] made a bog by refusing at first then said he was coming & then didn't come.

So that's the Garter for you.

It's the 19 June & there has been ONE day with no measurable rain so far. A bit much you'll agree. Everyone is getting edgy.

Heywood Hill Prize[4] today*. I'll report.

Much love, Debo

*Soggy lawn & yet another tent.

1 James Callaghan (1912–2005). Labour Prime Minister 1976–9. Married Audrey Moulton in 1938. Created life peer in 1987.

2 Edwin Bramall (1923–). Chief of the Defence Staff 1982–9. Created Field Marshal in 1982, life peer in 1987 and Knight of the Garter in 1990.

3 As Colonel of the 2nd Gurkha Battalion, Lord Bramall had a Gurkha soldier as his driver.

4 The party for the bookshop's annual literary prize was held at Chatsworth.

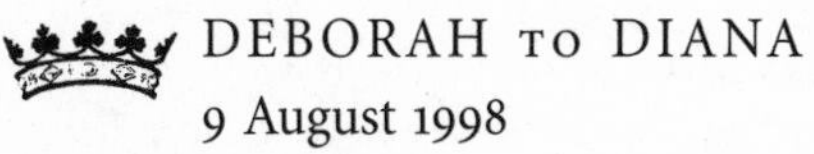

DEBORAH to DIANA
9 August 1998

Chatsworth
Bakewell

Darling Honks

Henry [Coleman] back from Lismore with a good tale of some of the American tenants – the host wished for a ghost so wonderful

Denis[1] whistled up one Mr Twigg (sec of the hunt!). He was dressed in a sheet, a night-cap, chains, carried a lantern, they fixed a fishing line to the chandelier in the dining room. When pulled it shook & rattled & then the apparition appeared through the windows.

One American woman nearly fainted, screamed like anything & said she must leave the castle *at once*, go anywhere, even the hotel . . . It took ages to persuade her that the ghost was Mr Twigg, he had to appear in the flesh . . . she was really horror-struck, the joke nearly went too far.

Much love, Debo

1 Denis Nevin; the butler at Lismore.

DIANA TO DEBORAH
11 December 1998

104 rue de l'Université[1]
75007 Paris

Darling Debo

When you think of the tiny Temple harbouring so much it is bewildering. Some of the furniture seems huge & some weeny, all quite unlike itself. Elo[2] & I did your room yesterday, not quite the Centre Bedroom I fear, nor the Red Velvet.[3]

I understand nothing, not the door or how people get in & I'm too deaf to hear buzzer or bell, have lost several keys & am altogether hopeless Granny. Don't hear telephone or fax, Elo speaks no French, altogether we are babes in the wood. I must learn how to do the cooker. So many things to learn & I'm too old & not an apt pupil.

Must get up for picture hanging.

Love darling, Honks

1 Diana had moved to a flat in the same street as her son Alexander and daughter-in-law Charlotte.
2 Consuelo Papasin; Diana's Filipino housekeeper.
3 The main spare bedrooms at Chatsworth.

DIANA TO DEBORAH *104 rue de l'Université, VII*
Ascension Day [13 May] 1999

Darling Debo

I haven't done my memo for Jan Dalley[1] but nobody is coming today so I'll have a try. As soon as it's done I'll send. She has got very silly adolescent letters from me to Jim,[2] apparently all his correspondence is in some American university, I suppose the whole lot was sold when he died, or do you think he sold them? Anyway the letters are available. One made me give an unwilling smile, apparently when Helleu died (and I was really *sad*), I wrote to Jim & said Nobody again will ever admire me as much as Helleu did. What a horrifying little beast I must have been.

I come out of the book a monster, can't be helped but what I'm trying to get changed is the part about Muv, lifted of course from Nancy's letters to Mrs Ham. Nancy's lies are almost worse than Decca's. Both stem from unhappiness (Decca's tragedies, Nancy's operation in 1941) but nobody realizes that except us.

Love darling, Honks

1 Author of *Diana Mosley, A Life* (1999).
2 James Lees-Milne had died on 28 December 1997, in his ninetieth year.

DIANA TO DEBORAH *104 rue de l'Université, VII*
13 June 1999

Darling Debo

'Your health, so precious to the hearts of us all' as Winston said in a toast to Stalin – but *your* health really *is* precious. Now darling please rest. You do far too much for others and nothing for yourself. So peaceful here. My charming fan[1] is coming anon for a chat, otherwise blank.

I've had lots of birthday cards, perhaps people think I'm ninety. I almost am. I've been reading about Evelyn [Waugh] again. I'm afraid he was a fiend in many ways and the snobbery so very silly not worthy of such a clever man. And the drunkenness. I think I had the best of him 1929–1930. He didn't drink, never seemed silly or snobbish, loved chatting and jokes and we had such fun here in Paris, delicious food. The Guinness flat was just near where I am now. What made him become so awful? The demon drink perhaps, also the war and its disillusions. Poor Laura what a fate. She died aged 57.[2]

Love darling, Honks

1 Jean-Noël Liaut (1966–). Anglophile writer who first met Diana in 1998 when he interviewed her for a biography of Hubert de Givenchy. They became close friends and saw each other several times a week until her death.
2 Laura Waugh died of pneumonia in June 1973.

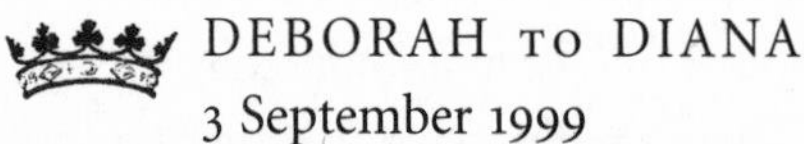

DEBORAH TO DIANA

3 September 1999

Chatsworth
Bakewell

Darling Honks

Michael's[1] funeral was in the most beautiful place, Compton Abbas between Shaftesbury & Blandford.

Short service, no address thank goodness. It set me thinking how strange it is that a man who had never set foot in his village church should wish to have his funeral service there. Churches are used 3 times it seems, wedding, christening & funeral. At the first two, solemn vows are made which people have no intention of keeping – at the last trump I suppose there's a glimmer of hope of everlasting life in a sort of heaven. Can you explain it? How do people expect a church to keep going for 3 occasions in a lifetime? A sort of superstition, a leftover from childhood? It soon won't be that as few children are taken to church in the way that our generation was.

Much love, Debo

1 Michael Tree (1921–99). Married Deborah's sister-in-law, Anne Cavendish, in 1949.

DIANA TO DEBORAH *104 rue de l'Université, VII*
9 September 1999

Darling Debo

What you say about Michael Tree's funeral – do you think only Christians should have funerals and weddings in church, where the words spoken are so beautiful and so much part of the best we have inherited from the past? I don't speak of christenings, I think it is too wicked to renounce in the name of the infant all the pomps & vanities of this wicked world and all the lustful joys of the flesh, which would include dinner at Maxim's or a visit to the National Gallery. But weddings and funerals are social occasions and I think myself they are beautiful and should quite like to have a little funeral at Swinbrook and my ashes near Woman's, but perhaps in view of what you say it would be better to get my sons to scatter my ashes *anywhere*, in the Bois de Boulogne would be easy for them. *I* don't mind a bit what happens but people like to say goodbye, at my age hardly any friends but masses of family. I do wonder if the people who say the creed every Sunday could really believe in the resurrection of the body? If they don't quite believe such an amazingly unlikely idea they shouldn't go to church and swear that they do. What would Runcie[1] say? He can't believe it, no rational human being could. It's no good saying this that & the other is symbolic, one cannot pick and choose between truth and symbol, the words are perfectly clear.

I don't want anyone at my cremation, they are so slow at Père Lachaise, unlike in England where it's 5 minutes. I went to Nanny's and to Gerald's, very easy but here it's too awful and takes forever. If you think Swinbrook unbearably hypocritical I will tell my sons what to do.

Love, Honks

1 Robert Runcie (1921–2000). Archbishop of Canterbury 1980–91.

DIANA to DEBORAH

104 rue de l'Université, VII

9 December 1999

Darling

I rather dread the (very easy) writing of all the labels for my 20 greats, they are only part of the task, there are Jonathan's three, and Louis, and various. I am so lazy, have never minded doing it before. Anyway I've got all the Xmas labels as well as 200 envelopes which will wend to you, I must ration my letters to you when you are so busy with real life.

The Law Courts are better than any theatre. So sensible of your gr children to go. I used to go often in Eaton Sq days. Tom would tell if a riveting case was on & he used to find me a good seat but I also went to the public gallery. I heard the Tavistocks' Restitution of Conjugal Rights case,[1] it was really about money, neither gave signs of wishing for conjugal rights but Lady T. wanted cash. And best of all was Farve, sued for slander by Andia, the wireless man. I went with Diana and Randolph C, and at the end she said 'It's so unfair, Cousin David was *bound* to win because he looks like God the Father'. Well one couldn't say that of Fayed or Hamilton.[2]

Love darling, Honks

1 In 1935, the Marquess of Tavistock, later the 12th Duke of Bedford, was sued by his wife for restitution of her 'conjugal rights', i.e. resumption of sexual relations. The Duke claimed that he was justified in denying them because Lady Tavistock was having an affair with their son's tutor.

2 The former Tory MP Neil Hamilton had brought a libel case against Harrods owner Mohamed Fayed who accused him of taking money in exchange for asking questions in the House of Commons.

DIANA to DEBORAH

104 rue de l'Université, VII

16 December 1999 [fax]

Darling Debo

Farve & Andia. Needless to say it started with Uncle Geoff at the Marlborough Club. He had heard of a wonderful S. American who was going to make millions with lovely ways of hiding a wireless, for example a sham Chinese pot which could take an honoured place among the old Famille Rose but which was in fact plastic, very cheap to turn out in thousands. In those days wirelesses and plastic were both rather go-ahead. Old Dave must meet him and *invest.* A luncheon arranged, Farve fell for the patter and invested. Some time later he began to have doubts (I expect Muv said no to a gothic casket for Asthall). When Lord Dulverton asked Farve whether he should invest in the Marquis of Andia's brilliant invention, Farve said 'First of all he isn't a marquis, and second don't invest and third I really don't think he is too honest'. A third member of the Marlborough, whose identity I can't remember, was told this in confidence and let it all out to the marquis while refusing to invest. Whereupon Andia sued Farve for slander.

Farve was wonderful under cross examination by a very bullying Counsel. I seem to remember it was Goddard, who became a very bullying judge. The judge of Farve's case was quite shamelessly on his side and treated Andia like a foreign black beetle, whereas he and Farve were brothers and Farve called him My Lord.

The case was dismissed and costs awarded to the defendant. Of course Farve had told Lord Dulverton everything that was alleged. But I suppose the judge thought he was quite right to warn Lord Dulverton about this obvious crook. That's where the millions he got for Batsford disappeared, and it was usually Uncle Geoff's fault. Farve was an innocent. All this circa 1926 or 27, I think. Diana Churchill hit the nail on the head for once.

Love darling, take care and get well, Honks

P.S. In those days wirelesses were HUGE and HIDEOUS.

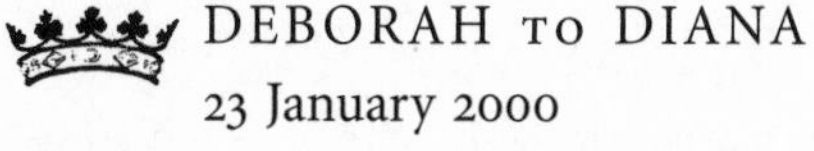

DEBORAH TO DIANA — *Chatsworth*
23 January 2000 — *Bakewell*

Darling Honks

Your letters of the last few days are so meaty I have to keep looking, forgetting (as I do now) & so looking again.

Now Decca. Muv's letter[1] is so sad & so generous & forgiving after what was a body blow. After 60 years it would still be a nightmare for a girl of 19 to disappear for 2 weeks (I remember it being longer but may be wrong, no I see Muv says 2 weeks) without any clue as to what had happened to her. I don't think she ever realized the effect it had on all at Rutland Gate. It was just as if someone young had died. No gramo (till then continuous). Silence, worry, sleepless, guessing what could have happened & then the whole story of the lies, deception & complete callousness of not thinking for one moment of what it wd be like for all of us. I felt betrayed. She was all to me, I could not believe that she could have done what she did. Of course I knew (as Muv did) that she was miserable at home but as I'd never heard of Esmond I had no idea that she would go, but it was the way she did it which was so cruel.

I once or twice asked her about it years later. She said it was the only way, she had to have time to get right away before being discovered & that if she had told me what would I have done? I must say I don't know the answer.

Decca was Nanny's favourite, I always thought, the adored curly haired favourite.

It was far the worst thing that happened to me, I was 16/17 & young for my age & very easily upset & the whole drawn out horror of it, the wondering what on earth had happened to her & then the cutting off with a knife seemed unbelievable.

There was a song of Harry Roy's (who we were all in love with) which went

Somebody stole my gal
Somebody stole my pal
Somebody came & took her away
She didn't even
Say that she was leavin . . .

'Gal' changed to 'Hen' & there it was, the whole story, often sung long after.

She was in Esmond's thrall and remained so till he died. I couldn't bear him, he had that effect, you either adored or hated. His death must have nearly killed her, oh poor Hen.

I don't think she ever saw Farve again (or did she, once, I don't know).

My goodness how it all comes back.

Decca softened & softened as the years went by, her letters show that. Not unusual. Do you remember when the Wife & Farve eventually met & she said something about expecting someone fierce & he said 'All the savagery has gone out of me'.

Much love, Debo

1 A letter written by Lady Redesdale at the time of Jessica's elopement, in which she begged her daughter to come home and blamed herself for Jessica's unhappiness, had been found by Mary S. Lovell while researching her biography, *The Mitford Girls* (2001).

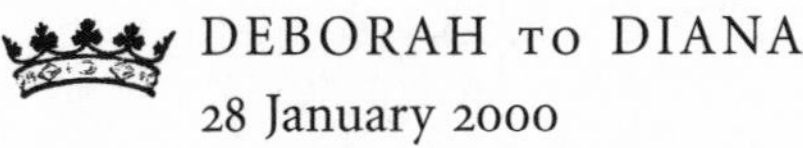

DEBORAH TO DIANA
28 January 2000

Chatsworth
Bakewell

Darling Honks

I've been looking at the ghoulishly embarrassing diaries of mine, 1938. I was so awful I can hardly read them. When Decca's baby died I just wrote a sentence saying so, & then went on about fishing with Farve at Swinbrook. Mind you I was suffering still from her departure & had had one or two awful times with Esmond when I went to see them in Bermondsey, & he was truly horrible about Muv etc.

I think Nancy was right that Decca was changed by him but she was ripe for change & it happened to be him, might have been anyone but he was such a strong personality & so violently against EVERYTHING.

There was no mention of going to see them after the tragedy of the baby, I suppose I'd have been kicked out by him & not much welcomed by her. There is a sad little note, 1938, from her saying 'We're going tomorrow' & at the end 'do write' but we had so cut off from each other by the time they went to America I couldn't think what to say, my life seemed so banal & so different from hers. The diary has some funny references to Pam Digby, funny in the light of her future career.[1]

Much love, Debo

1 In her diary, Deborah had described her contemporary as 'a tarty-looking girl' who had gained a reputation for getting drunk and 'playing the fool' early in the Season. Three times married, Pamela Digby was famous for her numerous lovers, who included Aly Khan, Gianni Agnelli and Elie de Rothschild.

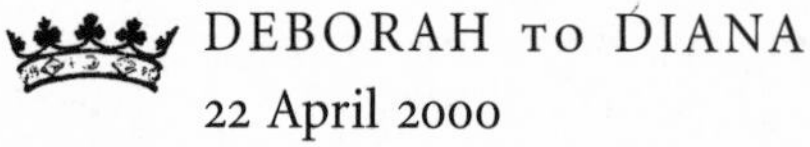

DEBORAH TO DIANA
22 April 2000

Chatsworth
Bakewell

Darling Honks

I bravely took 14 prs of specs to the Bakewell fellow who produces them because he's got a machine which tells which prescription each one is. I'm afraid he thinks I'm mad, said soothing things about how lots of people do the same but I'm not convinced. Anyway he noted on them whether they are for reading or distance & now I've got green & red cotton tied on them. Shall I remember green is for reading, red is for distance? I don't know.

I've found a lot of Granny's notes re this house & Hardwick. One wail starts 'Can someone tell me how many chimney stacks there are & to which rooms they belong?' I'm 'doing' the Back Passage here for Book,[1] good sport. I'll send when done.

More soon & you can't write too many letters. When I get back to The Pile I sift till I find yours – gold among the dross.

Much love, Debo

1 A revised edition of *Chatsworth: The House* (2002).

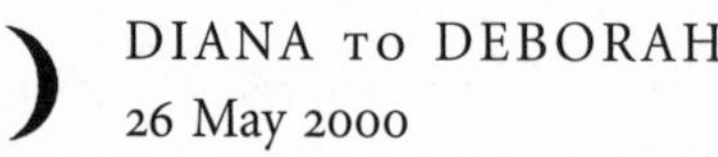

DIANA TO DEBORAH
26 May 2000

104 rue de l'Université, VII

Darling Debo

Very funny description of the Queen at the New Tate. She was steered away from the unmade bed and the bits of animals preserved in tanks of brine and allowed to look at a few bright abstracts.

My wonderful treat of laughing I had with the Kingsley Amis letters[1] has now stopped. He is a wild success with his novels and teaches at Cambridge & not Swansea, and worst of all he has fallen in love. The screams (mine) have died away. Love letters are always boring and he's no longer angry and seldom funny. However I shall go on reading because I want to see what happens, new wife etc.

Hymns have ceased to plague me. It was awful, their boring tunes & absurd words followed me even when walking in the street. I love 'Now The Day Is Over' but I must be careful not to get it in my head non-stop.

I thought Blair & his infant[2] would be the last nail in his coffin but I was quite wrong, he's gone up in the poll.

Love darling, Honks

1 The novelist's correspondence was published in 2000, edited by Zachary Leader.
2 The Prime Minister's youngest son, Leo Blair, was born on 20 May.

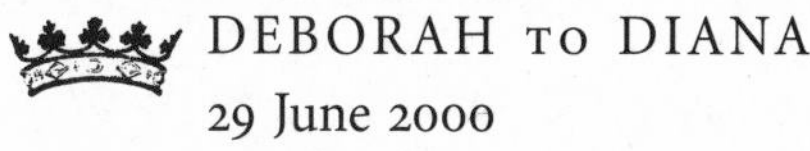

DEBOROAH TO DIANA
29 June 2000

Chatsworth
Bakewell

Darling Honks

I can't remember how much I've bored you with last wk-end.

We were hanging around the front door because the telephone said the car was just starting up the drive when a battered dirty thing arrived & it was Christopher Sykes.[1] V. comical. The shiny one followed with Queen,[2] her garden designer, lady in waiting & policeman & several tons of luggage in other cars.

The night before was very jolly, de la Rentas, Jayne W[rightsman], the Italian architect whom I love,[3] the ex Amb from France,[4] his friend,[5] the Roberts's,[6] he head of, & she drawings & prints, of the Royal collection, both *wonderful*, & beloved Neil McGregor[7] who was fearless in pulling the broodies off their nests when collecting eggs. So that was a goodly lot. We had really tried with flowers for the last three years so I thought we'd get some recs & eggs for the table to make a change. Alan[8] washed the huge Buff Cochin cock & a little black bantam hen & we put them in those glass accumulators out of the electric house on some hay. We piled up white & dark brown eggs in the Bachelor Duke's wildly decorated silver wine coolers with eagles round them and, as luck wd have it, some chicks had hatched in the farmyard in the morning so we filled 2 baskets with them (only put for ½ an hour in a warm hay heap). It had the desired effect & I don't think they'll ever get over it. The bantam laid an egg which put the lid on it.

No one coming this wk end thank heavens. I wish it could be sunny, it can't manage it.

Much love, Debo

1 Christopher Simon Sykes (1948–). Author and photographer.
2 Queen Sonja of Norway.
3 Federico Forquet, fashion designer, interior decorator and garden designer.
4 Jean Guéguinou (1941–). French ambassador to London 1993–8, to the Vatican 1998–2000, and Permanent Delegate to UNESCO since 2003.
5 Luc Bouniol-Laffont; chairman of the baroque ensemble 'Les Arts Florissants'.
6 Hugh Roberts (1948–). Director of the Royal Collection since 1996. Married Jane Low, Librarian and Curator of the Print Room at the Royal Library, Windsor, in 1975.
7 Neil McGregor (1946–). Director of the London National Gallery 1987–2002, and of the British Museum since 2002.
8 Alan Shimwell; a long-time chauffeur at Chatsworth.

DIANA TO DEBORAH

104 rue de l'Université, VII

18 August 2000

Darling Debo:

I've found letters from Woo ever since 1925. I can't tell you how it takes one back to Asthall. I am rather horrified by how *unfairly* strict Muv seems to have been. Poor Woo envying me because I was at Bexhill recovering from something, therefore I had no 'rows'. Oh how I hate rows. Are they an inevitable part of family life? I really don't think they need be. I think both Muv and Farve were in a way bored stiff without quite realizing what was wrong. It was not having enough to do. I have got nothing to do now, but feel so contented and spoilt and read all the time. But they were in their forties, and I'm ninety.

Love darling, Honks

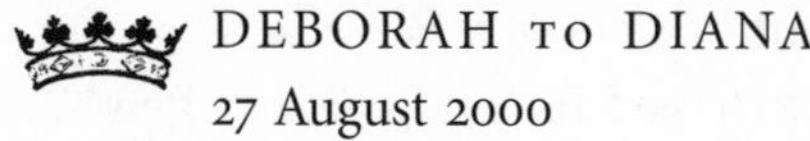

DEBORAH to DIANA
27 August 2000

Bolton Abbey
Skipton

Darling Honks

Re your letter from Woman in 1925 & Muv's strictness. What was she strict about? I suppose it is nearly impossible to remember the general carry on & the mad rules there were so long ago, I'm sure you remember events (like I do but not as well as you I know) but I wonder if she was stricter than the next mother of daughters. 76 years ago was another world, only just not Victorian. *Poor* Woman, she never wd have gone off the rails. She was 16? Awful age. I wonder if Muv believed in all the restrictions or if she was just doing the same as other people.

When I was 16 & 17 I think I was allowed to do more than my contemporaries like the Hermon-Hodges, Ogilvys, Gina Wernher & co. But I know everything had changed in those 14 or so years.

Rows. I know about them. You either have to retreat completely – & even then an 'atmosphere' remains – but if you stick to what you think, it ends in the banged door. Do you think Farve's terrifying temper was the result of ghoul experiences in the war, his brother killed & all that? I suppose Muv never would be a nondescript agree-er even before politics became such an issue.

You're right about them having nothing to do, well him really, she always seemed to be busy, but goodness knows how he spent the day & when you think how young he was when Woman wrote that letter, 46 I suppose. OH DEAR.

Much love, Debo

DIANA to DEBORAH
23 November 2000

104 rue de l'Université, VII

Darling Debo

A photocopy of Juliet's article arrived, so silly about *fond*.[1] The truth is anyone but a moron would have loved the opportunity to talk in private to Hitler, the man everyone spoke of, so powerful & unpredictable. Of course I often saw him in company, every evening at dinner at the Opera & often at his bistro, but what was fascinating was to get him alone and hear what he had to say. It wasn't often that this happened, but you can imagine how very interesting & fascinating. Nothing would ever make me pretend I was sorry to have had this unique experience. He is part of history, a terrible part, but very important, & he was usually surrounded by several people which makes chatting rather dull, always.

Poor Juliet is so upset. She's going to show her original article, so that I can see what was deleted. I just wish I'd refused the whole idea but she was so anxious to do it. Being hated means absolutely nothing to me as you know. I'm quite sure I would do the same again if I had the chance. But of course 'fond' has absolutely nothing to do with it. Just catty journalist nonsense. I only mind if it does *her* harm.

Love darling, Honks

1 Juliet Nicolson had interviewed Diana for the December 2000 issue of *Tatler* and quoted her as saying of Hitler, 'I was very fond of him. Very, very fond.'

DIANA TO DEBORAH *104 rue de l'Université, VII*
1 January 2002

Darling Debo

You have been so GOOD to continue writing despite your 31 guests.

Did you see Hardy's New Year poem in *D Telegraph*? It says God has ended a year and is beginning a new one 'In his unweeting way'.[1] I looked up unweeting and it's 'meaningless'. Oh Debo, exactly what I think. The Queen urges faith, but that too is unweeting unless you are able to feel it, which I am not. Some people feel it so strongly that they really hate those with a different faith. The Queen seems to say it doesn't much matter what the faith is about, so long as you've got it. Derek [Jackson] used to say 'Faith is believing what you know isn't true. If it were true, you wouldn't need faith'.

I do believe in hope. I hope all the time, but hope is not faith, it's a sort of wishful longing. I love seeing children because there's plenty of scope for hope. Katie's[2] children are adorable. They had sunshine for their Disney day, having motored here from Dordogne, rain & sleet all the way so far. Imagine luggage and 3 children in the back seat. What good parents. Fathers have become nannies, how will it all end?

Margaret Hudson writes to ask if I went to church on Xmas day. I would have at Edensor but not some dreary Mass in the local. Only for the music, to me it's all unweeting.

Jean-Noël [Liaut] is back, I really missed him. I'm going to list my bosom friends to end my poor book.[3] They must not be in any way exclusive, it was that which ruined my friendship with Evelyn [Waugh]. Bosom friends must all be allowed any number of other friends, and lovers. But they must be confidants, not relations. I can see, looking back, how important they have been to me. The two longest were Gerald [Berners], from when I was 22 until his death, and then the Count [de Baglion], from when I was 41 until his death. Now I've got Jean-Noël and he is 60 years younger than me. It's more laughing at the same things than anything else, plus fondness. And of course books. Gerald told me what to read, so have all of them. Robert Skidelsky is another bosom friend but too busy really, rushing round the world, for the job. I dread my book, the muddle I am in. But I must force myself to clear it up. It's really so short and easy, but I sometimes feel terribly old and paralysed. Jasmine says she'll bring her baby[4] & we will have a five generation photograph. Quelle idée!

Well darling you won't have got as far as this.

Happy new year and ALL LOVE Honks

1 Thomas Hardy, *New Year's Eve*, the last verse of which reads:

> 'He sank to raptness as of yore,
> And opening New Year's Day
> Wove it by rote as theretofore,
> And went on working evermore
> In his unweeting way.'

2 Katie Law (1960–). The daughter of Nancy's friend Joy Law and deputy literary editor of the *Evening Standard* since 1989. Married Andrew Campbell in 1990. Their children, Nell, Archie and Constance, were nine, eight and five years old respectively.

3 A new edition of *A Life of Contrasts*, published by Gibson Square Books (2002).
4 Jasmine Guinness (1976–). Diana's great-granddaughter had given birth to a son, Arthur Elwood.

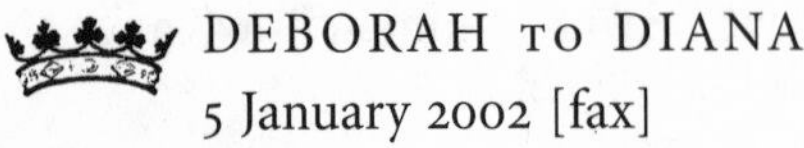

DEBORAH TO DIANA
5 January 2002 [fax]

Chatsworth
Bakewell

Darling Honks

So thrilled with two from you this A.M. Keep at it but please make the ghoul effort & finish yr book for OUR SAKES. I've just written you a long letter but this is to say we're still alive in the snow & cold. THEY give a thaw but God seems to think otherwise in his unweeting way.

I wish he'd weet a bit.

Hurrying over the ice to the post in the village.

Much love, Debo

*

At the end of July 2003, during the intense heat that enveloped France that summer, Diana suffered a small stroke. She refused to be hospitalized or accept any treatment that might stabilize her condition. Her four sons, several grandchildren and Deborah made their way to Paris to say goodbye, and she died peacefully at home on 11 August, aged ninety-three. She was cremated at Père Lachaise cemetery and the following week her ashes were buried next to Unity's in the churchyard at Swinbrook, after just the sort of simple service she had wanted. With her death, the extraordinary correspondence between the Mitford sisters came to an end.

ACKNOWLEDGEMENTS

My greatest debt of gratitude is to Deborah Devonshire, the last surviving Mitford sister, and to the late Diana Mosley, who allowed me unrestricted access to their correspondence, some of which they had not seen for eighty years. Their encouragement and help has been invaluable. I am also very grateful to Constancia Romilly and Benjamin Treuhaft, Jessica Mitford's children, for their generous cooperation.

I am lastingly indebted to Helen Marchant who, with the help of Andrew Peppitt, undertook the Herculean task of photocopying the letters at Chatsworth, which enabled me to work in conditions rarely afforded to an editor. I am also grateful to the following: Emma Tennant and her husband Eddie for their help in sorting the letters; Anne Pauline de Castries for her typing skills and encouragement; Jonathan Moyne for reading the manuscript and clarifying some obscure references; Elva Griffiths and Geoffrey Smith of Rare Books and Manuscripts at Ohio State University Libraries for their assistance; Diane Naylor, Chatsworth Photo Librarian; Gill Coleridge, my agent; and Courtney Hodell, my editor, for her perceptive observations.

I would like to thank the Rare Books and Manuscripts at Ohio State University Libraries for the use of Jessica's letters.

The following also kindly gave me their time, help or ideas: Lee and Emily Brown, Manuel Burrus, Simon Courtauld, Peter Day, Emmanuel Ducamp, Desmond Guinness, Peggy and Sebastian Guinness, Simon Head, Catherine Hesketh, Jean-Noël Liaut, Mary S. Lovell, Peter Miller, Rosaleen Mulji, Sybil and Henri d'Origny, and Hugo Vickers.

Index

Page numbers in *italic* refer to illustrations.
Titles and ranks are generally the latest mentioned in the text.